AF668834

Limca

LIMCA BOOK *of* RECORDS

India at Her Best

2023

INDIA AT HER BEST
75
YEARS OF INDEPENDENCE

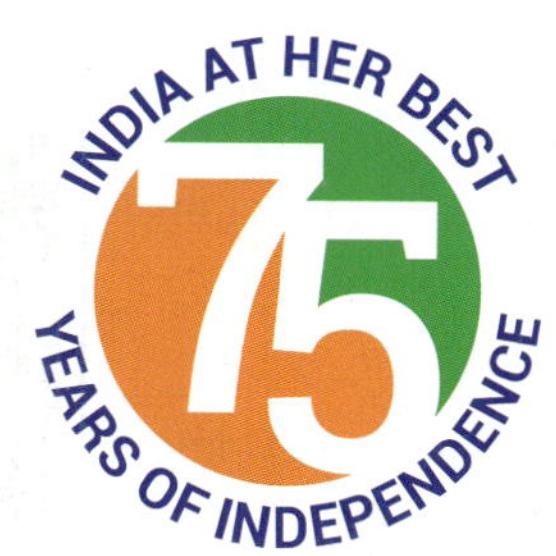

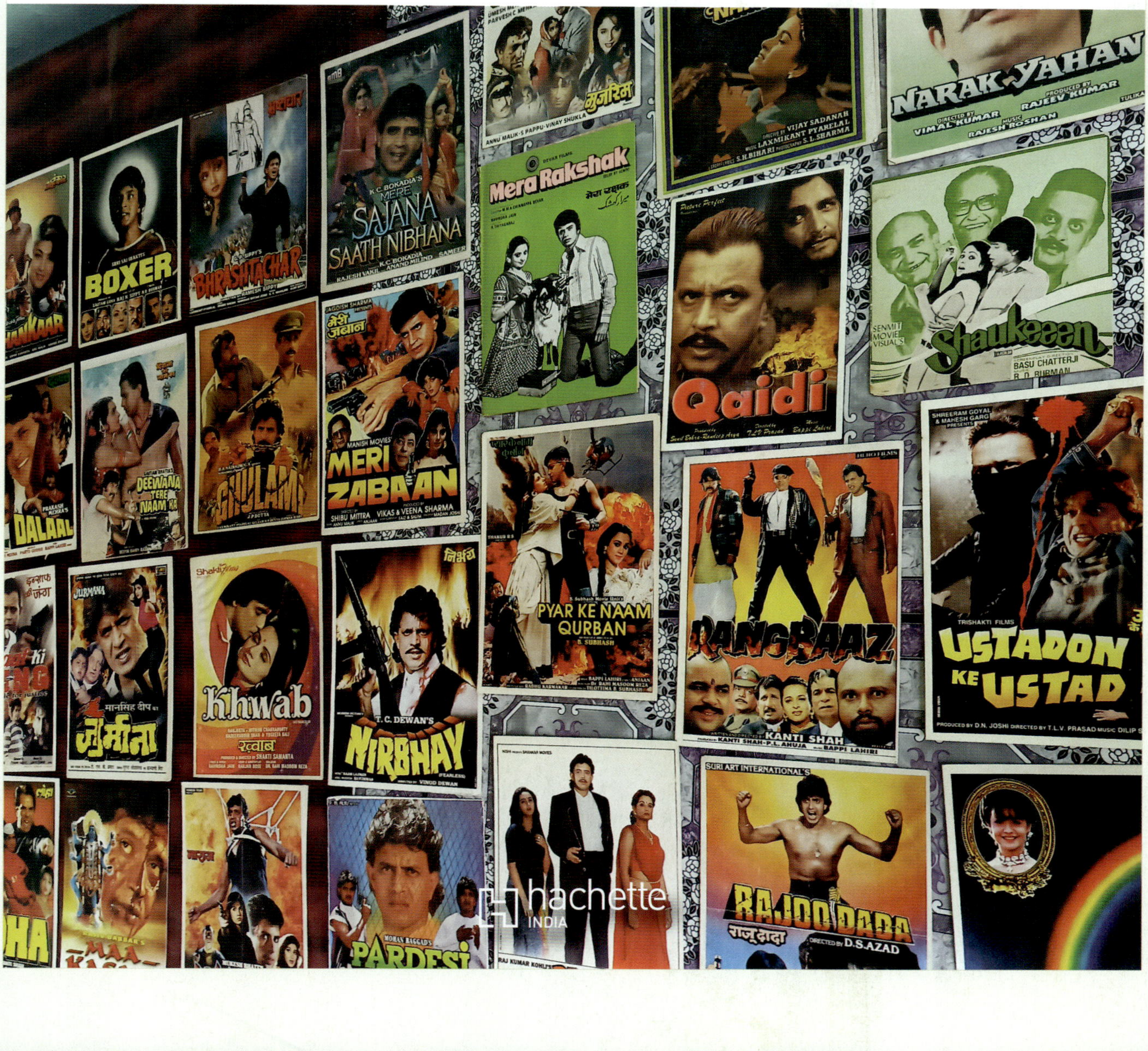

hachette INDIA

First published in 2022 by Hachette India
(Registered name: Hachette Book Publishing India Pvt. Ltd)
An Hachette UK company
www.hachetteindia.com

1

Information in the book has been updated to 31 August 2022, except in the Business and Economy, States and Union Territories and Sports chapters, where select information relates to later dates.

All maps in this work are pictorial representations, not to scale, and are not meant to represent exact political boundaries. They are for general illustration only, and are not intended to be used for reference purposes or reproduction elsewhere. It is clarified that the representation of a particular theme, or data set across regions with colour demarcations do not reflect political boundaries. It is also reiterated that such pictorial maps do not either represent or contradict India's national sovereignty, jurisdiction or the recognition of political regions as mandated by the Surveyor General of India for maps showing political boundaries.

Old place names (such as Madras, Calcutta and Bombay) may have been used to retain the historicity of the information as well as avoid confusion with earlier presidencies and provinces of the same name.

All efforts have been made to verify the copyright ownership of photographs as well as the correctness of the information included in this edition. Any omissions are unintentional and regretted, and, following written communication, will be rectified in the next edition.

Reprint specifications may be subject to change including but not limited to finishes, paper, text colour and colour sections.

ISBN 978-93-93701-47-3

Hachette Book Publishing India Pvt. Ltd
4th & 5th Floors, Corporate Centre
Plot No. 94, Sector 44, Gurugram 122003, India

Designed and typeset
by Syed Salahuddin

Printed and bound in India
by Manipal Technologies Limited

Dear Readers,

We are delighted to bring to you yet another exciting edition of the *Limca Book of Records*.

In a remarkable way, India has shown great courage and enterprise as it recoups and bounces back from the aftermath of what have been some of the most challenging years for the world. In these unprecedented times, the people of this country have proved to be tenacious champions of hope – committed to moving ahead, come what may. For more than 30 years, the *Limca Book of Records* has honoured exactly this indomitable quality in the people of India, honouring their feats and masterstrokes. As we continue to appreciate their fortitude, we are proud to have aligned Limca's new brand campaign with the prevailing resilience – #RukkMatt – to celebrate this 'unstoppable' spirit.

It is a privilege to witness the sheer will of the individuals and groups of people who put themselves through challenges and rise above the rest to make records. Coming from different corners of the country and fuelled by resolve, these record-setters bring out the best in themselves and those around them.

Along with millions of Indians, we are celebrating 75 years of India's independence by uncovering the most incredible tales of excellence. As people across the nation participated in the 'Har Ghar Tiranga' campaign, the tricolour was sent to the edge of space and unfurled at an altitude of over 30 km above Earth. Cities such as New Delhi and Lucknow witnessed mesmerizing drone shows with music and laser lights as part of Republic Day and other occasions. In sports, young Neeraj Chopra continued to shine brighter than ever, becoming the first Indian track-and-field athlete to win an Olympic gold medal.

The skies were literally not the limit for Mumbai's Captain Mayuri V. Deshmukh, as she became the first woman offshore pilot-in-command in the country. Down south, India awaits the inauguration of the longest railway platform in the world, which stretches a whopping 1,505 m in Hubballi, Karnataka. The waste-collection drive by the Maharashtra Navnirman Paryavaran Sena, with its 13,194 registered volunteers, expressed the power of the common people working towards the goal of collecting the most waste in a beach clean-up. Raising the bar in the field of art, Dr Radha Shankarnarayanan from Bengaluru created a 58.06 sq. m mandala artwork, the largest by an individual. In education, Soyeb Aftab from Rourkela became the first to score a perfect 720/720, garnering the all-India rank no. 1 in the National Eligibility cum Entrance Test (NEET) 2020 (UG). The Government's endeavour to provide better and faster technology to India brought forth 5G services in the country. The list of triumphs goes on.

In line with our constant effort to showcase the best of India, this edition is packed with thousands of records, along with interesting information, infographics and tables. Comprehensively mapping superlatives across different fields, the *Limca Book of Records* carries forward its mandate as an essential chronicle, both inspired and inspiring. We welcome our readers to participate enthusiastically in this celebration of our nation as we continue to share amazing stories from across India.

LBR Marketing Team
Coca-Cola India

EDITOR EMERITUS
Vijaya Ghose

HACHETTE INDIA LBR EDITORIAL TEAM

Editor: Vatsala Kaul Banerjee

Managing Editor: Anirban Sarkar

Senior Project Executive: Shubhali Chopra

Editorial Assistant: Debomitra Ghosh

CONSULTANTS

THE HUMAN STORY
Vijaya Ghose

ADVENTURE
Ajeet Bajaj

CINEMA
Diptakirti Chaudhuri

COMMUNITY DEVELOPMENT AND NATURE
Usha Rai

EDUCATION
Dr Alpana Neogy

MEMORY
Squadron Leader Jayasimha Ravirala

SPORTS
Jaydeep Basu: Football

Kamesh Srinivasan: Shooting, Tennis

K. Arumugam: Hockey

Meenakshi Pahuja: Swimming

Rakesh Rao: Badminton, Chess, Golf, Table Tennis

Suresh Kumar Lau: Archery, Basketball, Boxing, Cue Sports, Gymnastics, Kabaddi, Powerlifting, Weightlifting, Wrestling, General Sports

Vimal Kumar: Cricket

Hariprasad Chattopadhyay: Statistics

LAST DATE FOR NEW ENTRIES (COMPLETE WITH DOCUMENTATION) FOR THE *LIMCA BOOK OF RECORDS* 2024 EDITION:

31 MAY 2023

Please see the revised and updated Rules and Guidelines section for details.

Limca Book of Records does not have any branch offices or representatives.

General and Sales enquiries: **sales@hachetteindia.com**

Dear Readers,

As the world stares down at year three of the global pandemic that has affected so many lives on an unimaginable scale, we proudly bring to you another incredible edition of the book which embodies the spirit of courage, endeavour and triumph – exactly what millions of people of India and around the globe exhibited as they rose up to the challenges of post-pandemic life. As the world moves on, new challenges will arise, and we might have to face more showdowns, but the essence of resilience and grit will help us make our way to a new dawn.

In the spirit of moving forward, we are happy to celebrate India's 75 years of Independence with this special edition. We are thrilled to pay our tribute by showcasing the exuberant, diverse essence of our country and its people who are driven by ambition. Together, we marvel at the achievements of our nation and witness India at her best!

It is especially rewarding for the team to go through numerous applications and entries that come from all corners of our country, showing the sheer excellence, vivacity and dedication of the people of this nation, who continue to inspire and impress. All these records are utterly unique. It never ceases to amaze us, how with each passing year, new records set a higher bar to surpass – little by little pushing the level of endurance, degree of risk and originality to reach new heights of victory.

With two years of exciting news and the most enthralling records, this edition is packed with stories of champions from all walks of life. The range and diversity of the records attempted and attained by the record holders in the book are sure to leave a mark in your hearts and minds. From demonstrating new human endeavours to making leaps in environmental conservation; from pushing the limits in adventure sports to building the largest of structures; from painting their way into history to performing medical marvels; from entering a new era of technology to discovering amazing phenomena in space – these people have made the unthinkable a reality. Excelling in the fields of education, sports, science, agriculture, defence, politics, media, culture and the arts, these people have left a long praiseworthy list of feats that is both engrossing and laudatory.

We offer heartfelt congratulations to those who have made it into this edition of the book – your robust readiness and resolve are what keep the *Limca Book of Records* going strong. For those who did not make it this time, we offer our gratitude for your efforts; there is always a next time and a next edition to look forward to. Please do read our revised and updated *Rules and Guidelines* section carefully – we try to streamline the parameters continuously, so that they are finely defined and clearly understood, for others to be able to set new records. We look forward to your participation and enthusiasm for the next edition. Your passion, your dreams and your courage make this book special, and bring out the best in our nation.

Thank you for your continued support.

Vatsala Kaul Banerjee
Editor, *Limca Book of Records*
Publisher, Reference Division, Hachette India

Vijaya Ghose: First Lady of LBR

This year Vijaya Ghose (or Viji as she's known to everybody) decided to lay down her pen after being first editor and then editor emeritus of the *Limca Book of Records* (*LBR*). Viji is as much an institution as the book itself, starting her innings with it in 1991.

I can still remember the day I first met Viji, and that meeting was of tremendous import – for me personally and for *LBR*.

But I get ahead of myself...

Let's get back to the beginning – the first chapter – a human story, if you will. Research work had started on the book way back in 1987 (the story of how the book began is there in the earlier editions) and I joined the *LBR* team planning the book the following year. There were four of us as a stable unit doing the research in a set of two office cabins in a soft drink factory in West Delhi. There was Viraf Sutaria, Anna Usha Abraham, yours truly, and heading up the research was T.K. Thomas (TKT) – formerly of All India Radio and a veritable polymath in all matters of general knowledge.

▲Vijaya Ghose in recent times, with her signature cheerful smile

It was all research and no editing then. Merely 12 rough chapter buckets we had into which we dumped our findings. Remember, the *LBR* was unknown, so nobody was sending in entries. Everything had to be manually researched, collated and then manually typed up – yes, the office didn't have a computer then – and filed in big box files.

▲Thomas Abraham (*right*) was mentored by Vijaya Ghose from right across the table

When the typescript was nearing readiness, TKT's contract ended and the management wanted a professional editor to look at it. Viji was retained as a freelance editor, and I had the pleasant task of editing the book with her at her sprawling house in South Extension, New Delhi. That's where I cut my teeth on editorial, and Viji patiently taught me everything from editorial and proofreading mark-ups to how to devise a house style, and from which were the best books to read for editing to how to write for different kinds of readers. The work was done quickly over a few months and the final typescript (I still have my copy of it – see top photo on facing page). This rarer than the original first edition – which in itself is a rarity today – was readied.

The first edition – *LBR* 1990 – was released to much fanfare with star-studded launch events in six cities, but if you can get hold of the book – that first edition with its (to me) rather bilious green cover is a collector's rarity – you might notice that the book has no editor credited, merely a lot of people acknowledged. Anyway, the book was a huge success and it was decided that *LBR* would be formalized as a separate division with our own office space and a larger team. And, yes, we would now get not only a computer but a state-of-the-art one and an in-house desktop publishing (DTP) unit rather than having to queue up to get the pages typed by the office stenographers. We were among the first in the country to get a swank new Apple Mac.

However, the bigger issue was that we needed an editor for the book now that it was to be a regular annual. I remember being asked who would best fit the bill and I unhesitatingly said, 'Viji, if we can get her'. She was then working at a major media house as a senior editor. What followed is probably a record by itself – I was asked to go and discuss things with her and find out her remuneration expectations. This is possibly the first and only time someone has recruited their own boss including locking in their salary!

To cut a short story shorter, Viji agreed and came aboard to take charge of the *LBR* division. The amazing thing about Viji is the ethos she creates from being the incredible human being she is. And the years that followed saw that in plenty. She continued her mentoring of me and my colleagues, and the *LBR* teams that followed. Seeing my interest in books and publishing, she encouraged me to look for a career in regular publishing. It was her advice that made me move to publishing as an editor with Oxford University Press, with subsequent stints at Dorling Kindersley, Penguin India, and now at Hachette India. It is wonderfully serendipitous that 30 editions later things have come full circle and Hachette India is today the publisher of the *LBR*, but it is also personally a bittersweet moment in saying goodbye to Viji as a colleague, though mentor and friend she will continue to be.

At 85 years young, she is still full of beans, but one can understand why she wants to move away from the working life, and spend time on people and interests she has perhaps not had as much time with – mainly 'her animals and other family'.

Viji's passion and indomitable courage matches that of the record holders she has editorially celebrated. Her love of animals is legendary, and her support of institutions that look after sick or ageing animals is incredible. She carries her countless acts of kindness and dauntlessness lightly. Not many of her thousands of *LBR* readers would know of her drive to re-teach herself speech (after a stroke cost her the ability to speak) from scratch, a painstaking and determined effort that was nothing short of inspirational. It is that inspiration that has been evident all these years – in over 30 editions – and will remain as long as the *LBR* stays in print.

Thomas Abraham
Managing Director, Hachette India
(He began his career with *LBR* in 1988.)

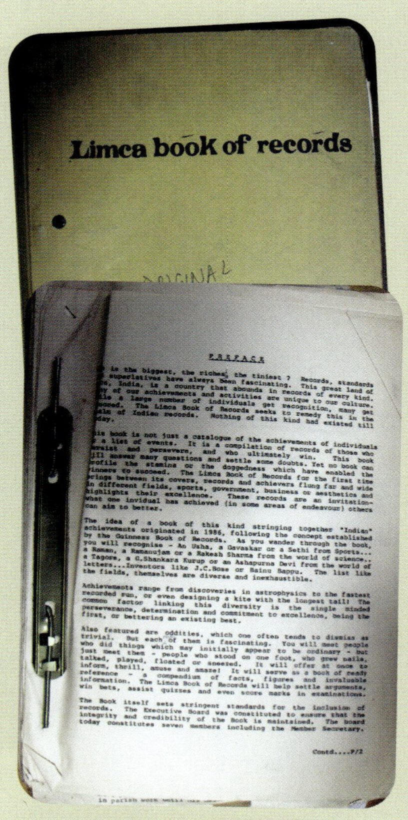

PREFACE

... is the biggest, the richest, the tiniest ? Records, standards ... superlatives have always been fascinating. This great land of ...s, India, is a country that abounds in records of every kind. ...y of our achievements and activities are unique to our culture. ...ile a large number of individuals get recognition, many get ...ecoed. The Limca Book of Records seeks to remedy this in the ...als of Indian records. Nothing of this kind had existed till ...day.

...is book is not just a catalogue of the achievements of individuals ... a list of events. It is a compilation of records of those who ...ersist and persevere, and who ultimately win. This book ...ill answer many questions and settle some doubts. Yet no book can ...rofile the stamina or the doggedness which have enabled the ...inners to succeed. The Limca Book of Records for the first time ...rings between its covers, records and achievers flung far and wide ...n different fields, sports, government, business or aesthetics and ...highlights their excellence. These records are an invitation- what one invidual has achieved (in some areas of endeavour) others can aim to better.

The idea of a book of this kind stringing together "Indian" achievements originated in 1986, following the concept established by the Guinness Book of Records. As you wander through the book, you will recognise - An Usha, a Gavaskar or a Sethi from Sports... a Raman, a Ramanujam or a Rakesh Sharma from the world of science.. a Tagore, a G.Shankara Kurup or an Ashapurna Devi from the world of letters...Inventors like J.C.Bose or Bainu Bappu. The list like the fields, themselves are diverse and inexhaustible.

Achievements range from discoveries in astrophysics to the fastest recorded run, or even designing a kite with the longest tail! The common factor linking this diversity is the single minded perseverance, determination and commitment to excellence, being the first, or bettering an existing best.

Also featured are oddities, which one often tends to dismiss as trivial. But each of them is fascinating. You will meet people who did things which may initially appear to be ordinary - but just meet them - people who stood on one foot, who grew nails, talked, played, floated or sneezed. It will offer at once to inform, thrill, amuse and amaze! It will serve as a book of ready reference - a compendium of facts, figures and invaluable information. The Limca Book of Records will help settle arguments, win bets, assist quizzes and even score marks in examinations.

The Book itself sets stringent standards for the inclusion of records. The Executive Board was constituted to ensure that the integrity and credibility of the Book is maintained. The board today constitutes seven members including the Member Secretary.

Contd....P/2

▲ **The carefully preserved typescript of the very first edition of the *Limca Book of Records***

▼ **Vijaya and Thomas *(both on the right)* at one of the many initial star-studded *LBR* events**

Novy Kapadia: A Life in Sport

2 April 1952–18 November 2021

I first came to know of Novy circa 1987 when I joined *Target*, the iconic children's magazine from the India Today Group, as a rookie journalist–writer. Despite it being a small magazine, we somehow had the best of writers and experts contributing to it, and Novy was at the time doing a series of articles on football with savvy tips for young football enthusiasts. One of the toughest things in sports is to get such advice across in print, but Novy was nothing if not passionate about football and determined to bring it closer to people, and he managed this difficult task with ease.

Over the years, I kept reading about him and from him. A professor of English literature at SGTB Khalsa College, University of Delhi, he served as the university's deputy proctor from 2003 to 2010. From 1980 onwards, as a sports journalist, he covered several international championships, including the FIFA World Cup (nine of them!) and the Olympics, and all major domestic tournaments. Novy won the Wills Award for Excellence in Sports Journalism in 1986.

While he covered many multi-sport events, his favourite path in life always passed through football fields. He started the Ashoka Football Club in Delhi, where he was coach and secretary at different times. A mentor, consultant and a veritable living archive of information about football, he would reel off records and milestones in meticulous detail. His sports commentaries were informed, admired and applauded.

Novy contracted a rare type of motor neurone disease and was confined to his house for the last two years of his life. Having been associated with the *Limca Book of Records* since the 1990s, he was a valued consultant and chief coordinator for the chapter on sports.

My interactions with him regarding the *Limca Book of Records* were marked by his steersmanship, efficiency and attention to the smallest details in the many sections he covered, ranging from football and hockey to athletics, badminton and squash. In the last edition he worked on, unable to use the laptop, he dedicatedly sent me updates on the phone. His final two months required life support and he left us all too soon, while still only in his sixties.

▲ **Novy (*left*) in conversation with Sunil Chhetri**

Novy's legacy lives on in the role he played in many sporting lives and in his books, ranging from one reflecting his Parsi heritage to those about football. Besides *Barefoot to Boots: The Many Lives of Indian Football* (Penguin Random House India, 2017), he published two comprehensive and popular FIFA World Cup guides with Hachette India – *The Football Fanatic's Essential Guide* in 2014 and its updated version in 2018.

We at the *Limca Book of Records* are deeply grateful that we had him as part of the team for so many years, and truly miss him, his authoritative knowledge and his expert advice.

Life and death are adjoining fields
And the ball is the spirit of the sport –
It stays in play
Oblivious of the end;
And we know you are seeing it all
From the commentator's box
Up in the sky,
Down here in our hearts...
In a limitless turf without boundary
Your voice echoes in the arena –
As the game goes on...
The beautiful game.

– Vatsala Kaul Banerjee

CONTENTS

THE HUMAN STORY

STRUCTURES

AGRICULTURE

32

3

15

60

84

88

83

GOVERNMENT

DEFENCE

THE NATURAL WORLD

TRANSPORT

MEDICAL SCIENCES

SCIENCE AND TECHNOLOGY

EDUCATION

MEDIA AND COMMUNICATIONS

LITERATURE

220

224

249

253

260

234

CONTENTS

INDEPENDENCE SPECIAL

VISUAL ARTS

BUSINESS AND ECONOMY

PERFORMING ARTS

SPORTS

ADVENTURE

417

318

335
COMMONWEALTH GAMES 2022

348

419

CONTENTS

STATES AND UNION TERRITORIES

433

436

439

453

THE HUMAN STORY

MEMORY

Fastest to identify the flags of all the countries of the world

Taha Ammar Kheyroolla (b. 7 November 2013) from Chennai, Tamil Nadu, identified the flags of all the countries (195) of the world in 3 mins 1 sec. on 16 May 2021.

Fastest to identify all the bones in the human body

Kudrat Kukreja (b. 23 February 2000) from Shimla, Himachal Pradesh, set a new record by identifying all the bones in the human body in 1 min. 53 secs on 21 August 2020 at Hotel Siddharth, Ram Bazar, Shimla.

Most dinosaurs identified – 1 minute

Reyaansh Paradeshi (b. 11 September 2015) from Doha, Qatar, correctly identified 85 dinosaurs by name in 1 min. on 28 May 2021 at the Indian Cultural Centre (ICC), Doha.

Fastest memorization followed by calculation*

A. Jayaprakash Reddy (b. 8 July 1983) from Chittoor, Andhra Pradesh, memorized a random 50-digit number, multiplied it with 25 and gave the answer in 4 mins 15 secs on 27 June 2019.

* This is an old record being featured for the first time.

Taha Ammar Kheyroolla: fastest to identify the flags of all the countries of the world

Kudrat Kukreja: fastest to identify all the bones of the human body

Reyaansh Pardeshi: most dinosaurs correctly identified by name in a minute

YOGA

Longest *padma mayurasana*

Mangal Raj (b. 11 August 1991) from Sitamarhi, Bihar, performed *padma mayurasana* (lotus in peacock pose) for 4 mins 14 secs from 5:49 p.m. to 5:54 p.m. on 19 November 2021 at Raj Classic Park, Versova, Mumbai.

Longest *mayurasana* – with one hand

Mangal Raj (b. 11 August 1991) from Sitamarhi, Bihar, performed *mayurasana* (peacock pose) with one hand for 56 secs on 4 February 2022 at Raj Classic Park, Versova, Mumbai.

Longest *purvattanasana*

Sandeep Krishna Murthy Karupakala (b. 27 January 1982) and Aruna K.S. (b. 2 January 1987) from Chintamani, Karnataka, held *purvattanasana* (upward plank pose) for 2 mins 10 secs on 10 April 2021 at Lalitha Nivas, Chintamani.

Longest *mandukasana*

Swapan Kumar Sur (b. 24 February 1974) from Faridabad, Haryana, performed *mandukasana* (frog pose) for 47 mins 11 secs from 8:33 p.m. to 9:21 p.m. on 14 April 2021 in Chhinamore, Hoogly, West Bengal.

Longest *niralamba ushtrasana*

Dr Narendra Kumar Sharma (b. 30 March 1978) from Jaipur, Rajasthan, performed *niralamba ushtrasana* (unsupported camel pose) for 10 mins 38 secs on 30 May 2021.

Longest *bakasana*

Virendra Vikram Singh (b. 2 December 1954) from Balrampur, Uttar Pradesh, performed the *bakasana* (crow pose) for 5 mins from 6:10 p.m. to 6:15 p.m. on 16 May 2022 at the M.P.P. Inter college, Balrampur.

Most rounds of *agnisar kriya* – 1 hour**

Jaishree Kaushik (b. 18 August 1953) from Gwalior, Madhya Pradesh, performed 272 rounds of *agnisar kriya* in 1 hr from 6:25 a.m. to 7:25 a.m. in the grounds of Shri Gauri Shankar Higher Secondary School, Gwalior.

Longest *janu sirsasna*

Virendra Vikram Singh (b. 2 December 1954) from Balrampur, Uttar Pradesh, performed *janu sirasana* (head to knee pose) for 60 mins from 9:00 a.m. to 10:00 a.m. on 24 February 2021 at Late Ravinder Memorial.

Mangal Raj: longest *padma mayurasana*

Mangal Raj: longest *mayurasana* – with one hand

Dr Narendra Kumar Sharma: longest *niralamba ushtrasana*

** This is a one-time category. Further and future claims for this category will not be accepted.

ENDEAVOUR

Most tennis balls held – one hand with palm down**

Shripad Vaidya (b. 5 May 1969) from Nagpur, Maharashtra, held 8 tennis balls in one hand with his palm facing downwards for 47 secs on 7 December 2020.

Shripad Vaidya: most tennis balls held – one hand with palm down

Most countries travelled – group

Sujoy Kumar Mitra (b. 8 July 1983) and his wife Sharmistha Dey (b. 2 May 1986) travelled to 154 countries together from 9 December 2011 to 2 April 2021. During the travel period of 2019–2021, they visited 21 countries including Iceland (Europe), Yemen (Asia), Venezuela (South America), Antigua and Barbuda (North America), Eritrea (Africa) and Somalia (Africa). The total travel duration is 9 years 115 days. Their ultimate goal is to travel to 193 UN Member countries.

(*Right* and *bottom*) Sujoy Kumar Mitra and Sharmistha Dey: most countries travelled – group

Most hits on the hip by the heels while performing *sirsasana***

Lieutenant Colonel Laxmi Dhar Bhuyan (b. 4 May 1971) from Balasore, Odisha, performed 13,725 hits on the hip by the heels in 1 hr 7 mins 10 secs while also performing the *sirsasana* on 15 January 2021 at Gyani Stadium, Nashik, Maharashtra.

** This is a one-time category. Further and future claims for this category will not be accepted.

Manisha Satyajit Dange: longest basketball shot

SKILLS

Longest basketball shot

Manisha Satyajit Dange (b. 8 December 1979) from Thane, Maharashtra, made a 21.4 m long basketball shot twice in 2 secs 72 millisecs at 10:03 a.m. on 22 May 2021 at the Central Railway Sport Complex, Parel, Mumbai, Maharashtra.

Most tennis ball touches on palm – 1 minute**

Vinod Kumar Chaudhary (b. 15 March 1980) from Sultanpuri, Delhi, bounced a tennis ball on his palm 235 times in 1 min. between 12:43 p.m. to 12:44 p.m. on 24 January 2021 at MD Memorial Public School, Sultanpuri.

Most juggling patterns on a balance board

Jaykishan Vimalbhai Hingu (b. 3 March 2000) from Jetpur, Gujarat, performed 28 juggling patterns using 3 balls while balancing on a balance board on 5 May 2021 at Radha Park, Jetpur. The patterns were: cascade, columns, fake columns, the machine, crossed columns, one going over the top, half shower, false shower, behind the back, box, clawed catches, Mangham's mangle, 'M', infinity, reverse infinity, Georgian shuffle, real tennis, tennis, yo-yo, oy-oy, outside throws, Statue of Liberty, shower, Ripley's rainbow, wiper, 'W', the weave and Mill's mess.

Jaykishan Vimalbhai Hingu: most juggling patterns on a balance board

Rotating the tongue 360 degrees**

Ansh Niren Maniar (b. 11 December 2006) from Rajkot, Gujarat, has the unique ability of rotating and rolling his tongue 360 degrees for over a minute. He performed this feat for 1 min. on 13 May 2021 in Rajkot.

Longest time spinning a basketball on fingers**

Priyanka Singh (b. 30 September 1996) from Lucknow, Uttar Pradesh, spun a basketball on her fingers, switching between two fingers continuously for 19 mins and 10 secs on 30 May 2021 at her residence.

MOST

Varieties of mini tarts

The School of Hospitality Management at IMS Unison University, Dehradun, Uttarakhand, organized a culinary challenge where a team – 'Fantastic 36' – headed by Chef Abhay Chamoli and Chef Devashish Pandey, prepared the most varieties of mini tarts on 21 April 2022. The event showcased 550 varieties of tarts with popular international types of fillings and toppings. The shells, prepared from shortcrust

OUNGSTERS KABADDI CLUB
KENDA
SCOTT

Bharath Kumar Urs (b. 8 February 1983) from Bengaluru, Karnataka, made the following records:

Longest time balancing a bicycle – one hand

He balanced a bicycle with one hand for 3 mins 34 secs on 7 November 2021 using only his right hand (with his left hand bent back) at Sadashiv Nagar, Bengaluru.

Longest time balancing a bicycle – with one hand on a 1.5 ft step**

He balanced a bicycle with one hand for 1 min. 29 secs on a 1.5 ft step on 8 February 2022 at the Corporation Ground, Bengaluru, Karnataka.

** This is a one-time category. Further and future claims for this category will not be accepted.

Varieties of mini tarts

pastry, was filled with both sweet and savoury vegetarian and non-vegetarian fillings. Abhay and Devashish along with team 'Fantastic 36', made 1,100 mini tarts, each measuring 4 in., with two pieces of each kind. Assembling the mini tarts took 2 hrs 30 mins from 11:00 a.m. to 1:30 p.m. at IMS Unison University, Dehradun.

Varieties of chaat

Team 35, coordinated by Chef Ashish Spencer, made 503 varieties of chaat in 2 hrs 20 mins from 10:25 a.m. to 12:45 p.m. on 12 March 2022 at Dewan VS Institute of Hotel Management, Meerut, Uttar Pradesh. The chaats involved innovation and the fusion of the ingredients into crunchy sweet and savoury chaat. The varieties of chaat included *sabudana papad sevpuri, khatta meetha bhel*, *dum aloo* masala *bhel*, *aloo paneer* chaat, coconut *puchka* chaat and pineapple chaat, among others.

Varieties of chaat

Varieties of pastries

Varieties of pastries

The Department of Hospitality and Tourism Management at Assam Down Town University, Guwahati, Assam, assembled 517 assorted pastries in 3 hrs 44 mins from 9:30 a.m. to 1:14 p.m. on 11 May 2022 on the university campus. A team of 25 in-house chefs comprising students and faculty, headed by Chef Jyotirmay Choudhury and Chef Mridu Pawan Rabha, made the pastries. These included pistachio and blackcurrant pastry, chocolate red velvet pastry, pineapple and mango pastry, and litchi and mixed fruit pastry, among others.

Varieties of biryani

Varieties of biryani

The Institute of Hotel Management Catering Technology and Applied Nutrition, Hyderabad, Telangana, prepared 75 varieties of biryani in 8 hrs on 5 April 2022 in the university premises. The varieties included *goemchi* chicken biryani, Goan shrimp biryani, bhatkal biryani, *mawa ki* biryani and *bharwan gosht ki* biryani, among others.

Varieties of rice dishes

A team of eight chefs and 32 students from the University Institute of Tourism and Hospitality Management, Chandigarh University, led by Chef Dev Raj, made 2,139 rice preparations in 3 hrs 16 mins from 2:00 p.m. to 5:16 p.m. on 14 September 2019 on the university premises.

Varieties of lassi

These dishes included red rice with beetroot, black rice with Thai guava, biryani, pulao, meat masala rice, and Schezwan chicken rice, among others.

Varieties of lassi

A team of seven chefs and 38 students led by Chef Gaurav Khurana, Dean of the Institute of Hotel Management, Guru Kashi University, Talwandi Sabo, Bathinda, Punjab, prepared 1,813 varieties of lassi on their campus on 13 August 2021. The different flavours used included mango, apple, savoury flavours, vegetables, herbal plants and sweets.

Varieties of beverages

Graphic Era (deemed to be university), Dehradun, Uttarakhand, prepared 560 varieties of beverages, all dairy-based, in 1 hr 15 mins between 11:20 a.m. to 12:35 p.m. on 21 May 2022 at the Chanakya Block in the university premises. The event was called 'Milk Mania' and involved 16 team members.

Varieties of dim sum

Amar Prakash Dabral, Mohsin Khan, Sunil Kumar Lal, Yogesh Upreti and 'Team Incredible of 26' from the Department of Hospitality Management, Graphic Era Hill (Deemed to be) University, Dehradun, Uttarakhand, assembled 624 varieties of dim sums as part of their event, 'The Dim Sums Quest'. A total of 2,496 dim sums were assembled in 1 hr 47 mins 6 secs between 11:10 a.m. and 12:57 p.m. on 6 May 2022 at the Chanakya block on the university premises.

Varieties of dim sum

Above: varieties of wraps

Below: varieties of quiche

Varieties of wraps

A team of seven chefs and 32 students led by Chef Gaurav Khurana, Dean of Institute of Hotel Management, Guru Kashi University, Talwandi Sabo, Bathinda, Punjab, prepared 1,348 varieties of wraps on their campus on 12 August 2021. The different fillings and sheets were chicken, mutton, fish, vegetables, dairy products and sweets.

Varieties of *phirni*

The students and faculty of the School of Hotel Management, Airlines and Tourism (SOHAD), CT University, Ludhiana, Punjab, in collaboration with Amul under the Gujarat Cooperative Milk Marketing Federation Ltd, prepared 1,101 different types of *phirni* on 11 January 2021. A total of 167 ingredients were used to prepare the varieties of *phirni.*

Varieties of *basundi*

Amity School of Hospitality, Jaipur, Rajasthan, made the most varieties of *basundi* on the university premises on 25 May 2022, under the guidance of Chef Dr Saurabh Sharma, associate professor, Amit School of Hospitality, along with Prof. Sanjvee Pal, Chef Adity, Dr Yashwant, Dr Sushil, Dr Jai, Chef Himmat Singh, four staff members and 21 students. They made 515 varieties of *basundi* in 3 hrs 29 mins. The *basundi* was served to all guests, faculty, staff, and students of Amity University.

Varieties of quiche

A team of students and faculty members from the Department of Hospitality Management of the Graphic Era Hill (Deemed-to-be) University, Haldwani, Uttarakhand, prepared 251 savoury quiche varieties in 1 hr 45 mins between 11:00 a.m. to 12:45 p.m. on 24 May 2022 on the university campus. These included chicken and basil quiche, mushroom quiche, broccoli and salmon quiche, and leek and chillies quiche, among others.

SMALLEST

Spinning wheel

Jayant Natthuji Tandulkar (b. 11 October 1976) from Nagpur, Maharashtra, designed the smallest charkha (spinning wheel to spin yarn) measuring 3.20 mm in length, 2.68 mm in width, 3.06 mm in height and weighing 0.04 gm in 10 hrs from 8:00 a.m. to 6:00 p.m. on 28 June 2020. He used materials such as wooden sticks, steel wire and cotton thread to make it. The charkha was measured using a vernier calliper and digital scale.

VADA MANIA

Most varieties of vada

The Savoy, Mussoorie team led by Chef Rajeev Badola, Chef Varinder Singh Rana, Chef Smriti Sarin Hari and Junior Chef Khyati Hari prepared 551 varieties of vada on 7 September 2021. Regional varieties of vada including *medu* vada, *keerai vadai*, *thavala*, masala vada and *kanji* vada, were prepared in front of guests and the general public. To spread the message of sustainable cuisine, regional *pahadi* vadas were prepared using local ingredients. The vadas were served to the guests and staff.

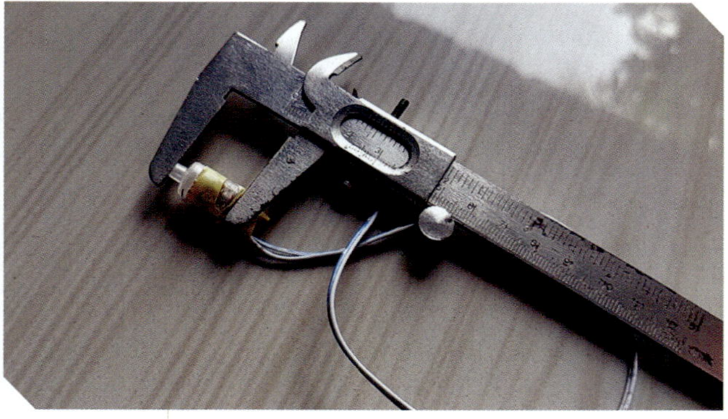

Above: smallest water-level controller; *Right*: smallest vacuum cleaner

Smallest electric bike

Functioning water-level controller printed circuit board

Pranav Ramesh Rokde (b. 30 October 1995) from Nagpur, Maharashtra, made the smallest functioning water-level controller printed circuit board (PCB) with dimensions of 28 mm x 28 mm x 15 mm in 2021 at his residence. The water-level controller encompasses electronic components such as NPN (negative-positive-negative) and PNP transistors, capacitors, a few resistors, a diode and a relay for switching water motor pump on and off.

Vacuum cleaner

Nithin Kumar T.S. (b. 6 January 1999) from Pathanamthitta, Kerala, made the smallest vacuum cleaner of 2.1 cm height and 1.1 cm width on 25 April 2021. He took 28 mins from 12:32 p.m. to 1:00 p.m. to make it at his residence.

Smallest electric bike model

Santhosh (b. 7 May 1974) from Mysuru, Karnataka, made the smallest electric bike model, named Moosshiqk-3. It measures 145 mm, with a 130 mm wheelbase, its total length being 230.4 mm. It weighs 2.5 kg, with a payload of 64 kg.

BIGGEST

Thali – dishes

The Institute of Hospitality, Management

Thali – dishes

STYLING SAREES

Kalpana Bhagwandas Shah (b. 30 November 1948) from Mumbai, Maharashtra, performed the following saree-draping feats:

Marathon saree-draping

She draped 226 saree styles in 21 hrs 10 mins between 11:30 a.m. on 9 April 2022 to 11:30 a.m. on 10 April 2022 at FTC Media, Mumbai. Her total break time was 2 hrs 50 mins.

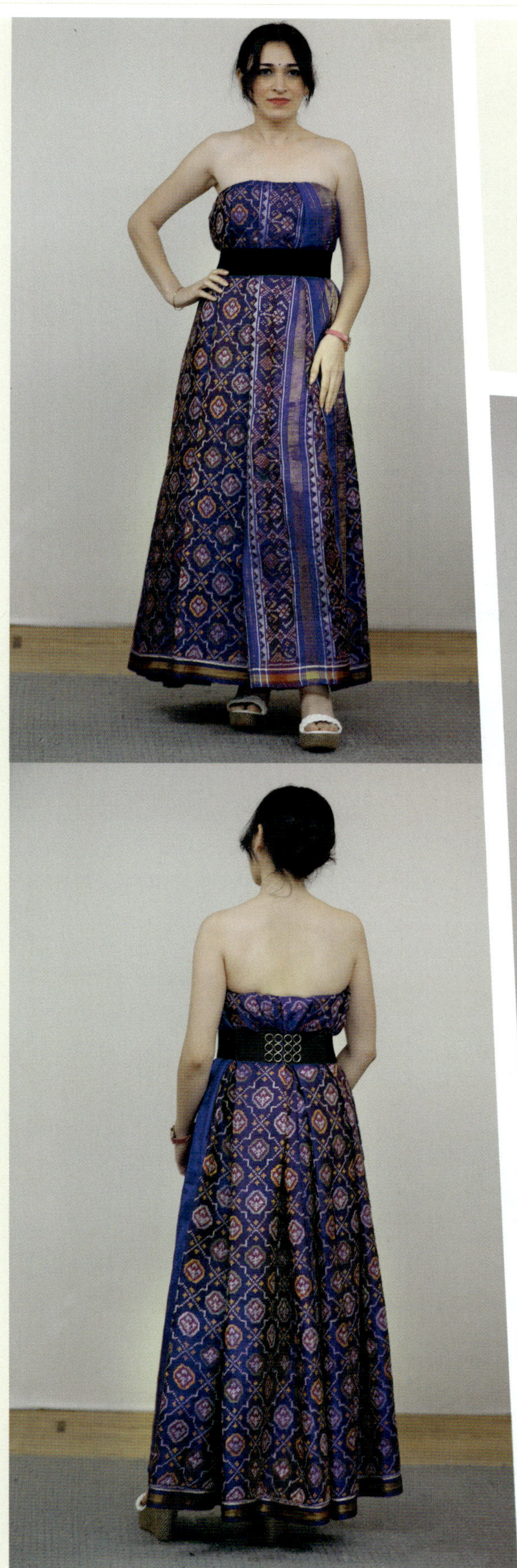

Most saree styles draped

She draped a total of 226 unduplicated saree styles. The sarees used varied from chiffon to georgette and crepe to Banarasi silk. A total of 3,914 ft of saree material was draped in total. The fastest saree drape was done within 1 min.

and Sciences, Kotdwar, Uttarakhand, made the biggest thali with 301 dishes from various states. The event involved 57 participants, 49 students and eight faculty members making the dishes in 2 hrs 15 mins on 15 May 2022 on the college premises.

Umbrella

The Rural Development and Research Center, Haryana, made the biggest umbrella, measuring 52 ft in height and having a diameter of 84 ft, at Aastha Science Park, Rewari, Haryana. The umbrella, made using GI.S.S. fabric, tensile, with a cement-concrete base, weighs 100 tonnes and covers an area of 5,760 sq. ft. Inaugurated on 19 March 2022, it has a digital lighting system and can be folded easily.

LONGEST

Sandwich

The St Soldier Institute of Hotel Management and Catering Technology, Jalandhar, Punjab, made the longest sandwich on 22 December 2021. Led by Sandeep Lohani, the principal, five faculty chefs and 15 students prepared a sandwich, measuring 223 ft 2.4 in. in length and 8 in. in width, in 35 mins from 11:13 a.m. to 11:48 a.m. They used 123 slices of loaf spread with a combination of vegetables, noodles, cheese, pasta and dressings for it.

Tallest *shivling* (temporary)**

Kebab

NIMS University-Jaipur in Jaipur, Rajasthan, made a kebab measuring 49 ft 8.4 in. in length with a team of 45 participants under the supervision of Prof. Manoj Srivastava in 9 hrs 53 mins on 6 April 2022. The vegetarian *tawa* kebab was made on a customized *tawa*, 50 ft long and 2.5 ft wide, using seven industrial gas cylinders with 4 mm hot plate *tawa* with rail burners underneath. It was displayed at the Sundervan Garden of NIMS University. The kebab was made with 16 kg potatoes, 5 kg chickpea flour, 2 kg green peas, 2 lt of ghee, 1 kg mint leaves, 5 kg onion garlic paste, 2 kg capsicum, 1 kg green chillies, 5 kg soya nuggets, 7 kg spinach and 900 gm ground garam masala.

TALLEST

Tallest *shivling* (temporary)**

Daffodils Public School, Mirzapur, Uttar

** This is a one-time category. Further and future claims for this category will not be accepted.

Largest single-piece floral structure – group

The Institute of Hotel Management Catering Technology and Applied Nutrition, Hyderabad, Telangana, created the largest single-piece flower structure using 53,516 flowers between 6:38 a.m. to 12:45 p.m. on 7 April 2022 on the university premises. They used spray chrysanthemums, orchids, birds of paradise, roses, and pink and white gladioli to make the floral structure.

FOOD FOR CHAMPIONS

The New Cochin Bakery, Kozhikode, Kerala, made the following records related to largest food items:

Largest *ela ada*

A Kerala delicacy, the largest baked *ela ada* measured 5 ft in length and 0.5 ft in width. Weighing 5 kg, it was prepared at 7:00 p.m. on 30 January 2020. Made of rice flour spread on a banana leaf, it was stuffed with freshly scraped coconut, sugar, cardamom, cashew nuts and raisins, and baked on a *tawa*. Two chefs baked the *ela ada* in roughly 4 hours.

Longest *unnakaya*

The longest *unnakaya* measured 1.5 ft in length and weighed 3 kg when prepared on 29 January 2020. A special-occasion dish of the Kerala Malabari families, the *unnakaya* is now a popular teatime snack. The main ingredients were banana with sugar, raisins, cashew nuts, cardamom and oil. Two chefs made the *unnakaya* in 3 hours.

Largest *erachipathiri*

The largest *erachipathiri* measured 5 ft x 2.5 ft and weighed 22 kg when prepared on 30 January 2020. A morning delicacy in parts of Kerala, this pancake-like dish is stuffed with meat of one's choice in multiple layers, each with unique toppings. Three members made the *erachipathiri* in 4 hours.

Bread

The largest stuffed bread measured 10 ft x 0.34 ft and weighed 8 kg when prepared on 29 January 2020. Its main ingredients were 8 kg *maida*, margarine, yeast, soya and flour. It was stuffed with a filling of 1.5 kg chicken along with vegetables and oil. Three chefs made the stuffed bread in 5 hours.

Largest *chatti pathiri*

The largest *chatti pathiri* measured 2 ft in diameter and weighed 10 kg when prepared on 30 January 2020. The main ingredients were 1 kg *maida*, 5 eggs, 2.4 kg sugar, 1.2 kg coconut milk, corn flour, raisins, nuts and ghee, among others. Three chefs made it in 4 hours.

Largest patty

The largest patty measured 8 ft x 0.33 ft and weighed 5 kg when prepared on 30 January 2020. The main ingredients were 2.5 kg *maida*, vegetable fillings like carrot, cabbage, potato, beetroot, onion, coconut scrapes, green peas, andvegetable masala and milk as topping. Two chefs made the patty in 4 hours.

Pradesh, made the tallest *shivling* (temporary) for the Mahashivratri Utsav in the school. He made the 43 ft *shivling* from 3:00 p.m. to 7:00 p.m. on 11 March 2021.

COLLECTIONS

A–Z: Coasters

Abhay Sharad Phatak (b. 21 February 1968) from Thane, Maharashtra, has a collection of 39 coasters from 17 countries (with names starting from A to Z) up to May 2022.

A–Z: Water-bottle labels

Abhay S. Phatak (b. 21 February 1968) from Thane, Maharashtra, has 52 water bottle labels (with names starting from A to Z) from 26 countries, a collection started in 2016.

A–Z: Inkpots

Ninad Jadhav (b. 11 July 1977) from Chhindwara, Madhya Pradesh has an A–Z collection

Above: A–Z coasters

Below: A–Z water-bottle labels

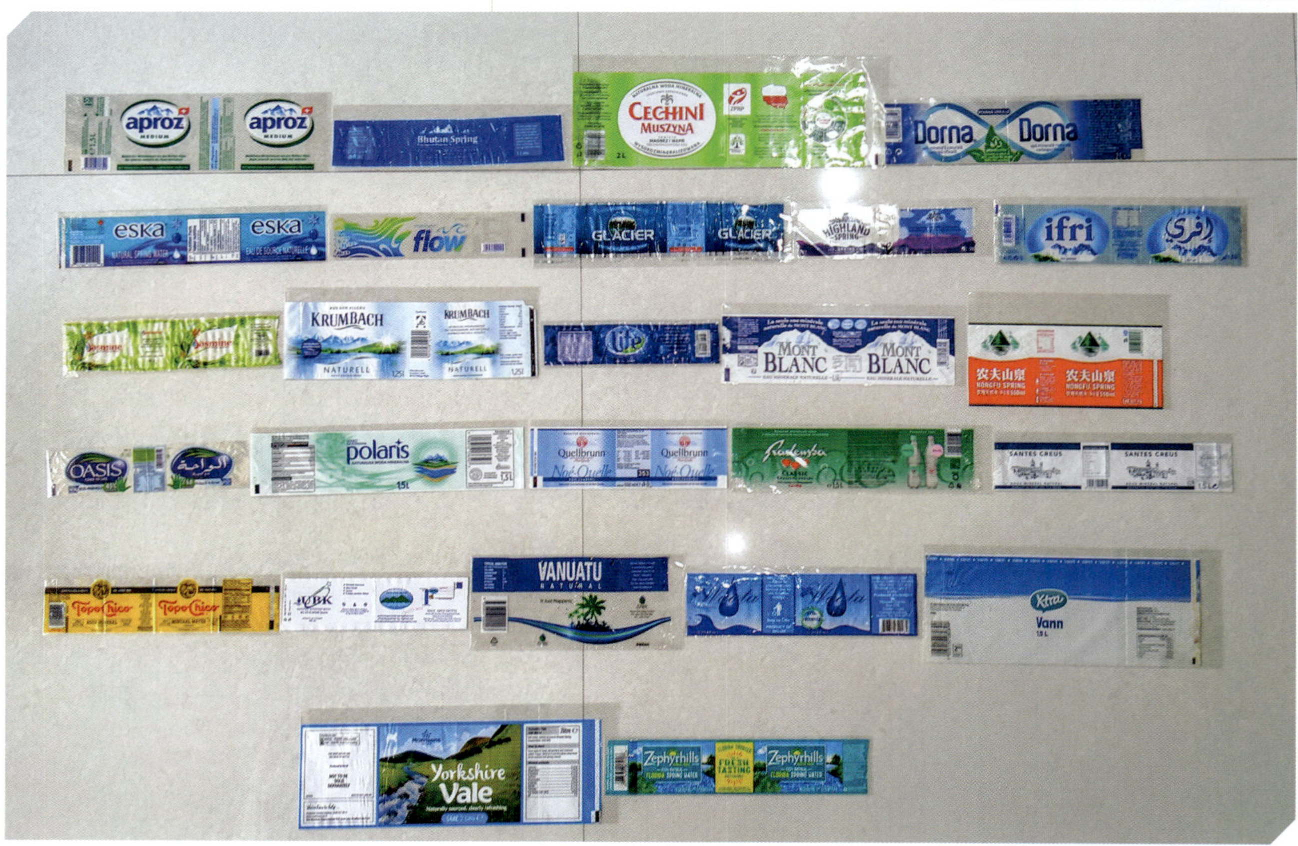

Erasers

Khushboo Marda Malani (b. 10 March 1980) from Delhi has curated a collection of 14,663 unduplicated erasers from over 40 countries till 20 May 2022. The erasers are in different shapes, sizes and colours, and are categorized into various themes, such as prominent persons, monuments, sports, animals, food, electronics, transportation, educational items and stationery, furniture and household equipment, and arms and ammunition, among others.

of 131 inkpots from 33 different companies (with names from A to Z). The collection includes perfumed ink, limited edition and special edition inkpots, among others.

A–Z: Airline air sickness bags

Abhay S. Phatak (b. 21 February 1968) from Thane, Maharashtra, has airline air-sickness bags from 18 different countries (with airline names from A to Z), a collection started in 2016.

A–Z: Foreign newspapers

Sudhir Jain (b. 7 October 1954) from Satna, Madhya Pradesh, has A–Z foreign newspapers in different languages from 26 countries (with names from A to Z).

Sudoku

K.S. Rao (b. 10 August 1940) from Hyderabad, Telangana, started collecting 'very hard' and 'evil' Sudoku puzzles and solving them from 2009 onwards. By 25 May 2022, he had added 977 puzzles, and the final tally was 12,145.

WR Credit cards

Manish Kumar Dhameja from Lucknow, Uttar Pradesh, has a collection of 1,638 valid credit cards from 25 banks. His first credit card was issued by the State Bank of India in 2014. The collection includes prepaid cards and add on/supplementary cards. His collection was exhibited from 10:00 a.m. to 11:00 a.m. on 30 August 2022 at the TCIL southern regional office, Hyderabad, Telangana.

Mandala artefacts (handmade)**

Gurdeep Kaur (b. 24 May 1981) from Delhi, has the largest collection of handmade mandala artworks on different materials including wine glasses, glass bottles, mugs, stones and ivory sheets. She started creating the items on 14 July 2020, and by 14 September 2021, she had completed 208 such mandala artifacts.

Wedding envelopes

V. Aishwarya Lakshmi (b. 3 December 2004) from Ramanathapuram, Tamil Nadu, has 535 unique wedding gift envelopes, a collection started in June 2021. On 3 December 2021, she exhibited her collection from 11:00 a.m. to 12:30 p.m. at the Collectorate, Ramanathapuram, Tamil Nadu.

The first coloured souvenir coins on the Panchatantra were released by Finance Minister Nirmala Sitharaman on the 17th foundation day of the Security Printing and Minting Corporation of India Ltd.

Manish Kumar Dhameja: largest collection of credit cards

** This is a one-time category. Further and future claims for this category will not be accepted.

BUTTERFLY FRENZY

Hardik Bhammar (b. 3 December 1985) from Bolangir, Odisha, has 6,055 items featuring butterflies, the largest such collection, which he started around 2018. His collection has phillumeny (match-related items), fusilately (phone cards or calling cards), cartophily (cigarette cards), vitolphilia (cigar bands), tea cards, philately (stamps, postcards, envelopes, first-day covers, special covers, postal stationery), and many other such items.

Obituaries – from a single family

Ninad Jadhav (b. 11 July 1977) from Chhindwara, Madhya Pradesh, has the most obituary news clippings of the Kapoor family (of Hindi cinema) from 272 multi-language newspapers. The obituaries are of Shammi Kapoor (111), Shashi Kapoor (68), Rishi Kapoor (19) and Kapoor (74).

Cinema press booklets – on a single personality

Ninad Jadhav (b. 11 July 1977) from Chhindwara, Madhya Pradesh, has a collection of 105 cinema press booklets on actor Mithun Chakraborty. The oldest booklet is of the film *Mera Rakshak* released in 1978.

Autographs of Ajit Laxman Wadekar

Satish Laxman Chaphekar (b. 5 February 1957) from Dombivli, Maharashtra, has 39 autographs of the late cricketer Ajit Laxman Wadekar, who played 39 international matches during his career including 37 Tests and two ODIs. Satish collected Wadekar's signature on various objects like photographs, bats, balls and gloves, among others.

Magazines – Hindi

Dr Jawahar Karnavat (b. 12 August 1959) from Bhopal, Madhya Pradesh, has 93 Hindi magazines, a collection started in 2002. The oldest magazine in his collection is the *Indian Opinion* published in 1903 in South Africa in Gujarati, Tamil, English and Hindi. In all, there are 25 weekly, three fortnightly, 40 monthly, 18 quarterly and seven half-yearly magazines. The Deepawali special issue of *Shanti Doot* published from Fiji contains as many as 120 pages.

Above: Cinema press booklets on a single personality; *Below*: Autographs of Ajit Laxman Wadekar

Seer (Indian weights)

Ranjeet Kumar Jha (b. 26 January 1989) from Bhopal, Madhya Pradesh, has a collection of 250 'seer' or 'ser', old Indian weighing scales in various shapes from different Indian princely states like Bhopal, Gwalior, Mewar, Agra, Rajkot and Indore. In total there are 25 kinds of seer. The scales carry different state seals with different values in different languages.

Dot portraits (handmade)**

Biman Das (b. 15 December 1981) from Howrah, West Bengal, has been drawing dot portraits of famous personalities who dedicated their lives for the well-being of humanity, since 2004. Using a crowquill nib and gel, he has made all 177 dot paintings in 8 in. x 6 in. frames.

** This is a one-time category. Further and future claims for this category will not be accepted.

Origami butterfly (handmade)**
Nidhi Bansal (b. 6 June 1989) from Fatehgarh Sahib, Punjab, has a collection of 750 origami butterflies. Starting with a 2 cm paper square, she made butterflies measuring 1 cm in size in various colours. It took her a total of 60 hrs from April 2020 to May 2021 to create this collection.

Soap covers of a single brand

Soap covers – single brand
Mohanan Vareeth Vattapparuthayl (b. 25 May 1972) from Eranakulam, Kerala, who has been using only Medimix brand soap at home, started a collection of the soap covers in 1994. Since then he has collected as many as 1,300 soap covers up of that single brand till 10 December 2021.

Maps
Ravindranath Vishnu Newadkar (b. 22 August 1960) from Thane, Maharashtra, has a collection of 365 maps up to 31 May 2022. These include 100 maps of various countries and 265 maps of different cities.

Magazine posters – *Sportstar* magazine**
Shabbir Salam (b. 6 September 1977) from Noida, Uttar Pradesh, has a collection of 1,420 unduplicated posters from *Sportstar* magazine up to 11 May 2022. The collection includes posters featuring sportspersons such as Martina Hingis, Leander Paes, Ken Doherty and Michael Jordon, among others.

Maps

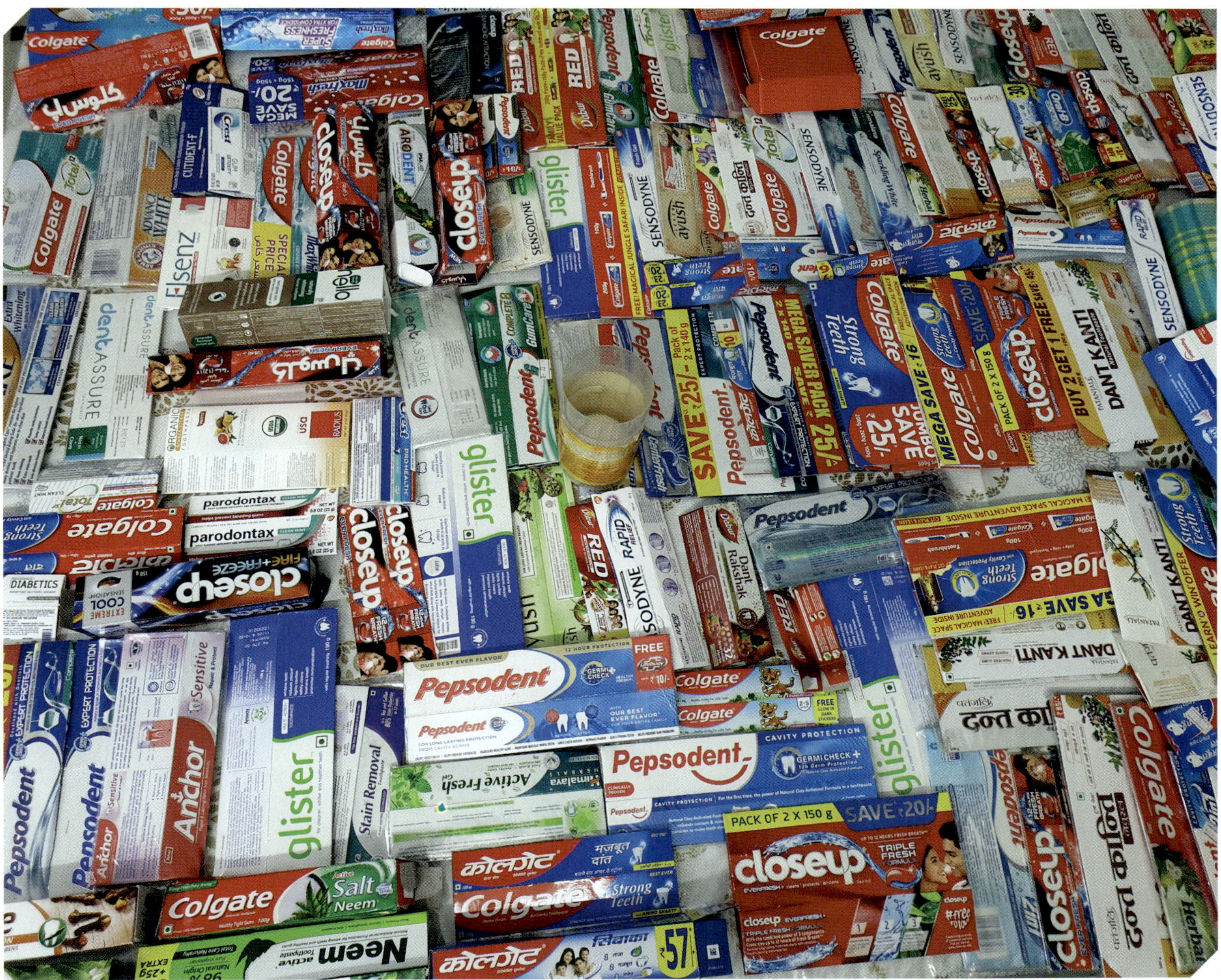

Toothpaste wrappers

Newspaper clippings – featuring Lata Mangeshkar

Gaurav Sharma (b. 24 November 1980) and Manju Lata Sharma (b. 5 June 1947) have collected 11,505 news clippings on the late singer Lata Mangeshkar. The oldest press clipping dates back to 1955. There are various original press articles on her from 1959 onwards in various languages – Hindi, Marathi, Odia, Bangla, Gujarati, Konkani, Tamil, Telugu, Assamese, Malayalam, Punjabi, Urdu and English. There are also original newspaper articles on her from Finland, the UK and Bangladesh.

Newspaper clippings – featuring Mahatma Gandhi

Shiju Thomas (b. 25 February 1976) from Bengaluru, Karnataka, has a collection of 860 news clippings on Mahatma Gandhi in various Indian languages.

Toothpaste wrappers

Mankeerat Kaur (b.11 October 2006) from Gurgaon, Haryana, has toothpaste wrappers from different countries, a collection started in April 2020. She has 178 unduplicated toothpaste wrappers from India, the UAE and the USA. Her complete collection comprises 204 wrappers.

Pradhan Mantri Yojana matchboxes

Alok Mehrotra (b. 16 October 1970) from Kanpur, Uttar Pradesh, has a collection of 1,550 matchboxes of 21 Pradhan Mantri Yojanas including the Awas Yojana, the Amrit Kosh Yojana, the Garib Kalyan Yojana, the Sukanya Samriddhi Yojana, the Namami Gange programme, the Swaach Bharat Mission, the Aarogya Yojna, the National Sports Talent Yojana, the Umang Yojana, the Jal Shakti Yojana and the Gold Yojana, among others. He started his collection in 2019.

Headgear

Ananta N. Joshi (b. 20 February 1968) from Kalyan, Maharashtra, has a collection of caps, turbans, armour and shields, a hobby started in August 1975. By 31 May 2022, his collection had grown to 2,930 headgear items.

200 items from a fine silver collection from Denmark and India will be jointly exhibited at the National Museum in New Delhi in March 2023.

** This is a one-time category. Further and future claims for this category will not be accepted.

Railway canteen coupons – ending with 786**

N. Krishnamoorthy (b. 14 October 1961) from Mumbai, Maharashtra, an employee of the Central Railway Matunga Workshop, has 180 railway canteen coupons ending with the number 786, a collection started in 2002.

Badges – political theme

Ranjeet Kumar Jha (b. 26 January 1989) from Bhopal, Madhya Pradesh, has 250 political badges of different years, shapes, sizes, material and logos of political parties, such as the Congress, BJP, BSP and AAP, among others, in his collection, which was started on 9 April 2003 and completed on 9 April 2021.

Antique matchbox labels – uncut sheets

Samirkumar Hasmukhbhai Arya (b. 16 December 1977) from Valsad, Gujarat, has a collection of 225 uncut antique matchbox labels.

Above: Badges – political theme

Below: Antique matchbox labels – uncut sheets

Coins – Covid-19 theme

CURRENCY, COINS AND STAMPS

Currency notes – denomination 100 and above

Sreehari Vishnu G. (b. 11 October 1996) from Alappuzha, Kerala, has 150 high-denomination currency notes from 100 to 100 trillion – from 53 countries, a collection made over 12 years. He displayed his collection of these high-denomination currency at an exhibition on 9 April 2021 at Gowri Resorts, Alappuzha.

Currency notes from most countries – denomination 1,000

Anup Kumar Gupta (b. 2 July 1980) from Bilaspur, Chhattisgarh, has currency notes of denomination 1,000 from 85 countries, a collection since 1 August 2021.

Commemorative currency notes – from most countries

Mitesh Dilipkumar Dave (b. 20 March 1989) from Morbi, Gujarat, has commemorative currency notes from 155 countries, a collection started in 1999.

Inset currency notes issued by the Reserve Bank of India (RBI)

Surender Kumar Saini (b. 19 July 1967) from Kaithal, Haryana, has 3,322 different inset currency notes issued by the RBI from 1950–2020, a collection of over 50 years. The amount of the currency note collection adds up to ₹2,80,852. The RBI governors who signed them were Sir B. Rama Rau, H.V.R. Iyengar, P.C. Bhattacharya, L.K. Jha, B.N. Adarkar, S. Jagannathan, K.R. Puri, M. Narasimham, I.G. Patel, Dr Manmohan Singh, Amitav Ghosh, R.N. Malhotra, S. Venkitaramanan, Dr C. Rangarajan and Dr Bimal Jalan.

Coins of denomination 1 – unduplicated

Monika Jain (b. 7 November 1984) from Gurugram, Haryana, has a collection of 169 different coins of denomination 1 issued by the RBI and the pre-independence British government, up to May 2022.

Coins – Definitive series

Rikha Indrapraksh Upadhyay (b.16 December 1998) from Mumbai, Maharashtra, has a collection of 1,087 different mint-wise and year-wise arranged definitive coins of the Republic of India.

Coins – Experimental

Ravikumar K.S. (b. 27 March 1978) from Chennai, Tamil Nadu, collects coins minted by the Indian government for experimental purposes. Since they minted only a few experimental coins, the collection is rare. These coins have EXP or EXPT stamped on the coin. He has seven experimental coins: three ₹5 coins from the Mumbai mint (featuring the Dandi march) ; two ₹1 coins from Calcutta; one ₹1 coin from the Mumbai mint; and one ₹2 coin from the Hyderabad mint.

Coins – Covid-19 theme

Pusta Krishna Kameswar (b. 1 August 1977) from Amalapuram, Andhra Pradesh, collected 18 coins from 15 countries – Australia, Egypt, France, Gibraltar, Hungary, Israel, Italy, Lithuania, Malta, Niue, Russia, Samoa, San Marino, Transnistria, Ukraine – one coin each from 12 countries and two coins each from three countries on the Covid-19 theme, released in 2020 and 2021.

Coins – environmental themes

Parvathina Venkata Narayana (b. 1 July 1971) from Yeditha, Andhra Pradesh, a teacher by profession, has a collection of coins on environmental themes since 2001. He has 613 coins from 145 countries in his collection. Every coin in this theme features at least one tree. The coins have captions like 'Protect Our World', 'Save the Environment', 'Forestry for Development', 'Forestry of Prosperity', 'Biodiversity', 'For a Better Environment', 'Preserve Planet Earth', 'Water for life' 'Endangered Animal Species' and many more in English and other foreign languages.

Coins – most denominations**

Late Bhudev Prakash had a collection of all 28 denominations – 1 paisa, 2 paisa, 3 paisa, ½ anna, 1 anna, 2 anna, one quarter anna, 12 anna , 5 paisa, 10 paisa, 20 paisa, 25 paisa, 50 paisa, 1 rupee, 2 rupee, 5 rupee, 10 rupee, 20 rupee, 50 rupee, 60 rupee, 75 rupee, 100 rupee, 125 rupee, 150 rupee, 200 rupee, 250 rupee, 350 rupee and 1000 rupee. At present, the coin collection is with Bhudev's wife Veena Devi and daughter Meenakshi Garg.

2004

The Reserve Bank of India (RBI) Monetary Museum was established in Mumbai, Maharashtra.

** This is a one-time category. Further and future claims for this category will not be accepted.

Coins – Indian from foreign mints

Ravikumar K.S. (b. 27 March 1978) from Chennai, Tamil Nadu, has 21 Indian coins issued from foreign mints. The collection has 19 foreign mint coins issued between 1985 and 2000 from the Royal Canadian Mint, Canada; the Heaton Press Mint, UK; the British Royal Mint Llantrisant, UK; the Taegu Mint, Korea; Oeschger Maslach and Co, Mexico City Mint, Mexico; the Kremnica Mint, Slovak Republic; the Seoul Mint, South Korea,; the Pretoria Mint, South Africa, the Tower Mint, UK; the Moscow Mint, Russia; and two foreign mint rare error coins from the Moscow Mint, Russia.

Most sets of Indian coins from foreign mints

Dr Vijay Naithani (b. 8 February 1974) from Panchkula, Haryana, has 100 complete sets of Indian coins that were minted in 10 foreign mints between 1985 and 2001 in various denominations: Canada – 4, Slovakia – 4, South Korea – 3, Russia – 3, the United Kingdom – 3, Mexico – 1 and South Africa – 1.

Coins from most countries – featuring images of horse riders***

Dina Nath (b. 19 July 1947) from Delhi has a collection of coins featuring images of horse riders from 50 countries. These include images of Queen Elizabeth II on horseback on her coronation, and wedding anniversaries; army generals; warriors and other riders on horseback in war scenes; victory processions; and equestrian sports.

Commemorative coins

Rikha Indraprakash Upadhyay (b. 16 December 1998) from Mumbai, Maharashtra, has a collection of the complete mint-wise and year-wise collection of all 406 different commemorative coins of the Indian Republic.

Commemorative coins – ₹2

Ravikumar K. S. (b. 27 March 1978) from Chennai, Tamil Nadu, has a collection of 60 unduplicated commemorative coins of denomination 2. This includes 55 mint-wise coins, four error and one non-circulation coin.

Commemorative coins – ₹5

Ravikumar K.S. (b. 27 March 1978) from Chennai, Tamil Nadu, has 175 unduplicated commemorative coins of denomination 5 from the Republic of India by mint-wise, error and Mule coin, a collection started in 2010. The first coin in his collection is of former prime minister Indira Gandhi in 1985 and the latest was of south Indian actor and politician MGR (Maruthur Gopalan Ramachandran) in 2019. The collection includes the rare Tilak design error coin; and the extremely rare 1996 Crop Science Congress coin and 1991 Commonwealth and Tourism Year coin, among others.

Commemorative coins – ₹100

Ashish Rajesh Ramrakhiani (b. 19 June 1988) from Thane, Maharashtra, has 68 commemorative coins of ₹100 issued by different mints between 1980 and 2020.

A–Z: Special covers

Ninad Jadhav (b. 11 July 1977) from Chhindwara, Madhya Pradesh, has an alphabetical collection of 421 special covers released by the Department of Posts. The covers have themes such as Indian mythology, sports,

26 stamps were issued by India Post in 2022 up to November.

A–Z special covers

*** This record is featured from an earlier edition, with modifications.

Philatelic material – literature theme

Dr Upender Vennam (b. 14 December 1971) from Hyderabad, Telangana, a passionate philatelist since many years, has 1,073 items of philatelic material from 100 countries exclusively on famous poets, writers and authors, including all Nobel laureates in literature up to 2017 along with a few Jnanpith Award winners.

Indian Railways, Indian cinema, and famous personalities such as Swami Vivekananda, Subhas Chandra Bose and many more.

Postage stamps

Dr Jawahar Verhomai Israni (b. 22 August 1943) from Delhi has the largest collection of 51,682 postage stamps, all singles, from 245 countries. He has held regular exhibitions of his postage stamp collection in various places – including schools, colleges, offices and factories – for many years. The collection has different themes such as leaders, colleges, poets, statues, sculptures, dances, birds, animals, cats, butterflies, ships and dams, among others.

Philatelic material – Mother Teresa theme

Harbandhu Amarnath Mittal (b. 5 August 1960) from Vadodara, Gujarat, has a collection of 513 philatelic items on Mother Teresa. He has 122 stamps, 184 miniature sheets, 68 first-day covers, special commercial covers, Full sheets/block of 4, Errors and postal stationery from 89 countries as of 13 January 2021.

Stamps – featuring Princess Diana

Stamps – featuring Princess Diana

Vivekanand Devarajan (b. 28 April 1980) from Alampalayan, Tamil Nadu, has 100 stamps featuring Princess Diana totalling 100 from 17 countries. This collection started from 2019.

Stamps from most countries – featuring Mahatma Gandhi

Ajay Garg (b. 1 October 1979) from Dholpur,

19 Philatelic exhibitions were organized in line with the celebrations of India@75 by December 2021.

Philatelic material – Mother Teresa theme

Rajasthan, has a collection of 950 stamps featuring Mahatma Gandhi, from 170 countries.

Stamps – painting theme

Shubham Ghansham Kumawat (b. 20 July 1995) from Ahmednagar, Maharashtra, has a collection of 2,508 stamps of different paintings.

Meghdoot cards

Jaagruthi Nithin Adka (b. 23 October 2005) from Bengaluru, Karnataka, has 1,018 Meghdoot cards which were issued for the first time in 2002 by India Post. These cards are on consumer themes, private company advertisements, entertainment and public awareness. She has an entire rare set of 112 cards in 16 different languages issued in 2008.

Jaagruthi Nithin Adka: largest collection of Meghdoot cards

Stamps from most countries – bird theme

Pushpa Khamesra (b. 19 March 1968) from Udaipur, Rajasthan, had 7,265 postage stamps featuring birds from 354 countries up to 28 December 2021.

Stamps – Cats and Dogs

Vivekanand Devarajan (b. 28 April 1980) from Alampalayan, Tamil Nadu, has the following stamp collections:

Stamps – featuring dogs: He has 529 stamps from 69 countries. The collection has used stamps, unused mint stamps and miniature sheets. The smallest stamp in his collection measures 1.8 cm x 2.3 cm and the longest stamp in his collection measures 3.1 cm x 7.2 cm. This collection started from 2012.

Stamps – featuring cats: He has 274 stamps from 53 countries. The collection includes used stamps, unused mint stamps, and used and unused mint miniature stamps. This collection started in 2014.

Greeting envelopes from India Post – with pre-printed postage stamp

Jaagruthi Nithin Adka (b. 23 October 2005) from Bengaluru, Karnataka, has collected 259 greeting envelopes with pre-printed postage stamps issued by India Post from 2000 till May 2022.

Indian advertising postcards

Dinesh Sharma (b. 29 November 1970) from Ghaziabad, Uttar Pradesh, has the maximum number of advertising postcards, which were displayed in an exhibition, the Canberra Stamp Show 2020 (organized by the Philatelic Society of Canberra, Australia) during 13–15 March 2020. He displayed 290 Indian advertising postcards of 15 paisa, in chronological order from 1975 to 2000.

THIS AND THAT

Most art forms on a saree *pallu***

Rakhi Gupta (b. 12 June 1986) from New Delhi, made a 'saree of unity', depicting 60 art forms from Indian art and culture on a 2.50 m (8 ft 2.45 in.) saree *pallu* over a period of

Most art forms on a saree *pallu*

** This is a one-time category. Further and future claims for this category will not be accepted.

Waistcoat made of square nuts**

Vikas Sikharam (b. 6 July 1992) from Bengaluru, Karnataka, made a waistcoat using 5,468 square nuts supported by silicon ties without any lining. Weighing around 15 kg, the waistcoat measures 69 cm in length and the front and back width was 57 cm each. The total measurement was 114 cm (44 in.). It was made in 30 hrs during 1–31 January 2021.

STACKING IT UP WITH COINS

Shripad Vaidya (b. 5 May 1969) from Nagpur, Maharashtra, holds the record for performing the coin-stacking feats listed below. He does not use glue or adhesive to make these structures of coins.

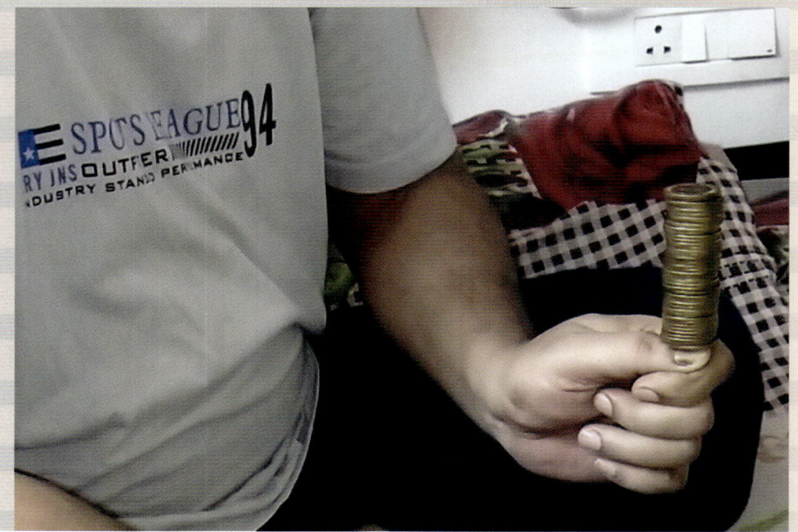

Most ₹10 coins stacked on the thumbnail**

42 coins of ₹10 were stacked on his thumb nail in 3 mins 37 secs on 10 September 2020.

Biggest coin-stacked hollow partially hanging structure**

He made the biggest coin-stacked partially hanging hollow structure with 968 coins, measuring 6 in. in length, 4 in. in width and 5.5 in. in height in 3 hrs on 24 April 2021. He used coins of denomination 1, 2 and 10 for making the structure.

Most ₹10 coins standing vertically to display the word 'Superhuman'**

He used 123 coins for this feat in 3 hrs on 20 September 2020.

Most coins stacked to depict a Ganesha image**

He stacked 1,325 coins to depict an image of Lord Ganesha on 5 October 2020. He used coins of denominations ₹1, ₹2 and ₹5.

Most coins stacked to make the mirror image of the word 'Superhuman'**

He stacked 1,093 coins to depict a mirror image of the word 'Superhuman' in 2 hrs 30 mins on 28 September 2020.

Most coins stacked on the arm to spell 'Superhuman'**

He stacked 84 coins of denomination ₹1 to spell 'Superhuman' in 1 hr on his arm on 14 September 2020.

** This is a one-time category. Further and future claims for this category will not be accepted.

40 days from 25 February to 5 April 2021. Some of the art forms are *alpana* (Bengal), *aari* work (Jammu, Jammu and Kashmir and Gujarat), Thangka (Sikkim), *shamilami* art (Manipur) Sanganeri block art (Rajasthan), *phulkari* (Punjab), mirror work (Gujarat), *kasuti* (Karnataka), and *manjusha* art (Bihar).

Currency related to movie stars**

Himanshu Tiwari (b. 4 October 2000) from Sonipat, Haryana, has Indian currency notes that depict the Bollywood history of actor Amitabh Bachchan from the first to his 221st movie and of actor Akshay Kumar from the first to his 132nd movies. Serial numbers of movies, release dates of movies, age of Bachchan and Kumar in movies and all important dates are portrayed by serial numbers on currency notes of denomination 10. His total collection is of 42,000 currency notes and was started in 2016.

Anand S.: most side-jump push-ups – 1 min.

PHYSICAL FEATS

Most full-contact kicks on a kick-pad – alternate legs – 1 hour

Naman Bhardwaj (b. 6 February 2002) from Ghaziabad, Uttar Pradesh, did 6,170 full-contact kicks in 1 hr from 10:20 a.m. to 11:20 a.m. on 26 May 2021 at Vasundhara Taekwondo Academy, Ghaziabad, Uttar Pradesh.

Most side-jump push-ups – 1 minute

Anand S. (b. 18 May 1993) from Chennai, Tamil Nadu, performed 42 side-jump push-ups in 1 min. from 1:00 p.m. to 1:01 p.m. on 20 October 2021.

Most superman push-ups – 1 minute

Kuwar Amritbir Singh (b. 4 November 2001) from Gurdaspur, Punjab, performed 52 superman push-ups in 1 min. from 12:05 p.m. to 12:06 p.m. on 5 May 2021.

Naman Bhardwaj: most full-contact kicks on a kick-pad

*** This is a one-time record. Further and future claims for this category will not be accepted.

JACK OF ALL JUMPS!

Here's a look at the existing jumping jack records from previous editions:

	Record category	Record detail
1	Most jumping jacks – 1 minute (men)	127
2	Most jumping jacks – 1 minute (women)	115
3	Most people performing jumping jacks simultaneously	2,988

Most jumping jacks – 1 hour

Jasjeet Singh (b. 21 March 1990) from New Delhi performed 4,479 jumping jacks in 1 hr from 9:12 a.m. to 10:12 a.m. on 17 February 2021.

Jasjeet Singh: most jumping jacks – 1 hour

ONLINE FEATS

Longest conference

The Institute of Green Engineers (IGEN), Chennai, Tamil Nadu, organized the longest conference lasting 16 hrs 46 mins between 7:00 a.m. on 8 August 2020 and 12:05 a.m. on 9 August 2020 on Zoom. The conference was held to celebrate Environment Day and featured speakers from 20 countries.

Most participants in a training/ workshop

The Department of Management Studies, B.K. Birla College of Arts, Science and Commerce, Kalyan, Maharashtra, organized a training session on basic self-defence with 291 participants from 10:15 a.m. to 10:50 a.m. on 8 March 2021 on Microsoft Teams. The session was led by Revati Hunswadkar and the participants were taught three attack kicks, two defence blocks and three punch types.

Longest lesson

Rajashri Sanjay Kabra (b. 21 July 1998) from Washim, Maharashtra, conducted the longest online lesson for 16 hrs 25 mins from 7:45 a.m. to 11:32 p.m. on 5 May 2022. The total break time was 1 hr 10 mins. The event was conducted on Google Meet from Deogiri College, Aurangabad, Maharashtra. The lesson was on Physics and targeted topics for preparation for competitive exams such as BARC, IIT, JAM, GIS, CSIRNET and TIFR, among others.

Most people cooking together

Kamlesh Ashok Salve (b. 25 February 1980) from Mumbai, Maharashtra, organized an event with 1,165 participants cooking together. The event was held on Zoom from 11:00 a.m. to 11:45 a.m. on 15 August 2020.

Top and *right*: most people cooking together

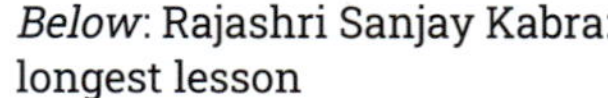

Below: Rajashri Sanjay Kabra: longest lesson

Most toys donated – single day

Children's University, Gandhinagar, Gujarat, has donated 5,100 toys on a single day, 12 May 2022, on its campus between 9:00 a.m. and 11:00 a.m. The toys were distributed to eight organizations and schools, as well as NGOs working with children. The donation drive was organized by the University's Departments of Toy Innovations and Social Work, and around 30 people participated in the drive.

Most people doing the hula hoop together

Youth Zone Dance Academy, Mumbai, Maharashtra, conducted an online session with 110 participants doing the hula-hoop together for 2 mins on 25 October 2020 on Zoom.

Longest seminar

Dr Geetha Challa (b. 28 June 1971) from Hyderabad, Telangana, conducted an online seminar from 7:00 a.m. to 8:45 p.m. on 10 October 2020 with 140 participants. The seminar lasted for 12 hrs 19 mins with a total break time of 1 hr 26 mins. The seminar was on the effects of COVID- 19 on mental health and coping mechanisms for the same.

Most people doing the hula hoop together

COMMUNITY DEVELOPMENT

Most benches donated – 1 year

The Ghanshyamdas Saraf Trust, a charitable trust in Mumbai, Maharashtra, donated 127 three-seater RCC pink benches to temples and police stations in and around Mumbai, between July 2021 and July 2022. A team of eight people were employed in making the benches and it took a week to make 20 benches.

Most ramps constructed – single day

J.K. Cement Ltd, Uttar Pradesh, set a record by constructing 249 cemented ramps for the specially-abled on 5 August 2021 at different government schools around Jaipur, Rajasthan. The ramps were constructed by around 2,000 people working under the guidance of civil engineers and contractors. The ramps were constructed for government schools of Jotwara City and Rural and Sanganer City and Rural.

Longest distance covered for awareness – geared bicycle – solo

Srinivasan B. (b. 28 December 1975) from Chennai, Tamil Nadu, covered 3,677 km in 14 days 3 hrs from 6:20 a.m. on 12 February 2022 to 9:21 a.m. on 26 February 2022 on the Kashmir to Kanniyakumari route. He began his ride from Ghanta Ghar, Srinagar, Jammu and Kashmir, and ended it at Kanniyakumari Beach, Kanniyakumari. His ride was to raise awareness against plastic bag usage and promotion of cycling to reduce pollution. He carried a placard with the message, 'Avoid Plastic Bags Usage' on his bicycle and conversed with motorists and general public en route to create awareness.

Longest ride for awareness by differently abled riders – retrofitted scooters – group

Ameer Siddiqui (b. 13 January 1980), founder of the Eagle Specially Abled Riders, Delhi, coordinated and led a 3,500 km ride on retrofitted scooters from India Gate in Delhi to the Gateway of India in Mumbai and back to India Gate from 1 October to 15 October 2019. There were 16 differently abled participants in this longest awareness ride on the importance of education for the differently abled. They travelled through 34 cities of seven states, viz, Delhi, Haryana, Rajasthan, Gujarat, Maharashtra, Madhya Pradesh and Uttar Pradesh.

As per the Edelgive Hurun India Philanthrophy List 2022, industrialist Shiv Nadar is the 'most generous' and donates ₹3 crore a day!

Longest seminar

STRUCTURES

EARLY TIMES

Earliest structures

The oldest structures excavated in Koldihwa in Allahabad (now Prayagraj) District, Uttar Pradesh, date to the first half of the seventh millennium BCE. Archaeological evidence has indicated that the site had circular huts made of timber posts and thatch, and a cattle pen.

Earliest village settlement

A 4,000 -year-old village settlement of the Chalcolithic period (Copper Age), along with remnants of subsequent Iron Age occupation, was unearthed at Balathal near Udaipur, Rajasthan. It included a massive mud rampart. It is the oldest village settlement in India outside of Harappan sites.

First architect

Maha Govinda, mentioned in the Buddhist work *Dhammapada*, is the first architect on record, who designed many north Indian cities in the fifth century BCE. Another treatise on housing architecture from the same period is the *Mayamata*, authored by the 'divine' architect Maya.

Earliest extensive drainage system

The Harappan towns of Lothal in Gujarat and Mohenjo-daro (now in Pakistan) , with rectangular houses, chessboard streets, brick-lined bathrooms, drainage pipes and cesspits, are unique in the ancient world. The toilets were flushed with water chutes carrying dirty water away to covered street drains. The main sewer, about 1.5 m (4 ft 11 in.) deep and 91 cm (2 ft 11 .8 in.) across, connected to north-south and east-west sewers.

Oldest known dockyard

Harappan civilization ruins include the oldest dockyard at Lothal in Gujarat. Built in 2300 BCE, it was about 16 km from the nearest port. A broad mud-brick embankment, almost 20 m (65 ft 7 in.) wide, surrounds a settlement 230 m x 170 m (754 ft 7 in. x 557 ft 9 in.) with an entrance to the south. The dock measures 218 m x 37 m (715 ft 3 in. x 121 ft 5 in.). It bears testimony to the knowledge of the Harappans as boats docked at Lothal till the 1850s.

Earliest known fortified city

The remains of rubble masonry and mud bricks, excavated at the Harappan site of Kalibangan in Rajasthan, have been dated to 3000–2500 BCE. These excavations show that Kalibangan was a fortified city with a stone

A brick-lined burial site at Rakhigarhi, Haryana

Rakhigarhi: The Harappan Civilization Highlighted Again

The ancient Harappan Civilization never stops being in the news! This time round, the Archaeological Survey of India (ASI), during an excavation at the 32-year-old Rakhigarhi site in Haryana, found an advanced drainage system, wide roads and multi-storey residential buildings, not to forget what is considered to be a jewellery-making unit! They also discovered graveyard sites with around 60 burial grounds, terracotta toys, clay seals and pots. Rakhigarhi has gained in importance as a source of information about this incredible civilization, as other key sites such as Harappa and Mohenjo-daro are now part of Pakistan. Giving a nod to its significance, Union Finance Minister Nirmala Sitharaman mentioned in her 2020 budget speech that all Harappan excavation sites will house an 'on-site' museum to showcase India's ancient legacy and cultural heritage.

Lothal, Gujarat: oldest known dockyard

The Indus Valley Civilization was first identified in 1921 at Harappa in the Punjab region and in 1922 at Mohenjo-daro, near the River Indus in the Sindh region. Both sites are now in Pakistan.

citadel, and surrounded by a massive rampart of mud bricks.

Earliest *stambha*

The oldest surviving examples of the *stambha* or pillar belong to the period of Emperor Ashoka (r. c. 268 to 232 BCE). The best known is the pillar and its edict at Sarnath near Varanasi, Uttar Pradesh, ordered by him 26 years after his coronation, to convey the teachings of the Buddhist scriptures.

Earliest open-air theatre

The third century BCE brick structure at Nagarjunakonda in Guntur District, Andhra Pradesh – similar to ancient Greek and Roman amphitheatres – has a pit with tiers on all four sides, which could seat at least 1,000 spectators. It encloses a rectangular room of 16.5 m x 13.7 m (54 ft 1.5 in. x 44 ft 11.4 in.). The structure has good acoustic properties.

First known example of ancient hydraulic engineering

A first century BCE site in Singraur (Sringaverapura) near Allahabad (now Prayagraj), Uttar Pradesh, revealed the remains of a large rectangular brick tank, a unique example of ancient hydraulic engineering. Water from the River Ganga was brought through a feeding channel into a silting chamber, from which clean water flowed into a main tank.

Oldest rust-free iron pillar

The iron pillar in the Qutub (Minar) complex in Delhi has stood strong since the fifth century CE when it was erected by King Chandra Varman. A solid iron shaft, 7.32 m (24 ft) high, it has six lines in Sanskrit inscribed on it.

Oldest palace site excavated

Kumrahar in Patna, Bihar, dating to 250 BCE, is said to be one of Emperor Ashoka's palaces. The remains of the columns at the site indicate that the palace had an 84-pillar hall, originally made of wood.

Oldest man-made lake

Sudarshan Lake at the foot of Girnar Hills in Junagadh District, Gujarat, was built during the reign of Chandragupta Maurya (c. 321–297 BCE), according to the epigraph engraved on the Ashokan pillar a kilometre from the lake. It was restored by Emperor Ashoka around 273 BCE. Now the lake has shrunk due to silt and debris.

Only swastika-shaped well

A 1,200-year-old well at Thiruvellarai near Manachanallur in Tiruchirappalli District, Tamil Nadu, is shaped like a swastika with steps on four sides. It was dug by Pallava ruler Dantivarman in c. 800 CE. It was later developed and built in the form of a swastika by Alambakathu Vijayanallulan Thambi Kamban Arayan.

Only natural arch

The Silatoranam, a 7.62 m x 3.05 m (25 ft x 10 ft) natural arch at the Tirumala Hills, about 1 km north of the Venkateswara Temple in Tirumala town in Tirupati, Andhra Pradesh, is the only one of its kind in Asia. It is also a notified national geo-heritage monument.

Largest stupa

The great stupa at Sanchi in Madhya Pradesh, built with bricks by Emperor Ashoka between 273 and 232 BCE, was later enlarged and enclosed within another stone stupa. In its present form, the stupa now has a diameter of 37 m (121 ft 5 in.) and a height of 16 m (52 ft 6 in.).

The Sanchi stupa, Madhya Pradesh: largest stupa

Deepest step well
Chand Baori, located at Abhaneri in Dausa District, Jaipur, Rajasthan, is the deepest step well in India, extending to 30 m (98 ft 5 in.) down from the ground. It is also considered to be the largest ancient step well in the country and among the oldest wells in the world. Its oldest parts were constructed in the eighth century by King Chand and the upper storeys were built during the reign of the Mughals in the 18th century. The step well has 13 levels and 3,500 narrow steps. The temperature at the bottom of the well remains 5-6°C lower than the temperature at its surface.

MEDIEVAL AND MODERN ERAS

First garden tomb
The tomb of Sikandar Lodi (r. 1489-1517) of the Lodi dynasty, is located in Lodi Garden near Lodi Road in New Delhi and was built during 1517-18 by his son Ibrahim Lodi.

Earliest known monumental tomb
The Sultan Garhi tomb in Delhi was built over a *garhi* (cave) in 1231 for Prince Nasiruddin Mahmud by his father Iltutmish, the third sultan of the Slave dynasty, who ruled in Delhi (r. 1210-36). The octagonal tomb is like a fortress with a courtyard-like layout, uncommon for a tomb.

Tallest brick minaret
The Qutub Minar in Delhi, made in fluted sandstone carved with verses from the Quran, is 72 m (236 ft) high with 379 steps inside leading to the top. It is a tapering tower of five storeys, with a base diameter of 14.3 m (47 ft), which reduces to 2.74 m (9 ft) at the top. Its construction began under Qutbuddin Aibak in 1193 CE and his successor Iltutmish added three storeys. Firuz Shah Tughlaq completed the last storey in 1383 CE.

Longest corridor
The corridor in the Ramanathaswamy Temple in Rameswaram, Tamil Nadu, which is dated to the 17th century, is 1,220 m (4,002 ft) long. Though it has 1,212 sculpted and painted pillars, it is popularly known as the 'corridor with a thousand pillars'.

WR Largest corbelled cornice dome
The Gol Gumbaz, built in 1659 in the tomb complex of the Adil Shahi sultans at Bijapur in Karnataka, features a dome that measures 42 m (137 ft 9.5 in.) in diameter. Its corbelled cornice (the ornamental projection that crowns a building) projects more than 3 m (9 ft 10 in.). The dome is the largest of its kind in the world.

Largest silver article
A 1.8 m (5 ft 11 in.) tall silver jug at the City Palace in Jaipur, Rajasthan, was made for the maharaja of Jaipur to store drinking water during his visit to England in 1901 for the coronation of King Edward VII.

Largest vaulted hall
The Bara Imambara in Lucknow, Uttar Pradesh, is not only India's but also Asia's largest hall without any external support of wood, iron or stone beams. The hall measures 49.4 m x 16.2 m (162 ft x 53 ft 2 in.). The ceiling is more than 15 m (49 ft 2.5 in.) high.

Largest bas-relief
The 'Descent of the Ganga' bas-relief, also known as 'Arjuna's Penance', in Mamallapuram

A night view of the Dashashwamedh Ghat, Varanasi

Kashi Vishwanath Corridor: The New Path of Faith
Thousands of pilgrims throng Varanasi, Uttar Pradesh, one of the oldest continuously inhabited cities in India, with a religious, educational and cultural history going back many millennia. The Kashi Vishwanath Corridor project aims to facilitate the thousands of pilgrims who visit the city's temples and ghats by easing their movement through the congested areas of the holy town, especially from the revered Kashi Vishwanath Temple, one of the 12 main Jyotirlingas, to the ghats of the River Ganga. Under the project, which is estimated to cost over ₹800 crore, more than 300 properties have been acquired and around 1,400 owners rehabilitated. During the first phase of the project, over 40 ancient temples were rediscovered and restored. The plan envisages 23 buildings including a tourist facilitation centre, a Vedic Kendra, a Mumukshu Bhavan (for those desiring salvation), a Bhogshala, a city museum, a viewing gallery and a food court, along with wider and cleaner pathways, better street lighting and other amenities.

'Arjuna's Penance' or the 'Descent of the Ganga', Mamallapuram, Tamil Nadu: largest bas-relief

in Chengalpattu District, Tamil Nadu, is 27 m (88 ft 7 in.) long and 9 m (29 ft 6 in.) high. Created during the Pallava period in the seventh century CE, it features over 30 large and small sculptures of animals, humans, sages and gods.

There are 3,693 centrally protected monuments/sites under the ASI in India. Uttar Pradesh (745), Karnataka (506) and Tamil Nadu (413) have the highest number of sites maintained by the ASI.

Largest maze

The Bhul-bhulaiya, which is a set of passages on the top terrace of the Bara Imambara building in Lucknow, Uttar Pradesh, is a labyrinth of over 1,000 interconnected passages that can be approached through a narrow flight of steps but seem to lead nowhere. These passages reduced the load on the walls, which support the massive 4.88 m (16 ft) thick roof with an estimated weight of about 20,000 tonnes.

Oldest known British inscription

The Fort St George cemetery in Chennai, Tamil Nadu, has a tombstone reportedly belonging to one Elizabeth Baker, dating back to 1632.

FORTS AND PALACES

Oldest fort

The Kalinjar Fort in Banda District of Uttar Pradesh has several temples dating to the rule of the Gupta dynasty from the third to the fifth centuries. Built on a hill at one end of the Vindhya mountain range, at 367 m (1,204 ft), this enduring fort was used by several of the ruling dynasties of Bundelkhand, including the Chandela dynasty of Rajputs in the 10th century, and the Solankis of Rewa.

Fort on three hills

Gingee Fort, located about 100 km from Chennai, Tamil Nadu, is built on three hills – Krishnagiri, Chandragiri and Rajagiri – forming a triangle. Together they form a fort complex, each with its own citadel. The fort walls are 13 km long and the three hills are connected by walls enclosing an area of around 11 sq. km. Built by the Konar dynasty in 1190 CE, the fort was then improved upon by the Cholas and subsequently modified in Vijayanagara times.

Oldest extant marble structure

The white marble structure over Hoshang Shah Ghori's tomb, built by his son, at Mandu, Dhar District, Madhya Pradesh, is the oldest extant marble structure known.

WR Fort with largest metal ordnance

The Bijapur Fort in Bijapur District, Karnataka, houses the famous bell-metal cannon Malik-e-Maidan ('lord of the battlefield'), the largest piece of medieval bell-metal ordnance, which is 4.45 m (14 ft 7 in.) long, with a diameter of 1.5 m (4 ft 11 in.). It weighs 55 tonnes and has a bore of 0.71 m (2 ft 4 in.) from which an iron ball of over a tonne could be fired.

Only fort with a tiger reserve

The 'forest fort' of Ranthambore, a classical *vana durg*, is located in Ranthambore National Park, Sawai Madhopur District, Rajasthan. Built between 944 and 1110 CE by a Chauhan ruler whose name is disputed, it towers over the park from atop a hill.

Only 'palace' with just a facade wall
Hawa Mahal ('the palace of winds') in Jaipur, Rajasthan, has a facade built on to a wall of the main palace compound. Royal ladies seated in its 953 niches and windows could look down at the street below.

Only palace with a bird sanctuary
The Bharatpur Palace in Rajasthan houses the Keoladeo National Park (earlier Bharatpur Bird Sanctuary) within its site. It is the only nature reserve in India whose owner, the maharaja of Bharatpur, augmented the water supply in 1760 with an irrigation canal to create the habitat that became a stopover for the migratory Siberian crane. It was converted into a bird sanctuary in 1956 and a national park in 1981.

Only surviving mud fort
Gaur citadel in Malda District, West Bengal, once led into a *mahi durg* (mud fort) of dynasties including the Guptas and the Palas. Its ramparts – which are 9.65 km (31,660 ft) long, 9.14 m (30 ft) high and 54.86 m (180 ft) thick at the base – are now in ruins. It was once hidden by a dense jungle.

Only undefeated marine fort
Janjira Fort is a *jala durg* (sea fort) near Murud Village in Raigad District, Maharashtra. It is the only undefeated fort along the western coast of India, despite attacks by the Dutch and British East India Companies. It was built by Malik Ambar, an Abyssinian minister of the Nizam Shahi dynasty. Built at the end of the 17th century, the fort is almost entirely intact.

Palace with the largest chandelier
The durbar hall of Jai Vilas Mahal of Gwalior, Madhya Pradesh, has two chandeliers, each 12.5 m (41 ft) high and weighing 3.5 tonnes. It is said that three (or eight!) elephants were hoisted to the roof (or suspended from it!) to make sure it would withstand the weight of the chandeliers.

Highest gateway
Buland Darwaza, the highest gateway in India, is 53.5 m (175 ft 6 in.) high. It was built by Mughal emperor Akbar (r. 1550–1605) at Fatehpur Sikri, about 40 km from Agra in Uttar Pradesh, and commemorated his conquest of Ranthambore Fort and Khandesh.

Oldest medieval amphitheatre
The Rang Ghar, about 3 km from Sivasagar in Assam, was built during the reign of Swargadeo Rudra Singha (1696–1714) with bamboo and wood. It was rebuilt in brick by Swargadeo Pramatta Singha during 1744–50. It was the royal sports pavilion where Ahom kings watched cockfights and bullfights.

Longest fortification wall
A 36 km (118,110 ft) long fortification wall was built by Rana Kumbha (r. 1433–68) along the Aravallis in Rajasthan to protect his kingdom of Mewar. It enclosed 34 fortresses. At its widest sections, the wall is 15 m (49 ft) thick, and has stone-brick masonry and decorative flourishes along the top.

Palace with a thousand doors
Hazar Duari ('thousand doors'), the palace of Nizam Humayun Khan (r. 1824–38) in the Kila Nizamat premises in Murshidabad, West Bengal, has 1,000 doors, of which 100 are false. It was designed by the Scottish architect, Duncan McLeod.

The country's largest reclining Buddha statue being built

Bodhgaya's Reclining Buddha Statue
India houses some of the world's tallest and most beautiful statues. To add to the list, a statue of Lord Buddha in the reclining pose is being constructed at Amwan Thokar at Bodhgaya, Bihar, the place of the Buddha's enlightenment and a major hub for Buddhist devotees. Built by Buddha International Welfare Mission (in whose premises it will lie), this statue will be 30.48 m (100 ft) long and 9.1 m (30 ft) high, making it the largest reclining Buddha statue in the country. The length was decided to be 80 ft (for 80 years of the Buddha's life), but the length of the altar made it 100 ft. Work on this colossus started in 2019 and is expected to be complete by early 2023. The statue is being built in fibreglass by the well-known sculptor Mintu Pal and his team of 22 artisans from Kolkata, West Bengal. A reclining Buddha is an important iconographic motif in Buddhism, showing the Buddha lying down on his right side with his head resting on a cushion or his folded right arm, about to enter *parinirvana* following his last illness.

Taj Mahal: Most Visited Monument

The Taj Mahal in Agra, Uttar Pradesh, continued to be the most visited monument in India, raking in over ₹25 crore in financial year (FY) 2022, despite a 73 per cent decrease in revenue compared to FY20 (nearly ₹97 crore) due to COVID-related restrictions. Earnings from the Taj Mahal were over five times more than those from Delhi's Red Fort and 10 times more than those of the Mamallapuram monuments in Tamil Nadu and the Sun Temple in Konark, Odisha. According to official data, the Taj Mahal attracts about 7–8 million visitors annually, with more than 0.8 million from overseas. Given the higher ticket prices for foreign visitors, they make up a larger share of the Taj's earnings. Due to COVID-related restrictions, foreign arrivals had dropped to just about 100,000 in 2021 from over 0.9 million visitors before the pandemic. However, by May 2022, foreign tourist arrivals improved to over 0.4 million, showing a consistent increase from the pandemic lows.

The Taj Mahal continues to mesmerize tourists

Longest time taken to build a mausoleum

The Taj Mahal, one of the Seven Wonders of the World, was built by Mughal emperor Shah Jahan (r. 1627–58 CE) as a mausoleum for his wife Mumtaz Mahal, on the banks of the River Yamuna in Agra, Uttar Pradesh. It took 22,000 workmen 22 years (1631–53) to complete it. It is built on a 29 sq. m (312 sq. ft) marble platform on a sandstone base.

First restoration of a fort

In 1986, Aman Nath, a designer, and Francis Wacziarg, a former French diplomat, along with businessmen O.P. Jain and L. Poddar, bought the 15th-century ruins of the Neemrana Fort, built by local chieftain Nimola Meo, on the Delhi–Jaipur highway. They restored it and opened it as a hotel with 12 rooms in 1991.

RELIGIOUS STRUCTURES

Earliest extant structural temple

A third century BCE circular brick-and-timber shrine excavated at Bairat (now Viratnagar) in Jaipur District, Rajasthan, is considered to be the earliest surviving structural temple. The shrine, with a diameter of 8.23 m (27 ft), was built with lime-plastered panels of brickwork alternating with 26 octagonal wooden pillars. The shrine, portico and a 2 m (6 ft 6.7 in.) wide ambulatory were enclosed in a rectangular compound that measures 305 m x 21 m (1,000 ft 7.8 in. x 68 ft 10.7 in.).

Earliest extant Hindu temples

The Gupta period temples in Sanchi and Tigawa near Jabalpur in Madhya Pradesh belong to the fifth century CE. The Kankali Devi Temple in Tigawa is well preserved.

Earliest mosques

- The Cheraman Jama Masjid in Kodungallur, Thrissur District, Kerala, is said to have been built in 629 CE.
- The Adhai Din Ka Jhonpra in Ajmer District, Rajasthan, was one of the earliest examples of an Indo-Islamic mosque. It was commissioned by (the later Delhi sultan) Qutbuddin Aibak in 1192 CE, on the orders of Muhammad Ghori. It was built reportedly from the remains of dismantled temples, according to the Archaeological Survey of India.

First single-aisle mosque

The Bara Gumbad Mosque, a single-aisle mosque in Delhi's Lodi Garden, was constructed by Sikandar Lodi in 1494 CE.

First revolving minaret

The minaret of the 55-year-old Masjid-e-Chini Ki Burj also known as Chhoti Masjid in Jaipur, Rajasthan, was the first revolving minaret in India. The 10-tonne dome of the 30.5 m (100 ft) high minaret, with a 3 m (9 ft 10 in.) diameter, completed one round in a minute, running on a 1.5 HP motor.

First Baha'i house of worship

The Baha'i house of worship or 'Lotus Temple' in Kalkaji in New Delhi, the first such structure in Asia, is built on 26 acres (10.52 hectares) of land. Built between 1980 and 1986, it is

The Martand Sun Temple,
Jammu and Kashmir

Heritage First

INDIA AT HER BEST 75 YEARS OF INDEPENDENCE

Preserving heritage buildings is a thorny task due to the demand for space by ever increasing and rapid urban development, which expands into historical places and threatens the 300 m peripheral jurisdiction for protected monuments. Keeping this in view, the National Monuments Authority (NMA) has laid down a 101 Heritage By-Laws (HBLs) during the COVID-19 period (from 2019 onwards), which is a record of sorts. These by-laws embrace 126 centrally protected monuments. In the preceding decade, only five HBLs covering 31 centrally protected monuments were finalized.

The NMA was established under the provisions of the Ancient Monuments and Archaeological Sites Remains (AMASR) (Amendment Validation) Act, 2010, and invested with granting permissions to applicants for conservation-related activity in centrally prohibited and regulated areas.

The necessary regulations to protect and preserve monuments are realized in these HBLs by the NMA, which not only communicates them on its website but also welcomes the local population's feedback on the HBL's content. This response is taken into consideration before the HBLs are modified and sent to the Ministry of Culture, and further on to the Parliament for ratification.

Notably, the by-laws were finalized for the 14th century Vishnu Temple in Manipur; Jagannath Temple in Puri; Chausath Yogini Temple, Jabalpur; and the Jagatgrama Ashwamedha site and Lakha Mandal group of Shiva temples in Uttarakhand. As per the last update, draft HBLs were awaited from the ASI for finalization before sending them for approval from the Parliament for monuments such as the Taj Mahal, Agra; Qutub Minar, Delhi; Dwarkadheesh Temple, Dwarka; Hemis Gompa, Leh; and Martand Temple, Anantnag.

designed as a blossoming lotus. The main structure has three folds of nine concrete petals, each covered with Grecian marble. The temple rises to 35 m (114 ft 10 in.) and is surrounded by pools of water.

Oldest extant temple with a shikhara

The earliest known extant temple with a rudimentary shikhara or pinnacle is the Vishnu Dashavatara Temple, belonging to the Gupta period (320-550 CE), at Deogarh in Jhansi District, Uttar Pradesh. It is one of the earliest to draw on the stories of Rama and Krishna to decorate the panels.

Oldest Buddhist monument

A stupa, which was estimated to be 2,500 years old, was excavated in 1898 in Piprahwa in Siddharthnagar District, Uttar Pradesh, by British colonial engineer and landowner W.C. Peppe. The solid brickwork stupa was 7 m (23 ft) high and its cupola measured 35 m (114 ft 10 in.) in diameter. Most of the other surviving stupas are from the reign of Emperor Ashoka (c. 273 to 232 BCE).

Oldest leaning temple

Built in the 17th century by Baliar Singh of the Chauhan dynasty, the 10.6 m (34 ft 9 in.) tall Shiva Temple at Huma, a village on the banks of the River Mahanadi in Sambalpur District, Odisha, leans at an angle of 13.8 degrees. Its smaller shrines, bull pillar and *shivalinga*, all lean at different angles and in different directions.

Oldest *yogini* temple

The Chausath Jogini Temple at Hirapur, around 20 km from Bhubaneswar, Odisha, is the earliest extant *yogini* temple, dated to the ninth century CE. Its inner diameter is 7.6 m (25 ft) and outer circumference is 27 m (88 ft 7 in.). In the middle of the enclosure is a rectangular open *mandapa* 2.8 m x 2.4 m (9 ft 2 in. x 7 ft 10 in.). The niches in the inner enclosure feature images of yoginis and the outer surface has nine images of Katyayani, one of the nine forms of the Hindu goddess Parvati.

Oldest church

St Thomas Syro-Malabar Church, located in Palayoor in the Thrissur District of Kerala, is dated to 52 CE. According to tradition, it was established by St Thomas. It was rebuilt in the 17th century by the Reverend Fenichi. The original altar survives.

Oldest active synagogue

The Paradesi Synagogue in Mattancherry in Kochi, Kerala, was built by the descendants of the European Jews in 1568 CE. The synagogue is also the first one known to be built in a Commonwealth country.

Biggest bathing tank

The Brahma Sarovar at Thanesar in Kurukshetra District, Haryana, is 1,370 m x 762 m (4,495 ft x 2,500 ft) and attracts thousands of pilgrims during solar eclipses. Its ancient water reservoir finds mention in the Mahabharata.

Biggest queue complex

The Vaikuntam queue complex at the Venkateswara Temple complex, Tirumala, Tirupati, Andhra Pradesh, permits the free flow of around 35,000 pilgrims daily. It has a two-tier seating gallery, two corridors and a floor at the ground level with amenities within a semicircular length of 238 m (781 ft). A new complex was added later for *sarvadarshan* or free entry of devotees.

Biggest temple bell

The 110-year-old bronze bell at Tirumala Devaswom, Kochi, Kerala, is more than 1.8 m (5 ft 11 in.) high and weighs over 3 tonnes. The bell is suspended from a huge wooden frame that rests over four massive granite pillars.

Vishnu Dashavatara Temple, Deogarh, Jhansi, Uttar Pradesh: oldest extant temple with a shikhara

Biggest temple lamp

A lamp with 1,000 wicks at the Chettikulangara Devi Temple in Alappuzha District, Kerala, is made of 1,500 kg of gunmetal. It is 3.3 m (10 ft 10 in.) high with 13 tiers like banyan branches. The lowest rung is 2.1 m (6 ft 10.7 in.) in circumference and holds 101 wicks. The topmost is over 1 m wide with 53 wicks.

Only Nataraja temple

The Thillai Nataraja Temple in Chidambaram in Cuddalore District, Tamil Nadu, built by a succession of kings and devotees between the 10th and the 17th centuries CE is unique because Shiva is worshipped here not as a *lingam* but as Nataraja, the Lord of Dance. The temple has four *gopurams* (monumental

The Ancient Monuments and Archaeological Sites and Remains (Amendment) Bill, 2017, was introduced in the Lok Sabha by the minister of tourism and culture, Dr Mahesh Sharma.

The ASI has identified **138** monuments as must-see monuments. Information about them is available at https://asimustsee.nic.in/.

entrance towers) carved with 108 dance postures described in the *Natyashastra*, the ancient Hindu text on the performing arts.

Only rat temple

The 575-year-old temple of Karni Devi (one of the nine incarnations of goddess Durga) has a large number of rats called *kaba*, believed to be the offspring of the presiding deity. Located at Deshnok, 35 km from Bikaner, Rajasthan, this temple is devoted exclusively to the 'holy' rats, which have the run of the place.

Only temple with an apsidal sanctum

The Durga Temple at Aihole in Bagalkot District, Karnataka, is a peripheral structure with a semicircular *garbhagriha* (sanctum sanctorum). The 18 m (59 ft) long and 11 m (36 ft) wide temple has a 7 m (23 ft) verandah. The flat roof, 9 m (29 ft 6 in.) above the ground, is surmounted by a *gopuram*. The temple is built on an earlier Buddhist *chaitya* hall.

Only quadrangular *yogini* temple

The 10th century CE, Chausath Yogini Temple in the famous Khajuraho complex in Madhya Pradesh is the only quadrangular *yogini* temple in the country. Built entirely of coarse granite, the temple stands on a terrace that is 7.6 m (25 ft) high and has peripheral shrines.

Most sculptures in a temple

The Meenakshi Sundareswar Temple in Madurai, Tamil Nadu, has more than 30 million sculptures in its shrines, halls and colonnades. It covers an area of 243 m x 228 m (797 ft x 748 ft).

WR Largest cave temple complex

The cave temples in Ellora in Aurangabad District, Maharashtra, were built between the fifth and 10th centuries CE. There are 12 Buddhist, 17 Hindu and five Jain cave temples and monasteries. The Kailasa or Kailasanatha Temple in cave 16 is the largest single monolithic rock excavation in the world.

Largest sun temple

Built by Narasimha Deva I in 1200 CE, the Sun Temple in Odisha represents a huge chariot with 12 pairs of ornamental wheels, drawn by seven horses rearing up to the east. The original temple consisted of a sanctum sanctorum with a lofty curvilinear shikhara, a 34.14 m (112 ft) long and 38.4 m (126 ft) high *jagmohana* (assembly hall), and a dance hall. Along with many subsidiary structures, the Sun Temple, which is now the largest extant sun temple, was enclosed within a compound wall 264 m (866 ft) long and 165 m (541 ft) wide, with three gates.

Largest collection of temples

There are as many as 1,000 Jain temples and 12,000 idols in the Shatrunjai Hills of Palitana in Bhavnagar District of Gujarat.

Largest church

The 76.2 m x 55 m (250 ft x 180 ft 5 in.) Se Cathedral at Old Goa, around 10 km from Panaji, is the largest in India. It was constructed between 1562 and 1619, and consecrated in 1640. It had two towers, but one collapsed in 1776 and was not rebuilt.

Largest mosque

The Taj-ul-Masjid or Taj-ul-Masajid in Bhopal, Madhya Pradesh, was built by Sultan Shah Jehan Begum between 1868 and 1901. Constructed over decades, the mosque was completed in 1985 by Maulana Sayed Hashmat Ali Sahab and Allama Mohammad Imran Khan Nadwi Azhari. Its name means 'The Crown of

The Se Cathedral, Goa: largest church

INDIA AT HER BEST 75 YEARS OF INDEPENDENCE

SPECTACULAR STATUES

1 Statue of Unity
182 m/597 ft

India's Statue of Unity is the world's tallest statue. It represents Indian freedom movement leader Sardar Vallabhbhai Patel, who led the unification of Indian states after Independence. Situated on the river island Sadhu Bet in Rajpipla in Gujarat, 3.2 km from the Narmada Dam, it was completed in 2018.

3 Lord Hanuman
52 m/171 ft

Built near the River Vamsadhara in Madapam, Andhra Pradesh, this world's tallest statue of Lord Hanuman was completed in 2020.

4 Muthumalai Murugan
44.5 m/146 ft

Consecrated at the Sri Muthumalai Murugan Thirukovil at Puthiragoundampalayam in Attur taluk in Salem District, Tamil Nadu, this statue was completed in 2022.

5 Maa Vaishno Devi
43 m/141 ft

This statue, dating from 2010, is located in Vrindavan, Uttar Pradesh. It is a highlight of the Vaisno Devi Dham temple complex.

2 Statue of Equality
65.8 m/216 ft

The Statue of Equality is the statue of the 11th-century Vaishnavite philosopher and social reformer Ramanuja or Ramanujacharya, situated in Muchintal village in Rangareddy District in Telangana. Built to mark Ramanujacharya's thousandth birth anniversary, it was completed in 2022.

6 Veera Abhaya Anjaneya Hanuman Swami

41 m/135 ft

This beautiful white statue of Lord Hanuman, built in 2003, is located in the town of Paritala, near Vijayawada in Andhra Pradesh.

8 Tathagata Tsal

39 m/128 ft

This 60-tonne copper statue in the Buddha Park of Ravangla (or Tathagata Tsal) in Sikkim is part of the Rabong Monastery complex, and was built between 2006 and 2013, to mark the 2,550th birth anniversary of the Buddha.

9 Dhyana Buddha

38.1 m/125 ft

This meditative Buddha statue is located in Amaravati on the banks of the River Krishna in Guntur District of Andhra Pradesh. Completed in 2015, the statue is decorated with sculptural work from the Amaravati school of art, which flourished in the region from 200 BCE to 200 CE.

7 Thiruvalluvar

40.5 m/133 ft

Thiruvalluvar, who lived between the first century BCE and the sixth century CE, was a Tamil poet and philosopher, who is best known for his legacy work, *Tirukkural*, a collection of couplets on wide-ranging topics such as ethics, politics, economics and love. His statue stands on an island in Kanniyakumari town, where the Bay of Bengal, the Arabian Sea and the Indian Ocean meet. The stone sculpture stands on a 11.5 m pedestal.

10 Padmasambhava

37.5 m/123 ft

The Padmasambhava was a Buddhist master, who is also known as Guru Rinpoche ('the Precious Master') in Tibet. This colossus, located on a mountain above Rewalsar Lake, sacred to Hindus, Sikhs and Buddhists alike, in Mandi District of Himachal Pradesh, was completed in 2012.

Mosques' and it has an interior area of 23,000 sq. m (247,570 sq. ft). The mosque is made of red stone and can accommodate 175,000 worshippers.

Largest synagogue
Located on Moledina Street in Pune, Maharashtra, the Ohel David Synagogue is a 30 m (98 ft 5 in.) high tower, built in the Gothic style with a spire and four giant clocks. Its foundation was laid on 5 November 1863 by David Sassoon, the leader of the Jewish community in Bombay (now Mumbai), Maharashtra, and it was completed in five years. The interior is 19.4 m (63 ft 7.7 in.) long, 13.75 m (45 ft 1 in.) wide and 9.4 m (30 ft 10 in.) high.

Largest monastery
The largest Buddhist monastery in the country, and a functioning one, is located in the city of Tawang in Arunachal Pradesh. The three-storey structure spread over 140 sq. m (1,507 sq. ft) has 65 residential buildings that can house up to 450 lamas. This monastery's Tibetan name – Galden Namgey Lhatse – translates as 'celestial paradise on a clear night'.

Largest *chaitya* hall
The Karla Caves near Lonavala, Maharashtra, house the largest known *chaitya* (Buddhist prayer hall) cave. Its dimensions are 37 m x 14 m x 14 m (121 ft 5 in. x 46 ft x 46 ft).

Heaviest and highest single-stone shikhara
The 80-tonne single-piece granite shikhara atop the Brihadeeswarar Temple at Thanjavur, Tamil Nadu, is the largest and heaviest single-stone object on top of any temple in the world, and is a marvel of engineering. The temple was constructed from 1004 CE, during the reign of Rajaraja Chola, to 1009 CE. It is the world's first temple built with granite. Its vimana (a pyramidal tower built over the central shrine of a temple) is also the highest, at 66 m (216 ft 6 in.).

Only mosque of marble
Moti Masjid, built by Mughal emperor Aurangzeb during 1659–60 CE within the Red Fort in Delhi, is made entirely of marble.

Only shaking minarets
At the Sidi Bashir Mosque in Ahmedabad, Gujarat, the minarets, which are three storeys high and have carved balconies, are known as the *jhulta* or shaking minarets. Dated to 1452 CE, the mosque was built either by Sidi Bashir, a slave of Sultan Ahmed Shah, or by Malik Sarang, a noble in the court of Sultan Mahmud Begada. The shaking of either minaret results in the other minaret vibrating after a few seconds, a fact that was first observed in the 19th century by an Englishman and Sanskrit scholar, Monier M. Williams. One minaret has been partly taken down to prevent it from falling over.

Highest gurdwara
The gurdwara at Hemkund–Lokpal in Chamoli District, Uttarakhand, at a height of 4,328.16 m (14,200 ft) above the mean sea level, finds mention in the Guru Granth Sahib and in Guru Gobind Singh's memoir, *Bachittar* (or *Bichittar*) *Natak*.

Highest monastery
The Tangyud Monastery at Komic Village near Hikkim in Spiti Valley, Himachal Pradesh, is India's highest monastery at an altitude of around 4,572 m (15,000 ft). Built like a fortified castle, it lies on the edge of Kibber Wildlife Sanctuary.

Tallest temple tower
The 13-storey Sri Ranganathaswamy Temple, built between 1982 and 1987 at Srirangam in Tiruchirappalli District, Tamil Nadu, has a 72 m (236 ft) high *rajagopuram* (main gateway).

Tallest church
The Gothic-style Basilica of Our Lady of Dolours, known locally as Puthanpally, is a minor basilica of the Syro-Malabar Catholic Church in Thrissur, Kerala.

The ASI has unearthed a Buddhist monastery, believed to be at least 900 years old, buried in a hilly area of Hazaribagh District of Jharkhand.

Brihadeeswarar Temple, Thanjavur, Tamil Nadu: heaviest and highest single-stone shikhara

The Global Vipassana Pagoda, Gorai, Maharashtra: tallest hollow stone structure

Its construction started in 1929. Its two front towers are 45 m (147 ft 8 in.) tall and the central tower is 79 m (259 ft 2 in.) tall.

WR Tallest hollow stone structure

The Global Vipassana Pagoda at Gorai in Mumbai, Maharashtra, is one of the world's largest structures enshrining the relics of the Buddha, donated by the Sri Lankan government and the Mahabodhi Society, Bodhgaya, Bihar. Inaugurated on 8 February 2009, it contains the largest and tallest pillar-less hollow stone pagoda in the world. The height of the dome is 29 m (95 ft 1.7 in.) and the height of the building is 96.12 m (315 ft 4.2 in.) It took around 11 years and 2.5 million tonnes of stone to complete it.

STATUES AND IDOLS

WR Tallest statue

A 182 m (597 ft) 'Statue of Unity' of Sardar Vallabhbhai Patel, inaugurated on 31 October 2018, stands on Sadhu Bet river island in the River Narmada near Rajpipla, Gujarat. Designed by sculptor Ram V. Sutar, it took nearly four years to build and cost an estimated ₹29.89 billion (2,989 crore).

WR Tallest monolithic statue

The Gommateshwara statue at Shravanabelagola, Karnataka, is the world's tallest monolithic statue. Dedicated to Bahubali and venerated by the Jains, it is 17.37 m (57 ft) high. It was carved from a single block of granite rock and weighs 80 tonnes. It was built between 978 and 993 CE by Chavundaraya, a minister of the Western Ganga dynasty.

WR Largest bird sculpture

Jatayu, the largest bird sculpture in the world, is located at the Jatayu Earth's Center (also known as Jatayu Rock or Jatayu Nature Park) in Chadayamangalam, Kollam, Kerala. The sculpture, conceptualized and built by sculptor and film-maker Rajiv Anchal, is 60.96 m (200 ft) long, 45.72 m (150 ft) wide and 21.33 m (70 ft) high. It houses a digital museum and a multidimensional theatre, making it a 'functional' sculpture.

WR Tallest *shivalinga*

The tallest *shivalinga* in the world was created by Maheswaram Sri Sivaparvathi Temple Trust, Thiruvananthapuram, Kerala. It measures 33.85 m (111 ft) and was constructed in six years and one day between 31 December 2012 and 31 December 2018.

Jatayu Centre, Chadayamangalam, Kerala: largest bird sculpture

WR Tallest Shani Dev statue

The Shani Dev Sewa Samiti, Shani Dham, Jammu, built and installed the world's tallest Shani Dev statue, which is 11.88 m (39 ft) high, including its 1.83 m (6 ft) base, in Jourian Village, Akhnoor District, Jammu and Kashmir. It weighs a round 2,100 kg.

Tallest Ganesha Idol

A 6 m (19 ft 8 in.) high and 3.35 m (11 ft) wide Ganesha, weighing 190 tonnes and carved out of a single block of stone, was installed at the Mundhi Vinayagar Temple at

Puliakulam, Coimbatore District, Tamil Nadu. Its *abhisheka* ritual needs 3 litres of oil and is performed using a ladder.

Tallest Durga structure

Nuruddin Ahmed from Bishnupur Village in Chirang District, Assam, built the tallest Durga structure, measuring 30 m x 14.5 m x 8 m (98 ft 5 in. x 47 ft 7 in. x 26 ft 3 in.), using only bamboo materials (including 5,000 bamboo sticks). No other material was used except cotton cloth as rope. It was made to promote the bamboo sector in Assam.

WR Largest bust

Inaugurated on 24 February 2017, the 34.1 m (112 ft) tall 'Adiyogi' Lord Shiva statue made of steel and located in Coimbatore, Tamil Nadu, at the Isha Yoga Centre, has been funded by the Isha Foundation, founded by Sadhguru Jaggi Vasudev. Built over eight months, the structure weighs a reported 500 tonnes. Its height signifies the 112 chakras in the human system to explore the 112 dimensions of life.

Largest Nandi statue

Nandi is the sacred bull and Lord Shiva's vehicle in Hindu mythology. The Nandi statue, about 200 m (656 ft) from the Veerabhadra Temple at Lepakshi Village in Anantapur District, Andhra Pradesh, is 4.57 m (15 ft) tall and 8.23 m (27 ft) long, and is carved from a single piece of granite.

Largest *shivalinga*

Located in Bhojpur, on the outskirts of the city of Bhopal in Madhya Pradesh, the Bhojeshwar Temple, built by Raja Bhoj (r. 1010–53 CE), houses the largest *shivalinga*, 5.5 m (18 ft) high and 2.5 m (8 ft 2 in.) in circumference.

BRIDGES

First iron bridge

The first iron bridge was built by Jessop and Company Limited in 1815 over the River Gomti in Lucknow in Uttar Pradesh. Designed by engineer Rennie, it was made at Butterfly Iron Works, England, for the nawab of Awadh.

First cable-stayed road bridge

The Akkar Bridge in Jorethang, over the River Rangit in Sikkim, is an all-concrete, cable-stayed road bridge built in 1988. It spans a 1.5 km (4,921 ft) wide and nearly 20 m (65 ft 7 in.) deep valley. The bridge consists of two 77 m (252 ft 7 in.) symmetrical spans supported from a single central pylon. With 17 pairs of cable stays, the 55 m (180 ft) high pylon supports the decking 21 m (69 ft) above the river bed.

'Adiyogi' Lord Shiva statue, Coimbatore, Tamil Nadu: largest bust

Longest cable-stayed bridge

The Vidyasagar Setu in Kolkata, West Bengal, popularly known as the second Hooghly Bridge, is over 1 km long, and is made of steel and reinforced concrete. Holding it up are 152 cables sheathed in high-density plastic. Work on the bridge began in 1977 and it was declared open for traffic and pedestrians in 1992.

Longest balanced cantilever bridge

The 3,015 m (9,892 ft) road bridge across the River Brahmaputra at Tezpur, Assam, called Kolia Bhomora Setu, is the longest bridge that has been provided with a central suspended span of 15 m (49 ft 2.5 in.) length because of its geographical location in a seismic zone. The bridge consists of 24 spans of 120 m (393 ft 8 in.) each and two shore spans of 67.5 m (221 ft 5 in.) each. With a carriageway of 7.5 m (24 ft 7 in.) width, it was constructed between October 1981 and April 1987.

Longest Bailey bridge

The 182.8 m (600 ft) long suspension bridge over the River Chubi in Wokha, Nagaland, connects the Mokokchung District and the Dimapur District of Nagaland.

Longest sea bridge

The Bandra–Worli Sea Link (also known as the Rajiv Gandhi Sea Link) in Mumbai, Maharashtra, the longest sea bridge in India, is 5.6 km (18,373 ft) long. It connects Bandra in the western suburbs of Mumbai to Worli in south Mumbai, across Mahim Bay. This cable-stayed bridge, which carries eight lanes of traffic, was inaugurated on 30 June 2009.

Biggest cantilever bridge

Howrah Bridge (or Rabindra Setu) is India's biggest cantilever bridge. It spans the River Hooghly in Kolkata, West Bengal, and is 457 m (1,499 ft) long. It was completed in 1943.

Pamban rail bridge, India's first sea bridge was opened, connecting the town of Mandapam in mainland India with Pamban Island, and Rameswaram in Tamil Nadu.

10 LONGEST BRIDGES

Godavari Fourth Bridge–Bypass Bridge, Andhra Pradesh
4,135 m/13,566 ft
Road
River Godavari

Arrah–Chhapra Bridge, Bihar
4,350 m/14,272 ft
Road
River Ganga

Digha–Sonpur Bridge, Bihar
4,556 m/14,948 ft
Rail-cum-railroad
River Ganga

Vembanad Rail Bridge, Kerala
4,620 m/15,157 ft
Rail
Vembanad Lake

Vikramshila Setu, Bihar
4,700 m/15,420 ft
Road
River Ganga

Bogibeel Bridge, Assam
4,940 m/16,207 ft
Rail-cum-road
River Brahmaputra

Bandra–Worli Sea Link, Maharashtra
5,600 m/18,373 ft
Road
Mahim Bay

Mahatma Gandhi Setu, Bihar
5,750 m/18,865 ft
Road
River Ganga

Dibang River Bridge, Arunachal Pradesh
6,200 m/20,341 ft
Road
River Dibang

Bhupen Hazarika Setu, Assam
9,150 m/30,020 ft
Road
River Lohit

Only bascule bridge

The only bascule bridge in the country is constructed on Tolly's Nullah (or Adiganga) at Khidirpur in Kolkata, West Bengal. Operated by the Kolkata Port Trust, it is built in two halves, each of which goes up to allow ships to pass through. The bridge has a span of about 35 m (114 ft 10 in.) and was built by Wagner Biro AG, Austria. It was commissioned on 5 November 1966, and replaced a swing bridge built in 1892.

Tallest bridge

The 64 m (210 ft) high Panval Nadi viaduct near Ratnagiri, Maharashtra, is the tallest bridge in the country.

WR Highest rail bridge

In August 2022, India finally completed the world's highest and much anticipated railway bridge in the form of the Chenab Bridge, which is placed 359 m (1,177 ft 10 in.)) above the level of the river bed, some 35 m (115 ft) higher than the Eiffel Tower in Paris, France. The rail bridge is part of the Udhampur-Srinagar-Baramulla rail link project (USBRL). Located in the Reasi District of Jammu and Kashmir, the bridge is 1,315 m (4,314 ft 3.6 in.) long and is aimed at boosting connectivity to the Kashmir Valley. The rail bridge is designed to withstand high wind speed of up to 266 kmph and bear strong earthquake forces of the highest intensity seismic zone-V in India. The height of its cable crane's pylon at the Srinagar end is 127 m, which is much taller than the Qutub Minar, which is 72 m (236 ft) high. Connecting Bakkal (Katra) and Kauri (Srinagar), the bridge was constructed using 24,000 tonnes of blast-proof steel by the Indian Railways in collaboration with the Defence Research and Development Organization (DRDO).

Highest suspension bridge

At a height of 4,144 m (13,596 ft) above sea level, the Chicham Bridge is built over a deep gorge and connects Kibber and Chicham in Himachal Pradesh.

Highest Bailey bridge

The highest Bailey bridge in the country is at a height of 5,602 m (18,380 ft) at Khardung La in Ladakh. The 30 m (98 ft 5 in.) long bridge rests on ice. It consists of square diamond-braced panels that can be assembled on approach and then pushed or pinned together at the corners to form a girder. It was designed and built by Lieutenant Colonel S.G. Vombatkere of the Border Roads Organization in August 1982.

Mahatma Gandhi never visited the USA, but it has the most number of statues of him – more than 15 – outside India.

Busiest bridge
With nearly 60,000 vehicles a day and countless pedestrians, Howrah Bridge, also called Rabindra Setu, in Kolkata, West Bengal, is India's busiest bridge.

Longest bridge over water
The Bhupen Hazarika Setu, also referred to as the Dhola–Sadiya Bridge, connecting Dhola and Sadiya in Dibrugarh District and Lakhimpur District respectively in Assam, is the longest bridge over water. The 9.15 km (30,020 ft) long bridge on the River Brahmaputra was inaugurated on 26 May 2017 by Prime Minister Narendra Modi. It is named after Bhupen Hazarika, a well-known Assamese musician and film-maker who died in 2011.

Longest road-and-rail bridge
Bogibeel Bridge on the River Brahmaputra, between Dhemaji and Dibrugarh Districts, Assam, is the longest road-and-rail bridge, with a length of 4.94 km. Its construction was started in April 2002 and it was completed in December 2018. The bridge has a double-line 1.676 m (5 ft 6 in.) broad-gauge railway on the lower deck and a three-lane road on the upper one. It is India's first bridge with fully welded steel–concrete support beams to bear earthquakes of magnitudes of up to 7 on the Richter scale.

DAMS

Earliest canal system
Canal systems have existed since the pre-Harappan era (around 2500 BCE). Excavations at Dholavira in Gujarat have revealed ingenious systems for diverting water from seasonal nullahs.

Earliest dam and canal
The earliest dam discovered was built on Sudarshan Lake in Junagadh (then Girinagar) in Gujarat. It dates to 326 BCE.

Longest canal
The Indira Gandhi Canal or Rajasthan Canal, which starts in Punjab and ends in Rajasthan, is 959 km long, and the world's second longest canal. Its schemes include 6,308 km of distributary canals.

Oldest extant dam
The Grand Anicut Dam, also known as the Kallanai Dam, built on the River Kaveri, 24 km from Tiruchirappalli in Tamil Nadu, is the oldest extant dam known in India. This masonry dam, which was built in the second century CE by the Chola king Aditha Karikalan (or Aditya II), is 330 m (1,083 ft) long, 5.49 m (18 ft) high and 12–18 m (39–59 ft) wide. The ancient dam was remodelled, repaired and fitted with sluice gates during 1899–1902. For centuries, it has irrigated more than a million acres (0.4 million hectares) of land.

The Indira Gandhi or Rajasthan Canal: longest canal

Oldest cement masonry dam
The Khadakwasla Dam on the River Mutha, 20 km from Pune in Maharashtra, was built on the suggestion of Colonel Fife of the Royal Engineers and civil engineer N.G.K. Murti. It was started in 1869 and completed in 1879. The dam has since been rebuilt.

First hydroelectric project
Shivanasamudra in Chamarajanagar District, Karnataka, opened in 1902 and involved the harnessing of the Kaveri Falls to supply electrical energy to run the machinery at the Kolar goldfields. The power station is still a functioning one.

Longest ancient dam
The 16 km (52,493 ft) long Veeranam embankment dam in Cuddalore District, Tamil Nadu, was built in 1037 CE and is still in use.

Longest breakwater
The V.O. Chidambaranar Port (earlier Tuticorin Port) North Breakwater in Tamil Nadu is the longest at 4.14 km.

Largest water reservoir
Indirasagar Dam is a multipurpose project on the River Narmada in the East Nimar District of Madhya Pradesh. The reservoir has a capacity of 12.2 billion cubic m (9,890,701 acre

Currently, there are **5,254** completed large dams in India.

DISTRIBUTION OF LARGE DAMS (DECADE-WISE)

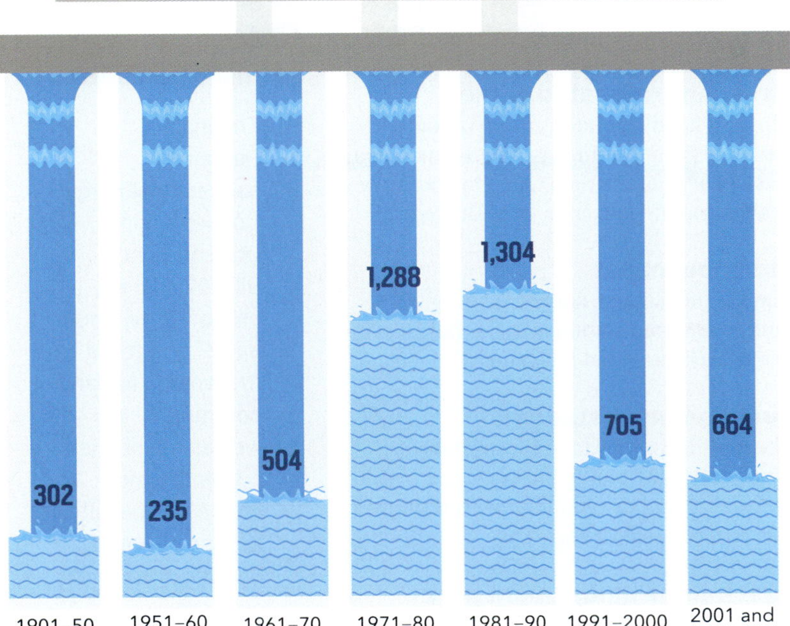

Year of construction unavailable: 194; Under construction: 437
Source: National Register of Large Dams, Central Water Commission, Government of India

feet) and, in terms of water storage, stands as the largest reservoir in India.

Largest river dam

The Sardar Sarovar Dam is a gravity dam on the River Narmada near Navagam in Surat District, Gujarat. One of 30 dams planned on the River Narmada, it is the largest such structure to be built and among the largest dams in the world. Four Indian states - Gujarat, Madhya Pradesh, Maharashtra and Rajasthan - receive water and electricity supplied from the dam.

Lighthouse in Thalassery, Kerala: first unmanned lighthouse

Largest barrage

The Farakka Barrage on the River Ganga was opened in 1972 to help maintain navigable depths in Syama Prasad Mookerjee Port (earlier Kolkata Port). Its length of 2,245 m (7,365 ft 6 in.) contains 108 gated bays of 18 m (59 ft) and two 8 m (26 ft) fish locks.

Highest earth-fill dam

The Pong Dam or Beas Dam, is an earth-fill embankment dam on the River Beas in Himachal Pradesh and the highest of its type at 133 m (436 ft 4 in.). Maharana Pratap Sagar Lake, created by the dam, is a bird sanctuary.

LIGHTHOUSES

Oldest lighthouses

In 1766, two signal houses were built, one on Old Woman's Island (now part of Colaba) and the other at Malabar Point, in Bombay (Mumbai), Maharashtra. The former was replaced by the first proper lighthouse built during 1768–71. This threw a beam seven leagues seaward in clear weather at 45.72 m (150 ft). It was repaired in 1828 and 1853, but stopped operating when the Prongs Lighthouse was installed in 1874.

Oldest functional lighthouses

- The lighthouse built in 1821 on Sagar Island, at the mouth of the River Hooghly in West Bengal, was renovated in 1911. Its elevation from the mean sea level is 26 m (85 ft 4 in.) and the tower is 25 m (82 ft) high. Its flashing light has a range of 31 km in clear weather.
- The Prongs Lighthouse in the Colaba area in Bombay (now Mumbai), Maharashtra, is recorded to have been constructed in 1874 by Thomas Ormiston. The beam of the lighthouse can be seen at 30 km and it is still operational. Its height is 41 m (135 ft) and range is 43 km.

First unmanned lighthouse

Near Thalassery (earlier Tellicherry) in Kannur District, Kerala, stands the first unmanned lighthouse. It was built in 1835 and renovated in 1924. It is at an altitude of 27 m (89 ft) from the mean sea level and its range is 8 km.

Tallest lighthouse (from mean sea level)

The tallest lighthouse from the mean sea level is at Dolphin's Nose at Visakhapatnam, Andhra Pradesh. Its masonry tower rises 19 m (62 ft

4 in.) up from the ground level and it has an elevation of 173 m (567 ft 7 in.), which is 192 m (630 ft) from the mean sea level.

Tallest lighthouse

The Jakhau Lighthouse in Gujarat is the tallest at 46 m (151 ft). It was established in 1957 and the present tower was built in 1965. Located on the main quay of Jakhau, a fishing port in western Kachchh, the lighthouse has a range of 33 km.

Lighthouse farthest from shore

The lighthouse farthest from shore is on the Vengurla rocks, 20 km from Vengurla in the Sindhudurg District of Maharashtra.

AMUSEMENT ZONES

Largest amusement park

Spread over 138 acres (56 hectares), Imagica is located off the Mumbai-Pune Expressway at Khopoli, Maharashtra. It has India's largest theme park, a water park, India's largest snow park, and first theme park hotel. It also features the longest, tallest and fastest roller coaster, 40.2 m (132 ft) high with over 853.4 m (2,800 ft) of track length and a speed of 120 km/hr. It also has 'I for India', the country's first simulation ride and India's longest flume ride of 470 m (1,542 ft).

WR Largest adventure park

The world's largest adventure park was opened by the Indian Air Force Station, Bagdogra, Darjeeling, West Bengal, under the Eastern Air Command, Indian Air Force, and the Directorate of Adventure Sports in August 2018. Spread over 860 acres (348 hectares), the park at the Bagdogra Air Force Station has 62 land, air and water adventure sports, like skydiving, parasailing and rappelling.

First amusement park

Appu Ghar at Pragati Maidan, New Delhi, the first family entertainment centre in India, opened during the 1982 Asian Games in Delhi. It was named after the Games' mascot – Appu the elephant. Shutting down in 2008, it reopened in Gurugram, Haryana, with projects in The Great India Place mall and Worlds of Wonder amusement and water-theme park in Noida, Uttar Pradesh, as well as at Metro Walk and Adventure Island in Rohini, Delhi.

First indoor amusement play station

Funky Orbit at Ansal Plaza Mall on Khel Gaon Marg in New Delhi was launched on 15 June 2000 by Panoramic Entertainment Pvt. Ltd. The multi-tiered play station had an 8.53 m (28 ft) long curly slide and a ball pool.

MECHANICAL AND GENERAL STRUCTURES

First elevator

The first elevator was installed at Raj Bhavan, in Calcutta (now Kolkata, West Bengal) in 1892. It used Otis's first design of an electric lift.

First hand-operated crane

The first hand-operated crane was built by Jessop & Company in 1850. The 5-tonne crane was installed at the then Calcutta Port (now Syama Prasad Mookerjee Port) Customs.

First houseboat

The first houseboat, named Victory, was built in 1888 and stationed at the Dal Lake in Srinagar, Jammu and Kashmir.

First floating restaurant

The first floating restaurant was built at Sirhind, Punjab, on the Bhakra Canal in 1979. The eight room air-conditioned restaurant was part of a tourist complex.

First marine amusement park

In 1998, Dolphin City was set up by Amusements and Picnic Resorts Pvt. Ltd in Chennai, Tamil Nadu, with three performing dolphins and a performing sea lion show. Following the death of the performing dolphins, the marine amusement park featured sea lion performances, underwater viewing and leisure boating.

First live entertainment, theatre and leisure destination

Kingdom of Dreams in Gurugram, Haryana, is India's first live entertainment, theatre and leisure destination. Spread over 6 acres (2.4 hectares), it is run by the Great Indian Nautanki Company (GINC), a joint venture of Apra Group and Wizcraft. The destination consists of two theatres, Nautanki Mahal and the Showshaa Theatre, and a cultural and cuisine area known as Culture Gully.

First revolving restaurant

Neelkanth Patang at Ahmedabad, Gujarat, was the first revolving restaurant at 67.4 m (221 ft) above ground level. Opened in 1984, it has a 90-minute rotation, which unfolds a view of the old and new city of Ahmedabad.

First space-frame concrete structure

The first space-frame structure in reinforced concrete was the Hall of Nations at the Trade Fair Authority of India exhibition grounds in Pragati Maidan, New Delhi. Built during

The Indian Parliament passed the Energy Conservation (Amendment) Bill 2022, which proposes minimum use of non-fossil fuel energy for large commercial as well as residential buildings, and imposes a penalty in case of non-compliance.

TOP 10 TALLEST BUILDINGS*

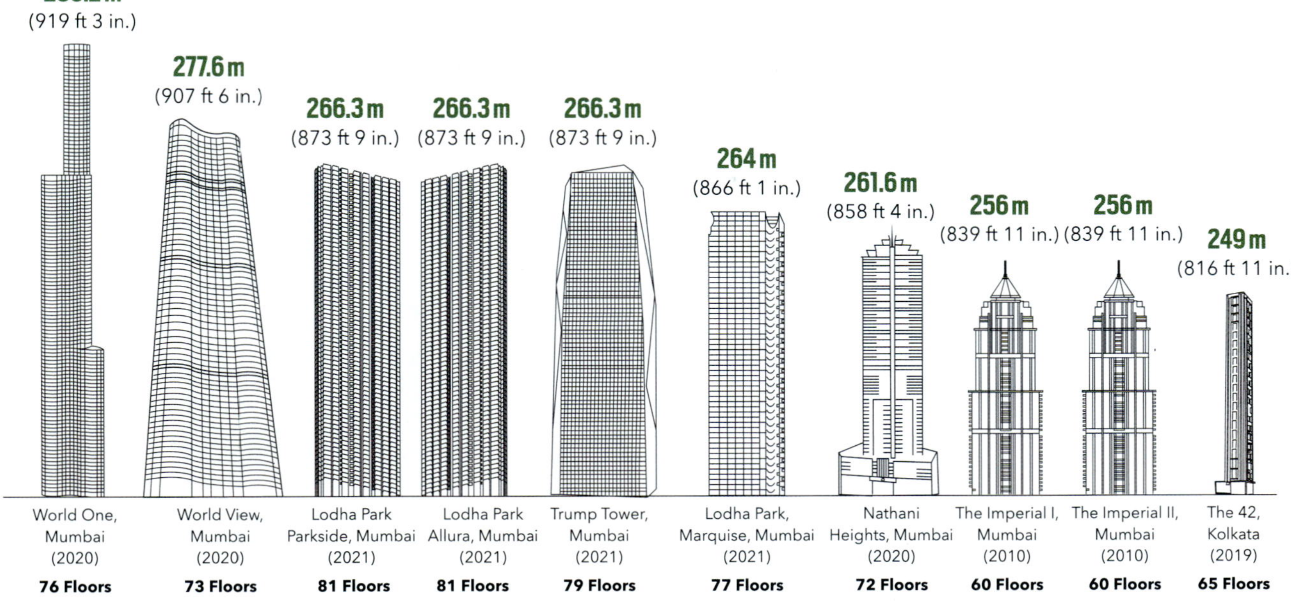

* All residential buildings. Source: Council of Tall Buildings and Urban Habitat

India has 126 tall buildings of above 150 m.

1971–72, the hall offered an uninterrupted exhibition area of 6,700 sq. m (72,120 sq. ft) in a 82 m x 82 m x 27 m (269 ft x 269 ft x 88 ft 7 in.) pyramid supported at eight points.

First water park

Shanku's Water Park on the Ahmedabad–Mahesana Highway in Gujarat was launched by Shankarbhai Chaudhary in 1993, on a 75-acre (30.35 hectares) campus. It introduced a giant 15.24 m (50 ft) speed slide that ended in a shallow water pool, a spiral ride, a wave pool that simulated sea waves, and a kids' corner.

Largest glasshouse

A glass-covered hall in Davanagere, Karnataka, completed in 2018, covers 7,334 sq. m (78,942.5 sq. ft). It houses a horticultural information centre and a botanical garden.

Rashtrapati Bhavan, New Delhi: largest official residence

Largest official residence

The Rashtrapati Bhavan in New Delhi, the official residence of the president of India, has 340 rooms, 18 staircases, 74 lobbies, 37 salons, 1 km of corridors, 37 fountains and 190 acres (76.9 hectares) of gardens. The residence covers 50 acres (20.2 hectares) of a 330-acre (133.5 hectare) estate.

Largest auditorium

The Sri Shanmukhananda Hall, inaugurated on 22 August 1963 in Bombay (now Mumbai), Maharashtra, has a total capacity of 3,012 seats. The ground floor seats 1,552, the first balcony 896 and the second balcony 564 people. The stage has a depth and width of 16 m (52 ft) and a height of 6.4 m (21 ft).

Largest table

The teakwood table in the Banquet Hall at the Rashtrapati Bhavan in Delhi can seat 104 people at a time.

Largest cooking vessel

The original *badi deg* (big vessel), christened Deg-i-Chittor-Kusba or the 'Chittor-conquering vessel', said to be presented by the Mughal emperor Akbar to the *dargah* of Khwaja Moinuddin Chishti in Ajmer, Rajasthan, could hold 4,000 kg of food at a time – enough for 12,000 people.

Largest retractable roof

Kunta International Ltd, Noida, Uttar Pradesh, designed, built, installed and commissioned an electrically driven retractable roof on a reusable structure on the presidential dais on Rajpath, New Delhi, for Republic Day 2018. Made of steel and polycarbonate sheets with inbuilt sensors, it was 30.5 m (100 ft) wide and 6.4 m (21 ft) deep.

Largest cinema multiplex

Mayajaal in Kanathur in Chennai, Tamil Nadu, has the largest movie multiplex with 16 screens and a seating capacity of 2,600. It is part of an entertainment centre that houses a shopping mall, a sports complex and a resort.

Longest conveyor

The longest single-belt international conveyor stretched from near Shella, East Khasi Hills District, Meghalaya, in India to a cement factory at Chhatak in Sunamganj District, Bangladesh. It was about 17 km long (7 km in India and 10 km in Bangladesh) and conveys limestone and shale at 960 tonnes/hr. The conveyor was engineered by AUMUND France and Larsen & Toubro, and installed on-site by Beltpro. Its rollers are unusually designed to deal with both horizontal and vertical terrain curves.

Most names engraved on a monument

India Gate in Delhi carries the names of 13,516 British and Indian soldiers of the British Indian Army, who died during 1914–21 at various fronts of the First World War and the Third Anglo Afghan War. This constitutes the largest number of names inscribed on a monument. Designed by architect Edwin Lutyens, the arch was completed in 1921. It is 42.3 m (139 ft) high and 9.1 m (30 ft) wide.

Longest underground pipeline

The Hazira-Bijapur-Jagdishpur (HBJ) gas pipeline was India's first cross-country gas pipeline. This project by GAIL (India) Ltd began in 1986 to supply gas to fertilizer plants in Uttar Pradesh. The first phase, consisting of a non-branched 1,750 km grid, was later expanded to supply gas for industrial and domestic use in Rajasthan, Haryana and the National Capital Territory (NCT). This extended the grid length to 3,474 km.

The first skyscraper

Usha Kiran, an apartment building of 26 storeys in Bombay (now Mumbai), Maharashtra, was the first of high-rise buildings. It was built between 1964 and 1967.

Tallest chimney

The 275.2 m (903 ft) tall chimney of the Reliance Dahanu Thermal Power Station in Dahanu in Palghar District of Maharashtra is India's tallest RCC chimney. The base diameter of the chimney is 7 m (23 ft).

Oldest ice-skating rink

The ice-skating rink near Lakkar Bazaar in Shimla, Himachal Pradesh, was founded in 1920 by one Mr Blessington. Initially out of bounds for Indians during British rule, it is now managed by the Shimla Ice-skating Club and is open for skating between the winter months of December and February.

MODERN STRUCTURES

First honorary doctorate in architecture

Joseph Allen Stein, a US-born architect who came to India in 1952, was conferred an honorary doctorate, the first in architecture, by Anna University, Chennai, Tamil Nadu, in September 1999.

First architect to win the Pritzker Prize

Dr Balkrishna Vithaldas Doshi (b. 26 August 1927) won the famed Pritzker Architecture Prize on 12 March 2018, the first Indian to do so in the award's 40-year history. The Pritzker Prize is referred to as the Nobel Prize in architecture.

First concrete building

The Golconde dormitory at Sri Aurobindo Ashram in Pondicherry (now Puducherry) was designed by Czech-American architect Antonin Raymond (1888–1976) and completed in 1948. All its features evolved from a study of the local climatic conditions and the occupants' needs.

The national emblem sculpture atop the new Parliament building in New Delhi

The Parliament Gets a Makeover

The iconic Parliament House in New Delhi, designed by British architects Sir Edwin Lutyens and Herbert Baker, took six years to build from 1921 to 1927. It is believed that the circular building was inspired by the Chausath Yogini Temple in Morena, Madhya Pradesh. As the demand for space increased significantly, in 1956, two floors were added, and in 2006, the Parliament Museum was built.

With a view to the number of Lok Sabha seats increasing from the current total of 545 after 2026, an expansion of the Parliament House is expected to solve the issues of cramped seating, lack of seating in joint sessions of the two Houses, and security concerns. The new structure, work on which began in 2020, will be a four-storey building with a seating capacity of 1,224. Costing an estimated ₹970 crore, the triangular building will display three important leitmotifs: the national flower – the lotus, the national bird – the peacock and the national tree – the banyan.

Rock Garden, Chandigarh

Where Rocks Come Alive

The Rock Garden of Chandigarh is a true miracle that has withstood the threats of demolition and vandalism, and survived. It was the secret and enduring work of one passionate man, Nek Chand Saini (1924–2015), who was an ordinary government official.

Nek Chand began to build this 'garden' in 1957, with scrap collected from various sources, including industrial sites and homes. At the time, the area he chose to work in was a forest buffer zone, so his work was illegal. When it came to light, he had already spent 18 years creating his 'kingdom of Sukrani', bustling with people, animals, dancers and musicians, and was able to garner support for it and get funding to expand it. He was appointed as the subdivisional engineer at the Rock Garden, and continued his work.

Now, the Rock Garden's 40 acres (16 hectares) near Sukhna Lake house waterfalls and thousands of sculptures made from waste, including discarded washbasins, pots, crockery, bangles and what not. It is visited by thousands of visitors every day. The 2021 movie *Shershaah* featured a few scenes filmed here.

India's Biggest Demolition

Two illegally constructed towers at the Supertech Emerald Court Housing Society in Sector 93A, Noida, Uttar Pradesh, made headlines on 28 August 2022. The 103 m (338 ft) high towers were demolished by the 'waterfall implosion' technique in a mere 12 seconds! The demolition of these twin residential towers was ordered by the Supreme Court and carried out by a Mumbai-based company, Edifice Engineering, along with South African firm Jet Demolitions as their expert partner. With the grounding of Apex (32 storeys) and Ceyane (29 storeys) towers, India joined the club of countries that have razed buildings taller than 100 m (328 ft). Edifice Engineering and Jet Demolitions had earlier demolished four residential complexes in Maradu municipal area of Kochi, Kerala, using the same technique, but the scale of operations was smaller.

The highlights of the demolition were:

- **Six** months were spent in planning the operation.
- The Allahabad High Court ordered the demolition in **2014**, after which the case was referred to the Supreme Court, which gave the final verdict in August 2021.
- Over **9,000** accurately placed holes were drilled for **3,700** kg of explosives.
- **Seven thousand** residents, with **150** pets and **2,500** vehicles were moved out of the immediate and near vicinity as the closest buildings were only 8 m (26 ft) away.
- Approximately **80,000** tonnes of debris resulted from the demolition, of which a quantity of **50,000** tonnes was used to fill the basements of the demolished buildings, and the rest was to be reprocessed on-site and then taken to waste-processing centres.
- The cost of the demolition exceeded **₹20** crore was, and it was insured for **₹100** crore.

First underground market

Palika Bazaar, the air-conditioned underground market at Connaught Place (now Rajiv Chowk) in New Delhi, was set up in 1978.

First all-steel building

The ICICI headquarters in Mumbai, Maharashtra, designed by Raja Aederi and built in 1995, have a superstructure area of 39,948 sq. m (430,000 sq. ft) with two-level basements of 21,368 sq. m (230,000 sq. ft) and a structural area of 14,000 sq. m (150,700 sq. ft).

First permanent crafts market

Delhi Haat in Delhi opened in 1994.with 62 stalls selling handicrafts from all over the country, and 25 food stalls.

Tallest building

World One, a 280.2 m (919 ft 3 in.), 76-floor

Supertech Twin Towers, Noida, Uttar Pradesh: biggest demolition

skyscraper in Mumbai, Maharashtra, is the tallest completed building in India. Developed by the Lodha Group, the building was completed in 2020.

Tallest escalator

The Janakpuri West metro station on the Magenta Line of the Delhi Metro features India's tallest escalator. The escalator is 15.6 m (51 ft 2 in.) high.

SPECIALIZED STRUCTURES

Oldest slide

The rock-cut slide at Mamallapuram in Chengalpattu District, Tamil Nadu, is said to be the world's oldest children's slide.

Most elaborate step well

The Rani Ki Vav ('queen's step well') at Patan, Gujarat, was built by Rani Udayamati, the queen of King Bhimadeva I (r. 1022–64 CE) of the Chalukya dynasty, in memory of her husband. It measures 65 m x 20 m (213 ft 3 in. x 65 ft 7 in.) and is over 28 m (91 ft 10 in.) deep. Originally, over 800 sculptures decorated it.

First floating cottages

Kabeer Khader and M.R. Narayanan's Floatels India in 1999 launched 20 floating cottages at Poovar Island Resort in Thiruvananthapuram District, Kerala. Designed by architect N. Mahesh, they are built on laminated ferro-cement platforms.

First igloo stay

Keylinga's Manali Igloo Stay, near Sethan Village, about 16 km from Manali in Himachal Pradesh, was opened in 2017 by Vikas Kumar and Tashi Dorje of Keylinga Himalayan Adventures. Starting with two fully functional igloos, the duo provide guests sleeping bags with extra fleece, and hot-water bottles.

First igloo cafe

India's first cafe in the shape of an igloo opened in Gulmarg, Jammu and Kashmir, on 24 January 2021, at an altitude of 2,650 m (8,694 ft) in the Pir Panjal Range of the Himalayas. A part of the Kolahoi Green Group of Hotels and Resorts, the cafe is a 4.5 m (14 ft 9.17 in.) high structure completed by a team of 20 members in 15 days, and has a diameter of 7.3 m (23 ft 11.4 in.). The igloo cafe accommodates four tables that can seat around 16 people at a time and is currently the biggest igloo cafe in Asia.

First eco-hotel

Asia's first certified eco-hotel, The Orchid, opened in Mumbai, Maharashtra, in 1997.

Largest tent structure

The largest permanent tent structure stood at the Osho International Commune in Pune, Maharashtra. Oval in shape – with a 62.75 m (205 ft 10 in.) major axis and a 32.8 m (107 ft 7 in.) minor axis – it had a floor area of 1,582 sq. m (17,029 sq. ft). The roof, which was 3.9 m (12 ft 9.5 in.) high, was a free-spanning, tensile structure on a three-hinged steel arch covering 45.5 m (149 ft 3 in.). It used nylon reinforced PVC material, weighing 1,990 kg.

WR Largest gazebo

Nirmala Nilayam Retirement Community at Theetipalayam near Siruvani in Coimbatore District, Tamil Nadu, completed the largest gazebo on 20 March 2021. It measures 242.25 sq. m (2,607.59 sq. ft). The gazebo serves as a yoga hall, a seminar hall, a space for art and music sessions, and a meditation space.

WR Largest dome

The World Peace Monument is located at the Maharashtra Institute of Technology's World Peace University (MIT -WPU) campus at Loni Kalbhor near Pune, Maharashtra. At a height of 29 m (95 ft), the world's biggest pillar-less dome is built on top of the World Peace Prayer Hall and Library, and has a diameter of 48.7 m (160 ft), compared with the Vatican's Dome's 42.5 m (139 ft 5 in.). Completed in 2018, the dome has a bell hanging from the centre.

Largest underground aquarium

The Bagh-e-Bahu Aquarium at the Baghe-Balm Garden that surrounds Bahu Fort in Jammu in Jammu and Kashmir, is the largest underground aquarium in India. At more than 220 m (721 ft 9 in.) in length, this fish-shaped aquarium has freshwater and saltwater fish species in 24 caves with 13 smaller caves.

Highest and longest ropeway

The Gulmarg Gondola, a gondola lift that covers 2,540 m (8,333 ft), is a joint venture of the Jammu and Kashmir government and the French firm Pomagalski SA. Its first stage transfers people from Gulmarg at 2,600 m (8,530 ft) to Kongdori Station in Kongdori Valley. The second stage goes to 3,747 m (12,293 ft) on Kongdori Mountain, with the highest point at 4,200 m (13,780 ft).

Longest river ropeway

A 1.8 km (5,906 ft) long ropeway was opened in August 2020 across the River Brahmaputra in Guwahati, Assam. It connects the southern and northern parts of the city, cutting down travel time from an hour to eight minutes.

Longest transportation railway tunnel

The 11.21 km long Pir Panjal or Banihal Railway Tunnel is the longest transportation tunnel in India. It connects Bichleri Valley, Banihal, to Qazigund in the Kashmir Valley. Th e first train here was flagged off on 26 June 2013.

Representative image

Going for Green Buildings

Green architecture is being hailed as the way of the future by which we can balance the proliferation of urban and other structures with urgent environmental concerns. Green structures follow an ecologically friendly design and use natural resources in all the processes involved in a building's entire lifetime. The principles of sustainability, energy efficiency and low carbon footprint are to be adhered to throughout. The broad guidelines are:

- All the natural features of the site, such as the direction of the sun, the flow of wind, trees, vegetation and landforms, should be conserved and integrated into the design.
- Optimal methods should be implemented to decrease the use and wastage of water, along with including a rainwater harvesting system and a wastewater recycling plant.
- The building should have low-energy operations and low maintenance costs, and use renewable energy sources, such as natural light, waterbodies and solar heaters.
- The architecture must ensure healthy indoor areas with enough natural light and ventilation, and avoid building materials, such as paints, that have toxins and pollutants.
- The building must be accessible to persons with disabilities.
- The structures should use local and sustainable materials (such as bamboo and rammed mud), techniques and resources.
- The process should have minimum wastage, along with segregation of waste.
- The building should use technology and innovations that reduce the carbon footprint, such as LED lights and energy-saving cooling and heating systems.

In India, green buildings are rated by two main organizations: the Indian Green Building Council (IGBC), established in 2001 under the Confederation of Indian Industry (CII), which is aligned with the LEED certification of the US Green Building Council, a globally recognized green building rating system; and the Green Rating for Integrated Habitat Assessment (GRIHA), which was formed by the Government of India in 2007.

AGRICULTURE

GENERAL

First nationwide farm loan waiver

The first nationwide farm-loan waiver in independent India was implemented in 1990 by the V.P. Singh government. It cost the exchequer ₹10,000 crore.

Biggest farm loan waiver

The then Maharashtra chief minister Devendra Fadnavis announced a farm loan waiver of ₹340 billion (34,000 crore) in June 2017. This unprecedented waiver was intended to provide relief to 8.9 million (89 lakh) farmers in the state.

First agricultural theme park

N.K. Kurian, a civil engineer is the person behind Mango Meadows, India's first man-made agriculture-themed park spread on 12 hectares (29.65 acres) of land, in Kottayam, Kerala. Work on the park began in 2004 and it was opened to the public in December 2016. With saplings and seeds collected from 15 countries, currently the park has 4,500 species of plants, including 1,900 medicinal plants, 700 trees and 900 flowering plants.

First fruit train

A train exclusively carrying fruit – 980 tonnes of locally grown bananas – was flagged off from Tadipatri railway station in Anantapur District, Andhra Pradesh, to the Jawaharlal Nehru Port in Mumbai, Maharashtra, on 31 January 2020. The train was laden with 43 refrigerator containers of bananas that had been despatched for export to international markets.

First State/UT to enact a law on contract farming

Tamil Nadu became the first state in the country to pass a law on contract farming, titled the Agricultural Produce and Livestock Contract Farming and Services (Promotion and Facilitation) Act, in February 2019. Contract farming enables more transparency, and legally safeguards the interests of farmers, producer companies and purchasers. The Act covers the produce of agriculture, sericulture, horticulture, apiculture, animal husbandry and forest activities.

First fully organic state

Sikkim was declared India's first fully organic state on 18 January 2016. It has succeeded in converting around 75,000 hectares (185,329 acres) of its agricultural land to certified organic land by implementing organic practices as per the guidelines of the National Programme for Organic Production.

First state/UT to regulate crops

Telangana has become the first state in the country that will stipulate for its farmers when and how much of which crops to grow. From the beginning of the kharif season in 2020, the state decided to regulate the cropping pattern with the help of a detailed cropping map and a seed regulation authority. The emphasis is to drive supply according to the market demand.

HISTORY

Earliest cotton cultivation

The earliest evidence for cotton production comes from the Harappan civilization (2500–1700 BCE). The first sample of cotton material, discovered by archaeologist Daya Ram Sahni during 1921–22, was a small fragment of cotton from Mohenjo-daro (now in Pakistan), clinging to the side of a vase and dyed red with madder pigment (*Rubia tinctorum*).

A Budget for Farmers

While presenting the Budget 2022–23, Finance Minister Nirmala Sitharaman announced that Kisan drones will be promoted and used for crop assessment, digitization of land records, and spraying of insecticides and nutrients. States will also be encouraged to revise the syllabuses for agriculture universities to gear them towards contemporary farming methods, better management, zero budget and organic farming. This initiative is part of the government's objective of making farming free of chemicals. Other measures to promote the agricultural sector include facilitating a fund through National Bank for Agricultural and Rural Development (NABARD) for start-ups involving agriculture and rural enterprises for the farm produce value chain, and a plan for policy and legislative steps to promote agroforestry and private forestry. The ministry also said that this rationalized and comprehensive scheme will help to increase domestic production of oil seeds and reduce dependence on their import.

TOP 5 STATES WITH AREA UNDER ORGANIC FARMING
(Area in Hectares)

	State	Under NPOP Certification	Under PGS Certification	Total Area
1	Madhya Pradesh	1,020,017.98	175,560	1,195,577.98
2	Maharashtra	371,722.62	25,160	396,882.62
3	Rajasthan	298,686.29	123,000	421,686.29
4	Gujarat	147,866.41	2,000	149,866.41
5	Odisha	92,694.81	44,800	137,494.81

NPOP: National Programme for Organic Production and PGS: Participatory Guarantee Systems.
Source: *Agricultural Statistics at a Glance*, Ministry of Agriculture and Farmers' Welfare; Data provided by the APEDA from accredited Certification Bodies under NPOP on Tracenet and NCOF as per the details available on the PGS portal for PGS certification.

2,142,718 farmers have been registered under the Pradhan Mantri Kisan Maandhan Yojana.

Earliest irrigation
Evidence of irrigation on agricultural land in the Indian subcontinent dates to the Chalcolithic period (3000–1000 BCE). The Inamgaon area of Maharashtra has a prehistoric mud embankment structure with a stone foundation. This was connected to the River Ghod by a number of channels. Floodwater was used effectively to irrigate the surrounding regions by storing it and then distributing it during the dry months.

Earliest ploughed field
Archaeologists B.B. Lal and B.K. Thapar of the Archaeological Survey of India (ASI) found a ploughed field dated to c. 2450–2300 BCE during excavations at Kalibangan in Pilibangan Tehsil in Hanumangarh District, Rajasthan.

First famine commission
The Famine Commission set up in 1880 with Sir Edward Buck as its secretary and provincial agencies under his guidance, was the first famine commission in the country. It was a forerunner of the later Ministry of Food and Agriculture of the government after India became independent.

William Carey: founder of the Agri-Horticultural Society of India, the first agricultural society

First agricultural society
William Carey, a British Christian missionary, social reformer, translator and anthropologist, founded the Agri-Horticultural Society of India in September 1820 in Calcutta (now Kolkata, West Bengal) to help disseminate scientific information among the people.

First society of soil sciences
The Indian Society of Soil Sciences was formed on 22 December 1934 in Calcutta (now Kolkata, West Bengal) with 28 members, and it was formally inaugurated on 3 January 1935 at the Presidency College (now Presidency University). Sir Bryce C. Burt, the then agricultural commissioner in the Imperial (now Indian) Council of Agricultural Research (ICAR), was its first president and Prof. J.N. Mukherjee, its first secretary.

First agricultural research institute
The Imperial Agricultural Research Institute, established in 1905 at Pusa, Samastipur District, Bihar, was India's first agricultural research institute. After the building was damaged in an earthquake in 1934, the institute was shifted to New Delhi in 1936. It is now known as the Indian Agricultural Research Institute (IARI) and is the oldest agricultural institute in India.

First pollen cryobank
The first pollen cryobank (frost bank) was established in 1983 at the Indian Institute of Horticultural Research, Bangalore (now Bengaluru), Karnataka, to conserve genetic biodiversity among plants and to support the work of crop breeders.

First agricultural university
The G.B. (Govind Ballabh) Pant University of Agriculture and Technology (GBPUA&T), also known as Pantnagar University, was the first agricultural university in India. It was inaugurated on 17 November 1960 as the Uttar Pradesh Agricultural University (UPAU). Later, in 1972, its name was changed to Govind Ballabh Pant University of Agriculture and Technology after the first chief minister of Uttar Pradesh and Bharat Ratna recipient Pandit Govind Ballabh Pant.

First spices research institute
The regional station for spice research, set up at Kozhikode, Kerala, in 1975, which later evolved into the Indian Institute of Spices Research in 1986, is the apex research organization for spices in the country.

WR Oldest desert locust control programme
The Locust Warning Organization (LWO), set up in 1939 in Karachi (now in Pakistan) by the British, is the oldest locust control programme in the world. In 1946, the LWO moved to Delhi under the Directorate of Plant Protection, Quarantine and Storage, Ministry of Agriculture and Farmers' Welfare, Government of India. It surveys locust populations and issues bulletins.

WR Oldest tea research station
Set up in 1911, the Tocklai Experimental Station in Jorhat, Assam, is the world's oldest and largest tea research station. Its many contributions include the invention of tea machinery and the development of 30 vegetative clones. The transfer of innovative

Central Tuber Crops Research Institute, Sreekariyam, Kerala: only research centre for tropical tuber crops

technology to its member estates is carried out through its advisory network that covers 1,076 tea estates occupying 341,049 hectares (842,750.4 acres) of land spread over the Brahmaputra Valley, the Barak Valley, Tripura, the Dooars, Darjeeling and the Terai areas. Tocklai has its regional R&D centre at Nagrakata in Jalpaiguri District, West Bengal.

WR Only research centre for tropical tuber crops

The Central Tuber Crops Research Institute at Sreekariyam in Thiruvananthapuram District, Kerala, is the only institute in the world dedicated to research on tropical tuber crops. It was established in 1963.

WR Only weed research centre

The Directorate of Weed Science Research (DWSR), Jabalpur, Madhya Pradesh, set up the National Research Centre for Weed Science on 22 April 1989 – the only one in the world for weed management research.

WR Largest groundwater irrigation system

India has the largest groundwater irrigation system in the world, with 39 million hectares (96.4 million acres) of land under this kind of irrigation. Besides groundwater, India's irrigation depends on canals from rivers, well-based systems, tanks and other rainwater harvesting. About two-thirds of farmlands in the country still depend on the monsoon.

Research institute located at the highest altitude

The Defence Institute of High Altitude Research (DIHAR), situated at 3,505 m (11,499 ft) in Leh, Ladakh, is a laboratory of the Defence Research Development Organization (DRDO). It was established in 1962 to help Indian defence troops as well as farmers of the region with appropriate agro-animal technologies.

AWARDS AND HONOURS

First Indian scientist to receive the Ramon Magsaysay award

Geneticist Dr M.S. Swaminathan received the Ramon Magsaysay award in 1971 for community leadership, becoming the first Indian scientist to do so. Known as the 'Father of the Green Revolution' for his leading role in food self-sufficiency in India, he was the director of the Indian Agricultural Research Institute (IARI) in Delhi at the time. Dr Swaminathan advocates environmentally sustainable agriculture as well as preservation of biodiversity, culminating in what he has termed an 'evergreen' revolution.

INCREASE IN INDIA'S NET IRRIGATED AREA (in Lakh Hectares)

Source: PIB AKAM series, Press Information Bureau, Government of India

INDIA AT HER BEST 75 YEARS OF INDEPENDENCE

A branch of ICICI bank

ICICI Bank Becomes the First to Use Satellite Data to Grant Farm Loans

ICICI Bank has announced that they will use satellite data to ascertain the credit worthiness of prospective customers who belong to the farming sector. The bank will be the first in India and among a few in the world to use satellite data to measure parameters such as land, crop patterns and irrigation. This will lead to quicker lending decisions reducing the assessment time from the industry standard of 15 days to just a few days. The contactless assessment is also a welcome method in the post-pandemic world and helps in reducing travel costs for the bank. Currently, they are using the technology in over 500 villages of Maharashtra, Madhya Pradesh and Gujarat, with plans to scale up to 63,000 villages across the country. The bank works with agri-fintech companies to build analysis with over 40 parameters to help existing and new customers for Kisan Credit Card loans.

Indian spices and spice products were exported to 180 destinations across the world.

First Indian fellow of the Royal Society

Dr Benjamin Peary Pal, the first director of the Indian Council of Agricultural Research (ICAR), was also the first Indian agricultural scientist to become a Fellow of the Royal Society of London, UK, while in office, in 1972. He was also awarded the top national civilian awards: the Padma Shri (1959), the Padma Bhushan (1968) and the Padma Vibhushan (1987).

First Indian president of the International Society of Soil Sciences

Dr J.S. Kanwar was elected president of the International Society of Soil Sciences for the period 1978–82. The Society was founded in 1924, mainly by European agro-pedologists interested in establishing standardized methods of soil analysis.

First winner of the World Food Prize

So far, eight Indians have won the World Food Prize. This global award is given to outstanding individuals who have advanced human development by improving the quality, quantity or availability of food in the world. The first Indian winner of this award was agronomist, agricultural scientist and plant geneticist Dr M.S. Swaminathan in 1987, and the most recent was Dr Rattan Lal, an India-born British scientist from the USA, in 2020.

FARMLANDS AND PRINCIPAL CROPS

Largest single farm

The Central State Farm at Suratgarh in Rajasthan, with an area of 6,296 hectares (15,557.8 acres), is said to be the largest farm in Asia.

Largest average farm holdings in a state/UT

Nagaland has the largest farm holdings, with 4.87 hectares (12.03 acres) as the average size of an operational unit as per the 2015–16 Agricultural Census.

Smallest average farm holdings in a state/UT

The average size of an operational farm in Kerala is 0.18 hectares (0.49 acres) as per the 2015–16 Agricultural Census.

WR First hybrid Basmati rice

The IARI, New Delhi, developed and released RH-10 in 2001, the first hybrid superfine-grained aromatic rice in the world. The optimum yield of this variety of rice, with typical Basmati traits, is 7 tonnes/hectare.

WR First pigeon pea hybrid *(arhar)*

The International Crops Research Institute for Semi-Arid Tropics (ICRISAT) released the world's first hybrid pigeon pea, ICPH-8, in 1991. This variety recorded a yield potential of 2,057 kg/hectare.

Only genetically modified crop approved for commercial cultivation

Bt *(Bacillus thuringiensis)* cotton was the first genetically modified (GM) crop approved for commercial cultivation in 2002 by the Government of India. The Genetic Engineering Appraisal Committee (GEAC) has also approved confined field trials of 20 GM crops, viz., cotton, mustard, brinjal, okra, sorghum, groundnut, maize, potato, tomato, chickpea, pigeon pea, banana, castor, papaya, watermelon, sugar cane, wheat, rice, rubber tree and Indian wormwood, for generation of bio-safety data from both private and public sector institutions.

First cotton hybrid
The first commercial cotton hybrid in the country, named H-4 or Sankar-4, was developed at the Gujarat Agricultural University in 1970 by agricultural scientist Dr Chandrakant T. Patel.

First tea estate
In 1837, the British East India Company set up the first tea estate at Chabua in Dibrugarh District, Assam. Now the estate is owned by Amalgamated Plantations Private Ltd. The first Tea Committee in India was set up in 1834 by the then Governor General of India, William Bentinck.

State/UT with maximum cold storage capacity
Uttar Pradesh has 14,834,695 tonnes of cold storage capacity as on 31 January 2022.

Tallest paddy plant
Tanaji Nikam, a farmer in Vannur Village in Kolhapur, Maharashtra, grew a paddy plant 2.8 m (9 ft 2 in.) tall in 2005 using organic manure.

Tallest sugar cane
Vedant Rajendra Yadav (b. 28 January 1998) from Fursungi Village in Pune District, Maharashtra, grew a sugar cane plant that was 13.1 m (43 ft) in height in January 2021.

Tallest jowar
Dodda Ramachandra Reddy (b. 20 January 1951) from Peddapalli, Karimnagar District, Telangana, grew a jowar plant that was 5.3 m (17 ft 4 in.) high as on 27 October 2018. It took 161 days to grow to this height.

Largest number of organic producers in the world
According to the World of Organic Agriculture Report 2022, India has the largest number of organic producers in the world. With 1,599,010 certified organic producers, the country is home to more than 47.02 per cent of the total number of organic producers (3.4 million) worldwide. However, when it comes to the total area under certified organic cultivation, India only has 1.5 per cent of its entire agricultural area under organic cultivation.

Only producer of five commercial silk varieties
India is the only producer of all five commercial varieties of silk, viz., mulberry, oak tussore, tropical tussore, *eri* and *muga*. Golden *muga* is produced only in India. During 2018–19, India produced 31,906 tonnes of raw silk.

RISE IN HORTICULTURAL PRODUCTION IN THREE DECADES
(in Million Tonnes)

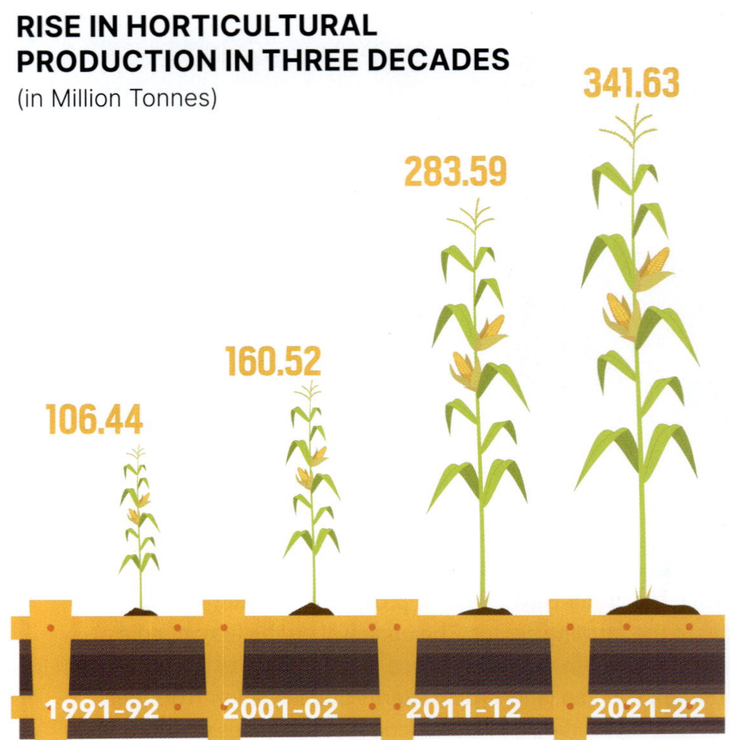

Source: PIB AKAM series, Press Information Bureau, Government of India

Highest tea garden
The Korakundah Tea Estate of the United Nilgiri Tea Estates Co. Ltd, near Coonoor in the Nilgiris in Tamil Nadu, has its highest tea garden at an altitude of 2,471 m (8,107 ft).

HORTICULTURE

First seed company
The National Seeds Corporation, set up in 1963 by the Government of India, undertakes the production of certified seeds of nearly 600 varieties of 60 crops through its 8,000 registered seed growers.

First vanilla cultivation
The first cultivation centres of vanilla were set up more than a century ago at the Kallar Fruit Research Station, Thiruvananthapuram District, and the Ambalavayal Horticultural Research Station, Wayanad District, Kerala.

First non-narcotic poppy
Sujata, a poppy variety developed in 1998 at the Central Institute of Medicinal and Aromatic Plants, Lucknow, Uttar Pradesh, was the first poppy variety free of opium and opium alkaloids.

First coconut hybrids
Researchers at the Coconut Research Station, now called the Central Plantation Crops Research Institute (CPCRI), Kasaragod, Kerala,

The total poultry population in India is **851.81** million as per the 20th Livestock Census (2021).

Representative image

Future-Ready: India's Global Agri-Horticultural Gene Bank

Featuring an array of over 4.6 lakh agri-horticultural crops, the world's second-largest refurbished advanced gene bank at the ICAR-National Bureau of Plant Genetic Resources, New Delhi, was inaugurated by the Union minister of agriculture and farmers' welfare, Narendra Singh Tomar, in August 2021. The refurbished unit will benefit not only farmers but also academicians and researchers in both the public and private sectors. The bank, which has the capacity of housing another 10 lakh germ plasm accessions, focuses on conserving a heterogeneous mix of indigenous crops and those from across the globe. Revolutionary in scope, the bank, along with its 10 regional units across the country, focuses on preserving in-situ and off-site germ plasm. The seeds stored in the facility are accumulated via a very specific set of exploratory missions and programmes, and then preserved in a controlled environment with the required temperatures and humidity settings.

Longest ash gourd

produced the first coconut hybrids between the tall and dwarf palms in 1932, with two to three times more nuts than in each of the parent palms.

First mustard hybrid

In 2008, NRC Sankar Sarson (NRCHB 506), an Indian hybrid of mustard, was developed by a team of scientists led by Dr K.H. Singh at the National Research Centre on Rapeseed-Mustard (NRCRM; now called the Directorate of Rapeseed Mustard Research) in Bharatpur, Rajasthan.

Highest vineyard

At 1,585 m (5,200 ft) above the mean sea level, Kookkal Vineyards (Domaine Kookkal) at Kookkal Village, near Udhagamandalam, Tamil Nadu, are the highest commercial-scale vineyards in the country.

WR Tallest papaya plant

Jhantu Paul from Kolkata, West Bengal, owns the tallest papaya tree (*Carica papaya*) measuring 14.07 m (46 ft 2 in.) as verified on 22 January 2017.

Heaviest jackfruit

Kaithakkoli Kurichiya's family found a jackfruit weighing 57.9 kg in their compound in Thallappuzha, Wayanad District, Kerala, in May 2020. The jackfruit was 67 cm (26 in.) long, with a circumference of 1.35 m (4 ft 5 in.).

Longest ash gourd

Dr Johnson Nayankara (b. 1 August 1981) from Mapranam in Thrissur District, Kerala, has grown the longest ash gourd as verified on 11 November 2020. It was 47.3 cm (18.62 in.) long, with a 6.2 cm (2.4 in.) stalk.

Longest and biggest coconut

Dr Dilip Kumar Vitthaldas Patil, a scientist at the Central Institute for Cotton Research, Nagpur, Maharashtra, preserved for 12 years, the largest and biggest coconut (and the longest preserved) seen in India. Dr Patil found this giant coconut in a farm in Pilicode Village, Kasaragod District, Kerala. Even in the dried state, it was 27 cm (10.63 in.) horizontally, 67.5 cm (26.57 in.) long (technically known as equatorial length) as against normal green coconuts, which are 14 to 20 cm (5.51 to 7.87 in.) horizontally and 25 to 45 cm (9.84 to 17.72 in.) long. In its dried state the coconut weighed 1,450 g against an average of 300–500 g.

WR First onion hybrid

The world's first onion hybrid was developed at the Indian Agricultural Research Institute, New Delhi, in March 2002 with a potential of increasing yield by 20 per cent.

First castor hybrid

The Castor and Mustard Research Station in Sardarkrushinagar in Banaskantha District, Gujarat, developed the first castor hybrid named GCH 3 and released it in 1968–69 on a commercial scale. GCH 7, released in 2006, has the highest potential productivity (3,000 kg/ hectare) in India.

Hottest chilli

The *bhut jolokia*, or 'ghost chilli', is the hottest chilli in India. Rated at 1,041,427 Scoville heat units (SHUs), this variety is cultivated in the north-eastern states of Arunachal Pradesh, Assam, Nagaland and Manipur.

Largest producer of spices

India is the largest producer of spices and spice products. In 2020–21, India produced 16.6 million tonnes of spices.

Largest producer of coconuts

India produces 34.73 per cent of the global production of coconuts. As per 2020–21 reports, the area and production of coconuts in the country is 2.18 million hectares (5.8 million acres) and 14.57 million tonnes, respectively. The four southern states of Kerala, Tamil Nadu, Karnataka and Andhra Pradesh account for 88.97 per cent of the area under coconut cultivation and 89.67 per cent of the coconut production in the country.

Largest producer of mangoes

According to the first estimates for 2020–21, India's mango production stood at 20.82 million tonnes. Andhra Pradesh turned out to be the top mango-producing state with the production of 5,001,740 tonnes of mangoes.

ANIMAL HUSBANDRY

Early vet research

Research on animal healthcare began with the setting up of the Imperial Bacteriological Laboratory at Poona (now Pune), Maharashtra, on 9 December 1889, with Dr Alfred Lingard as the first bacteriologist in 1890. It was moved to Mukteshwar, Uttarakhand, in 1895. The Indian Veterinary Research Institute (IVRI) later began in 1913 at Izatnagar, Bareilly District, Uttar Pradesh.

First veterinary surgeon

William Moorcroft (1767–1825), a Britisher who was appointed veterinary surgeon in 1808 at the Pusa Stud Farm, Bihar, is the first one on record in India.

First dairy research institute

Established in 1923 as the Imperial Dairy Institute of Animal Husbandry and Dairying in Bangalore (now Bengaluru), Karnataka, it was renamed National Dairy Research Institute (NDRI) after Independence. In 1955, its headquarters were shifted to Karnal, Haryana. It undertakes research, teaching and extension activities in dairy development.

First frozen semen bank for bulls

The first frozen semen bank for bulls was established in 1963 in Mattupatti, Kerala, with Indo-Swiss collaboration, with the objective of evolving a new breed of cattle adapted to the local environment. The

bank dealt with the collection, processing, storage and transportation of the semen of bull breeds.

First artificial insemination in bulls

Artificial insemination was successfully attempted for the first time in 1939 by Sampath Kumaran, who crossed the Indian Hallikar breed with Holstein Friesian bulls.

First calf cloned from frozen semen

In July 2014, a male cloned calf named Rajat was produced by the National Dairy Research Institute (NDRI), Karnal, Haryana, using a donor cell from the frozen semen of a highly ranked Murrah buffalo bull. This was the first time when frozen semen was used for cloning a farm animal.

First lamb from frozen embryo

Scientists at the Central Sheep and Wool Research Institute in Avikanagar in Tonk District, Rajasthan, implanted a cryo-preserved Bharat Merino embryo into a Kheri surrogate ewe, which birthed a lamb on 20 January 1999.

Most piglets in a single litter

An artificial insemination field project by scientists at the National Research Centre on Pig in Guwahati, Assam, achieved the largest litter size of 19 piglets in a single delivery in 2012.

First cloned pashmina goat

Noori, the first cloned pashmina goat, was born at the Faculty of Veterinary Sciences and Animal Husbandry, Sher-e-Kashmir University of Agricultural Sciences and Technology, Srinagar, Jammu and Kashmir, on 9 March 2012. With a birthweight of 1.3 kg, she was produced by a team headed by Dr Riaz Ahmad Shah, using somatic cell nuclear transfer technique.

First test-tube yak calf

The first test-tube yak calf in the

Bhut jolokia: hottest chilli

Floriculture covered a total area of 0.33 million hectares (0.82 million acres) with a production of 2.61 million tonnes of flowers in 2020–21.

The National Dairy Research Institute Turns 100

Initially set up in Bangalore (now Bengaluru), Karnataka, in 1923 as the Imperial Institute of Animal Husbandry and Dairying, the National Dairy Research Institute (NDRI, renamed after Independence) shifted its headquarters to Karnal, Haryana, in 1955. The institute gained further significance in 1970 when it started functioning under the Indian Council of Agricultural Research, and later in 1989 when it acquired the status of a Deemed University. The NDRI is responsible for carrying out research and developing a curriculum to enhance various aspects of dairy production, processing and management. Moreover, it specializes in providing human resources for dairy development while ensuring that knowledge and developments from laboratories reach the farmers.

On 1 July 2022, the Union minister for agriculture and farmers' welfare, Narendra Singh Tomar, initiated the beginning of the centenary year celebrations of the institute. The year-long celebrations will also include the adoption of 100 villages under the NDRI, wherein the rural population will be acquainted with various aspects of enhancing animal husbandry and dairy farming.

Milk production

Representative image

world, a male yak calf weighing 19 kg, was born at the Nyukmadung farm of the National Research Centre on Yak (NRCY), Dirang Dzong, West Kameng District, Arunachal Pradesh, on 15 July 2013. The yak calf was named Norgayal.

First and largest cattle farm

The District Livestock Farm in Hosur in Krishnagiri District, Tamil Nadu, which is spread over 664 hectares (1,641 acres), is India's and Asia's largest cattle farm. A horse-rearing centre during British rule in the 19th century, it was given over to the Agricultural Department of India in Madras (now Tamil Nadu) in 1924 to be run as a cattle-breeding station. Its mandate was to maintain pure native milk breeds, such as the Red Sindhi, and to conduct research on cattle.

First cross-bred cow

The first cross-bred cow breed in India, called Taylor, was named after an Englishman, William Taylor, who was the one to initiate cattle cross-breeding in Patna, Bihar, in the mid-19th century.

WR First cloned buffalo

On 6 February 2009, a team of six scientists – S.K. Singla, M.S. Chauhan, R.S. Manik, P. Palta, R.A. Shah and A. George – all from the Animal Biotechnology Centre at the National Dairy Research Institute (NDRI) in Karnal, Haryana, produced the first female water buffalo calf in the world by cloning from a year-old buffalo of the Murrah breed. Although the calf died five days later, the team of scientists succeeded in testing the cloning and other technologies that helped them achieve one of their objectives of getting the desired gender of the cloned animal.

WR First cloned female buffalo by hand-guided technique

In June 2014, scientists of the National Dairy Research Institute (NDRI) in Karnal, Haryana, produced the world's first female cloned buffalo calf through 'hand-guided' cloning, using a donor cell from the ear of a high-yielding Murrah buffalo. The calf was named Lalima.

Most calves cloned from a single bull

The Central Institute for Research on Buffaloes (CIRB), located in Hisar, Haryana, achieved the production of seven clone calves from a single superior breeding bull, named M-29, between October 2019 and January 2020.

WR First buffalo-milk powder

The Kaira District Cooperative Milk Producers Union (Amul Dairy), Anand, Gujarat, produced whole and skimmed milk powder from buffalo milk in 1955. They were also the first in the world to commercially produce cheese and baby food from buffalo milk in 1960.

Only camel farm

The National Research Centre on Camel (NRCC), also a camel-breeding farm, was set up in Bikaner, Rajasthan, in 1957 for conducting scientific research on camels. The centre aims to study ways of optimizing the working capacity of camels. It is the only camel farm in the country.

WR Largest population of livestock

India had the largest population of livestock,

INDIA'S POSITION IN WORLD AGRICULTURE

Grains

1. Total Cereals: Third, after China and the USA.
India: 324.30 MT; **World**: 2,963.81 MT; **Percentage Share**: 10.94

2. Rice: Second, after China.
India: 177.65 MT **World:** 749.19 MT; **Percentage Share:** 23.71

3. Wheat: Second, after China.
India: 103.60 MT; **World:** 764.98 MT; **Percentage Share:** 13.54

4. Pulses: First
India: 21.54 **World:** 84.69 **Percentage Share:** 25.44

AREA (in million hectares)

Total Area: Seventh, after the Russian Federation, Canada, the USA, China, Brazil and Australia.
India: 328.73; **World:** 13,497.30; **Percentage Share:** 2.44

Land Area: Seventh, after the Russian Federation, China, the USA, Canada, Brazil and Australia.
India: 297.32; **World:** 13,030.09; **Percentage Share:** 2.28

Arable Land: Second, after the USA
India: 156.07; **World:** 1,383.35; **Percentage Share:** 11.28

Oilseeds

5. Groundnut: Second, after China.
India: 6.73 MT **World:** 49.54 MT
Percentage Share: 13.58

6. Rapeseed: Third, after Canada and China.
India: 9.26 MT; **World:** 49.54 MT;
Percentage Share: 12.88

Rapeseed

Groundnut

Commercial Crops

7. Sugarcane: Second, after Brazil.
India: 405 MT; **World:** 1,955 MT; **Percentage Share:** 20.73

8.Tea: Second, after China.
India: 1.39 MT; **World:** 6.76 MT; **Percentage Share:** 20.56

9. Coffee (green): Eighth, after Brazil, Vietnam, Colombia, Indonesia, Ethiopia, Honduras and Peru.
India: 0.32 MT; **World:** 10.03 MT; **Percentage Share:** 3.19

10. Jute: First.
India: 1.71 MT; **World:** 3.38 MT; **Percentage Share:** 50.52

11. Vegetables: Second, after China.
India: 137.40 MT; **World:** 1,129.67 MT; **Percentage Share:** 12.16

12. Fruits: Second, after China.
India: 104.05 MT; **World:** 882.16 MT; **Percentage Share:** 11.79

13. Onions: Second, after China.
India: 22.82 MT; **World:** 99.52 MT; **Percentage Share:** 22.93

14. Potatoes: Second, after China.
India: 50.19 MT; **World:** 354.81 MT; **Percentage Share:** 14.15

Tea
Coffee
Sugarcane
Potato
Fruits
Vegetables

Livestock

15. Cattle: Second, after Brazil.

India: 193.46 MH*; **World:** 1,511.11 MH; **Percentage Share:** 12.80

16. Buffaloes: First.

India: 109.85 MH; **World:** 202.45 MH; **Percentage Share:** 54.26

17. Camels: Nineteenth, after Chad, Somalia, Sudan, Kenya, Niger, Ethiopia, Mauritania, Mali, Pakistan, UAE, Saudi Arabia, Mongolia, Yemen, Algeria, China, Eritrea, Nigeria and Oman.

India: 0.25 MH; **World:** 38.16 MH; **Percentage Share:** 0.66

18. Sheep: Second, after China.

India: 74.26 MH; **World:** 1,240.31 MH; **Percentage Share:** 5.99

19. Goats: First.

India: 148.88 MH; **World:** 1,108.97 MH

Percentage Share: 13.43

20. Chickens: Seventh, after the USA, China, Indonesia, Brazil, Pakistan and Iran.

India: 807.89 MH; **World:** 33,235.54 MH; **Percentage Share:** 2.43

Dairy Products

21. Milk: First.

India: 187.63; MT **World:** 876.83 MT; **Percentage Share:** 21.40

22. Eggs: Third, after China and the USA.

India: 6.29 MT; **World:** 90.38 MT; **Percentage Share:** 6.96

23. Meat: Fifth, after China, the USA, Brazil and the Russian Federation.

India: 8.14; **World:** 335.46; **Percentage Share:** 2.13

*MH = million heads

with an estimated 536.76 million heads of cattle by 2019, making up as much as 31 per cent of the world's livestock population.

Largest dairy development programme

Project Operation Flood, launched in 1970 by the National Dairy Development Board (NDDB) and led by Dr Verghese Kurien, general manager and later chairman, AMUL, and chairman, NDDB and the Institute of Rural Management Anand (IRMA), Gujarat, involved forming a National Milk Grid that connected milk producers to consumers in over 700 towns and cities in India.

Top milk-producing country

India has led the world in milk production since 1997. Milk production in the country increased to 209.96 million tonnes during 2021. India contributes 21 per cent of the global milk production. The top milk-producing states are Uttar Pradesh, Rajasthan and Madhya Pradesh.

Heaviest and highest-priced bull

In March 2018, Haryana's first Murrah Ratan Award was won by a buffalo called Shahenshah, which weighed between 1,100 and 1,200 kg and was owned by Narender Singh from Didwari Village, Panipat, Haryana.

Heaviest goat

Asif Ali from Bhopal, Madhya Pradesh, reared the heaviest goat named King on his R.K. Goat Farm. King weighed 171 kg on 25 July 2019.

State with the most veterinary institutions

Rajasthan leads Indian states and UTs with 7,897 veterinary institutions (31 March 2018).

Highest stud farm

The Zanskar Pony Breeding and Training Centre at Partapur in Nubra Block, Ladakh, is located at 3,146 m (10,321 ft) above the mean sea level.

Oldest cow

Ruby, a cow owned by Dr Dipa Panjuani of Pune, Maharashtra, crossed 35 years in 2017. It was milking till six months before it turned 32 years old.

POULTRY AND FISHERIES

First broiler chicken variety

B-77, the first broiler variety of chicken, was released by the IVRI in Izatnagar in Bareilly District, Uttar Pradesh, in 1977.

Largest dairy development programme

WR First transgenic rohu fish

During 2004–05, a team of scientists led by Dr T.J. Pandian at the Madurai Kamaraj University, Madurai, Tamil Nadu, developed a genetically modified rohu fish that could grow 6–7 times faster than a normal one.

First deep-sea fishing station

The Deep-Sea Fishing Station, Mumbai, Maharashtra, was set up in October 1946. It was renamed the Exploratory Fisheries Project (EFP) in 1974 when it systematically surveyed the coastal and offshore waters up to a depth of 70 m (230 ft). Engaged in oceanic surveys of Exclusive Economic Zones, it was renamed the Fishery Survey of India in 1979.

First pearl culture

The first cultured pearls, using the Akoya pearl oyster, were produced in 1973 at the Tuticorin Research Centre at the Central Marine Fisheries Research Institute (CMFRI) in Thoothukudi, Tamil Nadu, in collaboration with the Tamil Nadu State Fisheries Department.

First and only licensed fisherwoman

In 2017, K.C. Rekha from Thrissur, Kerala, became India's only licensed deep-sea fisherwoman. Rekha accompanies her husband Karthikeyan to work every day.

First research institute for freshwater aquaculture

The Central Institute of Freshwater Aquaculture, Bhubaneswar, Odisha, began in the Pond Culture Division of the Central Inland Fisheries Research Institute, at

The Department of Revenue and Agriculture and Commerce was set up in pre-Independence India.

FISH PRODUCTION IN INDIA
(in Million Tonnes)

Year	Inland	Marine	Total
1950-51	218	534	752
1960-61	280	880	1,160
1970-71	670	1,086	1,756
1980-81	887	1,555	2,442
1990-91	1,536	2,300	3,836
2000-01	2,845	2,811	5,656
2010-11	4,981	3,250	8,231
2019-20	10,437	3,727	14,164

Source: Department of Fisheries, Ministry of Fisheries, Animal Husbandry and Dairying

Cuttack, Odisha, in 1949. The division was later upgraded as the Freshwater Aquaculture Research and Training Centre in 1976. It became an independent institute on 1 April 1987.

First marine aquarium for ornamental fish
An aquarium for ornamental fish breeding and multiplication was established in 1998 in Vizhinjam near Kovalam in Kerala.

Ground-breaking Nano Urea for Indian Farmers

Dr Ramesh Raliya, a biotechnology scientist, who lives and works in India and the USA, has developed nano urea in liquid form to improve farm yields and prevent damage to crops due to indiscriminate use of agrochemicals. The patented nano urea can be sprayed directly on to leaves during the growth stages. This is better absorbed than the conventional urea through soil. A 500 ml bottle of this nano urea is said to be equivalent to a 45 kg bag of urea, making the process cheaper and more effective. Raliya licensed the nano urea to the Indian Farmers Fertilizer Cooperative Limited (IFFCO) for free so that they may get access to it at lower costs. In 2019, he set up a nanotechnology research and development centre at Gandhinagar, Gujarat, and the first nano urea plant was set up in Kalol in May 2022.

Dr Ramesh Raliya with a bottle of the nano urea developed by him

Oldest fisheries research institutes
The oldest fisheries research institutes are the Central Marine Fisheries Research Institute (CMFRI), established in 1947, and the Central Inland Capture Fisheries Research Institute (CICFRI), also set up in 1947 under the name of Central Inland Fisheries Research Institute (CIFRI) in Calcutta (now Kolkata, West Bengal).

Largest poultry company
Suguna Foods Private Ltd, which achieved a sales turnover of over ₹8,700 crore (87 billion) during 2019–20, is the largest broiler chicken company in India. Based in Coimbatore, Tamil Nadu, it ranks among the top 10 poultry enterprises worldwide and operates in 18 states in India, covering over 40,000 farmers in over 15,000 villages. Its products and services include hatcheries, feed mills, processing plants, value-added eggs, and broiler and frozen chicken.

Biggest hen egg
A hen at the Dev Research and Breeding Farms of Sukhbir Singh of Ramrai Khera in Jind, Haryana, laid an egg weighing 167 g on 28 September 2014. It was 8.35 cm (3.3 in.) long and 5 cm (2 in.) wide.

Top shrimp-producing state/UT
Andhra Pradesh led with 634,672 million tonnes, followed by West Bengal with 35,392 million tonnes, in 2020–21.

FERTILIZERS, PESTICIDES AND MACHINERY

First biocontrol agents
The ladybird beetle of Australia was introduced in 1898 to control mealy bugs on fruit crops.

Earliest soil treatment experiments
The earliest methods to find out the effects of inorganic fertilizers on the soil – its physical, chemical and biological properties vis-à-vis crop yields – were started at the Agricultural College and Research Institute, Coimbatore, Tamil Nadu, in 1909.

First fertilizer factory
The first SSP (single superphosphate) factory that produced fertilizer mixtures, insecticides and fungicides was set up in 1906 in Ranipet District in Tamil Nadu by East India Distilleries Parry Ltd.

First pesticide
Benzene hexachloride (BHC) was first

commercialized by the Imperial Chemical Industries Ltd (ICI) in 1952 at Rishra in Hooghly District, West Bengal. A factory was set up in Calcutta (now Kolkata, West Bengal).

First institute for farm machinery training and testing

The Central Farm Machinery Training and Testing Institute (FMTTI), established in 1959 in Budni, Sehore District, Madhya Pradesh, was the first of the four FMTTI centres in India. Since its inception and up to March 2020, the centre has trained a total of 69,056 trainees from across India.

First synthetic pesticide

DDT (Dichlorodiphenyltrichloroethane) was introduced in 1946 for vector control and used in 1948. Its use was banned in May 1989.

First neem-based biocide

The first neem-based biocide was tested and commissioned by the National Tree Growers Cooperative Federation during 1997–98.

State/UT with the highest use of chemical pesticides and biopesticides

Maharashtra was the highest consumer of chemical pesticides (13,175 million tonnes) and biopesticides (934.44 million tonnes) in 2020–21.

State/UT with the highest use of fertilizers per hectare

With a total consumption of 312.04 kg/hectare in 2021, Puducherry is the largest consumer of fertilizers (N, P & K).

First use of lift irrigation

In 1926, an experimental lift irrigation system on 1,012 hectares (2,500 acres) of wasteland was started in the Rachna Doab region of Gangapur Village in Punjab (now in Pakistan) by Sir Ganga Ram, a member of the Regional Commission on Agriculture.

First agri-plane

Hindustan Aeronautics Ltd's HA-31 Basant monoplane was built in 1972 for agricultural needs. Its use was discontinued in 1980.

Earliest use of tractors

Sardar Sir Jogendra Singh (1877–1946) experimented with steam tractors for wasteland reclamation in 1914 at Aira estate in Lakhimpur, Uttar Pradesh, and at Iqbal Nagar (now in Pakistan) in Punjab.

First semi-autonomous tractor

In April 2018, Mahindra and Mahindra Ltd rolled out a high-tech tractor, the Pack 1. This is an 'intelligent' tractor with a driver-assist system.

Neem leaves and fruit: The first neem-based biocide was commissioned during 1997–98

WR Largest seller of tractors

Mahindra and Mahindra Ltd is the largest-selling tractor brand in India, with total sales of 337,052 units in the financial year ended March 2022. It exported 17,646 units in the same period.

Most sold farm equipment with largest market share

Tractors have the biggest share of the farm machinery market in India, at 80 per cent. In 2020–21, overall tractor sales in the country were 842,266 units.

State/UT with most tractor exports

Maharashtra with exports worth US $186 million is the state with the most tractor exports in the year 2019–20. According to Directorate General of Commercial Intelligence and Statistics data, Punjab exported tractors worth US $178 million in 2019–20 while Tamil Nadu exported tractors worth US $156 million.

Tractors: farm equipment with the largest market share

GOVERNMENT

HISTORICAL PERSPECTIVE

Earliest republic on the subcontinent

Vrijji, a *mahajanapada* ('republic') of ancient India, dating to the sixth century BCE, is believed to be the earliest republic on the Indian subcontinent. It did not have a monarch, but instead a popular assembly of elders carried on the business of state. Vrijji was formed by the union of several clans, including the Lichchhavis, Jnatrikas and Videhas. Its capital was at Vaishali, in the present-day region of Mithila, Bihar.

Early administration

During the time of the Mauryan rulers (322–180 BCE), the state maintained a vast bureaucracy with important functionaries called *tirthas*. The top administrators were the minister (*mantri*), the high priest (*purohita*), the commander (*senapati*) and the prince (*yuvaraja*). An elaborate machinery was in place for taxation too.

First Indo-European alliance

Chandragupta Maurya met Alexander III of Macedon in 327 BCE – after the battle with Porus (or Puru) and the capture of Punjab – and teamed up with him for the capture of Magadha in what may be termed the first Indo–European treaty.

First woman ruler

In 1236 CE, Razia Sultan of the Mamluk dynasty ascended the Delhi throne, making her the first and only female ruler of the Delhi Sultanate and the first woman ruler in India.

First colonial rule

Colonial rule in India took seed with the establishment of the first European trading centre in Quilon (now Kollam), Kerala, in 1502 by the Portuguese. Dom Francisco de Almeida was appointed the first Portuguese viceroy in India by King Manuel I of Portugal in 1505.

First War of Independence

The country's First War of Independence, which British historians called the Sepoy Mutiny or the Rebellion of 1857, was the first organized fight against the colonial rulers, and an important milestone in the long struggle for independence.

First design of the national flag

The 'Flag of Indian Independence' was raised by freedom fighter Bhikhaiji (or Bhikaji) Rustam Cama (1861–1936) from Bombay (now Mumbai), Maharashtra, on 22 August 1907 at the International Socialist Conference in Stuttgart, Germany. It was based on the 'Calcutta flag', which was one of the first unofficial flags of India, designed by Sachindra Prasad Bose and Hemchandra Kanungo, and hoisted on 7 August 1906 at Parsi Bagan Square, Calcutta (now Kolkata, West Bengal). Cama's flag featured three colours: the top band was green, the middle one was saffron and the bottom one was red. The upper band had eight lotuses, symbolizing the eight provinces of British India. The middle band had the words '*Vande Mataram*' in Devanagari script, and the lower band had a crescent and a sun, representing Islam and Hinduism respectively. The flag went through many versions before reaching its present form.

First rendition of the national song

'*Vande Mataram*', India's national song, composed by Bankim Chandra Chatterjee and published for the first time in his work *Anandamath*, was first sung at the Indian National Congress session in 1896 in Calcutta (now Kolkata, West Bengal).

First rendition of the national anthem

'Jana Gana Mana', India's national anthem composed by Rabindranath Tagore, was sung for the first time on 27 December 1911 at the Calcutta (now Kolkata, West Bengal), session of the Indian National Congress. The song was formally adopted in its Hindi version by the Constituent Assembly as India's national anthem on 24 January 1950.

First satyagraha

In 1917, Mahatma Gandhi organized the first satyagraha, a non-violent protest, in Champaran, Bihar, for indigo cultivators, against British laws governing the cultivation of the plant.

First Republic Day parade

India became an independent nation on 15 August 1947, and declared itself a sovereign and democratic republic with the promulgation of the Constitution of India on 26 January 1950. The first Republic Day parade was held five years later in 1955 at Rajpath (now Kartavya Path), New Delhi, which became its permanent venue.

Shortest reign

Following the death of Alauddin Khilji (Khilji dynasty) in 1316, Malik Kafur captured the

Dom Francisco de Almeida: first Portuguese viceroy in India

Tantia Tope's soldiery: first War of Independence

Amrit Kaal: The Next 25 Years

Several times in the past year, the phrase 'Amrit Kaal' has cropped up, such as in the speeches of Prime Minister Modi and Finance Minister Nirmala Sitharaman. It refers to a blueprint of the vision and hope for the country as it moves towards 100 years of Independence. The prime minister described this broadly as excellence in every field, but in a more detailed way, the objective of this is to improve the lives of all citizens, bridge the developmental, social and financial divide between villages and cities, reduce government intervention in public life, cut down overlapping compliances, and increase focus on energy transition and climate action, using the latest technologies. It also includes Prime Minister Gati Shakti, a national master plan for multi-modal connectivity. This is a digital platform to bring 16 ministries together for integrated planning and coordinated execution of infrastructure connectivity projects to ensure the smooth movement of people, goods and services from one mode of transport to another. This will ease the last mile connectivity of infrastructure and reduce travel time for people.

There have been **15** presidents and **14** prime ministers of India since Independence.

throne of Delhi. His reign lasted between 25 and 30 days. He was ousted by Alauddin's son, Shihabuddin Omar.

Longest colonial rule

Goa, Daman and Diu were under colonial rule for the longest period in Indian history – over 450 years. For over a decade after the British had left India, the Portuguese ruled these pockets as 'Estado da India Portuguesa' (the Portuguese State of India). They were liberated by the Indian Army on 19 December 1961.

PARTIES AND ELECTIONS

First political organization

The first recorded political organization in the country was the Zamindari Association of Calcutta (now Kolkata), West Bengal. Formally launched in 1838, it was a body of landlords, which changed its name to Landholders' Association shortly after its inception. Its principal organizers were Radhakanta Deb and Prasanna Kumar Tagore. Set up to defend the landlords against the so-called pro-peasant policies of the government, it became defunct in 1851.

Oldest political party

Allan Octavian Hume, a member of the Imperial Civil Service, initiated the events that led to the formation of the first political party in India. Speaking out against British policies in India, in 1883, he exhorted Calcutta University graduates to form their own national political movement. This led to the first session of the Indian National Congress in Bombay (now Mumbai), Maharashtra, in 1885.

First party constitution

The first constitution of the Indian National Congress was drawn up in 1908, after the split in the party between the moderates and the extremists in the 1907 session held in Surat, Gujarat.

First woman to address a session of the Indian National Congress

Kadambini Ganguly, who was the first Indian woman doctor, was the first woman to address an open session of the Indian National Congress held in Calcutta (now Kolkata, West Bengal), in 1901, when she moved the vote of thanks.

First woman president of the Indian National Congress

British socialist and women's rights activist Annie Besant, who was elected president of the Indian National Congress in 1917, was the first woman to head the party.

First communist party

According to the Communist Party of India (Marxist), M.N. Roy, Virendranath Chattopadhyay and Abani Mukherjee set up a communist party in Tashkent, Uzbekistan, in 1920. However, the Communist Party of India goes by the belief that the first communist party in India was established by Satyabhakta, a left-wing Congressman, in Kanpur, Uttar Pradesh, in December 1925.

Longest-serving president of the Indian National Congress

Sonia Gandhi, the Italian-born Indian politician and wife of former Indian prime minister Rajiv Gandhi, was the longest-serving president of the Indian National Congress.

She headed the party from 1998 to 2017. With her at the helm, the Congress-led United Progressive Alliance (UPA) was victorious in the 2004 and 2009 general elections.

First chief election commissioner

Sukumar Sen (1898–1963) was India's first chief election commissioner from 21 March 1950 to 19 December 1958. Under his leadership, the Election Commission of India conducted India's first two general elections during 1951–52 and 1957. He also administered the first parliamentary elections in Sudan in 1953.

First general election

India went to the polls as an independent country for the first time during 1951–52, with 314 constituencies with one seat, 86 constituencies with two seats, and one with three seats. There were also two nominated Anglo-Indian members. At the time, the Election Commission of India recognized 14 political parties as multi-state parties and 39 parties as state parties. Voting in the election was based on the 'balloting system', i.e., casting votes in ballot boxes allotted to the respective candidates.

Longest tenure as chief election commissioner

K.V.K. Sundaram, India's second chief election commissioner, served for eight years, nine months and 11 days, from 20 December 1958 to 30 September 1967.

Shortest tenure as chief election commissioner

V.S. Ramadevi, the first woman chief election commissioner (acting) of the country, held the post of chief election commissioner for only 17 days from 26 November 1990 to 12 December 1990.

First use of single ballot paper and single ballot box

The general election of 1962 introduced the single ballot paper system, in which the voter had to mark one choice from the candidates and drop the paper in a ballot box. Earlier, during the 1951–52 and 1957 Lok Sabha elections, there were separate ballot boxes for each candidate with their name and party symbol on them.

First use of indelible ink

Indelible ink was used for the first time in the third Lok Sabha elections in 1962. Mysore Paints and Varnish Ltd, based in Mysore (now Mysuru), Karnataka, was authorized to manufacture the ink. The company continues to supply this ink to this date.

First electronic voting machines

Electronic voting machines (EVMs) were used for the first time in the assembly by-elections in Kerala in April 1982. The machines were introduced by the Electronics Corporation of India Ltd (ECIL).

First app launched for voter vigilance

For the first time in elections, an application called 'cVIGIL' was launched for citizens to report any malpractice or violation of the model code of conduct before or during elections. This app includes a combination of live photo/ video and time-stamping with auto-location. A government official is bound to respond within 100 minutes. Launched in July 2018, the app was rolled out across India before the 2019 Lok Sabha election.

First 'Others' category of voters

A third gender category of voters, called 'Others', was introduced in the electoral rolls in 2014. As many as 28,314 voters enrolled in this category in 2014 and 38,970 voters in 2019.

First teenage vote

The 61st amendment of the Constitution of India in 1989 lowered the voting age for election to the Lok Sabha and the state legislatures from 21 years to 18 years. As a result, 35.7 million voters in the age group of 18–21 years voted.

First NOTA option

The 2014 general elections were the first to offer Indian voters the option of choosing 'None of the Above' (NOTA), also known as the 'against all' or a 'scratch' vote internationally. The NOTA option provides a neutral vote to those electors who do not wish to vote for any candidate on the electoral ballot. Around 1.04 per cent of voters polled NOTA in the 2019 elections.

First EVMs/ postal ballot papers with photographs of candidates

For the first time in the history of elections in India, the EVMs/postal ballot papers carried the photographs of all the candidates in the constituency. This was done to enable the voters to identify the political leaders and to avoid confusion between candidates with similar names.

Sukumar Sen: first chief election commissioner

Though India became independent in August 1947, the last of the British troops left India only in February the next year.

President Droupadi Murmu: Setting an Example

President Droupadi Murmu

The National Democratic Alliance (NDA) nominee, Droupadi Murmu, made history in the presidential election held on 18 July 2022, when she defeated opposition candidate Yashwant Sinha and became the 15th president of India, She is not only the second woman president of the country, but also the first from a tribal community – and the youngest of all Indian presidents to date.

Born to a Santhali farming family on 20 June 1958, in Uparbeda Village in the Baidaposi area of Rairangpur, Odisha, she was named Puti Biranchi Tudu, but a schoolteacher renamed her 'Droupadi'. She studied in the village school and then in Bhubaneswar city. She worked as a junior assistant in the State Irrigation and Power Department from 1979 to 1983, and then as a teacher at Sri Aurobindo Integral Education Centre at Rairangpur till 1997. In that year, she was elected as the councillor of the Rairangpur Nagar Panchayat as an independent candidate from a reserved seat for women. She then joined the Bharatiya Janata Party (BJP). Before she became the president of the country, she served as the ninth governor of Jharkhand between 2015 and 2021, as a member of the Odisha Legislative Assembly between 2000 and 2009, and as the minister of state for fisheries and animal resources development in Odisha between 2000 and 2002. She was awarded the Nilkanth Award for the Best MLA in 2007 by the Odisha Legislative Assembly.

First transgender election ambassador

Gauri Sawant, a transgender activist from Mumbai, Maharashtra, was appointed as the first transgender election ambassador in the country in 2019.

Highest voter turnout in the Lok Sabha general election

The 2019 general election had the largest voter turnout to date with 613,136,854 voters, constituting 67.1 per cent of the total electorate of the country.

Lowest voter turnout in the Lok Sabha general election

In the 1951–52 general election, which was the first election to be held in independent India, only 44.87 per cent of the electorate was recorded as having cast their votes.

Fewest women elected in a general election

Only 19 women were elected in the 1977 general election, which was the fewest ever in the history of general elections.

Most female candidates in a Lok Sabha general election

The 2019 general election registered a total of 723 female candidates.

Most women elected in a Lok Sabha general election

Seventy-eight women were elected in the 2019 Lok Sabha general election, making it the election with the highest number of successful female candidates.

Most independent candidates elected in a general election

In the history of Indian elections, independent candidates had the most successful run in the 1957 general election, winning 42 seats.

Most independent candidates in a general election

The 1996 general election had a total of 10,636 independent candidates, the highest ever to date.

Fewest independent candidates elected in a general election

Only three of the 3,235 independent candidates in the 2014 general election were successful, the lowest win by independents in the history of general elections in India.

WR Largest electorate

The number of voters in the 2019 general election was 908,722,153, making India the largest (most populous) democracy in the world.

WR The most expensive election

The 2019 Lok Sabha election was estimated to be the most expensive election in the world. An estimated ₹55,000 crore (550 billion) was spent during these elections, according to a report brought out by the Centre for Media Studies.

Voter-verifiable paper audit trail in all constituencies for the first time

The Election Commission of India set up the voter-verifiable paper audit trail or VVPAT system in all constituencies in 2019. The VVPAT prints a slip with the serial number, name and symbol of the candidate for whom the vote was cast.

TOP BILLING

Here's an account of the number of bills passed by both houses of Parliament, ever since they were formed.

Year	Number of sittings: Lok Sabha	Number of sittings: Rajya Sabha	Bills passed by both Houses of Parliament
1952	103	60	82
1953	137	100	58
1954	137	103	54
1955	139	111	60
1956	151	113	106
1957	104	78	68
1958	125	91	59
1959	123	87	63
1960	121	87	67
1961	102	75	63
1962	116	91	68
1963	122	100	58
1964	122	97	56
1965	113	96	51
1966	119	109	57
1967	110	91	38
1968	120	103	67
1969	120	102	58
1970	119	107	53
1971	102	89	87
1972	111	99	82
1973	120	105	70
1974	119	109	68
1975	63	58	57
1976	98	84	118
1977	86	70	48
1978	115	97	50
1979	66	54	32
1980	96	90	72
1981	105	89	62
1982	92	82	73
1983	93	77	49
1984	77	63	73
1985	109	89	92
1986	98	86	71
1987	102	89	61
1988	102	89	71
1989	83	71	38
1990	81	66	30
1991	90	82	63
1992	98	90	44
1993	89	79	75
1994	77	75	61
1995	78	77	45
1996	70	64	36
1997	65	68	35
1998	64	59	40
1999	51	48	39
2000	85	85	63
2001	81	81	61
2002	84	82	86
2003	74	74	56
2004	48	46	18
2005	85	85	56
2006	77	77	65
2007	66	65	46
2008	46	46	47
2009	64	63	41
2010	81	81	43
2011	73	73	36
2012	73+1	73+1	32
2013	63	63	29
2014	67	64	38
2015	72	69	36
2016	70	72	43
2017	61	61	44
2018	63	65	29
2019	67	65	49
2020	33	33	39
2021	59	58	51

Oldest winning candidate
Bharatiya Janata Party (BJP) leader Lal Krishna (L.K.) Advani was 86 years old when he won the Gandhinagar seat in Gujarat in the 2014 general elections.

Youngest winning candidate
Biju Janata Dal (BJD) member Chandrani Murmu was only 25 years old when she contested and won the Keonjhar seat in Odisha in the 2019 general election.

State/UT with the largest electorate
Uttar Pradesh had the largest electorate in the 2019 general election, with 145,858,999 eligible voters.

State/UT with the smallest electorate
The Union Territory of Lakshadweep had the smallest electorate in the 2019 general election, comprising a total of 55,057 eligible voters. The UT also holds the record for being the constituency with the smallest electorate in the country.

State/UT with the largest voter turnout
Madhya Pradesh had the largest voter turnout in terms of the percentage of the total number of voters in the 2019 general election, with a turnout of 71.2 per cent. In terms of number of voters, Uttar Pradesh, with 86,481,398 voters, led all states.

State/UT with the smallest voter turnout
In terms of percentage turnout, Jammu and Kashmir (before Ladakh was separated from it) had the smallest voter turnout in the 2019 general election, with 29.39 per cent of the voters turning out to vote. In terms of the number of voters, Lakshadweep, with 47,009 voters registered the smallest voter turnout.

Most voter IDs distributed – 1 hr
The district administration of Allahabad (now Prayagraj), Uttar Pradesh, led by District Magistrate Sanjay Kumar and Chief Development Officer Andra Vamsi, conducted the largest ever voter ID distribution camp on 16 February 2017, distributing 12,594 voter ID cards in one hour. The distribution event took place from 11:00 a.m. to 12:00 noon at the Parade Ground in the city.

WR Highest polling station
The polling station at Tashigang in Spiti Valley, Himachal Pradesh, situated at an altitude of 4,650 m (15,256 ft), is the highest polling station in the world. The polling station has 47 registered voters. In October 2021, the bypoll registered 52 votes as five local officials obtained permission to vote at Tashigang.

PRESIDENTS AND VICE PRESIDENTS

First presidential election
The first presidential election in the country was held in 1962 when former vice president Dr S. Radhakrishnan (1888–1975) became the president of India. He held the post till 1967.

First vice president
Dr S. Radhakrishnan was vice president of India during 1952–62. He also had the longest tenure as vice president, that of 10 years, a record he shares with Hamid Ansari, who was in office from 11 August 2007 to 11 August 2017.

First woman president
Pratibha Patil (in office: 25 July 2007–25 July 2012) became the first woman to be appointed the president of India. Earlier, Pratibha Patil had held the office of governor of Rajasthan during 2004–07. She was affiliated with the Indian National Congress.

Oldest to become president
On 25 July 1997, K.R. Narayanan (1920–2005) assumed the office of president of India when he was 76 years and 271 days old, making him the oldest president to assume office.

L.K. Advani: oldest winning candidate in a general election

Dr S. Radhakrishnan (*left*): first vice president

Aadhaar: Keeping It Secure

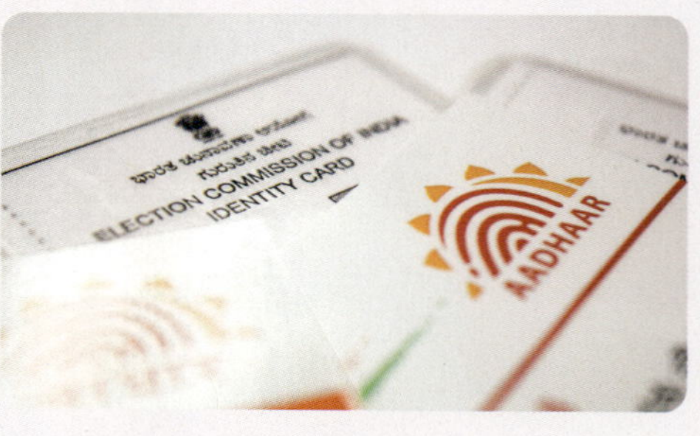

Following confusion over whether citizens should give photocopies of their Aadhaar cards to unlicensed private institutions which retain them, the Unique Identification Authority of India (UIDAI) asked citizens not to download e-Aadhaar copies on public computers. When they do, they must delete all downloaded copies from the device. The Aadhaar has become a key identity document for a number of operations including opening a bank account or investing in a government scheme.

Oldest vice president to assume office

Bhairon Singh Shekhawat (1923–2010) became vice president on 19 August 2002, when he was 79 years of age.

Youngest to become president

Droupadi Murmu (b. 20 June 1958) became the youngest president of India when she assumed the office of president of India on 25 July 2022 at the age of 64 years and 35 days. The earlier record was held by former president Dr Zakir Husain who became president at 64 years and 67 days.

Shortest tenure as president

Dr Zakir Hussain (1897–1969), the third president of India, held the office of president from 13 May 1967 until his death, for a little less than two years. Dr Husain was also the first president to die in harness.

Dr Rajendra Prasad: longest tenure as president

Longest tenure as president

Dr Rajendra Prasad (1884–1963), a lawyer and freedom fighter, was appointed as the first president of India on 26 January 1950, a post he occupied for 12 years, three months and 18 days until 13 May 1962.

V.V. Giri: shortest tenure as vice president

Shortest tenure as vice president

V.V. Giri (1894–1980) was vice president for two years during 1967–69, making his tenure the shortest for a vice president. He was elevated to the post of (acting) president on 24 August 1969, following the death of Dr Zakir Husain.

Most presidents from a state

With three presidents to date, Tamil Nadu is the state that has given the country the most number of presidents. They are: S. Radhakrishnan, R. Venkataraman and A.P.J. Abdul Kalam.

- Dr S. Radhakrishnan, the first vice president and second president of India, held the position of president during 1962–67.
- R. Venkataraman, the eighth president of India, held office during 1987–92.
- A.P.J. Abdul Kalam, the 11th president of India, held the presidential office during 2002–07.

Sardar Vallabhbhai Patel: first deputy prime minister

PRIME MINISTERS

First prime minister

Jawaharlal Nehru became the first prime minister of India on 15 August 1947. Previously, he headed the interim government as prime minister, starting 2 September 1946. He served as prime minister until he died on 27 May 1964.

First and only woman prime minister

Indira Gandhi, the first and only woman to become prime minister of India, was in office from 1966 until 1977. She was re-elected in 1980 and her second tenure lasted four years, until her assassination in 1984.

First prime minister to die in harness

- Jawaharlal Nehru, the first prime minister of India, passed away on 27 May 1964, after serving the office for 17 years. He was the first prime minister of India to die in harness.
- Jawaharlal Nehru's successor, Lal Bahadur Shastri, died at Tashkent, Uzbekistan, on 11 January 1966. He was the first prime minister of India to die in harness abroad.
- Indira Gandhi was the first Indian prime minister to be assassinated while in office, on 31 October 1984.

First prime minister to resign

Morarji Ranchhodji Desai (1896–1995) was the first prime minister of India to resign from the office. He assumed office on 24 March 1977 and resigned from his post on 28 July 1979, following a split in the Janata Party, which he was heading at the time.

First deputy prime minister

Sardar Vallabhbhai Patel was sworn in as the first deputy prime minister of India on 15 August 1947 in the first cabinet of independent India, which was headed by the then prime minister Jawaharlal Nehru.

Oldest to become prime minister

Morarji Ranchhodji Desai, a freedom fighter during India's struggle for Independence, became prime minister at the age of 81 years and 24 days on 24 March 1977. Earlier he had held many offices, such as those of minister of home affairs, deputy prime minister and finance minister. He was also the chief minister of undivided Bombay state from April 1952 to October 1956.

Youngest to become prime minister

Rajiv Gandhi assumed office on 31 October 1984, when he was 40 years and 72 days, following the assassination of his mother, Prime Minister Indira Gandhi.

Shortest tenure as prime minister

- Chaudhary Charan Singh (1902–87) was prime minister for 171 days from 28 July 1979 to 14 January 1980, making him the shortest-tenured prime minister on record.

- Gulzari Lal Nanda had two shorter tenures as acting prime minister, once from 27 May to 9 June 1964, after Jawaharlal Nehru's death, and again from 11 to 24 January 1966, following Lal Bahadur Shastri's demise.

THE PARLIAMENT

First session of Parliament

The first session of Parliament in free India was held on 13 May 1952 with Jawaharlal Nehru as prime minister and Dr Rajendra Prasad as president.

First Speaker of the Lok Sabha

Freedom fighter 'Dadasaheb' G.V. Mavalankar was the first Speaker of the Lok Sabha, holding the post from 15 May 1952 to 27 February 1956.

First deputy Speaker of the Lok Sabha

On 30 May 1952, Madabhushi Ananthasayanam Ayyangar was elected as deputy Speaker of the Lok Sabha.

First visually impaired member of Parliament

Sadhan Chandra Gupta (1917–2015), an Indian lawyer and politician, became the first blind member of Parliament (MP) in 1953. He later served as the advocate general of West Bengal. Gupta was elected to the Lok Sabha from the Calcutta (now Kolkata), West Bengal, South-east constituency in a 1953 by-election on a Communist Party of India (CPI) ticket.

First woman secretary general of Rajya Sabha

V.S. Ramadevi was the first woman to be appointed as the Secretary General of the Rajya Sabha on 1 July 1993, for three years. She was also acting chief election commissioner for some time in 1990.

First representative in the British House of Commons

The 'Grand Old Man of India', Dadabhai Naoroji, was the first Indian-origin and non-white member of the British House of Commons, when he was elected as a Liberal Party member of Parliament in London from Central Finsbury in July 1892, by a bare majority of three votes. He held the position till 1895.

First couple in Parliament

Joachim and Violet Alva from Karnataka were the first couple in Parliament. While Violet was elected to the Rajya Sabha in 1952, Joachim became a Lok Sabha member in the same year.

Srinagar, Jammu and Kashmir

Jammu and Kashmir Aces e-Governance Parameters

Among all the Union Territories, Jammu and Kashmir topped in e-Governance services delivery with an overall compliance of nearly 90 per cent, as mentioned in the National e-Governance Service Delivery Assessment (NeSDA) report 2021, prepared at the initiative of Department of Administrative Reforms and Public Grievances (DARPG) in the Union Ministry of Personnel. The Union Territory enabled savings of around ₹200 crore annually, which used to be incurred in the carriage of 300 truckloads of physical files during the Annual Durbar move between the two capital cities of Jammu and Srinagar. The operationalization of two secretariats in Jammu and Kashmir using e-Office also enabled an uninterrupted work culture without any official break of six weeks for organization of files in the two cities, which was the earlier practice. Jammu and Kashmir became the first UT to have the Good Governance Index and the first to launch the District Good Governance Index for 20 districts.

First state legislative assembly

The maharaja of Travancore, Sree Moolam Thirunal Rama Varma, constituted an eight-member assembly in March 1888. A bicameral system was introduced on 28 October 1932 by King Chithira Thirunal Balarama Varma, who abolished the existing council and set up the Sree Moolam Assembly (Lower House) and the Sree Chitra State Council (Upper House).

First woman legislator

Dr S. Muthulakshmi Reddy was a social worker, educationist and physician, with many firsts to her credit. In 1926, she became the first woman legislator (Madras Legislative Council member) and in 1930, by way of the All India Women's Conference, pushed through the Child Marriage Restraint Act. She was also the first woman alderman of the Madras Corporation in 1937.

Dr S. Muthulakshmi Reddy: first woman to be elected to a legislative body

First Lok Sabha dissolution

The fifth Lok Sabha was dissolved by Indira Gandhi in 1971, for the first time in the history

There are currently **52** ministries and **57** departments under the Union government.

of the Indian Parliament. The second Lok Sabha dissolution came in 1979 under Charan Singh, and the third was the ninth Lok Sabha on 6 March 1991 under Chandra Shekhar.

First hung Parliament

A hung parliament is a situation where no single political party has an absolute majority of seats in the Parliament. For the first time in nine general elections, India's electorate did not give a decisive verdict in 1989. The Congress (I) was ousted in the north and the ruling regional parties were similarly ousted in the south.

Longest tenure as Rajya Sabha chairman

Dr S. Radhakrishnan, the second president and first vice president of India, had the longest tenure as chairman of the Rajya Sabha, from 1952 to 1962.

Longest term as Speaker

Balram Jakhar served as Speaker from 1980 to 1989, for eight years and 329 days in two terms, becoming the Speaker with the longest tenure.

Shortest term as Speaker

Neelam Sanjiva Reddy was Lok Sabha Speaker from 26 March to 13 July 1977, thus serving the shortest term as Speaker. He was the sixth president of India, from 1977 to 1982.

Shortest Lok Sabha term

The 12th Lok Sabha lasted from 10 March 1998 to 26 April 1999, a duration of around 13 months, due to the withdrawal of support by the All-India Anna Dravida Munnetra Kazhagam (AIADMK) from the National Democratic Alliance (NDA) government led by Atal Bihari Vajpayee.

Shortest session of state legislative assembly

There was a one-minute session of the Rajasthan Legislative Assembly from 11:00 a.m. to 11:01 a.m. on 14 August 1972, the shortest session of a legislative assembly on record.

Lok Sabha with highest average age

The average age of the elected MPs in the current 17th Lok Sabha is 54 years, making it the Lok Sabha with the highest average age in the history of the Indian Parliament.

Lok Sabha with lowest average age

The first Lok Sabha (1952–57) had the lowest average age of 46.5 years.

Maximum bills passed in a year

The Parliament passed 118 bills in 1976, which is the highest number of bills ever passed by it in a single year.

National party with most votes

The Congress (I) secured a record 115,221,078 votes (78.5 per cent of the total votes) and won 412 out of the 513 parliamentary seats in the elections held in December 1984. This is the largest victory margin of any political party on record.

UNION GOVERNMENT

First non-Congress government

The Janata Party, led by Jayaprakash Narayan, overthrew the Indira Gandhi government in the 1977 general election to form the first non-Congress government in the history of independent India. Morarji Desai was appointed prime minister of the government formed by the Janata Party.

First electoral win by an Indian political party

In the elections held under the provisions of the Government of India Act, 1935, the Indian National Congress formed governments in seven states, in addition to a coalition ministry in Assam. They lasted till October–November

INDIA AT HER BEST 75 YEARS OF INDEPENDENCE

GENERAL ELECTION STATISTICS

Year	Number of Contesting Candidates	Number of Polling Stations	Number of Registered Voters (in millions)	Voter Turnout (in percentage)
1951	1,874	196,084	173.2	45.7
1957	1,519	220,478	193.7	47.7
1962	1,985	238,031	216.4	55.4
1967	2,369	243,693	250.2	61.0
1971	2,784	342,918	274.2	55.3
1977	2,439	373,910	321.2	60.5
1980	4,629	436,813	356.2	56.9
1984-85	5,492	506,058	400.3	64.0
1989	6,160	580,798	498.9	62.0
1991-92	8,749	591,020	511.5	55.9
1996	13,952	767,462	592.6	57.9
1998	4,750	772,681	605.9	62.0
1999	4,648	774,651	619.5	60.0
2004	5,435	687,473	671.5	58.1
2009	8,070	830,866	717.0	58.2
2014	8,251	927,553	834.0	66.4
2019	8,054	1,037,848	912.0	67.4

Source: *Electoral Statistics Pocket Book* 2021, Election Commission, Government of India

THE PRIME MINISTER'S VISITS IN 2022

International Visits

Denmark
Uzbekistan
Nepal
Japan
Germany
France
United Arab Emirates

1939, after which they unanimously resigned in protest against the inclusion of Indians in the Second World War.

First woman full-term finance minister
Nirmala Sitharaman became the first woman to be a full-fledged finance minister of India on 31 May 2019. She is the second woman finance minister after former prime minister Indira Gandhi, who held the finance ministerial office for some time while she was prime minister during 1970–71. Sitharaman was also the first woman minister with defence as her sole portfolio from 2014 to 2019.

First Union minister to die in harness
Sardar Vallabhbhai Patel, India's first home minister and first deputy prime minister, who died on 15 December 1950, was the first Union minister to die while in office.

First Union minister to resign
Dr Syama Prasad Mookerjee resigned from the Union cabinet on 19 April 1950. After leaving the Nehru government and the Congress party, he founded the Bharatiya Jana Sangh in 1951.

Longest serving cabinet minister
Babu Jagjivan Ram was a Union minister for over 28 years from 15 August 1947 to 25 July 1979 with a break from 31 August 1963 to 24 January 1966. Some of the portfolios held by him included the Ministry of Labour, the Ministry of Defence, and the Ministry of Transport and Communications.

Shortest tenure of a cabinet minister
Justice H.R. Khanna was in office as the minister for law and justice in the Charan Singh ministry for five days from 30 July to 3 August 1979.

First woman cabinet minister
Vijaya Lakshmi Pandit was elected to the provincial legislature of the United Provinces as minister for local government and health in 1937, making her the first woman cabinet minister. Later, she was president of the United Nations General Assembly from September 1953 to September 1954.

Babu Jagjivan Ram: longest serving cabinet minister

Domestic Visits

1. Madhya Pradesh
2. Uttar Pradesh
3. Kerala
4. Karnataka
5. Gujarat
6. Haryana
7. Punjab
8. Tamil Nadu
9. Jharkhand
10. Bihar
11. Andhra Pradesh
12. Himachal Pradesh
13. Maharashtra
14. Telangana
15. Nagaland
16. Assam
17. Jammu and Kashmir
18. Goa
19. Uttarakhand
20. Manipur
21. Tripura

The Government of India divided the country into 14 states and six Union Territories under the State Reorganization Act.

First use of Hindi at UN

Atal Bihari Vajpayee (1924–2018), former prime minister of India, gave a historic speech in Hindi at the United Nations General Assembly in 1977 as India's minister for external affairs, the first to do so. This was the first time when any Indian leader had given a speech in Hindi at any international platform. It was translated into English by an Indian diplomat. Vajpayee spoke again in Hindi in 1978.

THE STATES

First linguistic state (pre-1947)

The Orissa (now Odisha) province that was formed as a result of the division of the Bihar and Orissa province in 1936, was the first to be formed on a linguistic basis.

First chief minister elected abroad

M.G. Ramachandran (popularly known as 'MGR') was elected chief minister of Tamil Nadu while he was admitted in a New York hospital. His nomination papers for the Andipatti assembly constituency were flown in from the USA and he was elected in absentia. He was sworn in on 10 February 1985, forty-three days after the election.

First linguistic state (post-1947)

The Telugu-speaking Andhra state was carved out of Madras state on 1 October 1953, with its capital at Kurnool. It was later merged with the Telugu-speaking areas of Hyderabad state to form Andhra Pradesh on 1 November 1956.

First modern Indian states

The Indian states of Bihar and Orissa (now Odisha) were the first to be formed in British India. The Bihar and Orissa province of Bengal Presidency was carved out as a separate province on 1 April 1912, which included the present-day states of Bihar, Jharkhand and parts of Odisha. On 1 April 1936, the then Bihar and Orissa province was divided into the separate provinces of Bihar and Orissa.

State sharing borders with most states

Uttar Pradesh shares its borders with nine Indian states – Rajasthan, Haryana, Himachal Pradesh, Delhi, Uttarakhand, Bihar, Madhya Pradesh, Jharkhand and Chhattisgarh.

State with the largest area

With an area of 342,239 sq. km, Rajasthan is the largest state. It covers around 10.4 per cent of India's total area.

State with the smallest area

Goa is India's smallest state with a total area of 3,702 sq. km.

Kerala Government Secretariat

Kerala Tops in IT-powered Government Services

According to the latest National e-Governance Service Delivery Assessment (NeSDA) 2021, Kerala ranked first in the country in providing public services by utilizing information technology. They also topped the category of 'Single Window Access to Information and Service Links'. Kerala Chief Minister Pinarayi Vijayan took to Twitter to announce the achievement of the state and the ruling Left Democratic Front (LDF) government. As per the NeSDA report, submitted by the DARPG, Kerala managed government services excellently, providing efficient public service delivery through e-governance in a variety of areas, including finance, employment, education, local government, social welfare, the environment and tourism.

State with the longest coastline
Gujarat has the longest coastline of 1,214.7 km, followed by Andhra Pradesh with a coastal length of 973.7 km.

State with the longest international border
West Bengal shares a 2,216.7 km long border with Bangladesh, making it the state with the longest international border.

Shortest term as chief minister
- Jagdambika Pal was chief minister of Uttar Pradesh for one day – on 21 February 1998.
- Harish Rawat's second term as chief minister of Uttarakhand lasted a day – 21 April 2016.

Youngest state
Telangana was formed on 2 June 2014, after its separation from the state of Andhra Pradesh.

First woman chief minister
India's first woman chief minister was freedom fighter Sucheta Kripalani (1908–74). She was the chief minister of Uttar Pradesh (1963 to 1967).

First state under president's rule
President's Rule was imposed on Punjab from 20 July 1951 to 17 July 1952. The proclamation came after the resignation of the Congress ministry headed by Dr Gopichand Bhargava.

WR First elected communist government in power
On 5 April 1957, the Communist Party of India in Kerala formed the first communist government in the world to come to power by voting. It was led by E.M.S. Namboodiripad. It was dismissed by the Centre in 1959.

First 'film star' chief minister
M.G. Ramachandran or 'MGR' was the first film star to become chief minister when he assumed office in Tamil Nadu on 4 July 1977.

Oldest chief minister
Mizoram's chief minister Zoramthanga (b. 13 July 1944) is the oldest serving chief minister of a state.

Most chief ministers in a year
Haryana had four chief ministers in nine months from November 1989 to July 1990: Devi Lal (November 1989), Om Prakash Chautala (December 1989), Banarsi Das Gupta (May 1990) and Hukam Singh (July 1990).

Youngest chief minister
- M.O. Hasan Farook Maricar, three-time chief minister of Pondicherry (now Puducherry), was the youngest chief minister when he came to power at 29 years in 1967. He died in office in 2012 as Governor of Kerala.
- Pema Khandu, elected as chief minister of Arunachal Pradesh in 2016 at the age of 38 years, is the youngest serving chief minister of a state.

Chief minister with the longest tenure and most consecutive terms
Pawan Kumar Chamling (former chief minister of Sikkim) has been India's longest-serving chief minister, having served in that post for five terms from 12 December 1994 to 26 May 2019 (24 years, 165 days). He has surpassed the record of Jyoti Basu, who held the office of chief minister of West Bengal from 1 June 1977 to 6 November 2000 (23 years, 137 days).

GOVERNANCE

First Indian in the Imperial Civil Service
Satyendranath Tagore, elder brother of Rabindranath Tagore, was the first Indian to join the service in 1863. He was recruited into the Covenanted Civil Service (later named the Imperial Civil Service). His first posting was in the Bombay Presidency (which included parts of present-day Maharashtra, Gujarat and Sindh).

First Indians in the Privy Council
In 1907, K.G. Puta and Syed Hussain Bilgrami were admitted to the Privy Council of India, the supreme appellate authority in British India, which advised the British monarchy.

First municipalities
Municipal corporations for civic amenities were set up first between 1880 and 1884, when Lord Rippon was the viceroy of India.

First Public Service Commission
The Public Service Commission was first constituted under the chairmanship of Sir Charles Umpherston Aitchison, governor of Punjab, in 1926.

First panchayats
Panchayats were first established in villages under the Panchayat Act in 1912, but with little success. It was in 1952 that a new Panchayat Act revived the system.

First woman ambassador
Vijaya Lakshmi Pandit, the sister of India's first prime minister, Jawaharlal Nehru, was India's first woman ambassador, to the erstwhile USSR from 1947 to 1949. She also served as

Pema Khandu: youngest serving chief minister

Vijay Lakshmi Pandit (*extreme right*): first woman ambassador

The number of women MPs in the Lok Sabha has risen from **5** per cent in the first Lok Sabha to **14** per cent in the 17th Lok Sabha.

ambassador to the USA and Mexico (1949–51) and in Ireland (1955–61). She held a post in the cabinet in pre-Independence India, the first Indian woman to do so. Her longest tenure was in London, as high commissioner to the UK, serving from 1954 to 1961. Her last posting as ambassador was in Spain. She served as governor of Maharashtra from 1962 to 1964 and as member of the Lok Sabha from 1964 to 1968.

First woman career diplomat
Chonira Belliappa Muthamma from Coorg (now Kodagu), Karnataka, qualified for the Indian Civil Service and joined the foreign service in 1949. She served in France, the UK and Burma (now Myanmar), and later as ambassador to Hungary and Ghana.

First woman IAS officer
Anna Rajam George (b. 17 July 1927) from Calicut (now Kozhikode), Kerala, was the first woman to qualify for the Indian Administrative Service (IAS) in 1950. She was posted as a subdivisional officer in a small town in Tamil Nadu in 1951.

First woman mayor
Tara Cherian (1913–2000) was appointed mayor of Madras (now Chennai), Tamil Nadu, in 1957. She received the Padma Bhushan in 1967.

Youngest governor
Swaraj Kaushal was appointed governor of Mizoram in February 1990 when he was 37 years and seven months old.

AADHAAR STATISTICS
(in Crores)

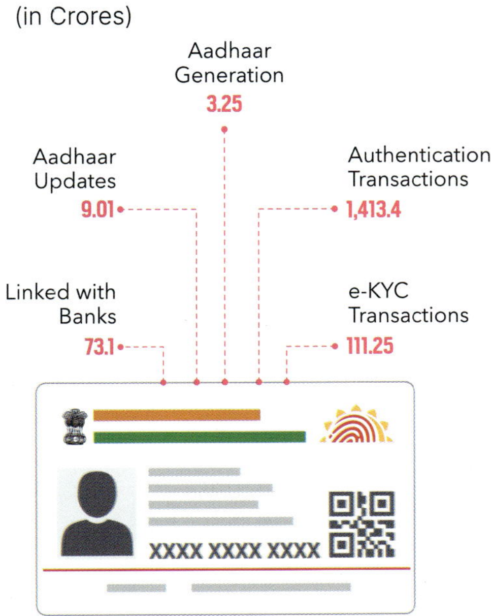

Data from 2020–21. Source: *UIDAI Annual Report* 2020–21

Youngest mayor
Arya Rajendran (b. 12 January 1999), the Left Democratic Front councillor from the Mudavanmugal ward, became the mayor of Thiruvananthapuram Corporation, Kerala, in December 2020 when she was 21 years old.

First woman sarpanch
Chhavi Rajawat, the first woman sarpanch (head of the village panchayat) in India, looks after Soda, a village in Tonk District, Rajasthan. She assumed office in February 2010 at the age of 30 years. She is an alumna of Rishi Valley School, Madanapalle, Andhra Pradesh; Mayo College Girls' School, Ajmer, Rajasthan; and Lady Shri Ram College, New Delhi. She also holds an MBA degree from Balaji Institute of Modern Management, Pune, Maharashtra. She left her corporate job to work in rural India.

Youngest sarpanch
Anant Parag Khadilkar, the youngest sarpanch in India, secured the post in Nagargao Sattari Village in Goa in 2017 when he was only 21 years old. He was then a graduate in commerce.

Youngest woman sarpanch
Twenty-one-year-old Asruni Khan was elected as the sarpanch of Chulhera Village in Bharatpur District, Rajasthan, in January 2020.

AADHAAR

State/UT with least Aadhaar coverage
Nagaland, with a low saturation percentage of 60.70 per cent, has the lowest Aadhaar saturation among all states and Union Territories in India, on the basis of total projected population (31 August 2022).

State/UT with maximum Aadhaar coverage
Delhi, with an saturation percentage of 107.46 per cent, has the maximum Aadhaar coverage. The saturation percentage is calculated as the percentage of the number of Aadhaar cards assigned, upon the total projected population for the year (31 August 2022).

LAW AND ORDER

First Indian sheriff
Manackjee Rustomjee, a Parsi businessman and judge from Bombay (now Mumbai), Maharashtra, was appointed as the sheriff of Calcutta (now Kolkata, West Bengal) in 1873, the first Indian to be appointed to the position.

First all-woman police station
The first all-woman police station in the country was started in October 1973 at Calicut (now Kozhikode) in Kerala. Sub-inspector Padmini was in charge of it.

WR First fingerprint bureau
The first fingerprint bureau in the world was set up in Calcutta (now Kolkata), West Bengal, in June 1897. A murder case in 1898 in Jalpaiguri is reported to be among the first in which the culprit was incriminated on the basis of dactyloscopy, which is the science of fingerprint identification.

First forensic science laboratory
In 1853, the Government Examiners' Laboratory was established in Calcutta (now Kolkata), West Bengal, followed by labs in Madras (now Chennai), Tamil Nadu, Bombay (now Mumbai), Maharashtra, Lahore (now in Pakistan) and Agra, Uttar Pradesh. At present, there are seven central forensic science labs in India, viz., Hyderabad, Kolkata, Chandigarh, New Delhi, Guwahati, Bhopal and Pune.

First Indian director of the Intelligence Bureau
T.G. Sanjeevi Pillai took over as the first Indian director of the Intelligence Bureau, Ministry of Home Affairs, from Sir N.P.A. Smith in April 1947 and held office till July 1950.

First open prison
The first open prison in India, Durgapura Open Camp, was started in Rajasthan in 1956 by the then governor, Dr Sampurnanand, in the Government Agriculture and Research Centre campus at Jaipur. Prisoners who had spent six years behind bars could live with their families and go out in the day to earn.

First Police Act
The Police Act of 1861 led to the creation of a police service. This Act introduced a uniform system applicable to entire British India.

First police dog squad
The Madras City Police Dog Squad, now called the Chennai City Police Dog Squad, was started in 1952 by a sub-inspector of police, Kanniah Naidu, in Chennai, Tamil Nadu. It was the first police dog squad in India.

High court with the most judges
Allahabad High Court has the largest sanctioned strength of 160 judges, but has never held its full complement. As on 1 November 2020, it had 59 permanent judges and 41 additional judges.

Largest prison complex
Tihar Prisons, which started with the Central Jail in 1958, now includes nine central jails, apart from a district jail at Rohini, New Delhi, making it the largest prison complex in Asia. Starting with a capacity of 1,273 prisoners, it now houses 13,183 prisoners against the sanctioned capacity of 5,200 prisoners.

First transgender sub-inspector
India's first transgender sub-inspector, K. Prithika Yashini, joined the Tamil Nadu Police force on 2 April 2017. She was posted to Dharmapuri District in Tamil Nadu after a legal battle with the Madras High Court ruling in her favour.

First woman IPS officer
Kiran Bedi (b. 9 June 1949) was the first woman to join the Indian Police Service (IPS) on 16 July 1972. She retired in 2007 and was later the lieutenant governor of Puducherry (May 2016–February 2021).

Biggest cryptocurrency crime
India's biggest cryptocurrency crime involving US $300 million through a multilevel bitcoin marketing scam allegedly perpetrated by Amit Bhardwaj, director of Gain Bitcoin, was registered in Pune, Maharashtra. The victims allegedly claimed that the bitcoin investment company duped them into investing in bitcoins for higher returns. Bhardwaj had allegedly fled India and was traced to Bangkok, Thailand, before his arrest at Delhi airport in April 2018.

NUMBER OF CASES IN COURTS

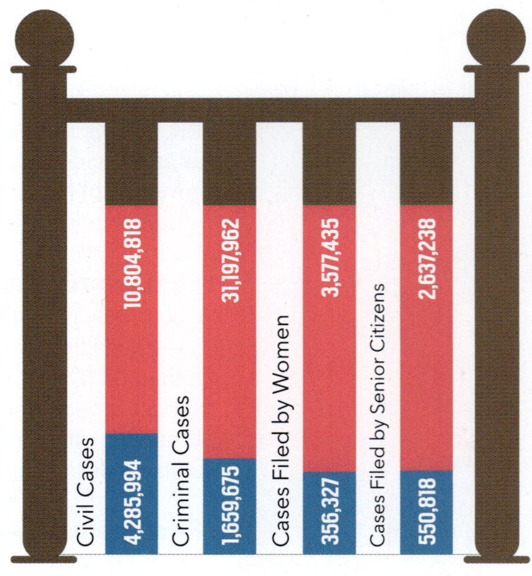

Source: National Judicial Data Grid, Department of Justice; Data extracted on 24 September 2022

LEGAL MATTERS

First British Indian Code
The East India Company's proposal for separate civil and criminal courts in districts on 15 August 1772 in Calcutta (now Kolkata, West Bengal), was the first British Indian Code.

First Penal Code
The Indian Penal Code (IPC) and the Criminal Procedure Code (CrPC), which were introduced in Bengal in 1862, were drafted on the recommendations of the first Law Commission of India set up in 1834, chaired by British historian and politician Thomas Babington Macaulay.

First public prosecutor
S. Subramania Iyer (1842–1924), jurist and freedom fighter, was appointed public prosecutor in Madras (now Chennai), Tamil Nadu, in 1887.

First woman advocate
Cornelia Sorabji (1866–1954) was the first woman to graduate in law in 1894. However, law being a male bastion then, she was

S. Subramania Iyer: first public prosecutor

Looking for a Government Scheme Is Easier Now

Easing Indian citizens' access to various government schemes, the Centre has launched 'myScheme', a platform (https://www.myscheme.gov.in/), which provides a one-window search portal where people can check their eligibility for various schemes. Launched by Prime Minister Modi at the Digital India Week 2022 at Gandhinagar, Gujarat, the platform is developed, managed and operated by the National e-Governance Division (NeGD), with the support of the Ministry of Electronics and Information Technology (MeitY) and the Department of Administrative Reforms and Public Grievance (DARPG) in partnership with other Central and state ministries/departments. This government–user interface for government schemes facilitates the discovery of the appropriate scheme suitable for a user, and helps with the application process, obviating the need to check multiple websites. The three-step process requires users to enter their attributes, such as demographics, income and social details, among others. In the next step, the portal finds the relevant schemes from the many schemes available; and in the third and final step, the user can select from the list of schemes and gather further information from the dedicated scheme page.

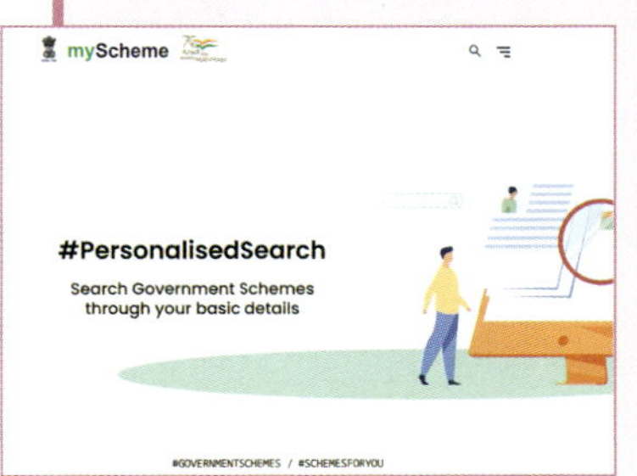

Number of Schemes in Different Areas*

Category	Number of Schemes
Agriculture, Rural and Environment	10
Banking, Financial Services and Insurance	39
Business and Entrepreneurship	17
Education and Learning	45
Health and Wellness	22
Housing and Shelter	8
Public Safety, Law and Justice	2
Science, IT and Communications	3
Skills and Employment	22
Social Welfare and Empowerment	71
Sports and Culture	3
Transport and Infrastructure	4
Travel and Tourism	2
Utility and Sanitation	15

*As on 20 September 2022; Source: Press Information Bureau

There are 25 high courts in India, with six having control over more than one State/UT.

enrolled in the Allahabad High Court Bar only in 1923.

First barrister-at-law

Gyanendramohan Tagore (1826–90) passed the barrister-at-law examination from Lincoln's Inn in England on 21 June 1862, becoming the first Indian to do so. In November 1865, he was enrolled into the Calcutta High Court in Bengal Presidency (now in Kolkata, West Bengal) as the first Indian barrister.

First high court judge

Shambhunath Pandit, a Kashmiri domiciled in Calcutta (now Kolkata, West Bengal), was appointed judge at the Calcutta High Court on 2 February 1863. His tenure ended in 1867.

First woman chief justice

Justice Leila Seth (1930–2017) was appointed the chief justice of Himachal Pradesh on 5 August 1991, becoming India's first woman chief justice of a high court.

First woman judge of the Supreme Court

Meera Sahib Fathima Beevi (b. April 1927) was appointed as a judge of the Supreme Court in October 1989, the first Indian woman to hold this post. She was also the second woman in the world to hold such a position.

First chief justice of India

India's first chief justice was Justice Sir Harilal J. Kania (1890–1951), who held the position from 26 January 1950 to 6 November 1951.

First Indian president of the International Court of Justice

Dr Nagendra Singh (1914–88) was the first Indian president of the International Court of Justice, serving from 1985 to 1988. He was also the first Indian to be a judge of the court. He received the Padma Vibhushan in 1973.

First woman judicial officer

Anna Chandy (1905–96), a member of the Travancore Legislative Council during 1923–24, graduated in law in 1930 and was appointed munsif by the erstwhile state of Travancore in 1937. She became a district and sessions judge in 1948, and a judge of the Kerala High Court in 1959.

First Indian woman on the United Nations law board

Neeru Chadha, an international law expert, became the first Indian to be appointed to the

International Tribunal for the Law of the Sea (ITLOS), being elected to the UN body in June 2017.

First citizen to have a 'no caste, no religion' certificate

M.A. Sneha Parthibaraja, a lawyer from Tirupattur, Tamil Nadu, became the first Indian citizen to win the right to not have a caste or religion, on 5 February 2021. She was granted the certificate after a nine-year-long court battle.

First transgender lawyer

Sathyasri Sharmila, a lawyer in the Bar Council of Tamil Nadu and Puducherry, is the first transgender lawyer in India. Although she completed her education in 2007, she enrolled as an advocate after the NALSA (National Legal Services Authority of India) judgment of 2014, which recognized the third gender.

First transgender judge

Joyita Mondal Mahi, India's first transgender judge, was appointed as a judge in the Lok Adalat in West Bengal in 2017. She was 29 years old at the time.

Oldest civic body

The Greater Chennai Corporation, Tamil Nadu, was inaugurated under a royal charter issued by King James II of England, on 29 September 1688, as the Corporation of Madras. It is the oldest civic body in the country and the second oldest in the world.

Oldest high court

The Calcutta High Court, established on 1 July 1862, under the Indian High Courts Act, 1861, is the oldest high court in India. It also has jurisdiction over West Bengal, and the Union Territory of Andaman and Nicobar Islands. Its building was designed by British architect Walter Granville, who based it on the Cloth Hall at Ypres in Belgium. The seat of the high court is Kolkata. It also has a permanent circuit bench in Port Blair, the capital of the Andaman and Nicobar Islands. It has a sanctioned strength of 72 judges. Thottathil B. Radhakrishnan is its current serving chief justice.

THE CENSUS

First census

The first all-India census was conducted in 1872 in British India. However, the first regular census in the country was conducted in 1881, and then every ten years. The last census was conducted in 2011. The census is conducted by the registrar general and the census commissioner under the Ministry of Home Affairs, Government of India.

Most populated state*

Uttar Pradesh is India's most populated state, with a population of 199,812,341.

Most populated Union Territory

Delhi is India's most populated Union Territory with a population of 16,787,941.

Least populated state

Sikkim is India's least populated state, with 610,577 persons.

Least populated Union Territory

Lakshadweep, with a population of 64,473, is the least populated UT.

Most densely populated state

Bihar has a population density of 1,106 persons per sq. km, making it the most densely populated state in India.

Most densely populated Union Territory

The national capital Delhi, with a population density of 11,320 persons per sq. km, is the most densely populated UT.

Least densely populated state

Arunachal Pradesh, with a population density of 17 persons per sq. km, is the least densely populated state in India.

Least densely populated Union Territory

Andaman and Nicobar Islands have a population density of 46 persons per sq. km, making it the least densely populated UT.

State/UT with the highest sex ratio

Ladakh has the highest sex ratio at birth among states and UTs, with 1,125 females per 1,000 males.

State/UT with the lowest sex ratio

Dadra and Nagar Haveli and Daman and Diu have a sex ratio at birth of 817 females per 1,000 males.

Under the e-Courts Mission Mode Project, monitored and funded by the Department of Justice, Ministry of Law and Justice, the data of 3,256 court complexes across the country is now available online.

Calcutta High Court: oldest high court

* All population statistics are based on the 2011 Census

DEFENCE

ARMY

PERSONNEL

First Indian commander-in-chief

General (later field marshal in 1986) K.M. Cariappa (1899–1993) took over from the British commander-in-chief (C-in-C), General Sir Roy Bucher, on 15 January 1949 and held office till 14 January 1953. The only other C-in-C was General M. Rajendra Sinhji Jadeja, who took over as the first chief of army staff (CoAS) in April 1955, after which the post of C-in-C was abolished.

First field marshal

S.H.F.J. (Sam) Manekshaw, the then general, became field marshal in 1973. He was honoured with the Padma Bhushan in 1968 and the Padma Vibhushan in 1972.

First chief of integrated defence staff

On 1 October 2001, Lieutenant General Pankaj Joshi was appointed the first chief of integrated defence staff (CIDS) in the country, reporting to General Sundararajan Padmanabhan, chairman of the Chief of Staff Committee at the time.

First chief of defence staff

On 31 December 2019, after demitting office as chief of army staff, General Bipin Rawat (1958–2021) took over as India's first chief of defence staff (CDS), serving as a tri-services chief and principal military adviser to the defence minister on all matters related to the army, navy and air force. He also headed the Department of Military Affairs created within the Ministry of Defence.

First commissioned officer

Major General K. Bhagwati Singh (ID I-O-No. 1) passed out of the Indian Military Academy (IMA) in 1934, with his batchmate (and later field marshal) Sam Manekshaw.

First women in the army

The first batch of 25 women outside the Army Medical Corps (AMC) was commissioned in the Indian Army on 6 March 1993 at the Officers Training Academy in Madras (now Chennai), Tamil Nadu. They were inducted into non-combat departments, such as supply, legal, education and logistics.

First woman lieutenant general

Dr Punita Arora from Saharanpur, Uttar Pradesh, was promoted to the rank of lieutenant general on 1 September 2004. She was the first woman in any of the four services (army, navy, air force and coast guard) to reach a three-star rank.

First women in Military Police

On 25 April 2019, the Indian Army issued a formal notification inviting women applicants for the post of soldier – general duty. This was the first time that the army opened its ranks to women for personnel below officer rank (PBOR). The soldiers were to be inducted into the Corps of Military Police (CMP) to investigate offences like theft, molestation and rape. Their portfolio also included assisting civil police and the prevention of breach of regulations by army personnel.

MEDALS AND HONOURS

First Victoria Cross

The first Indian to be awarded the Victoria Cross was Sepoy (later Subedar) Khuda Dad Khan of the 129 Baluchis, on 31 October 1914, for gallantry at Hollebeke, Belgium, in the First World War.

Youngest to receive the Victoria Cross

At nineteen, Sepoy Kamal Ram of the Royal Indian Army was the youngest Indian to receive the Victoria Cross in 1944. Born in Bholupura Village of Karauli District, Rajasthan, he was with the 3rd Battalion of the 8th Punjab Regiment during the Second World War.

First George Cross

Havildar Nandlal Thapa of Gurkha Rifles received the George Cross in 1935 for exceptional courage and devotion to duty. He was about 32 years old at the time, and was serving in the 2nd Battalion of the 8th Gurkha Rifles.

First prisoner of war and first Kirti Chakra recipient

Flying Officer Ulrich Anthony D'Cruz, whose aircraft was shot down by ground fire on 1 December 1947 in the 1947–48 Kashmir war, was taken prisoner by Pathan tribesmen and later by the Pakistan Army, and released after a year. He was awarded the Kirti Chakra in 1952 for bravery during captivity.

First Param Vir Chakra

Major Somnath Sharma, heading a detachment of the Kumaon Regiment at Badgam, Jammu and Kashmir, laid down his life in the effort to save Srinagar city and airport from a Pakistani attack during the Kashmir operations in 1947. He was given the award posthumously in 1950.

General Bipin Rawat: first chief of defence staff

5 girl cadets are set to join the Rashtriya Indian Military College in Dehradun, Uttarakhand, for the first time in its history of 100 years, as announced on 12 March 2022.

A stamp commemorating Major Somnath Sharma: recipient of the first Param Vir Chakra for the Indian Army

Indian Army's New Combat Uniform

Indian Army's new uniform

Republic Day 2022 saw the Indian Army showcasing its new combat uniform, which features a 'digital disruptive' pattern. Specially designed for it by the National Institute of Fashion Technology (NIFT), the new uniform sees changes in all aspects, including the fabric, the weight and the camouflage pattern. The olive green of the earlier uniform has been replaced with earthier shades, making the uniform more versatile for different terrains such as rocky mountains, green hills and sandy deserts. The new weave that allows for quick drying is also lighter and more durable, besides being comfortable in both summer and winter.

First Ashok Chakra

Naik Nar Bahadur Thapa of 5 Gurkha Rifles was awarded the Ashok Chakra Class I (now known as the Ashok Chakra). On 15 September 1948, during the Hyderabad police action, as the No. 2 Platoon of the A Company came under fire on the banks of the River Tungabhadra, he dashed across the 100-yard open ground and single-handedly silenced the gun crew.

First Republic Day commander and first army officer to receive the Padma Bhushan

The first Republic Day parade of independent India, which featured inter-service contingents from the army, navy, air force and police forces, was held on 26 January 1950, and was commanded by Brigadier (later Lieutenant General) Joginder Singh Dhillon, a Bengal Sapper. On 24 November 1965, as lieutenant general, he became the first Indian Army officer to receive the Padma Bhushan.

A *subedar* (*left*) of the Mahrattha Light Infantry: oldest infantry unit

First Indian peacekeeper to win the United Nations Military Gender Advocate Award

Major Suman Gawani, an Indian Army officer, was awarded the UN (United Nations) Military Gender Advocate of the Year award on 29 May 2020 in a virtual ceremony, becoming the first Indian peacekeeper to receive the honour. She served as a peacekeeper in a UN mission in South Sudan (UNMISS) in 2019.

Most decorated regiment

The Sikh Regiment has to its credit the highest number of gallantry awards, i.e., 1,652. These include two Param Vir Chakras, eight Maha Vir Chakras, 64 Vir Chakras and four Ashok Chakras, among other decorations.

UNITS

First artillery company

- The first artillery company was raised temporarily in 1748 in India under British rule with Indian troops, and was called the Gun Lascars.
- A company of Bombay Artillery, which still exists as 5 Bombay Mountain Battery, was raised on 28 September 1827, which is celebrated as Gunners' Day.

First artillery unit

On 15 January 1935, A Field Brigade (now 1 Field Regiment SP), with four batteries of horse-drawn guns, was raised at Bangalore (now Bengaluru), Karnataka. This date was adopted by the Regiment of Artillery as its raising day.

First administrative unit

The Army Service Corps (ASC) was established in 1748 when Stringer Lawrence, commander-in-chief in India, appointed Robert Clive as commissary. It was formally set up in 1760 in the Bengal, Madras and Bombay Presidencies, and became a formal Supply and Transport Corps in 1901. The ASC was the oldest administrative component of the East India Company and was then known as the Commissariat.

Oldest infantry brigade

5 Mountain Brigade was raised in September 1939. Deployed in the Along (now Aalo) sector of Arunachal Pradesh, its area of responsibility comprises a frontage of more than 460 km.

Oldest infantry unit

Raised on 4 August 1768, the 1 Maratha Light Infantry or Jangi Paltan is the only unit that does not hang captured enemy flags upside down in its mess. It is also the only unit that was in constant battle for 20 years after it was raised, and in this duration, it earned 18 battle honours and five theatre honours.

First cavalry unit
The first Indian cavalry unit was raised in 1787 as 5 Regiment of Madras Native Cavalry. It became 1 Regiment in 1788 under Major Tonyn. Renamed 26 Light Cavalry in 1903, it was amalgamated with 30 Lancers in 1922 and became the 8th Light Cavalry.

First cavalry regiment
The first cavalry regiment before India's independence, the Scinde Horse, was raised in 1838 as the Scinde Irregular Horse by Captain Ward in Hyderabad (in Sind, now in Pakistan) under the command of Captain John Jacob. It last paraded its horses in April 1938 at Rawalpindi (now in Pakistan).

First rifle regiment
The rifle regiment as a tactical unit was introduced in 1841 and the first such unit was the 4 Bombay Native Infantry, which till 1947 was 1 Battalion of Rajputana Rifles and is now 3 Guard. They were issued Enfield muzzle-loaders and 577 bullets.

First tri-services affiliation
Bengal Sappers has been affiliated with the Indian Navy and Indian Air Force since 2002. Originally known as the Bengal Sappers and Miners, and headquartered in Roorkee (now in Uttarakhand), it has won 80 battle honours and 11 theatre honours.

First Special Operations Division
India's first Special Operations Division was announced on 15 May 2019. At its peak, this tri-services division will have around 3,000 commandos from the Indian Army's special forces, the Indian Air Force's Garud force and the Indian Navy's MARCOS commando units. The raising is the first step for counterterrorism operations. Major General A.K. Dhingra, from the 1 Para Special Forces Regiment, was the first chief of the division.

EQUIPMENT

First gun foundry
The Board of Ordnance was constituted in April 1775, but it took 27 years to establish a factory at Cossipore in Calcutta (now Kolkata), West Bengal, on 18 March 1802 as the Gun Carriage Agency. In 1830, it was renamed the Gun Foundry and, in 1905, this name was changed to Gun and Shell Factory.

First and oldest extant armament checker
The Proof and Experimental Establishment in Chandipur in present-day Odisha, called the Proof Department, was set up on 7 November 1895. It has been associated with major armament developments. Included under the Defence Research and Development Organization (DRDO) in 1958, it had Lieutenant Colonel B.N. Mitra as its first Indian director.

First rifle factory
A rifle factory, set up at Ichhapore, Bengal (now Ishapore, West Bengal), began production on 20 September 1904. It produced the .303-inch Bolt action rifles in large quantities for the First and Second World Wars.

Earliest tanks
The first three tanks of the Indian Army were two varieties of Medium-D tanks brought in 1920 before Indian independence. Fifty Vickers MkII-B light tanks were acquired for use in India in 1933.

First indigenous tank
The first military tank that was made in India, named Vijayanta,

Within the last five years India's defence exports have grown by 334 per cent, and the country is now exporting its defence products to over 75 countries.

Vijayanta: first indigenous tank

Women in the Indian Army
Representative image

A Step Towards a Gender-Neutral Army

In an initiative towards equal opportunities, gender equality and gender neutrality in the defence forces, the Indian Army's selection board granted a timescale promotion to five women officers to the post of colonel – a promotion that was previously reserved only for female officers serving in the Judge Advocate General Department, the Army Education Corps and the Army Medical Corps. The five women officers promoted – Lt Col. Sangeeta Sardana (Corps of Signals), Lt Col. Navneet Duggal and Lt Col. Sonia Anand (Corps of EME), and Lt Col. Ritcha Sagar and Lt Col. Reenu Khanna (Corps of Engineers) – have paved the way for the promotion of female officers from the Corps of Signals, the Corps of Engineers, and the Corps of Electronics and Mechanical Engineers. The promotion was granted after 26 years of 'reckonable service' to their corps.

The Border Roads Organization (BRO) was established.

rolled out of the assembly line on 12 December 1965 at the Heavy Vehicles Factory in Avadi in Madras (now Chennai), Tamil Nadu. It entered service on 29 December 1965.

First flying spy

Unmanned aerial vehicles (UAVs) were used first in the Kargil conflict in 1999 to detect the movement of enemy troops and locate bunkers. UAVs were brought in to counter Pakistan's Gultari guns and the US-made AN/TPQ-36-37 gun-locating radars.

First indigenous armoured personnel carrier

In 1987, the first BMP-2 infantry fighting vehicle, Sarath, was assembled at the ordnance factory at Shankarapally, Andhra Pradesh (now in Telangana), from Soviet-supplied components. Sarath was made indigenously subsequently in 1991.

First indigenous training simulator

On 20 February 2002, the Simulator Development Division, Secunderabad (now in Telangana), introduced the aiming training simulator (ATS) for infantry combat vehicles.

First indigenous revolver

In 2002, the research and development wing of the Ishapore Rifle Factory in Barrackpore, near Kolkata in West Bengal, after around two years of research, developed a low-cost and high-tech revolver, which weighs barely 380 g. The .22-in. automatic revolver had a range of 20 m (65 ft 7 in.).

First bulletproof helmets

In July 2017, the army obtained bulletproof helmets for the first time. The 1.2 kg to 1.4 kg lightweight helmets are being made in Kanpur, Uttar Pradesh, by MKU Systems, which is manufacturing them for the Indian Army for the first time. The company had earlier manufactured such helmets for the UN and the North Atlantic Treaty Organization (NATO) forces.

First indigenously manufactured bulletproof vests

Shantanu Bhowmik, professor at the Department of Aerospace Engineering at the School of Engineering, Amrita University, Coimbatore, Tamil Nadu, designed the first indigenous bulletproof vest for the armed forces in 2017. The 20-layer vest, made with indigenous ultramodern lightweight thermoplastic technology, is being developed in collaboration with DRDO. The vest is effective up to a temperature of 57°C and weighs 1.5 kg while the earlier jacket weighed 15 kg.

Lightest towed artillery

On 18 May 2017, the Indian Army received the first batch of two M-777 A-2 ultralight howitzers (ULH) from the USA. These ULHs, with a maximum range of 30 km, manufactured by BAE Systems, were test-fired in Pokhran, Rajasthan. The 155 mm, 39-calibre guns are equipped to fire Indian ammunition.

First robot sentry

In 2017, the Indian Army built Robot Sentry, a mobile robot specifically meant for patrolling and surveillance applications in urban campuses of the army. Another robot, the Snake, has 14 active joints for lateral undulation, sidewinding and rolling. These help the robot to navigate difficult passages.

First indigenous sniper rifles

SSS Defence, based in Bengaluru, Karnataka, has developed the country's first indigenous sniper rifle prototypes with 7.62 mm x 51 mm calibre and .338 Lapua magnum platforms. The barrel length ranges from 20 to 24 in. (50.8 to 60.96 cm) based on use environments and specific missions.

MADE-IN-INDIA DEFENCE

As part of the AatmaNirbhar Bharat Abhiyan, the Indian Army, the DRDO, the Defence Public Sector Undertakings (DPSUs) and Indian industry have developed various indigenously manufactured equipment and systems that will modernize the army. Union defence minister Rajnath Singh handed these to the Indian Army on 16 August 2022, a day after India celebrated its 75 years of independence. Here are a few of the equipment and systems.

1 Future Infantry Soldier as a System (F-INSAS)

This is a combination of three subsystems.

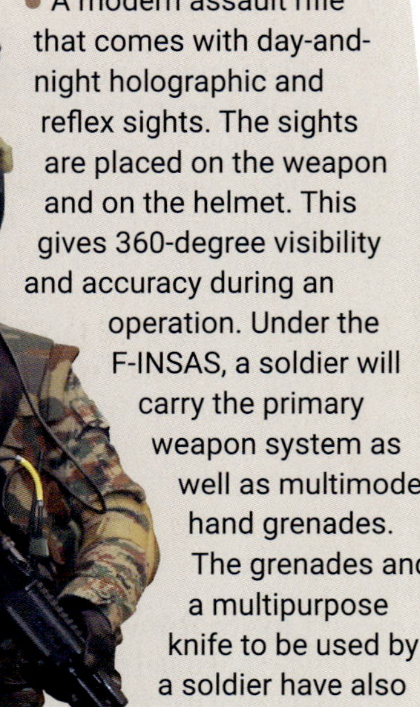

- A modern assault rifle that comes with day-and-night holographic and reflex sights. The sights are placed on the weapon and on the helmet. This gives 360-degree visibility and accuracy during an operation. Under the F-INSAS, a soldier will carry the primary weapon system as well as multimode hand grenades. The grenades and a multipurpose knife to be used by a soldier have also been created indigenously.
- Then comes a protection system. This includes a specially designed helmet and a bulletproof jacket.
- The third part is a communication and surveillance system. This subsystem is capable of being further upgraded by incorporating real-time data connectivity too.

State-of-the art. high-mobility infantry protected vehicles and assault boats were among the other significant forms of defence equipment that the minister handed over to the Indian Army on this occasion.

2 Nipun

This is a new-generation anti-personnel mine. The Armament Research and Development Establishment, Pune, and Indian industry worked together to develop this mine. It will provide better protection to the troops than the vintage NMM 14 mines, which the Indian Army has been using for a long time.

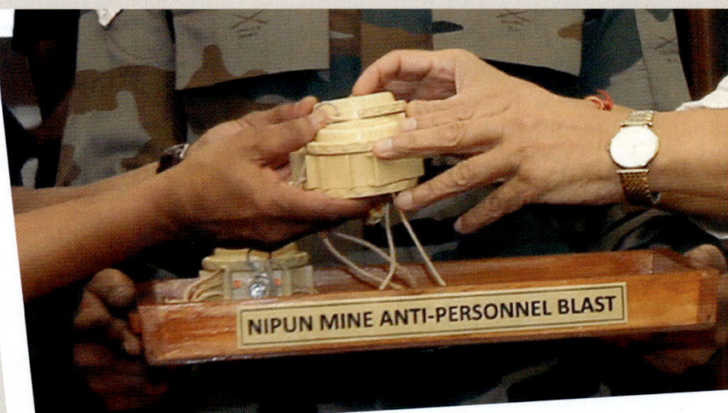

3 Hand-held Thermal Imager (Uncooled)

This is a surveillance and detection equipment that will give visibility to Indian soldiers both during the day and at night as well as during adverse weather conditions. Detecting enemy movements and their other activities has become easier than before.

India's first set of next-gen AERVs

First set of next-gen Armoured Engineer Reconnaissance Vehicle

Indian Army chief General Manoj Mukund Naravane flagged off and inducted the first set of indigenously developed next-generation Armoured Engineer Reconnaissance Vehicles (AERVs) at Bombay Engineering Group (BEG) on 21 December 2021. The AERV, which can match the speed of tanks, will upscale the existing engineer reconnaissance capabilities of the Indian Army significantly, keeping in view the possibility of future conflicts.

Longest-range nuclear missile

On 26 December 2016, India successfully test-fired Agni-V, a surface-to-surface nuclear-capable missile with the longest range, from Abdul Kalam Island off the Odisha coast. Designed and developed by DRDO, this 17 m (55 ft 9 in.) long missile can carry a nuclear warhead of about 1.5 tonnes reportedly over 5,000–8,000 km. India is the sixth country after France, China, Russia, the USA and the UK to have a missile with a range of over 5,000 km.

Agni-V: nuclear missile with the longest range

OPERATIONS

First heli-lifted battalion

The First Guards (2 Punjab), raised in 1762 as 10 Battalion of the Coastal Sepoys and redesignated 18 times since, was heli-lifted during the counter-insurgency operations in Nagaland during 1969–70.

First heli-borne operations

In 1971, the Indian Army used helicopters to capture the 7,000-strong Sylhet garrison in East Pakistan (now Bangladesh). The 5 Gurkha Rifles (Frontier Force), which were led by Major M.M. Malik, landed with the first sortie of seven helicopters at Mirpara on the banks of the River Surma.

First para-regiment in action

The 17 Para Field Regiment supported operations at Tangail in Bangladesh in 1971 by sending 49 Para Field Battery, a sub-unit of the regiment along with 2 Para.

First use of air cavalry

In May 2018, during Exercise Vijay Prahar carried out in the Mahajan Firing Range near Suratgarh, Rajasthan, Indian troops worked on the first use of the concept of air cavalry unleashed by the US Army in Vietnam during 1955–73. In these operations, weaponized attack helicopters carried out combined action against the 'enemy' in coordination with tanks and mechanized ground forces, while conventionally helicopters are called in only when ground forces cannot neutralize ground targets. This requires very precise coordination but speeds up the operation.

WR Highest battleground

Siachen is a 76.8 km river of ice abutted by knife-edged, fluted, serrated ridge lines, sometimes exceeding 6,400 m 21,000 ft) where temperatures dip to as low as –55°C. Army posts at altitudes from 4,572 m to 6,096 m (15,000 ft to 20,000 ft) face bitterly cold 200 km/hr blizzards.

WR Highest tank battle in the world

On 1 November 1948, an Indian brigade group, supported by the 7th Cavalry (using Stuart Tanks), broke through the Himalayan range at Zoji La in Jammu and Kashmir at 3,528 m (11,575 ft) to drive out a group of invaders from Pakistan intermixed with Pakistan-occupied Kashmir (PoK) battalions and tribal groups.

GENERAL

First army veterinary school

A veterinary school was started at Kirkee in Poona (now Pune) District, Maharashtra, in 1862, for officers and men of artillery, cavalry and mounted police. Similar schools also came up in Hapur (1877, now in Uttar Pradesh), Lahore (1882, now in Pakistan), Ambala (1889, now in Haryana) and Simla (1891, now Shimla in Himachal Pradesh).

First military intelligence school

Opened in Karachi (now in Pakistan) on 20 January 1945, the first military intelligence school moved to Mhow (Dr Ambedkar Nagar) in Madhya Pradesh, and was renamed the Intelligence Corps Training School and Depot. On 29 February 1984, its name was changed to Military Intelligence Training School and Depot.

First military dog school

The War Dog Training School was opened in 1959 at the Indian Army Remount and Veterinary Corps Centre and School (now RVC Centre and School) in Meerut, Uttar Pradesh. Training for avalanche rescue operations began here in September 1976.

First board of ordnance

The Board of Ordnance was set up in 1775 at Fort William, Calcutta (now Kolkata), West Bengal. Currently, the Indian Ordnance Factories Organization – a set of 41 ordnance factories under the aegis of its corporate headquarters, the Ordnance Factory Board (OFB), Kolkata – has more than 200 years of experience in the development and marketing of a range of land, sea and air defence systems. At present, the OFB has nine training institutes, three regional marketing centres and four regional controllers of safety under it.

First counter-insurgency school

The Counter-Insurgency and Jungle Warfare School was established at Mynkre, Meghalaya, in 1967. It was relocated to Vairengte in Mizoram on 1 May 1970.

First high-altitude warfare school

Instituted as a formation ski school at Gulmarg, Jammu and Kashmir, the High Altitude Warfare School came into being on 8 April 1962. The courses at this institute include those on skiing and mountaineering.

Longest bridge built during war

The Indo-Pakistan war in 1971, termed the Sappers War, saw the construction of a 421.8 m (1,384 ft) composite bridge across the River Madhumati in East Pakistan (now Bangladesh) in a matter of 34 hours. It was the longest 'war' bridge to be constructed by India after the Second World War and the longest operational bridge constructed during a war involving India.

First nuclear shelter

DRDO, the Pune-based research and development laboratory, introduced an integrated battlefield shelter for all three services in 2002 to withstand nuclear or chemical strikes for up to 96 hours. The portable shelter, 28 m (91 ft 10 in.) long and with a diameter of 2.5 m (8 ft 2 in.), had chemical toilets, water tanks, pumps for sewage disposal and two power generators. It could accommodate 30 people and could be used as a command post, an observation post and a communication centre.

First National War Memorial

The armed forces first proposed a National War Memorial way back in 1960. On 25 February 2019, the memorial, designed by the Chennai-based WeBe Design Lab, led by Yogesh Chandrahasan, was inaugurated near India Gate, New Delhi. Covering over 40 acres (16.2 hectares), it has the names of Indian soldiers martyred in 1947–48 (Kashmir), 1961 (Goa), 1962 (China), 1965 and 1971 (Pakistan), 1987 (Siachen), 1987–88 (Sri Lanka), 1999 (Kargil) and other operations. It has concentric circles, with the Amar Chakra (Circle of Immortality) and an Eternal Flame in the centre. Around it are the Veerta Chakra (Circle of Bravery), a gallery depicting iconic battles and the Rakshak Chakra (Circle of Protection). The circles represent the *chakravyuh* or

First National War Memorial at India Gate, New Delhi

The National Florence Nightingale Award 2020

Brigadier S.V. Saraswati

Hailing from Chittoor, Andhra Pradesh, Brigadier S.V. Saraswati, deputy director general of the Military Nursing Service (MNS), was awarded the National Florence Nightingale Award in September 2021 by the then president Ram Nath Kovind, for her remarkable contribution and professionalism as the nurse administrator of the MNS. Brigadier Saraswati has not only refined the drape kits and suture packing for cardiac surgeries and enhanced pedagogical material, besides training residents, nursing trainees of the operation room and auxiliary staff, but she has also helped in more than 3,000 emergency as well as life-saving surgeries. Over the 35 years of her service, an array of national and international forums have seen Brigadier Saraswati representing the Military Nursing Service. In addition to serving at different army hospitals across the country, Brigadier Saraswati also served with the United Nations Peacekeeping Forces in the Congo in Africa. For her exemplary professionalism in the nursing profession, along with her commendable services to soldiers and their families, Brigadier Saraswati was also bestowed with the Chief of the Army Staff Commendation in 2015, the United Nations Medal in 2007 and the General Officer Commanding-in-Chief Commendation in 2005.

Killer Squadron Receives the President's Standard

To mark the golden jubilee of the inception of the 22nd Missile Vessel Squadron or the 'Killer Squadron' and to honour its contribution to protecting the nation on its seas, the then president of India, Ram Nath Kovind, presented the President's Standard to it on 8 December 2021. The squadron gained its name, the Killer Squadron, after the determined attacks – codenamed Operation Trident – that it carried out in the Indo-Pak War of 1971 (the year the unit was established), which saw no casualties in Indian forces. Ever since, the squadron has led in an array of operations including Operation Vijay and Operation Parakram, and after the Pulwama attack, it was deployed at a striking distance off the coast of Pakistan. It has also received illustrious battle honours – one Maha Vir Chakra, eight Nausena Medals and seven Vir Chakras.

traditional Indian war formation. The Param Yodha Sthal has busts of 21 recipients of the Param Vir Chakra.

First win at International Scout Masters Competition

Held in India for the first time, the host Indian Army team, trained by the Southern Command, won the Fifth Army International Scout Masters Competition (ISMC). Part of the International Army Games, it was held at Jaisalmer Military Station, Rajasthan, during 6–14 August 2019 and included five stages of competitions. Participants included teams from the armies of Armenia, Belarus, China, India, Kazakhstan, Russia, Sudan and Uzbekistan.

First Bactrian camels join the army

Since February 2017, the Bactrian camel was put through the paces at the Defence Institute of High Altitude Research (DIHAR), a DRDO laboratory in Leh, Ladakh. Bactrian camels are used to patrol the Line of Actual Control (LAC) in Ladakh and carry loads for the army.

First Indian dog breed in active duty

The Indian Army began to use dogs for active duty in 1959, the preferred breeds being the Labrador retriever, the Great Swiss Mountain dogs and the German shepherd. In 2017, the Remount and Veterinary Corps introduced the first Indian breed, the Mudhol hound (or caravan hound), a sight hound used as a hunting hound first in Central Asia and later in the Deccan region, especially Karnataka. It is known for its courage, speed and loyalty.

NAVY

PERSONNEL

First naval pilot

Lieutenant Y.N. Singh of the Royal Indian Navy was deputed to England in 1941 for basic training and later to Canada where he obtained his wings in 1944 before serving in the escort carriers of the Royal Navy in the Second World War.

First commander-in-chief

- The first commander-in-chief of the Royal Indian Navy was Admiral Sir Edward Parry in August 1948.
- Rear Admiral I.T.S. Hall was the first post-Independence commander-in-chief of the Royal Indian Navy. The word 'Royal' was dropped on 26 January 1950.

First chief of naval staff

- Admiral Sir Mark Pizey was the first chief of naval staff in 1955.
- The first Indian chief of naval staff was Vice Admiral Ram Dass Katari in 1958.

First four-star admiral

Admiral A.K. Chatterji (1914–2001) became a four-star admiral on 1 March 1968. He joined the Royal Indian Marines as a cadet in 1933 and became chief of naval staff in 1966.

First woman maritime reconnaissance pilot

Shubhangi Swaroop became the first woman pilot in the navy who was trained to fly maritime reconnaissance aircraft in 2017. Three other women cadets – Astha Segal, Roopa A. and Sakthi Maya S. – passed out with her in the first batch of women officers from the Indian Naval Academy, Ezhimala, Kerala, on 22 November 2017, and were inducted into the naval armament inspection (NAI) branch. The Indian Navy had inducted its first woman officer in 1991. Its aviation branch had women working as air traffic control officers and as observers in aircraft.

First woman pilot of naval aircraft

On 2 December 2019, 24-year-old Sublieutenant Shivangi Singh graduated with two other trainee officers from the Seventh Dornier Conversion Course (DOCC) at Kochi, Kerala. Originally from Muzaffarpur, Bihar, this Short Service Commission pilot entry scheme officer was commissioned into the Indian Navy in June 2018 and underwent a year of flying training at the Air Force Academy (AFA), Dundigal, Telangana, and Indian Naval Air Squadron (INAS) 550 and INS *Garuda* in Kochi. During training, she flew aircraft such as Pilatus PC 7 MkII, a basic trainer, at AFA before the Dornier Conversion Course.

First woman officers as 'Observers'

Sublieutenant Kumudini Tyagi and Sublieutenant Riti Singh graduated as 'Observers' (airborne technicians) in the Indian Navy's stream of helicopters to be deployed on warships for short- or long-term missions. They were awarded their wings in a graduation ceremony held at INS *Garuda* on 21 September 2020.

UNITS

First navy air squadron

On 17 June 1959, the Fleet Requirement Unit was commissioned as the Indian Naval Air Squadron 550. INS *Vikrant*, formerly HMS *Hercules*, joined the Indian Navy on 16 February 1961 as the first aircraft carrier and saw action during the Goa liberation struggle in December 1961. It has flown 14 types of aircraft, starting with Sealands to the Dornier maritime reconnaissance aircraft flown currently.

First unmanned aerial vehicle squadron

The navy's first unmanned aerial vehicle (UAV) squadron, intended to patrol the seas, was commissioned on 6 January 2006, with 12 UAVs from Israel. The Intensive Flying and Training Units were based in Kochi, Kerala.

Only training command

The Southern Naval Command is the only training command of the Indian Navy. It was augmented by INS *Magar*, which arrived at Kochi, Kerala, on 10 April 2018 to join the first Training Squadron for sea training of officers.

First exclusive naval base

INS *Kadamba*, inaugurated on 31 May 2005 near Karwar in Karnataka, is India's third operational naval base after Mumbai and Visakhapatnam, and the first under the sole control of the navy. Signifying another first, the inauguration speech was read out in Sanskrit. Sanctioned in 1985 as Project Seabird, its foundation stone was laid in 1986.

EQUIPMENT

First cruiser and flagship

HMS *Achilles*, a 7,030-tonne battleship, formerly of the Royal Navy, was commissioned as HMIS *Delhi* on 5 July 1948 in England,

DEFENCE ALLOCATION (BUDGET ESTIMATES) 2022–23
IN ₹ CRORE

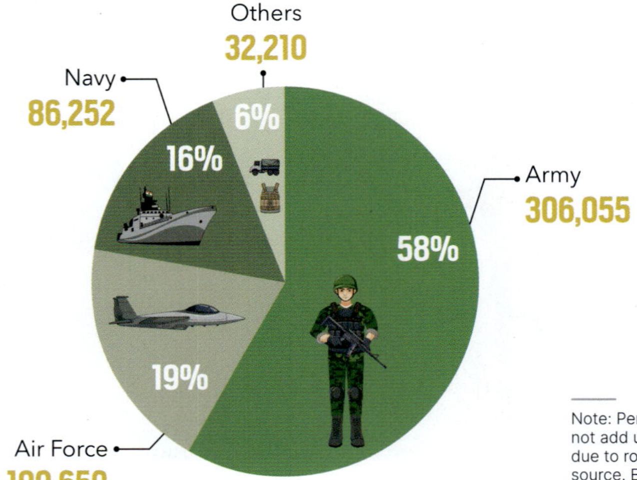

Note: Percentages may not add up to 100% due to rounding off at source. Expenditure for the army includes expense on Border Roads Organization, and Jammu and Kashmir Light Infantry. Expenditure for the navy includes expense on Coast Guard. Sources: Expenditure Budget, Union Budget 2022–23

TOTAL DEFENCE ALLOCATION
525,166

Guard of honour at the Southern Naval Command: only training command

Representative image

The New Pathway to the Armed Forces with the Agnipath Scheme

In order to increase the opportunities for the youth to join the armed forces and serve the nation, the Cabinet Committee on Security approved Agnipath, a recruitment scheme for the armed forces, on 14 June 2022. Under the scheme, young people, to be called Agniveers, will be recruited into the armed forces for a service period of four years, and on the realization of the services, the Agniveers will be entitled to 'Seva Nidhi' – a one-time tax-exempt package. While the Agniveers, unlike the other standard recruits, will not have access to any benefits associated with gratuity or pension, the forces have ensured a provision of a non-contributory life insurance cover of ₹48 lakh for their service engagement period.

Out of the selected applicants, 25 per cent will be allowed to continue their services as a regular cadre with a minimum engagement period of service of 15 years under the already prevailing rules and regulations, and terms and conditions. The training the Agniveers receive will ensure that a further newly skilled, technologically informed, disciplined as well as motivated workforce enters the newer industries with zeal, teamwork and an elevated sense of patriotism. The scheme envisages the induction of 100 officers and 1,000 other young recruits, between 18 and 25 years old, in the Indian military.

INS *Chakra*: first nuclear submarine

and became the first cruiser and flagship of the Indian Navy. It arrived at Bombay (now Mumbai), Maharashtra, on 15 September 1948. HMIS *Delhi* (renamed INS *Delhi*) was 169.1 m (554 ft 9 in.) long and 16.77 m (55 ft) across its beam, with a speed of 32 knots. Its armaments included six 152 mm guns, eight 102 mm guns, fifteen 40 mm guns, four anti-aircraft three-pounders and eight torpedo tubes.

First missile boat

INS *Vinash*, a Soviet OSA 1 commissioned on 21 January 1971, was fitted with four SS-N-2A surface-to-surface missiles and four 30 mm guns. With a complement of 30 crew, it could reach speeds exceeding 35 knots.

First submarine depot ship

INS *Amba*, an ex-Soviet Ugra-class ship with a displacement of 6,750 tonnes, is a submarine tender and was commissioned on 28 December 1968. INS *Amba* has two cranes (6 tonnes and 10 tonnes) and it can accommodate 750 personnel.

First indigenous patrol boat

Godavari-class frigate INS *Ajay*, commissioned on 21 September 1960, is a front-line warship equipped with missiles, guns and anti-submarine equipment, as well as early warning navigation and electronic warfare systems. Built by Garden Reach Shipbuilders and Engineers (GRSE) Ltd, it could carry two Sea King helicopters.

First submarine base

On 19 May 1971, INS *Virbahu*, the Indian Navy's first submarine base, was commissioned near Visakhapatnam, Andhra Pradesh.

First submarine rescue ship

INS *Nistar* was converted from a fleet minesweeper to a submarine rescue ship and commissioned on 29 March 1971. An ex-Soviet Valday-class ship, it features a diving bell, a recompression chamber, two rescue chambers and a lift of 10 tonnes.

First indigenous submarine

INS *Shalki*, the first of SSK Type-1500 submarines, built at Mazagon Dock Ltd, Bombay (now Mumbai), Maharashtra, was commissioned in February 1992. It has a displacement of 1,450 tonnes and carries 14 AEG SUT torpedoes.

First nuclear submarine

INS *Chakra*, the navy's first nuclear-powered submarine belonging to the Victor 1 SSN class had a speed of 32 knots and a dive displacement of 5,000 tonnes. It carried 90 sailors. On lease from the USSR, it was commissioned on 3 February 1988 and sent back in 1991.

First missile corvette

INS *Kora*, the first indigenously built missile corvette, was commissioned on 10 August 1998. Capable of operating in nuclear, biological and chemical confrontation zones, it had a displacement of 1,300 tonnes and an overall length of 91.16 m (299 ft). INS *Kora* had two indigenous fuel-efficient diesel engines and could touch 26 knots. Along with a helipad for

INS VIKRANT: A FORCE MULTIPLIER

INS *Vikrant*, India's first indigenous aircraft carrier, aptly named after the country's distinguished first aircraft carrier *Vikrant* (a veteran of India's war against Pakistan in 1971), was commissioned on 2 September 2022 in Cochin Shipyard Ltd in Kochi, Kerala. With this, India joined the elite group of nations to have developed an aircraft carrier indigenously, viz., the USA, Russia, China, France and the UK.

INS *Vikrant* was designed by the Warship Design Bureau (WDB), an in-house organization of the Indian Navy, and built by Cochin Shipyard Ltd, a PSU under the Ministry of Ports, Shipping and Waterways, in Kerala. It took nearly 17 years to design and develop INS *Vikrant*.

The aircraft carrier is the largest ship ever built in India's maritime history and the flight deck is comparable to two football fields. It houses a physiotherapy clinic, an ICU (Intensive Care Unit), an isolation ward and laboratories.

The steel used in the construction of INS *Vikrant* was indigenized through the Steel Authority of India Ltd (SAIL) in collaboration with the Defence Research and Development Laboratory (DRDL) and the Indian Navy. INS *Vikrant* is being viewed as a prime example of 'AatmaNirbhar Bharat' in the defence sector as a majority of the components and materials used in its construction have been sourced from within the country.

Built as a cost of around ₹20,000 crore, INS *Vikrant* furthers India's ambition of a blue-water navy.

Key Features

Specifications: 262 m x 62 m (860 ft x 203 ft)
Displacement: Approx. 43,000 tonnes when fully loaded
Maximum speed: 28 knots
Endurance: 7,500 nautical miles
Crew size: 1,600
Compartments: 2,200 (also has specialized ones for women officers and sailors)
STOBAR: INS *Vikrant*'s flight deck incorporates the STOBAR (Short Take-Off But Arrested Recovery) operation mode, which allows aircraft to take off with a short runway with help of a ski jump. Landing and recovery is aided by arrester wires.
Aircrafts Hosted: INS *Vikrant* can operate a flight deck with 30 fighter aircraft (currently MiG 29K) and a mix of Kamov 31 AEW helicopters. It can also host MH-60R multi-role helicopters and Dhruv advanced light helicopters (marine version).
Weapons: It can carry high-tech weapons such as the Barak-8 surface-to-air missile system.

Background: INS *Vikrant*; *below:* INS *Vikrant* being undocked at Cochin Shipyard Ltd

THE INDIAN NAVY'S NEW ENSIGN

Prime Minister Narendra Modi unveiled the New Naval Ensign (Nishaan) on 2 September 2022 during the commissioning of INS *Vikrant*. The Naval Ensign is a maritime flag used by naval ships of various countries to denote their nationality. The Naval Ensign can be the same as the national flag of the country that it represents, or it can be different from it. In the case of India, the Naval Ensign used by the Indian Navy differs from the country's national flag.

Before Independence (1928–50) The Indian Navy has changed its ensign multiple times during the colonial era and also after Independence.

On **26 January 1950**, the Royal Indian Navy was renamed the Indian Navy, and its crests and flags were changed. For the ensign, the Union Jack was replaced with India's national flag in the canton.

In **2001**, the Saint George's cross was done away with and the ensign featured the crest of the Indian Navy on a white background, with the flag of India placed in the canton.

Following complaints from sailors about the Indian Navy's Crest not being distinguishable from the sky, in **2004**, the Government of India again used the Saint George's Cross, but with the addition of the national emblem of India at the intersection of the cross.

In **2014**, a further version of the ensign was made with the inclusion of the Indian national motto 'Satyameva Jayate' in the Devanagari script below the national emblem.

In **2022**, a new ensign was launched, with the Indian national flag in the upper canton, a blue octagon encasing the national emblem atop an anchor to depict steadfastness, placed on a shield with the Navy's motto 'Sam No Varuna' (a Vedic mantra invoking the god of seas) in Devanagari. The octagon indicates the eight directions and has been included as a symbol of the Navy's 'multidirectional reach and multidimensional operational capability'. The golden frames of the octagon have been inspired by the seal of Maratha emperor Chhatrapati Shivaji Maharaj.

INS *Talwar*: one of the first multi-warships

advanced light helicopters and Chetaks, it had a complement of 11 officers and 110 sailors.

First indigenous modern warship
INS *Nilgiri*, which was commissioned on 3 June 1972, was the first modern warship built at Mazagon Dock Ltd, Bombay (now Mumbai), Maharashtra. INS *Nilgiri*, based on the British Leander-class frigates, had a hangar with a telescopic extension to take Alouette III helicopters. It was decommissioned on 31 May 1996.

First ocean minesweepers
INS *Pondicherry* and INS *Porbandar*, built at the Isora Yard, Leningrad, USSR (now Russia), were given to the Indian Navy in 1978. These Natya-1-class sweepers have steel hulls with active mine detection sonars.

First dedicated cadet training ship
INS *Tir* (A86), named after HMIS *Tir*, a River-class frigate of the Royal Indian Navy that had served in the Second World War as HMS *Bann* (K256), was the first dedicated cadet-training ship built at Mazagon Dock Ltd. It was the senior ship of the First Training Squadron under the Southern Naval Command. Commissioned on 21 February 1986, it carried 120 cadets and 20 instructors.

The Defence Research and Development Organization launched a supersonic and missile-assisted torpedo system.

First anti-ship missile
On 2 March 2017, the first anti-ship missile was fired from an indigenously built Kalvari-class submarine, the first in a series of Scorpene-class submarines being built in India. The submarine was stationed in the Arabian Sea and the missile successfully hit a surface target.

First fast attacker
INFAC-T-80 (Indian Navy's extra-fast attack craft), commissioned at the Naval Dockyard in Mumbai, Maharashtra, on 24 June 1998, was the first fast-attack high-speed vessel and the first of an Indo-Israeli defence project. This aluminium-hull vessel could sustain 45 knots and it was the smallest ship in the Indian Navy.

First multi-warships
INS *Talwar* was launched in May 2000, INS *Trishul* in November 2000 and INS *Tabar* in May 2001. These Talwar-class guided missile frigates were designed and built by Russia.

First indigenous fleet replenishment tanker
INS *Aditya*, built by GRSE, Calcutta (now Kolkata), West Bengal, was commissioned at Visakhapatnam, Andhra Pradesh, on 3 April 2000. Manned by 16 officers and 140 sailors, the 172 m (564 ft) long fleet tanker has a deadweight tonnage of 1,700. It can touch a speed of 24 knots with an endurance of 10,000 nautical miles, and load six ships simultaneously on the high seas. It also carries a Sea King helicopter.

First Integrated Automatic Aviation Meteorological System
On 28 March 2017, the then chief of naval staff, Admiral Sunil Lanba, inaugurated the first Integrated Automatic Aviation Meteorological System (IAAMS) at INS *Rajali* (informally also known as the Arakkonam naval air station) in Tamil Nadu. The IAAMS has been established with the objective of modernizing the meteorological infrastructure and aviation safety of the nine naval air stations of the Indian Navy through automated monitoring of weather.

First indigenous ammunition
The Indian Navy received its first made-in-India 30 mm ammunition for AK-630 rotary cannons fitted on warships, as reported on 29 August 2022. The production of AK-630 guns was carried out by M/s Economic Explosives Ltd (EEL), Nagpur, Maharashtra, a subsidiary of Solar Industries India Ltd.

First Indigenously developed naval anti-ship missile
India's first Indigenously developed naval anti-ship missile for the Indian Navy was test-fired om 18 May 2022. The missile was launched aboard a Seaking 42B Naval Helicopter from the Integrated Test Range (ITR) at Balasore in Odisha.

First 'green' ship
In February 2017, the survey vessel INS *Sarvekshak*, based at the Southern Naval Command in Kochi, Kerala, became India's

first naval ship to go green by installing a zero-maintenance solar power system that can generate 5.4 kW of electricity. It replaces the ship's emergency diesel alternator. The customized power-generating system has flexible, razor-thin solar panels on the canopy of the retractable helicopter deck, which use no-fume solid electrolyte batteries and are maintenance-free for 24 years. The solar-power-generating system can be used to run communication equipment and on-board lights, and charge batteries. With an annual carbon emission of 60,225 kg, it will replace about 22,995 litres of diesel.

Largest aircraft carrier

INS *Viraat*, commissioned on 12 May 1987 at Devonport, UK, is the second and largest aircraft carrier of the Indian Navy. The 28,700 tonne INS *Viraat* (R-22), earlier called HMS *Hermes*, was launched in 1953 as the flagship of the South Atlantic Task Force in the Falklands War in 1982. The Indian Navy is among eight navies in the world to have aircraft carriers.

Longest serving warship/aircraft carrier

INS *Viraat* – the second Centaur-class aircraft carrier in service – served India for 30 years after 27 years of service in the Royal Navy of the UK as HMS *Hermes*. The UK Royal Navy commissioned it in 1959 and it was later sold to the Indian Navy in 1986. It was decommissioned on 6 March 2017.

GENERAL

First modern shipbuilder

In 1736, the East India Company invited Lowji Nusserwanji Wadia to build the first shipyard in Bombay (now Mumbai), Maharashtra. Since then, seven generations of the Wadias have built ships, including HMS *Minden* (the first constructed outside of Great Britain), HMS *Trincomalee* and HMS *Cornwallis*.

First modern shipbuilding yard

Garden Reach Shipbuilders and Engineers (GRSE) Ltd, located on the eastern bank of the River Hooghly in present-day Kolkata, West Bengal, dates to 1884. The company's name was changed to Garden Reach Workshop in 1916 and on 1 April 1960, it was taken over by the Government of India. The name was changed back to Garden Reach Shipbuilders and Engineers on 1 January 1977. It builds a range of ships, including warships, sophisticated commercial vessels, harbour craft and fast, powerful patrol vessels for the Indian Navy and the Coast Guard. It built INS *Ajay*, India's first indigenous patrol boat, in 1960.

First naval dockyard

The Naval Dockyard at Bombay (now Mumbai), Maharashtra, started with the Bunder Pier in 1693. A tiny dry dock was constructed in 1750. The old Bombay Dock and the Duncan Dock were built in 1765 and 1810 respectively. A wet basin was constructed in 1892. The largest naval dockyard today, it is the premier maintenance facility for ships and submarines of the navy.

INS *Sarveskshak*: first 'green' ship

First naval school

The Signal School on INS *Venduruthy* was established at Bombay's Carnac Bunder in 1919 in Maharashtra. The next year, it was shifted to the Naval Dockyard, Bombay (now Mumbai), Maharashtra, and in 1941, to HMIS *Talwar*, also in Bombay. In 1946, it finally moved to Kochi, Kerala.

First naval academy

The first naval academy was established in Kochi, Kerala, in January 1969. The first batch of cadets graduated in December 1970. Commander K. Ramdas was the first officer-in-charge. Earlier, cadets used to be trained in England.

First floating dry dock

The floating dry dock at Port Blair, Andaman and Nicobar Islands, commissioned in 1987, has a lifting capacity of 11,500 tonnes and can accommodate vessels that have a deadweight of up to 30,000 tonnes.

First indigenous floating dock

On 20 June 2017, FDN-2, the first indigenously designed and constructed floating dock of the Indian Navy was launched at the Larsen & Toubro Ltd shipyard at Kattupalli in Chennai, Tamil Nadu. The

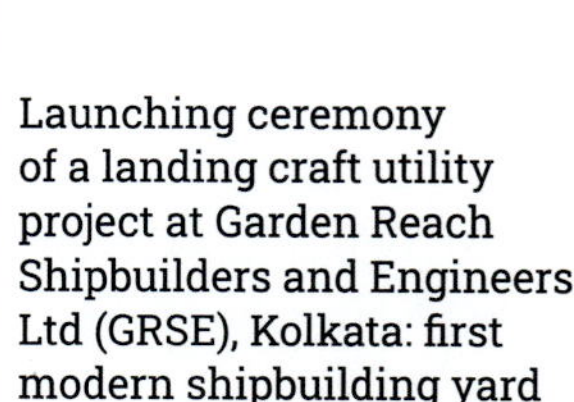

Launching ceremony of a landing craft utility project at Garden Reach Shipbuilders and Engineers Ltd (GRSE), Kolkata: first modern shipbuilding yard

The Directorate General Defence Estates has developed an AI-based software which can detect change on ground, including identifying unauthorized constructions and encroachments on land under defence use, using satellite imagery.

185 m (607 ft) long and 40 m (131 ft 3 in.) wide platform has best-in-class machinery and control systems. It accommodates up to 8,000-tonne ships with draught up to 7 m (23 ft), including submarines.

First aircraft carrier dry dock

On 28 September 2019, the first aircraft carrier dry dock was inaugurated at the Naval Dockyard in Mumbai, Maharashtra. The largest dry dock of the Indian Navy, it can accommodate INS *Vikramaditya* (IAC-I), the indigenous aircraft carrier under construction at Cochin Shipyard Ltd, and ships with a tonnage of up to 90,000 tonnes. Started in 2010, the completed dock is 281 m (921 ft 11 in.) long, 45 m (147 ft 8 in.) wide and 17 m (55 ft 9 in.) deep. Unlike most dry docks that are made by excavating land, this one is built into the sea, for which 38 caissons or watertight steel sections drained out seawater before construction could begin.

First unified theatre command

Vice Admiral Arun Prakash took over as the first commander-in-chief of the Andaman and Nicobar Command in 2001, with operational control of all three services and the Indian Coast Guard in the Andaman and Nicobar theatre.

First helicopter training school

INS *Rajali* at Arakkonam, Tamil Nadu, houses the Indian Naval Air Station (INAS), which is a base for training helicopter pilots.

First deep-sea submarine rescue system

On 12 Dec 2018, the Indian Navy's first flyaway Deep-Sea Submarine Rescue System was inducted by Admiral Sunil Lanba at the Naval Dockyard, Mumbai, Maharashtra. The system has a non-tethered Deep Submergence Rescue Vehicle (DSRV) and associated equipment, which give the navy the capability to search, locate and rescue crew. The rescue system can be mobilized from the naval base at Mumbai, to the nearest mobilization port by air, land or sea to expedite rescue. On 5 June 2019, an entirely Indian crew conducted its first full submarine rescue drill on the Kilo-class submarine, INS *Sindhudhvaj*, off the eastern coast of India.

Vice Admiral Arun Prakash (*right*): first unified theatre command

First combat management system

A combat management system (CMS) for indigenous aircraft carriers has been developed by the Indian Navy along with the Tata Power Strategic Engineering Division (TPSED), in collaboration with the Weapon and Electronics System Engineering Establishment and MARS, Russia. On 28 March 2019, it was handed over to the navy. All tests and trials conducted on its hardware and software were successful. This is the first CMS developed by a private company for the Indian Navy.

First all-woman crew to circumnavigate the world

On 21 May 2018, a six-member all-woman crew completed circumnavigating the globe in 254 days on-board INSV *Tarini*, becoming the first Indian all-woman crew to do so. The journey ended at INS *Mandovi* jetty in Panaji, Goa, from where they had set sail on 10 September 2017. The crew included Lieutenant Commanders Vartika Joshi, Pratibha Jamwal, P. Swathi, and Lieutenants S. Vijaya Devi, B. Aishwarya and Payal Gupta. The 17 m (56 ft) sailing vessel was captained by Lieutenant Commander Joshi. The crew was mentored by Commander Dilip Donde, who became India's first solo circumnavigator in 2010.

Longest expedition with a mixed crew

INSV *Mhadei* and INSV *Tarini* set sail for the Bay of Bengal Offshore Sailing Expedition on 22 February 2020 from the Indian Naval Ocean Sailing Node in Goa. The crew comprised five naval officers, including two women officers in each boat, covering 6,100 nautical miles over 55 days. Captain Vipul Meherishi, the skipper of INSV *Tarini*, led the expedition. Captain Atool Sinha was the skipper of INSV *Mhadei*. The sailing vessels had scheduled halts at Colombo (Sri Lanka), Yangon (Myanmar), Chittagong (Bangladesh) and Phuket (Thailand).

First virtual reality centre

On 12 April 2019, Admiral Sunil Lanba

inaugurated the first virtual reality centre (VRC) at the Directorate of Naval Design (Surface Ship Group). This centre boosts the design of indigenous warships, and collaborative design reviews between designers and end-users of warships. It has developed 19 warship designs.

AIR FORCE

PERSONNEL

First Indian pilots

- Lieutenant Indra Lal Roy from Calcutta (now Kolkata), West Bengal, was the first Indian pilot with the Royal Flying Corps and later in the Royal Air Force during the First World War. He claimed 10 victories in air combat, all within two weeks in July 1918. He was killed in action when only 19 years old and was posthumously awarded the Distinguished Flying Cross.
- The only other Indian pilots known to have flown in the First World War were Sardar Hardit Singh Malik, Lieutenant S.G. Welingkar, Lieutenant Errol Sharat Chandra Sen and Lieutenant Naoroji.

First air chiefs

Air Marshal Subroto Mukerjee became the first Indian chief of air staff when he succeeded Air Marshal Sir G.E. Gibbs on 1 April 1954. However, the IAF chief's rank was only equivalent to that of a lieutenant general of the Indian Army at the time. The IAF got its first air chief marshal only in 1966 when Air Marshal Arjan Singh was promoted to the post in recognition of the IAF's role in the 1965 war with Pakistan.

First Indian station commander

Wing Commander Subroto Mukerjee was given command of the airbase RAF Kohat (now in Pakistan), the first all-Indian station with only Indian Air Force (IAF) squadrons, in 1944.

Longest tenure as air chief

Air Marshal Subroto Mukerjee served the longest tenure as air chief, from 1 April 1954 to 8 November 1960.

First marshal

On 26 January 2002, former chief of the Indian Air Force, Air Chief Marshal Arjan Singh, was given the rank of marshal, equivalent to a field marshal. Arjan Singh was also a recipient of the Distinguished Flying Cross.

First woman flight commander

Wing Commander Shaliza Dhami was the first woman to become a flight commander in the IAF. She was commissioned to the position on 26 August 2019 and took command of a Chetak Helicopter Unit at Hindon Airbase, Ghaziabad, Uttar Pradesh. She is also the first woman to be granted a permanent commission and the first to be an authorized instructor for IAF helicopters.

First woman air marshal

Air Marshal Padmavathy Bandopadhyay, AVSM, VSM, (b. 4 November 1944) took over as the director general of medical services (Air) on 1 October 2004. Having joined the IAF in 1968, she was also the first woman to reach the rank of air vice marshal in 2002.

First squadron commander

Flight Lieutenant Subroto Mukerjee took over command of 1 Squadron on 3 September 1939 – later becoming the first officer to command a flight, a squadron, a station and finally the IAF.

First commissioned woman pilot by order of merit

Squadron Leader Priya Nalgundwar (b. 28 November 1970) was commissioned in the Indian Air Force in the Flying Branch on 17 December 1994 as part of the first batch of seven women pilots and stood first in the order of merit in her batch. She received her wings from the then chief of air staff Air Chief Marshal S.K. Kaul.

GLOBAL MILITARY SPENDING* TOP 5 COUNTRIES

WORLD TOTAL SPENDING

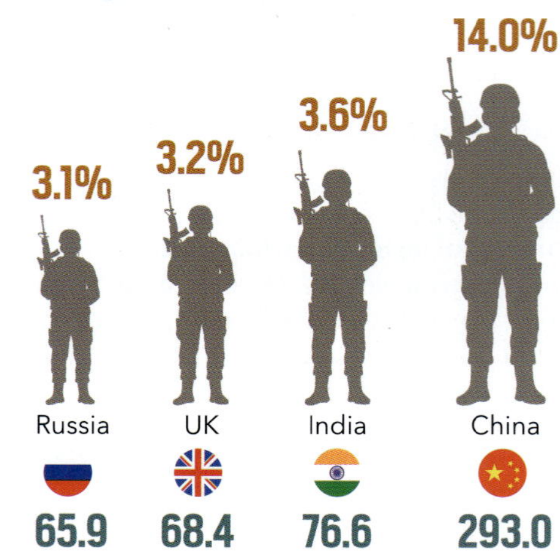

* 2021 data; Source: sipri.org

Air Marshal Subroto Mukerjee: first Indian chief of air staff

The fly-past during the conclave organized to commemorate 60 years of the Chetak helicopter's service to the nation

A Diamond Jubilee for Chetak

The oldest helicopter of the Indian Air Force – the Chetak – completed 60 years of service in April 2022. With its origins in France (Alouette III), the first licence-produced Chetak was delivered to the IAF in 1965. Operated by all three armed forces along with the Indian Coast Guard, the Chetak weighs over two tonnes, has a speed of 185 km/h and a range of 500 km, with the capacity of holding five people, excluding the two pilots. Over the years, the chopper has not only been utilized for training newly commissioned helicopter pilots but has also been vital in times of war, evacuations associated with casualties, relief missions and VIP flying. Due to its size and design, the helicopter can easily access various terrains and locations including the Siachen Glacier and warships, and has the ability to land in small areas. To mark the diamond jubilee of the chopper, the IAF, at its Hakimpet station in Hyderabad, Andhra Pradesh, organized a conclave, the '*Yashaswat Shat Dashakam*', to pay tribute to the Chetak.

The Indian Air Force received new uniforms for both the ground personnel and combat teams as they celebrate **90** years of the defence service in 2022.

First women combat pilots

In July 2016, for the first time, women combat pilots were inducted into the Indian Air Force with the then defence minister Manohar Parrikar commissioning Mohana Singh, Avani Chaturvedi and Bhawana Kanth.

First woman medical officer

Dr Vijayalakshmi Ramanan (later, wing commander), an army doctor, was inducted into the IAF in 1955.

First helicopter pilot

On 28 March 1954, Flight Lieutenant A. Neil Todd and his co-pilot Squadron Leader S.K. Majumdar flew the then prime minister, Jawaharlal Nehru, from Palam, Delhi, to Tilpat Range in Faridabad, Haryana, and back.

First chief of foreign air force

Air Commodore K. Jaswant Singh, who was on deputation to Ghana to plan and establish the Ghana Air Force, took charge on 25 March 1959 as its air chief.

First technical officer

Harjinder Singh, one of 19 Hawai Sepoys recruited to the IAF in 1931 (who later became air vice marshal), was promoted to the rank of warrant officer in 1941 and became a flying officer in 1942. He was 41 years old when he learned to fly, earned his wings and became the air officer commander-in-chief of the then newly formed Maintenance Command in Kanpur, Uttar Pradesh, in 1955.

First woman in the Defence Services Staff Course

Padmavathy Bandopadhyay (later air marshal) joined the Indian Air Force as a medical officer. Bandopadhyay was also the first woman to attend the prestigious Defence Services Staff Course (DSSC) in 1978; the first woman in Asia to specialize in aerospace medicine; and the first Indian woman to visit the North Pole (1989–90).

First woman pilot to lead the Republic Day fly-past

Flight Lieutenant Swati Rathore became the first woman pilot to lead the Republic Day fly-past on 26 January 2021. She flew an Mi-17 V5 with the IAF flag in a formation of four choppers. Flight Lieutenant Bhawana Kanth also participated in the Republic Day fly-past. A total of 38 IAF and four Army aircraft were part of the parade.

MEDALS AND HONOURS

First couple to be awarded the Vishisht Seva Medals

Flight Lieutenant (Dr) Sati Nath Bandopadhyay and his wife Flight Lieutenant Padmavathy Bandopadhyay were honoured with the Vishisht Seva Medal (VSM) at the same investiture ceremony by Air Chief Marshal O.P. Mehra for their service to the nation in the 1971 Bangladesh operations. They are the only Indian Air Force couple to be awarded such a commendation.

First woman to be awarded the Yudh Seva Medal

Squadron Leader Minty Aggarwal, a woman fighter controller who essayed a stellar role in intercepting retaliatory air attacks by the Pakistan Air Force after the Indian Air Force's Balakot air strikes in February 2019, was awarded the Yudh Seva Medal on 15 August 2019. Aggarwal thereby became the first woman in India's military history to be awarded the medal for distinguished service of a high order during war, conflict or hostilities. Aggarwal was among seven fighter controllers on duty in an underground bunker at the Ambala airbase. She joined the air force in 2011.

First Param Vir Chakra

Flying Officer N.J.S. Sekhon of 18 Squadron is the only Indian Air Force officer to have been decorated with the Param Vir Chakra, the highest gallantry award. It was given posthumously after he was killed in an air battle over Srinagar in Jammu and Kashmir on 14 December 1971.

First and only Sarvottam Yudh Seva Medal

On 15 August 1999, Air Marshal Vinod Patney was awarded the Sarvottam Yudh Seva Medal (SYSM) for his exemplary leadership during the Kargil conflict in 1999. The award is the highest wartime distinguished service decoration. The medal has been conferred thrice to date and he is the only IAF officer to receive it.

UNITS

First squadron

1 Squadron was formed on 1 April 1933 at Karachi's Drigh Road Airfield with Royal Air Force (RAF) officer Flight Lieutenant C.A. Bouchier as the first commanding officer. The first six Indian officers commissioned into the IAF were: Subroto Mukerjee, H.C. Sirkar, A.B. Awan, Bhupendra Singh, Amarjeet Singh and J.N. Tandon, along with 19 technicians who formed the complement. The six officers were pilots except Tandon, who was commissioned as first ground duty officer.

First bomber squadron

The 5 Squadron (Tuskers) was raised on 2 November 1948 on the Consolidated B-24 Liberator bomber. It is now equipped with Jaguar IS and based in Ambala, Haryana.

First transport squadron

The first transport squadron of the IAF was raised with Spitfire fighter aircraft under the command of Squadron Leader S. Sajad Haider at Kohat (now in Pakistan). It moved to Bhopal, Madhya Pradesh, in 1946 and converted to Dakotas, which it flew till 1954, when it then converted to Packets, a twin-engine cargo aircraft.

First squadron to have a jet bomber

106 SPR Squadron, though technically tasked with photo reconnaissance work, was the first unit to fly the famous English Electric Canberra in April 1957. The first squadron to have a jet bomber role again was No. 5 Squadron that took charge of the bomber variant of the Canberra in September 1957.

First heavy-lift transport squadron

44 Squadron, known as 'Himalayan Geese', was raised in 1961 and equipped with the An-12 four-engine turboprop transport aircraft. In the 1980s, it was renamed the 'Mighty Jets'.

First attack helicopter squadron

125 Helicopter Squadron (also known as Gladiators) is a fighter squadron that was formed on 1 November 1983 with the Mil Mi-25 attack gunships. It was re-equipped with Mi-35 helicopters in April 1990. The squadron saw action in Sri Lanka during the operations of the Indian Peacekeeping Force (IPKF) between 1987 and 1990. It is currently based at the Pathankot air force station, Punjab.

EQUIPMENT

First supersonic aircraft

1 Squadron (The Tigers) was equipped with the Dassault MD-452 Mystere Iva in February 1957. The Mystere could break the sound barrier in a dive. However, the first squadron to fly a level-flight-capable supersonic aircraft was the 28 Squadron, raised in October 1963 on the MiG-21F. Aptly christened First Supersonics, 28 Squadron also has the honour of being the first squadron to fly a Mach 2-capable fighter.

First aircraft

The biplane aircraft Westland Wapiti with a maximum speed of 362 km/hr was inducted into the IAF on 1 April 1933. Fitted with two machine guns, this aircraft could carry a load of 263 kg. Four Wapitis, which are believed to have been procured for 10 pounds sterling each, formed the A Flight of 1 Squadron, commanded by Flight Lieutenant C.A. Bouchier of the Royal Air Force (RAF).

First jet

The British single-seat Vampire was inducted in 1948, making India the first Asian country with jet fighters. In 1950, India entered into a licence agreement with de Havilland Aircraft Company Ltd, UK, and the first Vampire built by Hindustan Aeronautics Ltd (HAL) flew on 21 February 1952. Vampires were phased out in 1975.

First jet bomber

The twin-engine English Electric Canberra, which is a long-range and reconnaissance aircraft, was inducted into the Indian Air Force

A stamp honouring Flying Officer Nirmal Jit Singh Sekhon: recipient of the first Param Vir Chakra for the Indian Air Force

The proposed new airbase in the Changthang Wildlife Sanctuary in the Ladakh region will be spread across over 500 hectares (1235.53 acres) of land within the reserve. The approval for the project underlines many conditions that the IAF has to fulfil to mitigate damage and impact on the fragile ecology of the area.

The single-seat Vampire: first jet

in 1957. Six IAF Canberras of 5 Squadron served with the UN forces on the Congo peacekeeping assignment in October 1961.

First indigenous aircraft (trainer)

The HT-2-piston-engined elementary trainer was designed at HAL. It made its maiden flight on 5 August 1951 and was in operation from 1953 to 1990. It replaced the Tiger Moth and was used to train over 5,000 Indian and foreign pilots.

First indigenous fighter aircraft

The single seat Mach-2 combat jet fighter HF (Hindustan Fighter)-24 MkI (Marut Ground Attack Fighter), with two single-shaft turbojet engines, was designed at HAL, Bengaluru. It took its maiden flight on 17 June 1961.

First Gnat

The first Gnat or Ajeet, a single-seat, light fighter bomber, about a third in size and half the weight of a conventional fighter, was inducted into the IAF in 1958. The first Gnat, made by HAL, flew on 18 November 1959. It won the IAF its only Param Vir Chakra, and was in front-line service for more than three decades.

Tejas: first indigenous light combat aircraft

First indigenous light combat aircraft

Tejas is the first advanced fly-by-wire light combat aircraft (LCA) designed, developed and manufactured indigenously by HAL, DRDO, NAL (National Aerospace Laboratories) and ADA (Aeronautical Development Agency). It is a lightweight single-seat multi-role jet fighter, and pegged as the world's smallest and lightest supersonic fighter. It is equipped with a satellite-aided inertial navigation system, a digital computer-based attack system and autopilot mode. Tejas can fire air-to-air missiles, and carry bombs and precision-guided ammunition with a reach of over 400 km. It is mainly for use in close air-to-ground operations.

First indigenous advanced light helicopter

The naval version of the advanced light helicopter (ALH), developed by HAL, took its first flight from INS *Viraat* on 8 March 1998. It had an integrated dynamic system, hinge-less main rotor and composite blades, bearing-less tail rotor, advanced cockpit and high-power engines with electronic control. It could exceed a speed of 250 km/hr.

First indigenous tandem-seat jet trainer

The intermediate jet trainer (IJT) was designed in India, with the fastest design-to-first-flight time, and flown officially by Squadron Leader Baldev Singh for 20 mins on 21 March 2003. With a 10 m (32 ft 10 in.) wingspan and an overall length of 11 m (36 ft), the 3,500 kg aircraft can touch 750 km/hr. However, the credit of being the first tandem-seat jet trainer used for intermediate flying training in the IAF goes to the Polish PZL TS-11 Iskra.

First indigenous AEW&C class of aircraft

On 14 February 2017, the IAF was given its first indigenous Airborne Early Warning and Control (AEW&C) System class of aircraft in initial operational configuration (IOC) by DRDO, during Aero India 2017, a biennial air show and aviation exhibition, at the Yelahanka airbase in Bengaluru, Karnataka. It is built on an Emb-145 platform, and has an air-to-air refuelling capability to enhance surveillance time.

First AESA radar for IAF

The IAF gave the nod in July 2017 for the first Active Electronically Scanned Array (AESA) radar to be integrated into its aircraft. The radar is fitted on to Jaguar fighter aircraft. In conventional radars, the antenna is moved manually to scan enemy targets. The AESA radar moves electronically and rapidly, tracking multiple and long-distance targets, while also jamming enemy communications and radars.

First Apache helicopters

On 3 September 2019, eight Boeing-made Apache Guardian attack helicopters were inducted into service at the Pathankot air force station. The AH-64E (I) Apache helicopter

STRONG SKIES

Of the total aircraft strength of the Indian Air Force, 38.4 per cent are fighters, 15.2 per cent are transport aircraft, 18.5 per cent are trainers and 26.6 per cent are helicopters, with the remaining 1.3 per cent being tankers or aircraft on special missions. Here are a few of the IAF's fighter, transport and trainer aircraft*.

Fighters

HAL Tejas

This indigenously made single-engine, delta wing, light multi-role fighter, designed by ADA in collaboration with the Aircraft Research and Design Centre (ARDC) of HAL for the Indian Air Force and Indian Navy, received its final operational clearance in 2019.

MiG-27 (from the Soviet Union)

The Mikoyan MiG-27 was built for air-to-ground attack. First manufactured by the Mikoyan-Gurevich Design Bureau in the Soviet Union, it was later built under licence in India by HAL, and named 'Bahadur'.

Sukhoi 30 MkI (from Russia)

This all-weather, long-range fighter joined the IAF in 2002, and the first assembled-in-India Sukhoi 30 MkI was inducted into the IAF in 2004.

Jaguar (from France and the UK)

This jet assault aircraft's many roles include supersonic performance and functioning as a nuclear delivery platform.

MiG-29 (from the Soviet Union)

A twin-engine aircraft, the Mikoyan MiG-29 is a multipurpose fighter that can carry out a number of different operations, along with deploying a range of air-to-surface ammunition.

MiG-21 (from the Soviet Union)

This a supersonic jet fighter and interceptor aircraft from the Mikoyan-Gurevich Design Bureau is used by several nations even 60 years after its first flight.

Dassault Mirage 2000 (from France)

This lightweight single-engine, multi-role fourth-generation jet fighter is manufactured by Dassault Aviation.

Dassault Rafale (from France)

This twin-engine fighter aircraft designed and manufactured by Dassault Aviation has canard delta wings.

Transport

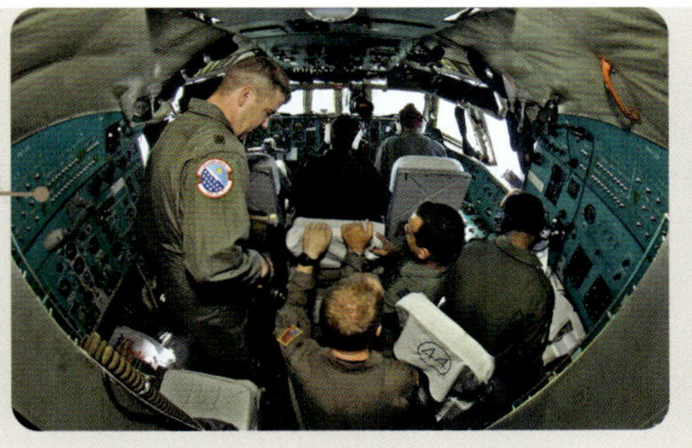

Ilyushin Il-76 (from the Soviet Union)

This aircraft is a multipurpose airlifter from the Ilyushin Design Bureau. It was designed to deliver heavy machinery to remote areas.

Hawker Siddeley HS 748 (from the UK)

This 40-seater turboprop feeder liner has a short take-off and advanced landing capabilities.

Boeing 737 (from the USA)

This carrier has seen many modifications since its first flight in 1967. It was the highest-selling aircraft before the Airbus 320.

McDonnell Douglas/Boeing C-17 Globemaster (from the USA)

A big military transport aircraft, this was designed for the US Air Force by aerospace manufacturing company McDonnell Douglas from the 1970s to the 1990s. It is deployed for airlifts of troops and cargo.

Lockheed Martin C-130J Super Hercules (from the USA)

A versatile turboprop military transport aircraft, it is used for assault in the air, search and rescue, scientific and weather research, airborne refuelling, firefighting and patrolling. It can land on and take off from unbuilt runways.

Dornier DO 228 (from Switzerland)

This twin-turboprop aircraft was designed and made by Dornier GmbH. In 1983, HAL manufactured the aircraft in Kanpur, Uttar Pradesh, under licence.

Antonov (AN-32) (from Ukraine)

A turboprop twin-engine transport aircraft, this can bear extreme weather conditions.

Trainers

BAE Hawk (from the UK)

This is a single-engine, jet-powered advanced trainer aircraft.

HAL Kiran (HJT-16)

Indigenously designed and manufactured by HAL, this is a two-seater jet-powered trainer aircraft.

Pilatus PC-7 (from Switzerland)

Able to perform training functions including aerial acrobatics, and tactical and night flying, the Pilatus PC-7 Turbo Trainer is a tandem-seat training aircraft.

*The images are for representational purposes only and to show the aircraft type, and based on the availability of images, the aircraft shown here are not necessarily or all from the IAF.

has been built keeping in mind the high mountainous terrain that the IAF operates in. It can also carry out precision attacks. This helicopter can receive and transmit images from the ground to its weapon systems and likewise transmit images from its weapon systems to the ground. The air crew and ground crew were trained to operate the helicopter at the US Army base, Fort Rucker.

First indigenous anti-radiation missile

Rudram-1, a new-generation air-to-surface anti-radiation missile (NGARM), developed by DRDO for the Indian Air Force was test-fired on 9 October 2020 on a radiation target on Wheeler Island off the coast of Odisha. The missile Rudram-1 was fired from a Sukhoi-30 MkI fighter aircraft, the potential launch-source aircraft for the same. With its ability to detect radio sources from 100 km away, the missile can disarm enemy radars and target the range of emitters. Its strike range is between 100 and 250 km.

First S-400 air-defence system

The Indian Air Force has deployed the first S-400 Triumf air defence missile system in the Punjab sector near Pakistan border, as reported on 21 December 2021. The deployment is to take care of any aerial threat from either Pakistan or China, using its capability to shoot down enemy fighter aircraft and cruise missiles at a long range (400 km).

OPERATIONS

First active operation

In September 1937, the 1 Squadron operated from Miranshah in North Waziristan (now in Pakistan) against hostile tribesmen. The IAF men lived inside a fort for safety and had to wheel in their aircraft into the fort every evening. Flying Officer (later Air Marshal) Aspy Merwan Engineer was the first officer to be Mentioned-in-Dispatches for the operations.

First airlift of Indian troops

During the Kurdish uprising in April 1923, the Royal Air Force flew 280 Sikh troops from Kingarban to Kirkuk, Iraq. Covering the distance that would normally require a five-day march, the flight covered 120.7 km in 10 hours.

First indigenous fighter aircraft

The single seat Mach-2 combat jet fighter HF (Hindustan Fighter)-24 MkI (Marut Ground Attack Fighter), with two single-shaft turbojet engines, was designed at HAL, Bengaluru. It took its maiden flight on 17 June 1961.

First flight to the true North Pole

The IL-76 aircraft of the 44 Squadron, representing the IAF, flew over the true North Pole in Exercise Cope Thunder-03 in Alaska, USA, with 14 crew members. The mission was launched on 19 June 2003 at 8:15 p.m. IST from USA's Eielson air force base, south-east of Fairbanks, Alaska, and the crew flew over the true North Pole on 20 June 2003 at 00:16 a.m. IST. The aircraft returned to base on 20 June 2003 at 5:51 a.m. IST after a flight lasting 9 hrs 36 mins.

Rudram-1: first indigenous anti-radiation missile

Highest helipad operation

In January 2003, the IAF conducted high-altitude trials in the Siachen Glacier area. They airlifted an artillery gun to an elevation of 5,600 m (18,372 ft) and a snow scooter to Point Sonam (6,400 m/21,000 ft). This was the first time a helicopter of this class had operated at such altitudes.

Biggest rapid airlift

On 18 December 2018, the Western Air Command of the IAF airlifted a record 463 tonnes from the Chandigarh airbase and dropped the load in Ladakh. The massive airlift was done in a single wave and proved the IAF's rapid airlift capability. The feat was completed by 16 fixed-wing transport aircraft including the C-17 Globemaster, the Ilyushin-76 Gajraj and the medium-lift tactical aircraft, Antonov-32. The airdrop was done in less than six hours.

GENERAL

Only vintage flight

A vintage aircraft flight was raised in Palam, Delhi, in 1988 for heritage aircraft, such as the Howard, Tiger Moth and Dakota planes.

First forward surgical centre

During an IAF military exercise, Gaganshakti-2018, from 8 to 22 April 2018, the IAF set up a Forward Surgical Centre (FSC) at Naliya air force station in Gujarat. An FSC can be used for life- and limb-saving surgeries as also to help stabilize a patient.

First mobile health app launched by a defence service

MedWatch, a mobile health application, was launched by the IAF on 8 October 2018 for the IAF's 85th anniversary. With content from the

All 33 Sainik Schools started admitting girls from the academic session 2021–22. The Ministry of Defence approved 21 new Sainik Schools in partnership mode from the academic year 2022–23.

Union defence minister Rajnath Singh at the 'AI in Defence' exhibition

The First-Ever 'AI In Defence' Symposium

The Ministry of Defence, as part of the *Azadi ka Amrit Mahotsav* celebrations, introduced more than 75 recently developed artificial intelligence technological developments devised and created by various services, including the District Rural Development Agency, Defence Public Sector Undertakings (DPSUs) and Innovations for Defence Excellence start-ups in the first-ever symposium and exhibition – 'AI in Defence or AIDef' – held in July 2022. Union defence minister Rajnath Singh launched a book with details of the relevant products developed over the last four years in the AI industry and emphasized the need for amalgamating AI in providing effective solutions for the defence forces during warfare.

A wide range of technological changes have been adopted by the forces already, such as remotely piloted and unmanned aeronautical vehicles, and the focus is now on moving to domains such as radio frequency spectrum management, underwater domain awareness satellite image analysis and the Identification Friend or Foe (IFF) system. In addition to these, reportedly around a hundred other projects are currently in the pipeline.

The products launched during the symposium included AI-platform automation; human behavioural analysis; lethal autonomous weapon systems and block chain–based automation, among several others. Three AI products created by the DPSUs were highlighted during the symposium for their business potential: the Driver Fatigue Monitoring System by Bharat Earth Movers Ltd; the AI-enabled voice transcription or analysis software by Bharat Electronics Ltd; and the AI-enabled evaluation of welding decks in X-rays of non-destructive testing by Garden Reach Shipbuilders and Engineers Ltd.

Directorate General of Medical Services (Air), it was developed in-house by the Directorate of Information Technology (DIT) and is available on the Android platform for users. It provides a range of health information, reminders and utility tools. The app shares important web links and helpline numbers along with a body mass index (BMI) calculator and health record cards.

COAST GUARD

PERSONNEL

First director general of the Indian Coast Guard

Vice Admiral V.A. Kamath, PVSM, was the first director general of the Indian Coast Guard (ICG) from 19 August 1978 to 31 March 1980.

First woman pilot

Assistant Commandant Monica Seth joined the Indian Coast Guard on 5 June 1998. She flew a total of 1,500 hours during her tenure. She flew on missions during the Kargil conflict in Jammu and Kashmir in 1999 and also for earthquake relief in Gujarat in January 2001.

First woman hovercraft pilot

In 2017, Assistant Commandant Sneha Khatayak became the first woman hovercraft pilot in India.

First women combatants

In 2017, the Indian Coast Guard became the first Indian armed forces service to deploy women in combat roles on-board ships. Assistant Commandants Anuradha Shukla, Sneha Khatayak, Shirin Chandran and Vasundhara Chouksey were trained at the Indian Coast Guard station at Mandapam, Tamil Nadu.

First and only Integral ICG contingent operating abroad

An ICG Dhruv helicopter – CG 853 – has been operating in Maldives along with an ICG contingent. Since its induction, the helicopter has aided in 168 medivac (medical evacuation) missions, saving 178 lives.

MEDALS AND HONOURS

First Yudh Seva Medal

Deputy Commandant S.P.S. Basra and Deputy Commandant B.A.S. Bhar were awarded the Yudh Seva Medal (YSM) on 26 January 1989. Commanding the Indian Coast Guard ships ICGS *Ahalya Bai* and ICGS *Tara Bai*, respectively, they prevented the infiltration of the Liberation Tigers of Tamil Eelam (LTTE) in the Palk Bay.

First to receive President's Tatrakshak Medal

Commandant A.K. Dey received the award for his efforts in firefighting during the construction of an Indian Coast Guard ship, and preventing an oil spill off the coast of Goa in June 1994.

EQUIPMENT

First vessels

ICGS *Kuthar* and ICGS *Kirpan* (formerly of the Indian Navy) were commissioned on 19 August 1978 under Commander N.S. Achreja and Commander V.K. Tuli respectively.

First indigenous offshore patrol vessel

On 21 February 2019, ICGS *Sachet*, the first indigenous offshore patrol vessel (OPV) of the Indian Coast Guard was launched at Goa Shipyard Ltd (GSL). This OPV is part of an indigenous project that was launched on 13 November 2016. Designed in-house, these OPVs will be used for protecting the Exclusive Economic Zone. The vessel weighs 2,400 tonnes and is equipped with features like quick-response boats for rescue and anti-piracy, gunnery simulators and many more advanced features.

Latest training vessel

On 24 October 2018, ICGS *Varuna*, an indigenously designed training vessel built by Reliance Naval and Engineering Ltd (RNAVAL), was launched at the Pipavav Shipyard, Gujarat. ICGS *Varuna* is a 105 m (344 ft 6 in.) long vessel with a crew of 242 officers and sailors. It is powered by twin diesel engines and can reach a speed of 20 knots. It has ultra-modern navigation and communication systems. This is the largest ship built yet for the Indian Coast Guard.

OPERATIONS

First and longest deep-sea passage by hovercraft

On 13 January 2015, Indian Coast Guard Air Cushion Vehicle (ACV) H-198 undertook area deployment from New Mangaluru, Karnataka, to Androth Island in the Lakshadweep Islands, across the Arabian Sea. The ACV hovercraft, piloted by Commandant Amitabh Banerjee and Deputy Commandant Konark Sharma, covered 142.5 nautical miles (264 km) in five hours. The ACV H-198 is the only hovercraft in India to venture into the lagoon islands of Lakshadweep. The return run of 146 nautical miles (270.39 km) was made on 22 January 2015.

First underwater clean-up

On 5 June 2019, celebrated as World Environment Day, the Indian Coast Guard (Eastern Region) conducted an underwater debris clean-up exercise in the Bay of Bengal near the Chennai (Tamil Nadu) coast, in association with Dive India. The operation lasted two hours during which nearly 500 kg of trash was collected. This was the first underwater clean-up in India to remove debris, nets and plastic from the ocean.

GENERAL

Youngest defence service

The Indian Coast Guard or Sea Police, was constituted as India's fourth defence force under the Coast Guard Act on 18 August 1978, for the preservation and protection of the 2.01 million sq. km Exclusive Economic Zone. The force is under the direction and control of the director general, Indian Coast Guard.

First hovercraft berthing platform

In 2001, the first hovercraft berthing platform was built at Haldia, West Bengal, in eight months by the Military Engineer Services.

Largest integrated shipbuilding facility

Reliance Naval and Engineering Ltd (RNAVAL), known earlier as Reliance Defence and Engineering Ltd and Pipavav Shipyard Ltd, headquartered in Mumbai, Maharashtra, is one of the largest shipbuilding yards of its kind in the world. RNAVAL is the first private sector company in India to earn a licence and contract to construct warships. It has India's largest integrated shipbuilding facility with the shipyard located in Pipavav, Gujarat. Its dry dock measures 662 m x 65 m (2,172 ft x 213 ft). It has the only modular shipbuilding facility in India.

Indian Coast Guard: youngest defence service

THE NATURAL WORLD

PHYSICAL FEATURES

Longest land mountain range

The Himalayan range is the loftiest and most rugged mountain barrier in Asia. Out of the 7,300 mountain peaks in the world, 96 are in the Himalaya–Karakoram range. The range stretches over 2,500 km and varies from around 500 km in width in Jammu and Kashmir to around 200 km in Arunachal Pradesh. Some of the higher ranges are composed of 600-million-year-old Precambrian rocks.

Highest peak

Kangchenjunga, with its base partly in India and partly in Nepal, is 8,586 m (28,169 ft) high. Yalung Kang (also on the India–Nepal border) is second at 8,505 m (27,903 ft) and Nanda Devi comes third at 7,816 m (25,643 ft).

Largest glacier

Siachen Glacier, near the India–Pakistan border, is India's largest glacier. It is 75.6 km long and 2–8 km wide. It is also the second longest glacier in the nonpolar regions of the earth.

Only cold desert

Ladakh, at an average altitude of 4,878 m (16,004 ft), is the only cold desert in India.

Longest river

The 2,525 km long River Ganga is the longest river in the country. Its source is in the western Himalayas in Uttarakhand, from where the river flows south and east through the Gangetic Plain and Bangladesh, finally merging into the Bay of Bengal.

Largest river system

Of the total river discharge in India, 65 per cent is from the Himalayan group of rivers. The Rivers Ganga, Indus and Brahmaputra are part of this river system.

WR Largest delta

The triangular land mass formed by the River Hooghly, the Rivers Ganga–Padma–Meghna combined, and the Bay of Bengal is called the Bengal Delta. Two-thirds of this 57,000 sq. km delta is in Bangladesh and the rest lies in West Bengal, India.

Largest catchment area

The Ganga–Brahmaputra–Meghna system is the biggest river system in the country, with a catchment area of 272 million acres (110 million hectares), more than 43 per cent of the catchment area of all the major rivers of the Indian subcontinent.

Kangchenjunga: the highest peak, with its base partly in India and partly in Nepal

Largest crater

The Lonar meteorite crater in the Buldhana District of Maharashtra is India's largest and the world's third largest meteoric crater. It measures 1,800 m (5,906 ft) across and is 170 m (558 ft) deep. It is estimated that it was formed 50,000 years ago by a meteorite that was around 100 m (328 ft) in diameter, weighed a million tonnes, and was travelling at a speed of around 90,000 km per hour.

Largest freshwater lake

Wular Lake, India's largest freshwater lake, has an area of 260 sq. km. It is in Bandipora, Jammu and Kashmir.

Largest brackish-water lagoon

Chilika Lake in Odisha has an area of around 1,100 sq. km.

Largest cave

Amarnath Cave, about 44 km from Pahalgam in Jammu and Kashmir, is a popular pilgrimage. It is a natural cave at an altitude of 3,800 m (12,467 ft). The cave is 50 m (164 ft) wide and

India occupies **2.4** per cent of the world's land.

Lonar crater: largest crater, filled with water

The Ministry of Environment, Forest and Climate Change notified the Plastic Waste Management Amendment Rules, 2021, prohibiting identified single-use plastic items, which have low utility and high littering potential, by 2022.

5 m (82 ft) high. A remarkable stalagmite in the cave is worshipped as a *shivalinga.*

Largest desert
The Thar Desert stretches over an area of about 200,000 sq. km in India and spreads over four states: Punjab, Haryana, Gujarat and Rajasthan. It is interspersed with hillocks, gravel plains, salt marshes and lakes.

WR Largest island – freshwater
The island of Majuli, with an area of 352 sq. km, on the River Brahmaputra in Assam, is the largest freshwater island in the world.

Largest island – ocean
The island of Middle Andaman (1,523 sq. km) in the Andaman and Nicobar Islands is the largest ocean island in India.

Largest meteorite shower
On 14 July 1860, a heavy meteorite shower fell at Dharamshala (32°14′N, 76°28′E) in Kangra District, Himachal Pradesh. It consisted of many stones, the largest of which weighed 150 kg.

Barren Island: only active volcano

Highest waterfall
Kunchikal Falls in Nidagodu Village near Masthikatte in Shivamogga District of Karnataka falls down a total height of 455 m (1,493 ft), making it the highest waterfall in India.

Minimum rainfall area
Jaisalmer in Rajasthan receives an average rainfall of only about 200 mm (around 7.87 in.) in a year.

Maximum rainfall
Mawsynram, a village in the East Khasi Hills District, Meghalaya, about 65 km from Shillong, gets an average mean annual rainfall of 11,873 mm (467 in.) in about 147 days in a year. Earlier the record for the highest average rainfall was held by Cherrapunji (now Sohra) in the same district.

Highest temperature
On 19 May 2016, India recorded its highest ever temperature – 51°C – in Phalodi town in Jodhpur District in Rajasthan.

Highest surface salinity
The surface salinity in the Gulf of Kachchh, off the coast of Gujarat, varies from a maximum of 45.5 psu (practical salinity units), which is equivalent to parts per thousand, near the head of the gulf to 36.6 psu at the mouth.

WR Longest natural sandstone cave
The world's longest sandstone cave, with a length of about 24.58 km, Krem Puri in East Khasi Hills District, Meghalaya, is also known for its dinosaur fossils from 66–76 million years ago. Krem Puri is 6 km longer than the previous record holder – Venezuela's 18.2 km long Cueva Del Saman sandstone cave in Edo Zulia.

Lowest temperature
The lowest temperature recorded in Dras, Ladakh, was -60°C on 9 January 1995, making it the coldest inhabited place in India.

Lowest surface salinity
Salinity near the surface in the northern Bay of Bengal can be as low as 31 psu, because the bay receives fresh water as rain as well as run-off from the Rivers Ganga, Brahmaputra, Irrawaddy and others.

Only active volcano
Barren Island, which lies 110 km north-east of Port Blair in the Andaman and Nicobar Islands, is India's only active volcano. On 10 April 1991, it blew up nearly two centuries after it erupted in 1803. It last erupted in 1995.

FOSSILS

Oldest dinosaur fossil discovery

The first dinosaur fossils in India were discovered by a British palaeontologist, W.H. Sleeman, in Jabalpur, Madhya Pradesh, in 1828. The specimens were lost in 1877 and found in 2013 in the office of the Geological Survey of India, Kolkata, West Bengal.

RISE IN FOREST COVER

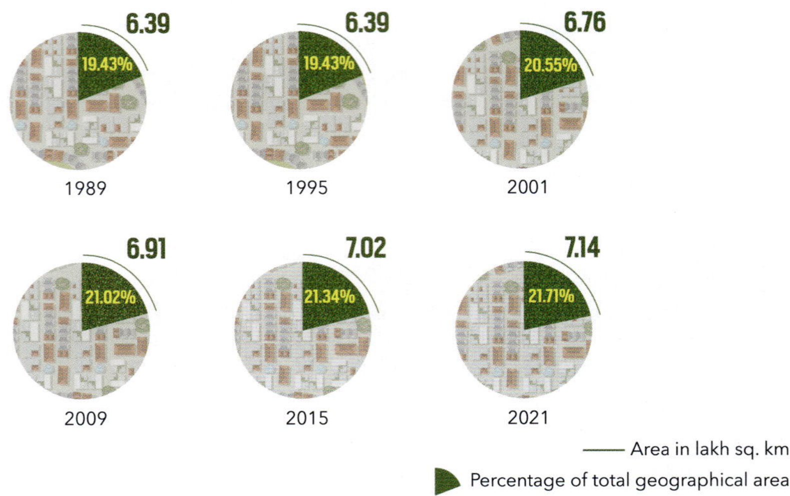

Source: PIB AKAM series, Press Information Bureau, Government of India

MAMMALS

Oldest living mammal

One of the oldest living mammals is the Indian one-horned rhinoceros (*Rhinoceros unicornis*). The Indian and Javan rhinoceroses first appeared in the fossil record of Asia 1.6–3.3 million years ago, though the species may have diverged much earlier, around 11.7 million years ago.

Smallest mammal

- *Land:* The white-toothed pygmy shrew (*Suncus etruscus*), which has a head-and-body length of 3–5.5 cm (1.18–2.17 in.) and a tail length of 2.5–3.2 cm (0.98–1.26 in.), is the smallest Indian land mammal by weight, weighing around 1.8 g. This shrew can be found across the Indian subcontinent, except in Jammu and Kashmir, and arid areas of Gujarat and Rajasthan.
- *Water:* The smallest water mammal in the country is the finless porpoise (*Neophocaena phocaenoides*), which is only 1.2–2 cm (0.47–0.79 in.) long. It is found in the waters of peninsular India.

Fastest mammal

- *Land:* The blackbuck (*Antilope cervicapra*), which is native to India, can run at a speed of up to 80 km per hour. It is found from Rajasthan to Punjab, and up to Odisha in the east and Tamil Nadu in the south; the cheetah (*Acinonyx jubatus*), recently introduced in India in Madhya Pradesh, can sprint at speeds of up to 120 km per hour.
- *Water:* The 2–2.5 m (6 ft 6 in.–8 ft 2 in.) long-beaked common dolphin (*Delphinus capensis*), found off the coast of peninsular India, swims at 30 knots or 55.5 km per hour.

Largest land mammal

The adult Asian elephant found in India (*Elephas maximus indicus*) belongs to the species of the largest land mammal *Elephas maximus.* An adult bull elephant averages 2.74 m (9 ft) in height at the shoulder and weighs around 4.5 tonnes. The female elephant or cow measures 2.35 m (7 ft 8.5 in.) at the shoulder and weighs around 3 tonnes. Elephants are found in four clusters in the plains of north, south, east and central India, and in the north-east.

Slowest mammal

- Land: The Bengal slow loris (*Nycticebus bengalensis*), which measures 30–40 cm (11 ft 10 in.–15 ft 9 in.), is the slowest land mammal in the country. It is found in Assam.
- *Water:* The slowest mammal in water is the 3.2 m (10 ft 6 in.) long dugong or sea cow (*Dugong dugon*), found in the Gulf of Kachchh, off the Malabar Coast and in the Andaman Islands.

Largest litter

The Indian mole rat (*Bandicota bengalensis*), found in most plains and forests, is known to have litters of over 12 young ones at a time.

The long-beaked common dolphin: largest mammal in water

Gibbons: only ape species

Fastest breeders

The Indian mole rat is the fastest-breeding mammal. The males mature in 58 days after birth and females in 90–100 days. Females have an average count of 11.32 pregnancies a year with a total break of 32.3 days in between. The female may produce as many as 70 young ones a year.

Slowest breeders

The elephant's main breeding season is the summer and when the monsoon begins. Only one calf is born at a time and at intervals of three years.

Longest-lived

- Humans are the longest living mammals.
- The average lifespan of a blue whale (*Balaenoptera musculus*) is 80–90 years.
- The Indian elephant follows with an average lifespan of around 60 years, but they can live up to 80–90 years.

Primate with the longest tail

The tail of the common langur measures an average of around 1 m (3 ft 3.4 in.).

Longest gestation

The elephant has a gestation period of about 20 months.

Rare Double-layered Dinosaur Egg Discovered in Madhya Pradesh

A new fossil discovery in Dhar District in Madhya Pradesh has furthered the research on the reproductive biology of dinosaurs. A team of researchers from Delhi University discovered a sauropod dinosaur nest consisting of ten eggs in June 2022. One of these eggs had another egg inside it – that is, it had two eggshell layers separated by a gap. This is a rare find and the first of its kind in fossil history. This egg-in-egg fossil, referred to as an 'ovum-in-ovo' egg, indicates that the reproductive system of dinosaurs was similar to those of birds and crocodiles. Prior to this discovery of the titanosaurid egg it was often concluded that the reproductive system of dinosaurs was similar to those of turtles and lizards.

A Titanosaurus reimagined

Shortest gestation

Rodents have a gestation period averaging a month.

The only apes

The western hoolock gibbon (*Hoolock hoolock*) and the eastern hoolock gibbon (*Hoolock leuconedys*) are the only ape species found in India, and they are the tallest primates too. Their average height, standing on hind legs, is about 0.9 m (3 ft).

WR The only camels that swim

The Kharai camels from the Kachchh region in Gujarat are the only ones of their kind in the world that can swim. They live with nomadic camel herders, who are indigenous to the region. The camels have padded hooves that help them navigate wet and salty coastal land and they can swim up to 3 km.

Only herbivorous marine mammals

Dugongs and manatees form the only group of herbivorous marine mammals. They are found in the Gulf of Mannar and the Palk Bay, where seagrass meadows provide them food. Highly endangered, dugongs are also found in the Gulf of Kachchh and near the Andaman Islands. They are 1 m to 3 m (3 ft 3 in. to 9 ft 10 in.) long and weigh around 400 kg.

WR Smallest feline

The world's smallest cat, about half to three-fourths the size of a domestic cat, is the rusty spotted cat *(Prionailurus rubiginosus)* found in southern and central India. The male has a head-and-body length of 35–48 cm (1 ft 2 in.–1 ft 7 in.) and the tail measures 15–30 cm (5.9–11.8 in.). It weighs about 1.5–1.6 kg (male) and 1.1–1.5 kg (female).

Largest/heaviest feline

Male tigers have a head-and-body length of 3.55–4.20 m (11 ft 7 in.–13 ft 9 in.). Females have a head-and-body length of 2.40–2.65 m (7 ft 10 in.–8 ft 8 in.). The height at shoulder is around 90–110 cm (35–43 in.). The average weight of males is 175–260 kg and for females, it is 100–160 kg.

Feline found at highest altitude

The snow leopard (*Panthera uncia*) is found at around 3,650–3,960 m (12,000–13,000 ft) in the Himalayan mountains.

Smallest bat

The Indian pygmy bat (*Pipistrellus tenuis*) has a head-and-body length of 3.3–4.5 cm (1.3–1.8 in.). Its tail is 3.5 cm (1.38 in.) and forearm is 2.5–3 cm (1.0–1.2 in.) long.

Largest bat
The large flying fox (*Pteropus vampyrus*) is the largest bat at 19.8–30 cm (7.8–11.8 in.) in the country, and is found in the Himalayas and peninsular India.

Rarest bat
Salim Ali's fruit bat (*Latidens salimalii*) found in southern India, and named after the famous ornithologist Salim Ali, is one of the rarest bats in India.

BIRDS

Largest round nests
The nests made by the megapodes (*Megapodius nicobariensis*) reach a height of 1.5 m (4 ft 11 in.) and have a circumference of 10 m (32 ft 10 in.).

Smallest and lightest
The Nilgiri flowerpecker (*Dicaeum concolor*) is only 7 cm (2.7 in.) long and weighs around 4.5 g.

Longest claws
The hind claw of the bronze-winged jacana (*Metopidius indicus*) measures around 6.5–7 cm (2.5–2.7 in.) long. Its leg (tarsus) is 6.5–6.8 cm (2.5–2.6 in.) in length.

WR Tallest flying bird
The sarus crane (*Grus antigone antigone*) is the world's tallest bird, standing 1.52 m (5 ft) tall. This greyish crane with a red head is common around the *jheels* of northern and central India. Of the 14–15 species of cranes in the world, six are found in India.

Smallest egg
The average size of the egg of the scarlet-backed flowerpecker (*Dicaeum cruentatum*) is 14 mm x 10.3 mm (0.55 in. x 0.4 in.).

Largest egg
The average size of the sarus crane's egg is 10.4 cm (4 in.) x 6.4 cm (2.5 in.).

Longest beak
The beaks of the rosy pelican (*Pelecanus onocrotalus*) and the Dalmatian pelican (*Pelecanus crispus*) are 43–45 cm (1 ft 4.9 in.–1 ft 5.7 in.) long.

Slowest
The Eurasian woodcock (*Scolopax rusticola*) flies at a speed of around 8 km per hour.

Swiftest/fastest dive
The peregrine falcon (*Falco peregrinus*) reaches speeds of over 320 km per hour. It can dive at a speed of up to 360 km per hour – faster than a moving racing car.

Saving Wolves in Ladakh
A community-based initiative has been launched to save the endangered Tibetan wolves across Ladakh. Herding and village communities have a confrontational relationship with wolves from whom they need to protect their livestock. Among the widely used traditional methods of entrapment are *shadongs* or pits with inverted funnel-shaped stone walls, usually built near villages or herder camps. A live bait is placed in the pit, and the wolves jump into it and then cannot jump out. The trapped wolves are then killed. Now with the community effort led by the Nature Conservation Foundation and the Snow Leopard Trust, an insurance scheme has been worked out to pay herders who may lose livestock to wolves. The people are building stupas next to the *shandongs* as a pledge towards conservation.

Himalayan wolf

Shortest legs
The crested tree swift (*Hemiprocne coronata*) has around 7–9 mm (0.27 –0.35 in.) long legs.

Longest legs
The legs (tarsus) of the sarus crane (*Grus antigone antigone*) measure 31–35 cm (1 ft 0.2 in.–1 ft 1.7 in.), making them the longest among birds.

Bearded vulture: largest wingspan

Black-necked crane

The Black-necked Crane Is Ladakh's Official Bird

In September 2021, the Union Territory of Ladakh declared the iconic black-necked crane (*Grus nigricollis*) and snow leopard as its official bird and animal respectively. This special status given to the black-necked crane and snow leopard will strengthen efforts to protect their habitats.

Smallest wingspan

The Nilgiri flowerpecker (*Dicaeum concolor*) male has a wingspan of 43–48 mm (1.69–1.89 in.). The female has an even smaller wingspan of 42–45 mm (1.65–1.77 in.).

Largest wingspan

The bearded vulture (*Gypaetus barbatus*) or the lammergeier, found along the lower Himalayas in Jammu and Kashmir, Himachal Pradesh, Uttarakhand, Sikkim, Assam and Arunachal Pradesh, has a wingspan of 2.31–2.83 m (7 ft 7 in.–9 ft 3 in.).

Common grass yellow butterfly

Butterfly Hot Spots in Delhi-NCR

For the regeneration of butterflies, 67 butterfly habitats have already been created in Delhi-NCR and more are being added. Some 50 species of host plants have been planted to attract egg laying by butterflies. The Bombay Natural History Society (BNHS) museum has been creating a corridor and butterfly hot spots by planting a variety of host plants in the gardens and parks of Delhi and adjacent areas. In the 2020 census by the BNHS, 75 species of butterflies were observed in Delhi, with the common species being the plain tiger, common grass yellow, the mottled emigrant and the common emigrant. There is concern about the decline in the butterfly population due to use of pesticides, de-weeding and the creation of ornamental gardens.

Rarest birds

Possibly, the rarest bird is the critically endangered Jerdon's courser (*Rhinoptilus bitorquatus*). The Nicobar megapode (*Megapodius nicobariensis*) or Nicobar scrub fowl, found in the Nicobar Islands, is also one of the rarest of Indian birds.

First bird hospital

The Charity Birds' Hospital in Chandni Chowk, Delhi, caters to about 20,000 birds a year and is the only exclusive hospital for birds in the country.

Only breeding ground for flamingos

The only known breeding ground in India for the lesser and greater flamingos is the Rann of Kachchh in Gujarat. Thousands of flamingos nest every year in the seasonal marshes of both the Great Rann and the Little Rann of Kachchh.

Most intricate nest

The weaver bird species, like the baya (*Ploceus philippinus*), makes the most intricate nests. Shaped like the pipe of a snake charmer, the nests have many chambers.

BUTTERFLIES

Smallest

The grass jewel (*Freyeria trochylus*) butterfly has a wingspan of only 1.5 cm (0.6 in.).

Largest moth

The Indian atlas moth (*Attacus atlas*) is possibly the largest in the world. The average length of males is 16.7–27.1 cm (6.57 –10.67 in.) and females are 14.2–26.2 cm (5.59–10.31 in.) long.

Biggest butterfly

The female of the golden birdwing (*Troides aeacus*) species has a wingspan of 19.4 cm (7.6 in.) and was recorded seen in Didihat, Uttarakhand. The male is much smaller with a wingspan of 10.6 cm (4.2 in.).

Butterfly at highest altitude

The blue Apollo (*Parnassius hardwickii*) is found at altitudes of 4,267–4,876 m (14,000–16,000 ft) in the Green Lake area at the base of Mt Kangchenjunga. This bluish white butterfly, with orange spots, has a wingspan of 4.5 cm (1.8 in.).

AMPHIBIANS

Smallest frogs

In February 2017, Indian scientists found seven new endemic species of *Nyctibatrachus*,

Cheetahs Are Back in India

Seventy years after their extinction in India in 1952, cheetahs have returned to the subcontinent. This move to bring cheetahs to India has been in the pipeline since the 1970s. Initially, the big cats were to be relocated from Iran, which did not work out due to various reasons. There are very few cheetahs left in Iran too, so Africa seemed a better place to acquire them from Namibia as it is home to the world's largest population of these felines, and that's where the cheetahs, all between four and six years, have come from.

On 17 September 2022, eight cheetahs arrived in Gwalior, Madhya Pradesh, after undertaking a transcontinental journey in a modified Boeing 747 passenger plane. A sum of ₹96 crore (960 million) was allotted for this project by the Government of India, and the Indian Oil Corporation provided an additional ₹50 crore (500 million). The release of the cheetahs into the wild coincided broadly with India's celebration of 75 years of Independence and specifically with Prime Minister Narendra Modi's 72nd birthday. The Kuno National Park in Madhya Pradesh, the new home for these eight cats, was equipped with the necessary facilities. Besides staff training, numerous public awareness campaigns were launched about these cheetahs. These campaigns deem the local communities as 'Cheetah Mitras' along with a local mascot named 'Chintu Cheetah'. Moreover, two elephants, called Siddhant and Lakshmi, have been brought to Kuno National Park from Satpura Tiger Reserve in Narmadapuram, also in Madhya Pradesh, to take charge of the cheetahs' security.

The five female cheetahs and three male ones have been christened as well. The Prime Minister named one of the female cheetahs 'Asha' ('hope' in Hindi), while the other female cats have been named Sasha, Tbilisi, Savannah and Siyaya. The two sibling male cheetahs have been called Freddie and Elton (after the singers Freddie Mercury and Elton John respectively), and the third male was christened Oban.

The cheetahs have made headlines. However, some experts have expressed concern regarding this move. They believe that the healthy survival of these wild cats requires huge grasslands for their habitation, which India has lost over the years.

Above and *below*: Photographed just after they were released in Kuno National Park, Madhya Pradesh, the cheetahs from Namibia try to find their bearings; *background*: A cheetah in Namibia

Geckos Named after Jackie Chan, Smaug and Balerion

Balerion forest gecko

Twelve new gecko species were found in the Western Ghats over the course of four years by a team of researchers from the Bombay Natural History Society (BNHS), Centre for Ecological Sciences (CES), Indian Institute of Science and the National Centre for Biological Sciences (NCBS), as reported in October 2021. Of these, ten are believed to be exclusive to the Indian subcontinent. With Saunak Pal as lead author, the study was conducted by Zeeshan Mirza, Princia Dsouza and Dr Kartik Shanker. All the geckos have been given interesting Latin names, such as *Cnemaspis jackieii* or Jackie's day gecko, because of the gecko's amazing agility, reminiscent of Hong Kong star Jackie Chan's stunts. Day geckos are among the most ancient reptiles from the Western Ghats, dating back to over 60 million years. Two of the other creatively named geckos are the Balerion forest gecko (*Cnemaspis balerion*), named after the dragon from the show *Game of Thrones*, and *Cnemapis smaug*, named after the dragon Smaug from J.R.R. Tolkien's book (and the series) – *The Hobbit*.

or night frogs, which make insect-like calls. Four species of these nocturnal amphibians, including Vijayan's night frog *(Nyctibatrachus pulivijayani),* were found in the Agasthyamala Biosphere Reserve (spread across many districts in Tamil Nadu and Kerala). They all measure around 12.2–15.4 mm (0.5–0.6 in.).

Largest frog
The Indian bull frog (*Hoplobatrachus tigerinus*), found all over the country, can grow up to 15 cm (5.9 in.). Some weigh as much as 1 kg.

Flying frog
The Malabar gliding frog *(Rhacophorus malabaricus),* found in Karnataka and the Wayanad District of Kerala, glides from the top of a tree to the base of another using its concave body and webbed feet as a parachute.

Rarest frog
The black, narrow-mouthed Malabar frog or Kerala Hills frog (*Melanobatrachus indicus*), found in the Anaimalai Hills of the Western Ghats, inhabits moist evergreen forests at 1,220 m (4,000 ft) and is considered one of the rarest frogs in the country.

REPTILES

LIZARDS

Largest lizard
The water monitor (*Varanus salvator*) reaches a length of 2.5 m (8 ft 2 in.) and can weigh up to 14 kg. It is a carnivorous lizard of the Sundarbans, Odisha and the Andaman Islands. Land monitor lizards (*Varanus bengalensis*) also grow to 61–175 cm (24–69 in.) from snout to tail end.

Longest tongue
The chameleon's tongue is three-fourths the length of the body (30 cm/11.8 in.) and has a viscid club-shaped tip. It can flick out its tongue and catch prey in 1/25th of a second.

Longest tail in relation to body
The long-tailed grass lacertid (*Takydromus sexlineatus khasiensis*) measures only 5 cm (2 in.), but its tail is 35 cm (13.7 in.) long – a ratio of 1 : 7. It is found in the Khasi Hills of Meghalaya.

Only flying lizards
Norvill's flying lizard (*Draco norvillii*), found in north-east India, and the Indian flying lizard (*Draco dussumieri*) from the Western Ghats and south India are endemic to India. Their average length is 23 cm (9 in.) and they can glide through the air for around 17 m (55 ft 9 in.).

Only legless lizard
The Asian glass lizard or Burmese glass lizard (*Ophisaurus gracilis*) is found at altitudes of 820–1,500 m (2,690–4,920 ft) in Darjeeling, West Bengal, and the Khasi Hills, Meghalaya. It crawls and uses its tongue in a snake-like fashion.

GECKOS

Smallest gecko
A 4 cm (1.6 in.) Persian sand dwarf gecko (*Tropiocolotes persicus*), or the dwarf or pygmy gecko, was recorded in Rajasthan in 2011.

The chameleon: longest tongue

Gharial Hatchlings in Odisha After a 45-year Wait

Forty-five years after the long-snouted gharials were introduced in the rivers of Odisha, the first batch of 28 hatchlings were spotted in May 2021 in the Baladamara area of the River Mahanadi, near the Satkosia Range. Around 50 foresters from six forest divisions had been patrolling the waterbody and spreading awareness across 30-odd villages close to the river, to protect the gharials. With the introduction of the gharials in 1975, Odisha became the only state to have all three species of the reptile – freshwater gharials, muggers and saltwater crocodiles.

There was an increase of 1540 sq. km in the forest cover and 721 sq. km in the tree cover of the country in 2021 as compared to 2019.

Largest gecko

The *Hemidactylus frenatus* or the common house gecko, found in Bihar, Bengal and north-east India, grows to around 34 cm (13.4 in.) in length. It feeds on insects, rats, birds and small snakes.

'Flying' gecko

The gliding gecko *(Ptychozoon kuhli)*, found in the Nicobar Islands and north-east India, can glide over 13 m (43 ft). It has skin flaps on the side of its head, body and tail, which help it glide when the animal launches into the air.

Rarest gecko

The golden hill gecko (*Calodactylodes avreus*), found in the Tirumala Hills of Andhra Pradesh, is a very rare species. Its body is golden yellow with brown spots.

CROCODILES

Shortest crocodile

The mugger crocodile (*Crocodylus palustris*), found in streams, is only 3 m (9 ft 10 in.) long. It is found almost all over India except at higher altitudes such as in the Himalayan mountains.

The mugger: shortest crocodile

Heaviest crocodile

The estuarine or saltwater crocodile (*Crocodylus porosus*) is the heaviest reptile in the country. The adult male crocodile may weigh around 1,000–1,300 kg while adult females weigh around 76 –100 kg.

Longest crocodile

The estuarine or saltwater crocodile grows to a recorded length of 7 m (23 ft). It is found in tidal estuaries, marine swamps and coastal waters in and around the Sundarbans, Odisha, and the Andaman and Nicobar Islands.

First known white crocodile

Gori, an albino white crocodile, was artificially hatched at the Bhitarkanika Dangamal Crocodile Research Centre in Odisha on 26 June 1975.

Rarest crocodile

The rarest of the three crocodile species found in India, the gharial (*Gavialus gangeticus*) grows to 6.25 m (20 ft 6 in.) and is the only living member of the family Gavialidae in India. The surviving population is found in the tributaries of the River Ganga–Girwa (Uttar Pradesh), Son (Madhya Pradesh), Ramganga (Uttarakhand), Gandak (Bihar), Chambal (Uttar Pradesh, Madhya Pradesh and Rajasthan) – and the River Mahanadi (Odisha). it is classified as critically endangered by the International Union for the Conservation of Nature (IUCN).

First/largest crocodile bank

The Madras Crocodile Bank Trust and Centre for Herpetology, 40 km from Madras (now Chennai), Tamil Nadu) was founded in 1976 by the naturalist Romulus Whitaker, and had over 8,000 crocodiles of 10 different species.

SNAKES

Longest sea snake

The yellow sea snake (*Hydrophis spiralis*) grows 1.8 m (6 ft) long. Specimens up to 3 m (10 ft) are not uncommon. It is found both in the Bay of Bengal and the Arabian Sea.

WR Longest snake

The reticulated python (*Python reticulatus*) is the longest snake in the world. It is found in the Nicobar Islands. The average length is between 3 and 6 m (10 and 20 ft). While the reticulated python prefers small mammals, it can take large animals up to the size of a full-grown wild boar.

Only snake that builds a nest

The female king cobra (*Ophiophagus hannah*),

BOUNTY OF BIODIVERSITY

The UNESCO's World Heritage Convention is a leading international programme to identify and acknowledge exceptional natural places in the world, highlighted by extraordinary biodiversity, ecosystems, geology or natural phenomena. The Convention has given recognition to around 3,500,000 sq. km in over 250 terrestrial and marine sites across more than 100 countries. India is home to seven such sites,

1 Kaziranga National Park

One of the very few areas in north-eastern India that has been left largely unmodified as representative of the flood plain of the River Brahmaputra, this national park is characterized by the world's largest population of one-horned rhinoceroses. The area also protects populations of other threatened species including the tiger, the Asian elephant, the wild water buffalo, the gaur, the Sambar deer, the hog deer, the capped langur, the hoolock gibbon and the sloth bear as well as aquatic species including the Ganges river dolphin. The vagaries of the river create an often shifting landscape of alluvial tall grassland and wide shallow pools skirted by reeds and deciduous to semi-evergreen woodlands. The park has one of the highest densities of tigers in the country and has been a tiger reserve since 2007.

Date of Inscription: 1985; **Property:** 42,996 ha (106,245 acres)

2 Manas Wildlife Sanctuary

At the foothills of the Eastern Himalayas, this park in Assam spans both sides of the River Manas, with alluvial grasslands hedged by forests. The monsoon and the Manas–Beki river system form four main habitats: Bhabar savannah, Terai tract, marshlands and riverine tracts. The sanctuary has around 60 mammal species, 42 reptile species, seven amphibians and 500 species of birds, of which many are globally threatened (such as the elephant, the tiger, the greater one-horned rhino, the clouded leopard and the sloth bear). It protects endemic species like the pygmy hog, the hispid hare, the golden langur and the Bengal florican. Plant diversity includes 89 species of trees, 49 of shrubs, 172of herbs, 36 of climbers, 15 of orchids, 18 of ferns and 43 of grass.

Date of Inscription: 1985; **Property:** 39,100 ha (96,618 acres)

3 Sundarbans National Park

Noted for having the largest area of mangrove forests in the world, along with tigers who are strong swimmers feeding on fish, crabs and other water animals, this park is a unique ecosystem, with 45 per cent wetlands and 55 per cent forest. Located at the mouths of the Rivers Ganga and Brahmaputra and traversing India and Bangladesh, it is characterized by tidal creeks, canals and an estuarine ecosystem. Amid its 78 species of mangrove, its abundant fauna includes the single largest population of tigers and threatened aquatic mammals such as the Irrawaddy and the Ganges river dolphins, reptiles including the king cobra and the endemic river terrapin, two very primitive horseshoe crabs, waterfowl and migratory birds.

Date of Inscription: 1987; **Property:** 33,010 ha (81,569 acres)

4 Nanda Devi and Valley of Flowers National Parks

Ensconced high in Western Himalayas, India's Valley of Flowers National Park is renowned for its meadows of endemic alpine flowers and stunning natural beauty. This richly diverse area is also home to rare and endangered animals, including the Asiatic black bear, the snow leopard, the brown bear and the blue sheep. The gentle landscape of the park complements the rugged mountains of Nanda Devi National Park. Together they make a unique transition zone between the mountain ranges of the Zanskar and the Great Himalayas, for both mountaineers and botanists.

Date of Inscription: 1988; **Significant modifications to the boundaries:** 2005; **Property:** 71,210 ha (175,964 acres); **Buffer zone:** 514,857 ha (1,272,239 acres)

5 Great Himalayan National Park Conservation Area

Located in the western Himalayas in Himachal Pradesh, this is an area of alpine peaks, meadows and riverine forests, enclosing altitude-sensitive ecosystems. It has mountain glacial and snow meltwater sources of many rivers and includes 25 forest types. The area has 805 vascular plant species, 192 species of lichen, 12 of liverworts and 25 of mosses, many of them endemic, besides over 30 species of mammals, 200 of birds, nine of amphibians, 12 of reptiles and 120 of insects. It also has many globally threatened mammals, birds and medicinal plants.

Date of Inscription: 2014; **Property:** 90,540 ha (223,729 acres); **Buffer zone:** 26,560 ha (65,631 acres)

6 Western Ghats

Around 30–50 km inland from the western coast and running parallel to it, this mountain chain stretches for over 1,600 km across the states of Kerala, Tamil Nadu, Karnataka, Goa, Maharashtra and Gujarat. Older than the Himalaya mountains, the Western Ghats display geomorphic highlights, exceptional biodiversity and many endemic species. One of the world's eight 'hottest hot spots' of biological diversity, the Western Ghats and their montane forests are very significant for the monsoon. The non-equatorial tropical evergreen forests are important sites of their kind. The Western Ghats house 229 plant species, 31 mammal species, 15 bird species, 43 amphibian species, five reptile species and one fish species that are globally threatened.

Date of Inscription: 2012; **Property:** 795,315 ha (1,965,266 acres)

7 Keoladeo National Park

This park in Rajasthan is right on the Central Asian migratory highway of birds and witnesses large gatherings of them coming from China, Afghanistan, Turkmenistan and Siberia, including pelicans, ducks and geese, over decades. Notably, it was the only known wintering site of the critically endangered Siberian crane and one of the sites for other globally threatened species such as the greater spotted eagle and imperial eagle. Some 364 species of birds have been recorded in the park, a duck-hunting ground for erstwhile maharajas. The landscape is a patchwork of grasslands, woodlands, woodland swamps and wetlands, encircled by human habitations. During the breeding season its heronry houses around 15 species of herons, ibis, cormorants, spoonbills and storks, where in a well-flooded year, over 20,000 birds nest.

Date of Inscription: 1985; **Property**: 2,873 ha (7,099 acres) which is found in the Western Ghats, parts of north India, eastern India, the North-east and the Andaman Islands, builds a 30 cm (11.8 in.) nest by scraping leaves, weeds and loose vegetation together.

Only 'flying' snake

The ornate flying snake (*Chrysopelea ornata*) is capable of gliding by launching itself from height. An instance of this species gliding for a distance of 50 m (164 ft) has been recorded. This snake inhabits the hilly forests of the south-west and the North-East, besides the Andaman Islands.

Fastest snake

Rat snakes and bronze-back tree snakes can reach a speed of 10 km per hour.

Loudest hiss

Russell's viper (*Daboia russelii*) hisses the loudest from among all Indian snakes – nearly as loud as the hiss of a pressure cooker.

Only snake with heat sensors

The pit viper (subfamily Crotalinae), found in the hilly parts of India, is able to locate warm-blooded prey using two heat sensors between its nostrils and eyes.

Snake at the highest altitude

No other species of snake has been found at an altitude higher than the Himalayan pit viper (*Gloydius himalayanus*). Herpetologist Frank Wall (1868– 1950), who lived in Sri Lanka and India, claimed to have seen one at an altitude of 3,658 m (12,000 ft) in Kashmir and one was captured at the foot of the glacier at Dharamshala at an altitude of 4,877 m (16,000 ft).

TORTOISES AND TURTLES

Largest rookery

The 12 km long sandy beach in the Gahirmatha region of Odisha is one of the largest rookeries for marine sea turtles. In February–March, olive ridley turtles (*Lepidochelys olivacea*) come out here in hundreds of thousands to mate and nest. The olive ridley is one of the seven endangered species of turtles in the world due to the disturbance and destruction of their habitat.

Largest terrapin

The Batagur terrapin (*Batagur baska*), found in the river estuaries of the Sundarbans, West Bengal, is the largest terrapin and a critically endangered species. The carapace of this terrapin is 59 cm (23 in.) long.

The king cobra: only snake that builds a nest

The leatherback sea turtle: largest turtle

Largest turtle

The leatherback sea turtle (*Dermochelys coriacea*) has a shell length averaging 2.5 m 8 ft) and weighs 700 kg. It feeds mainly on jellyfish.

Smallest tortoise

The Indian star tortoise (*Geochelone elegans*) grows to a length of only around 15 cm (5.9 in.).

Smallest carapace

The Cochin cane forest turtle (*Vijayachelys silvatica*) has a carapace that is 13 cm (5.1 in.) long.

Rarest freshwater turtle

India's rarest freshwater turtle is possibly the Assam leaf turtle (*Cyclemys dentata),* found in the hill streams of Assam. It grows to a length of around 24 cm (9.4 in.).

FISH AND MOLLUSCS

Oldest freshwater fish

Fossil remains of the Dipnoi subclass of fish or lungfish (*Ceratodus agassiz*) were found in the Maleri beds of the Godavari Valley in the late Triassic period (237–201.3 million years ago). The genus *Ceratodus* evolved in the northern hemisphere in the early Triassic period (251–247 million years ago).

400 Nagar Vans and 200 Nagar Vatikas have been planned with the objective to significantly enhance the tree cover outside forests.

Whale shark

'Save the Whale Shark' Campaign Takes off

The Wildlife Trust of India (WTI), headquartered in Noida, Uttar Pradesh, launched the 'Save the Whale Shark' Campaign in Karnataka on 30 August 2022. Aligned with the 'International Whale Shark Day', the campaign focuses on coastal Karnataka, Kerala and Lakshadweep islands. Its aim is to educate marine fishing communities as well as students about the whale shark and the need for its conservation. The whale shark is the largest fish on Earth – it grows to an approximate length of 18 m (59 ft) and can weigh around 21 tonnes. It has been declared 'endangered' by the IUCN. The biggest threat to these sharks has been entanglement in fishing nets.

Lightest/smallest fish

The dwarf pygmy goby (*Pandaka pygmaea*) is 1 cm (0.39 in.) long and weighs 4–5 mg.

Only fish with suction plates

The remora or suckerfish (family Echeneidae) can swim, but is usually found attached to sharks, turtles, dolphins and even ships. The first dorsal fin is modified into a suction apparatus, and the erection of the plate where the fish joins its host creates a vacuum, enabling the fish to stay attached.

Heaviest fish

The whale shark *(Rhincodon typus)* is the largest and heaviest shark in India, weighing up to 60 tonnes.

The banyan tree: longest lifespan

Only fish without a bony skeleton

Sharks (and their relatives, the guitar fish and swordfish) do not have a bony skeleton. They have cartilage or gristle. They are predominantly marine fish with a few freshwater representatives.

Only anadromous fish

Hilsa (*Tenualosa ilisha*) is India's only anadromous fish, which migrates from sea or estuarine waters up rivers for breeding. This fish is found mostly in the Gangetic estuary.

Only male fish producing young

Seahorses (Genus *Hippocampus*) are predominantly marine. The male fish carries a kangaroo-like pouch in its belly. The female passes her eggs to this pouch where the father incubates them. The young are thus born from the father.

Largest recorded subterranean fish

A fish measuring around 45 cm (17.7 in.) was discovered by Daniel Harries, a biologist from Heriot Watt University in Edinburgh, UK, in a cave in Meghalaya in February 2019.

Shortest-lived fish

Small fish such as the *Pandaka pygmaea*, and of the families Oreichthys and Gambusia (such as mosquito fish), live hardly for a year.

Longest-lived fish

The common carp, a freshwater fish that is found in ponds, lakes and large rivers, is said to live for over 50 years if left alone.

Largest clam

The giant clam (*Tridacna gigas*) grows to 1 m (3 ft 3.4 in.) long and weighs over 100 kg. This clam has been exploited throughout its Asia-Pacific range but is fortunately plentiful in the coral reefs of the Andaman and Nicobar Islands.

PLANTS

Oldest plant fossils

Fossils, which are 1.6 billion years old and appear to contain red algae, were found embedded in mats of cyanobacteria in phosphate-rich sedimentary rocks in Chitrakoot in central India, in May 2017. Until this discovery, the oldest known red algae were 1.2 billion years old.

Longest-lived tree species

The banyan tree (*Ficus benghalensis*), found in most parts of India, is known to have lived for more than 250 years.

Fastest-maturing trees
The eucalyptus and the subabul (*Leucaena leucocephala*) trees mature very fast and are both ready for cutting in 6–7 years.

Tallest trees
The fir (*Abies pindrow*) and deodar (*Cedrus deodara*) grow to an average height of 76.2 m (250 ft).

Biggest tree trunk
The deodar (*Cedrus deodara*) found in Jammu and Kashmir, Himachal Pradesh and Uttarakhand, have trunks with a circumference of around 12 m (39 ft 4 in.) or more.

Largest hollow tree
A baobab or monkey-bread tree (*Adansonia digitata*), which is a species of African origin, stands amid the ruins of the eastern part of the historic Golconda Fort near Hyderabad, Telangana. Reportedly, its 3.3 sq. m (35.5 sq. ft) hollow can comfortably fit in 10–12 people.

Largest tree canopy
A banyan tree identified in Anantapur District of Andhra Pradesh in 1988 by freelance photographer 'Regret Iyer' and K.S. Ramakrishna from Bangalore (now Bengaluru), Karnataka, was reported to have a canopy covering 2.1 hectares (5.19 acres) and was believed to be over 600 years old.

Tallest flower
- The gigantic Himalayan rhubarb (*Rheum nobile*) grows 0.9–1.2 m (3–4 ft) long. It is found even at 4,268 m (14,000 ft) in the Himalayan ranges.
- The corpse flower (*Amorphophallus titanum*) or 'titan arum', though not a native species, is the tallest flower (2.4 m/7 ft 10 in.) in India, and the largest by diameter (more than 1 m/ 3 ft 3.3 in.).

Longest creeper
The elephant creeper (*Argyreia nervosa*) grows to a length of 1.5 km, making it the longest creeper in the country and one of the longest in the world.

Largest family of plants
The Family Poaceae is the largest plant family in the country, and is represented by as many as 263 genera and 1,291 species. Poaceae or Gramineae is a ubiquitous family of monocotyledonous flowering plants known as grass. The Poaceae family includes cereal grass, bamboos and grasses of natural grasslands as well as the grasses of cultivated lawns and pastures.

Plants at the highest altitude
- The *Ermania himalayensis* grows at 6,000 m (19,685 ft) in the Himalayas.
- *Christolea himalayensis*, a herb usually about 10–15 cm (3.9–5.9 in.) tall, is found at 5,000–6,000 m (16,404–19,685 ft).

Rare flowering
Found in southern and eastern India, the talipot palm (*Corypha umbraculifera*) flowers once in 25–80 years and then dies.

Largest leaf
The leaf of the water lily (*Victoria amazonica*) may measure up to 1.5 m (5 ft) in diameter.

Heaviest fruit
The jackfruit tree (*Artocarpus heterophyllus*) is planted (but also grows wild) in the Western Ghats and elsewhere in India. The tree bears fruit of enormous size – weighing up to 40 kg.

Heaviest wood
Anjan (*Hardwickia binata*) wood is the heaviest, with a specific gravity of 0.61–0.73.

Lightest wood
Balsa (*Ochroma lagopus*) has a specific gravity of 0.12 to 0.15.

Tallest bamboo/grass
The tallest bamboo (*Dendrocalamus giganteus*), known as dragon bamboo, is found in Assam and West Bengal. It grows up to 40 m (130 ft) with a diameter of around 20–25 cm (8–10 in.).

CONSERVING NATURE AND WILDLIFE

Oldest zoos
- Raja Rajendra Mallick Bahadur started the Marble Palace Aviary and Zoo in Calcutta (now Kolkata, West Bengal) in 1854 specifically for the education and entertainment of the public.
- The Thiruvananthapuram Zoological Gardens in Kerala is said to have been set up by Maharaja Swathi Thirunal in 1859. Spread over 30 acres (12 hectares), it is the oldest extant zoo.

Oldest botanical gardens
The Acharya Jagadish Chandra Bose Indian Botanic Garden was established in 1787 in Shibpur, Howrah, near Kolkata in West Bengal, with about 12,000 living plants and 2.5 million dried plant specimens in the herbarium, from all over the world. The gardens cover 276.75 acres (112 hectares) in 25 sections.

The corpse flower: largest flower by diameter

Jackfruit: heaviest fruit

White tiger at Arignar Anna Zoological Park: largest zoo

The dugong has been categorized as vulnerable by the IUCN

India's First Dugong Conservation Reserve in Tamil Nadu

India's first Dugong Conservation Reserve was notified in Tamil Nadu on 21 September 2022 over an area of 500 sq km. in the Gulf of Mannar and the adjacent Palk Bay on the south-east coast of India. Dugongs, also called 'sea cows', are the only existing herbivore mammal that live exclusively in the sea and are categorized as vulnerable in the IUCN Red List of Threatened Species. The dugong population in Indian waters is estimated to be around 200 and is continuously decreasing. A challenge in the conservation of dugongs is their exclusive consumption of seagrass. One dugong can consume up to 40 kg of seagrass every day. Therefore, seagrass beds and their abundance play a vital role in their protection. Another cause of dugong mortality is accidental entanglement in fishing nets, as dugongs come up to the surface every four minutes to breathe.

First conservation organization

The Indian Board for Wildlife (IBWL), with S. Dharmakumar Sinhji as its vice chairman, was set up in 1952 by the Government of India. It was replaced by the National Board for Wildlife (NBWL) in September 2003.

First marine reserve

The Marine National Park and Sanctuary in Jamnagar District, Gujarat, forms the first marine reserve of India. Including Pirotan Island and other islands, it was given the status of a national park in 1980, and is rich in corals, octopuses, giant snails, sponges, crabs, lobsters and fish.

Largest zoological park

Arignar Anna Zoological Park at Vandalur near Chennai, Tamil Nadu, is the largest zoological park in South Asia. Spread over 602 hectares (1,487.57 acres), it has more than 100 species of birds, 50 species of mammals and 20 species of reptiles.

First wildlife magazine

Indian Wildlife was published by Jim Corbett in the 1930s.

First virtual herbarium

Since February 2017, a virtual digital herbarium of specimens preserved in the Kerala Forest Research Institute at Peechi in Thrissur District, Kerala, can be accessed at the URL *http://kfriherbarium.in*.

Highest national park

The Kangchenjunga Biosphere Reserve or the Khangchendzonga National Park in Sikkim is the highest national park at 8,585 m (28,166 ft) above the mean sea level.

Oldest NGO to be engaged in conservation and biodiversity research

On 15 September 1883, eight men established the Bombay Natural History Society at the then Victoria and Albert Museum (now Bhau Daji Lad Museum) in Bombay (now Mumbai, Maharashtra) to exchange information on natural history and exhibit interesting specimens. They were E.H. Aitken, Dr G.A. Maconochie, Dr D. MacDonald, J. C. Anderson, Colonel C. Swinhoe, J. Johnston, Dr Atmaram Pandurang and Dr Sakharam Arjun, along with H.M. Phipson.

State and UT with most wildlife sanctuaries

Andaman and Nicobar Islands have 96 wildlife sanctuaries (389.39 sq. km) and Maharashtra has 46 (7,592.3 sq. km).

State and UT with most national parks
Madhya Pradesh leads with 10 national parks, with 365,725 sq. km dedicated to them. Andaman and Nicobar Islands follow with nine national parks across 115,394 sq. km.

First national park
Jim Corbett National Park (earlier Hailey National Park and then Ramganga National Park), established in 1936, stretches over 521 sq. km across the two hill districts of Pauri Garhwal and Nainital, Uttarakhand, and is home to around 110 tree species, 50 species of mammals, 580 bird species and 25 species of reptiles. It was the first to come under the Project Tiger initiative. The elevation of the park ranges from 400 m to 1,200 m (1,300 ft to 4,000 ft).

Largest camera trap tiger census
India's tiger census of 2018 became the largest camera trap wildlife survey in the world. Camera traps (outdoor photographic devices fitted with motion sensors that start recording when an animal passes by) were placed in 26,838 locations across 141 different sites and surveyed an effective area of 121,337 sq. km as part of the survey. Individual tigers (excluding cubs), which were identified using stripe pattern recognition software from the photographs clicked by camera traps, numbered 2,461 by this method.

Highest number of leopards rescued by an individual*
Dr Arvind K. Mathur (b. 3 December 1969), veterinary officer, Nalagarh Biological Park, Jaipur, Rajasthan, has rescued 59 wild leopards and rehabilitated many of them in the wild. They were rescued over 12 years (8 October 2008 to January 2021) from deep wells, in human habitation, in jungles, sand dunes and from outside a temple.

Most snakes rescued in a year*
Pradip Khemchand Solanki (b. 16 June 1964), Manager, Baroda Gujarat Gramin Bank, Gandhinagar, Gujarat, a volunteer snake catcher, rescued 144 snakes from residential areas of Gandhinagar in 2020, and released them in forest areas. While 74 of the snakes rescued were poisonous, 70 were non-poisonous. The first snake caught on 2 January 2020 was a Russell's viper and the last on 30 December 2020 was a cobra.

Largest collection of bamboo species
Prashant Atmaram Date, a bamboo farmer and entrepreneur from Lakhalgaon Village, Nashik

Elephants at Jim Corbett National Park: first national park

Largest collection of bamboo species (partial photo)

RISE IN TIGER POPULATION

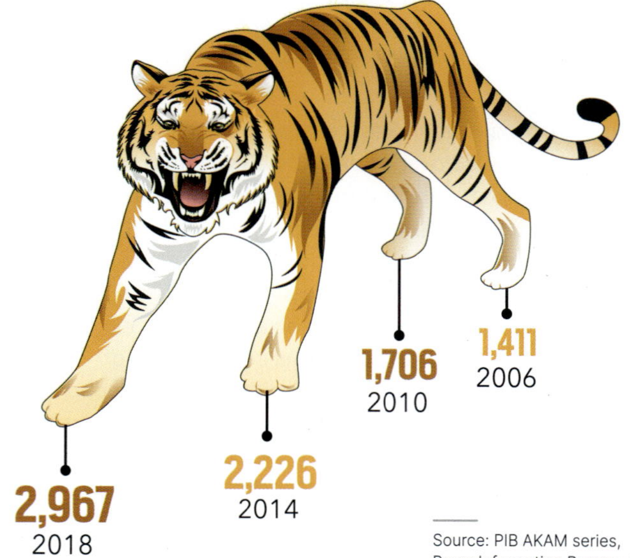

Source: PIB AKAM series,
Press Information Bureau, Government of India

*This is a one-time record. Further and future entries for this category will not be accepted.

Rajasthan's Desert National Park Reports 20 New Great Indian Bustard Eggs

The Great Indian Bustard has been deemed critically endangered on the IUCN Red List. Numerous conservation efforts have been made to stop their steady decline in the subcontinent. Therefore, the report that they have laid 20 eggs in the 2022 breeding season in the Desert National Park in Rajasthan made for joyous news. Moreover, four female bustards laid two eggs each. This was a major highlight as these birds generally lay one egg each in every breeding season. Heavy rainfall in 2022 led to the growth of luxuriant *sewan* grass, which the birds used as egg-laying grounds. The rainfall also contributed to the increase of insects and pests that the birds eat, thereby contributing to a protein-rich diet for them.

The great Indian bustard: a drawing by English naturalist Thomas Hardwicke

Taluk and District, has the largest collection of bamboo species in the country – totalling 94 species of 22 genera – in one place, called 'Date Bambusetum', where they are placed in flowerpots. Different species have been collected from bamboo-growing states for conservation away from their place of origin.

GARDENING

Tallest rose plant

Arunsinh Solanki grew a rose plant 11.88 m (39 ft) tall at his home in Godhra in Gujarat, as recorded on 13 May 2019.

Longest tapioca plant (partial photo)

Tallest prickly amaranth plant

In August 2017, T. Damodar and his wife Shobha T. Damodar from Belagavi, Karnataka, grew the tallest prickly amaranth plant (*Amaranthus spinosus*), which measured 4.03 m (13 ft 3 in.) in height. Normally this plant grows to a height of 0.3 m to 2.43 m (1–8 ft).

Tallest bougainvillea

Prof. Dr Ramesh Babu (b. 12 February 1957) has grown a 10.33 m (33 ft 11 in.) tall *Bougainvillea spectabilis* in his garden in Bengaluru, Karnataka. The over 16-year-old bougainvillea with white blossoms had a spread of 6.09 m (20 ft) and the girth at its base was 0.2 m (7.8 in.) as on 29 January 2020. Normally, the bougainvillea grows to an average height of 6.09 m (20 ft).

WR Tallest coriander plant

Dalbir Maan (b. 1 June 1982) grew a 2.28 m (7 ft 6 in.) coriander plant at his home in Melbourne, Australia, as recorded on 18 November 2020.

Longest tapioca plant

Satheesha Nayak (b. 16 July 1969), an anatomy professor at the Manipal Academy of Higher Education, Udupi, Karnataka, has grown the longest tapioca (cassava) plant, measuring 55 ft and 10 in. (16.76 m), as on 30 January 2022, in his kitchen garden. The plant is about three years old and was provided support on an adjoining mango tree.

Biggest lemon

K. Mohanchandran from Kothanur, Bengaluru, Karnataka, grew a lemon measuring 28 cm x 14 cm (11 in. x 5.5 in.) in his garden. The lemon had a circumference of 49 cm (19.2 in.) and weighed 2.365 kg on 22 February 2020.

Longest mango leaf

A mango tree with a leaf measuring 61 cm (2 ft) was found at the primary school of Budapur in Varanasi, Uttar Pradesh, by Dr Bhola Vishwakarma, one of the schoolteachers, on 30 October 2018.

Largest taro leaf

A taro (*Colocasia esculenta*) leaf measuring 76.0 cm x 64.5 cm (2 ft 5.9 in. x 2 ft 1.39 in.) was cultivated in Boudhgarh, Boudh District, Odisha, by Jayaram Rana on 7 January 2020.

Tallest drumstick tree

Prof. Dr Ramesh Babu from Bengaluru, Karnataka, has the tallest drumstick tree (*Moringa oleifera*) growing in his residential garden. On 20 June 2019, the 11-year-old tree was 8.2 m (26 ft 11 in.) tall with a spread of

3.66 m (12 ft) and a base girth of 47.6 cm (1 ft 6.74 in.) The average height of a drumstick tree is 6.1 m (20 ft).

Tallest musk mallow plant

A.K. Narayanan from Thrissur, Kerala, had a three-year-old musk mallow plant, 2.74 m (9 ft) tall as in June 2016, in his garden.

Tallest jamun tree

Prof. Dr Ramesh Babu from Bengaluru, Karnataka, has the tallest *jamun* tree (*Syzygium cumini*) in his garden. On 20 June 2019, the 15-year-old tree was 11.9 m (39 ft) tall with a spread of 6 m (20 ft) and a base girth of 1.04 m (41 in.) The average height of a jamun tree is 9.1–10.6 m (30–35 ft).

Longest green chilli

Krishnalal L.S. (b. 19 April 1982) of Thiruvananthapuram, Kerala, grew the longest green chilli, measuring 31 cm (12.1 in.) on his terrace garden in February 2020. He used a home-made nutrient mixture or organic and natural material for pest control while maintaining the nutrient grade of the soil.

Orchid blooms

Conserving Orchids for Two Decades

Ashis Kumar Roy, a teacher of life sciences at the Sri Narasingha Vidyapith, Darjeeling District, West Bengal, has been conserving the endangered epiphytic orchids in their natural habitat in the Dooars and Terai regions of West Bengal, with the help of students and local communities for over 20 years now, since 2000. He has created awareness about the importance of these native orchids that grow on trees and are now threatened by deforestation. His work is voluntary and Roy works with 50 to 60 students and community members who share his passion.

There are about 100 species of epiphytic orchids that grow on trees such as *sal*, *shisham*, *kadam* and mango. When a tree is to be cut, the community carefully takes orchids out of that tree and grow it on another tree. The transplanted orchids are watched and nurtured by the community.

ENVIRONMENT AND SUSTAINABILITY

First state/UT to place a ban on plastic bags

Sikkim became the first state to ban plastic bags in 1998. Local communities in Yuksom Village were upset by the harmful impact of plastics on the environment and formed the Khangchendzonga Conservation Committee (KCC), which banned plastic bags and bottles in 1996 and collected around 800 kg of plastic waste from trails and trek routes. Encouraged by their success, the state government announced a state-wide ban on plastic bags on 4 June 1998.

First forest healing centre

India's first forest healing centre was inaugurated on 7 March 2021 in Ranikhet, Uttarakhand. Spread across an area of around 13 acres (5.26 hectares), it was developed by the research wing of the Uttarakhand Forest Department as a space where visitors can take walks, hug trees and engage in calming activities like meditation and sky-gazing. The centre draws inspiration from the Japanese therapy of forest bathing (*shinrinyoku*) and ancient Indian traditions.

First green village

Khonoma Village, located in the Sechu-Zubza Subdivision of Kohima District, Nagaland, has become the country's first 'green village'. The first steps were taken by setting up the Khonoma Nature Conservation and Tragopan Sanctuary in 1998, leading to a ban on hunting in a 20 sq. km area. Ecological studies suggest that the village has 250 plant species, 204 species of trees, 45 varieties of orchids and 19 varieties of bamboo. The fauna includes 25 varieties of snakes, six kinds of lizards, 11 types of amphibians and 196 bird species, including the Blyth's tragopan, which is categorized as vulnerable on the IUCN Red List.

First Indian winners of the Champions of the Earth Award

Tulsi Tanti, chairman and managing director of the wind turbine manufacturer Suzlon Energy Ltd, was the first Indian recipient of the Champions of the Earth award in 2009 in the 'entrepreneurial vision' category. Since then, India has won five more awards. The latest recipients of the awards were Prime Minister Narendra Modi for policy leadership and the fully solar-powered Cochin International Airport for 'entrepreneurial vision' in 2018. The award is given by the United Nations Environment Programme.

The Government of India plans to work towards reducing India's total projected carbon emissions by one billion tonnes by the year 2030.

India is expected to meet **50** per cent of its energy requirements with renewable energy by **2030**.
The Ministry of Environment, Forest and Climate Change is going to launch the Swachh Vayu Sarvekshan to rank 131 cities in the country for implementing City Action Plans prepared as part of the National Clean Air Programme (NCAP) for reducing air pollution up to **40** per cent by 2025–26.

First country to have a cooling action plan

The India Cooling Action Plan (ICAP) is the first cooling action plan in the world. It addresses cooling requirements across all sectors to reduce direct and indirect emissions. ICAP aims to balance socio-economic and environmental needs while reducing refrigerant transition and cooling demand, enhancing energy efficiency and evolving better technology options.

First solar-heated tent

Considered to be the first in the world, a 10-seater portable tent that can be heated using solar panels was built by engineer and innovator Sonam Wangchuk along with the Himalayan Institute of Alternatives of Ladakh (HIAL) for the Indian Army. Built in four weeks at a cost of ₹5 lakh (0.5 million), the tent weighs less than 30 kg and was specifically developed for Indian soldiers and army personnel serving in areas with very low temperatures.

Most waste collected – beach clean-up – single day

The Maharashtra Navnirman Pariyavaran Sena, headquartered in Mutunga, Mumbai, Maharashtra, set three records in waste collection on 11 December 2021, based on data available from 16 local governmental bodies:

- *Most waste collected – multiple venues*: 13,194 registered volunteers, among others, collected 59.2 tonnes of waste from 37 locations in seven districts of Maharashtra.
- *Most waste collected – single venue*: Volunteers collected 27 tonnes of waste from a single location – Uttan Beach, Bhavander, Thane District, Maharashtra.
- *Most participants in a waste collection campaign – multiple venues*: The clean-up campaign saw the participation of 13,194 registered volunteers across 37 locations in seven districts of Maharashtra.

Plog run with most participants

The biggest plog run (combining jogging with picking up litter – from Swedish *plockaupp*) was organized on Gandhi Jayanti on 2 October 2018 from 55 locations of Bengaluru, Karnataka, and 6.5 tonnes (6,500 kg) of plastic waste, including bottles and litter, was collected by 6,518 participants in four hours from 7:00 a.m. to 11:00 a.m. The participants, representing five organizations – BBMP (Bruhat Bengaluru Mahanagara Palike); Go Native; Namma Nimma Cycle Foundation; Let's Be the Change, United Way Bengaluru – and an individual, Ramakrishna Ganesh, created awareness on urban cleanliness by proper disposal of waste, especially plastic.

Tallest scrap-metal structure – group

A group of 120 students, training to be fitters, welders, electricians, plumbers and painters at the Government ITI in Berhampur, Ganjam District, Odisha, created the tallest scrap metal structure, a 21.33 m (70 ft) tall guitar, over a period of three months from 17 July 2019. The 'Best out of waste' mission sought to integrate skill development with waste management in an eco-friendly manner. The guitar was exhibited at the open-air Scrap Sculpture Museum of the ITI, along with 10 other smaller sculptures, which were also all created from waste.

Tallest scrap-metal structure – solo

Sandeep Pisalkar from Vadodara, Gujarat, created a replica of the iconic Eiffel Tower, measuring 21.33 m (70 ft) in height, with 40 tonnes (4,000 kg) of automobile scrap. The three levels of the structure were created separately and then assembled with the help of a crane. The material used included petrol tanks from trucks, C-channels, angles and clutch plates. It was exhibited at the Waste to Wonder Park, New Delhi, in February 2019.

Most trees planted – 15 mins

Under the supervision the NSS Programme Officer Shyam Sunder of the Government Dungar College, Bikaner, Rajasthan, a total of 1,05,000 saplings were planted at three locations in Village Gajsukhdesar in 3 min 50 sec by a team of 15,000 participants comprising NSS volunteers, schoolchildren and villagers on 4 August 2008. The total land covered under the plantation was 1,200 *bigha*s (300 hectares).

Most trees planted – 1 hour

Green India Challenge, an initiative by Rajya Sabha Member of Parliament J. Santhosh Kumar, of Telangana planted 354,900 trees in 1 hr on 4 July 2021 in Durga Nagar, Adilabad, Telangana. The 16,900 people involved in the plantation drive planted 21 trees each.

Most trees planted – single day

The Department of Forests and Wildlife, Uttar Pradesh, planted 258,747,661 saplings in a day on 5 July 2020, with the participation of various departments of the state as well as the general public. Starting at 5:55 a.m., the plantation work at selected plantation sites in all 75 districts concluded at 6:00 p.m. This was part of their larger campaign for tree plantation.

Indore, Madhya Pradesh: cleanest city

Most trees planted – in a quarter

The Maharashtra Forest Department, with the support of individual volunteers, planted 351,376,361 seedlings across the state between 1 July and 30 September 2019. The plantation work was done by 951,963.5 million people at 23,986.8 million plantation sites. To integrate the work of the forest department, the government hosted a Plantation Monitoring Information System (PMIS) and captured the plantation data of forest and non-forest agencies.

 Most saplings distributed – single day

The Department of Environment, Forest and Climate Change and the Department of Tourism, Government of Uttar Pradesh, along with the District Administration, Prayagraj, Uttar Pradesh, distributed 76,824 saplings on 9 August 2019. This was part of their larger campaign for tree plantation.

Largest single rooftop solar plant – by area

On 17 May 2016, a rooftop solar power plant was inaugurated at the Dera Baba Jaimal Singh (Radha Soami sect) premises at Beas, Amritsar District, Punjab. Spread over 42 acres (17 ha), the plant is the largest single rooftop facility and can generate 11.5 MW of electricity. The solar panels are laid over 82 acres (33.18 hectares) on eight rooftops and the project is planned to cater to 8,000 households.

Largest biogas plant – by capacity

As a step towards clean and green energy, Asia's largest compressed biogas (CBG) plant with a total capacity of 33.23 tonnes CBG per day was commissioned on 12 August 2022 at Bhuttal Kalan village in Sangrur District, Punjab.

First railway station with Green Building certification

Kevadia railway station in Gujarat, from whose third-level platform one can view the Statue of Unity, is India's first railway station with a Green Building Certification by the Indian Green Building Council (IGBC). The railway station features LED lights and star-rated branded electrical appliances to save electricity; water management through rainwater harvesting; a sewage treatment plant; waterless eco-urinals; and drip irrigation. Additionally, the segregated green waste will be reused to produce fertilizers.

Cleanest state

The Swachh Bharat Mission, the Central government's annual cleanliness survey to promote urban sanitation standards, ranked Chhattisgarh the cleanest state of India in 2021, for the third consecutive year. Maharashtra and Madhya Pradesh were ranked second and third respectively.

Cleanest city

The Swachh Bharat Mission 2022 ranked Indore in Madhya Pradesh as the cleanest city of the country for the sixth time in a row, among cities with a population of more than 10 lakh (one million). Surat in Gujarat and Navi Mumbai in Maharashtra were ranked the second and third cleanest cities respectively in the same category. Among the country's smaller cities with a population between one and 10 lakhs, Tirupati in Andhra Pradesh was ranked first, followed by Mysuru in Karnataka and New Delhi (NDMC).

The Ministry of Environment, Forest and Climate Change observed the third International Day of Clean Air for blue skies as Swachh Vayu Diwas ('Swachh Vayu Neel Gagan') to raise awareness and facilitate actions to improve air quality under the National Clean Air Programme (NCAP).

TRANSPORT

AIR

First flight

On 18 February 1911, Henri Pequet flew a Humber-Sommer biplane carrying mail from Allahabad (now Prayagraj), Uttar Pradesh, to Naini Junction, about 10 km away. Proper and official civil aviation, however, began on 15 October 1932, when a 2,092 km long flight of the aircraft D.H. *Puss Moth*, flown by aviator and industrialist J.R.D. Tata, under the aegis of Tata Air Services, a division of Tata Sons, delivered mail from the Drigh Road Aerodrome in Karachi (now in Pakistan) to Juhu Aerodrome in Bombay (now Mumbai, Maharashtra) and then continued to Madras (now Chennai).

First pilot licence

Jehangir Ratanji Dadabhoy Tata, an aviator, entrepreneur and chairman of Tata Group, became the first licensed pilot in India when he received his pilot licence No. 1 in 1929.

First airline

Tata Airlines, set up by pioneering industrialist J.R.D. Tata soon after he piloted India's maiden civil flight in 1932, was later converted into a public company in 1946 under the name Air-India Ltd, with him as its chairman. In March 1953, it was raised to be a public corporation and became Air India. The state-run carrier was privatized under the Tata Group in 2021.

First airfield

The grass aerodrome at Juhu in Bombay (now Mumbai), Maharashtra, opened in 1932. It was the base for Tata Airlines.

First aircraft designer

S.V. Setty, an assistant engineer with the Public Works Department, Mysore (now Mysuru, Karnataka), in 1911–12, designed, piloted and helped manufacture planes at Avro (a British company). With an eight-cylinder engine, the Avro biplane had a 9.76 m (32 ft) span and weighed 362.8 kg without a pilot or passenger. The plane touched a speed of around 72–80 km/hr.

First helicopter school

Hindustan Aeronautics Ltd (HAL), based in Bangalore (now Bengaluru), Karnataka, established a training school on 1 May 2000 for potential aviators to obtain commercial as well as private helicopter pilot licences.

First flying club

The Aero Club was established in Bombay (now Mumbai), Maharashtra, by industrial magnate Sir Victor Sassoon in 1928. In September 1929, the club was affiliated to the Royal Aero Club, UK. It was recognized by the Government of India as the coordinating body for flying clubs in India, and in 1948, the club was affiliated to the Federation Aeronautique Internationale.

First aeronautical society

On 17 December 1948, the Aeronautical Society of India was inaugurated at Bangalore (now Bengaluru), Karnataka, to promote advancement in the field of aeronautics, and dissemination of knowledge about aeronautical science and aircraft engineering to the public.

First radio plane

The twin-engine de Havilland DH-89 Dragon Rapide, which was on the Karachi– Bombay–Colombo route, was equipped with wireless transmission facilities on 1 December 1937.

First cargo service

An air cargo service started on 21 May 1927, between Calcutta (now Kolkata), West Bengal, and Bagdogra in Darjeeling District of West Bengal, by West Bengal Air Transport, operated for only a week.

First air ticket booking office

The first air ticket booking office was opened in 1939 in a building in the Churchgate Reclamation area in Bombay (now Mumbai),

Kempegowda International Airport, Bengaluru, Karnataka

Kempegowda Airport Wins Skytrax Award

The Kempegowda International Airport, Bengaluru, Karnataka, won the best regional airport in India and South Asia title at the Skytrax World Airport Awards 2022. The award ceremony was held at the Passenger Terminal Expo in Paris, France, on 16 June 2022. The award is given on the basis of customer votes and ratings that are collected in a survey conducted globally. The ratings are based on key factors such as check-ins, transfers, security, arrivals, shopping experience, immigration services and departures.

The Air India mobile app generated a revenue of ₹179.50 crore in the financial year 2021–22 (till 31 December 2021).

The Ministry of Civil Aviation won the Rajbhasha Kirti Puraskar 2021 for excellent implementation of the official languages policy, by the Department of Official Language, Ministry of Home Affairs, Government of India.

Maharashtra. The space now houses the Asiatic Department Store.

First air freight service

Air Freight Pvt. Ltd was set up in 1945 as handling agents for Tata Airlines and Air-India International. It was also the first air cargo clearing agent.

First international flight

Malabar Princess (a Lockheed L-749 Super Constellation) of the Air-India International Corporation, with Captain K.R. Guzder in command, flew from Bombay (now Mumbai), Maharashtra, to London, UK, via Cairo, Egypt, and Geneva, Switzerland, on 8 June 1948, carrying 35 passengers.

First crash

On 17 July 1950, a DC-3 aircraft was recorded to have crashed near Pathankot, Punjab, tragically killing all 22 passengers.

First indigenously assembled plane

The first HS-748 was assembled at the Aircraft Manufacturing Depot, Kanpur, Uttar Pradesh, and delivered to Indian Airlines on 27 June 1967.

First all-jet carrier

In 1962, Air India became the world's first all-jet carrier when it replaced Super Constellation planes with a fleet of Boeing 707.

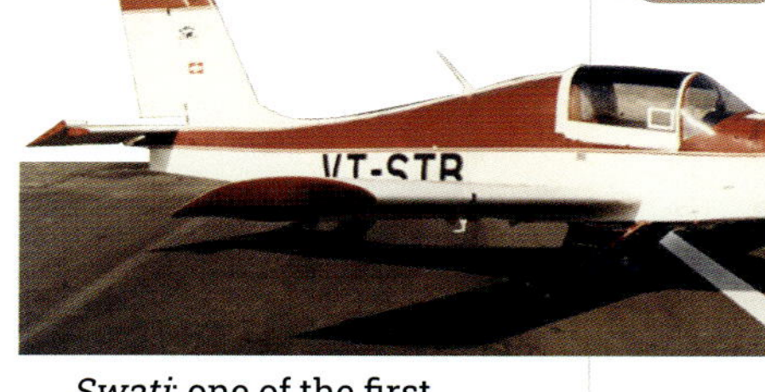

Swati: one of the first indigenous aircraft

First indigenous aircraft

- The Hindustan Trainer-2, built by Hindustan Aeronautics Ltd (HAL), Bangalore (now Bengaluru), Karnataka, made its maiden flight in August 1951. Meant for military use, it was also used by flying schools.
- *Swati,* a two-seater trainer for flying club pilots, was designed and built at Bharat Heavy Electricals Ltd (BHEL), Haridwar, Uttar Pradesh (now in Uttarakhand), by the Directorate General of Civil Aviation (DGCA). The aircraft's maiden flight was in November 1990 from Delhi.

First indigenous helicopter

The advanced light helicopter (ALH) was built at HAL, Bangalore (now Bengaluru), Karnataka, in 1992. The ALH was used both in defence and civil operations.

First Boeing 737-900 aircraft

Jet Airways acquired the first Boeing 737-900 aircraft in May 2003. Longest among the Boeing 737 family, the aircraft can seat 177–190 passengers and has a maximum flight range of 5,084 km. In 2018, Jet Airways took the delivery of the first 150 Boeing 737 MAX aeroplanes, becoming the first Indian carrier to fly the new variant.

First jet

Air India entered the jet age on 20 April 1960, when its Boeing 707 *Gauri Shankar* flew to London, UK. Soon after, on 14 May 1960, it flew to New York, USA. With this, India became the first Asian country to operate a transatlantic flight. The aircraft was written off after a landing accident at Bombay (now Mumbai, Maharashtra) on 22 June 1982.

First air taxi

India's first air taxi service started at Chandigarh Airport on 14 January 2021 under the UDAN-RCS (Regional Connectivity Scheme) of the Central government. With the capacity to seat a pilot and three passengers, the daily flight was 45-minute long and it plied on the Chandigarh–Hisar route at a cost of ₹1,755 per seat.

First air varsity

The Central Training Establishment in Hyderabad (now in Telangana), an independent training centre of Indian Airlines Ltd, was upgraded to a deemed university in 1997. The centre is equipped with infrastructure and training facilities for courses in civil aviation.

First air traffic control system

A state-of-the-art Air Traffic Control (ATC) system, supported by Raytheon flight data and equipped with radar-processing hardware, was installed at the Indira Gandhi International Airport (IGIA), New Delhi, on 14 January 1999. It provided three-dimensional radial, bearing and height information regarding the location and situation of any aircraft within a range of 250 nautical miles.

First heliport

India's first heliport was inaugurated in Rohini, Delhi, on 28 February 2017. Built by Pawan Hans Ltd, it is spread over an area of 25 acres (10.12 hectares) and has four hangars, nine parking bays and a terminal building that has a capacity of 150 passengers. The first such facility in South Asia, it helps in offshore transport, emergency medical services, promoting heli-tourism, and reducing the congestion on the IGI airport, Delhi.

First airport to install a body scanner

The first full-body scanner system was

installed on a trial basis at Terminal 1D of the Indira Gandhi International Airport, New Delhi, on 10 April 2010. Initially the system was used only on volunteering passengers and the scanning process took less than a minute. The scanning system, called SmartCheck, was built by American Science and Engineering (AS&E) and employed the X-ray backscatter technology.

First airport to install waste recycling machines

The Rajiv Gandhi International Airport (RGIA) in Hyderabad, Telangana, became the first airport in the country to instal waste recycling machines, launched as a pilot project in October 2017. Operated by GMR Hyderabad International Airport Ltd (GHIAL), the airport has equipment to crush and recycle plastic PET (polyethylene terephthalate) bottles, steel or aluminium cans and plastic bags into reusable raw material. These 'Swachh Bharat Recycling Machines' were designed and created by Mumbai-based company Wild West Media, and can be used to manufacture upcycled goods like bags, wallets and denim. Passengers may make a donation or claim discount coupons in return for submitting their waste plastic products. RGIA is also the first airport to have its own composting plant, which processes the food waste generated at the airport.

Highest commercial airport

Kushok Bakula Rimpochee Airport (or Leh airport) in Leh, Ladakh, is the highest commercial airport at 3, 256 m (10,682 ft) above the mean sea level. The airport is named after Kushok Bakula Rinpoche, whose Spituk Monastery is very close to the airfield. The Indian Air Force handed over the airport to the Airport Authority of India in 2016.

Largest passenger airport terminal

On 3 July 2010, Terminal 3 of the Indira Gandhi International Airport, New Delhi, became India's and South Asia's largest aviation hub, with the capacity to handle more than 40 million (four crore) passengers a year. The airport handled over 69.23 million (6.923 crore) passengers in 2018–19.

WR First fully solar-powered airport

The Cochin International Airport in Kochi, Kerala, became the first airport in the world to run completely on solar power, on 18 August 2015. The solar plant installed at the airport has 46,000 solar panels and can produce 50,000 to 60,000 units of electricity every day. The airport won the Champion of Earth Prize, awarded by the United Nations, in 2018.

First Boeing 787 Dreamliner

The Boeing 787 Dreamliner, a fuel-efficient aircraft that can carry up to 290 passengers and fly 15,750 km at a stretch, touched down for the first time at the Indira Gandhi International Airport, New Delhi, on 13 July 2011.

Oldest fleet

Founded in 1932 (then called Tata Airlines) and renamed in 1946 as Air-India Ltd, Air India has a fleet size of 125 aircraft (excluding subsidiaries), with an average age of 8.2 years, making it the oldest fleet in India. The airline has its headquarters in New Delhi.

Oldest to obtain a commercial pilot's licence

Captain Rajagopal Nagarajan (b. 25 April 1962) from Coimbatore, Tamil Nadu, joined the commercial pilot's course after retiring from the Indian Air Force. He obtained the commercial pilot's licence (CPL) from the Civil

The Indira Gandhi Rashtriya Uran Akademi (IGRUA) was established in 1985.

Kushok Bakula Rimpochee Airport, Leh, Ladakh: highest commercial airport

Akasa Air, newest airline

Newest Airline on the Block

Akasa Air, backed by late investor Rakesh Jhunjhunwala and aviation veterans Vinay Dube and Aditya Ghosh, received its operations certificate on 7 July 2022 from the Directorate General of Civil Aviation (DGCA). Its inaugural flight took place from Mumbai to Ahmedabad at 10:15 a.m. on 7 August 2022. The airline is set to to induct a fleet of 72 Boeing 737 Max aircraft over five years, and s set to become India's youngest and greenest fleet. Currently, it plies on 11 non-stop routes along eight cities including Ahmedabad, Bengaluru, Kochi, Chennai, Mumbai, Delhi, Guwahati and Agartala.

During 2021, scheduled domestic airlines operated 6.44 lakh scheduled flights carrying 71.6 million passengers.

Aviation Authority, Philippines, at 48 years on 11 December 2009.

WR Highest airfield

The Daulat Beg Oldi airstrip in Ladakh, at an altitude of 5,065 m (16,617 ft), is the highest airfield in the world. The Indian Air Force landed a C-130J Super Hercules aircraft at this airfield, reactivating it in 2013.

Most flights taken in a year

Ganesh Kumar Sukumaran Nair, managing director of Ayoki Fabricon Private Ltd in Pune, Maharashtra, set a record by taking a total of 234 flights from 1 January to 31 December 2018. Of these flights, 149 were on domestic routes and 85 were to international destinations.

Most air freight traffic

Indira Gandhi International Airport, New Delhi, handled over 737,000 tonnes of freight traffic by the end of financial year 2021.

WR Highest number of women pilots

In a report released by Air Line Pilots Association, International (ALPA) in 2018, India led the charts in the number of female pilots among all countries. Around 13 per cent of the pilots in the country are women whereas the global average is only 5 per cent. This means that out of every eight flights in India, one is flown by a woman. Airlines such as IndiGo, SpiceJet and Air India have the highest recruitment numbers for women pilots.

First woman commercial pilot

The first woman commercial pilot was Prem Mathur for Deccan Airways in 1951.

WR First woman Airbus commander

Captain Indraani Singh, who joined Indian Airlines in April 1986, was the first Indian and Asian woman to fly the Airbus A320 in 1989 and became the world's first woman commander of the wide-bodied Airbus A300 in August 1996.

First woman airbus pilot

On 14 May 1987, Durba Banerjee became the first woman to co-pilot a flight – Airbus A300 – on the Calcutta–New Delhi–Calcutta (now Kolkata, West Bengal) route.

First woman to obtain a pilot's licence

Urmila K. Parekh became the first woman to obtain a pilot's licence in 1930.

Longest length of runways

The Indira Gandhi International Airport, New Delhi, has the longest stretch of airport runways in the country, with a length of 4,430 m (14,534 ft).

First woman chief executive officer of an airline

Harpreet A. De Singh was appointed as the chief executive officer (CEO) of Alliance Air, a regional subsidiary of Air India, on 30 October 2020. Previously the executive director for flight safety at Air India, she became the first woman CEO of an airline. She was also the first woman pilot to be selected by Air India in 1988.

First woman chairperson of the International Civil Aviation Organization (ICAO) Aviation Security Committee

Shefali Juneja was elected as the chairperson of the ICAO Aviation Security Committee on 17 September 2021. A specialized agency of the UN, ICAO was formed to support and help nations with diplomacy and cooperation in air transport. India held the position 12 years ago. Shefali was also appointed as the representative in the council of ICAO in 2019.

First woman offshore pilot

Captain Mayuri V. Deshmukh (b. 11 November 1982) with CHPL 991 became the first woman offshore captain in the country when she flew from Juhu to Mumbai High, Mumbai, Maharashtra, as captain from 11:07 a.m. to 1:25 p.m. on 8 March 2022. She has complied with the syllabus laid down by the Directorate General of Civil Aviation (DGCA) and validated by Oil and Natural Gas Ltd.

Longest direct-route flight with an all-woman cockpit crew

Air India's flight AI-176 made history on 11 January 2021 when an all-woman cockpit crew flew a distance of 16,000 km from San Francisco, California, USA, to Bengaluru, Karnataka. The flight departed on 9 January 2021 and was flown by four pilots – Captain Zoya Aggarwal, Captain Papagari Thanmai, Captain Shivani Manhas and Captain Akansha Sonaware. The longest commercial flight to be operated by an Indian airline and the longest flight entering India, its flying time was 17 hours and its route remarkably included flying over the North Pole.

Largest passenger airline

IndiGo, with its headquarters in Gurugram, Haryana, is the largest passenger airline in India by passengers carried and fleet size. Since its inception in August 2006, it has grown from one plane to a fleet of 269 aircraft. It is also the largest individual Asian low-cost carrier in terms of jet fleet size. It has a destination count of 100 with 74 domestic destinations and 26 international ones.

WR First three-point disembarkation system

IndiGo, a leading Indian airline with its headquarters in Gurugram, Haryana, introduced a three-point disembarkation system in a global first on 4 August 2022. To mark its 16th anniversary, the airline introduced a disembarkation process that was carried out from two forward and one rear exit ramp. The new process will be implemented on IndiGo's A320 and A321 fleet for flights arriving at Delhi, Mumbai and Bengaluru airports initially and will be extended across the network subsequently.

RAIL AND METRO

First rail construction company

R.M. Stephenson, a British railway engineer, formed the East Indian Railway (EIR) Company in 1844 for the construction of railways. In a contract signed on 17 August 1849, the EIR and the Great Indian Peninsula (GIP) Railway Company, England, were authorized to construct and operate railway lines at Calcutta (now Kolkata), West Bengal, and Bombay (now Mumbai, Maharashtra).

First passenger train

India's first passenger train chugged away from Bori Bunder (later renamed Victoria Terminus, and then Chhatrapati Shivaji Maharaj Terminus) station in Bombay (now Mumbai) to Thane, Maharashtra, on 16 April 1853. It was pulled by three locomotives

LICENCES ISSUED

TYPE OF LICENCE

Category	Type of licence	Number of Licences issued
Aeroplane/Helicopter	Commercial Pilot Licence	863
Aeroplane/Helicopter	Air Transport Pilot Licence	485
Aeroplane/Helicopter	Private Pilot Licence	11
Aeroplane/Helicopter	Instrument Rating	889
FRTOL and FRTOL [R]	Flight Radio Telephony Operator	1,827
FATA - Initial	Flight Airscrew Temporary Authorization	21
FATA - Extension	Flight Airscrew Temporary Authorization	167
FIR	Flight Instructor Rating	16
AFIR	Assistant Flight Instructor Rating	56

Data for January–December 2021. Source: *Annual Report* 2021-22, Ministry of Civil Aviation, Government of India

World Travel Awards 2021

The World Travel Awards acknowledge and celebrate excellence across all sectors of the travel and tourism industry globally. Air India won Asia's Leading Airline – First Class award at the annual World Travel Awards held in December 2021. Nominated in the same category were Cathay Pacific, China Airlines, Japan Airlines, Korean Air, Malaysia Airlines, Singapore Airlines and Thai Airways. At the world level, the Adani Lounge International by TFS Performa at the Chhatrapati Shivaji International Airport, Mumbai, Maharashtra, won in the category of World's Leading Airport Lounge – First Class. Its fellow nominees were the first-class lounge at London City airport, England; the Skyteam lounge at Sydney Airport, Australia, and the Star Alliance lounge at Los Angeles International Airport, USA.

Air India wins Asia's Leading Airline award

From 1 January 2020, Indian Railways increased fares by 1 paisa/ km for non-AC classes, 2 paisa/ km in mail/ express non-AC classes and 4 paisa/km in AC classes on non-suburban routes.

named Sindh, Sultan and Sahib, and carried 400 passengers in 14 railway carriages. This historic journey, which was about 1 hr 15 mins long, was flagged off with a 21-gun salute.

First indigenous railway carriages

The first railway coaches made in India were built by two coach-building firms in Calcutta (now Kolkata), West Bengal: Steward and Company, and Seton and Company. John Hodgson was the chief engineer of the East Indian Railway Company then, and the coaches were employed for the first train journey from Howrah to Hooghly in West Bengal on 15 August 1854.

Fastest train

The fastest train in India is the Vande Bharat Express or Train 18, which reached a top speed of 180 km/hr during test runs. Its current operating speed is 130 km/hr. The train runs on four routes: New Delhi–Varanasi, New Delhi–Shri Mata Vaishno Devi Katra, Mumbai Central–Gandhinagar, New Delhi–Amb Andaura.

First double-decker train

India's first double-decker train was the Flying Ranee, a superfast train that runs between Mumbai Central and Surat station. It began operating in 1906, was halted in 1939 due to the Second World War, and resumed in 1950 as a daily service train.

First double-decker coaches

The Bombay, Baroda and Central India (BB&CI) Railway Company in Bombay (now Mumbai, Maharashtra), introduced the first double-decker coaches in 1862. These coaches had a seating capacity of 120 to 150 on the lower deck and 70 on the upper one.

The Deccan Queen: first deluxe train

First tramway company

The Calcutta Tramway Company was registered in London, UK, in 1880. The Government of West Bengal nationalized it in 1976.

First tramcars

A horse-drawn tramcar ran on a 3.8 km route between Sealdah and Armenian Ghat Street in Calcutta (now Kolkata, West Bengal), on 24 February 1873.

First superfast train

The Rajdhani Express, commissioned on 3 March 1969, runs between New Delhi and Howrah, West Bengal. It has an average speed of 130 km/hr.

First air-conditioned train

Prior to 1936, some coaches on the Bombay, Baroda and Central India (BB&CI) Railway Company, Bombay (now Mumbai, Maharashtra), had double walls lined with lead–zinc sheets filled with ice. The Frontier Mail (now renamed the Golden Temple Mail, which runs between Mumbai and Amritsar) was the first train to get air-conditioned (AC) coaches in 1934.

First deluxe train

The first deluxe train, the Deccan Queen, began between Victoria Terminus, Bombay (now Chhatrapati Shivaji Maharaj Terminus, Mumbai) and Poona (now Pune), Maharashtra, on 1 June 1930. It had 61 first-class, 156 second-class and 19 attendants' seats.

First electric train

The first electric train operated on the Harbour branch of the Great Indian Peninsula Railway from Victoria Terminus (now Chhatrapati Shivaji Maharaj Terminus) to Kurla in Bombay (now Mumbai, Maharashtra), over 16 km, on 3 February 1925.

First locomotive factory

The first locomotive factory in India was set up at Chittaranjan in Paschim Bardhaman District, West Bengal, in 1950. The first diesel locomotive, with an imported engine, was manufactured at the Varanasi Diesel Locomotive Works, Varanasi, Uttar Pradesh, on 4 January 1964.

First green corridor

The Manamadurai–Rameswaram stretch of the Southern Railway was inaugurated as India's first green corridor in July 2016, by installing bio-toilets in 150 coaches of 13 pairs of express and passenger trains on the 114 km long train route. Developed by Indian Railways and the Defence Research and Development Organization (DRDO), the toilets have zero human-waste discharge.

First Vistadome trains

A special seven-coach Vistadome passenger train was introduced on the Visakhapatnam–Araku route in Andhra Pradesh on 16 April 2017 by the Indian Railways. It has features such as see-through glass on all sides, glass roofs, LED lights, a GPS-based information system and an observation lounge that offers panoramic views throughout the journey.

First public–private partnership railway station

The Habibganj railway station in Bhopal, Madhya Pradesh, is the first railway station to be built under a public–private partnership and on par with international standards. The redevelopment work began in partnership with the Bansal Group on 9 June 2017. It lies on the main Jhansi–Bhopal–Itarsi route. The plan includes airport-like facilities, such as shopping complexes, forex kiosks and eateries, making it the first of its kind in the country.

WR Most locomotives produced in a year

The Chittaranjan Locomotive Works in Paschim Bardhaman District, West Bengal, produced 486 locomotives in the financial year 2021–22. They surpassed the Railway Board's production target for the period.

WR Most coaches produced in a year

The Integral Coach Factory, which is located at Perambur in Chennai, Tamil Nadu, manufactured 4,166 railway passenger coaches in 2019–20.

WR Oldest steam engine

The Fairy Queen, officially called the East Indian Railway Nr. 22, has the world's oldest working steam engine. This train started running in 1855 but was stopped in 1908. It was restored in 1997 by Perambur Loco Works in Perambur in Chennai, Tamil Nadu. In July 1997, this heritage train resumed its route between Delhi and Alwar, Rajasthan, and it still runs occasionally.

First woman train driver

Surekha Yadav Bhosale was the first woman to drive an Indian Railways train in 1988. She drove the first 'Ladies Special' local train, which started in April 2000 in Mumbai, Maharashtra. She was the first woman to join the Indian Railways as a trainee assistant driver in 1986. She also became Asia's first woman train driver in 2011, driving the Deccan Queen from Pune to Chhatrapati Shivaji Maharaj Terminus in Mumbai.

First stations

Bori Bunder, Byculla, Sion and Thane stations on the Bori Bunder–Thane line in Maharashtra, were the first railway stations built at the time of the inaugural run of the first passenger train from Bori Bunder to Thane in 1853.

WR Only railway station listed as a UNESCO World Heritage Site

The first train in the country was flagged off on 16 April 1853 from Bori Bunder (now Chhatrapati Shivaji Maharaj Terminus) in Mumbai, Maharashtra. The historic station is one of the busiest railway stations in India, and the only one declared as a UNESCO World Heritage Site. The building, featuring a Victorian Gothic style of architecture, was designed and constructed by draughtsman Axel Herman and architect Frederick William Stevens in 1888.

RailTel Corporation of India Ltd was established in 2000 to provide a communication network infrastructure to the Indian Railways. Currently, 6,052 stations are live with RailTel's RailWire Wifi.

Representative image

All Aboard the 'Bharat Gaurav' Train

Indian's first private train under the 'Bharat Gaurav' scheme chugged away for the first time from Coimbatore, Tamil Nadu, to Shirdi, Maharashtra, on 14 June 2022. The train departs at 6 p.m. on Tuesday and arrives at Shirdi at 7:25 a.m. on Thursday. The 'Bharat Gaurav' scheme aims at displaying India's historical landmarks, cultural heritage and pluralism. This train provides its passengers with a thorough darshan of the Sai Baba Temple at Shirdi. On the train journey to Shirdi, the train stops at seven stations, with the most notable stoppage being the one at Mantralayam Road. The train halts here for five hours in order to allow passengers to visit the Mantralayam Temple.

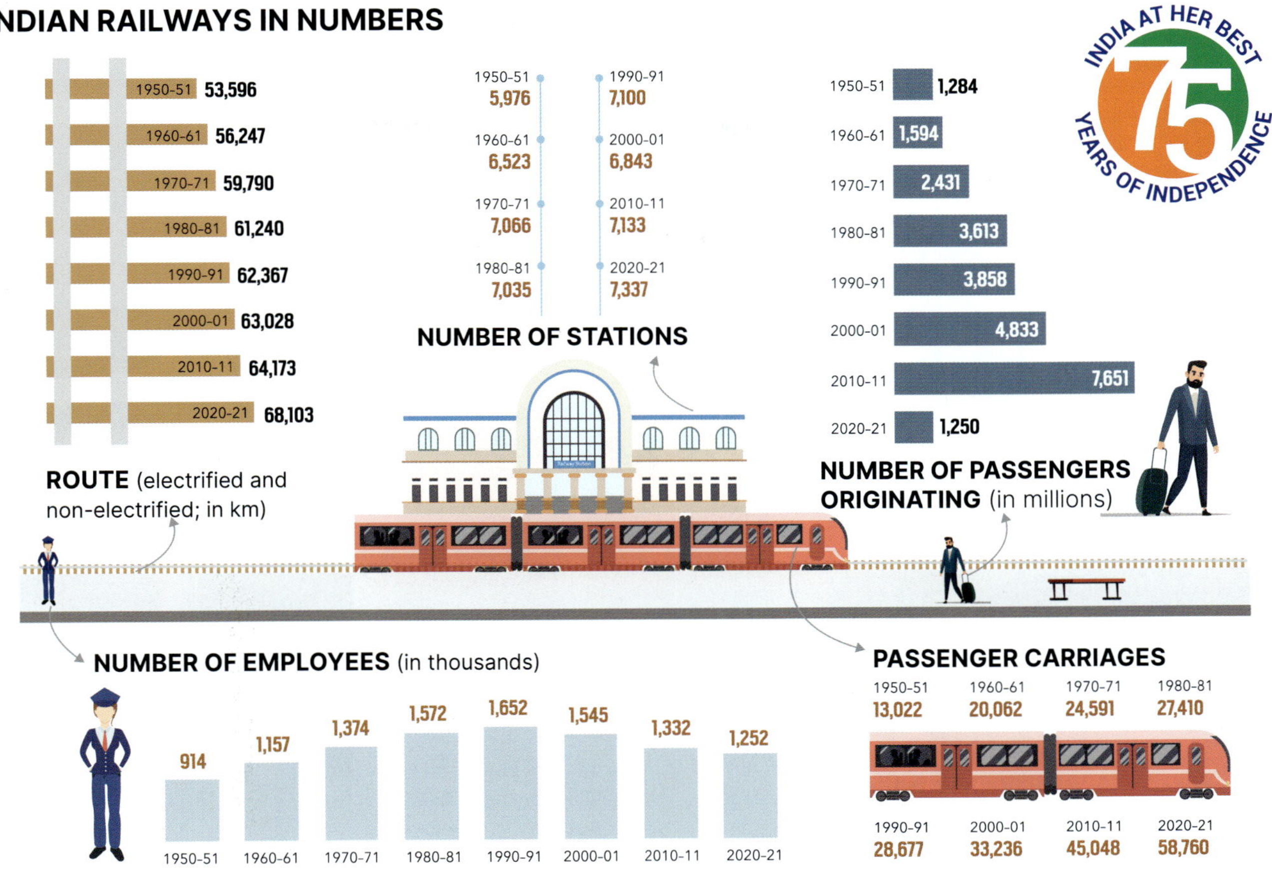

Source: Indian Railways Annual Reports and Accounts 2020–2021, Ministry of Railways, Government of India

The number of train accidents per million train km was

0.03

during the year 2020–21.

Station with most platforms

Howrah Junction, West Bengal, serves around one million passengers every day. It has 23 platforms, making it the station with the most platforms in India.

Busiest railway station

Kanpur Central station, Uttar Pradesh, is the busiest railway station in the country in terms of the number of trains that pass through it every day. As many as 230 trains pass through the station daily. This railway station also has the world's largest interlocking route system.

WR Station with the longest platform

Shri Siddharoodha Swamiji railway station in Hubballi, Karnataka, has completed the construction of the 1,505 m (4,937 ft 7.97 in.) long Platform No. 1, thus becoming the station with the world's longest railway platform. The platform is yet to be inaugurated.

WR Longest rails manufactured

The Bhilai Steel Plant, the largest plant of the Steel Authority of India Ltd (SAIL), became the only rail maker in the world capable of producing 260 m (853 ft) long rails, on 23 February 2005. It first manufactures 65 m (213 ft) long rails, which are welded together to form the 260 m tracks for high-speed trains.

Longest train route

The Dibrugarh–Kanniyakumari Vivek Express has the longest train route on the Indian Railways network, and the ninth longest in the world. It joins Dibrugarh in Assam to Kanniyakumari in Tamil Nadu, covering 4,286 km, while halting at 56 stations along the route. It starts at 11:05 p.m. and reaches at 9:50 a.m. on the fifth day, with a scheduled journey time of 82 hrs 5 mins.

Longest rail tunnel

The Pir Panjal railway tunnel or the Banihal railway tunnel, is 11.215 km long. Located in the Pir Panjal range of the Himalayas in Jammu and Kashmir, it opened in 2013.

First fully solar-powered railway station

The Guwahati railway station in Assam is India's first fully solar-powered station. Commissioned in 2017, the project has

Kolkata Metro

Mumbai Metro

INDIA AT HER BEST 75 YEARS OF INDEPENDENCE

TAKING THE METRO RAIL

Metro System	Commenced Operations in (Year)	Number of Stations
Kolkata Metro	1984	33
Delhi Metro*	2002	286
Namma Metro	2011	51
Mumbai Metro	2014	30
Chennai Metro	2015	32
Jaipur Metro	2015	11
Hyderabad Metro	2017	57
Kochi Metro	2017	22
Lucknow Metro	2017	21
Nagpur Metro	2019	24
Ahmedabad Metro	2019	6
Kanpur Metro	2021	9
Pune Metro	2022	10

Lucknow Metro

Namma (Bengaluru) Metro

Delhi Metro

Kochi Metro

Chennai Metro

Jaipur Metro

*Including NOIDA – Greater NOIDA Aqua line and Rapid Metro Gurugram

The Pune Metro began operations in 2022, becoming the latest metro system in the country.

2,352 solar panels on the roof. This solar project aims to make the railways environmentally responsible and reduce their carbon footprint. The panels have an average power generation capacity of 2,048 kWh per day.

First corporatized train

The Indian Railways launched the Tejas Express, India's first corporatized train, on 4 October 2019. The infrastructure is owned and run by the Indian Railway Catering and Tourism Corporation (IRCTC), a subsidiary of the Indian Railways, while the services on board are outsourced to private contractors. They include catering, housekeeping, ticketing and refund, among others. The train shuttles between Lucknow and New Delhi, and has only two halts – Kanpur and Ghaziabad. Running all week, except Tuesdays, it is contracted under the public–private partnership model.

First metro

A 16.3 km underground mass rapid transit system in the country was inaugurated on 24 October 1984 in Calcutta (now Kolkata), West Bengal, between Dum Dum and Tollygunge. The carrying capacity of this metro was 1.73 million passengers a day. The trains for the metro system were manufactured at the Integral Coach Factory, Perambur, Madras (now Chennai), Tamil Nadu, during 1981–82.

First to buy a Delhi Metro Smart Card and travel using it

Anil Marwah, with his son Ankit Marwah, became the first passenger to buy a Delhi Metro Smart Card and travel on all the then existing lines of the Delhi Metro when it commenced on 25 December 2002.

The Hauz Khas station, New Delhi: deepest metro station

Deepest metro tunnel

Delhi Metro Rail Corporation (DMRC) completed a metro tunnel at a depth of 45 m (147 ft 7 in.), and 20–25 m (65 ft 7 in.–82 ft) on 30 April 2009. The 1,556 m (5,105 ft) long tunnel below the underground Rajiv Chowk metro station in New Delhi is part of the 22.7 km long Airport Express Line.

Deepest metro station

The Hauz Khas station on the Magenta Line and the Yellow Line of the Delhi Metro is the deepest metro station, located at a depth of 32 m (105 ft).

Largest metro network*

The Delhi Metro, set up by the Delhi Metro Rail Corporation (DMRC), spread across 391 km, is the largest metro rail network in India in terms of both route length and ridership. It has 12 lines and 286 metro stations.

First underwater metro

The East-West corridor project, India's first underwater metro service under the Kolkata Metro Rail Corporation, is set to be completed by June 2023. The metro line will connect Salt Lake to Howrah via Kolkata with a 520 m (1,706 ft) stretch below the River Hooghly. The tunnels are built 33 m (108 ft) below the river bed. Of the 16.6 km route, the 9.30 km route between Sector V and Sealdah is operational.

First 'driverless' metro

The Magenta Line in the Delhi Metro became the first 'driverless' metro line in India. The 12.64 km long line started operating on 25 December 2017, and connected Kalkaji Mandir, New Delhi, to Botanical Garden, Noida, while halting at nine stations. The line was extended by 24.34 km to Janakpuri West in May 2018. Initially, it was run by an operator, with high levels of automation based on the Communication Based Train Control technology, and is planned to be 'driverless' in future.

ROAD

First state transport system

- In June 1932, the Nizam's State Railways Transport Department (NSRTD), Hyderabad (now in Telangana), set up a road transport service on a 24 km route, with 27 buses operating through three depots. Each bus could seat as many as 25 passengers.
- The first state-controlled road transport system in the country was introduced on 31 July 1948 by the Calcutta State Transport Corporation, headquartered in Calcutta (now Kolkata), West Bengal.

*Including NOIDA – Greater NOIDA Aqua line and Rapid Metro Gurugram

First highway

Lord William Bentinck, the then Governor General of India (1828–35), began metalling work on the 2,400 km long historic Grand Trunk Road from Calcutta (now Kolkata), West Bengal, to Peshawar (now in Pakistan) and beyond. During his tenure, the initial steps were taken to build a metalled road from Calcutta (now Kolkata), West Bengal, to Delhi.

First regular public transport

The first regular long-distance public road transport was introduced between Aligarh and Kanpur in Uttar Pradesh in November 1841.

First mail cart service

In 1845, mail bullock carts were running between Calcutta (now Kolkata, West Bengal), and Lahore (now in Pakistan), and from Bombay (now Mumbai, Maharashtra), to Surat, Gujarat. Bullocks were replaced by horses in 1850 and companies were formed to run this service. First among these was the Inland Transport Company of Tanti Mai in Kanpur in Uttar Pradesh.

First traffic police

The Traffic Department of Calcutta Police in Calcutta (now Kolkata, West Bengal), came into force in 1874 with 17 sepoys in its ranks.

Earliest route

In 1926, the Brihanmumbai (then Bombay) Electricity Supply & Transport Undertaking (BEST) purchased motor buses, choosing two points to try them out. The route covered present-day Afghan Church to Crawford Market through Dadar tram terminus, King's Circle, Opera House, Lal Bagh and Arthur Road in Mumbai, Maharashtra.

First car

The first motor car was reportedly imported in 1892 by the then maharaja of Patiala in Punjab. It was a De Dion Bouton car.

First trolley bus

Twelve trolley buses were imported to replace tramcars on the Gowalia Tank–Mazagon route in Bombay (now Mumbai), Maharashtra, on 11 June 1962. They were withdrawn in March 1971 in favour of buses.

First zero-emission electric car

REVAi, the environment-friendly electric car, is manufactured by the Reva Electric Car Company, Bengaluru, Karnataka, a joint venture formed by Amerigon Inc. of California, USA, and the Maini Group of Industries based in Bengaluru, Karnataka. This eco-friendly car was first flagged off from New Delhi in March 1998 and sold worldwide by 2011 in 26 countries. It was acquired by Indian conglomerate Mahindra & Mahindra in May 2010 and the company launched the electric hatchback e20 in 2013.

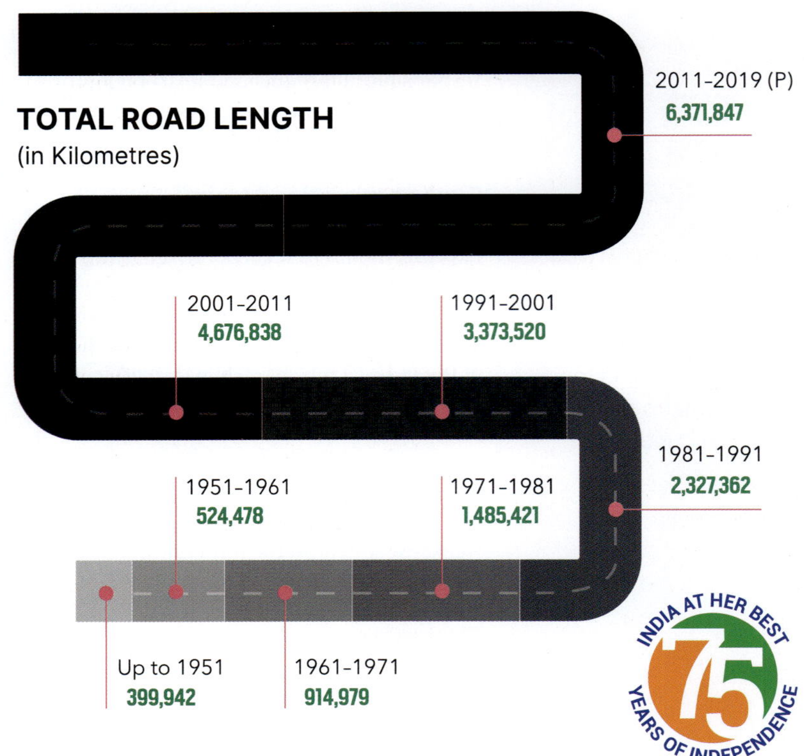

(P) = Provisional
Source: *Annual Report* 2021–22, Ministry of Road Transport and Highways, Government of India

First motor bus

The motor bus was introduced in Bombay (now Mumbai), Maharashtra, on the Afghan Church–Crawford Market route on 15 July 1926. With a cruising speed of 20 km/hr, it carried 24 passengers, with two to three standing ones. Twenty-six buses were bought for ₹12,000 each.

First stainless-steel bus

The first bus made of stainless steel was built at the Maharashtra State Road Transport Corporation workshop in Aurangabad, Maharashtra. It was inaugurated on the Bombay (now Mumbai)–Ratnagiri route, Maharashtra, on 12 February 1988.

First Indian car manufacturers

Hindustan Motors Ltd, registered in 1942 to manufacture vehicles, was followed by Premier Automobiles (1944) and Standard Motor Products of India Ltd (1948). The first Indian-built car, Hindustan 10, not fully indigenous but identical to the series M10 HP Morris, rolled out of the factory in 1946.

The length of national highways increased by over 50 per cent between 2014 and 2021.

The Ministry of Road Transport and Highways began the Good Samaritan scheme to provide legal assistance to those who offer immediate assistance to an injured victim in a road accident.

First indigenous payment eco-system for transport

The National Common Mobility Card (NCMC) based on the 'One Nation, One Card' model was launched in Ahmedabad, Gujarat, on 4 March 2019, by the Ministry of Housing and Urban Affairs, Government of India. It allows users to make payments across multiple transportation platforms like metros, toll taxes, buses and parking across India.

First satellite navigation system

Sanjay, a navigation system using a Global Positioning System (GPS) receiver and mapping software, was launched on 15 February 1999 in New Delhi. Once installed in the vehicle, the user could access Delhi's road map and get audio information about routes. It also tracks the vehicle from elsewhere. Developed indigenously at the I.B. Saxena Design Lab in New Delhi, it uses 24 satellites.

First battery-bus fleet

In 1987, for the first time, the Delhi administration introduced 76 battery-operated buses on 11 routes in Delhi, through the Delhi Energy Development Agency. Each bus had a laden weight of 3,800 kg, a cruising speed of 40 km/hr and a maximum speed of 60 km/hr.

Charging Ahead with E-vehicles

India is on its way to sustainable transit. The Union minister for road transport and highways Nitin Gadkari announced that the country currently has 1,334,385 electric vehicles (EVs) and 2,826 operational public charging stations as on 14 July 2022. These figures exclude the data of Andhra Pradesh, Madhya Pradesh, Telangana and Lakshadweep as these states are not included in 'VAHAN 4', which is an application that records data about vehicles in the country. As per his statement, 2,877 public EV charging stations in 68 cities and 1,576 charging stations across nine expressways and 16 highways have also been sanctioned under the Faster Adaptation and Manufacturing of Electric Vehicles (FAME) Phase-II scheme.

First electric bus

- The first electric bus service in India is reported to have commenced in Himachal Pradesh for Rohtang Pass, near Manali, at an altitude of 3,962.4 m (13,000 ft). The bus has been developed by Goldstone Infratech and the Automobile Research Association of India. It had the capacity to carry 30 passengers and can run 200 km on fully charged batteries.
- India's first electric double-decker bus was launched at Y.B. Centre in south Mumbai, Maharashtra, on 19 August 2022. The bus – the 'Switch EiV 22' – will be run by the Mumbai civic transport body. Two new electric buses, including the first air-conditioned double-decker bus in the country, will join the fleet of the Brihanmumbai Electric Supply & Transport Undertaking (BEST).

First electric cabs

Nagpur in Maharashtra is India's first city to have an electric mass mobility system. It has a fleet of 200 electric vehicles including taxis, buses, e-rickshaws and autorickshaws, owned by cab aggregator Ola. This multimodal electric vehicle project, the first of its kind in India, was inaugurated on 26 May 2017.

First CNG autos

Bajaj Auto Ltd launched the first of its Compressed Natural Gas (CNG) autorickshaws in Delhi on 29 May 2000. With a 3-kg CNG tank and a standby 3-litre petrol tank, it is powered by a 175 cc, four-stroke single overhead camshaft engine that gives 50 km per kg of CNG and meets the Bharat-II emission norms.

First fully electrical SUV

Hyundai launched India's first fully electric SUV, the Kona Electric, on 9 July 2019. The eco-friendly vehicle can cover approximately 452 km on a single charge and was introduced with four drive modes – Eco, Eco+, Comfort and Sport.

WR Highest filling station

The Indian Oil Corporation Ltd operates a filling station at Kaza, Spiti Valley, Himachal Pradesh, at an elevation of about 3,740 m (12,270 ft) above the mean sea level.

First 3D smart traffic lights

Students of Chitkara University in Rajpura, Punjab, designed the first 3D smart traffic lights in India, piloted by the Mohali Traffic Police on 2 August 2019. The new system, called 'Intelights', employs 3D technology and sensors to manipulate the green and red lights based on the actual number of cars that are present at the signal. This smart system of traffic lights was installed at Quark City near

NATIONAL HIGHWAYS (STATES AND UTs)

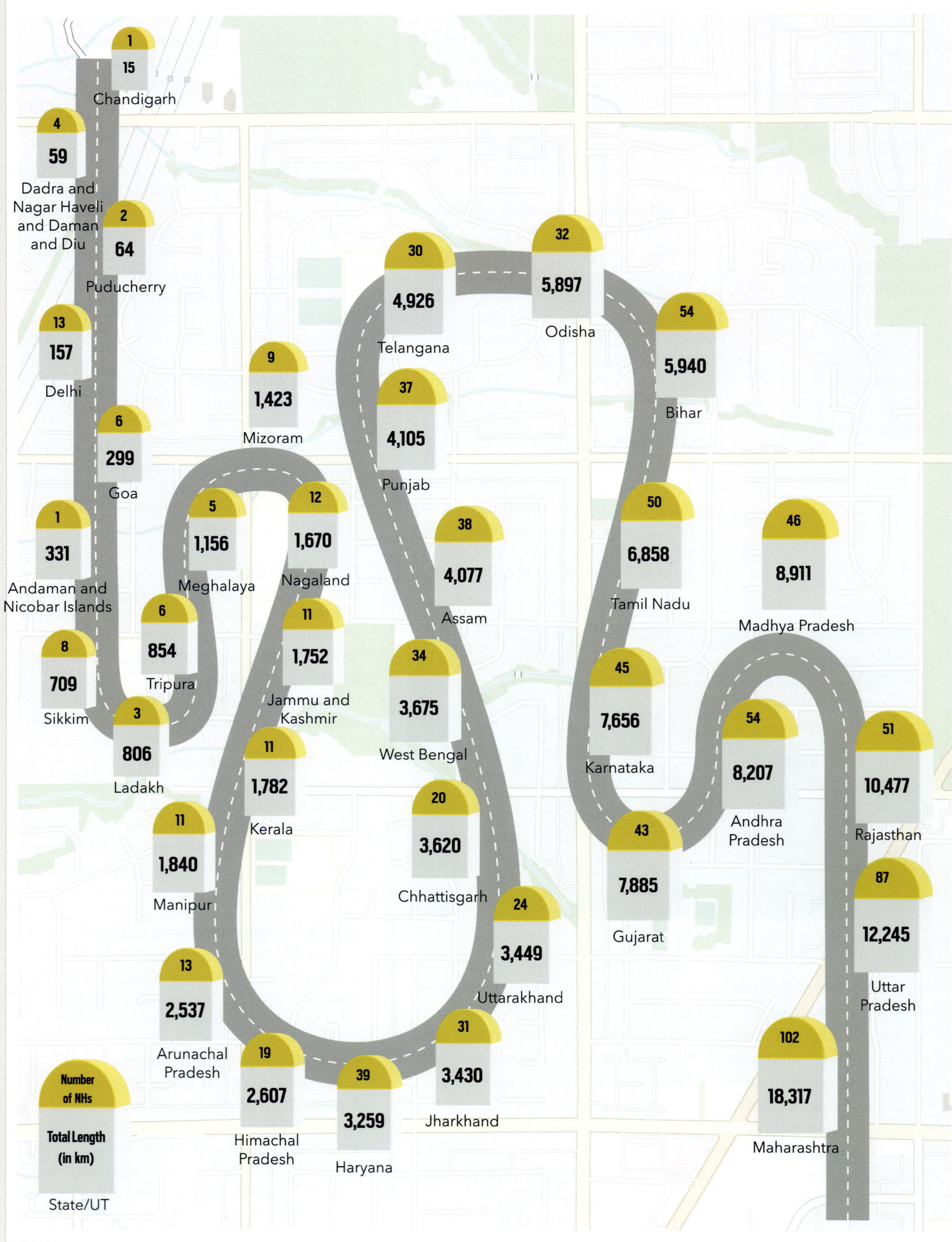

Source: *Annual Report* 2021–22, Ministry of Road Transport and Highways, Government of India

The Indian Road Congress (IRC) was registered as a society in 1937.

Airport Road in Mohali to enhance cost- and time-effective traffic management.

First Advanced Traffic Control system

The Delhi Police installed the first Advanced Traffic Control system at 47 intersections of the capital city in April 2000. The intelligent sensors in this high-tech system are equipped to assess the volume of traffic at each intersection and control the traffic light system accordingly.

Shortest national highway

National Highway 327 B, located in West Bengal, is the shortest national highway in India. Only 1.2 km long, it starts from its junction with NH-327 near Panitanki in Darjeeling District, connecting Mechi Bridge and terminating at the Indo-Nepal border.

Largest road network

India has a total road length of approximately 3,300,000 km, the second largest road network in the world, after the USA.

Largest automotive company

Tata Motors Ltd (earlier Tata Engineering and Locomotive Company), founded in 1945 and headquartered in Bombay (now Mumbai), Maharashtra, is the largest automotive company with a portfolio of cars, sports vehicles, buses, trucks and defence vehicles. Their consolidated net revenue for the fiscal year 2021 22 was ₹2,78,454 crore (₹2,784.54 billion) with 10,86,734 vehicles sold.

WR Highest national highway

The 490 km long Manali–Leh national highway has an average elevation of over 4,000 m (13,123 ft). Its highest elevation is 5,328 m (17,480 ft) at Tanglang La in Ladakh.

Most bituminous concrete poured – single day

Travelling over an approximate linear distance of 18,701 km, Hyderabad-based IJM (India) Infrastructure Ltd (IJMII) poured 15,656 metric tonnes (6,068.217 cu m) of bituminous concrete in 20 hrs 40 mins on 25 February 2021. The laying of the 26.82 km Solapur–Bijapur single lane of the four-lane NH-13 between Maharashtra and Karnataka was implemented under the National Highway Authority of India.

WR Longest highway tunnel

Atal Tunnel, a 9.2 km long tunnel on the Manali–Leh highway, was inaugurated on 3 October 2020. It cuts down the distance between Manali and Leh by 46 km and reduces travel time by four hours. Equipped with CCTVs and fire hydrants, the tunnel is the only one in India to have an emergency exit tunnel inside.

State/UT with the largest fleet of buses

Tamil Nadu State Transport Corporation (TNSTC) has a fleet of 22,000 buses. It is the largest government-owned bus transport corporation in the country (2019).

INTERNATIONAL CRUISE SHIP PASSENGERS HANDLED AT INDIAN PORTS

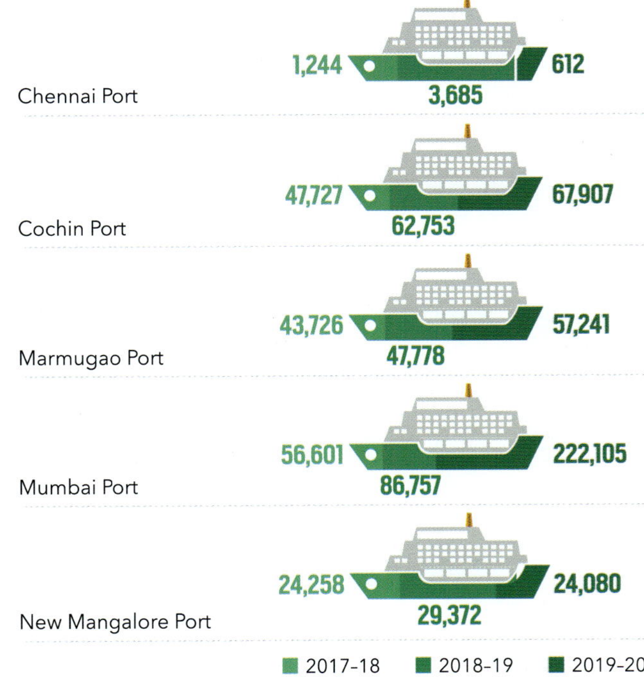

Source: *Annual Report* 2020–21, Ministry of Ports, Shipping and Waterways, Government of India

WATER

Earliest representation of ships

A rectangular seal portraying a vessel with a sharply upturned prow and stem was unearthed in an excavation at Mohenjo-daro (now in Pakistan). It was dated to 3000 BCE.

Earliest compass

According to the *Bombay Gazetteer*, Vol. XIII, Part II, Appendix A, a crude forerunner of the modern magnetic compass, the Matsya Yantra, was used around the fifth century CE. It featured an iron fish that floated in a vessel of oil, and pointed north.

Oldest ship

- Training ship HMS *Foudroyant* (*Trincomalee*), was built at the Bombay docks (now in Mumbai, Maharashtra) in 1817 and is now a museum ship in Hartlepool, UK. The *Trincomalee* carried 46 guns and displaced 1,065 tonnes.

- MV *Safeena* of Ellon Hinengo Ltd, Port Blair, Andaman and Nicobar Islands, built at the government dockyard in Rangoon (now Yangon), Myanmar, in 1942, is the oldest passenger ship.

First steamboat
The steamboat *Diana* was built in India in 1819 by Jessop & Co. Ltd in Calcutta (now Kolkata, West Bengal), and launched on 12 July 1823.

Oldest known dockyard
Remains of the Harappan civilization were discovered at Lothal near the Gulf of Cambay (now Khambhat) in Gujarat. Built in 2300 BCE, the dock is a rectangular tank, 218 m x 37 m (715 ft x 121 ft), and about 16 km from its nearest seaport. Boats docked at Lothal till the 1850s, a testimony to the knowledge of the Harappans.

First ship to sail from India
The first ship carrying the flag of an Indian Shipping Company, SS *Loyalty* of the Scindia Steam Navigation Company, sailed with a full complement of passengers from Bombay (now Mumbai), Maharashtra, to the British Isles. A hospital ship, *Loyalty* was bought on 17 February 1919 and converted to a passenger vessel. The day, 5 April, on which it undertook this voyage in 1919, is now observed as National Maritime Day.

First diesel engine ship
MV *Dwarka,* a modern D-class passenger and cargo ship of the British India Steam Navigation Company, entered service in 1947. Weighing 4,851 gross tonnes, it was 121.6 m (399 ft) long and 16.8 m (55 ft) wide. It had a service speed of 13.5 knots.

First shipping company
Freedom fighter V.O. Chidambaram Pillai set up the Swadeshi Shipping Company at Tuticorin (now Thoothukudi), Tamil Nadu, in 1906.

First woman marine pilot
Reshma Nilofer Naha (b. 4 February 1989) is the first and only Indian woman marine pilot in the country. She joined the Kolkata Port Trust in 2011 and became a trained marine pilot in January 2018. As a river pilot, she guides ships in and out of Sagar, and Haldia and Kolkata ports through the River Hooghly.

First solar ferry boat
The first solar-powered boat was launched in the country in December 2017. Named

Largest private port

Mundra Port in the Gulf of Kachchh, Gujarat, run by Adani Ports and Special Economic Zone Ltd (APSEZ), with its headquarters in Ahmedabad, is India's largest private port. It crossed the mark of 100 million tonnes of cargo handling in 2016, overtaking the government-owned Jawaharlal Nehru Port Trust near Mumbai, Maharashtra, as India's largest container port by capacity. Mundra Port is also India's biggest commercial port by volume handled.

Aditya, the boat is 21.18 m (69 ft 7 in.) long and 7.0 m (22 ft 11 inc.) wide. Constructed by the NavAlt Solar and Electric Boats Pvt. Ltd, it accommodates 78 rooftop solar panels and sails at a maximum speed of 7.5 knots. The boat seats 75 passengers and operates on the 2.5 km Vaikom–Thavanakadavu route in Kerala.

First hovercraft ferry
A diesel hovercraft service began between Surat and Ghogha Port in Gujarat on 10 December 1992, linking the two ports, 55 nautical miles (102 km) apart, in two hours.

First overseas cargo service
On 3 February 1948, a continental line for an overseas cargo service between India and European countries was inaugurated by the Scindia Steam Navigation Company, with the sailing of the cargo steamship SS *Jalabala* from Bombay (now Mumbai), Maharashtra.

Oldest operating port and largest riverine port
Calcutta Port, Bengal (formerly called Kolkata Port, and now renamed Syama Prasad Mookerjee Port, West Bengal), built by the East India Company and operating since 1870, is the oldest operating port in India. It is also the only major riverine port and the largest riverine port in the country.

First corporatized port
Ennore Port (now Kamarajar Port Ltd) on the Coromandel Coast, Chennai, Tamil Nadu, was the first Indian port that was a public company, and later became a corporatized port in 1999.

First private sector port
Pipavav Port in Gujarat, which was inaugurated in November 1996, has three dry cargo berths built as a single-length jetty of 725 m (2,379 ft), and a liquid cargo berth.

Largest covered dock
Hindustan Shipyard houses the largest covered dock at Visakhapatnam in Andhra Pradesh. The dock measures 240 m x 53 m x 11.25 m (787 ft x 174 ft x 37 ft) with an intermediate twin gate and undocking draft of 8 m (26 ft). It can accommodate ships of up to 80,000 deadweight tonnage.

First indigenous hovercraft
A twin-engine, air-cushioned hovercraft, made in 1987 by the Scientific Instrument Co. Ltd, Allahabad (now Prayagraj), Uttar Pradesh, had a 55 HP thrust engine for propulsion and an 8 HP engine for lift, with a payload capacity of 500 kg and a speed of 45 km/hr.

CAPACITY AT MAJOR PORTS
(in Million Tonnes)

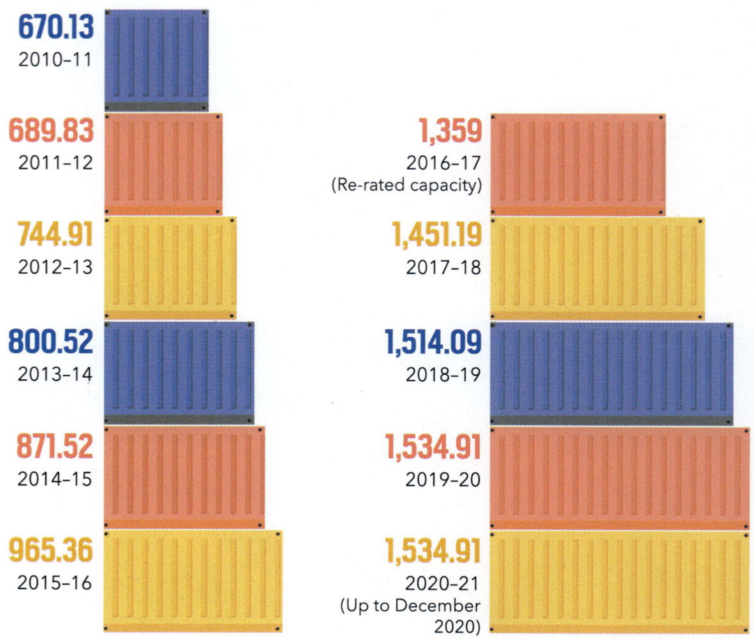

Data for 2010–21. Source: *Annual Report* 2020–21, Ministry of Ports, Shipping and Waterways, Government of India

First superfast catamaran service
A superfast catamaran service between Bombay (now Mumbai), Maharashtra, and Goa became operational from 14 November 1994. The 40 m long, 400-seater, twin-hull luxury catamaran was imported by Damania Shipping Ltd from Norway. It moved at 40 knots, covering 225 nautical miles (417 km) in 6 hrs 30 mins.

First roll-on–roll-off ferry service
A roll-on–roll-off ferry service began on 22 October 2017 between Ghogha Port and Dahej in Gujarat. The 31 km service reduces the travel time between the two towns from 7–8 hours to just over an hour. It can carry 1,000 passengers and 150 vehicles.

Only ship design and research centre
The National Ship Design and Research Centre (NSDRC) at Visakhapatnam, Andhra Pradesh, functions under the Ministry of Ports, Shipping and Waterways, Government of India. It was completed in April 1993 with help from the Netherlands.

Oldest shipping company
The Scindia Steam Navigation Company was started by Narottam Morarji, Walchand Hirachand, Lallubhai Samaldas and Kilachand Devchand on 27 March 1919.

At the end of 2021, India had a fleet strength of 1,463 vessels with a gross tonnage of 13,011,000.

MEDICAL SCIENCES

GENERAL

Earliest treatise on medicine
The Atharva Veda (1500 –1200 BCE), is the earliest known treatise on human diseases and medicine.

First Persian text on medicine
Ma'dan-i-Shifa-i-Sikandar Shahi was the first Persian text on the Unani and Ayurvedic systems of medicine, authored by Hakim Bahwa bin Khwas Khan during 1512–13 CE. It was printed in 1987 by Naval Kishore Press in Lucknow, Uttar Pradesh.

WR Largest healthcare scheme
Ayushman Bharat Yojana, announced as a universal healthcare plan by the Government of India in February 2018, is the largest healthcare scheme in the world. Aimed at providing free healthcare access to around 0.5 billion (50 crore) people in the country, the Ayushman Bharat Pradhan Mantri Jan Arogya Yojana (AB-PMJAY) was launched in September 2018. A paperless and cashless scheme, it involves e-cards being issued to beneficiaries and health insurance cover of up to ₹500,000 per family per year.

WR Largest survey sample
India's Annual Health Survey (AHS) is the first nationwide survey initiative to provide district-level fertility and mortality statistics. Begun with a baseline study in 2010–11 and a sample of 18.2 million people (3.6 million households), it is conducted in all 284 districts in eight Empowered Action Group (EAG) states, viz., Madhya Pradesh, Jharkhand, Bihar, Uttar Pradesh, Chhattisgarh, Uttarakhand, Odisha and Rajasthan. It reports vital indicators such as crude birth and death rates, sex ratios (at birth, 0–4 years and all ages) and mortality rates (maternal, infant, neonatal and under-five), separated by urban/rural and male/female data.

FERTILITY, CHILDBIRTH AND BABIES

WR Oldest IVF mother
On 12 October 2019, seventy-five-year-old Prabha Devi became the oldest woman to give birth, after conceiving through IVF. She delivered a baby girl, weighing 680 g, prematurely by caesarean section performed at Kinker Hospital, Kota, Rajasthan.

First IVF baby
Baby Harsha was born to Mani and Shyami Chawda on 6 August 1986 by the in vitro fertilization and embryo transfer (IVF-ET) method. This technique was used after three years of research by Dr Indira Hinduja of King Edward Memorial Hospital and Seth Gordhandas Sunderdas Medical College, Bombay (now Mumbai), Maharashtra.

First GIFT twins
The first twins, both of them male, born through the gamete intra-fallopian transfer (GIFT) technology, were born to Renuka and Vijay Thakkar on 5 September 1990 in Bombay (now Mumbai), Maharashtra.

First woman to give birth after a uterine transplant
Meenakshi Valand from Bharuch District, Gujarat, became the first Indian woman to deliver a baby after undergoing a uterine transplant on 19 October 2018 at Galaxy Care Hospital, Pune, Maharashtra.

Heaviest baby at birth
On 26 May 2016, Nandini, a 20-year-old mother, gave birth to a baby girl by caesarean section at a hospital in Hassan, Karnataka. The baby, whose birth weight was 6.8 kg, was reported to have been the heaviest one ever born in the country. The heaviest baby boy till then, who weighed 6.7 kg at birth, was recorded to have been born in November 2015.

Lightest baby
A premature baby girl, weighing 400 g and measuring 8.6 in. in length, was born by caesarean section on 15 June 2017 at Jivanta Children's Hospital in Udaipur. Rajasthan. She was kept in the neonatal intensive care unit (NICU) at the hospital for 210 days, under the care of Dr Sunil Janged, Dr Nikhilesh Nain and trained nursing staff, and was discharged when she weighed close to 2.4 kg.

MEDICAL INSTITUTIONS AND LABORATORIES

First hospital
The first modern hospital was established at Fort St George, Madras (now Chennai, Tamil Nadu), in 1664.

Oldest eye hospital
The Madras Eye Infirmary in Madras (now Chennai, Tamil Nadu) was set up in 1819. It is said to be the oldest eye hospital in India and Asia. It was renamed the Government

A first day cover commemorating the Ayushman Bharat Pradhan Mantri Jan Arogya Yojana

In the Economic Survey of 2022, India's public expenditure on healthcare stood at **2.1** per cent of the GDP in 2021–22 against **1.8** per cent in 2020–21 and **1.3** per cent in 2019–20.

A stamp publicizing the government's family planning programme

Ophthalmic Hospital in 1886, and is now called the Regional Institute of Ophthalmology and Government Ophthalmic Hospital. Locals refer to it as 'Ezhumbur Kanaaspatiri'.

WR First governmental family planning programme

India was the first country in the world to have government-sponsored family planning programmes, in 1952. The first private family planning clinic was opened even earlier in Mysore (now Mysuru, Karnataka) in 1930.

First medical college

Calcutta Medical College (now renamed Medical College and Hospital, Kolkata) in Calcutta, Bengal (now Kolkata, West Bengal), set up on 28 January 1835, was the first medical college to be established in India and Asia.

The number of undergraduate seats in government medical colleges have increased by 79 per cent and the number of postgraduate seats by 93 per cent since 2014.

First homoeopathic college

Dr L. Salzar from Austria began homoeopathic education in India in 1867. He influenced Dr P.C. Majumdar and Dr B.L. Bhaduri in Bengal, and in 1878, Dr Majumdar, with Dr D.N. Roy, Dr B.N. Banerjee and Dr Younan, set up the Calcutta Homoeopathic Medical College, Calcutta (now Kolkata, West Bengal), which was India's first homoeopathic college.

First homoeopathic company

M. Bhattacharya and Company Pvt. Ltd in Calcutta, Bengal (now Kolkata, West Bengal), was established in 1889 by Mahesh Chandra Bhattacharya from Comilla (now in Bangladesh), for making homoeopathic medicines.

First college of nursing

Christian Medical College and Hospital (CMCH), Vellore, Tamil Nadu, set up the first college of nursing in India in 1946.

A stamp commemorating he Tata Memorial Centre, Mumbai, Maharashtra, founded by Dr Darab Jehangir Jussawala, founder of the first cancer rehabilitation centre in Mumbai

First organized medical service

The Indian Medical Service was the formal collective name for the top echelon of the East India Company's and British Indian Army's medical service from the early 19th century up to 1896. Its three divisions – Bengal Medical Service, Madras Medical Service and Bombay Medical Service – were combined into a single service under government control in January 1897.

First dental college

Dr Rafiuddin Ahmed, the 'father of modern dentistry' in India, founded the Calcutta Dental College in Calcutta (now Kolkata), West Bengal, in 1920. By 1928, it was a well-known institution for scientific dental education in India.

First blood bank

Upendranath Brahmachari (1873–1946) set up a blood bank at Calcutta, Bengal (now Kolkata, West Bengal), in September 1939.

First medical school to offer oncology degrees

The Adyar Cancer Institute in Chennai, Tamil Nadu, is a non-profit cancer treatment and research centre set up in 1954 under the leadership of Dr Muthulakshmi Reddy. It was the first medical school in India to offer degrees in various sub-specialities of oncology, recognized by the Medical Council of India.

First centre for cancer rehabilitation

Dr Darab Jehangir Jussawala (1915–99) was a medical and surgical oncologist, medical writer, and director of the Lady Ratan Tata Memorial Centre in Bombay (now Mumbai), Maharashtra. Dr Jussawala was the co-founder of the Indian Cancer Society with Naval Tata in 1951 and established the Indian Cancer Rehabilitation Centre in Parel, Bombay (now Mumbai), Maharashtra, in 1956, which was the first such centre in India. He received the Padma Bhushan in 1975 from the Government of India.

First tribal medical college

A tribal medical college was founded in Attappadi, Palakkad District, Kerala, in 1993 with Achappan, a physician of the Kurichya tribe, as principal. Traditional knowledge of medicinal plants here has reportedly cured many people of conditions such as asthma, jaundice and blood pressure.

First corporate hospital

Apollo Hospitals, founded by Dr Prathap C. Reddy in Madras (now Chennai), Tamil Nadu, in 1983, was the first corporate hospital in the country.

First biotechnology department

Dr Indira Nath set up the first department of medical biotechnology at the All India Institute of Medical Sciences (AIIMS), New Delhi, for teaching and research in 1986.

First online clinic

Homoeopath Dr Mukesh Batra set up Dr Batra's Positive Health Clinic in Bombay (now Mumbai), Maharashtra, in 1982, which now has 230 clinics across 122 cities in India, Bangladesh, Dubai and the UK. He went online in 1997, which made him the first online medical consultant in the country.

First medical laser facility

India's first medical laser to destroy tumours with minimal blood loss was set up at the K.B. Bhabha Hospital in Bombay (now Mumbai), Maharashtra, in October 1993.

First sperm bank

Dr Aniruddha Malpani and Dr Anjali Malpani from Bombay (now Mumbai), Maharashtra, opened a sperm bank in 1990 to help infertile patients. It also had facilities for storing sperm of people who may be critically ill, for implantation at a later date.

First breast milk bank

Dr Armida Fernandez pioneered the establishment of Asia's first human milk bank at the Lokmanya Tilak Municipal General Hospital in Bombay (now Mumbai), Maharashtra, in November 1989.

First low-vision rehabilitation centre

L.V. Prasad Eye Institute, Hyderabad (now in Telangana), opened the Meera and L.B. Deshpande Centre for Sight Enhancement on 18 February 1997, to provide complete low-vision rehabilitation for patients by restoring optimal physical, psychological and social functioning.

First hormone replacement therapy clinic

A hormone replacement therapy (HRT) clinic was started by Urvashi P. Jha in March 1993 at the P.D. Hinduja National Hospital in Bombay (now Mumbai), Maharashtra, to deal with aspects of menopause.

First endoscopy lab

The first fully equipped endoscopy centre was established at the Bhatia General Hospital in Bombay (now Mumbai), Maharashtra, in October 1994. An endoscopy is performed to examine the interior of a hollow organ.

First indigenously developed vaccine

Rotavac, a rotavirus vaccine, was India's first indigenously developed vaccine, launched in 2015. Rotavirus is the most common cause of serious (often fatal) diarrhoea in children.

First department of minimal access surgery

Dr Pradeep Kumar Chowbey from Sir Ganga Ram Hospital, New Delhi, set up the first dedicated department of minimal access surgery (MAS) in Asia in 1995 and has trained nearly 1,000 doctors in laparoscopy in India and abroad.

First liver clinic

The first liver clinic opened at Sir Ganga Ram Hospital, New Delhi, in 2002 for treating patients with liver diseases.

First hospital with a stealth neuro-navigation system

The Sri Sathya Sai Institute of Higher Medical Sciences, Whitefield, Bangalore (now Bengaluru), Karnataka, set up in 2001, is the first in India and second in the world to acquire a stealth neuro-navigation system (for image-guided surgeries), which is one of the cutting-edge technologies in precision neurosurgery.

First hospital with a rooftop helipad

The eleven-storey Lakeshore Hospital and Research Centre, Kochi, Kerala, is the first super-speciality hospital in the country to have air, water and road ambulance services at its doorstep. Inaugurated in January 2003, this hospital with state-of-the-art medical services, has a helipad on its roof to facilitate heli-lifting of critically ill patients from airports in Kerala.

First rural medical college

Kasturba Health Society's Mahatma Gandhi Institute of Medical Sciences (MGIMS) in Sevagram, Maharashtra, was the country's first rural medical college. It was founded by Dr Sushila Nayar, a physician and politician, in 1969 and was affiliated to the Maharashtra University of Health Sciences.

52 per cent of all doctors in India are practising in just five states: Maharashtra, Tamil Nadu, Karnataka, Andhra Pradesh and Uttar Pradesh.

P.D. Hinduja National Hospital, Mumbai, Maharashtra: houses the first hormone replacement therapy clinic

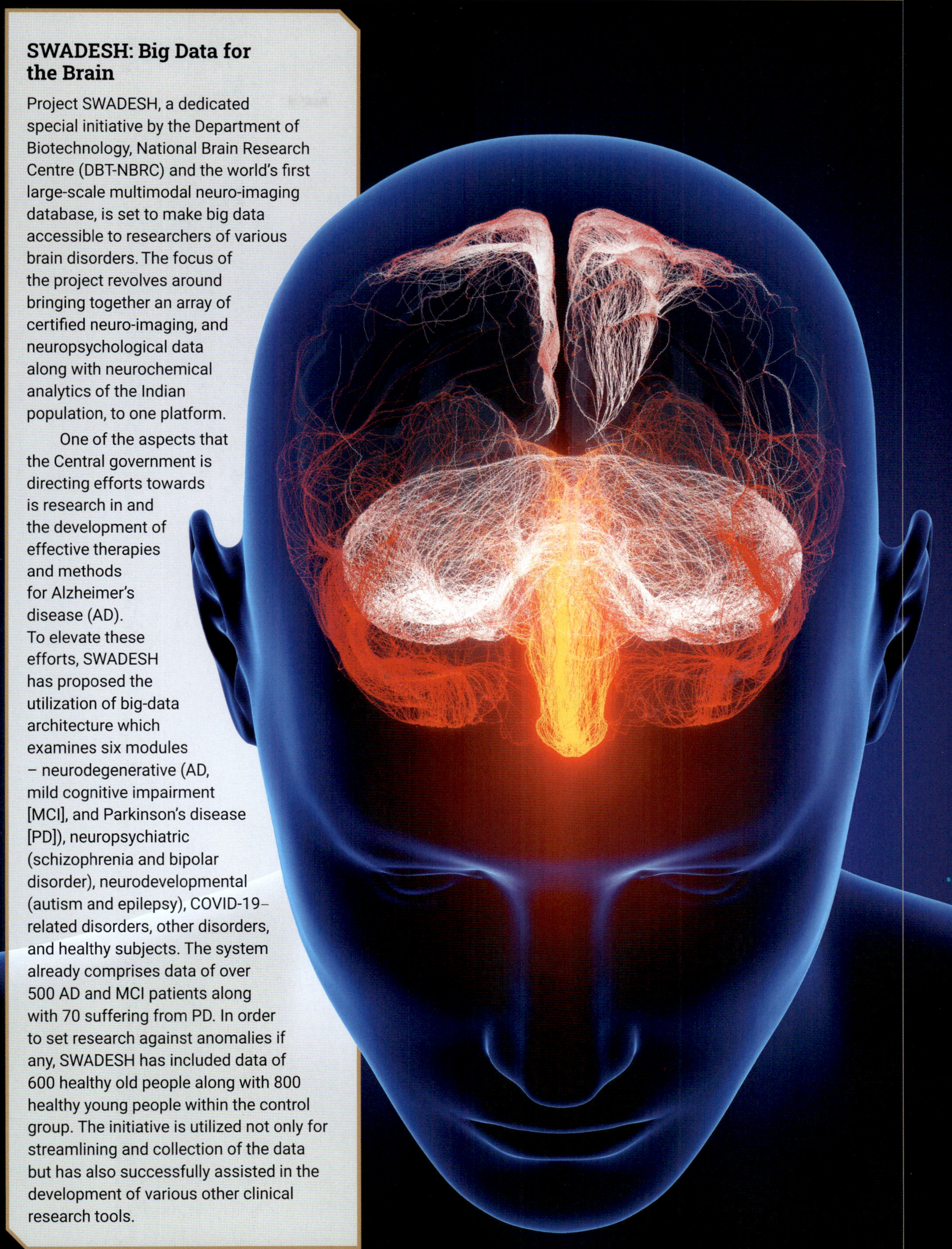

SWADESH: Big Data for the Brain

Project SWADESH, a dedicated special initiative by the Department of Biotechnology, National Brain Research Centre (DBT-NBRC) and the world's first large-scale multimodal neuro-imaging database, is set to make big data accessible to researchers of various brain disorders. The focus of the project revolves around bringing together an array of certified neuro-imaging, and neuropsychological data along with neurochemical analytics of the Indian population, to one platform.

One of the aspects that the Central government is directing efforts towards is research in and the development of effective therapies and methods for Alzheimer's disease (AD). To elevate these efforts, SWADESH has proposed the utilization of big-data architecture which examines six modules – neurodegenerative (AD, mild cognitive impairment [MCI], and Parkinson's disease [PD]), neuropsychiatric (schizophrenia and bipolar disorder), neurodevelopmental (autism and epilepsy), COVID-19–related disorders, other disorders, and healthy subjects. The system already comprises data of over 500 AD and MCI patients along with 70 suffering from PD. In order to set research against anomalies if any, SWADESH has included data of 600 healthy old people along with 800 healthy young people within the control group. The initiative is utilized not only for streamlining and collection of the data but has also successfully assisted in the development of various other clinical research tools.

Largest vaccine company

WR The Serum Institute of India in Pune, Maharashtra, founded by Cyrus Poonawalla in 1966, is the world's largest vaccine-making company by the number of doses produced and sold globally, with 1.2 billion vaccine doses supplied yearly to 147 countries.

First institute of advanced virology

The first Institute of Advanced Virology was inaugurated in February 2019 at Thiruvananthapuram, Kerala. It is affiliated to the Global Virus Network, which has 45 centres of excellence in more than 29 countries.

AIIMS: A hub of medical firsts

The All India Institute of Medical Sciences (AIIMS) is a public hospital and medical research university based in New Delhi. Established in 1956, it operates autonomously under the Ministry of Health and Family Welfare. It was:

- The first to start a medical toxicology lab in a medical college in 1986.
- The first to develop a DNA profiling lab in a medical college in 1990.
- The first Indian centre to perform a successful cardiac transplant in 1994.
- India's first minimally invasive surgery training centre.
- The first in the public sector to have an in vitro fertilization (IVF) facility, in February 2008.

First government-run department for disorders of sex development

The Postgraduate Institute of Medical Education and Research (PGIMER), Chandigarh, in July 2019, established the country's first government-run facility for children with disorders of sex development (DSD). The facility provides diagnosis of genetic and hormonal issues, surgical correction and psychological support for such children. Around 200 children per year can be treated here.

PUBLICATIONS

First to win a Pulitzer Prize for a health/medicine-related publication

Indian-origin American oncologist Siddhartha Mukherjee won the Pulitzer for General Non-fiction in 2011 for *The Emperor of All Maladies: A Biography of Cancer*, published in 2010 by Scribner, USA. The book was acclaimed as one of the 100 most influential books of the last 100 years by *Time* magazine and one of the 100 best works of non-fiction by the *New York Times Magazine*.

The Serum Institute of India, Pune, Maharashtra: largest vaccine company

DOCTORS

Father of plastic surgery

Sushruta is considered the 'father of plastic surgery'. He is believed to have lived around the sixth century BCE and pioneered the advancement of medicine in ancient India. His teaching of anatomy, pathophysiology and therapeutic strategies, featured in his *Sushruta Samhita*, were far ahead of his time.

First mention of leprosy

Susannah C.J. Kearns and June E. Nash, in an article for the *Encyclopaedia Britannica* (2008), stated that the first mention of leprosy is described in the Indian medical treatise *Sushruta Samhita* (c. sixth century BCE). However, *The Oxford Illustrated Companion to Medicine* holds that the mention of leprosy as well as ritualistic cures for it were described in the *Atharva Veda* (1500–1200 BCE), written before the *Sushruta Samhita*.

First doctors

- The first students to qualify as doctors were Bholanath Basu, Gopal Chandra Sheel, Dwarakanath Basu and Surajit Chakrabarti in 1839.
- Kadambini Ganguly (1861–1923) was the first South Asian female physician trained in Western medicine to graduate in South Asia in 1888 from the Calcutta Medical College (now Medical College and Hospital, Kolkata, West Bengal).

First psychosurgeon

M.S. Govindaswamy (1904–62) was the first psychiatrist to start psychosurgery in India. He combined psychological, medical, psychiatric and nursing aspects for holistic treatment.

First neurosurgeons

- Dr Jacob Chandy (1910–2007) started the department of neurology and neurosurgery in 1949 at Christian Medical College and Hospital, Vellore, Tamil Nadu. He initiated the first

The Indian medical tourism market was valued at US $2.89 billion in 2020 and is expected to reach US $13.42 billion by 2026.

Dr Jacob Chandy: first to start a department of neurology and neurosurgery

Representative image

Hope for Autism

A group of Indian researchers at the Jawaharlal Nehru Centre for Advanced Scientific Research (JNCASR), an autonomous research institute of the Department of Science and Technology (DST), Government of India, have shown the potential efficacy of 6BIO, a compound synthesized by them and tested for efficacy in a pre-clinical mice model, for a more effective way to treat Autism Spectrum Disorder (ASD) than current treatments. According to the authors of the study – Vijaya Verma, M.J. Vijay Kumar, Kavita Sharma, Sridhar Rajaram, Ravi Muddashetty, Ravi Manjithaya, Thomas Behnisch and James P. Clement – the compound shows tremendous potential for the enhancement of daily activities including but not limited to learning and remembering new tasks for those with ASD or intellectual disabilities (ID).

One of the primary problems is the lack of suitable genetic or pharmacological treatment for ASD or ID. Currently, the treatment is limited to addressing epileptic seizures or sleep problems. However, the introduction of 6BIO has proven to be useful in revitalizing neuronal function, learning and memory, sociability, and a decrease in epileptic seizures. The compound not only works as a catalyst for the restoration of neural functions during the human developmental stages (infancy and childhood) but also past the major brain development years (mid-childhood). The JNCASR team demonstrated that 6BIO can restore information processing and holds significant promise for therapies to treat ASD/ID using electrophysiology, which helps understand how neurons interact, and behaviour studies, which address general brain function.

training programmes in neurosurgery in 1958 and in neurology in 1962.

- Dr Subramanian Kalyanaraman (b. 1 January 1934) from Tiruchirappalli, Tamil Nadu, was the first Indian to receive a PhD in neurosurgery from the Royal College of Edinburgh, Scotland, in 1964.
- Dr Thanjavur Santhanakrishna Kanaka (1932–2018) was the first female neurosurgeon in Asia. She was also the first neurosurgeon in India to perform chronic electrode implants in the brain, having performed deep brain stimulation as early as in 1975.

First woman surgeon general

Mary Poonen Lukose (1886–1976) from Kerala graduated from the University of Madras (now in Chennai), Tamil Nadu, in 1909 and studied medicine in the UK. She became the first woman surgeon general of India in 1938 and was awarded the Padma Shri in 1975.

First woman aerospace doctor

Dr Parvathi Gopal from Bengaluru, Karnataka, joined the Institute of Aerospace Medicine in the Department of High Altitude Physiology in 1992. Her field of work included research and treatment to determine whether a fighter pilot is medically and mentally fit to fly.

Discovery of feeding centre in the hypothalamus

Prof. Bal Krishan Anand (1917–2007) was a famous physiologist and pharmacologist, born in Lahore (now in Pakistan). He was credited with the discovery of the 'feeding' centre in the hypothalamus in 1951 and regarded as the founder of modern neurophysiology in India.

First Lasker Award

Rustom Jal Vakil (1911–74) was the first Indian to receive the International Albert Lasker Award of the American Public Health Association in 1957 for the discovery of 'reserpine' extracted from the *sarpagandha* plant, used in Ayurveda to cure hypertension.

First doctor-to-doctor online session

A doctor-centric portal with the URL – *www.ranbaxyfordoctors.com*, hosted a discussion on 'Current trends in management of cardiac arrhythmia' on 28 August 2000, where 69 doctors chatted online. It was moderated by Prof. (Dr) K.K. Sethi, director, interventional cardiology and cardiac arrhythmia services, Sir Ganga Ram Hospital in New Delhi.

Most innovations by a medical professional

Dr Pankaj Garg (b. 27 December 1972), a colorectal surgeon from Panchkula, Haryana, has 16 innovations in the medical field to his name. Consisting of seven surgery procedures and nine treatment concepts, these have been published in national and international surgical journals from April 2015 to May 2019.

HEALTH CHECK-UPS AND SCREENING CAMPS

Most people screened – multiple venues

Lions Club International District 323 H-2,

under the leadership of district governor Mohinder K. Aggarwal and district activity chairperson Dr Sanjay Vora, organized a vision screening camp in 2015 in which 140,388 students were screened from 7:00 a.m. to 7:00 p.m. in 13 districts of Maharashtra on 8 October (World Sight Day).

Most people screened – single venue

An eye check-up camp organized by Netra Kumbh on 26 February 2019, at Prayagraj, Uttar Pradesh, from 8:00 a.m. to 5:00 p.m., saw a record visit of 6,660 people. The check-ups were done by ophthalmologists and optometrists from accredited hospitals from across India. Free spectacles were also distributed to many visitors.

MEDICINE AND SURGERY

Earliest cataract surgery

Ancient Indian physician Sushruta (c. sixth century BCE) had diagnosed that cataract was a disease of the eye lens, characterized by its opacity resulting in impaired vision, and had prescribed surgery as the only remedy. It was performed with a curved needle used to loosen the lens and push the cataract out of the field of vision. The eye would later be soaked with warm butter and then bandaged.

First medical symposium

The Vedic sage Bharadwaja, who is believed to have founded the Indian Ayurvedic system of medicine, presided over the first-ever symposium on medicinal plants in the seventh century BCE, possibly in the Himalayan region.

First conference

The first medical conference, inaugurated by the then viceroy of colonial India, Lord Elgin, was held in Calcutta, Bengal (now Kolkata, West Bengal), between 24 and 29 December 1894.

First international homoeopathic congress

The first International Homoeopathic Congress in India was held in 1967. It was organized and presided over by the renowned homoeopathic doctor Diwan Harish Chand. All the earlier ones, commencing from 1876, had been held in Europe and North America.

First separation of conjoined twins

Dr J. Dalal, paediatrics and neonatology specialist, surgically separated a set of conjoined twins (also known as Siamese twins) born to one Mrs Kambli on 11 August 1962 at Bhatia Hospital, Bombay (now Mumbai), Maharashtra.

Indian Scientists Find How Parasite Causing Black Fever Spreads

Scientists from Jawaharlal Nehru University, in a news-making breakthrough, have discovered how the Leishmania parasite, which causes black fever, targets and spreads faster in the body. Visceral leishmaniasis, also known as kala-azar or black fever, is a severe condition spread through bites from sandflies, which live in muddy areas and carry the *Leishmania donovani* parasite in their hair. If left undiagnosed and untreated, it can be fatal. In 2020, ten countries including Brazil, China, Ethiopia, Eritrea, India, Kenya, Somalia, South Sudan, Sudan and Yemen, accounted for more than 90 per cent of all new kala-azar cases reported to the WHO. The symptoms of kala-azar include anaemia, weight loss, spleen and liver enlargement, and irregular fever over many days.

The research shows that the Leishmania parasite takes control of SUMOylation, a critical regulator of many cellular, nuclear, metabolic and immunological processes, and lowers natural immune responses. The scientists were looking for a better understanding of the host–parasite interaction to find an efficacious and non-toxic therapeutic treatment for kala-azar. This discovery by the scientists will help facilitate further development of new medicines to manage this neglected but dangerous disease.

First open-heart surgery

Dr Reeve H. Betts, an American missionary, founded the first department of thoracic and cardiovascular surgery in 1948 at the Christian Medical College and Hospital, Vellore, Tamil Nadu, with cardiac surgical work beginning in 1950. Along with Dr N. Gopinath, he performed the first successful open-heart surgery here on a 12-year-old patient, Beulah, in 1961.

Dr N. Gopinath: first to perform open-heart surgery

Christian Medical College and Hospital's many firsts

Christian Medical College and Hospital (CMCH), Vellore, Tamil Nadu, is a private educational and research institute, which includes a network of primary, secondary and tertiary care hospitals. Founded in 1900 by an American missionary, Dr Ida S. Scudder, CMCH has many firsts to its credit:

- First reconstructive surgery for leprosy in the world (1948).

157 new medical colleges in the country have been approved in three phases and 72 are already functional.

- First department of neurological sciences (1948).
- First successful open-heart surgery in India (1961).
- First kidney transplant in India (1971).
- First virology department (1978).
- First bone marrow transplant (1986).
- First successful ABO incompatible (organ donated by a donor of a different blood type) kidney transplant (2009).

First heart-shrink surgery

Dr Naresh Trehan (b. 12 August 1946), a cardiovascular and cardiothoracic surgeon, performed the first successful heart-shrink surgery in India, which was also the first in Asia, with his team of cardiac surgeons, on a 50-year-old patient, Mani Ram Gurera, at the Escorts Heart Institute and Research Centre, New Delhi, on 21 May 1996.

First bloodless breast surgery

A team of doctors at the Dr B.R. Ambedkar Institute Rotary Cancer Hospital, AIIMS, New Delhi, carried out a major bloodless breast cancer surgery in September 1998, using ultrasonic waves.

First laser surgery on trachea

Dr Deepak Talwar, a leading pulmonologist, and his team at the Metro Hospital and Heart Institute, Noida, Uttar Pradesh, successfully opened up the lower part of a patient's windpipe. which had narrowed to 0.5 cm (0.2 in.) from the usual circumference of 2 cm (0.79 in.), in 1998. This was the first such surgery performed using laser technology.

First global telecast of surgery

On 11 June 1998, a team of doctors, led by leading cardiovascular and cardiothoracic surgeon Dr Naresh Trehan, operated upon six patients with heart ailments at the Escorts Heart Institute and Research Centre, New Delhi. The procedure was beamed live to 200 cardiac specialists and 1,000 delegates in San Francisco, USA. The back-end support was provided by the Medical Products Group at Hewlett-Packard.

Dr Kewal Kishan Talwar: implanted the first bi-ventricular pacemaker with Dr T.S. Kler

First cochlear implant

Dr Sandra Desa Souza was the first woman surgeon to perform a cochlear implant surgery in the human ear to treat complete deafness. The surgery was performed at Jaslok Hospital, Bombay (now Mumbai), Maharashtra, in November 1987.

First video-assisted heart surgery

Video-assisted thoracic surgery (VATS) was used for the first time in heart surgery at the B.M. Birla Heart Research Centre, Calcutta (now Kolkata), West Bengal, on several children suffering from a congenital heart disease called patent ductus arteriosus (PDA), in August 1994.

First craniopagus surgery

A team of 125 doctors and paramedical staff, led by Dr Deepak Kumar Gupta and Dr Ashok Kumar Mahapatra from the Department of Neurosurgery at the All India Institute of Medical Sciences (AIIMS), New Delhi, successfully separated 28-month-old twins Jagga and Kalia, who were joined at the cranium. The twins belong to Milipada Village in Odisha. The complex surgery was conducted in two stages, on 28 August 2017 (25 hrs long) and 25 October 2017 (20 hrs long).

First Maze III (atrial fibrillation) surgery

A heart surgery to cure arterial fibrillation (fast and irregular heartbeat) was performed for the first time in India by Dr Amit Banerjee, cardiothoracic surgeon, on 25-year-old Kiran Bir at the Govind Ballabh Pant Hospital, New Delhi, on 25 August 1994.

First coronary artery bypass surgery

Dr K.M. Cherian performed India's first successful coronary artery bypass surgery in 1975. He has pioneered several transplants at the Madras Medical Mission and Institute of Cardiovascular Diseases in Chennai, Tamil Nadu.

First bi-ventricular pacemaker

Prof. Kewal Kishan Talwar, cardiologist and former chairman of the Medical Council of India, New Delhi, and Dr T.S. Kler of Escorts Heart Institute and Research Centre, New Delhi, implanted bi-ventricular pacemakers on end-stage heart-disease patients on 8 May 2000 in two separate surgeries. This pacemaker ensures that all chambers of the heart contract and expand simultaneously.

Pioneering cataract removal

Cataract surgery was normally done through a 10–12 mm incision until 15 August 1998 when Dr Amar Agarwal pioneered the technique called Phakonit, in which a cataract was removed through a 0.9 mm incision at Dr Agarwal's Eye Hospital, Chennai, Tamil Nadu. This technique has now been adopted all over the world.

Smallest medical robot

The smallest medical robot measuring 120 nm (one nanometre is one-billionth of a metre) was created by Soutik Betal, a

INDIA AT HER BEST 75 YEARS OF INDEPENDENCE

AIIMS: THE PROMISE OF HEALTHCARE FOR ALL

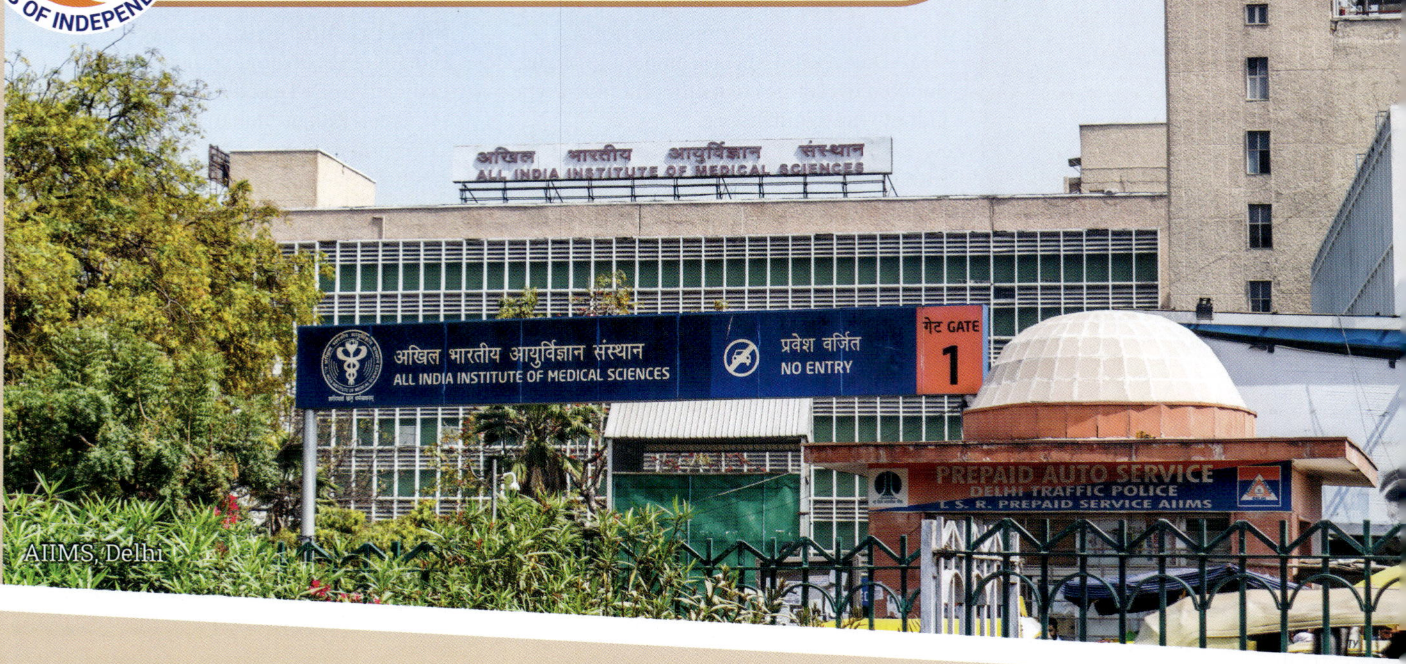

AIIMS, Delhi

Initiated as a pioneering and exemplary healthcare institution of independent India, the first AIIMS was proposed by the then prime minister, Jawaharlal Nehru, and set up in 1956 under the **All India Institute of Medical Sciences Act, 1956**. The original location for it was meant to be Calcutta (now Kolkata) in the form of modernizing an existing medical institute, but reportedly the then chief minister of West Bengal, Bidhan Chandra Roy, did not want the sponsorship of the Central government. Subsequently, Delhi became the chosen venue for this premier institute. Independent India's first health minister, Amrit Kaur, garnered funds for the institute from several quarters, including the Rockefeller Foundation, the Ford Foundation, and the governments of New Zealand, Australia, West Germany and the Netherlands.

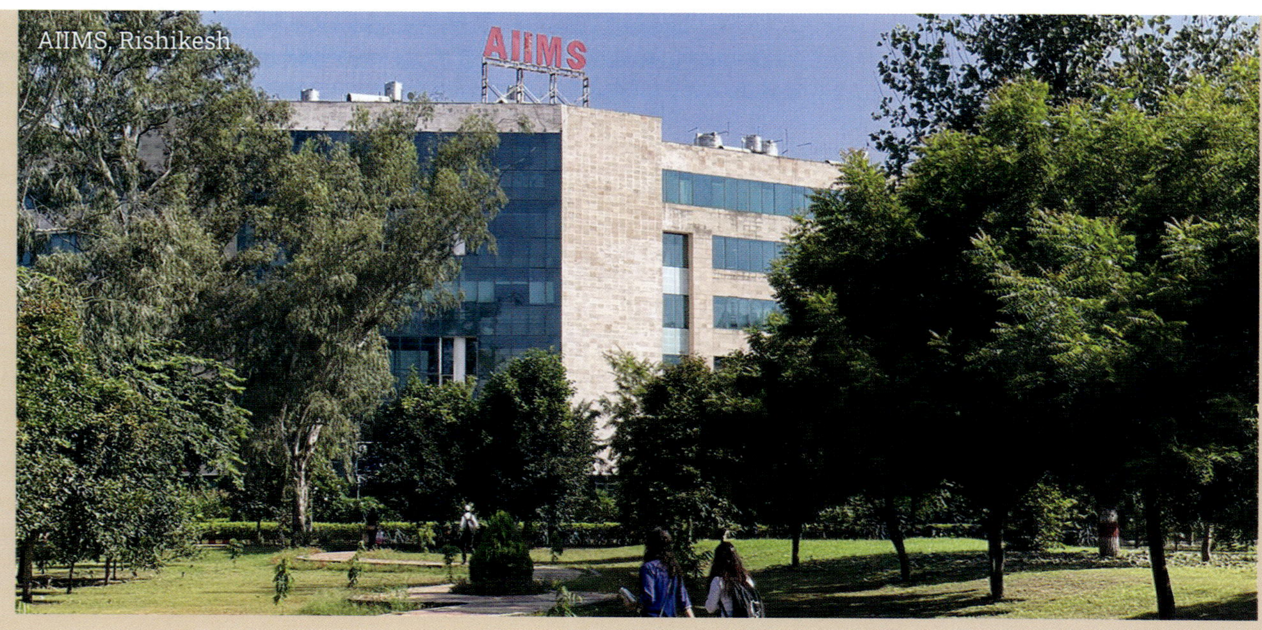

AIIMS, Rishikesh

AIIMS, Jodhpur

In 2003, the Government of India's Pradhan Mantri Swasthya Suraksha Yojana (PMSSY) initiative set out to ensure a more equitable access to affordable and quality tertiary healthcare across regions. However, it was only in March 2006 that, in Phase I, six medical institutes similar to AIIMS, Delhi were announced and executed through an ordinance from September 2012. These were **AIIMS, Bhopal** (Madhya Pradesh); **AIIMS, Bhubaneswar** (Odisha); **AIIMS, Jodhpur** (Rajasthan); **AIIMS, Patna** (Bihar); **AIIMS, Raipur** (Chhattisgarh); and **AIIMS, Rishikesh** (Uttarakhand), which are fully functional, along with being equipped with a block for treatment of COVID-19 patients and a COVID test lab.

In the second phase, **AIIMS, Rae Bareli** (Uttar Pradesh) was set up, after which the next phases saw four new AIIMS campuses: **AIIMS, Mangalagiri** (Andhra Pradesh) in 2014 and **AIIMS, Nagpur** (Maharashtra), in 2018; and later **AIIMS, Gorakhpur** (Uttar Pradesh), and **AIIMS, Kalyani**, in West Bengal, which started operations in 2019.

AIIMS, Bhopal

In February 2015, in Phase V, five more AIIMS were announced in the Union Budget speech, followed by two more in November the same year: **AIIMS, Avantipora,** and **AIIMS, Vijaypur** (Jammu and Kashmir), **AIIMS, Bilaspur** (Himachal Pradesh), **AIIMS, Bhatinda** (Punjab), **AIIMS, Guwahati** (Changsari, Kamrup District, Assam), **AIIMS, Madurai** (Tamil Nadu), and **AIIMS, Darbhanga** (Bihar), all completed between 2018 and 2020.

Phase VI of the initiative saw the announcement of two more AIIMS in the Union budget presentation in 2017: **AIIMS, Deoghar** (Jharkhand), and **AIIMS, Rajkot** (near Khandheri, Gujarat). **AIIMS, Deoghar,** began operations in 2019 and **AIIMS, Rajkot,** in 2020. In Phase VII, in December 2018, the Union cabinet approved the **AIIMS, Hyderabad** (Bibinagar, Telangana). It started functioning in August 2019. In February 2019, as part of Phase VIII, the Union Cabinet approved **AIIMS, Manethi** (in Rewari District, Haryana). New AIIMS hospitals have been announced to be located in Ranchi, Jharkhand, and Manipur. There are also proposals for establishing AIIMS campuses in Arunachal Pradesh, Goa, Karnataka, Kerala, Mizoram and Tripura.

doctoral research student from India, at the University of Texas, San Antonio, Texas, USA, on 10 November 2016. Capable of being remotely controlled electromagnetically and of interacting with biological cells, these robots may be used to advance research in cell-based therapy and for direct medication to cells for treating cancers and Alzheimer's disease.

TRANSPLANTS

First successful thumb transplant

Dr Tapeshwar Anand and Dr Mohan Das were part of a team of specialists who performed a 12-hr limb transplant surgery on a seven-hour-old baby Amy, at St Bart's Hospital, London, UK, on 24 March 2001. Her twin sister's thumb was transplanted on the hand of Amy (born thumbless) after the sister died at birth.

First successful liver transplant

The first successful liver transplant was performed at the Stanley Medical College in Chennai, Tamil Nadu, on 19 January 1996. It was the third transplant, the first two having been performed at Apollo Hospitals, Chennai, and AIIMS, New Delhi, respectively. In both cases, the patients died within a few days.

First womb transplant

Doctors at Galaxy Care Hospital, Pune, Maharashtra, successfully conducted India's first womb transplant on 18 May 2017 by transferring a woman's uterus to her 21-year-old daughter, who was unable to conceive. The procedure, which took 9 hrs using the laparoscopic technique, was performed by a team of 12 doctors.

First successful heart transplant

A team of doctors led by Dr P. Venugopal at the All India Institute of Medical Sciences (AIIMS), New Delhi, performed a successful heart transplant surgery in 5 hrs on 3 August 1994.

First paediatric heart transplant

On 14 June 1997, an 11-year-old boy underwent a successful heart transplant at the Institute of Cardiovascular Diseases, Madras Medical Mission, Chennai, Tamil Nadu. The surgery took three-and-a-half hours.

MEDICAL MARVELS

First scalp replantation

A completely avulsed scalp was replanted microsurgically on Gurkripal Singh by Dr Abraham Thomas and Dr Jaychandran of Christian Medical College and Hospital, Ludhiana, Punjab, in March 1985.

DISTRIBUTION OF HOSPITAL BEDS

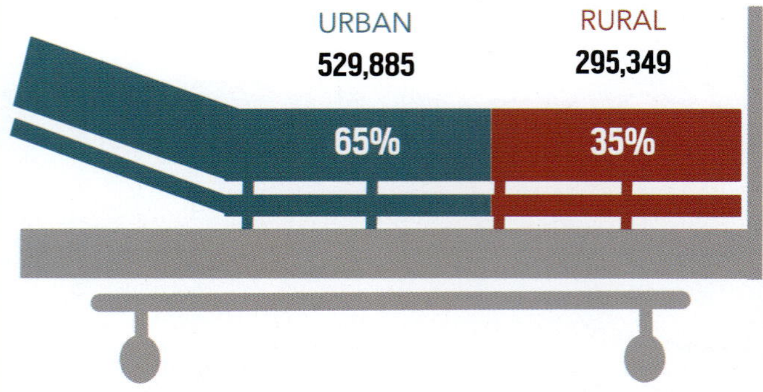

Source: National Health Profile India 2021, Ministry of Health and family Welfare, Government of India

First double (liver and kidney) transplant

Ganesh Nehru became the first recipient of a liver from his maternal uncle Mohan Ram and a kidney from his mother Hemlata simultaneously. The double transplant lasted 18 hrs on 17 April 2007, and involved 50 doctors and paramedics, besides intricate coordination between three operating theatres at Sir Ganga Ram Hospital, New Delhi. Dr A.S. Soin was the transplant surgeon in charge of the case.

Oldest to undergo hip surgery

- A team of doctors at the Postgraduate Institute of Medical Education and Research (PGIMER), Chandigarh, performed a hip replacement surgery on a 110-year-old woman (age based on her Aadhaar card), Manjauki, on 8 January 2020. The team comprised Prof. Vijay G. Goni, Dr Tanvir Samra, Dr Deepak, Dr Karan, Dr Pradeep and Dr Sumeet.
- Ram Lal, a 105-year-old patient, was the oldest to undergo a bipolar replacement of the right hip when he sustained a fracture around the hip joint. The surgery was carried out under Dr Sujoy Kumar Bhattacharjee, director, joint replacement surgery, at Metro Heart Institute with Multispeciality Hospital in Faridabad, Haryana, on 23 March 2018. The operation lasted 2 hrs 52 mins.

Oldest woman to deliver twins

Seventy-four-year-old Mangayamma Yaramati gave birth to a pair of twin girls on 5 September 2019 at the Ahalya Hospital, Guntur, Andhra Pradesh. Dr Sankayalla Uma Shankar delivered the babies by caesarean section. Conceived through IVF, the babies were the first children of the couple.

With a total of 1,317,594, Maharashtra has the highest number of healthcare workers, making up 13 per cent of all healthcare workers in the country.

Dr P. Venugopal *(right)*: led the first successful heart transplant surgery

COVID-19

First dedicated hospital

Reliance Industries Ltd (RIL) set up India's first dedicated COVID-19 hospital in a span of two weeks on 23 March 2020 in Mumbai, Maharashtra. Set up by Sir H.N. Reliance Foundation Hospital in collaboration with the Brihanmumbai Municipal Corporation (BMC), the facility at Seven Hills Hospital was a 100-bedded centre for COVID-19 patients. With all beds fitted with biomedical equipment such as ventilators and pacemakers, among others, the facility included a negative-pressure room that helped in preventing cross-contamination and infection.

First indigenous testing kit

A Pune-based diagnostic firm, Mylab Discovery, developed the country's first testing kit under virologist and research and development chief, Minal Dakhave Bhosale. The kit, which was named Patho Detect, was developed in just six weeks and reached the market on 26 March 2020. It gave the diagnosis in two-and-a-half hours compared to the six to seven hours taken by imported testing kits.

WR Largest repatriation exercise

An initiative launched by the Government of India, the 'Vande Bharat' mission was carried out to bring back Indians stranded in various parts of the world due to the restrictions imposed on air travel. Being pegged as the largest repatriation exercise in history, it was open to an Overseas Citizen of India (OCI) card holder, or any Indian who holds the citizenship of a foreign country, a valid visa of more than one year of that country or a green card, in accordance with the guidelines issued by the Ministry of External Affairs (MEA). Operating 64 flights to 12 countries from 7 May to 13 May 2020, Air India brought back around 15,000 Indians with the first two flights carrying 363 Indians from the Gulf to Kochi, Kerala. Carried out in 11 phases, Air India (including Air India Express) repatriated 2,113,972 inbound passengers on 13,997 flights and flew out 1,516,428 passengers on 13,989 outbound flights by 4 July 2021.

First clinical stem cell trial for COVID-19

Dr Abhijit Bopardikar, director, ReeLabs Pvt .Ltd, Mumbai, Maharashtra, conducted a Phase I clinical trial of intravenous administration of mesenchymal stem cells derived from the umblical cord and placenta in patients with novel COVID-19 virus pneumonia, with 17 patients at the LTMG Hospital and Medical College, Sion (West), Mumbai. The trial was conducted from 19 October 2020 to 15 May 2021.

Largest temporary hospital

By 9 July 2020, the Indian Army had established a temporary 1,000-bed hospital in Delhi under the guidance of CEO Operations, Major General S.S. Bhatia. Built by the Defence Research and Development Organization (DRDO) and TATA Sons Pvt. Ltd, it was manned by personnel from the Armed Forces Medical Services and had 250 ICU and 750 acute-care ward beds, with oxygen supply.

WR Largest lockdown

Around 1.3 billion people across India were asked by the Government of India to stay home for 21 days, starting 24 March 2020, making it the world's largest lockdown ever. While designated red and orange zones with high risk of infection had to limit movement to emergencies and essential goods and services, rules were eased in green zones with no confirmed COVID-19 cases. The lockdown was extended thrice up to 31 May, with a few relaxations.

India Leads Demand for COVID-Vaccine Equitability

After India and South Africa had led the campaign for temporarily suspending intellectual property limitations on COVID-19 vaccines and related technologies to provide developing countries access to them, at the 12th Ministerial Conference of the World Trade Organization (WTO) held in Geneva, Switzerland, a key deal was approved on 17 June 2022 by participating countries to waive off the intellectual property restrictions in part on the manufacture and production of COVID-19 vaccines for the next five years. The decision, which includes a patent waiver for the vaccines, was reached after nearly two years of discussions, negotiations and efforts. This will facilitate manufacturers in developing nations to access trade secrets about how to produce a viable COVID-19 vaccine. The agreement, however, excluded diagnostics and therapeutics, leaving many health advocacy groups and countries unhappy.

Longest object removed from the brain

Dr Rahul Prakash Modgi, neurosurgeon, and Dr Rajendra Gawatre, anaesthesiologist, operated on Pallavi Vijay Shelke, 17, at Shri Saibaba Hospital, Shirdi, Maharashtra, on 29 December 2012. They removed a 12 cm (4.72 in.) long iron rod, weighing 47 g, from her right fronto-temporo-parietal region.

Longest fistula removed

A 110 cm (43.30 in.) long fistula was removed from a patient by Dr Ashwin Porwal at Healing Hands Clinic, Pune, Maharashtra, on 10 May 2019. The surgery was conducted from 3:00 p.m. to 7:00 p.m. using the distal laser proximal ligation (DLPL) technique.

Largest small-intestinal tumour removed

A tumour measuring 21 cm x 19 cm x 13 cm (8.26 in. x 7.48 in. x 5.12 in.) was removed from the small intestine of a patient by Dr Karthik Babu Perumalla at Ramesh Sanghamitra Hospital, Ongole, Andhra Pradesh. The surgery was conducted on 1 March 2019 from 11:00 a.m. to 4:00 p.m.

Largest breast tumour removed

The largest breast tumour recorded, which measured 41 cm x 39 cm x 37 cm (16.14 in. x 15.35 in. x 14.57 in.), was removed from a patient by Dr Vikas Jain at the B.J. Hospital, Gondia, Maharashtra. The surgery was conducted on 25 July 2019 from 3:30 p.m. to 6:00 p.m. The tumour weighed 5.6 kg after it was removed.

Largest urinary bladder stone removed

Dr D.C. Patel operated on Maheshbhai Patel, a 49-year-old suffering from blocked urine, at Shree Sainath Surgical and Maternity Hospital, Dharampur, Gujarat, on 6 April 2017. Dr Patel removed a bladder stone 15 cm x 12 cm x 10 cm (5.90 in. x 4.72 in. x 3.94 in.) and weighing 1.365 kg. He was assisted by Dr Hemant Patel and Dr Nital Patel.

Heaviest ovarian tumour removed

WR • As per public domain information, the world's heaviest ovarian tumour, weighing 50 kg, was removed on 18 August 2020, at the Indraprastha Apollo Hospitals, New Delhi, from a 52-year-old patient, by a team of surgeons led by Dr Arun Prasad. The surgery lasted for three-and-a-half hours.

• *Malignant*: Kavita Khoiwal, assistant professor, Department of Obstetrics and Gynaecology, AIIMS, Rishikesh, Uttarakhand, along with her team of doctors, operated on a 24-year-old female patient on 21 August 2020 for the removal of the heaviest abdinopelvic mass. The weight of the cancerous ovarian mass was 41.1 kg, from which 36 litres of mucinous fluid was removed prior to removal and the remaining mass of 5.1 kg was removed subsequently. The size of the mass was approximately 60 cm x 50 cm x 40 cm (23.62 in. x 19.68 in. x 15.75 in.).

Heaviest kidney removed

Dr Puvvada Sandeep and three other doctors from his team at Ramaiah Medical College, Bengaluru, Karnataka, removed a kidney weighing 7.72 kg on 21 November 2019. Containing 3.12 litres of fluid, the kidney was

The telemedicine market is expected to reach US $5.5 billion by 2025.

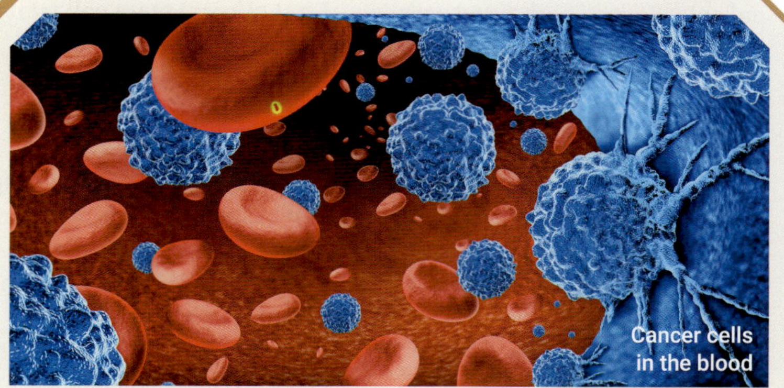

Representative image

AI-based Detection of Carcinogens

In an important breakthrough for the screening of novel drugs, researchers from the Indraprastha Institute of Information Technology (IIIT)-Delhi have developed an artificial intelligence-based model to detect carcinogens in chemical structures. The research on the software, named Metabokiller, was published in the journal *Nature Chemical Biology*. The research will be key because in the last many decades, many new drugs, as well as food items and cosmetics, have been later found to cause cancer. Also critical is the fact that, according to the study, approximately 5 per cent of cancers are heritable while around 95 per cent are caused by exposure to carcinogens (compounds) in the environment.

Gaurav Ahuja, assistant professor, Department of Computational Biology, IIIT-Delhi, along with Dr Debarka Sengupta, has developed six independent machine learning based models that meticulously scan every compound for carcinogen-associated properties. Other clinical and research institutes such as IIT-Ropar, Rajiv Gandhi Cancer Hospital and Research Centre, and the Institute of Genomics and Integrative Biology, under the Council for Scientific and Industrial Rearch (CSIR), New Delhi, have also participated in the research. What is unique about Metabokiller is that, unlike other machine learning where the reason for the prediction is obscure, it offers the underlying, interpretable reasoning for predicting carcinogens. The research team at IIIT-Delhi is now working on establishing a direct link between carcinogens and the mutations which they cause in the DNA.

VECTOR-BORNE DISEASES: NUMBER OF CASES

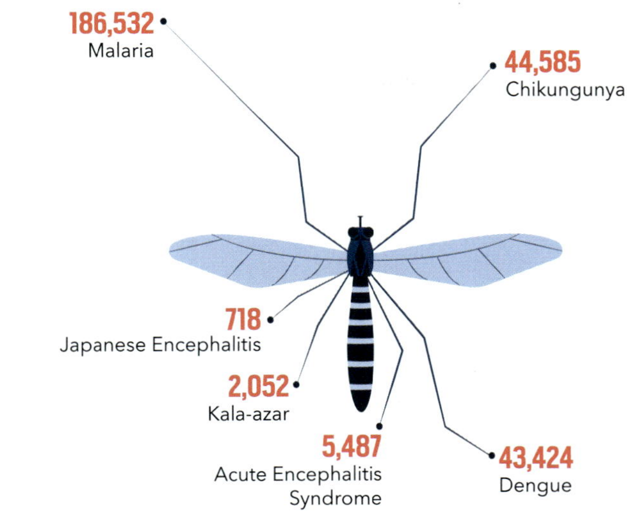

Source: National Health Profile India 2021, Ministry of Health and Family Welfare, Government of India

removed from a 53-year-old patient suffering from bilateral adult polycystic kidney disease (APKD) and chronic kidney disease.

WR Heaviest brain tumour removed

Dr Saraj Kumar Singh, Assistant Professor, AIIMS, Patna, Bihar, and his assisting team removed a brain tumour weighing 2.280 kg (2,280 g) from a 50-year-old male patient on 22 November 2021 at the hospital. The surgery to excise the tumour began at 12:26 p.m. and ended at 3:42 p.m., lasting 3 hrs 16 mins. The tumour measured 24 cm x 24 cm x 14 cm (9.44 in. x 9.44 in. x 5.51 in.).

Longest foreign body removed

Dr Sanjay Kolte, urologist and kidney transplant surgeon at Sparsh Urology and Kidney Hospital, Dhantoli, Maharashtra, removed a 154 cm (5 ft 0.6 in.) long soft electric wire from the urinary bladder of a patient by percutaneous cystoscopy extraction of foreign body surgery on 28 August 2012.

Largest bone tumour removed

Dr B.K.S. Sanjay, professor and head of orthopaedic surgery, Himalayan Institute of Medicine, Dehradun, Uttarakhand, removed a malignant bone tumour (chondrosarcoma) of the right femur, weighing 16.5 kg, from 35-year-old Naresh Kumar of Haridwar, Uttarakhand, on 10 June 2002. The tumour was 45 cm (17.71 in.) in length and 30 cm (11.81 in.) in width, with a circumference of 97 cm (38.19 in.) and a volume of 14,135 cubic cm.

Largest kidney stone removed

Dr Hemendra Shah at R.G. Stone Urological Research Institute, Mumbai, Maharashtra, removed a 13 cm (5.12 in.) wide kidney stone from a patient on 18 February 2004.

Largest urethral calculus removed

Dr Neeraj Kumar Agrawal removed a 5.6 cm (2.2 in.) long stone from a patient at Neeraj Lifecare and Stone Centre, Bareilly, Uttar Pradesh, on 21 August 2019.

Largest cystic tumour of the liver

Dr N. Bheerappa from the department of surgical gastroenterology at the Nizam's

STATE HEALTH INDEX

Top 5 Larger States

	States	Base Year (2018–19)	Reference Year (2019–20)	Incremental Progress
1	Uttar Pradesh	25.06	30.57	5.51
2	Assam	43.39	47.44	4.05
3	Telangana	65.74	69.96	4.22
4	Maharashtra	65.54	69.14	3.60
5	Jharkhand	44.16	47.55	3.39

Top 3 Smaller States

1	Mizoram	57.32	75.77	18.45
2	Meghalaya	25.35	43.05	17.70
3	Nagaland	23.57	27.00	3.430

Top 3 Union Territories

1	Delhi	40.17	49.84	9.67
2	Jammu and Kashmir	37.45	46.99	9.54
3	Lakshadweep	44.16	51.87	7.71

Source: NITI Aayog; There may be +/– 0.01 error in the Index score due to the difference in the variations in decimal points, but it does not affect the rank of States or UTs.

12,500 Ayush Health and Wellness Centres are planned in a phased manner for completion by 2023–24.

Institute of Medical Sciences, Hyderabad, Telangana, successfully removed the largest known cystic liver tumour (mucinous cystic neoplasm) in 2017. The 24-year-old female patient was operated on for a tumour measuring 40 cm x 28 cm x 15 cm (15.74 in. x 11.02 in. x 5.91 in.).

Largest thoracic tumour removed

The largest thoracic tumour was removed by a team of surgeons in December 2019 at the BLK Super Speciality Hospital, New Delhi, from a 54-year-old international patient from Tuvalu. The tumour, which measured 12 cm x 10 cm (4.72 in. x 3.93 in.), was removed through robotic intervention in a minimally invasive surgical procedure.

Largest oral (head and neck) tumour removed – in one piece

Dr Saurabh Gupta, assistant professor and consultant, Surgical Oncology, Max Superspeciality Hospital, Shalimar Bagh, New Delhi, as operating surgeon, removed a head-and-neck tumour from a 38-year-old male patient in a left commando surgery, which along with free alt flap reconstruction, took 11 hrs from 9:00 a.m. to 8:00 p.m. on 30 April 2020. The size of the tumour in this case of oral cancer was 18 cm x 12 cm x 8 cm (7.09 in. x 4.72 in. x 3.15 in.).

Largest kidney operated on

- Dr A.K. Hemal, Dr S.N. Wadhwa and their team from the Department of Urology, AIIMS, New Delhi, removed a non-functional kidney measuring 25 cm x 20 cm x 20 cm (9.84 in. x 7.88 in. x 7.88 in.), containing five litres of fluid, by laparoscopic nephrectomy in a unique operation with no incision, on 3 June 1996.
- A kidney measuring 40.5 cm x 22 cm x 12.5 cm (15.94 in. x 8.66 in. x 4.92 in.) and weighing 6.24 kg was removed by Dr Niket Kantilal Shah at Wanless Hospital, Miraj, Maharashtra, on 23 June 2017. It was removed from a 50-year-old patient suffering from adult polycystic kidney disease (APKD).

Most uterine fibroids removed

Dr Ravindra Keshavrao Shelmohkar removed 63 uterine fibroids from a 34-year-old female patient in an open abdominal myomectomy conducted on 14 April 2021 by him from 9:45 a.m. to 10:45 a.m. at PDEA's Ayurved Rugnalaya and Sterling Multispeciality Hospital in Nugdi, Pune, Maharashtra.

Surgery on heaviest woman

Forty-two-year-old Amita Rajani, weighing 300 kg, underwent bariatric surgery performed by Dr Shashank Shah at his hospital in Pune, Maharashtra, in 2015. She was bedridden for eight years before the surgery and had multiple risk factors. She lost 214 kg as a result of the surgery.

Rules for Pharma: Controlling Marketing Practices of Pharmaceutical Companies

The Central government has formed a five-member committee chaired and led by V.K. Paul, member (health) of NITI Aayog, to deliberate on an enforceable mechanism for regulating the marketing practices of pharmaceutical companies. The other members of the committee are: S. Aparna, secretary in the Department of Pharmaceuticals; Rajesh Bhushan, secretary in the Ministry of Health and Family Welfare (MoHFW); Nitin Gupta, chairman of the Central Board of Direct Taxes (CBDT); and a joint secretary (policy) from the Department of Personnel.

The committee will investigate related global best practices, existing provisions to regulate pharmaceutical marketing practices, and standardize and align mechanisms that can be implemented by the healthcare industry.

Current guidelines for pharmaceutical marketing are detailed in the Universal Code of Pharmaceutical Marketing Practices (UCPMP) issued by the Department of Pharmaceuticals that came into effect from January 2015. The Indian Medical Council (Professional Conduct, Etiquette and Ethics) Regulations, 2002, which comes under the Medical Council Act, 1956, elucidates the relationship between healthcare professionals and pharmaceutical companies. However, the UCPMP is voluntary and invites no legal penalty for violating the code. Meanwhile, the Supreme Court is in the process of hearing a plea seeking direction to the government to give the UCPMP a statutory basis.

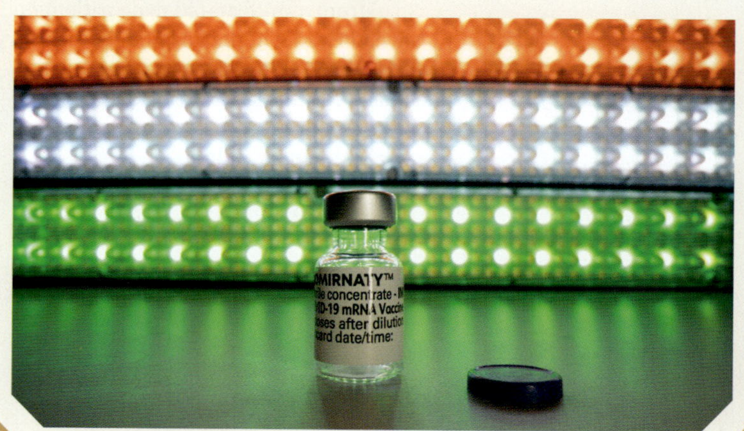

WR Surgery on world's heaviest teenager

Mihir Jain, then 14 years old, became the world's heaviest teenager to undergo bariatric surgery. He weighed 237 kg at the time, with a BMI of 92 kg/sq. m. The surgery was performed by Dr Pradeep Kumar Chowbey at Max Hospital, Saket, New Delhi, and a team of six doctors in 2 hrs 20 mins in July 2018.

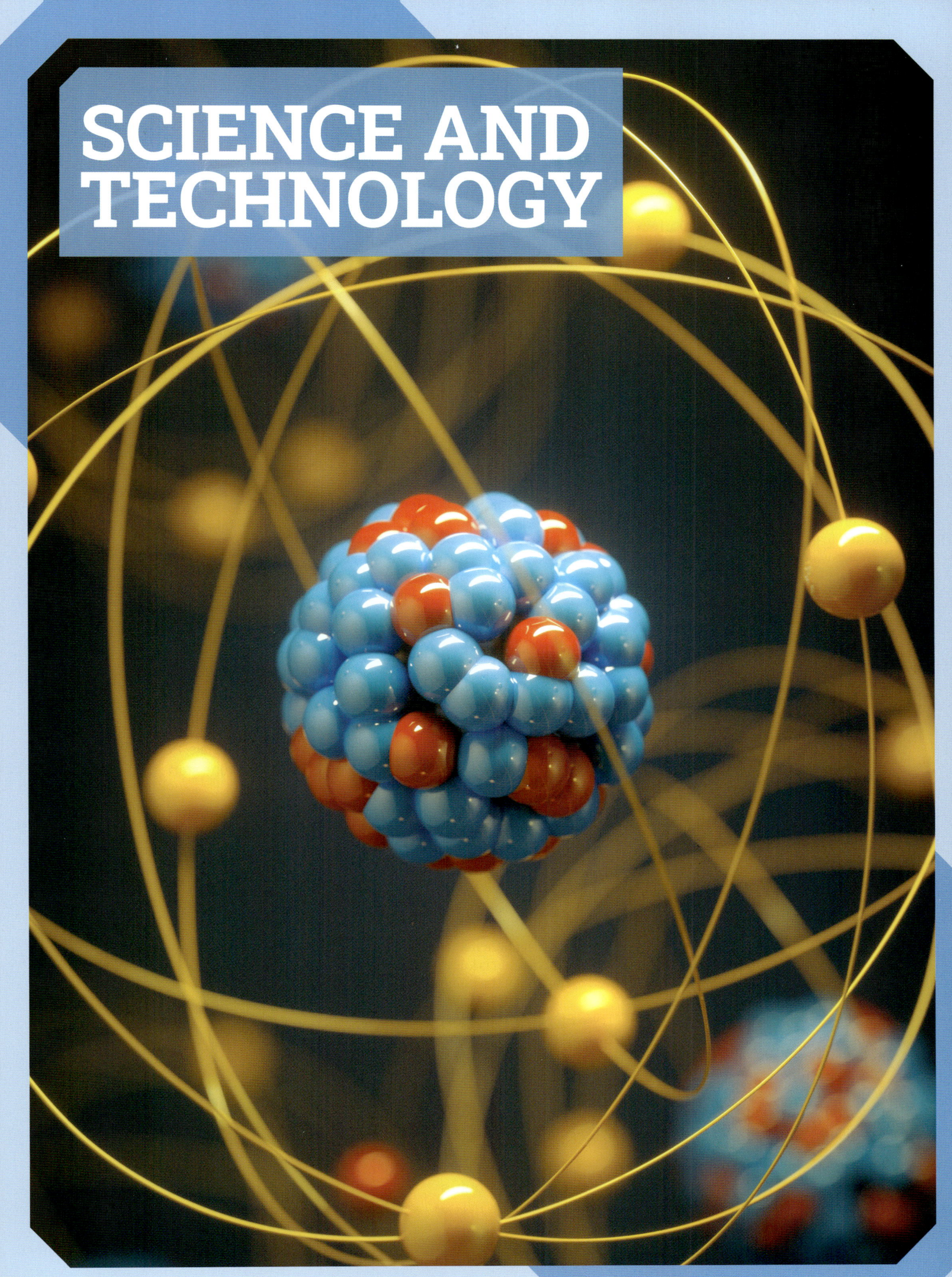
SCIENCE AND
TECHNOLOGY

FORMAL SCIENCES

MATHEMATICS

Earliest mention of mathematical series

Arithmetic and geometric series were mentioned in Vedic literature as early as 2000 BCE in the *Taittiriya Samhita* and in the *Panchavimsa Brahmana.*

Earliest treatise on geometry

The *Shulba Sutras* are the earliest known treatises that are related to geometry. Dating to the Vedic period, these texts are focused on the measurement and the building of altars. Baudhayana, who lived around 800 BCE, wrote the first *Shulba Sutra*.

Invention of algebra

Aryabhata (476–550 CE) from Kusumapura (Pataliputra) in Bihar is credited with the invention of algebra. He was also the first to approximate the value of π (pi) to 3.14159..., which is accepted today.

Earliest use of irrational numbers

The use of irrational numbers dates back to the *Shulba Sutras* (c. first millennium BCE).

First mention of geometry

In the first millennium BCE, Apastamba, the founder of a Vedic school, propounded practical geometry for the construction of sacrificial altars, which describes acute, obtuse and right angles.

Earliest magic squares

The oldest magic square that can be dated in India occurs in polymath Varahamihira's encyclopaedic work, the *Brihat-Samhita* (c. 550 CE). Varahamihira used a modified 4 x 4 magic square to indicate combinations and quantities of ingredients for making perfumes.

First to understand the idea of 'zero'

- Brahmagupta (c. 598–668 CE) was the first mathematician to treat zero as a number and present its mathematical operations.
- Bhaskara I (c. 600–680 CE) was the first mathematician to understand the properties of both zero and infinity, and to state that any number divided by zero equals infinity.

Earliest mention of the decimal system

Medhatithi, who lived around the ninth or 10th century CE, was the first to propound the concept of counting numbers in multiples of 10 and stated very high numerals in a systematic manner.

Earliest use of the decimal system

A Gupta inscription from 448 CE found in Allahabad (now Prayagraj) District, Uttar Pradesh, indicates that the decimal system was known in India at the beginning of the fifth century CE.

Use of sines and cosines in place of chords

In a significant contribution to trigonometry, Indian mathematicians changed the use of chords to sines and cosines, making the system much more convenient and the various theorems on triangles much neater. Starting with the *Arya-siddhanta* (c. fifth and sixth centuries CE), Aryabhata used a simple table for sines. Varahamihira gave the first clear statements of $\sin_2 A$ and $\sin_2 A + \cos_2 A$.

First study of infinite series

Founded in the 14th century by Madhava of Sangamagrama (c. 1340–1425 CE), who is said to have been born in present-day Irinjalakuda in Thrissur District, Kerala, the Kerala school of astronomy and mathematics (or the Kerala school) was responsible for notable contributions to the study of infinite series, trigonometry, geometry, algebra and calculus. The foundations for calculus laid by Madhava were further developed by his successors at the Kerala school, with many results that would later be repeated in Europe, including the infinite series for circular and trigonometric functions.

Earliest solution of the Brahmagupta–Bhaskara equation

Brahmagupta had nearly solved the indeterminate equation that is now referred to as the Pell equation. Bhaskara II (c. 1114–85 CE) had improved upon the solution long before Western mathematicians solved it. In Sanskrit, this equation is known as *varga prakriti* or the equation of the multiplied square.

First textbook on arithmetic

Ganita Sara Sangraha, written by the great mathematician Mahavira in 850 CE, is the first known textbook on arithmetic. The subject matter and its arrangement is said to be practically the same as that in present-day textbooks. It only lacks a chapter on decimals.

Discovery of differential calculus

Bhaskara II (c. 1114–85 CE), said to have been

India's biggest drone festival, the 'Bharat Drone Mahotsav 2022', was inaugurated by Prime Minister Narendra Modi at Pragati Maidan in New Delhi. The two-day event saw the participation of around 1,600 delegates including those from foreign embassies, armed forces, government officials, PSUs and drone start-ups.

born in Bijapur (now Vijayapura) in Karnataka, conducted mathematical operations that showed that he had invented calculus long before Isaac Newton and Gottfried Leibniz, who are considered its pioneers. He used calculus to determine the area and volume of a sphere and the daily motion of planets.

First to give the Gregory series

In 1502, Keḷallur Nilakantha Somayaji (1444–1545 CE) from Tirur in present-day Malappuram District, Kerala, devised the *Tantrasangraha* equation employed to give the approximate value of Π or pi (3.14159...). This is known today as the 'Gregory series' after it appeared in the works of later mathematicians James Gregory (1638–75) and Gottfried Leibniz (1646–1716).

D.R. Kaprekar, discoverer of the Kaprekar Constant

Discovery of the Kaprekar Constant

D.R. Kaprekar (1905–81) discovered in 1946 what is now known as the 'Kaprekar Constant' in mathematics. This is a constant (6174) that arises when one takes a four-digit number with at least two different digits and forms the largest and smallest numbers using its digits, and then subtracts the smaller one from the larger one. Continuing with this, one will always arrive at the number 6174.

Neelkantha Bhanu Prakash: fastest calculations by a human

Invention of the Mahalanobis distance

Pioneering statistician P.C. Mahalanobis (1893–1972) invented statistical tools such as the Mahalanobis distance and fractile graphical analysis in 1936. He was the first statistician to be elected a Fellow of the Royal Society, UK, in 1945.

First mathematical society

The Indian Mathematical Society (IMS) was the oldest organization in India devoted to the promotion of the study of and research in mathematics. With its headquarters in Pune, Maharashtra, it was founded by V. Ramaswamy Aiyer in April 1907. The society's first president was Dr B. Hanumantha Rao.

First to propose a theory on infinite dimensional representations

India-born American mathematician-physicist Harish Chandra (1923–83) created a theory for infinite dimensional representations in 1947, which first appeared in quantum mechanics when it was necessary to analyse the effect of symmetries on the motions of particles and waves.

WR Fastest human calculations

Twenty-year old Neelakantha Bhanu Prakash (b. 13 October 1999) became the fastest human calculator in the world after winning the gold for India in the Mental Calculation World Championship at Mind Sports Olympiad (MSO) in September 2020.

PHYSICAL SCIENCES

ASTRONOMY

Earliest observation of the Pole Star

Ancient astronomers Ashwalayana and Patanjali recorded observing the Pole Star (or *Dhruvatara*) in c. 1300 BCE.

The first astronomers

- Lagadha, who lived around 900 BCE near Srinagar, Jammu and Kashmir, was the first to systematize astronomy, the first to complete a text – *Vedanga Jyotisha* or *Jyotishavedanga* – on astronomy and the first to work out simple formulae to derive unknown quantities from known ones.
- Aryabhata was the first astronomer to deduce that the earth is round and that it rotates on its own axis, causing day and night.

First manual on the astrolabe

The astrolabe is an instrument for measuring the altitude of stars. Mahendra Suri (c. 1340–1400 CE), an astronomer, wrote a manual on the astrolabe in Sanskrit while under the patronage of ruler Firuz Shah Tughlaq of the Tughlaq dynasty.

First known record of an astrolabe

The Yantraraja, which was 276 mm (10.87 in.) in diameter, was designed and built in Ahmedabad, Gujarat, in 1607 for astronomer Damodara during the reign of the Mughal ruler Jahangir.

Evolution of the universe

Kapila, who lived around the eighth or seventh century BCE, was the first to think of and present a theory of the evolution of the universe. According to his philosophy called Samkhya, the existing universe evolved from an unmanifested, undifferentiated, infinite and eternal primordial ground state called *prakriti*.

WR First chain of observatories

About a century after European astronomers had verified Polish scientist Nicolaus Copernicus's theory that the Sun (and not Earth) was at the centre of the universe, Sawai Jai Singh II (1686–1743), the maharaja of the kingdom of Amber in Rajasthan, was the first in the world to build a chain of astronomical observatories, in Mathura, Varanasi, Delhi and Jaipur, from 1719 to 1737.

First modern catalogue of stars
The Madras or Taylor catalogue was made by T.G. Taylor, astronomer to the British East India Company, in 1844. The catalogue contained the positions of 11,015 stars, based on his observations of the night sky in Madras (now Chennai), Tamil Nadu.

First astronomical observatory
On 5 December 1786, William Petrie, an officer of the East India Company, made the first astronomical observations to calculate the latitude and longitude of the Masulipatnam Fort from his private observatory. This observatory on the terrace of his residence was fitted with an astronomical clock, a transit instrument and two or three telescopes. The first modern astronomical observatory, the Nizamia Observatory, was set up more than a century later in Hyderabad (now in Telangana) in 1908 by the Nizam's government.

First to observe a nova
Radha Gobinda Chandra (1878–1975) from Jessore (now in Bangladesh) was the first Indian astronomer to observe a nova. A nova is a transient astronomical event that causes the sudden appearance of a bright and seemingly 'new' star that slowly fades over weeks or months. He sighted the nova in the Aquila constellation on 7 June 1918. A pioneer of observational astronomy in Bengal (now West Bengal), Chandra was one of the first international members of the American Association of Variable Star Observers.

Oldest planetarium
The M.P. Birla Planetarium at Calcutta (now Kolkata), West Bengal, was established on 29 September 1962 by the Birla Education Trust. The planetarium coordinates the various activities of the Amateur Astronomers Association, which include telescope fabrication, astrophotography and organizing skywatching sessions.

Discovery of the Bappu–Wilson effect
Indian astronomer M.K.V. Bappu (1927–82), in collaboration with Colin C. Wilson at Mount Wilson and Palomar Observatories, USA, discovered a relationship between the luminosity of particular types of stars and their spectral characteristics. Known as the 'Bappu–Wilson effect', this helps determine the luminosity and distance of these types of stars. It was discovered in 1957.

Rings of Uranus discovered
- Prof. J.C. Bhattacharya and Sri Kuppuswamy from the Indian Institute of Astrophysics, Bangalore (now Bengaluru), Karnataka, discovered the rings of planet Uranus in 1976 at the Vainu Bappu Observatory in Kavalur, Tamil Nadu.
- Around the same time, US astronomer James Elliot and his team, aboard the airborne Kuiper Observatory, discovered the same rings during an occultation of a star by the planet.

Discovery of solar radio burst
In 1958, Prof. Govind Swarup (b. 1929) and A. Maxwell discovered a burst, called 'type U solar radio burst'. A pioneer of radio astronomy, Swarup was behind the concept, design and installation of the

Representative image

KIRAN: A Ray of Hope for Women in STEM
The issue of gender inequality in the field of science and technology has always been up for debate. To ensure that women make progress in the field, the Department of Science and Technology, Government of India, has initiated an exclusive scheme for 'Women in Science and Engineering-Knowledge Involvement in Research Advancement through Nurturing' (WISE-KIRAN). Various programmes of the KIRAN scheme have facilitated the careers of over 1,040 female scientists in the last three years along with 10,000 women from the grass roots and about 12,000 schoolgirls. Through the use of appropriate technology and the natural resources in their local environments, KIRAN aims to give economic and financial agency to women. Over the last three years, KIRAN has established many financial options for them, including 50 individual projects and 40 Women Technology Parks (WTPs).

Using the WISE value addition to the scheme, the government wants to help women in science to break the glass ceiling, be it in the form of representation in STEM (Science, Technology, Engineering and Mathematics) fields, academic and research associated assistance, upskilling at both national and international levels, or even something as small as mobility initiatives in case of relocations of employed female scientists, among others.

The First Five-Year Plan draft had a dedicated chapter on 'Scientific and Industrial Research'.

Ooty Radio Telescope near present-day Udhagamandalam, Tamil Nadu, and the Giant Metrewave Radio Telescope (GMRT) near Poona (now Pune) in Maharashtra.

Discovery of the variability of stars

In 1958, astrophysicist K.D. Abhyankar (1928–2007), professor of astronomy at the Osmania University in Hyderabad (now in Telangana), discovered the variability of two types of stars, called dwarf cepheid and the short period eclipsing binary BD-18 3477.

First university to teach astronomy

Osmania University, based in Hyderabad (now in Telangana), was the first educational institution in the country to start teaching astronomy and astrophysics at postgraduate and research levels in 1959. The Astronomical Society of India was also registered in Hyderabad, in 1972.

Largest optical telescope

The Vainu Bappu telescope of 2.34 m (7 ft 8 in.) diameter at Kavalur, Tamil Nadu, is the largest in Asia. It was built indigenously (including the mirror) in 1986 by the Indian Institute of Astrophysics, Bangalore (now Bengaluru), Karnataka.

WR Biggest sundial

The Samrat Yantra built by Sawai Jai Singh II, ruler of the kingdom of Amber in Rajasthan, in 1728 CE at Jaipur, Rajasthan, is the biggest sundial in the world. Its gnomon rises to 22.6 m (74 ft).

First discovery of an asteroid

R. Rajamohan (b. 1944), associate professor at the Indian Institute of Astrophysics, Bangalore (now Bengaluru), Karnataka, and his team discovered an asteroid (No. 4130) in 1988, through the optical telescope at Kavalur, Tamil Nadu.

Highest astronomical observatory

Established in 2001, the Indian Astronomical Observatory, under the aegis of the Indian Institute of Astrophysics, Bangalore (now Bengaluru), Karnataka, is located in Hanle (at Digpa-Ratsa Ri located atop Mt Saraswati) in Ladakh. It has the world's second highest optical telescope at 4,500 m (14,764 ft) above the mean sea level.

First woman president of the Astronomical Society of India

In 2019, the Astronomical Society of India elected its first woman president, Dr G.C. Anupama, a senior professor and dean at the Indian Institute of Astrophysics in Bengaluru, Karnataka. She has projects such as the Himalayan Telescope at the Hanle Observatory in Ladakh to her credit and is a member of an international team setting up a 30 m (98 ft 6 in.) telescope (TMT) in Hawaii, USA.

Osmania University, Hyderabad, Andhra Pradesh: first university to teach astronomy

First robotic telescope
India's first robotic telescope became functional on the night of 12 June 2018 at Hanle, Ladakh. It is the first one designed to observe dynamic or transient events in the universe. GROWTH-India, the facility at Hanle, is part of a multi-country collaborative initiative, known as the 'Global Relay of Observatories Watching Transients Happen' (GROWTH), to observe transient events in the universe.

PHYSICS

Earliest atomistic theory
Kanada, an ancient Indian natural scientist and philosopher, who lived between the sixth and second centuries BCE, composed the *Vaisheshika Sutra,* a text in which he explored and presented the relationship between cause and effect for the first time in relation to physics and philosophy.

WR First double radio source
Mrinal Kumar Dasgupta from the Institute of Radio Physics and Electronics, Calcutta (now Kolkata), West Bengal, discovered the first double radio source Cygnus A in 1953 in collaboration with R.C. Jennison at the Jodrell Bank Experimental Station in Cheshire, UK.

First solar heater
Prof. Shri Krishna Joshi from Almora, who lived in Allahabad (now Prayagraj), Uttar Pradesh, invented an apparatus for utilizing solar heat as a substitute for fire, named 'Bhanu Taap'. Also called the 'heliotherm', it was patented in 1900 and awarded a gold medal at the Industrial Exhibition of Calcutta (now Kolkata), West Bengal, in 1901.

First molecular distillation unit
Major General Sir Singh Sokhey of Haffkine Institute, in Bombay (now Mumbai), Maharashtra, installed the first molecular distillation unit in India to separate vitamin A from shark liver oil in the early 1940s. He was also the first Indian scientist to receive the Lenin Peace Prize in 1947.

First optical fibre
Narinder Kapary from the Imperial College, University of London, UK, invented the optical fibre in 1955. This is a thin and long fibre of glass through which light can travel without hindrance, whether it is bent or not. Optical fibres have a wide variety of applications in a range of fields, including medicine, computers, communications and the automotive industry.

WR First wireless demonstration
In 1894, scientist Jagadish Chandra Bose (1858–1937) at Presidency College, Calcutta, Bengal (now Presidency University, Kolkata, West Bengal), demonstrated the transmission of radio waves before Italian inventor Guglielmo Marconi did it in Europe, using very short radio waves or 'microwaves'.

First nuclear reactor
Apsara, the first Asian research reactor, at the Bhabha Atomic Research Centre (BARC) in Bombay (now Mumbai), Maharashtra, went critical in 1956. It was shut down in 2009.

First semiconductor laser
The Bhabha Atomic Research Centre, Bombay (now Mumbai), Maharashtra, developed a semiconductor laser in 1965.

First synchrotron radiation facility
The first synchrotron radiation facility in India was INDUS-1, set up in 2002. An advanced, indigenously built nuclear particle accelerator, it is part of the Centre for Advanced Technology at Indore, Madhya Pradesh.

First nuclear implosion
On 18 May 1974, India imploded its first nuclear device at Pokhran in Rajasthan. The test, code-named 'Smiling Buddha' was conducted at a depth of 107 m (351 ft). It yielded energy equivalent to 8–10 kilotonnes of TNT, and produced a 47 m (154 ft) wide and 10 m (33 ft) deep crater.

First prediction of hot superconductors
S.N. Ekbote and A.V. Narlikar from the National Physical Laboratory (NPL), New Delhi, were the first scientists to predict the presence of 'hot' superconductors based on their new theory of superconductivity formulated in

Jagadish Chandra Bose: first demonstration of transmission of radio waves

The Bhabha Atomic Research Centre, Mumbai, Maharashtra: housed the first nuclear reactor

1981, which challenged the then accepted Nobel Prize-winning theory.

First to measure ozone in the atmosphere

In 1985, M. Vivekananda and R.S. Arora from the Raman Research Institute, Bangalore (now Bengaluru), Karnataka, first measured the density and height distribution of ozone in the atmosphere over Bangalore by a simple ground-based technique using radio waves.

First advanced heavy water reactor

In 2016, the Bhabha Atomic Research Centre (BARC) in Mumbai, Maharashtra, designed an advanced heavy water reactor, which employed thorium instead of uranium as fuel. It was the centrepiece of India's nuclear power programme.

First Nobel Prize in physics

Sir Chandrasekhara Venkata Raman (1888–1970) from Tiruchirappalli, Madras Presidency (now Tamil Nadu), won the 1930 Nobel Prize in physics for his groundbreaking work in the field of the scattering of light, or the 'Raman effect'.

Only nuclear safety institute

With the inauguration of the Safety Research Institute at Kalpakkam, Tamil Nadu, on 20 February 1999, India became the second country after France to have such a facility.

Satyendra Nath Bose: first discovered bosons, with Albert Einstein

Google Honours Indian Physicist and Meteorologist: Anna Mani

Anna Mani

Google paid a tribute to Anna Mani in its Doodle on 23 August 2022 to mark her 104th birth anniversary. Born in 1918 in Peermade, Travancore (now in Kerala), Anna Mani was an avid reader, who went on to graduate from Pachaiyappa's College in Chennai (then Madras), Tamil Nadu, in physics and chemistry and win a scholarship to the Indian Institute of Science, Bangalore, to do research, and study meteorology at Imperial College, London, UK. She started her research career under the guidance of Sir C.V. Raman, the Nobel laureate. She made significant contributions to meteorological instrumentation and conducted research on solar radiation, atmospheric ozone and wind energy measurements. In this then male-dominated field, her work led to more accurate weather predications and the establishment of renewable energy. She went on to become the deputy director general of the Indian Meteorological Department (IMD) and, in 1987, was awarded the Indian National Science Academy's (INSA) K.R. Ramanathan Medal.

Discovery of the 'Krishnan effect'

In the 1930s, physicist Rappal Sangameswaran Krishnan (1911–99) from the Indian Institute of Science (IISc), Bangalore (now Bengaluru, Karnataka), discovered the 'Krishnan effect' – a new optical effect in the scattering of light. This led to the discovery of the presence of large clusters of molecules in liquid mixtures, glasses and colloidal solutions. It also helps in assessing the size of the scattering particles.

New method for thermal conductivity

Suresh Chand Jain (1926–2009), former director of the Solid State Physics Laboratory and Defence Research and Development Organization (DRDO), developed a new method known as the Jain–Krishnan method in 1952, which is now a standard method for measuring the thermal conductivity of solids at high temperatures.

Discovery of bosons

In the late 1920s, famous physicist and German Nobel Prize-winner Albert Einstein and Indian scientist Satyendra Nath Bose worked together on the Bose–Einstein equations, which pointed to a state of matter comprising particles, now known as 'bosons'. As researchers at the Joint Institute of Laboratory Astrophysics, Colorado, USA, they cooled thousands of atoms of rubidium to create the 'Bose–Einstein condensate'.

Discovery of mesons

Indian nuclear physicist Dr Homi Jehangir Bhabha and German physicist Dr Walter Heinrich Heitler presented the 'Cascade Theory of Electron Showers', called the 'Bhabha–Heitler Cascade Theory' in 1937 in Cambridge, UK, which explains the process of electron showers in cosmic rays. Bhabha recognized heavy electron particles in cosmic rays, which he named 'mesons'.

Discovery of helium isotope in cosmic rays

Dr K.M.V. Apparao (b. 1933), a scientist at the Tata Institute of Fundamental Research in Bombay (now Mumbai, Maharashtra), discovered an isotope of helium in cosmic rays, the energetic particles that fall down on Earth like a continuous rain from outer space, in 1961.

First carbon dioxide laser

Chandra Kumar Naranbhai Patel (b. 1938), an Indian-origin scientist in the USA, invented the powerful carbon dioxide laser in 1963, which resulted in making lasers a valuable tool in scientific research.

Indian Researchers Discover a Triple Active Galactic Nucleus

In a newly found galaxy, located quite close to ours, Indian researchers from the Indian Institute of Astrophysics, Bengaluru, Karnataka, along with an astrophysicist from College de France, Paris, have discovered black hole coalescence – three supermassive black holes from three different galaxies, forming a triple active galactic nucleus. Black holes do not emit any light, so it is very difficult to identify them. This rare space phenomenon was detected when the team was investigating an already recognized interacting galaxy pair. The team has successfully proved that the third cluster is a separate galaxy, and named it NGC7733.

A Galaxy Discovered in the Neighbourhood

At a distance of approximately 136 million light years from Earth, a faint but star-forming galaxy has been found by a team of researchers from the Indian Institute of Astrophysics, along with an astronomer from the College de France, Paris. The galaxy, which has a ghost-like appearance, had remained unnoticed due to its proximity and placement in front of a galaxy that is much brighter. The increasing strength of optical telescopes has made them sensitive enough to find incredibly faint galaxies, which account for up to 15 per cent of the universe's mass. Since data from the Ultraviolet Imaging Telescope (UVIT) on AstroSat assisted in the discovery of the galaxy, the team has given it the name UVIT J202258.73-441623.8 (or simply UVIT J2022).

PHOTOGRAPH: ESA/HUBBLE

Representative Image

The International Liquid- Mirror Telescope (ILMT) is located in the Devasthal Observatory, ARIES, Nainital

First and Largest Liquid-Mirror Telescope

Supernovae, gravitational lenses, space debris and asteroids are just a few of the many transients or variable objects that will be tracked by a new telescope facility atop a Himalayan mountain. India's first liquid mirror telescope – and the largest in Asia – sits at the Devasthal Observatory Campus of the Aryabhatta Research Institute of Observational Sciences (ARIES) in Nainital, Uttarakhand, and will be utilized to observe and examine the sky for galaxies and celestial objects. The innovative apparatus, created by astronomers from India, Belgium and Canada, collects and concentrates light through a revolving mirror with a diameter of 4 m (13 ft), constructed with a thin layer of liquid mercury.

The scientists involved, from all three nations, spun reflective mercury liquid until it curved into a parabolic surface form ideal for concentrating the light. Additionally, a thin translucent layer of Mylar was placed to ensure the protection of the liquid, and thereby the surface, from the wind. A sophisticated multi-lens optical corrector processes the reflected light to create clear pictures across a large field of vision, and uses a large-format electronic camera, positioned at the focus, to capture the images. The telescope will help not only in the detection of faint and diffused celestial objects but will also help in the collection of big data (of over 10 GB every night) that will further help understand the mysterious universe.

Presidency College, (now Presidency University), Kolkata, West Bengal: housed the first chemistry department at a university

Discovery of quantum Zeno paradox

Indian theoretical physicists Baidyanath Misra and E.C.G. Sudarshan, then conducting research at the University of Texas at Austin, USA, discovered the quantum Zeno effect (or paradox) in 1977. It is the quantum mechanical analogue of the proverbial adage 'a watched kettle never boils'. In 1989, the paradox was experimentally proven – 'Under continuous measurement, an unstable atomic nucleus that normally decays, was found not to decay.'

CHEMISTRY

First chemistry department

Chemistry was first taught as a subject in 1872–73 at Presidency College, Calcutta, Bengal (now Presidency University, Kolkata, West Bengal). Postgraduate courses were introduced in 1886. In 1889, chemist Prafulla Chandra Ray (1861–1944) set up the first organized laboratory here for research.

First heavy chemicals company

Behramji Sorabji Lalkaka (1880–1957) started the Pioneer Magnesia Works Ltd in 1915 at Kharagodha in the Little Rann of Kachchh, Gujarat, for the manufacture of magnesium chloride, the import of which was stopped from Germany due to the First World War. Magnesium chloride is used in a variety of ways in the chemical industry.

First chemicals company

In 1892, Prafulla Chandra Ray set up the Bengal Chemicals and Pharmaceutical Works Ltd at Calcutta (now Kolkata), West Bengal, using locally available materials, which led to the production of many chemicals and medicines indigenously. He was also the first person to synthesize ammonium nitrite (NH_4NO_2) in its pure form.

First Indian to receive the Chemical Landmark Plaque award

The Royal Society of Chemistry in 2011 honoured the life and work of Prafulla Chandra Ray with the first ever Chemical Landmark Plaque awarded to anyone from a country outside Europe.

First observation of spontaneous fission

Prof. Shyamadas Chatterjee (1909–95) from the Indian Physical Society in Calcutta (now Kolkata), West Bengal, first observed spontaneous fission – the splitting of a heavy nucleus on its own in uranium – in 1940, almost at the same time when scientists in Western countries reported its discovery.

First tokamak

The first Indian tokamak – essentially a magnetic bottle that can maintain conditions present inside the sun wherein enormous energy from nuclear fusion reactions is produced – named Aditya, was set up at the Institute for Plasma Research, Gandhinagar, Gujarat, in 1986.

First chain of national laboratories

Indian scientist and professor of chemistry Sir S.S. Bhatnagar proposed the setting up of national laboratories for research in individual fields and the Council of Scientific and Industrial Research (CSIR) approved five premier national laboratories. First among these were the National Physical Laboratory founded in 1947 in Delhi and the National Chemical Laboratory in Poona (now Pune, Maharashtra), in 1950.

Discovery of the isomerism of thiosulphuric acid

Prof. Priyada Ranjan Ray (1888–1982), director, Indian Association for the Cultivation of Science, Calcutta (now Kolkata), West Bengal, established for the first time the isomerism (compounds that have the same molecular formulae but different molecular structures) of thiosulphuric acid.

Discoveries in terpene chemistry

Dr Sukh Dev (b. 1923) from the Indian Institute of Technology, Delhi, discovered many new fundamental types of terpenoids, a class of naturally occurring organic compounds found in plants.

Discovery of phosphocreatine

In 1927, Dr Yellapragada Subbarow (1895–1948) from Bhimavaram, Madras Presidency (now in Andhra Pradesh), who went on to study at Harvard University, USA, and Cyrus H. Fiske of the same university, discovered the function of adenosine triphosphate, an organic phosphorous compound, as an energy source in the human cell, connected with the chemical mechanism of muscle contraction. He also discovered methotrexate (still used in chemotherapy) and diethylcarbamazine (DEC), which is used for effectively treating filariasis).

A Big Step towards Digitizing Biotechnology Ecosystems

INDIA AT HER BEST 75 YEARS OF INDEPENDENCE

In conjunction with the celebrations of the 75th year of India's independence, the Department of Biotechnology's Biotechnology Industry Research Assistance Council (BIRAC), has introduced special incentives for entrepreneurs in the field of telemedicine, artificial intelligence and digital health. The programme will determine 75 innovations to further R&D in the healthcare industry in the post-COVID world and find solutions to challenges that the pandemic has posed. BIRAC has deployed software on NICSI (National Informatics Centre Services Incorporated) to make the project proposal processes easier for transparency and good governance.

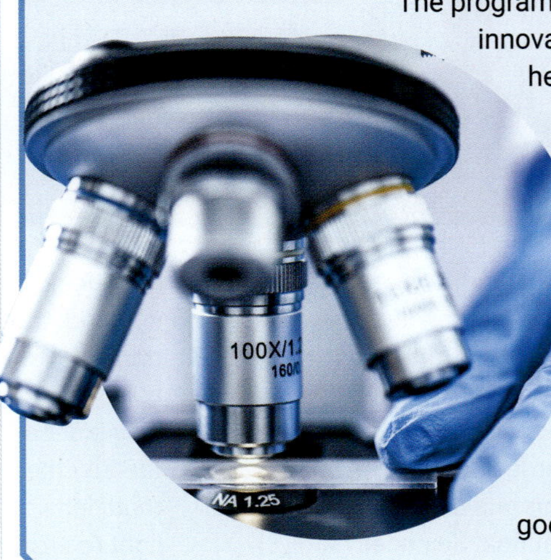

Largest scientific and industrial research organization

The Council of Scientific and Industrial Research (CSIR), which was set up in 1942, is India's largest research and development organization for scientific and industrial research for economic and environmental development.

Sir Shanti Swaroop Bhatnagar: first proposed India's National Laboratories

Discovery of tetracycline

Tetracycline, a life-saving drug, was discovered and developed in 1948 by a research group headed by Dr Yellapragada Subbarow at the Lederle Laboratories in New York, USA. An anti-plague drug, it helped save many lives in the 1994 plague epidemic in Surat, Gujarat.

GEOLOGY

First geologists

- Dr Henry Wesley Voysey, a doctor by profession, became the first professional

India's First Observatory to Monitor Space Activity to be Set Up in Uttarakhand

India's first commercial space situational awareness (SSA) observatory is set to be established in the Garhwal region of Uttarakhand. The project is being undertaken by Digantara, a space sector start-up. This observatory will be able to track objects as small as 10 cm (3.937 in.) that are orbiting the earth. It will also track space debris and military satellites hovering over the region. This will allow India to break into the space previously dominated by the USA with the latter's ability to monitor large spaces with multiple observatories. The data obtained by this observatory can contribute towards the reduction of potential collisions between satellites and spacecraft, thereby averting major losses.

geologist in India under British rule in 1818.

- D.H. Williams was officially deputed by the British in India to undertake the survey of coal-bearing areas in erstwhile Bengal in 1836.

First mention of seismological zones

Varahamihira, the ancient astronomer and scientist, was the first to mention seismological zones and the most earthquake-prone areas in his treatise *Brihat-Samhita* (c. 550 CE).

First geomagnetic observatory

The Colaba Geomagnetic Observatory in Bombay (now Mumbai), Maharashtra, was the first geomagnetic observatory to be set up in pre-Independence India. It was established in 1846 by the scientists of the East India Company to study the earth's magnetic field by using geomagnetic instruments.

First dinosaur fossils

- The Geological Survey of India (GSI) discovered dinosaur bone fossils from the Lameta formation of the late Cretaceous age (145 to 66 million years ago) at Raiyoli near Balasinor in the Kheda District, Gujarat, in 1981.
- Dinosaur egg clutches were also found at the site in 1982. Both the eggs and bones are preserved at the Indian Museum in Calcutta (now Kolkata), West Bengal.

Dr D.N. Wadia: first and only Indian to become president of the International Geological Congress

First megafossil from the Himalayas

In 1984, R.N. Lakhanpal, a scientist at the Birbal Sahni Institute of Palaeosciences, Lucknow, Uttar Pradesh, and his team discovered a leaf of the temperate palm *Trachycarpus*, the first definite megafossil record of the Miocene period (23 million to 5.3 million years ago) in Ladakh in the Himalayas.

First aeromagnetic survey of groundwater and minerals

The first aeromagnetic groundwater and minerals survey was undertaken as a collaboration between the Indian and Australian governments in March 1993.

First geoscientific data centre

The Geological Survey of India (GSI) set up a geoscientific data centre at Calcutta, Bengal (now Kolkata, West Bengal), on 3 November 1998. It is the largest repository of knowledge on earth sciences in Asia, Australia and Africa.

First underwater mining system

The National Institute of Ocean Technology, Chennai, Tamil Nadu, in collaboration with the University of Siegen, Germany, devised an underwater mining vehicle called the crawler, which extracts mineral-rich polymetallic nodules from the ocean floor. The mining system consists of a crawler, cutter and slurry pump. Mounted on board the ship ORV *Sagar Kanya*, its first test was conducted successfully on 14 March 2000 near Tuticorin (now Thoothukudi), Tamil Nadu.

First course in geology

Geology as a degree course leading to postgraduation was started at the Presidency College, Calcutta, Bengal (now Presidency University, Kolkata, West Bengal), for the first time in the country in 1892.

Largest mineral explorer

The Mineral Exploration Corporation Ltd, established in October 1972, is a public sector company with its corporate office at Nagpur, Maharashtra, and regional offices at Kolkata, Hyderabad, Ranchi, Jaipur and Nagpur. Its functions include mineral targeting, deposit assessment and mine development under the Ministry of Mines, Government of India.

WR Periodicity of geomagnetic reversals

J.G. Negi and R.R. Tewari from the National Geophysical Research Institute, Hyderabad (now in Telangana), put forward, in 1983, the theory that the flipping of the earth's magnetic field, i.e., the North Pole becoming the South Pole and vice versa, is related to variations in the gravitational force of the earth. They found that the frequency with which the earth's magnetic field flips is directly correlated to the periodicity of the orbit of the sun.

First official Indian geologist

Pramatha Nath Bose is considered to be the first official Indian geologist. He joined the Geological Survey of India (GSI) as an officer in 1880. He is known to have mapped the Vindhya Range as well as the igneous rocks of Raipur and Balaghat areas of what was then the Central Province.

First president of the International Geological Congress

Dr D.N. Wadia, president of the 22nd International Geological Congress, which was held in New Delhi in 1964, was the first and only Indian to become president of the International Geological Congress.

Discovery of iron ore deposits

Pramatha Nath Bose discovered the first iron ore deposit in Mayurbhanj region in present-day Odisha, in 1904, paving the way for the modern iron industry.

Discovery of vanadium

Abani Kumar Dey and J.A. Dunn discovered a new vanadium-bearing mineral in the Singhbhum–Mayurbhanj area, which is in present-day Jharkhand and Odisha, in the 1930s and called this mineral coulsonite (composition FeV_2O_4), the main source of vanadium in India. It is of strategic importance for making special steels. Abani Dey was the recipient of the First National Mineral Award in 1968.

OCEAN STUDIES

First course in oceanography

The first postgraduate course in oceanography was introduced in 1948 at Andhra University in Visakhapatnam in Andhra Pradesh.

First marine research institute

In 1974, the Central Marine Fisheries Research Institute was established at Mandapam in Ramanathapuram District, Tamil Nadu.

First oceanographic research vessel

RV *Gaveshani,* commissioned on 1 December 1975, was the first oceanographic research vessel. It carried teams of scientific personnel on various marine expeditions that could last from a few days to months.

Highest wave

Scientists on board the ship RV *Gaveshani* of the National Institute of Oceanography recorded a wave 13 m (42 ft 7.8 in.) high in the Arabian Sea off the coast of Goa in June 1979.

Representative image

Iron ore deposits: first discovered by Pramatha Nath Bose

First Antarctic expedition

Dr S.Z. Qasim, director, National Institute of Oceanography, Goa, reached Antarctica on 9 January 1982. The 21-member team left Mormugao Harbour, Goa, on 6 December 1981 on a Norwegian ship, MV *Polar Circle*, and returned on 21 February 1982. During the expedition, the team built Dakshin Gangotri, the first Indian scientific research base station in the Queen Maud Land area in Antarctica

Dr S.Z. Qasim: first to participate in an Antarctic expedition

First women on Antarctica

Structural geologist Sudipta Sengupta, and marine biologist and oceanographer Aditi Pant were the first Indian women to visit Antarctica, during the third Indian expedition to Antarctica from 3 December 1983 to 25 March 1984. The expeditions aimed to study atmospheric, biological, earth, chemical, and medical sciences in the region.

LIFE SCIENCES

BIOLOGY

Oldest biological fossils

Fossils of three-billion-year-old photosynthetic blue-green algae of the Archaean era (4 billion to 2.5 billion years ago) were discovered at Kashia in Orissa (now Odisha) in 1998 by scientists of the Birbal Sahni Institute of Palaeosciences in Lucknow, Uttar Pradesh. The latest find includes 1.6-billion-year-old red algae fossils in the Chitrakoot region of central India.

60 per cent of research and development institutions in the country belong to the private sector.

R.S. Paroda (left): established the first gene bank under the Indian Council of Agricultural Research

Discovery of earliest multicellular organisms

In October 1998, Pradip K. Bose, a professor at Jadavpur University, Calcutta (now Kolkata), West Bengal, found a site close to Churhat town in Sidhi District, Madhya Pradesh, where multicellular organisms with body fluid existed around 1.1 billion years ago. He discovered tracks on sandstone rock left by wormlike creatures about half a centimetre thick, while burrowing through the sea floor ages ago. This was the first evidence of macroscopic animals in India.

Rama Brahma Sanyal: first known zoologist

First zoologist

Rama Brahma Sanyal (1850–1908) joined the Calcutta Zoological Gardens in Calcutta (now Kolkata), West Bengal, in 1876. He wrote scientific papers on birds and sea snakes, and books on zoology.

First methane plant

Biomethane was first put to use in India in 1857 when a methane plant was installed in a colony near Bombay (now Mumbai), Maharashtra.

First anther culture

S.C. Maheswari and Sipra Mukherjee from Delhi discovered the anther culture technique in 1967, in which anthers (part of a stamen that contains pollen, in a plant) were placed on a synthetic culture medium.

Dr Kamaljit Bawa: first biologist in the world to win the Linnean Medal

First synthesis of a workable gene

India-born US resident Dr Har Gobind Khorana (1922–2011), using off-the-shelf chemicals, synthesized a total gene of the simple microbe *Escherichia coli* (which lives in the intestines of humans and animals) in 1976. He was awarded the Nobel Prize for physiology or medicine in 1968 for discovering the genetic code, which opened up the possibility of producing DNA in a laboratory. He shared the prize with US scientists Robert W. Holley and Marshall W. Nirenberg.

First to extract insulin from a plant

In the early 1980s, Pushpa Khanna, professor at the University of Rajasthan, Jaipur, was the first to extract an insulin-like substance from bitter gourd. That substance is an active ingredient called polypeptide-P, which lowers blood sugar in the body. Insulin is currently extracted from animal pancreas for the treatment of diabetes.

First national gene bank

R.S. Paroda, director general of the Indian Council of Agricultural Research, Delhi, established the first National Gene Bank in Delhi in 1985.

First biocentre

The M.S. Swaminathan Foundation, Chennai, Tamil Nadu, opened a biocentre in Pillayarkuppam Village in Pondicherry (now Puducherry) on 10 April 1999. This centre functions as a demonstration, training, information dissemination and service unit for sustainable food security.

First clone of hepatitis E virus

Dr S.K. Panda, professor of pathology, and his support team of scientists at the All India Institute of Medical Sciences (AIIMS), New Delhi, genetically engineered a clone of the hepatitis E virus in 1996.

First biologist to win the Linnean Medal

In 2018, Dr Kamaljit Bawa, president of the Ashoka Trust for Research in Ecology and the Environment (ATREE), and distinguished professor of biology at the University of Massachusetts, Boston, USA, was awarded the Linnean Medal for his pioneering research in the field of conservation biology. He researched biodiversity, the evolution of tropical plants, deforestation and non-timber forest products in Central America, the Western Ghats and the Himalayas.

First to isolate insulin-blocking enzyme

In 2013, India-born Kanwal Gambhir from Harvard University, USA, and his co-workers isolated an insulin-blocking enzyme. As insulin controls sugar levels in blood, this discovery had far-reaching implications in the control of diabetes, cardiovascular diseases and cancer.

Discovery of gymnosperms
In 1948, Birbal Sahni (1891–1949), a pioneering palaeontologist, discovered Pentoxyleae (gymnosperms), a plant group belonging to the Jurassic period (208 to 145 million years ago).

Discovery of the cholera exotoxin
S.C. Seal from the All India Institute of Hygiene and Public Health, Calcutta (now Kolkata, West Bengal), discovered cholera exotoxin in the early 1940s. The vaccine based on this helped in the eradication of cholera epidemics in India.

Discovery of seminal plasmin
Pushpa M. Bhargava and E.S.R. Reddy from the Regional Research Laboratory, Hyderabad (now in Telangana), discovered the protein seminal plasmin in the seminal fluid of a bull in 1979. This is a potent antimicrobial agent active on a wide range of micro-organisms, such as yeast.

First bamboo tissue culture
A.F. Mascarenhas, R.S. Nadgauda and V.A. Parasharami from the National Chemical Laboratory in Pune, Maharashtra, worked to produce a tissue culture of bamboo in 1990.

First human organ regeneration
In 2001, Dr Balakrishna Ganpatrao Matapurkar from Maulana Azad Medical College, New Delhi, was granted US Patent No. 6227202 (from 1995) for enabling regeneration of mammalian organs in the body at the site of old and diseased organs. He used unique stem cells in the body to regenerate organs like the uterus, urethra and ureters in animals, and large tendons in the human abdomen.

INTERDISCIPLINARY AND APPLIED SCIENCES

COMPUTERS

First indigenous chip
The Graphics and Intelligence-based Script Technology (GIST), developed by the Centre for Development of Advanced Computing (C-DAC), hit the market in the 1990s. While it was designed especially for land records departments based in different climatic zones, where protection from dust and other vagaries is not always available, it was also used by industries and public information systems.

First analogue computer
Biswaranjan Nag (1932–2004), former professor of radio physics and electronics at the Institute for Radio Physics and Electronics (IRPE), Calcutta (now Kolkata), West Bengal, built the first indigenous analogue computer (also called a differential analyser) in 1957.

First digital computer
The British-built HEC-2M installed at the Indian Statistical Institute in Calcutta (now Kolkata), West Bengal, in 1955. In 1964, the first indigenous computer, ISIJU-1, was developed by the Jadavpur University and the Indian Statistical Institute.

First indigenous palmtop computer
In 1995, a team of engineers working for Signals and Systems India Private Ltd, headquartered in Gurugram, Haryana, built the country's first indigenous palmtop computer suitable for a variety of industrial and field applications.

First Indian to obtain a PhD in computer science
Dr Raj Reddy (b. 13 June 1937), the dean of the School of Computer Science, Carnegie Mellon

India plans to launch its first mission to Venus in 2024 when Earth and Venus are aligned close enough for spacecraft to be put in the planet's orbit using the minimum amount of propellant needed for this.

HEC-2M: first digital computer

First Private Sector Space Launches

On 24 June 2022, the Indian Space Promotion and Authorization Centre (IN-SPACe) authorized Dhruva Space Pvt. Ltd, Hyderabad, Telangana, and Digantara Research and Technologies Pvt. Ltd, Bengaluru, Karnataka, to launch their payloads. This marked the beginning of private sector space launches in India. Dhruva Space's Dhruva Space Satellite Orbital Deployer (DSOD 1U), a technology payload, along with Digantara's ROBust Integrating Proton Fluence Meter (ROBI), a proton dosimeter payload, were carried onboard the PSLV Orbital Experimental Module (POEM).

In November 2020, the worldwide TOP500 project ranked India at number 111 in the world, based on the number of supercomputer systems it has.

University, Pittsburgh, USA, was the first Indian with a PhD in computer science, which he obtained in 1966 from Stanford University, USA. He was also the first person of Asian origin to receive the Association for Computing Machinery (ACM) Turing Award, in 1994, then the highest award in computer science, for his work in the field of artificial intelligence.

First powerful commercial computer

In 2001, Tata Consultancy Services (TCS) commissioned the 64-bit z-Series e-Server from IBM to become the first organization in South Asia to adopt the then latest technology being used in mainframe computing.

Fastest supercomputers

- In January 2018, India unveiled Pratyush and Mihir, an array of computers that are able to output a peak power of 6.8 petaflops (one petaflop is a million billion floating-point operations per second) across two sites – the Indian Institute of Tropical Meteorology, Pune, Maharashtra, and the National Centre for Medium Range Weather Forecast, Noida, Uttar Pradesh. The combination is dedicated to weather and climate research.
- A high-performance computing – artificial intelligence (HPC–AI) supercomputer, established under the National Supercomputing Mission (NSM), PARAM Siddhi–AI, was conceived by C-DAC, Pune, Maharashtra, and developed jointly with the support of the Department of Science and Technology, Ministry of Electronics and Information Technology, Government of India. Able to output a peak power of 6.5 petaflops, the supercomputer is used for research efforts in a wide range of areas such as healthcare, agricultural technology, cybersecurity, robotics and more. In November 2020, PARAM Siddhi-AI ranked 63rd among the top 500 most powerful supercomputers in the world.

First indigenous supercomputer

Developed by C-DAC in Pune, Maharashtra, in 1991, PARAM 8000 was capable of one billion calculations per second. The then director of C-DAC, Dr Vijay P. Bhatkar, under whom this project was conducted, is considered to be the architect of India's national initiative in supercomputing.

First supercomputer

On 25 March 1989, the Supercomputer Cray XMP-14 was installed as a key facility at the National Centre for Medium Range Weather Forecasting, New Delhi, to facilitate medium-range weather forecasting and agrometeorology programmes.

First powerful indigenous supercomputer

PARAM 10000, also developed by C-DAC under Dr Vijay P. Bhatkar's directorship, in 1998, was the first powerful indigenous supercomputer, capable of 100 billion calculations per second. It is housed at the National PARAM Supercomputing Facility (NPSF) at C-DAC, Pune, Maharashtra.

First to invent a new and speedy algorithm

In 1984, India-born mathematician Dr Narendra Karmarkar from Bell Laboratories in New Jersey, USA, introduced a new algorithm, called 'Karmarkar's algorithm', which solved linear programming efficiently, and helped computers find solutions to simultaneous inequalities very quickly. It solved problems 50 to 100 times faster than the methods known at the time.

First smallest multimedia notebook

In 1997, Bangalore-Ncore Technology's multimedia sub-notebook computer called the Yantra, which weighed just 2.1 kg, was the lightest laptop in the world. The Yantra occupied less than half of a briefcase, had a CD-ROM, a built-in sound blaster, two PCMCIA (Personal Computer Memory Card International Association) card slots and a small yet powerful battery built to last for more than three years.

First Super Fab Lab

The first super fab lab (fabrication laboratory) of the country was inaugurated via remote control from the Government Polytechnic College, Palakkad, Kerala, on 25 January 2020. Located at the Integrated Startup Complex of the Kerala Startup Mission (KSUM), Kalamassery, Kochi, the lab offers digital fabrication and computation, and was launched in collaboration with MIT (Massachusetts Institute of Technology, USA). The brainchild of Dr Neil Gershenfeld, director of the MIT Centre for Bits and Atoms, it aims to enable researchers, innovators and developers to do things beyond the purview of the existing fab labs of the country.

METALLURGY

WR Earliest zinc use

An artefact (No. 4189) containing 6.04 per cent zinc was found at the Harappan site of Lothal (dated to 2200–1500 BCE) in Gujarat. It indicated that the Harappan people could generate temperatures of above 1,000°C required for zinc metallurgy.

Earliest copper kiln

A copper smelting kiln, 35 cm (13.8 in.) high with an 18 cm (7 in.) rim diameter and 10 cm (3.9 in.) base diameter, was discovered at the Harappan site of Lothal (2200–1500 BCE) in Gujarat. Lothal copper was found to be very pure.

Earliest use of iron

Around 1000 BCE, iron was used in eastern Punjab, western Uttar Pradesh and Rajasthan. Excavations show that iron weapons such as arrowheads and spearheads were commonly used in western Uttar Pradesh from about 800 BCE. Iron is called *shyama* or *krishna ayas* (black/dark metal) in later Vedic texts.

First metallurgist to work with plutonium

Dr P.R. Roy, a scientist and director at the Bhabha Atomic Research Centre (BARC), Bombay (now Mumbai), Maharashtra, was the first Indian metallurgist to handle plutonium. He played a crucial role in India's first nuclear implosion at Pokhran, Rajasthan, in 1974.

First manufacture of steel

Indian smiths manufactured crucible steel, known as 'wootz', which was exported to many countries in medieval times. Indian raftsmen were known around the world at the time for their steel swords. After the British banned the production of weapons following the First War of Independence in 1857, wootz technology was lost.

New class of quasicrystals

In 1985, P. Ramachandra Rao and G.V.S. Sastry from the National Metallurgical Laboratory, Jamshedpur, now in Jharkhand, discovered a new class of quasicrystals composed of aluminium, manganese and zinc metals.

Earliest iron furnace

An iron furnace was found at Pandu Rajar Dhibi in Burdwan (later Bardhaman District), West Bengal, and was dated to 1100–800 BCE.

SPACE

First space venture

Launched from the base in Thumba near Trivandrum (now Thiruvananthapuram), Kerala, on 21 November 1963, a Nike-Apache rocket supplied by NASA kick-started the Indian space programme. Parts of this first sounding rocket launched by India were transported to the Thumba base on the carrier of a bicycle! St Mary Magdalene Church in Thumba is a preferred site for rocket launches because of its proximity to the magnetic equator. Quite fittingly, the church houses the Vikram Sarabhai Space Centre (VSSC) space museum.

First Indian space organization

India's space programme took off in 1972 with the Department of Space, Government of India, executing projects in space sciences, technology and activities through the Indian Space Research Organization (ISRO),

The Ministry of Home Affairs, Government of India, has decided to do away with over 300 awards given to scientists and medical researchers, and suggested instituting a Nobel Prize-like award, the Vigyan Ratna.

Cartosat-3 lifting off: imaging satellite with the highest resolution

SUPER SATELLITES

Since 1975, ISRO has launched 129 satellites of Indian-origin and 342 foreign satellites belonging to 36 countries, of which nearly 39 satellites are commercial satellites and rest are nanosatellites. Currently, India has a total of 53 operational satellites in space providing a range of services to the country. Here are some of the milestone moments in ISRO's satellite programme.

1975

Aryabhata

India's first fully indigenous satellite, Aryabhata, was launched into space from a Russian facility.

1979

Bhaskara-I

The first experimental remote-sensing satellite built in India was launched, with a TV and microwave cameras. The images sent by it are used for hydrology, forestry and oceanography.

Rohini Technology Payload

The satellite carried instruments to monitor the flight performance of SLV-3, the first Indian launch vehicle. However, it could not be placed into orbit.

1980

Rohini RS-1

India's first indigenous satellite launch. The satellite had an orbital life of nine months.

1981

Ariane Passenger Payload Experiment

ISRO's first indigenous, experimental communications satellite was launched by Ariane, a vehicle of the European Space Agency, from Guiana Space Centre, near Kourou in French Guiana.

Bhaskara-II

The second experimental remote-sensing satellite was launched.

1982

INSAT-1A

This was the first in a series of multipurpose communications, broadcasting and meteorology satellites providing communications and weather forecasting services for India with a host of ground stations throughout India (along with search-and-rescue services).

1983

Rohini RS-D2

Another satellite in the Rohini series, this one carried a sensor camera.

INSAT-1B

This communications and meteorology satellite served till 1990, returning around 36,000 Earth images.

1988

IRS-1A

This indigenous earth observation satellite was launched from the Soviet Cosmodrome at Baikonur, Russia.

1990

INSAT-1D

The third in the first-generation INSAT series served beyond its intended seven years, till 2002!

1991

IRS-1B

This remote-sensing satellite has completed 10 years of operation.

1992

SROSS-C

After two failed SROSS (Stretched Rohini Satellite Series) experiments, this satellite was launched for gamma-ray astronomy and ionospheric science.

1995

INSAT-2C

Its more powerful transponders improved communication facilities in remote areas like the North-East, and the Andaman and Nicobar Islands.

1997

IRS-1D

This satellite for earth observation built, launched and maintained by ISRO has returned higher quality images than its predecessors in its series.

1999

IRS-P4 OCEANSAT

This earth observation satellite carried a multifrequency scanning microwave radiometer (MSMR) and an ocean colour monitor (OCM).

2001

GSAT-1

This experimental satellite for the first developmental flight of GSLV-D1 was used for conducting communication experiments like digital audio broadcast, internet services and compressed digital TV transmission.

Technology Experiment Satellite (TES)

This experimental satellite was tasked with demonstrating technologies such as altitude and orbit control systems, high-torque reaction wheels, lightweight spacecraft structure, solid state recorder, X-band phased array antenna and two-mirror-on-axis camera optics, among other functions.

INSAT-3C

This satellite was designed to add to the existing INSAT capacity for communication and broadcasting.

2002

Kalpana-1 (METSAT)

The first dedicated meteorological satellite was launched by ISRO.

2003

RESOURCESAT-1 (IRS-P6)

This advanced remote-sensing satellite not only lends continuity to the remote-sensing data services of the IRS-1C and IRS-1D (which have served far beyond their mission lives) but also improves data quality in large measure.

2004

EDUSAT (GSAT-3)

The first dedicated 'educational satellite' was launched with two-way communication to classrooms for delivering educational materials.

2005

HAMSAT

This microsatellite facilitates amateur radio services to the Indian and international community of amateur radio operators.

CARTOSAT-1

This was the first Indian remote-sensing and earth observation satellite that could provide in-orbit stereoscopic images used for cartographic applications of global standards.

INSAT-4A

Used in direct-to-home (DTH) TV broadcasting, its transponders cover the Indian mainland and extended areas.

2007

CARTOSAT-2

Its pan-chromatic camera is used for imagery useful for cartography, urban and rural applications, land use and regulation, road network monitoring, water distribution, and other Land Information System (LIS) as well as Geographical Information System (GIS) applications.

SRE-1 (Space Capsule Recovery Experiment)

This test capsule demonstrated the technology of an orbiting platform for performing experiments in micro-gravity conditions.

2008

IMS-1

Earlier called TWSat (Third World Satellite), this was a low-cost microsatellite imaging mission.

2009

RISAT-2

This all-weather radar imaging satellite facilitates ISRO in disaster management applications.

ANUSAT

A research microsatellite, this was the first satellite built by students of an Indian university under the guidance of ISRO to demonstrate technologies related to store and forward communications. It was developed at Aerospace Engineering, Madras Institute of Technology, Chromepet, and Anna University. Students and faculty members of the Madras Institute of Technology and College of Engineering, Guindy, Tamil Nadu, were involved in the project.

2011

YOUTHSAT

This Indo-Russian mini-satellite mission saw the participation of university students at the graduate, postgraduate and research scholar levels to examine solar variability and thermosphere–ionosphere changes.

Megha-Tropiques

This is an Indo-French satellite mission to carry out research on the water cycle in the atmosphere, against the backdrop of climate change.

2016

INSAT-3DR

It is an advanced meteorological satellite with an imaging system and an atmospheric sounder. It can provide night-time pictures of low clouds and fog, and comparatively accurate estimation of sea surface temperature (SST).

SCATSAT-1

A miniature satellite to provide continuity to OceanSat-2 besides climate, tornado and other climate-tracking services.

2018

MICROSAT- TD

This demonstrator of first-in-class technology marked ISRO's 100th satellite.

GSAT-29

The mission of this communications satellite is to provide top-speed bandwidth to village resource centres in rural regions.

HySYS

This satellite mission provides hyperspectral imaging for agriculture, forestry and military applications.

ExseedSAT-1

This mini-communications satellite is the first to be privately funded.

GSAT-11

This geostationary satellite is India's heaviest yet.

GSAT-7A

This state-of-the-art communications satellite is for the use of the Indian Army and the Indian Air Force.

2020

EOS-01

An earth observation satellite to support applications in agriculture, forestry and disaster management.

2017

CARTOSAT-2D

This earth observation satellite was launched along with two Indian nanosatellites (INS-1A and INS-1B) and 101 nanosatellites from research facilities in the USA, Kazakhstan, Israel, the Netherlands, Switzerland and the UAE, the highest number of satellites (104) launched by a single launch vehicle at the time.

2013

SARAL

An Indo-French satellite mission for oceanographic studies, it carries out altimetric measurements related to ocean circulation and sea surface elevation.

IRNSS-1A

The first of seven satellites in the Indian Regional Navigation Satellite System (IRNSS).

GSAT-7 or INSAT-4F

The Indian Navy uses this multi-band military communications satellite.

2015

AstroSat

India's first dedicated Indian astronomy satellite mission includes a multi-wavelength telescope.

GSAT-15

This enhanced communications satellite carries GPS Aided GEO Augmented Navigation (GAGAN) payload.

2019

Microsat-R

This satellite was developed by the Defence Research and Development Organization (DRDO), for defence purposes.

KalamSAT-V2

This student-built satellite is the lightest in the world.

GSAT-31

This is a high-throughput telecommunication satellite, which provides Indian mainland and island coverage.

EMISAT

This satellite uses space-based electromagnetic intelligence (ELINT) for reconnaissance. It is used by the Indian Air Force.

CARTOSAT-3

This optical satellite is among those with the highest resolutions in the world.

with its headquarters in Bangalore (now Bengaluru), Karnataka.

First satellite centre

ISRO's Satellite Centre (ISAC), established in 1972, conducts research in satellite technology. Aryabhata, the first Indian satellite, Bhaskara I and II, and Rohini and APPLE satellites, were all designed and built at ISAC. The spacecraft of the Indian Remote Sensing satellite series and the Stretched Rohini satellite series were also designed at ISAC.

First weather-cum-communications satellite

Indian National Satellite INSAT-1A, launched on 10 April 1982 on an American Delta-3920 launch vehicle, was India's first satellite employed for meteorological observations over India and the Indian Ocean, as well as for domestic telecommunications, including nationwide direct TV broadcasting, TV programme distribution and meteorological data distribution.

First in space

- Squadron Leader Rakesh Sharma (b. 13 January 1949), then an Indian Air Force pilot, flew aboard spacecraft Soyuz T-11, launched on 2 April 1984, as part of the Intercosmos programme and spent over seven days orbiting Earth. He was the first Indian person to travel to space.
- Dr Kalpana Chawla (1962–2003), an American cosmonaut who was born in Karnal, Haryana, was the first woman of Indian origin in space. She zoomed into orbit aboard space shuttle Columbia on 19 November 1997 on a 16-day scientific mission, along with five fellow astronauts, and returned to Cape Canaveral on 5 December 1997. In 2003, Chawla was one of the seven crew members who died in the space shuttle Columbia disaster when it disintegrated during its re-entry into Earth's atmosphere.

First remote-sensing mission

IRS-1A, the first of a series of indigenous state-of-the-art remote-sensing satellites, was launched into a polar sun-synchronous orbit on 17 March 1988 from the Soviet Cosmodrome at Baikonur. It carried two cameras, LISS-I and LISS-II, with a swathe width of 140 km during each pass over India.

Highest-resolution imaging satellite

CARTOSAT-3, considered to be India's highest-resolution civilian satellite to date, was successfully launched into space along with 13 nano US nanosatellites by ISRO on 27 November 2019. Weighing 1,625 kg, the observation satellite lifted off from the Satish Dhawan Space Centre, SHAR (Sriharikota High Altitude Range), Sriharikota, Andhra Pradesh. It is an advanced imaging and mapping satellite with a mission life of five years and a panchromatic resolution of 0.25 m (9.8 in.).

First indigenous satellite series

Designed and built by ISRO, INSAT-2A was launched by the Ariane launch vehicle from Kourou, French Guiana, on 10 July 1992. INSAT-2B was also launched by Ariane on 23 July 1993. INSAT-2C, the third in this series of satellites, was launched on 7 December 1995 and put into operation in February 1996.

First indigenous satellite launcher

The PSLV-D3, developed by ISRO, hoisted a 930 kg Indian remote-sensing satellite (IRS-P3) into an orbit of 807 km from Earth, 17 minutes after it shot into space on 21 March 1996.

First flight of PSLV

With a lift-off weight of 294 tonnes, the 44.4 m (145 ft 8 in.) tall Polar Satellite Launch Vehicle (PSLV) is a four-stage vehicle that employs two solid and liquid propellant stages each. The first operational flight of PSLV took place on 29 September 1997, putting the satellite IRS-1D

The Council of Scientific and Industrial Research (CSIR), India's largest research organization, is now led by its 1st woman director general – Dr Kalaiselvi N., an electrochemical scientist.

Chandrayaan-1 lifts off on PSLV C11: first lunar probe

Gaganyaan Launch Postponed to 2024

India's debut human space flight mission, Gaganyaan, is now set to launch in 2024. Previously, it was scheduled to take off in 2022 to mark India's 75 years of independence. However, the training of astronauts in Russia and India was halted due to COVID-19. The first test flight for Gaganyaan will reportedly be taking place towards the end of 2022. After this, Vyom Mitra, a female-looking humanoid robot, is scheduled to fly to outer space in the spacecraft. Meanwhile, the potential crew will be prepared by ISRO to send two astronauts into a low earth orbit in 2024.

The Indian Space Research Organization (ISRO) was formed in 1969 and superseded the earlier space agency, the Indian National Committee for Space Research (INCOSPAR), set up in 1962 by the then Prime Minister Jawaharlal Nehru.

into a polar sun-synchronous orbit, from ISRO's SHAR (Sriharikota High Altitude Range) centre in Sriharikota, Andhra Pradesh.

First oceanographic satellite

IRS-P4 (OceanSat), the first satellite built for ocean applications, was launched into a polar sun-synchronous orbit, 720 km high, by the PSLV from SHAR, Sriharikota, Andhra Pradesh, on 26 May 1999. A 1,050 kg satellite measuring 2.8 m x 1.98 m x 2.57 m (9 ft 2 in. x 6 ft 6 in. x 8 ft 5 in.), the IRS-P4 orbited the earth in 99.31 mins. It completed its mission on 8 August 2010.

First flight of GSLV

India's first Geosynchronous Satellite Launch Vehicle (GSLV-D1) blasted off from the Satish Dhawan Space Centre, SHAR, Sriharikota, Andhra Pradesh, at IST 3:43 p.m. on 18 April 2001. The giant three-stage vehicle carried a 1,540 kg experimental communication satellite, GSAT-1, to be placed in the geosynchronous transfer orbit.

First lunar probe

Chandrayaan-1 was India's first lunar probe. It was launched by ISRO, using a PSLV-XL rocket on 22 October 2008 from Satish Dhawan Space Centre, SHAR, Sriharikota, Andhra Pradesh. It operated until August 2009. The mission included a lunar orbiter and an impactor.

First university for the study of and research on outer space

The Indian Institute of Space Science and Technology (IIST), located at Valiamala in Thiruvananthapuram, Kerala, was inaugurated on 14 September 2007 by G. Madhavan Nair, the then chairman of ISRO. A government-aided institute and deemed university, it is the first in Asia to be dedicated to the study of and research on outer space. It was set up by ISRO with former Indian president A.P.J. Abdul Kalam as its first chancellor. The university offers engineering undergraduate, postgraduate and doctorate programmes, focusing on space science, technology and their applications.

First interplanetary mission

On 5 November 2013, PSLV-C25, the 25th flight of PSLV (Polar Satellite Launch Vehicle) launched Mangalyaan, the Mars Orbiter Mission (MOM) spacecraft, from SHAR, Sriharikota, Andhra Pradesh. Under the aegis of ISRO, the mission was conducted to observe the physical features of Mars and the Martian atmosphere. With this mission, ISRO became the fourth space agency in the world to reach Mars. India is the first Asian nation to reach the Mars orbit, and the first nation in the world to do so in its first attempt.

WR Smallest spacecraft launched

On 23 June 2017, the world's smallest spacecraft, Sprites, was launched by ISRO's PSLV rocket and placed in the low earth orbit.

The 3.5 cm x 3.5 cm (1.38 in. x 1.38 in.) space probe weighs just 4 g and runs on sunlight.

First mission to land a rover on the moon

ISRO's plan to land on the moon with the ambitious Chandrayaan-2 mission, which included an orbiter, a lander and a rover, would have been the first-ever mission in the world to land a rover near the unexplored lunar south pole. Chandrayaan-2 was launched on 22 July 2019 and was expected to land on the moon on 7 September 2019. However, communication with the Vikram lander was lost when it was just 2.1 km away from the moon's surface. The orbiter, where 95 per cent of the experiments are placed, was not affected. Debris from the Vikram lander was located on the moon's surface by NASA's Lunar Reconnaissance Orbiter (LRO) camera on 3 December 2019. Located about 750 m (2,460 ft) north-west of the main crash site, the debris was initially spotted by Shanmuga Subramanian, a mechanical engineer from Chennai, Tamil Nadu, who then contacted the American space agency.

First dedicated commercial satellite mission

India's Polar Satellite Launch Vehicle PSLV-C51 successfully launched the satellite Amazonia-1, developed by Brazil, along with 18 co-passenger private satellites, from SHAR, Sriharikota, Andhra Pradesh, on 28 February 2021. The first dedicated commercial mission of NewSpace India Ltd (NSIL), under the Department of Space, Government of India, it was part of space reforms aimed at increasing the participation of private companies in the space sector. The co-passenger satellites included four from Indian National Space Promotion and Authorization Centre (IN-SPACe) and 14 from NSIL.

First private satellite launched

Exseed SAT-1, built by Exseed Space Innovations Private Ltd, founded by scientists Kris Nair and Asshar Farhan, became the first private Indian satellite to be launched in space. The amateur (ham) radio satellite hitched a ride on the Elon Musk-led company SpaceX's Falcon 9 rocket on 4 December 2018.

Heaviest satellite launched

GSAT-11, weighing 5,854 kg and laying claim to being the heaviest Indian satellite ever launched, was sent into space on 5 December 2018 from the Ariane Launch Complex at Kourou in French Guiana. The satellite is expected to help boost communication services across India.

WR Lightest satellite in orbit

Kalamsat-V2 was launched by ISRO on 24 January 2019 from the Satish Dhawan Space Centre, SHAR, Sriharikota, Andhra Pradesh. Weighing only 1.26 kg, it is said to be the world's lightest satellite to be put into orbit. It was made by students belonging to Space Kidz India, a Chennai-based aerospace start-up pioneering in design, fabrication and launch of small satellites, spacecraft and ground systems. The satellite will also serve as a communications device for ham radio transmission, which is a form of wireless communication used by amateurs for non-commercial activities. It took six days to make and cost around ₹12 lakh (1.2 million).

Most satellites launched in a single mission

ISRO launched an unprecedented 104 satellites, including India's earth observation satellite, on a single rocket from the spaceport in SHAR, Sriharikota, Andhra Pradesh, on 15 February 2017. Elon Musk's SpaceX surpassed this world record by launching 143 satellites on a single rocket on 24 January 2021.

GSAT-11 communications spacecraft: heaviest satellite

After two decades of research and development, ISRO developed India's first indigenous cryogenic engine for its launch vehicle programme.

EDUCATION

LITERACY

First state/UT with 100 per cent literacy

On 18 April 1991, also the 81st birthday of Dr Malcolm S. Adiseshiah, the doyen of adult education in India, Kerala was declared 100 per cent literate.

First 100 per cent literate district

In 1990, Ernakulam, Kerala, with a population of three million then, became the first completely literate district in the country, with a literacy rate of 98.34 per cent in the age group of 5–60 years.

First national education council

The All India Council for Secondary Education (AICSE) was set up in 1955.

State/UT with the highest literacy rate

Kerala, with 96.2 per cent, has the highest rate of literacy among all states, according to the 75th round of the National Sample Survey (NSS) conducted from July 2017 to June 2018.

State/UT with the lowest literacy rate

Andhra Pradesh, with 66.4 per cent, has the lowest rate of literacy among all states, according to the 75th round of the National Sample Survey.

State/UT with highest/lowest female literacy rate

The female literacy rate in Kerala was 95.2 per cent while Rajasthan recorded 57.6 per cent, according to the 75th round of the National Sample Survey.

State/UT with the highest percentage of graduates

Out of a total of around 68 million graduates in the country, Chandigarh, with 24.65 per cent, has the highest percentage of its population as graduates, according to the 2011 Census of India.

State/UT with the lowest percentage of graduates

Assam has the lowest percentage of graduate population, with only 4.83 per cent as per Census 2011.

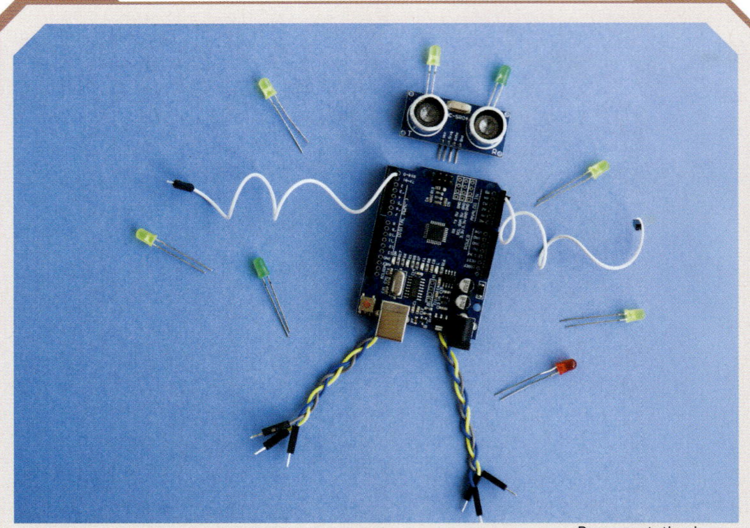

Representative image

Artificial Intelligence Goes to School in Madhya Pradesh

The State Board of Open School Education in Madhya Pradesh announced a new technology-based education curriculum in March 2022. This will allow students of classes VIII and IX to opt for artificial intelligence (AI) as a subject. The board signed a memorandum of understanding (MoU) with technology corporation Microsoft India. Based on this agreement, 53 schools will conduct AI classes. These 53 Education for All (EFA) schools have been provided with a 240-hour annual course and a book on AI by Microsoft India. Moreover, online classes on AI will be conducted for students by the Microsoft team. The teachers of classes VIII to XII will be trained by Microsoft as well. This initiative will allow students to be well-versed in skills and knowledge related to machine learning, data processing and sentiment analysis at an early stage.

SCHOOLS

Earliest schools for girls

- St Thomas School for Girls, which was founded in 1789 for the English-speaking community of Calcutta, Bengal (now Kolkata, West Bengal), was the first girls-only school in India.
- John Elliot Drinkwater Bethune (1801–51) established Calcutta Female School, the first school for girls, with the help of Raja Dakshinaranjan Mukhopadhyay, Ramgopal Ghosh and Pandit Madan Mohan Tarkalankar in 1849. Bethune was the law member of the Governor General's Council and became the president of the Council of Education. It was maintained from his private funds.
- The Church Missionary Society opened the first boarding school for girls in Tinnevelly (now Tirunelveli), Tamil Nadu, in 1821.

Oldest extant school

St George's Anglo-Indian Higher Secondary School, founded as the as the Military (later Madras) Male Orphan Asylum, was established in 1715 in Madras (now Chennai, Tamil Nadu).

First school for the hearing-impaired

Established in 1893, the Calcutta Deaf and

National Education Day was first celebrated on this day to mark the birth anniversary of Maulana Abul Kalam Azad, independent India's first minister for education.

The Kendriya Vidyalaya Sangathan headquarters, Delhi: largest chain of government schools

The National Testing Agency (NTA) conducted the Common University Entrance Test (CUET) in six phases for the academic year 2022–23. This is a new national, standardized test for students to get admission in **90** universities including Central, state and private universities.

Dumb School in Bengal (now in Kolkata, West Bengal) was the first school for the hearing-impaired.

Oldest extant institute for the blind

The Institute for the Blind – Andh Vidyalaya – was established in Lahore (now in Pakistan) in 1939 and shifted to Delhi after Independence in 1947.

First minister of education

Independent India's first minister of education was Maulana Abul Kalam Azad (1888–1958) during 1947–58. Besides establishing the first Indian Institute of Technology (IIT), the Indian Institute of Science (IISc), the School of Planning and Architecture (SPA) and the University Grants Commission (UGC), he set up key cultural and literary organizations – the Sangeet Natak Akademi, the Lalit Kala Akademi, the Sahitya Akademi and the Indian Council for Cultural Relations.

First Indian school abroad

The Indian High School, Dubai, set up in 1957, was the first Indian educational institution in a foreign country.

WR Largest open school

Set up as an autonomous institution under the Ministry of Human Resource Development in 1989, the National Institute of Open Schooling (NIOS) has a cumulative enrolment of 2.81 million students. It works through a network of 22 regional centres, two subregional centres, two NIOS Cells and over 7,000 Accredited Institutions and Accredited Vocational Institutions. These centres are located in various parts of the world, viz., India, Nepal and the Middle East.

Largest chain of government schools

The Kendriya Vidyalaya Sangathan, an autonomous body under the Ministry of Human Resource Development, Government of India, since 15 December 1963, administers 1,252 schools, including three abroad, with 1,425,215 students, as of October 2022.

First solar-powered school

Sri Aurobindo International Centre for Education in White Town, Puducherry, became India's first fully solar-powered educational institute in 2014. It was set up in 1943 by Mirra Alfassa, the spiritual collaborator of Sri Aurobindo.

Largest school science fair – single venue – single day

Science World, a science club formed by science communicators, in Prayagraj, Uttar Pradesh, in collaboration with Shri Mahaprabhu Public School, organized a science fair on 14 December 2019 at Delhi Public School, Prayagraj, in which 4,272 students from over 35 schools, participated.

Largest school science fair – multiple venues – single day

More than 22,500 students from 637 upper primary schools of Bastar District, Chhattisgarh, conducted more than 35,000 scientific experiments at 116 centres on 18 January 2017. Called Bastar Vigyan Mela, the annual event was organized by the Department of Education, Bastar District. The students demonstrated scientific activities and displayed innovative science models.

HIGHER EDUCATION

First steps

The first educational policy in colonial India was articulated in an 1854 dispatch sent by Sir Charles Wood to the then Governor General Lord Dalhousie. Sir Charles stressed the adoption of vernacular languages in local primary schools, Anglo-vernacular language in high schools and English-medium education in colleges.

First Sanskrit university

The Sampurnanand Sanskrit Vishwavidyalaya in Varanasi, Uttar Pradesh, was the first Sanskrit university in India and is said to have been established in 1791 as a Sanskrit college during Company rule. It has 628 affiliated colleges across India.

First modern university

William Carey, a British Christian missionary,

opened the first missionary college at Serampore, Bengal (now Srirampur, Hooghly District, West Bengal) in 1818. It was granted the status of a university in 1829.

First modern college

The first college to offer modern education in India was the Hindu College of Calcutta, Bengal (now Kolkata, West Bengal), established in 1817. Scottish watchmaker and philanthropist David Hare was its first principal. It was renamed Presidency College in 1855 and then rechristened the Presidency University on 7 July 2010.

First university act

The Indian Universities Act, 1904, was the first set of educational reforms, which stipulated that universities should offer more teaching and research opportunities, and exert more control over affiliated colleges.

Longest functioning ancient university

Nalanda Mahavihara, located about 95 km south-east of present-day Patna in Bihar, functioned uninterrupted as a university from the Buddha's time in the sixth century BCE up to the 13th century CE, when it was destroyed by Muhammad bin Bakhtiyar Khilji. The university's curriculum then included many subjects such as logic, medicine, metaphysics, grammar and the sciences. In an effort to emulate the ancient centre of learning, Nalanda University, an exclusively postgraduate and doctoral institution, was started in 2014 in Rajgir, Bihar.

First intermediate colleges

The University of Punjab (now in Chandigarh) and the University of Allahabad (now in Prayagraj, Uttar Pradesh) were the first to establish intermediate colleges, offering two-year courses between high school and a degree college, in 1917, as proposed by the Sadler Commission.

First five universities

The universities of Calcutta (now University of Calcutta), Madras (now University of Madras) and Bombay (now University of Mumbai), which were modelled on London University, were established in 1857 as non-teaching examining bodies. The universities of Punjab (now University of the Punjab in Lahore, Pakistan) in 1881 and Allahabad (in present-day Prayagraj, Uttar Pradesh) in 1887 followed after several years.

First five residential universities

In 1915, the Banaras Hindu University (BHU) was established as a teaching and residential university, followed by the Universities of Mysore (1916), Patna (1917) and Osmania (1918), and Aligarh Muslim University (1920).

Corridor of Presidency University: first modern college

First rural university

Mahatma Gandhi Chitrakoot Gramoday University, established in 1991 in Chitrakoot, Madhya Pradesh, to promote rural education, was the first rural university in the country.

First energy studies university

The University of Petroleum and Energy Studies in Dehradun, Uttarakhand, established in 2003, is India's first university specializing in petroleum, energy and power.

First virtual medical university

The first virtual medical university, Medvarsity, established in 2000, is an initiative of Apollo Hospitals Group.

First women's university

The Shreemati Nathibai Damodar Thackersey (SNDT) Women's University was established in Pune, Maharashtra, by D.K. Karve (its first principal) on 5 July 1916. Dr R.P. Paranjpye was its first vice chancellor.

First college for women

The Bethune School of Calcutta, Bengal (now Kolkata, West Bengal),

The University of Allahabad, Prayagraj: one of the first intermediate colleges

Bethune School building, Kolkata: it became the first college for women

set up in 1849, was reorganized after it merged with Banga Mahila Vidyalaya. In 1879, Bethune College classes started with one student, Kadambini Bose.

First college alumni association

Dr William Miller, principal of Madras Christian College, Madras (now Chennai), Tamil Nadu, formed the first alumni association in 1891.

First school of mines

The Indian School of Mines – now renamed the Indian Institute of Technology – in Dhanbad, Jharkhand, opened in 1926.

First institute to teach modern architecture

The first course in architecture can be traced to the founding of a draftsman's class at the Sir J.J. School (established in 1856) of Arts, Bombay (now Mumbai, Maharashtra) in 1896. In 1913, the course was reorganized, and an independent Department of Architecture was formed.

First technical university

The Thomason College of Engineering, established in 1847 at Roorkee (now in Uttarakhand), was India's first technical university. Its civil engineering department is the oldest one. It is now the Indian Institute of Technology (IIT), Roorkee.

First technical university for women

The Indira Gandhi Delhi Technical University for Women (IGDTUW), New Delhi, was founded in 1998.

First IIT

The first Indian Institute of Technology (IIT) was established in 1951 at Kharagpur, West Bengal, at the site of the Hijli Detention Camp. There are 23 approved IITs in India currently.

First metro technology institute

The Institute of Metro and Rail Technology (IMRT) opened in October 2013 in Hyderabad, Telangana. It offers short- and long-term courses to design, build and manage modern rail systems.

First railway university

The National Rail and Transport University was established on 5 September 2018 at the Pratap Vilas Palace in Vadodara, Gujarat. It provides education and training in the latest technological applications related to the railways, such as radio frequency identification, artificial intelligence and satellite-based tracking. It offers graduate degrees in subjects such as transportation management, transportation technology, rail infrastructural engineering, rail systems and communication engineering.

First college of nursing

The Christian Medical College (CMC) and Hospital, Vellore, is a private educational institute with a network of hospitals in and around Vellore, Tamil Nadu. It was started in 1902 by Dr Ida Scudder, a third-generation American missionary. In 1903, she began training women compounders and started the first school of nursing at CMC in 1909.

First and oldest extant medical college

William Bentinck (Governor General of India during 1828–35) founded Calcutta Medical College in Calcutta, Bengal (now Kolkata, West Bengal) on 28 January 1835.

Calcutta Medical College: first and oldest extant medical college

First college of veterinary science
The first college of veterinary science was established at Lahore (now in Pakistan) in 1882. Before this, lectures in veterinary science were given to civilians at the Agricultural College at Saidapet, Madras (now Chennai, Tamil Nadu) and at the College of Sciences in Poona (now Pune), Maharashtra.

First veterinary research institute
Established in 1889, the Indian Veterinary Research Institute (IVRI) at Izatnagar in Bareilly District, Uttar Pradesh, is India's premier advanced research facility in the field of veterinary medicine and allied branches. IVRI is currently under the Indian Council of Agricultural Research, New Delhi, and has six regional campuses for graduate, postgraduate and diploma courses.

First veterinary university
The Tamil Nadu Veterinary and Animal Sciences University (TANUVAS), which opened in 1989 in Madhavaram Milk Colony, Chennai, was the first veterinary and animal sciences university in Asia.

First statistical institute
The Indian Statistical Institute (ISI) was established in 1931 in Calcutta, Bengal (now Kolkata, West Bengal), by scientist and statistician P.C. Mahalanobis.

First university of fisheries and ocean studies
The College of Fisheries in Panangad, Cochin (now Kochi), Kerala, established in 1979, was a constituent college of the Kerala Agricultural University. The Kerala University of Fisheries and Ocean Studies (KUFOS) was established in 2010 with its headquarters at the College of Fisheries.

First institute of oceanography
The National Institute of Oceanography, which was founded on 1 January 1966, is an autonomous research organization that undertakes scientific research and studies of special oceanographic features of the northern Indian Ocean. The institute has its main campus in Dona Paula, Goa, and regional centres have been set up in Mumbai, Kochi and Visakhapatnam.

First institute for population sciences
The Institute for Population Sciences in Bombay (now Mumbai), Maharashtra, earlier known as the Demographic Training and Research Centre, was established in 1956 to prepare students for administrative, teaching, research and consultancy careers in population sciences.

University of Delhi

A Common University Entrance Test
The Ministry of Education has introduced the Common University Entrance Test (CUET [UG]-2022) for admission into all undergraduate programmes in all Central universities for the academic session 2022–23. CUET is a common platform and provides equal opportunities to students from across the country, especially those from rural and remote areas. A single examination will help candidates to be a part of the admission process to all the Central universities of the country.

First university for the study of outer space
The Indian Institute of Space Science and Technology (IIST) in Thiruvananthapuram, Kerala, is the first university in Asia to be solely dedicated to the study and research of outer space. It was set up by the Indian Space Research Organization (ISRO) under the Department of Space, Government of India, in 2007. The institute offers undergraduate, postgraduate and doctorate programmes with a focus on space science, space technology, geoinformatics, earth system sciences and their applications.

First gemmological institute
The Gemmological Institute of India (GII), a

GROWTH IN THE NUMBER OF UNIVERSITIES AND COLLEGES

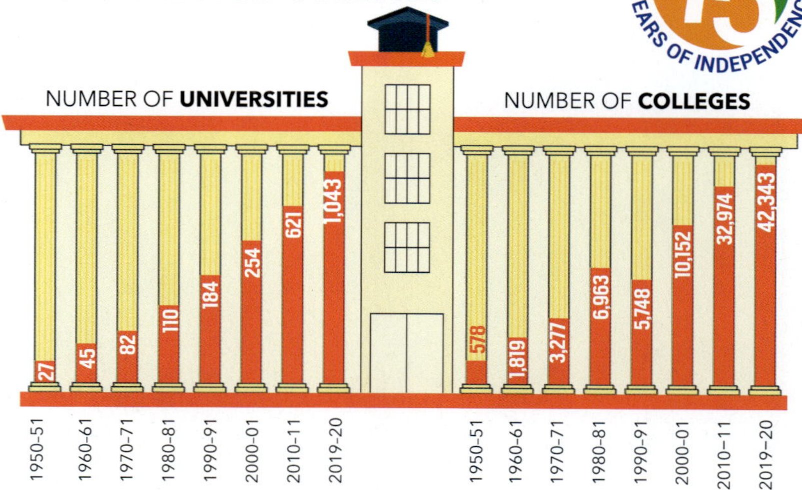

Year	Number of universities	Number of colleges
1950–51	27	578
1960–61	45	1,819
1970–71	82	3,277
1980–81	110	6,963
1990–91	184	5,748
2000–01	254	10,152
2010–11	621	32,974
2019–20	1,043	42,343

Source: PIB AKAM series, Press Information Bureau, Government of India

The Indian Sign Language Research and Training Centre (ISLRTC) launched the Indian Sign Language (ISL) digital content of NCERT textbooks of classes I–V and an ISL Dictionary app to celebrate International Sign Language Day.

non-profit public institution founded by the Gem and Jewellery Exporters Association, was established in Bombay (now Mumbai), Maharashtra, in 1971 to promote the scientific knowledge of gemmology.

First institute of mass communication

The first institute to provide a formal education in mass communication was the Indian Institute of Mass Communication (IIMC). Set up by the Government of India in 1965, it is now located in the JNU (Jawaharlal Nehru University) campus in New Delhi. In 1966, it was made an autonomous institution under the Ministry of Information and Broadcasting, and offers courses related to different media.

First home science college

Lady Irwin College, established in 1932 in New Delhi, was the country's first home science college.

First institute of fashion technology

The Ministry of Textiles, Government of India, set up the National Institute of Fashion Technology (NIFT) in Delhi on 24 August 1987 to provide professional human resources for the textile industry. There are currently 17 NIFT campuses in the country.

First institute for studying footwear design

The Footwear Design and Development Institute (FDDI), set up in 1986 at Noida, Uttar Pradesh, trains students in footwear technology, computer-aided designing and pattern making.

First law university

The National Law School of India University (NLSIU) in Bangalore (now Bengaluru), Karnataka, was established on 29 August 1987. Currently, there are 23 such national law universities in India.

First national institute of management

The Indian Institute of Management Calcutta (now in Kolkata), West Bengal) was established for the pursuit of postgraduate studies in management on 17 November 1961 by the Government of India, in collaboration with the MIT Sloan School of Management, USA, the Government of West Bengal, the Ford Foundation, and several Indian industries.

First model-training school

Catwalk, set up in Bombay (now Mumbai), Maharashtra, in 1990, by leading model Lubna Adams, was the first training school in India for fashion models.

First college of physical education

The YMCA College of Physical Education in Madras (now Chennai), Tamil Nadu, established in 1920 by Harry Crowe Buck of Pennsylvania, USA, was Asia's first college for physical education. It is now affiliated to the Tamil Nadu Physical Education and Sports University, and is considered a pioneer in the promotion of sports for persons with disabilities.

First radio jockey training academy

The Academy of Broadcasting in Chandigarh, set up in July 2003, was the first academy for training radio jockeys.

First yoga university

The Bihar Yoga Bharati in Munger, Bihar, an institute for advanced studies in yoga, set up in 1964, was the first of its kind in Asia.

First university for the disabled

The Jagadguru Rambhadracharya Handicapped University in Chitrakoot,

Representative image

A Bank Where Students Can Deposit Credit

The Academic Bank of Credit (ABC) proposed in the National Education Policy (NEP) 2020 was launched on 29 July 2021. The ABC will function much like a bank or repository for student credits. Students as account holders will be able to accumulate credits and redeem them. The ABC will make the process of changing courses and attaining degrees easier. This service will allow for an interdisciplinary or liberal education for students. Students will be able to transfer credits to other educational institutions, which would make their course structure and education more flexible. Moreover, this will allow students the freedom to choose their own pace for studies.

Uttar Pradesh, was established as a private university on 27 September 2001 to provide higher and professional education only to persons with disabilities in four categories: the visually impaired, the hearing-impaired, the mobility-impaired and the mentally impaired, as defined in the Persons with Disability Act, 1995.

First national institute for the visually impaired
The National Institute for the Visually Impaired was established in Dehradun, Uttarakhand, in 1979.

First college for the hearing-challenged
The St Louis Institute for the Deaf and Blind in Madras (now Chennai), Tamil Nadu, which opened on 8 September 1993, was the first college for the hearing-impaired in the country. It is affiliated to the University of Madras and offers graduate degrees.

First military school
The Prince of Wales Royal Indian Military College in Dehradun, Uttarakhand, now called the Rashtriya Indian Military College (RIMC), was inaugurated on 13 March 1922 by Prince Edward VIII, the Prince of Wales, to provide training to Indian boys to become officers in the armed forces.

First defence academy
The National Defence Academy at Khadakwasla, Maharashtra, was opened on 16 January 1955, to give its students a military orientation to join any of the three services of the Indian armed forces.

First college for sanitation workers
The Harpic World Toilet College, located in Aurangabad in Maharashtra, was established in August 2018. It is the first of its kind in the country and has trained more than 3,200 sanitation workers. It trains workers in the required skills and also makes them aware of the occupational hazards related to the job. It is run by British consumer goods company Reckitt Benckiser.

First university only for tribal students
The Kalinga Institute of Social Sciences, founded by Achyuta Samanta in Bhubaneswar, Odisha, became India's first exclusively tribal university when it was granted university status by the Ministry of Human Resources in 2017. It admits students only from tribal communities and is the only known university in the world to do so.

National Defence Academy, Khadakwasla, Maharashtra: first defence academy

First correspondence courses
The University of Delhi introduced non-formal education in 1962 with its first correspondence course.

First postgraduate degree
Calcutta University in Calcutta, Bengal (now Kolkata, West Bengal), conferred the first postgraduate degree (MA) in India in 1862.

First to obtain a PhD in library science
In 1957, the University of Delhi awarded the first PhD in library science to D.B. Krishna Rao for his study on 'Facet analysis and depth of agriculture classification' under Dr S.R. Ranganathan and Dr S. Dasgupta.

First engineer
Nilmani Mitra (1828–94) is considered the first Indian to obtain an engineering degree, from the Roorkee Engineering College (now IIT,

GROWTH IN THE NUMBER OF SCHOOLS IN INDIA

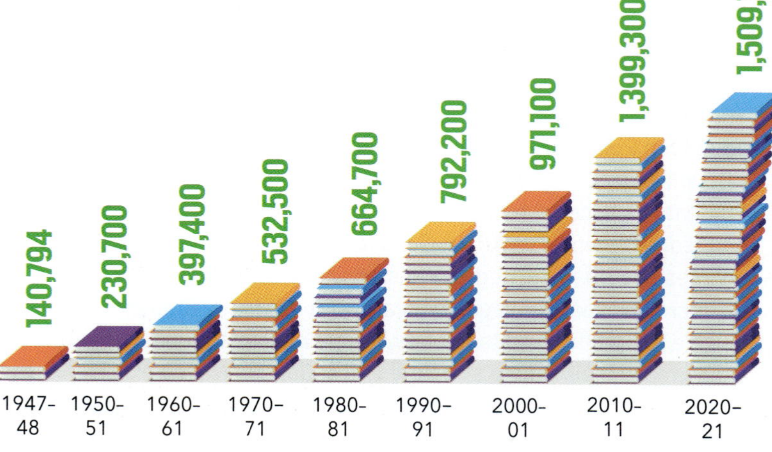

Sources: PIB AKAM Series

A decision was made to cancel the Class XII board examinations in the interests of the health and safety of students amid COVID-19. This was the first time these exams were cancelled in the history of the Central Board of Secondary Education (CBSE).

Roorkee), Uttarakhand. A civil engineer, he designed and built many famous mansions in 19th-century Calcutta.

First Indian to receive a PhD from a foreign university

Agostino Lourenco of Margao, Goa, is considered to have received his PhD in chemistry in Paris, France, in 1860.

First woman doctor

Kadambini Ganguly née Bose obtained the Graduate of Bengal Medical College degree to become the first woman doctor in 1888.

First woman vice chancellor

Hansa Jivraj Mehta (1897–1995) set a benchmark when she became the vice chancellor of the Maharaja Sayajirao University of Baroda, Vadodara, Gujarat, in 1949.

First Indian vice chancellor

In 1890, Gurudas Banerjee became the vice chancellor of Calcutta University, Bengal (now West Bengal).

First women graduates

Kadambini Ganguly and Chandramukhi Basu passed the BA examination from Calcutta University (now in Kolkata, West Bengal) in 1883.

First woman Bachelor of Medicine

Anandibai Joshi was the first Indian woman to obtain a Bachelor of Medicine degree in 1886 from the University of Philadelphia in the USA, but she did not practise medicine.

Kamala Sohonie: first Indian woman to receive a PhD in a scientific discipline

First woman law graduate

Cornelia Sorabji (b. 1866) graduated in law from the University of Bombay (now University of Mumbai) in 1894.

First to obtain a doctorate

In 1904, Annoda Prasad Sircar became the first to obtain a doctorate when the University of Allahabad (established in 1887) awarded him a DSc.

First woman to obtain a PhD

Sita Poovaiah of Coorg (now Kodagu, Karnataka) obtained a doctorate in dance from the University of Bombay (now University of Mumbai, Maharashtra) in the 1940s.

First woman to obtain a PhD in a scientific discipline

Kamala Sohonie (8 June 1912–28 June 1998), a biochemist, received her PhD at the Indian Institute of Science (IISc) Bangalore (now Bengaluru), Karnataka, in 1939, for her work on vitamins and the nutritive values of pulses, paddy and groups of food items consumed by the poorer sections of society.

First woman engineer

A. Lalitha (b. 1919) qualified as an electrical engineer from the College of Engineering, Guindy (CEG), University of Madras (now in Chennai, Tamil Nadu), in 1937.

First to pass the Indian Medical Service examination

Surjo Kumar Chakraborty (1826–74), MRCS (Member of the Royal College of Surgeons), was the first Indian to pass the Indian Medical Service (IMS) examination in 1855. He subsequently became the first Indian professor of Materia Medica at Calcutta Medical College.

First to score 100 per cent in NEET

Kota=based ALLEN Career Institute's student Soyeb Aftab scored 720/720 with All-India rank no.1 at the National Eligibility cum Entrance Test (NEET) 2020 (UG).

First gender-neutral certificate

The National Academy of Legal Studies and Research (NALSAR), Hyderabad, Telangana, issued the first gender-neutral graduation certificate in June 2015.

WR First chartered scientist in aviation

Dr Bishnujee Singh (b. 27 October 1972), the chief executive officer of Cayley Aerospace Inc., from Lynnwood, Washington, USA, became the world's first chartered scientist in aviation, with the Science Council, UK, in association with the Royal Aeronautical Society, on 26 September 2006.

Most Master's degrees obtained – men

Vandana Agrawal (b. 12 November 1954) from Alwar, Rajasthan, has 10 MA degrees, the highest number of postgraduate degrees attained by a woman in India.

Most postgraduate degrees obtained – men

Prof Dr V.N. Parthiban, former head, Department of Commerce, R.K.M. Vivekananda College, Chennai, Tamil Nadu, has 13 postgraduate degrees in humanities, eight postgraduate degrees in commerce and three in science subjects. He also has 12 postgraduate degrees in Law and eight dealing with subjects like financial management, logistic management and foreign trade, among others. He has 12 MPhil degrees in commerce,

DIGITAL HERITAGE

The Ministry of Culture, Government of India, has launched a project for the digitization of collections in museums and art galleries to both preserve them and bring them closer to the people, wherever they are located, in a National Digital Repository of Museums. It's possibly the first time that 10 national museums will be digitized and be available online on one portal! The digital collections would be created using the technical expertise of the Centre for Development of Advanced Computing (C-DAC), Pune, Maharashtra, and the Art Institute of Chicago, USA, employing the software JATAN: Virtual Museum Builder. The virtual museums would provide linking of digital content, online access to heritage information resources through mobile devices and kiosks, integration of documentation in multimedia formats, and 360-degree panoramas.

National Museum, New Delhi

Established in the President's House on 15 August 1949 by C. Rajagopalachari, the then Governor General of India, the museum's current building was begun in 1955 and completed in 1989. The museum holds approximately 200,000 objects, both Indian and foreign, covering over 5,000 years of heritage.

A painted shield at the National Museum, New Delhi

Indian Museum, Kolkata, West Bengal

Founded in 1814 by the Asiatic Society of Bengal with Danish botanist Dr Nathanial Wallich as the curator, the museum was variously known as the Asiatic Society Museum, and then the Imperial Museum, before finally being named the Indian Museum. It was the earliest and largest multipurpose museum of the time in the entire Asia-Pacific region. It houses around 1,002,600 exhibits.

Exhibits displayed at the Indian Museum, Kolkata

Victoria Memorial, Kolkata, West Bengal

Reportedly the world's largest monument to a monarch, the stunning building of the Victoria Memorial now houses a museum with more than 30,000 objects. Its 25 galleries include the royal gallery, the national leaders' gallery, the portrait gallery, the central hall, the sculpture gallery, the arms and armoury gallery, and the more recent Kolkata gallery (tracing the history of the city). Besides paintings, it has a collection of rare and antiquarian books.

Victoria Memorial Hall

National Gallery of Modern Art, New Delhi

National Gallery of Modern Art, New Delhi

This gallery, established in 1954, with later branches at Mumbai and Bengaluru, has more than 17,000 works by Indian and foreign artists, such as Raja Ravi Verma, Abanindranath Tagore, Rabindranath Tagore, Gaganendranath Tagore, Nandalal Bose, Jamini Roy, Amrita Sher-Gil, Thomas Daniell and Nicolas Roerich. Some of the works are from as far back as 1857.

National Gallery of Modern Art, Mumbai, Maharashtra

This gallery in Cowasji Jehangir Hall, Colaba, was opened to the public in 1996, with collections of more than 14,000 works by renowned artists and sculptors.

National Gallery of Modern Art, Mumbai

National Gallery of Modern Art, Bengaluru, Karnataka

Inaugurated in the year 2009, this gallery displays more than 500 exhibits by a large number of artists, including contemporary ones. Just as the other national galleries of modern art, the gallery organizes and hosts events on art and culture.

Salar Jung Museum, Hyderabad, Telangana

The Salar Jung Museum was established in 1951 and showcases the vast personal collections of Nawab Mir Yousuf Ali Khan, known as Salar Jung III. Shifted to its present building in 1968, the museum has a collection of more than 46,000 art objects, over 8,000 manuscripts and over 60,000 books, dating from the second century BCE to modern times, displayed across 38 galleries. A special gallery is devoted to the Salar Jung family.

Salar Jung Museum, Hyderabad

Allahabad Museum, Prayagraj, Uttar Pradesh

Located in the historic Chandrashekar Azad Park, this national-level museum's 16 galleries showcase art, antiquities, paintings, sculptures (including ancient ones from Bharhut and Bhumra), coins, ceramics, illustrated manuscripts, farmans, weapons, textiles, natural history specimens, photographs, prints and personality-based collections of leaders, poets and authors.

Nagarjunakonda Museum, Guntur District, Andhra Pradesh

This archaeological museum in an island location in Nagarjunakonda houses the excavated artefacts from Nagrajunakonda, rescued from being submerged due to the construction of the Nagarjunakonda Dam. Important exhibits include a memorial pillar depicting King Vasishthiputra Chamtamula and inscriptions of King Vijaya Satakarni.

Goa State Museum, Panaji, Goa

Also known as the State Archaeology Museum, it was established in 1977 at Adil Shah's Palace (Old Secretariat). It has more than 8,000 artefacts, including sculptures, art objects, paintings, manuscripts, rare coins and anthropological exhibits.

psychology, political science and international business, among others. He has nine MBA degrees, and two PhD degrees, taking the total of his postgraduate degrees to sixty-seven (67).

Postgraduate qualifications from most number of universities

Dr Anil Kumar Yadav (b. 4 June 1968) holds 32 postgraduate qualifications (PhD, MPhil and PG degrees and diplomas) from 20 universities across 17 states and Union Territories. His record begins with MA (Sociology) from Annamalai University in May 1995 and his latest degree is MA (Sociology) from the University of Mumbai, Maharashtra, in May 2022.

Youngest chancellor

Dileep K. Nair became the youngest chancellor of a university in the country when he took office at the North East Frontier Technical University (NEFTU) in Along (now Aalo), West Siang District, Arunachal Pradesh, in April 2017. He was 38 years old at the time.

Oldest school of art

Sir J.J. School of Art in Bombay (now Mumbai, Maharashtra), was founded by Sir Jamsetjee Jeejeebhoy in 1833.

Oldest course in pharmacy

The Portuguese introduced the first pharmacy course with a medical course in 1842 at an old Portuguese school, the 'Escola Medica de Goa'. It was renamed the Goa College of Pharmacy in 1963 and moved to its current premises, a former Portuguese school in Panaji. The college is now affiliated to Goa University and is run by the Government of Goa.

WR Largest open university

The Indira Gandhi National Open University (IGNOU) at Maidan Garhi, New Delhi, has the distinction of being the largest open university in the world, serving more than three million enrolled students through its 21 schools of studies, and a network of 67 regional centres, around 2,667 learner support centres and 29 overseas partner institutions.

ARCHIVES AND LIBRARIES

First library

Christian missionaries at Serampore, Bengal (now Srirampur, West Bengal) set up their first library (later the William Carey Library) in 1800, which became the hub of their educational activities. The Reverend John Fountain, sent to India in 1796 to assist William Carey, a missionary, was its first librarian.

Oldest library

The Calcutta Public Library (established in 1836) was merged with the Imperial Library (established in 1891) in 1903. In 1953, it was inaugurated as the National Library with B.S. Kesavan as its first librarian.

First online Braille library

Launched in 2012 by the National Institute for the Visually Handicapped (NIVH), Dehradun, Uttarakhand, to commemorate the birth anniversary of Louis Braille on 4 January, the online Braille library provides access to 12,000 books in 10 languages in a user-friendly format. The library can be accessed at http://nivh.gov.in/index.php/national-braille-library

First operational digital library network

DELNET was the first operational digital library network. It was started as a project of the India International Centre, New Delhi, in 1988 and registered as a society in 1992.

First classical library

The mission of the Murty Classical Library of

Sir Jamsetjee Jejeebhoy: founder of the oldest school of art

UNESCO declared 5 October as World Teachers' Day in 1994 to honour the adoption of the UNESCO–International Labour Organization's Status of Teachers recommendation that delineated the rights and responsibilities of teachers at the Paris Conference in 1966.

National Library, Kolkata, West Bengal: oldest library

The University of Calcutta, drawn by Francis Firth, late 19th century

The University of Calcutta: A Course in Firsts

Established on 24 January 1857, the University of Calcutta was the first multidisciplinary and Western-style educational institution in Asia. It was also the first university in Asia to teach European classics, English literature, Indian philosophy and Occidental and Oriental history. At the time of establishment, it had a catchment area ranging from Lahore to Burma (now Myanmar) and Ceylon (now Sri Lanka).

Here are some other highlights of the university:

- The first medical school, the Calcutta Medical College, was affiliated to the university in 1857.
- From 1836 to 1890, the Government Science College, Jabalpur, the first Indian science college, was affiliated with the university.
- The first university library began functioning here in 1870.
- The first college for women, Bethune College, established in 1879, was also affiliated to the university.
- Bankim Chandra Chattopadhyay and Jadunath Bose were the first graduates of the university in 1858. Kadambini Ganguly and Chandramukhi Basu were the first female graduates in 1882.
- Five Nobel laureates (the highest number in South Asia) are associated with the university. They are Sir Ronald Ross, Rabindranath Tagore, Sir C.V. Raman, Amartya Sen and Abhijit Vinayak Banerjee.

India is to present the pre-modern classics of Indian literature from the past two millennia – a part of world literature's treasured heritage – to a new generation. It began publishing classics in January 2015. The original Indic text, in the appropriate script, is accompanied by a modern English translation on the opposite page.

First mobile library

A bullock cart (in the shape of a small stall), laden with books at Melavasal, a village near Mannargudi in Tamil Nadu, on 21 October 1931, was possibly the first mobile library in the country. The brainchild of Rao Bahadur S.V. Kanagasabai Pillai, a Mannargudi-based engineer, the library was inaugurated by S.R. Ranganathan, called the father of library science in India. The mobile library carried books that dealt with beekeeping and other cottage industries, aimed at providing vocational training to farmers. The cart would visit neighbouring villages in the months when

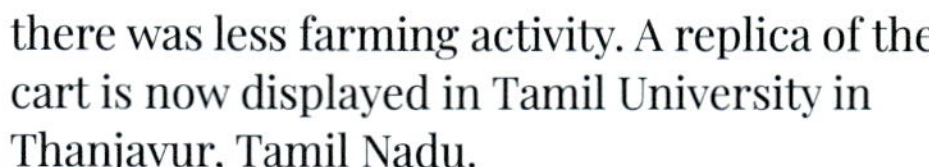

there was less farming activity. A replica of the cart is now displayed in Tamil University in Thanjavur, Tamil Nadu.

First sports library

The Kanga Library at Wankhede Stadium, Mumbai, Maharashtra, has a collection of 13,000 books on sports. Around 10,000 of these are on cricket, including the entire collection of Wisden Cricketers' Almanack from 1864.

Biggest public library system

The Delhi Public Library, started as a UNESCO project in 1951 by the Government of India, is the biggest public library system in India and reportedly the busiest set of public libraries in South Asia. The library network consists of a central library, three branch libraries, 20 sub-branch libraries, one community library, eight resettlement colony libraries, one Braille library, 100 mobile library service points (including 25 Braille mobile library points) and 33 deposit stations in the Union Territory of Delhi and the NCR. It has a collection of over 1.8 million books in English and other Indian languages.

Only underground library

Almost 128 km from Jaisalmer, Rajasthan, in Bhadriya Village in Jaisalmer District, is an underground library 16 ft (4.88 m) below ground level. Above this library is a temple of Devi Bhadariya Mata. The library can seat 4,000 persons and is maintained by the trustees of the temple. Housing around 900,000 books, the library was started by Harbansh Singh Nirmal, an avid reader, popularly known as Bhadariya Maharaj.

Largest university library

The Maulana Azad Library, the central library of Aligarh Muslim University in Aligarh, is the largest university library in Asia. The current seven-floor library houses about 1,400,000 books, periodicals, pamphlets, 43,000 e-journals and manuscripts, paintings and photographs. It was inaugurated by Jawaharlal Nehru, the first prime minister of India, in 1960.

Only bookshop-cum-library on a lake

Gulshan Books, a bookshop-cum-library set up in May 2016, has a reading room, a café and over 80,000 books. Located on Nehru Park Island on the Dal Lake in Srinagar, Jammu and Kashmir, it can be reached by a shikara.

Largest film archives

The National Film Archives were set up in

1964 in Poona (now Pune), Maharashtra, as a media unit of the Ministry of Information and Broadcasting, Government of India. Besides over 100,000 films, it has 157,687 photographs, 23,748 film posters, 14,210 song booklets, over 100,000 press clippings and more.

Largest library

- *By number of books:* The National Library, Kolkata, with more than 2.6 million books and over 500,000 manuscripts, is the largest library by number of books. The campus of the library is spread over 30 acres (12.14 hectares). However, the actual built-up area is around 1.5 lakh sq. ft (1.39 hectares).
- *By built-up area:* The Anna Centenary Library in Chennai, Tamil Nadu, is the largest in terms of constructed area – close to 330,000 sq. ft (3.07 hectares). It houses around 1 million books.

Anna Centenary Library, Chennai, Tamil Nadu: largest library by built-up area

A first-of-its-kind tram library

A specially designed tram library to run along Kolkata's College Street route was inaugurated on 1 October 2020. The tramcar has free Wi-Fi to help passengers read e-books while they travel. The library has books and magazines, including those on competitive examinations.

First transgender resources library

India's first transgender library was opened as part of the transgender resource centre in Viswanathapuram, Madurai, Tamil Nadu, in 2016. The centre focuses on providing materials to help people become aware of the non-binary gender and ambisexual people.

First boat library

The Young Readers' Boat Library was set up on a boat by the West Bengal Transport Corporation in collaboration with a heritage bookshop. It was launched on 26 January 2021, and houses a collection of over 500 titles in English and Bengali. The boat library conducts three-hour ferries on the River Hooghly, starting from Millennium Park to Belur Math Jetty and back. It also offers free Wi-Fi facilities and various readership activities, and conducts three trips on all weekdays.

MUSEUMS

First public museum in a university

Established in 1937, the Ashutosh Museum of Indian Art, located in the main campus of the University of Calcutta, West Bengal, is the first public museum in any university in India. It is named after Sir Ashutosh Mukherjee, the great educationist, who introduced the study of Indology – including Indian art and archaeology – at the university level, and was the vice chancellor of the university from 1906 to 1914 and 1921 to 1923. The museum houses more than 25,000 sculptures, paintings, folk-art objects, textiles and terracotta items, among other artefacts from various phases of Indian art, with special emphasis on the art of Bengal.

First museum of textiles

The Calico Museum of Textiles in Ahmedabad, Gujarat, was set up by Gautam Sarabhai, chairman of Calico Mills, in 1949, at the suggestion of the pioneering art historian and philosopher, Dr Ananda Coomaraswamy. The museum has a comprehensive collection of Indian textiles. The foundation of modern Indian textile studies was laid here and the catalogues of the Calico Museum textile collection are an indispensable reference.

First railway museum

Inaugurated by Kamlapati Tripathi, the then minister of railways, on 1 February 1977, the Rail Transport Museum at Chanakyapuri, New Delhi, was the first rail museum in India. it was renamed the National Rail Museum in 1995 and features historical exhibits and artefacts related to the history of rail transport in India.

First Partition museum

The Arts and Cultural Heritage Trust, set up on 24 October 2016 in Amritsar, Punjab, is the world's first museum on Partition of India. Housed in a restored portion of the Town Hall, it is dedicated to Partition of the subcontinent in 1947. The museum commemorates Partition's victims, its survivors and its legacy. On display are photographs, clothes, utensils and other memorabilia of the time.

14,500 schools across India will be developed under the PM SHRI Schools scheme, with a total project cost of **₹27,360** crores (273.6 billion) allotted for it in 2022 for five academic years starting from 2022–23.

Above: National Rail Museum, New Delhi: first railway museum

Below: Partition Museum, Amritsar, Punjab: first museum themed on Partition

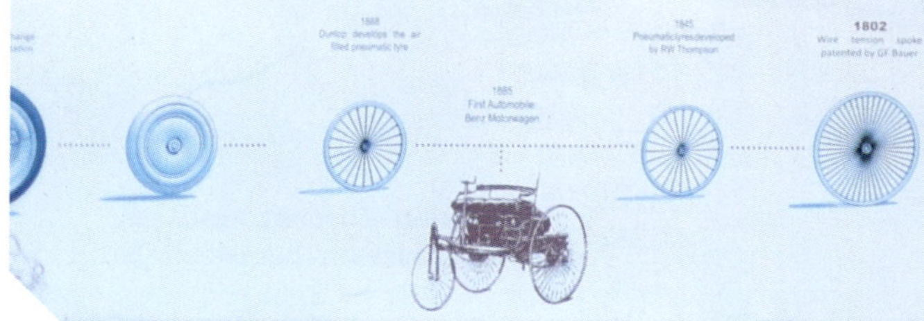

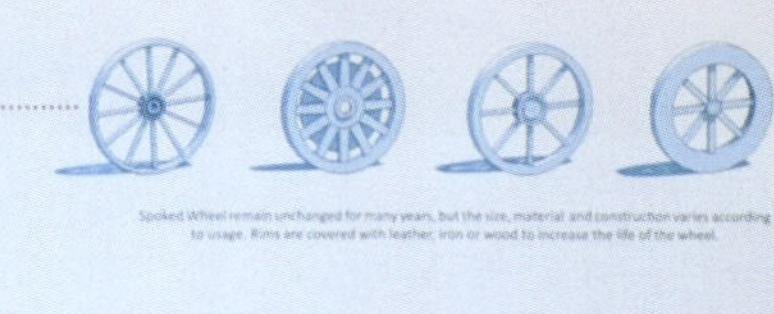

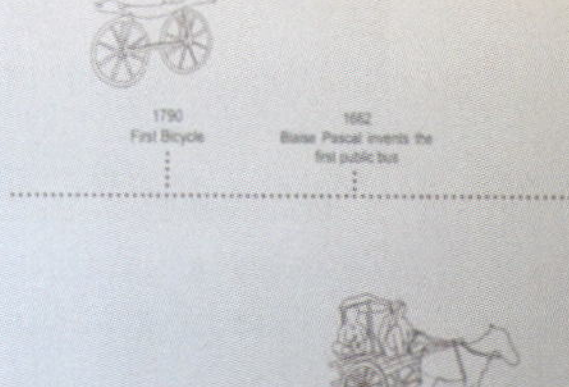

The Heritage Transport Museum, Tauru, Haryana: first transport museum

First national museum of Indian cinema

The country's first National Museum of Indian Cinema (NMIC) was inaugurated in Mumbai, Maharashtra, in January 2019. Conceived in 1997, it has been designed by the National Council of Science Museums and implemented by the Films Division, under the Ministry of Information and Broadcasting, Government of India. It is placed in a period 19th-century heritage bungalow called Gulshan Mahal, and extends to another new high-technology five-floor building with two mezzanine floors. On display are projectors, recording equipment, cameras, archival posters of old films, and biographies of actors and other film personalities.

First transport museum

Opened on 7 December 2013, the Heritage Transport Museum at Tauru, Nuh District, Haryana, has a rich collection of 2,500 objects, including howdahs, bullock carts, palanquins, a 1924 Ford, vintage scooters, a 1946 Piper aircraft, transport toys from the 1920s to now, and other related artefacts.

First kite museum

A museum dedicated to the rarest kites in the world is housed in Ahmedabad, Gujarat, a city popular for its annual International Kite Festival. Established in 1985, the museum was the brainchild of Bhanubhai Shah, who donated his rare collection of over 50 years to the Ahmedabad Municipal Corporation. The only kite museum in the country, it is located in the basement of Sanskar Kendra and boasts of kites of many shapes and sizes, with some that measure up to 6.7 m x 4.88 m (22 ft x 16 ft).

First underground museum

India's first underground museum opened in the Rashtrapati Bhavan on 2 October 2016. The museum showcases a collection of artefacts associated with each of the past presidents of

India, including their personal belongings and vehicles, with a range of materials highlighting the history of India's freedom struggle. The museum displays more than 2,000 artefacts in a sprawling 12,077.39 sq. m (130,000 sq. ft) space.

There are **2,442** rare manuscripts in the custody of the National Archives of India.

WR First museum of toilets

The Sulabh International Museum of Toilets at Mahavir Enclave in New Delhi, a museum dedicated to toilets, has 300 objects with a mix of originals, models and photographs. The museum traces 4,500 years of the history of toilets.

First election museum

Inaugurated in 2016, the Election Museum, located in the office premises of the chief electoral officer at Kashmiri Gate, Delhi, depicts the election journey of the largest democracy in the world. The four sections – library, audiovisual, photo gallery, and electoral management – display more than 200 archived photographs, maps, artefacts and references. Possibly the largest of its kind in the world, the museum showcases the electoral journey of India since the first general election in 1952.

First insect museum

An insect museum was unveiled by Tamil Nadu chief minister Edappadi K. Palaniswami, at the Tamil Nadu Agricultural University in Coimbatore, Tamil Nadu, in March 2018. Covering 621.61 sq. m (6,691 sq. ft), this museum displays insect specimens starting from the early 20th century. It has live butterflies in a natural setting, termite mounds, bee species and insect-eating plants, along with images, videos and models of their behaviour and habitats.

First interactive museum of music

The Indian Music Experience (IME), established in 2018 in Bengaluru, Karnataka, is a rare museum that offers an interactive musical journey during which the visitor is encouraged to touch and feel the instruments on display to create one's own music. IME features a Sound Garden with 10 playable musical sculptures. It also has touchscreens, musical instruments, small theatres and audio-video kiosks as well as a learning centre that offers music classes and workshops on a regular basis.

First wax museum

Madame Tussauds Delhi, located in the vintage Regal Theatre in Rajiv Chowk, New Delhi, was part of the famed international chain of wax museums, the first of which opened in London in 1835. Set up in December 2017, the Delhi wax museum had on display over 40 life-size wax sculptures of political leaders, and celebrities from sports and music, Bollywood and Hollywood. The 23rd location for Tussauds museums, it closed in December 2020.

WR First museum of utensils

Vechaar (Vishalla Environmental Centre for Heritage of Art, Architecture and Research), a museum that archives heritage utensils, including more than 5,400 pots, pans, serving vessels, nutcrackers and other kitchen equipment, is housed in a village-like complex called Vishalla in Ahmedabad, Gujarat. The museum was set up in April 1981 by its collector and owner, Surendra C. Patel, and anthropologist Jyotindra Jain.

First culinary arts museum

Michelin-starred Indian chef Vikas Khanna opened India's first living culinary museum, the Museum of Culinary Arts, at his alma mater, the Welcomgroup Graduate School of Hotel Administration in Manipal, Karnataka, in April 2018. Over 2,000 utensils and artefacts from all over India and dating back centuries are housed in the museum, which is the shape of a giant pot (similar to Harappan ones). It is spread over 25,000 sq. ft (2,322 sq. m), as a part of the Department of Culinary Arts.

First dinosaur museum

The Dinosaur Museum at the Balasinor Dinosaur Park in Raiyoli Village in Balanisor Taluka in Gujarat's Mahisagar District was inaugurated in June 2019. With an enhanced version of the Dinosaur Museum already existing there, the facility is equipped with modern technology like 3D projection, virtual-reality presentations, interactive kiosks and life-size dinosaur replicas. Its 10 galleries exhibit dinosaur remains and fossil records from the area as well as other regions of Gujarat and India, and show the history of these dinosaurs (such as the *Rajasaurus narmadensis*) from their origin to extinction.

First sports museum

Fanattic Sports Museum is located over 6,700 sq. ft (622.45 sq. m) at Ecospace in New Town, Rajarhat, around 25 km from central Kolkata. Opened in 2017, this multi-sports museum displays memorabilia from cricket, hockey, football, the Olympics and Paralympics. It houses memorabilia collected by cricket historian Boria Majumdar for over 25 years. Highlights include Sachin Tendulkar's glove, Lionel Messi's shoe, Didier Drogba's Chelsea jersey and many artefacts donated by Olympic gold medallist Abhinav Bindra, Paralympics silver medallist Deepa Malik and bronze medallist Devendra Jhajaria, among others.

First science museum

The first science museum was set up by the

Representative image

A Gender Equity Programme in Government Schools in Odisha

The Department of School and Mass Education of Odisha announced its partnership with the NGO Breakthrough and the Abdul Latif Jameel Poverty Action Lab (J-PAL), South Asia, on 8 August 2022. A memorandum of understanding (MoU) was signed to introduce a gender equity curriculum in the government schools of Odisha. This curriculum will be integrated into the social studies syllabus in over 18,000 middle and 5,000 secondary schools in the state. The Gender Equity Programme was launched to help Odisha achieve the Sustainable Development Goals (SDG) related to quality education and gender equality. Breakthrough is responsible for the contextualization and integration of this curriculum into the syllabus of students from classes VI to X. They will also oversee the training of teachers, conduct interactive workshops, engage parents in this programme and collect feedback. J-PAL will monitor all activities to verify that the objectives of the course are being achieved. The programme aims to engage adolescents in discussions about gender norms, roles and discriminatory practices, to help shape their outlook and gender attitudes.

Fanattic Sports Museum, Rajarhat, West Bengal: first sports museum

Science City Kolkata, under the National Council of Science Museums: largest chain of science museums

The *'Beti Bachao, Beti Padhao'* (*BBBP*) scheme was launched in the country on this date and in six years of its inception the Gross Enrolment Ratio (GER) of girls at the secondary level had improved from 77.45 per cent to 81.35 per cent by 2021.

industrialist Ghanshyam Das Birla at BITS (Birla Institute of Technology and Science), Pilani, Jhunjhunu District, Rajasthan, in 1954. Located in a hall (185 sq. m/1,991 sq. ft area) of the Tower Building, it depicts the industries and business enterprises of the Birla family. It is the only museum of industry and technology located inside a university campus.

Largest chain of science museums

The National Council of Science Museums (NCSM), under the Ministry of Culture, Government of India, is the largest chain of science centres/museums under a single administrative umbrella in the world. There are 24 science centres or museums and an R&D laboratory and training centre of NCSM, located in different states in India.

Largest and oldest museum

The Indian Museum in Kolkata, West Bengal, one of the oldest museums in the world, founded by the Asiatic Society of Bengal in 1814 has rare collections of antiques, armour and ornaments, fossils, skeletons, mummies and Mughal paintings.

QUIZZES

First live quiz on TV

Neil O'Brien, called the 'father of quizzing', brought the concept of quizzes to India in 1967, after watching them on TV in the UK in the 1960s. He moderated the Eddie Hyde Memorial Quiz Contest 1967 in the parish hall of the Church of Christ the King in Calcutta (now Kolkata, West Bengal) before an audience of forty. The open live quiz had four teams with members from all walks of life.

First quiz show on radio

On 12 April 1972, the *Cadbury Bournvita Quiz Contest* for high-school students became the first English quiz show to be broadcast on radio (Vividh Bharati) in India. It became one of India's famous quiz contests. It ran for over a decade and was later revived as a television quiz in June 1992. The original quizmaster on the radio show was Hamid Sayani, a prominent broadcast personality.

First national TV quizmaster

Raman Kumar was the first quizmaster on national television. He hosted *Mashoor Mahal* during 1985–86 in the quiz genre, featuring famous personalities.

Longest-running open quiz

Instituted in 1992 in Chennai, Tamil Nadu, by the Landmark Bookstores, the annual Landmark Quiz is the longest-running open quiz in the country. A preliminary round of about 40 questions that come up on a screen is held due to the huge turnout. The quiz is hosted by Dr Navin Jayakumar and his team (which included his mother) since its inception, with the exception of 2006 when Derek O'Brien was the quizmaster.

Longest-running school quiz

The *Cadbury Bournvita Quiz Contest* was a weekly televised show that started in 1992

Arna Jharna: The Extraordinary Thar Desert Museum

This museum in Rajasthan is an unusual one, celebrating desert landscapes and the folk culture of the people. Located in Moklawas Village, around 15 km from Jodhpur, Arna Jharna (which means 'forest and spring') was conceptualized by folklorist and ethnomusicologist Komal Kothari, whose enduring work of documenting folk music, culture and oral traditions for the Rupayan Sansthan is exhibited here. Established in 2000 using local architectural methods, the museum, which unconventionally displays objects without glass cases, houses artefacts from the communities of Rajasthan, including a peerless collection of unique folk musical instruments, such as the *kamaicha*, the *jogia sarangi*, the *nagfani* and the *narh*, which have sadly fallen into disuse. It also showcases 160 brooms, made of vegetal materials such as grasses, shrubs and bushes growing in *bajra*, maize and *jowar* crop zones. Using audio and video recordings and other exhibits, the museum builds a holistic picture of rural Rajasthani people and their interaction with their natural environment as a seamless landscape of their art and culture.

as the first televised school quiz in India. Anchored by reputed quizmaster Derek O'Brien, it ran continuously on Zee TV till 2001, after which it moved to the TV channel Sony, followed by Colors. Now, it is conducted in a mobile app format.

Longest-running televised quiz

Prashnottari, a twice-a-week (previously fortnightly) quiz, with participants from schools, colleges and a general live TV audience, was first telecast on Prasar Bharati's Jaipur Doordarshan Kendra on 23 July 1993. Hosted by former IAS officer Dr Mahendra Surana since it began, it continued without break on the same channel, completing 900 episodes on 15 March 2020.

Longest-running state-level quiz

Initiated in 1986 by Vijaya Bank, Karnataka's oldest quiz competition, titled VGenUth Quiz Contest (now called the Baroda Champ Annual Quiz Contest) is open to all high-school students across Karnataka. Its 34th edition was held on 2 February 2020 in Bengaluru, in which more than 400 students from over 200 schools participated.

Most participants in an online quiz – single day

An e-quiz based on the theme 'AatmaNirbhar Bharat: Strengthen the Future', organized by the School of Entrepreneurship Skills, Bharatiya Skill Development University in Jaipur, Rajasthan, and conducted in association with The Employers Association of Rajasthan and the Global Foundation for Skill Development and Entrepreneurship, had 5,058 participants on 1 June 2020. The purpose of this quiz was to disseminate knowledge about the AatmaNirbhar Bharat Abhiyan or Self-Reliance Movement.

Most participants in an online quiz – multiple days – up to a month*

An online quiz, to commemorate Asteroid Day 2021, organized from 21 June to 30 June 2021 by Smartcircuits Innovations Pvt. Ltd, Haryana, saw the participation of 15,754 students from Grade I to Grade XII.

Most participants in an online quiz – multiple days – up to a year

A school fitness and sports quiz launched in September 2021, as part of the Central government's celebration of 75 years of Independence. saw the participation of 36,299 students from 13,502 schools in the preliminary round, which completed on 25 January 2022. The quiz aimed to offer a national platform for students to show their knowledge and create awareness about India's sporting history.

Most participants in an offline quiz – multiple venues – single day

The Haryana Police organized an hour-long state-level quiz competition on 8 November 2016 on the theme of road safety. As many as 2,447,744 students participated in it.

A sum of ₹1,04,278 crore was allotted to the education sector in the Union budget for the financial year 2022–23.

*This is a one-time record. Future and further claims for this category will not be accepted.

MEDIA AND COMMUNICATIONS

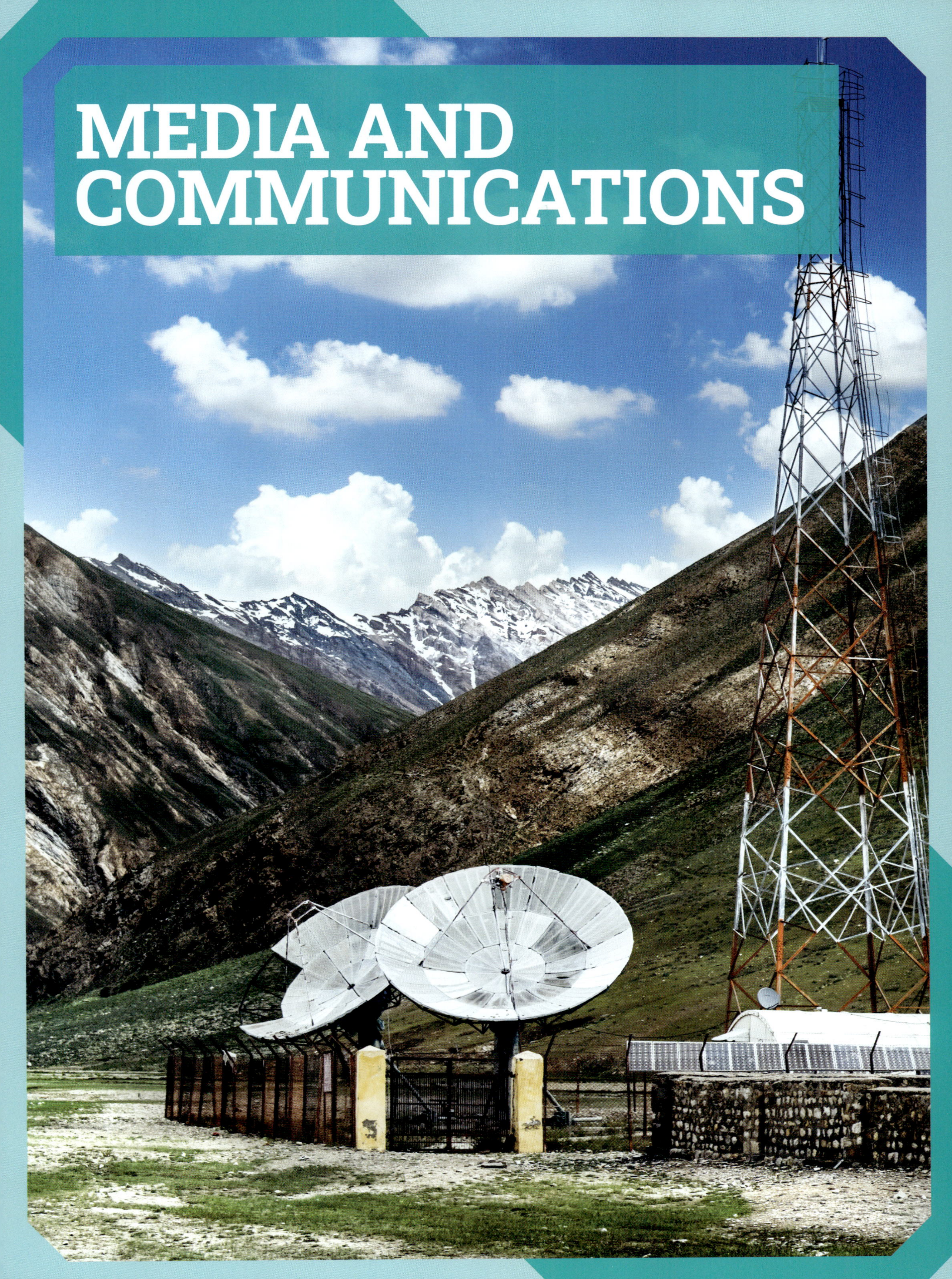

PRINT

First printing press
The first printing press came to India accidentally, in 1556, when the patriarch designate of Abyssinia (now Ethiopia, Africa) broke his journey at Goa and later died there. The printing press was left behind. The printers were a Spaniard called Joao de Bustamante and his Indian assistant, whose name is not known.

First paper-making machine
William Carey (1761–1834), a British Christian missionary, translator, social reformer and cultural anthropologist, who founded the Serampore College and University in Bengal, first set up a paper-making machine in Calcutta (now Kolkata, West Bengal) in 1830.

First lithographic printing
Lithographic printing was introduced by the Calcutta Art Studio in 1878 in Calcutta (now Kolkata), West Bengal.

First multilingual press
A multilingual press for all the main local Indian languages was first set up in Serampore, Bengal (now Srirampur, Hooghly District, West Bengal), in 1800 by Christian missionaries.

Earliest type
The first types in any Indian language were cast in Goa in 1577 by Joao Goncalves, reportedly assisted by Father Pero Luis, who was a Tamil Jesuit priest.

First typewriters
The first typewriters were imported into India in 1896.

First indigenous typewriters
- Godrej & Boyce Manufacturing Company Ltd manufactured India's first manual typewriter in 1955. It was designed and created entirely by Indian engineers.
- Blackwood India Ltd in Calcutta (now Kolkata), West Bengal, established in 1960 and then renamed J.K. Business Machines in 1961, were the first makers of portable typewriters in the country.
- The first indigenous electronic typewriters were manufactured by Hindustan Teleprinters Ltd in 1975.

First press regulation
The Censorship of Press Act of 1799 was the first regulation with an element of censorship to enforce wartime restrictions on the press. It was enacted by the then Governor General Lord Wellesley, who anticipated a French invasion of India. All news was scrutinized, including 'pre-censorship' before publication, by a special security administration unit with a view to preventing information leaks.

First newsprint factory
The first paper mill in India to manufacture newsprint was a factory at Nepanagar, Burhanpur District, Madhya Pradesh, set up in January 1955.

First news agency
The Press Trust of India (PTI), which is a non-profit-sharing cooperative of Indian newspapers, was established on 27 August 1947. It took over the Associated Press of India and the Indian operations of Reuters, and provided news, photographs, features and infographics from February 1949 onwards.

Press Trust of India office, New Delhi: first news agency

 First news agency to supply news in Urdu
On 5 June 1992, the United News of India (UNI) became the first agency in the world to supply Urdu news. It remains the only agency to do so.

First vernacular paper
Samachar Darpan was published in Bengali from Serampore, Bengal (now Srirampur, Hooghly District, West Bengal), by William Carey and John Clark Marshman from May 1818 onwards. Marshman was a British journalist, historian and publisher of the *Friend of India* from which *The Statesman* newspaper descended.

First newspaper
Hicky's Bengal Gazette or the *Original Calcutta General Advertiser*, India's and Asia's first newspaper, was launched on 29 June 1780 by James Augustus Hicky, an Irishman.

First non-English newspaper

In 1794, the Reverend Harutyun Shmavonyan edited and published *Azdarar* in the Armenian script in Madras (now Chennai, Tamil Nadu). This was the first Armenian journal in the world and the first non-English one in India.

The only handwritten newspaper

The Musalman, the oldest Urdu language daily newspaper, published in Chennai, Tamil Nadu, is the only handwritten newspaper in the world. It is a four-page evening paper handwritten by four calligraphers or *katibs*, and printed. Established in 1927 by Syed Azmatulla, it has not missed a single day's publication. The paper has correspondents all over India and sells at 75 paise a copy to around 25,000 subscribers.

First Hindi newspaper

Banaras Akhbar began in 1845, under the editorship of Govind Narayan Thatte, as the first Hindi newspaper.

First newspaper for the visually impaired

Swagat Thorat's *Sparshdnyan*, launched in February 2008, is India's first newspaper for the visually challenged. Its name means 'knowledge by touch', and it is published in Marathi on the 1st and 15th of every month.

INDIA AT HER BEST 75 YEARS OF INDEPENDENCE

IIMC, New Delhi

On the Course in Journalism

The Indian Institute of Mass Communication (IIMC) was set up in 1965 as an autonomous society and the national centre for teaching, training and research in mass communication, under the Ministry of Information and Broadcasting. With its headquarters in Jawaharlal Nehru University New Campus, New Delhi, it now has five regional campuses in Dhenkanal, Odisha; Kottayam, Kerala; Aizawl, Mizoram; Amaravati, Maharashtra; and Jammu, Jammu and Kashmir. Over the years, IIMC has developed an array of courses, such as a diploma course in development journalism, and postgraduate diploma courses in journalism (English/Hindi/Odia/Urdu/Marathi/Malayalam), radio and TV journalism, digital media, and advertising and public relations, among others.

Year	No. of Students Awarded a Diploma
1991	94
1995	147
2000	155
2007	258
2010	270*

*2010–11 report mentions 'testimonials'; Source: Ministry of Communications annual reports

First financial daily

The Economic Times, India's first financial daily, was launched by the Times of India Group in March 1961. Like the London-based *Financial Times*, it too was printed on salmon-pink paper.

First daily with an international edition

In February 1994, India's global newspaper, *The Asian Age*, was launched simultaneously from Delhi, Mumbai and London. It has a Kolkata edition too.

First magazine in Hindi

Saraswati, India's first Hindi monthly magazine, was published in January 1900. Its founder was the well-known printer and publisher Chintamani Ghosh and the magazine was published by the Indian Press, which was based in Allahabad (now Prayagraj, Uttar Pradesh).

First newspaper run entirely by women

Khabar Lahariya is the first newspaper in India that is entirely staffed, edited and published by women. The eight-page rural weekly in Hindi is sold in 600 villages in its print form and on multiple digital platforms. It was launched in 2002 in Chitrakoot District, Uttar Pradesh. In 2009, it was awarded the UNESCO King Sejong Literary Prize for its contribution to literacy.

First women's magazine in English

The Indian Ladies' Magazine was first published in English in 1901 by Kamala Satthianadhan in Madras (now Chennai, Tamil Nadu).

First women's magazine in an Indian language

Masik Patrika in Bengali, published from Calcutta, Bengal (now Kolkata, West Bengal), in 1854, was the first women's magazine in an Indian language.

First magazine for the visually challenged

White Print was the first lifestyle magazine in English in India for visually challenged people. It was launched in May 2013 by Upasana Makati, a former communications student from the University of Ottawa, Canada. This 64-page monthly, printed at the National Association for the Blind, Mumbai, Maharashtra, and circulated across India, features articles about sports, politics, culture, fashion and technology, besides short stories and reader contributions. *White Print* has also released Braille-tactile alphabet books in

Braille, both in English and Hindi, which are called 'Tactabet'.

First newspaper to be printed in colour

The Hindu, with its headquarters in Madras (now Chennai, Tamil Nadu), began as a weekly in 1878 and turned into a daily in 1889. A family-run newspaper, it was the first to be printed in colour in 1940. It was also the first Indian newspaper to own aeroplanes to distribute newspapers (1963), and the first newspaper to digitize and be available online (1995).

First feminist journal

Manushi, founded in 1978 in Delhi, and edited by Madhu Kishwar, was the first feminist journal in the country.

First vernacular periodical

Digdarshan, a Bengali monthly, first appeared in April 1818.

First Indian publication in the USA

India Abroad, the first Indian weekly in the USA, was launched by Gopal Raju, an India-born American publisher and editor, in 1970. It focused on news for the Indian diaspora.

First letters to the editor column

The letters to the editor column was introduced in the biweekly magazine *Calcutta Journal*, first published in 1878 in Bengal (now West Bengal).

Multi-edition daily with the largest readership

Dainik Jagran, which has its headquarters in Kanpur, Uttar Pradesh, leads with 37 editions across 11 states and a readership of 68,667,000 (2019 Q4; Indian Readership Survey [IRS]).

Daily (and Hindi daily) with the largest readership

Dainik Jagran, which is headquartered in Kanpur, Uttar Pradesh, has a readership of 68,667,000 (2019 Q4; IRS).

State/UT with the most Indian-language publications

Delhi leads among all states and UTs in publications in the maximum number of Indian languages, with publications in as many as 15 languages. It is followed by Maharashtra, Uttarakhand and Tamil Nadu with publications in 14 languages each. Gujarat comes after that with publications in 11 languages by 2020–21.

English daily with the largest readership

The Times of India, headquartered in Mumbai, Maharashtra, has a recorded readership of 17,344,000 (2019 Q4; IRS).

State/UT with the most publications

Uttar Pradesh, with 21,166 publications, leads with the maximum number of publications in India. It is followed by Maharashtra, with 19,796 publications, and Delhi with 16,351 of them by 2020–21.

Most circulated government publication

Employment News, an English weekly that is published from New Delhi by the Publications Division, Ministry of Information and Broadcasting, Government of India, has the highest circulation of 239,498 among government publications (as of 2019).

State/UT with most registered newspapers

Uttar Pradesh, with 21,166 registered publications, is the state with the most registered newspaper publications. It is followed by Maharashtra, with 19,796 publications, and Delhi, with 16,351 of them.

Largest read regional-language daily

Malayala Manorama, with its headquarters in Kottayam, Kerala, has a readership of 17,763,000 (2019 Q4; IRS).

Most read English magazine

India Today, a weekly published from Noida, Uttar Pradesh, by the India Today Group, has a readership of 9,493,000 (2019 Q4; IRS).

Most read Hindi magazine

India Today (Hindi), a weekly published from Noida, Uttar Pradesh, by the India Today Group, has a total readership of 6,641,000 (2019 Q4; IRS).

Most read magazine in a regional language

Vanitha, a Malayalam fortnightly magazine, published from Kottayam, Kerala, by the Malayala Manorama Group, has a readership of 5,886,000 (2019 Q4; IRS).

State/UT with most publications in a single language

Uttar Pradesh, with 16,557 publications in Hindi, leads among all states and UTs with the most publications in a single language (Hindi). It is followed by Madhya Pradesh, with 11,973 Hindi-language publications, and Maharashtra, with 9,982 publications in Marathi.

The Press Information Bureau released 31,349 press releases during 2020–21.

A magazine and newspaper stall in Uttar Pradesh

Gobind Behari Lal: first Indian-origin journalist to win the Pulitzer Prize

First Indian-origin journalist to win the Pulitzer Prize

Gobind Behari Lal (1889–1982), a science journalist in the USA, won the Pulitzer Prize in 1937.

Longest-running Indian women's magazine

Femina, which started in July 1959 with Frene Talyarkhan as its first editor, continues to be published. It is now published by Worldwide Media, which is owned by the Times Group. It was also the first lifestyle magazine of the country in English, and has the highest circulation in its category (108,560 in August 2019).

Oldest children's magazine

Chandamama, founded by Telugu film-makers B. Nagi Reddy and Aluri Chakrapani was launched in July 1947 in Telugu. It was edited by Kodavatiganti Kutumba Rao. The magazine ceased publication in 1998. In 2007, it was acquired by Geodesic Ltd. Its last edition came out in March 2013 and since then its status is unknown. In its heyday, *Chandamama* was published in 13 languages and had a readership of around 200,000 across the country.

TOP 10 LANGUAGES WITH MOST NEWSPAPERS*

Source: Press In India 2020–21, Office of the Registrar of Newspapers in India
* Only publications that filed annual statements

Oldest extant newspaper – regional language

The *Bombay Samachar*, now titled *Mumbai Samachar*, is the oldest continuously published newspaper in any language in India, and continues to be published. Launched on 1 July 1822 by Fardoonjee Marazban (1787–1847), the daily is published in both Gujarati and English. Marazban, who was from Bombay (now Mumbai, Maharashtra), was a printer and a newspaper editor. He established vernacular journalism in India and initiated the production of Gujarati types.

Oldest extant newspaper – English

The Times of India began on 3 November 1838 as a biweekly, initially called *Bombay Times and Journal of Commerce*. It was renamed *The Times of India* in 1850, with J.E. Brennan as its editor.

Longest career as a journalist

B.P. Sharma, a journalist from Jammu and Kashmir, who died in 2005 at the age of ninety-seven, was an active journalist for over 70 years. He established the Jammu station of Radio Kashmir (All India Radio) and was its first director. He also worked with the news agency Reuters, *The Times of India, Hindustan Times* and *The Tribune*. Later, he served as the principal information officer of Jammu and Kashmir.

Longest spell as editor

Tushar Kanti Ghosh (1898–1994) was editor of the *Amrita Bazar Patrika*, based in Kolkata, West Bengal, for 64 years. He had founded the newspaper in 1928.

Daily newspaper column appearing over the longest period

Prem Kumar Sharma (b. 19 November 1958) has been writing a daily horoscope column in *HT City*, a supplement of the *Hindustan Times* since 3 October 1999. Up to 19 January 2021, he had completed 21 years and 3 months as a daily columnist.

Longest letter to the editor

Vinod Chandrashekhar Dixit (b. 1 December 1964) from Ahmedabad, Gujarat, wrote the longest letter to the editor on the topic 'Bank of India Celebrating 116 Years of Trusted Relationship', which was published in *Free Press*, Ahmedabad, Gujarat. Its word count was 3,093 and it was published on 8 September 2021.

Most letters to the editor

Vinod Chandrashekhar Dixit (b. 1 December 1964) from Ahmedabad, Gujarat, has written the most number of letters to the editor in the span of a year. He wrote a total of 1,769 letters between 1 April 2016 and 31 March 2017, and they were published in different newspapers and magazines.

Most articles published in a year

Vinod Chandrashekhar Dixit (b. 1 December 1964) from Ahmedabad, Gujarat, holds the record for publishing the most number of articles in newspapers and magazines in a year. The total number of articles published by him between May 2019 and April 2020 was 742.

Most pages in a newspaper supplement

Kannada daily *Vijayavani*'s Mysuru edition brought out a special issue with 320 pages in 10 volumes on 25 March 2020. This supplement was dedicated to Shri Mayakara Madappa, a social reformer and spiritual leader of the 16th century. The newspaper was sold at a price of ₹4.

Most pages in a newspaper

Dainik Bhaskar's Indore edition brought out a special issue with 128 pages on 17 September 2020. This newspaper was on the theme 'AatmaNirbhar Indore'.

RADIO

First private radio station

On 10 September 1935, Akashvani Mysore, a private radio station, was set up in present-day Karnataka by Dr M.V. Gopalaswamy, professor of psychology and principal of the Maharaja's College, at his residence.

Largest media organization

All India Radio (AIR) today reaches almost the entire population across the length and breadth of the country and nearly 92 per cent of the total area, making it the largest media organization by reach. It broadcasts in 23 languages and 179 dialects. Programmes of its External Services Division are broadcast in 11 Indian and 16 foreign languages.

First direct relay

A historic occasion, the first direct relay coincided with India's 'freedom at midnight' from British colonial rule. The ceremonies for the transfer of power from Britain to an independent India on the night of 14–15 August 1947 at the Central Hall of the Parliament House in Delhi were relayed by AIR.

First frequency modulation (FM) service

- AIR inaugurated the first ever FM service from Madras (now Chennai), Tamil Nadu, on 23 July 1977.
- Delhi started an FM stereo station on 19 March 1988.

First private FM broadcaster

Times FM from The Times Group commenced operations in 1993 from Ahmedabad, Gujarat. It ran till June 1998 and was relaunched as Radio Mirchi in 2000. Over the years, Radio Mirchi has expanded its presence across 63 cities in India and multiple stations in the UAE and the USA.

First private FM station

Radio City Bangalore, based in Bengaluru in Karnataka, started on 3 July 2001, becoming

Akashvani Bhavan, New Delhi, the headquarters of All India Radio

Uttar Pradesh Launches Its Own Radio Service

With a view to promoting the rich heritage, history and distinctive culture of Uttar Pradesh, the state's Department of Culture launched a community radio – Radio Jaighosh – on the anniversary of the Kakori Train Action at the recently renovated Sangeet Natak Akademi in Lucknow on 9 August 2022. Available at 107.8 MHz, Radio Jaighosh is available on both social media as well as the smartphone application of the radio. The shows include *Parakram* – stories of the unsung heroes of both pre- and post-independence India; *Shaurya Nagar* – a programme revolving around the oral traditions and legends of the state's 75 districts; *Kala Yatra*, focusing on the arts of the region; *Rajya ki Raftaar*, which shares information about government schemes; *Rajya Ki Rasoi* — which showcases local delicacies; and weekly educational programmes, among others.

Red FM launched its station in Leh, Ladakh.

the country's first private radio station, after the Government of India opened up the FM broadcasting industry to private companies and competition.

First controller of broadcasting

Lionel Fielden took over as the first controller of broadcasting for the Indian State Broadcasting Service (ISBS) on 30 August 1935 in British India. A senior BBC producer, he spent five years in India, establishing a countrywide radio service. On 8 June 1936, the ISBS was renamed All India Radio.

First broadcasting service

The Madras Presidency Radio Club, under the stewardship of C.V. Krishnaswamy Chetty, started a broadcasting service in 1924, using a tiny 40-watt transmitter with an effective range of only 8 km.

First broadcast

In June 1923, the Radio Club of Bombay made the first ever broadcast in the country from Bombay (now Mumbai, Maharashtra). This was followed by the setting up of the Calcutta Radio Club in West Bengal around five months later.

First broadcasting company

The Indian Broadcasting Company (IBC) was set up in Bombay (now Mumbai, Maharashtra), on 23 July 1927, with a medium-wave transmitter that had a range of 50 km.

First national programme of plays

On 15 August 1956, AIR first aired a play that was broadcast countrywide.

First national programme of music

AIR broadcast its first national music programme on 20 July 1952 with sitar maestro Pandit Ravi Shankar as the music conductor.

First sponsored programme

A musical programme, *Saridon Ke Saathi*, sponsored by Saridon, was aired on 3 May 1970 on the Mumbai–Pune–Nagpur network.

First news bulletin

On 19 January 1936, AIR aired its first news bulletin. The Central News Organization (CNO) was formed in August 1937. AIR came under the Department of Information and Broadcasting four years later.

First national programme of talks

On 29 July 1953, AIR aired the first national programme of talks in English.

First cricket commentary

On 1 January 1936, Bertie Meyer provided commentary for a match between the All-India XI and the maharaja of Patiala's Australian XI, from Bombay (now Mumbai) station, Maharashtra, from 12:46 p.m. to 1:00 p.m.

First phone-in programme

Phone-in programmes were introduced on 10 January 1993 at AIR, Delhi.

First radio *sangeet sammelan*

All India Radio held its first Radio *Sangeet Sammelan* (festival of music on radio) in 1954.

First relay between radio stations

On 18 January 1939, an inter-station relay took place between Delhi and Bombay (now Mumbai, Maharashtra).

WR Highest radio station

The Himbotingla station of AIR in Ladakh, located at an altitude of 4,053.84 m (13,300 ft) above the mean sea level, is the highest radio station in the world. The 10 kW, high-power transmitters were inaugurated on 25 September 2021.

Most commercial radio programmes anchored

The legendary radio announcer and programme anchor Ameen Sayani started his broadcasting career in 1951. During his career, he compèred more than 10,000 commercial radio programmes, and voiced 12,000 spots and jingles. He produced more than 38,920 publicity programmes for feature films.

Longest running commentary

Melville de Mellow's running commentary on the last journey of Mahatma Gandhi on 31 January 1948, a day after his assassination, lasted for more than seven continuous hours.

Longest running DX (digital transformation) Net broadcast on ham radio

Muthuvama Sanil Deep (b. 17 January 1959) from Kozhikode, Kerala, operates the longest running broadcast DX Net on Ham radio. The network was started on 27 November 1988 on 7085 kHz at 8:30 a.m. He has been single-handedly operating the network from 1990 till date. The network operates from 8:30 p.m. to 9:30 p.m. on Sundays, on which he shares information regarding radio channels across the world. His radio network also disseminates vital updates during natural disasters. His individual call sign is VU3 SIO.

Most consecutive wins in a ham radio contest*

Muthuvama Sanil Deep (b. 17 January 1959) from Kozhikode, Kerala, has won prizes in the Lake City Contest every year consecutively for 14 years from 2007 to 2020. Hosted by the Quilon Amateur Radio League, the Lake City Contest is organized to celebrate World Amateur Radio Day and the contest is held for ham radio operators in South Asia. As part of the contest, Ham radio operators are to maintain wireless contact with maximum ham radios in and out of India in one day.

Top FM Broadcaster

Radio Mirchi is heard by over 40 million people across the country. It led in 25 cities in India, including the top six metros – Delhi (42.9 lakh/4.29 million), Mumbai (34.6 lakh/3.46 million), Pune (16.3 lakh/1.63 million), Kolkata (9.6 lakh/0.96 million), Hyderabad (7.6 lakh/0.76 million) and Ahmedabad (7.6 lakh/0.76 million), by the end of 2019.

TELEVISION

First telecast

The first experimental telecast was carried out in Delhi on 15 September 1959 from a makeshift studio with the help of a single transmitter of 500W, which carried signals up to 25 km for an operational time of an hour a day. The studio was relocated to Rajpath for the first live telecast of the Republic Day parade in 1960.

First national telecast

Doordarshan started nationwide telecasts on 15 August 1982 from its TV studio in Mandi House in New Delhi.

First simultaneous tele-broadcast

Om Namah Shivay, directed by Dheeraj Kumar, was the first tele-serial to be telecast and broadcast at the same time on television and radio from March 1999.

First colour TVs

In 1982, the year India hosted the Asiad (Asian Games), colour TVs were introduced in India.

First colour transmission

An experimental telecast was conducted from the Madras TV station (in present-day Chennai, Tamil Nadu) on 18 July 1980 for one hour. It was transmitted to Delhi viewers.

First programme for rural areas

Krishi Darshan, a TV programme aimed at disseminating useful information on farming to rural areas and agricultural communities, started on 26 January 1967 on DD National and still continues on the channel as well as on DD Kisan. It is considered to be the longest-running non-fiction TV series.

First TV station to get a second channel and multi-channels

Delhi was the first TV station to get a second channel on 17 September 1984. Doordarshan introduced five new channels on 15 August 1993 via Insat-1B.

First satellite linkage

The first satellite linkage experiment was launched on 1 August 1975 in six states in the country for one year. Later, satellite channels were available for the first time in 1991 to a select few who had access to the powerful dish antennas in embassies and five-star hotels.

First central production centre

Set up in 1989 at the Siri Fort Complex, New Delhi, the Central Production Centre began with two large studios equipped with modern facilities to produce high-quality, well-researched programmes.

First private channel

Zee TV, the first private television channel in the country, was launched in October 1992 in collaboration with Star TV and Zee Telefilms Ltd.

First business channel

Asia Business News International (ABNI), a 24/7 business channel, was launched on

9 TV channels were taken off air between 2017 to 2022 owing to programme and advertising code violations.

*This is a one-time category. Further and future claims for this category will not be accepted.

NDTV: first private producer of national news

14 February 1996 by the Hinduja Group in collaboration with Asia Business News (ABN) and TV18.

First private producer of national news

In February 1995, New Delhi Television Ltd (NDTV) became the first private producer of national news with the show titled 'The News Tonight', which was hosted by Prannoy Roy at 8:00 p.m. They were the first private broadcasters for news on Doordarshan.

Aaj Tak: first private satellite channel

First private satellite channel

Aaj Tak was the first private satellite channel permitted in 2000.

First 24-hour news channel

Star News, India's first 24-hour news channel, started on 3 February 1998, with news updates every hour from 6:00 a.m.

First infotainment channel

DD-3, which was Doordarshan's dedicated channel for infotainment, was launched on 14 November 1995.

First teleshopping programme

Shopping through TV was introduced on 1 January 1995, with an hour-long home-shopping show on Doordarshan's Metro channel in Delhi.

Top 10 TV Channels*

	Channel	Ratings (Average)
1	Sun TV	2408.38
2	Star Maa	2281.08
3	Star Plus	2276.85
4	Goldmines	2126.89
5	Dangal	2100.26
6	Colors	1576.42
7	Star Pravah	1509.02
8	Star Vijay	1469.30
9	Zee TV	1428.96
10	Sony Sab	1418.04

Source: Broadcast Audience Research Council India (BARC); *Ratings are for Week 39 (2022), All India

First serial

Teesra Rasta was the first fiction serial telecast from Doordarshan Kendra, New Delhi, starting from 2 May 1962.

First video film

Teri Meri Kahani, the first video film, was produced by B.R. Chopra in 1981.

First telefilm

Satyajit Ray's *Sadgati* was telecast on the national network on 13 April 1981. This 52-min. telefilm was based on Munshi Premchand's short story. Produced by Doordarshan, it starred well-known actors, such as Om Puri and Smita Patil.

First major TV series produced

Doordarshan produced the first major TV series, *Ramayan* and *Mahabharat*.

First telefilm in sign language

Nishabda Kanasugalu, a five-episode serial about a deaf girl, produced in Kannada by Ivan Nigli, was telecast from 8 January 1995 by Doordarshan Kendra, Bangalore (now Bengaluru), Karnataka.

First soap opera on Indian TV

Hum Log was the first soap opera on television in India. Its 154 episodes were telecast between 7 July 1984 and 17 December 1985.

First sci-fi serial

Space City Sigma, produced by Studio Ifekt, was telecast from 21 May 1989.

First Indian animation serial

Featuring Ghayab, the do-gooder ghost, *Ghayab Aya* was the first fully 'made-in-India' serialized animation film telecast on Doordarshan in 1986. The animator director was the well-known painter-illustrator Suddhasattwa Basu.

First director general of Doordarshan

P.V. Krishnamoorthy became the first director general of Doordarshan on 1 April 1976, the day Doordarshan and AIR were each given separate status.

First newsreader

Doordarshan began a five-minute news bulletin in 1965 with Pratima Puri as the first TV newsreader.

First high-definition channel

The first high-definition (HD) channel was introduced in India by Discovery Communications in March 2010.

First DTH service

Launched on 2 October 2013, Dish TV was the first Direct-to-Home (DTH) service in India.

Tallest TV tower

The tallest TV tower in India is located in Rameswaram, Tamil Nadu. The height of the tower is 323 m (1,060 ft). The tower was built in 1995 and is used by Doordarshan for television broadcasting. It is made of reinforced cement concrete and the mast is of lattice steel.

Most watched daily soap

Anupamaa, starring Rupali Ganguly and Sudhanshu Panday, is the most watched daily soap in India, according to the Broadcast Audience Research Council (BARC) between 21 and 27 October 2021. It was followed by *Taarak Mehta Ka Ooltah Chashma* and *Kaun Banega Crorepati* 13.

Broadcast Seva Portal Launched

On 4 April 2022, the Ministry of Information and Broadcasting launched the Broadcast Seva Portal in New Delhi. An online portal to aid the filing and processing of applications from broadcasters for licences, registrations and permissions of all kinds, the portal was launched by Anurag Singh Thakur, the Union minister of information and broadcasting. Aiming to benefit over 900 satellite TV channels, 70 teleport operators, 1,700 multi-service operators, 350 community radio stations and 380 private FM channels, the service will make the payment system efficient and transparent.

POST AND PHILATELY

Earliest postal communication

- In India, the earliest evidence of a systematic mail service is found during the reign of Chandragupta Maurya (r. 321–297 BCE), who ruled from Magadha (now in southern Bihar). In his empire, confidential reports were dispatched from the emperor to the outlying provinces, and from the provinces back to the ruler.
- The first recorded mention of a postal service was made by Ziauddin Barani, who wrote that Alauddin Khilji (r. 1296–1316) organized a regular foot-runner service, called *harkara*, as early as 1296. These *harkaras* carried a baton with bells and ran across allotted territory, carrying mail in a relay system with the runners changing every mile.
- Sikandar Lodi (r. 1488–1518), a ruler of the Lodi dynasty set up small posts across his kingdom and sent firmans daily to his armies.
- Babur (r. 1483–1530), the founder of the Mughal Empire, set up horse couriers from his capital at Agra up to Kabul, maintaining a regular 'postal' system.

Birds and animals as carriers of mail

- **Bullock mail:** Between 1846 and 1904, bullock carts were used along the Grand Trunk Road between Allahabad (now Prayagraj, Uttar Pradesh), and Delhi to deliver mail. By 1875, as many as 41 government bullock 'trains' operated in the north-west provinces and Punjab. With the coming of the railways, bullock routes were used less and the last line from Ambala in Haryana to Simla (now Shimla) in Himachal Pradesh was shut down in October 1904.
- **Camel post office:** A mobile post office on camelback was started at Mithariya, Bikaner District, Rajasthan, on 27 October 1977. The postmaster here was given a special allowance for maintaining the camel. The office was later converted into a stationary post office.
- **Pigeon post:** The Odisha Police used pigeons as messengers till 2004. The force had a strength of around 900 homing pigeons.

Post under British rule

- The first superintendent of post offices was appointed in Allahabad (now Prayagraj, Uttar Pradesh), in 1870.
- British India became the first non-founding member of the General Postal Union in 1876.

First mail by steamboat

In 1828, mail was sent by a steamboat service between Calcutta (now Kolkata, West Bengal) and Allahabad (now Prayagraj, Uttar Pradesh), along 1,266 km of the River Ganga, the earliest instance of mail delivery by steamer in Asia.

First postal training centre

Established on 2 April 1951, the postal training centre at Saharanpur, Uttar Pradesh, was the first training centre in Asia, set up exclusively for postal and telegraph personnel.

First pigeongram

The first pigeongram in India was carried from Asansol to Calcutta (now Kolkata) on 18 February 1931 in Bengal (now West Bengal), with 42 homing pigeons carrying missives over 212.43 km. There were 21 military and 21 civilian pigeons, two of which were named Amy Johnson and Akash Ranee, carrying messages for Lady Ezra and David Ezra respectively.

Pigeon post

Representative image

First electronic Indian Postal Order

On 22 March 2013, the first electronic Indian Postal Order (E-IPO) was introduced for

India Post covers **100** countries under the International Speed Post service, as on 8 October 2021.

Indian nationals living abroad. On 14 February 2014, the service was also extended to all Indian citizens.

Largest postal network

With a network of 156,434 post offices, the Indian Department of Posts has the world's largest postal network as recorded till 31 March 2021.

Longest time taken for domestic delivery

A postcard sent from Lucknow, Uttar Pradesh, on 18 May 1981 to a trading company at Raja Darwaza, Varanasi, Uttar Pradesh, reached its destination after over seven years on 1 December 1988.

First postcard

The Postal and Telecommunications Department issued the first postcard on 1 July 1879.

First value payable post service

Sending inland parcels by value payable post (VPP) was introduced in the country from 1 December 1877, on demand from the traders' community of Calcutta (now Kolkata, West Bengal).

First window delivery of letters

The Madras General Post Office or GPO (now in Chennai, Tamil Nadu) began the window delivery of letters from 1 June 1786 in the then Fort St George Square.

First hot-air balloon carrying mail

A special postal cover was carried in a hot-air balloon carrier of India Post from Sakthi Mills Ground, Pollachi, Coimbatore District, Tamil Nadu, to the postmaster of Kovipalayam, Pollachi, on 3 January 2016.

First postmen

Postmen or delivery peons were first engaged on a security bond with a specific responsibility, as part of postal reforms carried out in Bengal in 1840. They were dressed in uniform and wore badges supplied by post offices. They were allowed to earn baksheesh of 2 pies (1 pie = 1/192 of a rupee) on each letter delivered, in addition to the collection of postage due to the post office.

First Indian postmaster general

- *Man:* Rai Bahadur Saligram became the first Indian postmaster general for the North-Western Provinces in 1881.
- *Woman:* Sushila Chaurasia, who was born in Bijapur, Karnataka, in 1923, became the first woman to become postmaster general in the country. She assumed charge of the Madhya Pradesh circle on 24 May 1979.

First woman postal inspector

R. Santhakumari, who was from the Thiruvananthapuram postal division, Kerala, passed the inspector's examination in 1968 to become the first woman postal inspector.

First postwoman

K. Padmakshy Amma, who worked in the Thiruvananthapuram postal division in Kerala, joined service on 19 February 1959 as the country's first postwoman.

First letter by airmail

The first airmail letter was introduced in the country in November 1944. Priced at six annas, the airmail letter was called an 'aerogramme' and could be sent to the UK and other countries under the British Empire.

First insured mail service

The system of insurance post for letters and parcels, which was then called the 'insured mail service', was introduced on 1 January 1878.

First all-woman post office

- Avinashilingam Home Science College post office at Coimbatore, Tamil Nadu, which opened in January 1966, was the first all-woman post office in India.
- A post office, which started functioning at Manoramaganj in Indore, Madhya Pradesh, on 31 March 1976, is also fully run only by women employees.

First express mail service

Speed Post was introduced by the Government of India on 1 August 1986, connecting seven cities in the country, and five other countries to India.

First dead letter office

A post office for undelivered, unclaimed letters and letters with incomplete addresses was set up during 1834–37 in Benson Town in Bangalore (now Bengaluru, Karnataka). It was also called a Returned Letter Office.

First post office savings bank account

The post office savings bank, which started on 1 April 1882, introduced the then revolutionary concept of banking with a post office instead of a bank, which had been the usual method of keeping one's savings.

First computerized registration centre

The first computerized registration centre

(CRC) was opened in June 1996 at the Market Road wing of the New Delhi General Post Office (or GPO).

First mobile post office
On 1 November 2011, the Department of Post, Government of India, launched the Post Office on Wheels initiative with its first mobile van running in Pune, Maharashtra. The van worked from 8:00 a.m. to 8:00 p.m. daily covering 30 locations in a week, stopping at each location for two hours. The van offered all types of postal services, including e-enabled services, selling postcards, opening a new savings account and selling postal life insurance, among others. The services were resumed during the COVID-19 related lockdown in 2020 to deliver pensions and provide mobile services in states such as Kerala and Uttar Pradesh.

First drive-in post office
A drive-in post office was inaugurated on 11 November 1975 in Pune, Maharashtra.

First online post office
The Head Post Office located at Sansad Marg, New Delhi, became fully computerized on 24 June 1998.

Stamps from most countries in honour of a person
Stamps in honour of Mahatma Gandhi have been issued from over 150 countries up to 2019.

First letter boxes
A great reform in the history of Indian post took place in October 1854 with the introduction of letter boxes located away from post offices.

First parcel service
Originally known as Bhangy post, parcel service was introduced on 2 December 1884. Its name came from the *bhangy* or bamboo stick with parcels on either end that the parcel carriers balanced on their shoulders.

First registered mail service
The first mention of a system of registration being adopted by a post office to secure the safety of coins or documents in transit was found in an advertisement published on 20 February 1795. Actual registered post was introduced in Bombay Presidency on 1 November 1849 with a postal notice on 16 October 1849. In Bengal, it was established at Calcutta GPO on 1 January 1851 and later at Madras GPO. The fee was eight annas for registering a letter.

First automatic mail processing centre (AMPC)
The first AMPC was launched at the Mumbai GPO, Maharashtra, on 29 April 1993, and a second one was established at Chennai, Tamil Nadu, in October 1995.

WR First airmail
India became the first country in the world to send mail by plane when 6,500 letters and postcards were flown from Allahabad to Naini (a distance of only 18 km!) in Uttar Pradesh in a Humber-Sommer biplane by Henri Pequet on 18 February 1911. A pictorial postmark showing the aeroplane was used.

Mahatma Gandhi: stamps from most countries in honour of a person

First stamp
The Scinde Dawk (Provincial), India's first half-anna stamp, was issued with the help of Edward Lees Coffey, the postmaster of Karachi, on 1 July 1852 in Scinde District, Karachi (now in Pakistan). It was embossed on circular red wafers used as seals on letters, with the East India Company emblem and the legend Scinde District Dawk around the circumference. It was Asia's first ever adhesive stamp. It was withdrawn in 1854.

First letter to post office in space
According to reports in 1992, Reagan Jones sent a letter from Vandiperiyar P.O. to the Russian consul general in Chennai, Tamil Nadu, who further sent it on to Moscow, Russia. Using radio waves, Moscow sent the message – greetings for space scientists – to the post office in space.

The average area served by a post office is **21.36** sq. km

9 October

World Post Day is observed as the anniversary of the establishment of the Universal Postal Union in 1874 in Bern, Switzerland.

Longest-serving postmaster

Brother K.V.S.J. Peter, who received a Padma Shri in 1983, was the longest-serving postmaster, for 68 years. He took charge of the Shenbaganur post office in Dindigul District, Tamil Nadu, on 12 September 1913, and was in service till 8 February 1982.

Earliest official stamps

India issued stamps in 1866 and the State of Hyderabad issued stamps in 1873. The stamps had 'service', 'official' or '*sarkari*' over-stamped.

First state to issue a stamp (pre-1947)

Kathiawar state in Saurashtra (later Gujarat) issued a one-anna stamp in November 1864 with the inscription 'Saurashtra Post 1864–65'.

First Indian stamp featuring a woman

The Indian saints and poets series, issued on 1 October 1952, featured Mirabai, the 16th-century bhakti poet-saint.

First stamp of independent India

A 3.5-anna stamp with the inscription 'Jai Hind' was issued on 21 November 1947.

First sportsperson on a stamp

A stamp that portrayed pioneering cricketer Sir Ranjitsinhji Vibhaji Jadeja (1872–1933) was issued on 27 September 1973. He was the first Indian to play Test cricket for England.

First aromatic stamp

India introduced its first aromatic stamp, a ₹15 stamp fragrant with the scent of sandalwood, in 2006.

Only living persons on Indian stamps

Only eight persons have been featured on stamps in their lifetime: social reformer Dr D.K. Karve (1958); statesman and scholar Dr M. Visvesvaraya (1960); India's first president Dr Rajendra Prasad (1962); second president Dr S. Radhakrishnan (1967); fourth president V.V. Giri (1974); Mother Teresa (1980); former prime minister Rajiv Gandhi (1985); and cricketing legend Sachin Tendulkar (2013).

First differently shaped stamps

- **Polygonal:** The four-anna indigo-and-red stamp of India, issued on 15 October 1854, was polygonal, with the top and side panels raised from the main frame, which was slightly curved.
- **Circular:** The earliest circular stamp was the Scinde Dawk, though only the first printing was circular in the true sense since the later versions were issued on sheets that were usually cut square. It was the first circular stamp issued not only in India but in all of Asia. Later, the states of Indore (1889) and Jammu and Kashmir (1866–78) issued similar circular stamps.
- **Oval:** The half-anna red stamp, issued by the Indian state of Bhor (now in Maharashtra) in 1879, was oval in a horizontal format. It was imperforate and had to be cut out.
- **Triangular:** Stamps of this shape were issued on 10 October 1985 by the Border Roads Organization.
- **Diamond-shaped:** Depicting Raja Rammohun Roy, these stamps were issued on 27 September 1964.
- **Trimmed:** These revenue stamps, reissued for postal use in 1866, had their inscriptions cut off at the top and bottom.
- **Octagonal:** A set of six octagon-shaped commemorative stamps to mark the 150th birth anniversary of Mahatma Gandhi was released on 2 October 2019 for the first time.

First customization of stamps

Initially introduced in India during the World Philatelic Exhibition 'INDIPEX-2011', 'My Stamp' is the scheme for personalized sheets of postage stamps of India Post. Such a sheet has a thumbnail image, e.g., the customer's photograph, logos of institutions, artwork, famous tourist places, historical cities, heritage buildings and wildlife, among others, on a selected template sheet featuring postage stamps. The facility is available for both non-corporate and corporate entities.

First stamp to be jointly issued with another country

India and erstwhile USSR issued a set of two stamps on the Festival of India in the USSR, which was held in August 1990. Both countries issued the stamp with the same design.

First foreigner on a stamp (post-1947)

Henry (also Henri) Dunant featured on a 15-paisa Red Cross centenary stamp issued on 8 May 1963. A Swiss businessman and social activist, he co-founded the International Red Cross and was the first recipient of the Nobel Peace Prize.

First centenary stamp

A commemorative stamp was issued on 1 October 1954 to celebrate the first centenary of Indian postage stamps.

First commemorative stamps

A set of six stamps was issued on 9 February 1931 on the laying of the foundation of New Delhi as the new capital of India. These

POST IT HERE!

First post office

The East India Company set up its first post office in Calcutta, Bengal (now Kolkata, West Bengal), in 1727. It was later merged with the General Post Office, Kolkata. The building was designed in 1864 by Walter B. Grenville, a consultant architect. In one end of the building is the Philatelic Bureau.

First floating post office

The Floating Post Office, located on a shikara at Dal Lake, Srinagar, Jammu and Kashmir, is the world's first and only floating post office. Inaugurated in 2011, it housed a philately museum and a souvenir shop, and also offered Internet facility along with international phone calls.

First Indian post office outside India

Set up in 1983, the first Indian post office outside Indian territory was located at the scientific base of Dakshin Gangotri, Antarctica, during the third Indian expedition to Antarctica and became operational on 24 February 1984. On 26 January 1988, the Dakshin Gangotri P.O. was set up under the Department of Post in north Goa. Scientist G. Sudhakar Rao, a member of the Seventh Indian Scientific Expedition to Antarctica in 1987, was appointed its first honorary postmaster. Dakshin Gangotri was decommissioned in 1990.

Largest post office

With an area of 11,148 sq. m (120,000 sq. ft), India's busiest and biggest post office is the Mumbai General Post Office. With 101 business counters, it caters to more than 50,000 address sites and handles around 25,000 customers daily.

Highest post office

The highest post office in India is located at an altitude of 4,440 m (14,567 ft) in Hikkim Village in Spiti Valley, Himachal Pradesh. For nearly 40 years since the post office opened on 5 November 1983, Rinchen Chhering has been the postmaster. Since June 2022, the post office has been housed in a new structure shaped like a letter box! The motorable road to Hikkim goes on to the highest motorable village Komic, and the Hikkim Branch Post Office serves around 430 people in Hikkim, Komic and other neighbouring villages, besides tourists.

were the first pictorial stamps depicting the important landmarks of the city.

First private printing of commemorative stamps

A set of four stamps on Mahatma Gandhi was first printed by Courvoisier, who was a Swiss printer, and issued in 1948.

First autograph-inscribed stamp

A stamp issued on 7 May 1961 to commemorate the birth centenary of Nobel laureate Rabindranath Tagore had his signature inscribed on it.

First one-rupee charity stamp

The first charity stamps were issued on 26 January 1950. Three 'Healthy India' charity stamps were brought out in denominations of one anna, four annas and one rupee.

First stamp designer (pre-Independence)

Captain H.E.L. Thuillier, the deputy surveyor general of India, who was then stationed in Calcutta, Bengal (now Kolkata, West Bengal), designed the first lithographic stamps, which were issued in 1854 and said to be engraved by an artist called Munirooddin.

First miniature sheet

To commemorate the India International Philatelic Exhibition 1973 in Delhi, a miniature sheet with a face value of ₹4.65 was issued on 14 November 1973.

First philatelic society

The Philatelic Society of India, the country's first philatelic society, was formed in Bombay (now Mumbai, Maharashtra), on 6 March 1897.

First stamp featuring wildlife

The first Indian stamp depicting an animal was released in 1962, and it was a 15-paisa stamp showing the Indian rhinoceros. Next year, five more such stamps came out, featuring the Indian gaur (10 paise), the red panda (15 paise), the Indian elephant (30 paise), the Bengal tiger (50 paise) and the Asiatic lion (one rupee).

First Indian president of Federation Internationale de Philatelie (FIP)

Late D.N. Jatia, a reputed philatelist, was elected president at the 59th Congress of the FIP in London, UK, on 14 May 1990.

First Indian to design a stamp for the United Nations

Dipok Dey (b. 1938) from Calcutta (now Kolkata, West Bengal), was the first Indian to design a stamp for the UN in 1985. The stamp was based on the theme of child survival.

Largest philatelic bureau

Mumbai General Post Office Philatelic Bureau in Maharashtra, also an international philatelic bureau, is the largest in the country.

First national philatelic museum

The National Philatelic Museum of India was established in New Delhi on 6 July 1968. It has large collections of postage stamps printed and issued by India and former princely states of India, early essays, proofs and colour trials, Indian stamps used abroad, early Indian postcards, postal stationery and other thematic collections. It also has a philatelic bureau and postal objects such as letter boxes from Victorian times.

First philatelic exhibition

The Philatelic Society of Bengal held an exhibition of postage stamps at the art gallery of the Government School of Art (now renamed the Government College of Art and Craft) in Calcutta, Bengal (now Kolkata, West Bengal), in December 1894.

First international stamp exhibition

'India 80' was the first international stamp exhibition held in Asia under the patronage of the Federation Internationale de Philatelie (FIP), held from 25 January 1980 to 3 February 1980.

A Golden Gesture

To honour Neeraj Chopra's historic gold medal at the 2020 Tokyo Olympics in the men's javelin event, India Post installed a landmark golden letter box in his hometown, Khandra, Haryana, while the letter box of the Head Post Office, Panipat, Haryana, was also painted golden. Chopra's victory not only got him the title of 'Golden Boy' but also made him the first Indian sportsperson to get a gold medal in athletics at the Olympics. India's Department of Post and Telegraph usually commemorates achievements with special postage stamps; the golden letter box is a unique initiative. The dedication in Hindi on the letter box reads: 'Mr Neeraj Chopra: In honour of javelin throw gold medal winner Tokyo Olympics 2020'.

National Phliatelic Museum, New Delhi

Dakiya Dak Laya!

Launched on 28 June 2022 by Ashwini Vaishnav, minister of communications, railways, electronics and IT, and Devusinh Chauhan, state minister of communications, the Dak Karamyogi is an initiative created with the aim of enhancing the skills of the Gramin Dak Sewaks. The portal, a Department of Post initiative, not only offers standardized content in 12 Indian languages to ensure accessibility but also perfectly blends the offline mode of learning (at various department units across the country) with online training modules. The content includes resources that focus on soft-skills enhancement and procedural professional development of a workforce that comprises 165,873 departmental employees and 240,478 Gramin Dak Sewaks.

TELECOM

Last money order

In April 2015, India Post discontinued the traditional money order service, which was more than a century old.

Last telegram

Inda's 163-year-old telegram service ended at 11:45 p.m. on 14 July 2013. Its last message was booked at the Central Telegraph Office, Janpath, New Delhi, by Ashwani Mishra, who sent telegrams to Congress leader Rahul Gandhi and the director general of DD news S.M. Khan.

First Indian radio telegraphy company

The Indian Radio Telegraphy Co. was established in 1923, which ushered in the era of wireless telegraphy.

First submarine cable link

Madras (now Chennai, Tamil Nadu), was linked to Penang, Malaysia, in 1886 with a submarine telegraph cable.

First fibre-optic link

India's first fibre-optic link was made in 1979 when Hindustan Cables Ltd's office at Shivaji Nagar, Pune, Maharashtra, was linked to the Cotton Telephone Exchange, a distance of 4 km.

First Indo-European telegraph line

The first independent double line of telegraph from London, UK, to Karachi (now in Pakistan) via Tehran, Iran, which was constructed by M/s Siemens and Co., was opened for operations on 31 January 1870.

First director general of the telegraph service

Sir William O'Shaughnessy was appointed as chief superintendent of telegraphs in 1857 in colonial India.

First manufacturer of telephones

- A telecommunication maintenance and repair shop was set up at Alipore, Calcutta (now Kolkata, West Bengal) in 1860. The manufacture of minor components that were needed for the Baudot Telegraph and Line stores was initiated at the P&T workshop in 1913.
- The Indian Telephone Industries Ltd was established at Doorvaninagar near Bangalore (now Bengaluru), Karnataka), in July 1948 for manufacturing automatic and carrier equipment. The local assembly of phones from imported parts began in 1948 and the first phone off-the-line was produced on 26 January 1949.
- The first telephone with indigenous components was made in 1951.

First STD service

The facility for subscriber trunk dialling (STD) was first started between Lucknow and Kanpur in Uttar Pradesh on 26 November 1960.

First ISD service

The Arvi earth station for satellite communication, set up in 1971 in Arvi near Poona (now Pune), Maharashtra, marked the introduction of the first operator-dialled service to international subscribers. The first intercontinental telephone exchange was commissioned in 1973 and the first international subscriber dialling (ISD) telephone service was introduced between Bombay (now Mumbai), Maharashtra, and London, UK, in 1976.

First known use of SOS signal

On 1 November 1977, the duty operator in the astral wireless station at Ennore, near Madras (now Chennai), Tamil Nadu, received a weak SOS call from a cargo ship in the Bay of Bengal; its engine room was on fire. The call was acknowledged and rescue ships reached in an hour.

First radio phone link
On 1 May 1933, Sir Samuel Hoare, the then Secretary of State for India under British rule, spoke from London, UK, to Sir Frederick Sykes, governor of Bombay, on radio phone, thus establishing a communication network between Britain and India.

First push-button telephone
The first Indian firm to manufacture electronic push-button phone answering machines was Bharti Telecom Ltd. It was also the first Indian company to launch cordless phones that were called 'Beetel'.

First automatic telephone exchange
The first automatic telephone system in the country was commissioned at Simla (now Shimla, Himachal Pradesh), in 1914. The exchange had 400 working lines and another 300 lines in reserve.

First call using a mobile phone
On 31 July 1995, the then Union telecom minister Sukh Ram and the then chief minister of West Bengal Jyoti Basu spoke to each other using hand-held mobile phones, over Modi Telstra's MobileNet service.

First Internet telephony service
On 25 July 2018, government-owned Bharat Sanchar Nigam Limited (BSNL) launched India's first Internet telephony service that allows users to dial any phone number in India through its mobile app.

First SMS provider
Hutchison Max offered a global text messaging service (SMS) in India in 2001.

First circle launch
In 1996, Bharti Mobile Ltd, which was a joint venture of Bharti Enterprises with Telia Company of Sweden, launched Airtel, the first to provide services in a circle (outside metros) in Himachal Pradesh.

First cellular operators' association
The Cellular Operators Association of India (COAI), Delhi, was set up in 1995.

First national/international roaming service
- On 12 September 1997, the Department of Telecommunications (DoT), Ministry of Communications, Government of India, cleared a national automatic roaming facility for cellular operators in Delhi, Mumbai, Calcutta (now Kolkata) and Chennai.
- International roaming facility was approved on 12 January 1998.

BSNL: launched the first Internet telephony service

First carrier to demonstrate 5G service capability
Bharti Airtel became the first carrier to successfully demonstrate live 5G service over a commercial network on 28 January 2021 in Hyderabad, Telangana. The carrier was capable of delivering 10x speed, 10x latency (the time it takes for data to pass from one point on a network to another) and 100 x concurrency (the execution of multiple instruction sequences at the same time) in comparison with existing technologies.

Service area with largest access subscriber base
Uttar Pradesh (East), with 98.14 million (9.814 crore) wireless and wireline subscribers, has the largest subscriber base (September 2020).

First net fax service
Satyamfax, launched by Satyam Infoway on 25 April 2000 at Chennai, Tamil Nadu, in technical association with Singapore Telecom, was the first to provide fax to fax, web to fax, email to fax, and PC desktop to fax services.

First telephone exchange
In 1881, the Government of India licensed the Oriental Telephone Company to set up telephone exchanges in Calcutta (now Kolkata), Bombay (now Mumbai), Madras (now Chennai), and Karachi (now in Pakistan). A 50-line exchange was set up in Calcutta in 1881 as one of the oldest exchanges in the world. It was set up only five years after the invention of the telephone.

First cellular service
Modi Telstra, a joint-venture company of the B.K. Modi Group and the Telstra Corporation of Australia, inaugurated the first commercial cellular service in India on 23 August 1995. The network was constructed by Telecommunication Engineering Centre and the Modi Telstra team.

89.33
million subscribers applied to avail the mobile number portability facility during 2020–21.

India Launches 5G Services

The fifth generation of mobile networks, 5G was launched in India on 1 October 2022 by Prime Minister Narendra Modi. The launch took place at the sixth edition of India Mobile Congress (IMC), India's flagship technology festival, held at Pragati Maidan in New Delhi. The 5G services were announced for roll-out in 13 cities in the first phase. Of these, four cities – Delhi, Kolkata, Mumbai and Chennai – will have access to the service by end of October 2022. Airtel, Reliance Jio and Vodafone Idea – the three major telecom operators of the country – showcased the use of 5G technology at IMC. The service is set up to function at 10 Gbps at its peak compared with 4G, which offered 100 Mbps. Thus, 5G is nearly 100 times faster. To use this service, one does not require a new SIM card; however, a smartphone that can enable 5G will be needed. The service is also expected to enhance the facilities of the health sector, smart farming and disaster management.

Overall tele-density in 2020–21 was 88.17 per cent.

Mobile tower at the highest altitude

Installed by BSNL with the help of the Indian Army's Trishul Signallers, the highest mobile tower is located at 4,877 m (16,000 ft) in Chongtash in Ladakh. With this tower, even the remotest regions of Ladakh are connected by a communication link.

Largest wireline service provider

BSNL was the leading operator in wireline service, with 6,649,439 subscribers and 32.85 per cent of the market share as on 31 March 2021.

Largest wireless service provider

Reliance Jio was the leading wireless service provider with 422.92 million subscribers, followed by Bharti Airtel with 352.39 million subscribers, up to March 2021.

Hotmail: first free email service

State/UT with highest tele-density

Delhi had 273.14 per cent tele-density (number of fixed [landline] telephone connections per 100 people in a specified area) up to 30 September 2020.

Service provider with number of rural subscribers – wireless

Reliance Jio has 179.31 million rural subscribers, which amounts to 33.47 per cent of total wireless rural subscribers. It is followed by Bharti Airtel with 168.63 million rural subscribers and Vodafone Idea with 149.93 rural subscribers up till March 2021.

INTERNET, SOCIAL MEDIA AND APPS

First provider of Internet services

Videsh Sanchar Nigam Limited (VSNL), under DoT, Ministry of Telecommunications, Government of India, was the first provider of Internet services in the country. It was launched on 15 August 1995.

First private Internet service provider (ISP)

Satyam Infoway (Sify) became the country's first private Internet service provider company on 22 November 1998.

WR First free email service

Conceived by Sabeer Bhatia (and colleague Jack Smith), Hotmail was the first free email service that took the whole world by storm in 1996. Bhatia was a Bengaluru-born Indian-American businessman and led Hotmail as its president and CEO, until its eventual acquisition by Microsoft in 1998.

First 3G operators

- The public sector telecom service provider Mahanagar Telephone Nigam Limited (MTNL) first provided 3G mobile service in parts of Delhi on 11 December 2008.
- Tata Docomo launched its 3G mobile service in many states – Rajasthan, Uttar Pradesh (West), Gujarat, Maharashtra (except Mumbai), Haryana, Punjab, Kerala, Karnataka and Madhya Pradesh – on 5 November 2010, becoming the first private 3G operator in India.

First mobile app store

Airtel App Central was the first Indian mobile application store in the country. It was launched by Bharti Airtel Ltd on 9 February 2010.

Top Internet subscription – service areas – both wired and wireless

The highest-subscription service areas in the country are the states of Uttar Pradesh (East+ West) (87.88 million/8.78 crore), Maharashtra (61.42 million/6.14 crore), Andhra Pradesh (56.73 million/5.67 crore), Tamil Nadu

(50.42 million/ 5.04 crore) and Madhya Pradesh (47.23 million/4.72 crore).

First Aadhaar-based payment app

The Government of India launched Bharat Interface for Money (BHIM) app, an Aadhaar-based mobile app for digital payments, on 30 December 2016.

Largest WhatsApp user base in the world

India remained WhatsApp's biggest market with 400 million (40 crore) monthly active users, who exchange around 60 billion (6,000 crore) messages daily (July 2019). The country has been the biggest market for WhatsApp since November 2015.

Most viewed Indian video on YouTube

'Phonics Song with TWO Words', an alphabet learning video by ChuChu TV has garnered 4,348,214,171 views on YouTube as on 14 December 2021. The video was posted on 7 March 2014.

Highest data consumption

India has the highest data consumption of 11 Gb/month per user on an average.

Most popular mobile operating system

The favourite mobile operating system in India is Android with 62 per cent usage; next is Windows with 19.4 per cent usage.

Largest Facebook user base

With 310 million (31 crore) active users, India emerged as Facebook's largest country audience in July 2020.

Most number of mobile app downloads

India had the most number of mobile app downloads on the Apple iOS Appstore as well as on Google Playstore in the second quarter of 2020 with 7 billion (700 crore). It is followed by USA with 3.75 billion (375 crore) and Brazil with 3 billion (300 crore).

Most popular browser

The most popular browser in India is Google Chrome, with a share of 51.91 per cent among all browsers.

Fastest 4G service provider

Vodafone Idea Ltd is the provider of the fastest 4G network in the country with a download speed of 13.74 Mbps and an upload speed of 6.19 Mbps. It is followed by Bharti Airtel and Reliance Jio.

Most popular search engine

Google, with a user base of 93.4 per cent, is the favourite search engine in India.

Most downloaded mobile application

Aarogya Setu, a COVID-19 contact-tracing app launched by the Government of India became the most downloaded application in India and the seventh most downloaded application in the world. It recorded 127.6 million (12.76 crore) installations up till July 2020.

First and only 4G, all-Internet protocol network

Reliance Jio, which revolutionized the mobile Internet market in India when it rolled out 4G services in 2016, is the only network in the world to rely solely on 4G Long-Term Evolution (LTE) network, based on Internet telephony, without the backing of the legacy 3G/2G services.

Most subscribed YouTube channel

T-Series (Super Cassettes Industries Pvt. Ltd), a music record label and film production company, became the first YouTube channel in the world to reach 100 million subscribers in May 2019. As of October 2022, it had 226 million (22.6 crore) subscribers.

Highest concurrent video viewership

In the ICC Cricket World Cup 2019 semi-final between India and New Zealand, Hotstar scaled a new global peak in concurrent viewership, with 25.3 million (2.53 crore) users tuning in to the video-streaming platform during the 49th over on 10 July 2019. This surpassed the platform's earlier peak of 15.6 million (1.56 crore), recorded on 16 June 2019 during the India–Pakistan match. That game had also attracted a cumulative single-day reach of 100 million (10 crore). The ICC Cricket World Cup was streamed across six languages: English, Hindi, Bengali, Tamil, Telugu and Kannada.

Largest social network penetration

India is the world's second largest market with 349.97 million (34.997 crore) users in 2020. While there are many apps available to the Indian public, YouTube leads with an 82 per cent market penetration. It is closely followed by Facebook (76 per cent), WhatsApp (70 per cent), Instagram (64 per cent) and Facebook Messenger (53 per cent), according to the 2019 Q3 figures.

The Internet subscriber base in the country was 825.301 million users, as on 31 March 2021.

Android OS: most popular mobile operating system

LITERATURE

THE WIDE WINDOW
THE ERSATZ ELEVATOR
THE VILE VILLAGE
THE HOSTILE HOSPITAL
THE SLIPPERY SLOPE
LITTLE WOMEN
JANE EYRE
THE SECRET GARDEN
TED DEKKER
THE BRIDE COLLECTOR
TED DEKKER
THE CIRCLE
SINNER
DEKKER
A TALE of TWO CITIES
Charles Dickens
THE HUNCHBACK OF NOTRE DAME
Victor Hugo
LES MISÉRABLES
Victor Hugo
WISE WORDS
Leithart
C.S. LEWIS
The Big Book of Riddles, Puzzles and Enigmas
HOUSE
PERETTI
DEKKER
SELZNICK
THE INVENTION OF HUGO CABRET
SCHOLASTIC PRESS
SKELTON
ENDYMION SPRING
DELACORTE PRESS
HAMLET
RESPECTABLE SINS
BRIDGES
HOLD FAST
COOPER
The REASON for GOD
WHAT IS MARK KIERANSKY
THE AGE OF FABLE
BULFINCH
GREAT CASES of SHERLOCK HOLMES
BONHOEFFER THE COST OF DISCIPLESHIP
Life Together
DIETRICH BONHOEFFER Meditating On The Word
Bonhoeffer — PRISONER FOR GOD — Macmillan
BOYD
Heaven is for
CARSON
How Long, O Lord?
YOU CAN CHANGE
CHESTER
THE MASTER'S WAY OF PERSONAL EVANGELISM
COLEMAN
THE HOLE IN OUR HOLINESS
DEYOUNG
JUST DO SOMETHING
DEYOUNG
BUSY
GELISSEN & MACADAM
Billy Graham
Death and the Life After
WEIRD
GROESCHEL
WHY NOT WOMEN?
CUNNINGHAM HAMILTON
TIMOTHY KELLER JESUS THE KING
TIMOTHY KELLER
PRAYER
PRODIGAL GOD
The Prophet and the Age of the Caliphate
C.S. LEWIS
THE FOUR LOVES
C.S. LEWIS
WOUNDED by God's People
GRAHAM LOTZ
ASHAMED OF THE GOSPEL
MACARTHUR
MARTIN
Hostage to the Devil
INTO the DEN of INFIDELS
10 Answers for Skeptics
BLUE LIKE JAZZ
"I CAN" Evangelism
How to Be a Muslim
AN AMERICAN STORY
MARY C. NEAL, MD
Questioning Evangelism
Newman
COVENANTAL APOLOGETICS
crucial conversations
EVANGELISM & THE SOVEREIGNTY OF GOD
PACKER
Abounding Grace
M. SCOTT PECK, M.D.
COUNTER CULTURE
PLATT
don't waste your life
piper
FOR THE FAME OF GOD'S NAME
EVANGELISM Handbook
REID
THE FATHER GLORIFIED
THE PEACEMAKER
SANDE
THE JESUS MISSION SCOTT
SPIRITUAL EQUIPPING for MISSION
STROBEL
THE CASE FOR FAITH
MIRACULOUS MOVEMENTS
TROUSDALE
i am n
ONE THOUSAND GIFTS
VOSKAMP
SPIRITUAL WARFARE
Warner
NO LONGER A SLUMDOG
YOHANNAN
REVOLUTION IN WORLD MISSIONS
CAN MAN LIVE WITHOUT GOD
RAVI ZACHARIAS

BOOKS

Oldest living language

Tamil, which belongs to the Dravidian group of languages, is the oldest living language of India. *Tholkappiyam,* the oldest known work in Tamil, is a work on Tamil grammar. It has been dated to between the second century BCE and the fifth century CE.

Oldest manuscript

The oldest manuscript among contemporary Indian languages is that of a bilingual Tulu-Greek comedy titled *Sariti,* currently housed at the Bodleian Library at Oxford, UK. The manuscript dates to the first century CE.

Oldest surviving book

The oldest surviving Indian book is the Tamil work *Christiya Vanakkam,* a revised edition of the *Doctrina Christiana.* It was first published in 1560 in Goa, and followed by its Tamil version published in 1564.

Earliest known grammar text

The Sanskrit grammar treatise *Ashtadhyayi,* which was composed around 500 BCE by Panini, a grammarian, is said to be the earliest formalized book on Sanskrit grammar. It contains 4,000 precise rules of grammar in as many *sutra*s, expounding an array of topics such as syntax, root derivatives and moods.

First known printed book

The first known printed book in India, titled *Conclusoes e Outras Coisas,* was printed in Portuguese in Goa by Joao de Bustamante, a Christian missionary.

Earliest known anthology

Therigatha, the ninth book of the *Khuddaka Nikaya,* is the earliest known anthology. This Buddhist scripture, written in Pali, consists of short poems recited by the early members of the Buddhist sangha. It has 73 poems, which are organized into 16 chapters, and the text comprises 522 stanzas.

Earliest known Tamil work

Tholkappiyam, a treatise on the grammar of the Tamil language, which has been dated to between the second century BCE and the fifth century CE, is the earliest extant work in Tamil. The authorship is loosely attributed to the sage Tholkappiyar.

Earliest known Malayalam work

Samkshepa Vedartham, a catechism book by the Reverend Clement Pianius, was printed in movable type in Rome in 1772.

Earliest original Odia work

Lavanyavati, the first Odia epic, was an original work featuring the love story of a prince of Karnataka and a princess of Sri Lanka, by Upendra Bhanja (1680–1720), who belonged to a ruling feudatory family in Ghumsar in Bhanjanagar in present-day Odisha. Called *'Kavi Samrat',* he is said to have written many books.

Earliest known Kannada works

- The earliest extant work in Kannada, the second oldest living language in India, is the *Kavirajamarga,* which was written (possibly in parts) by a Rashtrakuta king – Nrupatunga Amoghavarsha I (r. 814–78 CE). It is a work on the rhetoric, poetics and grammar of Kannada.
- The Kannada text in prose, titled *Vaddaradhane* (sixth to ninth century CE), which is believed to have been written by Shivakotiacharya, consists of inspiring stories of 19 great Jain saints.

Earliest known Gujarati works

- The earliest work in Gujarati prose was *Balavabodha,* written by Tarunaprabha and dated to 1355 CE.
- *Prithvichandra Charita*, written by Manikyasundara in 1422 CE, is a great example of old Gujarati prose, and said to be reminiscent of Banabhatta's *Kadambari.*

Earliest known Marathi works

- *Viveka Sindhu* was written by Mukundraj (1128–1200 CE) in Marathi verse, and preached

Instituted in 1961, the Jnanpith Award is given only to Indian writers writing in Indian languages included in the Eighth Schedule of the Constitution of India and English, with no posthumous awards conferred.

First Novel in an Indian Language to Win the International Booker Prize

Tomb of Sand by Hindi writer Geetanjali Shree became the first Indian-language (Hindi) novel to win the prestigious International Booker Prize in 2022. Translated from *Ret Samadhi* into English, it is set in north India and follows the story of an 80-year-old woman. It is the first of Shree's books to be published in the UK in English by Tilted Axis Press in August 2021. The original in Hindi was published by Rajkamal Prakashan, and the translation was published by Tilted Axis Press and Penguin Random House India. Six books were shortlisted from among which Shree's novel was chosen. The prize money of £50,000 (₹46 lakh approximately) was shared between Shree and her English translator, Daisy Rockwell.

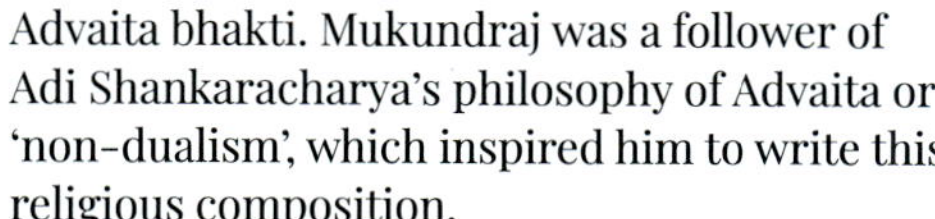

Authors from as many as 11 European nations participated in the 'Long Night of LiteratureS' on 23 September 2022 at the Instituto Cervantes in New Delhi.

William Shakespeare's First Folio

Advaita bhakti. Mukundraj was a follower of Adi Shankaracharya's philosophy of Advaita or 'non-dualism', which inspired him to write this religious composition.

- *Leela Charitra* by Mahim Bhat is a biography of Chakradhara, a 13th-century saint who founded the Mahanubhava sect and socio-religious movement. The work contains more than a hundred stories on the subject.

Earliest known Telugu work

The first printed prose work in Telugu, which was a part of the New Testament, was translated by the Reverend Benjamin Schultze in the early 18th century.

Earliest English work

Cavelly Venkata Boriah's *Account of the Jains,* published in 1809, is the first extant evidence of Indian writing in English.

Only Shakespeare folio

A rare copy of Shakespeare's First Folio (1623) was found at the Mahatma Gandhi Central Library, University of Roorkee, Uttar Pradesh (now IIT-Roorkee, Uttarakhand). The 900-page volume titled *Mr William Shakespeare's Comedies, Histories and Tragedies* was found in an old trunk in the librarian's office. It contains 36 of Shakespeare's 37 plays.

First known printed books in local languages

- **Assamese:** An early translation of the New Testament, titled *Dharmapustak,* printed by the Serampore Mission Press, Serampore, Bengal (now Srirampur, West Bengal), in 1813.
- **Bengali:** *Regulations for the Administration of Justice in the Courts of Dewanee Adaulat,* popularly known as the Regulation Impey Code, published by the East India Company's Press, Calcutta (now Kolkata, West Bengal), in 1792.
- **Devanagari/Hindi:** *Grammar of Sanskrit and Grammar of the Hindustani Language,* published by the Chronicle Press, Calcutta (now Kolkata, West Bengal), in 1796.
- **Dogri:** *Valmiki Ramayana,* published by Sri Saraswati Press, Jammu and Kashmir, in 1858.
- **Gujarati:** *Dabestan-e-Mazaheb,* the Gujarati translation of a Persian book, published by Fardoonjee Marazban in Bombay (now Mumbai, Maharashtra), in 1815.
- **Kannada:** *A Grammar of the Karnatic Language* by William Meckerell, published by the Serampore Mission Press, Serampore, Bengal (now Srirampur, West Bengal), in 1820.
- **Konkani:** *Doutrina Crista,* printed at the Society of Jesus Press, Goa, in 1556.
- **Maithili:** *Krishna Janma,* edited by Grierson, published by Vidyapati Press, Laheriasarai, Bihar, in 1936.
- **Malayalam:** *The Bible,* printed at the Courier Press, Bombay (now Mumbai, Maharashtra), in 1811.
- **Odia:** A translation of the New Testament by Pandit Mrityunjaya Vidyalankar, printed at the Serampore Mission Press, Serampore, Bengal (now Srirampur, West Bengal) in 1807.
- **Tamil:** *A Book of Prayers,* published by the Society of Jesus Press, Goa, around 1560.
- **Telugu:** *A Grammar of Telugu,* printed at the Serampore Mission Press, Serampore, Bengal (now Srirampur, West Bengal), in 1813.
- **Urdu:** Hallhead's Urdu translation of Kannada laws, published by Honourable Company Press in Calcutta (now Kolkata, West Bengal) in 1792.

First poet in English in India

Henry Louis Vivian Derozio (b. 18 April 1809), assistant headmaster of Hindu College, Calcutta (now Presidency University, Kolkata, West Bengal), is considered to be the first Indian poet who wrote in English. The poems that he submitted to the newspaper *India Gazette* under the pseudonym 'Juvenis' were published as a collection in 1827. The second edition of the collection was released in the following year and included his most famous poem, 'The Fakeer of Jungheera', which featured aspects of life in colonial India.

First pseudonym

'Sujatha' was the pseudonym of the popular Tamil author S. Rangarajan (1935–2008), who wrote more than 100 novels, 250 short stories, ten books on science, ten stage plays and a volume of poems. He was a regular contributor to topical columns in Tamil periodicals such as *Ananda Vikatan, Kumudam* and *Kalki.* He served for a brief period as the editor of *Kumudam,* and also wrote screenplays and dialogues for Tamil movies.

First sign language dictionary

Bridging the gap for the deaf and speech-disabled communities, *The Indian Sign Language Dictionary,* a first-of-its-kind book, was launched on 23 March 2018. Developed by the Delhi-based Indian Sign

Language Research and Training Centre (ISLRTC), it contains 3,000 words in Hindi and English, and their corresponding graphic representations. Available in both print and video formats, it brings uniformity to the various sign languages used. It divides the words into five categories – Everyday, Legal, Academic, Medical and Technical Terms.

Longest novel

Avakasikal, written by M.K. Menon in Malayalam, runs into 3,958 pages, in four volumes, making it the longest novel in any Indian language. He received the Sahitya Akademi Award in 1981 and the Vayalar Award in 1983 for the novel.

WR Scripture in the largest format

A special edition of the Bhagavadgita at the ISKCON temple in New Delhi is the world's largest-sized scripture. The book measures 2.8 m x 2 m (9 ft 2.2 in. x 6 ft 6.7 in.) and has 670 pages. Weighing 800 kg, it was printed in Milan, Italy, on YUPO synthetic paper, making it untearable and waterproof. It was unveiled on 26 February 2019.

Smallest book

B. Jameela from Madras (now Chennai), Tamil Nadu, had a copy of the Quran, which is 27 mm (1.06 in.) long, 19 mm (0.74 in.) wide and 10 mm (0.39 in.) thick, and weighed only 4.4 g.

Thickest book

Povitr Pustokantlem Bhanddar – Roman Konkani Biblical Concordance is the thickest book. It is 149.09 cm (58.7 in.) thick, and measures 30.5 cm (12 in.) in length and 43.2 cm (17 in.) in width. The book was launched on 28 February 2021 at the Our Lady of Carmel Chapel, Navelim, Goa. The copyright owner of the book is Ives Joaquim Tavares.

Most translated Indian work

The most translated Indian work is the Bhagavadgita, which is an integral part of the Mahabharata. The Bhagavadgita was first translated into English in 1785 by British typographer and founder of the Asiatic Society, Charles Wilkins. Since then, it has been translated into as many as 55 languages.

Largest sales for a children's book – hardback

Harry Potter and the Cursed Child (Parts One and Two) is the official script book for the play of the same name written by J.K. Rowling, John Tiffany and Jack Thorne. It is the eighth story in the Harry Potter book series. Released in India by Hachette India, Gurugram, Haryana, in July 2016, it sold 259,537 print copies (as of October 2017), making it the largest-selling children's book in India.

Largest sales on release for a fiction title – hardback

Dan Brown is a bestselling American author of thrillers. His book *Origin* was the fifth in his Robert Langdon series, following *Angels & Demons, The Da Vinci Code, The Lost Symbol* and *Inferno.* It was released in India on 3 October 2017 by Penguin Random House India, with an initial subscription of 125,000 copies, breaking all records in the fiction hardback category.

Largest-selling bilingual dictionary

The *English–English–Malayalam* Dictionary by T. Ramalingam Pillai was first published in May 1983. Published by DC Books, based in Kottayam, Kerala, it is in its 55th impression now. As on September 2019, around 2.4 million copies had been sold.

Largest lifetime sales – hardback

The Secret by Rhonda Byrne, published by Simon and Schuster, USA, in 2006, is a bestselling self-help book, based on the pseudoscientific 'law of attraction', which claims that a person's thoughts can change the world directly. The book has sold over 700,000 copies in India and has also been translated into 50 languages.

Largest adult non-fiction seller – hardback

Cricket legend Sachin Tendulkar's autobiography, *Playing It My Way,* co-authored with Boria Majumdar, was published in India by Hachette India, Gurugram, Haryana, and released on 6 November 2014. It broke all previous records in the adult non-fiction (hardback) category with 150,289 copies confirmed on order subscriptions.

Anthology in most languages

An international multilingual anthology of poetry, titled *Amaravati Poetic Prism* 2019, edited by Padmaja Iyengar-Paddy and published by the Cultural Centre of Vijayawada and Amaravati, Andhra Pradesh, features 1,303 poems in 120 Indian and foreign languages by poets from across India and the world.

WR Longest audiobook

The longest audio book, titled *Shree Haricharitramrut Sagar*, was voiced by Gyanjivandasji Swami - 'Kundaldham' and Ishwarcharandasji Swami - 'Kundaldham', and published on 27 October 2017. The audiobook is 146,444 mins 52 secs long.

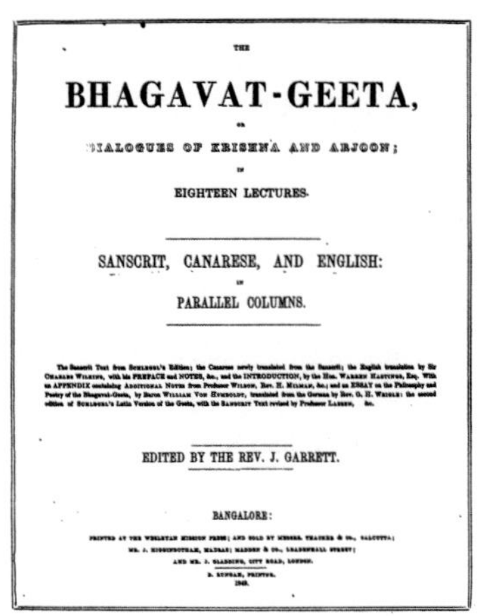
THE

BHAGAVAT-GEETA,

OR

DIALOGUES OF KRISHNA AND ARJOON;

IN

EIGHTEEN LECTURES.

SANSCRIT, CANARESE, AND ENGLISH:

IN

PARALLEL COLUMNS.

EDITED BY THE REV. J. GARRETT.

BANGALORE:

The Bhagavadgita: most translated Indian work

India ranks **3rd** after the USA and UK in English-language publishing in terms of market share.

The ISBN system switched from a 10-digit to a 13-digit format.

BOOK SELLING AND PUBLISHING

First book fair

The First International Book Fair opened at New Delhi's Pragati Maidan on 18 March 1972 during the International Book Year. Around a hundred Indian publishers took part, displaying about 10,000 books in English and local Indian languages. Foreign participants included those from the USSR, the USA, France, New Zealand, Turkey and Sri Lanka.

First book café

Café Turtle in the Full Circle bookshop in Khan Market, New Delhi, was among the first book cafés in India when it opened in 1999.

First children's literary festival

Co-founded by Swati Roy, Jo Williams and Venkatesh M. in 2008, Bookaroo was the first children's literary festival in India, with its first edition held in New Delhi.

First virtual literary festival

LitFest X, organized between 23 October and 1 November 2015 was the country's first virtual literary festival. The event used multiple platforms like YouTube, Google Hangouts, Facebook and Twitter to present the interactive sessions to readers.

First literary agency

Neville Tuli of Osian, Rajasthan, set up the first professional agency for authors on 9 April 2007. The first author they signed on was Omair Ahmad on 1 June 2007. The literary agency was a division of Osian's Connoisseurs of Art Pvt. Ltd.

College Street, Kolkata, West Bengal: largest book market

First independent publisher

The first Indian publisher to set up a press was Gangakishor Bhattacharya in 1821 in Calcutta (now Kolkata, West Bengal), a former employee of the Serampore Press, Serampore, Bengal (now Srirampur, West Bengal). He published 18th century ballads in Bengali and adaptations from classics.

First feminist publishing house

Kali for Women, a not-for-profit trust, publishing a wide variety of books by women and on women, was started in 1984 by Urvashi Butalia and Ritu Menon in New Delhi.

First comic book convention

The Annual Indian Comic Book Convention (Comic Con) was organized for the first time on 19 February 2011 by Twenty Onwards Media at Dilli Haat, New Delhi. Fifty publishers participated in it, bringing together writers, gamers, cosplayers, games and films.

First book village

- Bilhar, located in Satara District of Maharashtra, was identified as the first book village in India on 4 May 2017. Known as '*Pustakanch Gaav*', the village has genre-specific libraries in 25 locations, housing more than 15,000 books, mostly in Marathi. The village is decorated with murals, paintings and artworks on the theme of books. The aim of the initiative is to share a passion for books and an appetite for knowledge.
- The Bappuji Smaraka Vayanasala and the Kerala State Library Council have turned Perumkulam in Thiruvananthapuram District, Kerala, into a village of books, as announced by Jnanpith Award winner M.T. Vasudevan Nair in June 2019. Ten boxes with 50 books each were set up for anyone to take books from and replace with others.

Oldest bookshop

Higginbothams, the oldest bookshop in the country, was opened in 1844 by Abel Joshua Higginbotham in Madras (now Chennai, Tamil Nadu). It has a subscription division that helps educational institutions, corporate bodies and professionals to get journals and periodicals from more than 3,000 publishing houses abroad.

Largest book market

College Street in Kolkata, West Bengal, is the venue of the largest book market in the country and possibly the largest used-books market in the world. Known locally as *boi para* (the neighbourhood of books), this 1.5 km long street sees a large number of book lovers and buyers every day. The street suffered major damage due to cyclone Amphan in May 2020, but crowd funding efforts and the resilience of the shopkeepers brought it back in business.

Biggest retail bookshop chain – high street

Crossword Bookstores Ltd, a wholly owned subsidiary of Shoppers Stop Ltd, is the largest high-street bookstore chain in India. Established in October 1992, the company had 80 stores, including franchises, across India in December 2022, including in Mumbai, Bengaluru, Ahmedabad, Gurugram, Delhi, Kolkata, Chennai, Pune, Nashik, Vadodara, Jaipur, Bhopal, Kanpur, Panaji, Thrissur, Kottayam, Thiruvananthapuram, Siliguri, Lucknow, Kohima, Ghaziabad, Raipur and Hyderabad.

Largest bookshop

Sapna Book House in Gandhinagar, Bengaluru, Karnataka, was started in 1967 by Suresh C. Shah. Spread over 3,716 sq. m (40,000 sq. ft), it has more than 220,000 titles covering many genres and topics. Sapna Book House has four more branches in Bengaluru and Mysuru – adding up to retail space of about 9,290.3 sq. m (100,000 sq. ft).

Most travel bookshops

Wheeler (A.H. Wheeler and Co. Pvt. Ltd) owns a bookstore chain co-founded by Emile Moreau and T.K. Banerjee in Allahabad (now Prayagraj, Uttar Pradesh) in 1877, with around 900 popular bookshops selling magazines and books at as many as 264 railway stations.

Largest trade publishing house

Penguin Random House India is the subcontinent's largest English-language trade publisher. It publishes more than 250 new titles every year and has an active backlist of 3,000 titles.

Largest literary publisher

DC Books in Kottayam, Kerala, started in 1974 by Dominic Chacko Kizhakemuri, is considered the publishing hub of south India. The translation programme of DC Books is considered to be the largest in India. It publishes around 1,400 books in a year (2019).

Largest literary festival

The Jaipur Literature Festival, founded in 2006, is an annual literary festival in Jaipur, Rajasthan, which brings together some of the most prominent thinkers and writers from across the world, every January. The festival directors are authors Namita Gokhale and William Dalrymple, and it has been produced by Sanjoy Roy of Teamwork Arts since 2008.

Most prolific translator – published literary works

Prof. Bibek Debroy, an economist, policymaker and author, has translated into English, the Mahabharata (2.25 million words), *Harivamsha* (160,000 words, published in 2016), the *Valmiki Ramayana* (0.5 million words, published in 2017) and the *Bhagavata Purana* (0.5 million words, published in December 2018). He is the third person (after Kisari Mohan Ganguli [published between 1883 and 1895] and Manmatha Nath Dutt [1855–1912]) to translate the unabridged version of the Mahabharata into English. His translation was published in 10 volumes (2010–14), and a box set released in 2015 by Penguin Random House India.

The Sahitya Akademi was established by the Government of India to preserve and promote literature in Indian languages.

Kolkata to Host a Literature Festival on Sweets

Kolkata is all set to host a litfest on sweets. It will be a three-day festival from 9 to 11 December 2022. The organizers have said that Oxford University professor Dr Kunal Basu, painter Jogen Choudhury and former Prasar Bharati CEO Jawhar Sircar (currently, a Rajya Sabha member) are a few of the many participants in the unique literary meet. This festival will be organized across 10 venues that will bring together traditional homes, art galleries and modern institutions of Kolkata. Furthermore, reportedly each venue will have the world's largest tables of *mishti* (sweets) with over 60 varieties. The festival will witness one of the largest gatherings of writers, historians, food aficionados, and stalwarts from the world of cinema and theatre.

TOP 10 FRONT-LIST TITLES* 2021

	Title	Author	Volume
ADULT FICTION	*400 Days*	Chetan Bhagat	66,455
	A Touch of Eternity	Durjoy Datta	23,650
	Last Queen	Chitra Banerjee Divakaruni	17,249
	You Only Live Once: One for Passion Two for Love Three for Friendship	Stuti Changle	13,146
	Write Me a Love Story	Ravinder Singh	10,651
	Turn a Blind Eye: William Warwick Novels	Jeffrey Archer	10,254
	Over My Dead Body: William Warwick Novels	Jeffrey Archer	9,633
	Whereabouts: A Novel	Jhumpa Lahiri	8,778
	Can't Quarantine Our Love	Sudeep Nagarkar	6,490
	That Night: Four Friends. Twenty Years. One Haunting Secret	Nidhi Upadhyay	6,447
ADULT NON-FICTION	*Karma: A Yogi's Guide to Crafting Your Destiny*	Sadhguru	112,614
	Atmasiddhi Shastra: Six Spiritual Truths of the Soul	Pujya Gurudevshri Rakeshji	43,338
	Unfinished: A Memoir	Priyanka Chopra Jonas	32,661
	Do Epic Shit	Ankur Warikoo	29,647
	My Life in Full: Work, Family, and Our Future	Indra Nooyi	29,240
	Twelve and a Half: Leveraging the Emotional Ingredients Necessary for Business Success	Gary Vaynerchuk	17,947
	Karma: Why Everything You Know About It Is Wrong	Prashant Acharya	16,601
	Believe: What Life and Cricket Taught Me	Suresh Raina and Bharat Sundaresan	16,418
	The Everyday Hero Manifesto	Robin Sharma	15,674
	The Almanack of Naval Ravikant: A Guide to Wealth and Happiness	Eric Jorgenson	15,057
CHILDREN'S FICTION	*Diary of a Wimpy Kid: Big Shot* (Book 16)	Jeff Kinney	15,598
	Rowley Jefferson's Awesome Friendly Spooky Stories	Jeff Kinney	9,514
	All-Time Favourites for Children	Ruskin Bond	8,824
	How the Earth Got Its Beauty	Sudha Murty	6,962
	How to Be a Writer	Ruskin Bond	4,521
	Amar Chitra Katha Folktales Collection	Christopher Baretto and Preeti Vyas	4,399
	The Sage with Two Horns: Unusual Tales from Mythology	Sudha Murty	3,747
	The Christmas Pig	J. K. Rowling	3,199
	Daughter of the Deep	Rick Riordan	3,186
	Illustrated Ramayana for Children: Immortal Epic of India	Shubha Vilas	2,439
CHILDREN'S NON-FICTION	My Encyclopedia of Space: What? Why? How? When?	Om Books International	2,830
	Becoming: Adapted for Younger Readers	Michelle Obama	1,433
	Two-Epics-in-One (The Girl Who Chose; The Boys Who Fought)	Devdutt Pattanaik	906
	They Found What?/They Made What?	Shweta Taneja	660
	How We Know What We Know: Fascinating Stories of Discovery and Invention	Shruthi Rao	612
	Unlocking the Universe	Stephen Hawking and Lucy Hawking	446
	Postbox Kashmir: Two Lives in Letters	Divya Arya	321
	Favourite Stories from Hindu Myths	Arshia Sattar	273
	Quirky History: The Swan Car of Nabha and Other Unusual Stories from History	Mini Menon	269
	Knowledge Encyclopaedia: Wars – World History	Wonder House	252

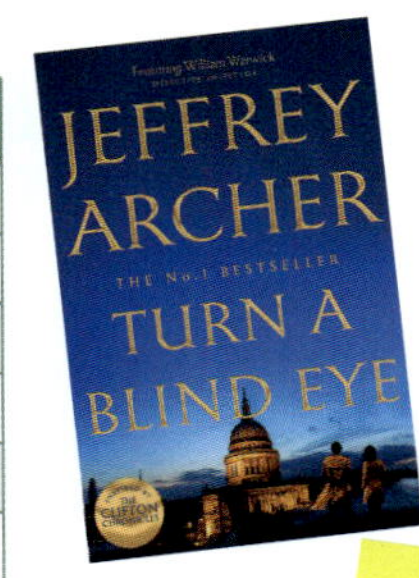

*NOTE: Titles published between 1 January and 31 December 2021. Data sourced from Nielsen BookScan retail panel market and © Nielsen BookData. Volume indicates the number of copies sold.

FIRST AND LATEST AWARD WINNERS

Benyamin

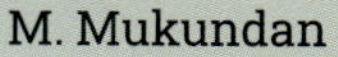
M. Mukundan

Award	First Winner(s)	Latest Winner(s)
Jnanpith Award	G. Sankara Kurup for *Odakkuzhal* (*The Bamboo Flute*), 1950	Damodar Mauzo, 2021
DSC Prize for South Asian Literature	Jeet Thayil for *Narcopolis*, 2013	Amitabha Bagchi for *Half the Night Is Gone, 2018*
JCB Prize for Literature	Benyamin for *Jasmine Days*, 2018	M. Mukundan for *Delhi: A Soliloquy, 2021*
Hindu Literary Prize	Manu Joseph for *Serious Men*, 2010	Mirza Waheed for *Tell Her Everything* and Santanu Das for *India, Empire, and First World War Culture: Writings, Images and Songs*
Kamaladevi Chattopadhyay NIF (New India Foundation) Book Prize	Milan Vaishnav for *When Crime Pays: Money and Muscle in Indian Politics*, 2018	Dinyar Patel for *Naoroji: Pioneer of Indian Nationalism*, 2021

Dinyar Patel

Manu Joseph

Santanu Das

AWARDS AND HONOURS

First Sahitya Akademi Bhasha Samman Award

The Bhasha Samman Awards are given annually for contribution towards the development of a language. The first of these awards were given in 1996 to:

- Dharikshan Mishra for Bhojpuri.
- Bansi Ram Sharma and M.R. Thakur for Pahari (Himachali).
- K. Jathappa Rai and Mandara Keshava Bhat for Tulu (Karnataka).
- Chandra Kanta Murasingh for Kokborok (Tripura).

Nayantara Sahgal (*right*): first Indian winner of the Commonwealth Writers' Prize

First recipients of the Sahitya Akademi Award

- *Man*: Makhanlal Chaturvedi (1889–1968), a Hindi poet, was the first person to receive this award for *Him Tarangini* (Hindi) in 1955.
- *Woman*: The Punjabi poet and writer Amrita Pritam (1919–2005) received the award in 1956, the year after its inception, for *Sunehre* (Punjabi), a collection of poems.

Punjabi and Hindi writer and poet Amrita Pritam: first woman to receive the Sahitya Akademi Award

First recipients of the Jnanpith Award

The Jnanpith Award is presented annually by the Bharatiya Jnanpith to an Indian author for his/her contribution to literature.

- *Man*: Malayalam poet G. Sankara Kurup (1901–78) was the recipient of the first Jnanpith Award in 1965, the year of its inception, for his anthology of poems, *Odakkuzhal.*
- *Woman*: • Ashapurna Devi (1909–95), Bengali novelist and poet, was the first woman author to receive the Jnanpith Award in 1976 for her novel *Pratham Pratishruti* (which was published in 1965), the first of a trilogy that included *Subarnalata* and *Bakul Katha.*

Malayalam poet G. Sankara Kurup: first recipient of the Jnanpith Award

First Indian citizen to win the Booker Prize

Arundhati Roy (b. 24 November 1961) won the prestigious Booker Prize in 1997 for her first novel, *The God of Small Things.*

- Two other Indian-origin authors had won the Prize before her – Salman Rushdie for his novel *Midnight's Children* in 1981 and Sir V.S. Naipaul for *In a Free State* in 1971 (he also won the Nobel Prize in literature in 2001).
- Kiran Desai won the laurel for her novel, *The Inheritance of Loss,* in 2006.
- Aravind Adiga won the Booker Prize in 2008 for his novel, *The White Tiger.*

First Indian winner of the Commonwealth Writers' Prize

Author Nayantara Sahgal (b. 10 May 1927) won the Commonwealth Writers' Prize for Best Book in 1987, for her novel *Plans for Departure.*

First Indian winner of the Neustadt Prize

The Neustadt International Prize (given for an author's body of work) is one of the few international prizes for which poets, novelists and playwrights are all eligible. Raja Rao was the first Indian to win it in 1988. Indian-Canadian writer Rohinton Mistry won the prize in 2012.

First Indian winner of the Ondaatje Prize

Sports journalist Rahul Bhattacharya's *The Sly Company of People Who Care* won the Royal Society of Literature Ondaatje Prize 2012. It also won the Hindu Literary Prize (2011) and was the Kirkus Fiction Book of the Year in the USA.

First Indian recipient of the UNESCO International Book Reading Award

Dina Nath Malhotra started Hind Pocket Books and became a book consultant to UNESCO in 1971, before being awarded the Book Reading Award. His son Shekhar Malhotra later started the Full Circle publishing house and bookshop in New Delhi.

First Sahitya Akademi Fellowship

Former Indian president and eminent scholar Dr S. Radhakrishnan (1888–1975) was the first to receive this honour in 1968 for his contribution to Indian thought and universal humanism. The first woman to be elected Fellow of the Akademi was the poet Mahadevi Varma in 1979.

First winner of Grinzane Cavour award

Anita Desai won the lifetime achievement award of the Grinzane Cavour Prize in Piedmont, Italy, on 18 July 2005.

First Indian winner of Newbery Medal

- Dhan Gopal Mukerji (1890–1936), who was born in a village near Calcutta (now Kolkata, West Bengal) and later went to the USA, was the first Indian winner of the Newbery Medal for his novel, *Gay-Neck, the Story of a Pigeon,* in 1928.
- The most recent winner of the award is

Indian-origin writer Veera Hiranandani for her work *The Night Diary* in 2019.

First to win the DSC Prize for South Asian Literature

Poet and novelist Jeet Thayil won the DSC Prize for South Asian Literature 2013 for his novel *Narcopolis* (Faber & Faber).

First Indian-origin winner of the Pulitzer Prize – fiction

Jhumpa Lahiri's *Interpreter of Maladies* (Mariner Books/Houghton Mifflin) won the Pulitzer Prize for Fiction in 2000.

First winners of the Rabindranath Tagore Literary Prize

The Rabindranath Tagore Literary Prize, started in 2018, is awarded annually for valuable contributions to literature and poetry.

- Kabir (awarded posthumously) for *One Hundred Poems* of Kabir in 2018.
- Rana Dasgupta for *Solo* (2010) in 2019.
- Raj Kamal Jha for *The City and the Sea* (2019) in 2020.

Jhumpa Lahiri: first Indian-origin winner of the Pulitzer Prize for fiction

Freedom to Read: After 75 Years

INDIA AT HER BEST 75 YEARS OF INDEPENDENCE

The Government of India in association with the Ministry of Culture is in the process of reviving interest in Indian literature that was banned during British rule. The Ministry has identified poems, writings and publications banned due to their patriotic fervour, and put together as catalogues for audiences. These literary works are in different Indian languages, including Bengali, Hindi, Urdu, Kannada, Punjabi, Sindhi, Telugu, Gujarati and Tamil. One of the features is Union ministers reciting poems from their regions on video. These videos showcase '*Daridra Nian*' by Odia poet Gangadhar Mishra, poem '*Kasumbi No Rang*' from the book *Sindhudo* by poet Jhaverchand Meghani and '*Bharatha Matha Geetham*' by Telugu poets Vaddadhi Seetharaamanjaneyulu and Pudipeddhi Kashi Viswanatha Sastri.

Highest monetary prize

- The JCB Prize, established in 2018, is the most valuable prize in Indian literature, amounting to ₹25 lakh (2.5 million). Funded by JCB, a British manufacturing firm, the prize is awarded to the best work of fiction by an Indian citizen in English or translated from another language into English. Each of the five shortlisted books is awarded ₹1 lakh (0.1 million) and a separate prize of ₹5 lakh (0.5 million) is given if the winning entry is a translation. Mita Kapur, founder and CEO of Siyahi literary consultancy now serves as the JCB Prize's literary director.
- The richest prize for non-fiction writing is the New India Foundation Prize, valued at ₹15 lakh (1.5 million).

Rabindranath Tagore is the only Indian to have been awarded the Nobel Prize for literature, in 1913, for his anthology of poems, *Gitanjali*.

INDIA AT HER BEST

75

YEARS OF INDEPENDENCE

Celebrating Our Nation

The Government of India organized a year-long programme, *Azadi ka Amrit Mahotsav*, with five main themes: The freedom struggle; Ideas @75; Resolve@75; Actions@75; and Achievements@75. The series of events commenced on 12 March 2021 with a 75-week countdown to the 75th anniversary of Independence and will culminate on 15 August 2023. Here are a few highlights...

Images for POSTerity: Commemorative Stamps

Several stamps were issued to celebrate *Azadi ka Amrit Mahotsav*. The Department of Posts, Ministry of Communications, released thematic stamps to capture the various facets of Indian culture. Commemorative stamps were also released by 22 postal circles across India to honour the unsung heroes of the Indian freedom struggle. The launch events were held at the birthplaces of these heroes. Many other events such as the golden jubilee of ICRISAT (International Crops Research Institute for the Semi-Arid Tropics), 50 years of statehood of Tripura, Meghalaya, Manipur and Arunachal Pradesh, the centenary celebrations of the University of Delhi, 200 years of the publication of *Mumbai Samachar*, the 44th Chess Olympiad, Right to Free Legal Aid, and the journey of the national flag were commemorated with stamps. The contribution of healthcare workers and the scientific community to the development of the Covaxin vaccine was also acknowledged through the launch of a stamp. Additionally, stamps were issued to honour the defence forces for milestones such as the President's Fleet Review 2022, the centenary year of the Rashtriya Indian Military College (RIMC) and the permanent commission of women officers in the Indian Army.

Several Bharat Ratna award winners, such as Dr P.V. Kane and Sri Guru Tegh Bahadur Ji (400th anniversary) were also honoured with stamps.

Commemorative stamps and first day covers released during *Azadi ka Amrit Mahotsav*

Coins for Collectors

To commemorate 75 years of India's independence, Prime Minister Modi launched special coins. They included the denominations of ₹1, ₹2, ₹5, ₹10, and ₹Rs 20. These coins have the logo of the *Azadi ka Amrit Mahotsav* on them, and a unique and progressive feature is that they can be easily identified by visually impaired people.

Prime Minister Narendra Modi released commemorative coins

Historical Clicks

For the last seven decades, the Lalit Kala Akademi, the premier government institution involved with visual arts, has supported and nurtured artists in the field of painting, graphic design, ceramics, sculpture and photography, among others. The Akademi organized several events and activities for the *Azadi ka Amrit Mahotsav*, including a photography exhibition on World Photography Day (19 August), portraying different themes such as the Indian freedom struggle along with Indian forts, ancient temples, mountains, and other heritage sites. The exhibition received 1,603 entries from 423 photographers, out of which 135 photographs were selected by the jury for display. The exhibition was inaugurated by Padma

1,000 Make-in-India drones made different formations during the Beating the Retreat ceremony in New Delhi

The national flag was unfurled 30 km above Earth by Space Kidz India

Shri award winner Raghu Rai, and Uma Nanduri, the chairman of the Lalit Kala Akademi.

Lighting the Sky with the Colours of Freedom

The largest Indian drone show portraying the First War of Independence in 1857 was organized at the Residency in Lucknow, Uttar Pradesh, on 20 December 2021. With the help of a team of Russian drone engineers, 500 drones performed aerial acrobatics in the sky, accompanied by a light-and-sound show. It displayed the tale of India's freedom struggle from 1857 to 1947. This event also marked 100 years of the Chauri Chaura incident in Gorakpur District in the then United Provinces (now Uttar Pradesh). The police there had fired upon a number of protesters participating in the non-cooperation movement, causing them to attack a police station and set fire to it. The resulting death of three civilians and 22 policemen led Mahatma Gandhi to call of the non-cooperation movement countrywide The drone show also included a display of the 1925 Kakori Train Action along with drone portraits of freedom fighters such as Subhas Chandra Bose, Rani Lakshmi Bai and Mangal Pandey. The mega drone show was organized by the Union Ministry of Culture and the Department of Tourism and Culture, Uttar Pradesh.

Another mega drone show lit up the skies during the Beating the Retreat ceremony in New Delhi on 29 January 2022, when 1,000 drones made indigenously under the Make in India initiative displayed several formations such as the *Azadi ka Amrit Mahotsav* logo, the national flag and the map of India, among others.

'Rang Swadheenta' – Honouring Indian Freedom Fighters

To commemorate the 75th anniversary of India's independence, the Sangeet Natak Akademi held 'Rang Swadheenta' from 27 to 29 August 2022, a festival honouring Indian freedom fighters. The programme focused on diverse folk music and singing styles from across the country. The audience witnessed a variety of songs and styles including Dhimaryai, Ragini, Oggukatha and Dhadi. The guests of honour included Amita Prasad Sarbhai, joint secretary in the Ministry of Culture, and Uma Nanduri, chairman of the Lalit Kala Akademi and joint secretary in the Ministry of Culture. Nearly a hundred artistes from nine different states and 12 teams participated in this festival.

Out of This World Flag

As part of the *Azadi ka Amrit Mahotsav* and the '*Har Ghar Tiranga*' campaign, the Indian national flag was unfurled 30 km above Earth by Space Kidz India, an Indian aerospace start-up that designs, fabricates and launches small satellites, spacecraft and ground systems. The flag was sent to an altitude of 106,000 ft above Earth on a balloon that unfurled it. Space Kidz India also launched a satellite named AzadiSAT into the low earth orbit. This satellite was developed by 750 girl students from across the subcontinent.

ISRO's Virtual Space Museum

As part of the celebrations for the 75th anniversary of Indian independence, the Indian Space Research organization (ISRO) launched their first virtual space museum, SPARK. This platform showcases digital content describing their missions in an interesting way. It comprises documents, videos and images relating to launch vehicles, missions and satellites. It was launched by the chairman of ISRO.

Pradhan Mantri Sangrahalaya: A Tribute to Prime Ministers

The Pradhan Mantri Sangrahalaya was inaugurated on the 131st birthday of Dr B.R. Ambedkar by Prime Minister Narendra Modi as part of the celebrations for the 75th anniversary of India's independence. It is a homage to all the prime ministers of India since Independence. The building includes Teen Murti Bhavan along with newly constructed areas in New Delhi. It has 43 galleries and covers an area of 15,600 sq. m. Its logo show Indians holding the Dharma Chakra, which symbolizes the nation and democracy. The design of the building incorporates sustainable and energy conservation practices. It has displays of the freedom struggle, the framing of the Constitution of India and the journey of all the prime ministers in the past.

An Iconic Museum on Wheels

A museum on wheels located inside two trams cars of Kolkata, West Bengal, was inaugurated by Firhad Hakim, the transport and housing minister of West Bengal, on Independence Day 2021. The Museum on Wheels has been curated by the Arts and Cultural Heritage Trust in collaboration with the West Bengal Transport Corporation (WBTC). The first car highlights the key moments during the opposition to British rule from 1900 to 1947, and how borders were drawn to divide Bengal and Punjab each into two. The second car portrays the migration and rehabilitation of people that took place after Partition and explores the humanitarian aspects of the separation. The museum was on display at Esplanade (Central Kolkata) till December 2021. On 1 January 2022, it began travelling to different parts of the city.

'Har Ghar Tiranga'

In conjunction with the *Azadi ka Amrit Mahotsav* celebrations, Prime Minister Narendra Modi launched the *'Har Ghar Tiranga'* campaign to encourage Indian citizens to hoist the Tricolour at home. The purpose of this campaign was to evoke a feeling a patriotism in the people. Union Territories, states, ministries and even several NGOs and self-help groups took part in this campaign. During this campaign a total of 5,885 people collected at a cricket stadium in Chandigarh to create the largest image of a waving national flag. This event was organized by the NID foundation along with Chandigarh University.

As a part of the *'Har Ghar Tiranga'* campaign, around six crore selfies were uploaded to the Har Ghar Tiranga website. To ensure the campaign was a success, the government made sure there was an ample supply of flags.

A flag 'march' on water in Chandigarh

A Step Towards Digitizing Biotechnology Research

In conjunction with the celebrations of India's 75 years of independence, the Biotechnology Industry Research Assistance Council (BIRAC) introduced a scheme of special incentives to aid 75 start-ups in the fields of telemedicine, artificial intelligence and digital health. The goal is to identify 75 innovations that further research and development in the healthcare industry in the post-COVID world and find solutions to problems posed by the pandemic. BIRAC has also promoted Startup India and Make in India to enhance the growth of biotechnology. To ensure that the project was in line with the Digital India Mission, BIRAC deployed the e-Office Lite software on the National Informatics Centre Services Incorporated (NICSI) server to make processes such as project proposals easier, and foster transparency and good governance.

A Star for a Star!

Jitendra Singh, Union minister of state for science and technology, launched a mentorship programme titled 'DBT-Star College Mentorship Programme' to promote scientific thinking in young innovators. The initiative aims to have a 'Star College' in every district, supported by the Department of Biotechnology (DBT) and offering strong undergraduate science courses. The programme is set to facilitate networking and outreach, and provide support, which includes the acquisition of equipment, training of faculty and staff, lectures by renowned scientists and visits to research institutes. It also includes activities such as workshops and discussions, along with outreach initiatives to support government schools and institutions, particularly in rural areas. This is to ensure that the institutions under the scheme will have the resources to meet the needs of the programme. Currently, there are 278 undergraduate colleges under the scheme.

'Vigyan Sarvatra Pujyate' – Celebrating India's Achievements in Science and Technology

'Vigyan Sarvatra Pujyate' was a week-long programme organized as a part of the National Science Week in 75 cities across India. It was done as a part of the *Azadi ka Amrit Mahotsav* celebrations. Its purpose was to celebrate the scientific and technological contributions of various governmental organizations in partnership with other agencies in the past 75 years. It provided a platform to these organizations to highlight their projects and how they helped find answers in different sectors such as space, defence, astronomy, health and agriculture, among others. The programmes were categorized under four themes, titled 'From the Annals of the History of S&T', 'Milestones of Modern S&T', 'Swadeshi Paramparik Inventions and Innovations' and 'Transforming India'. The National Science Book Fair was also organized as a part of this programme with the goal to communicate scientific concepts through poetry, theatre, folk forms and cultural shows.

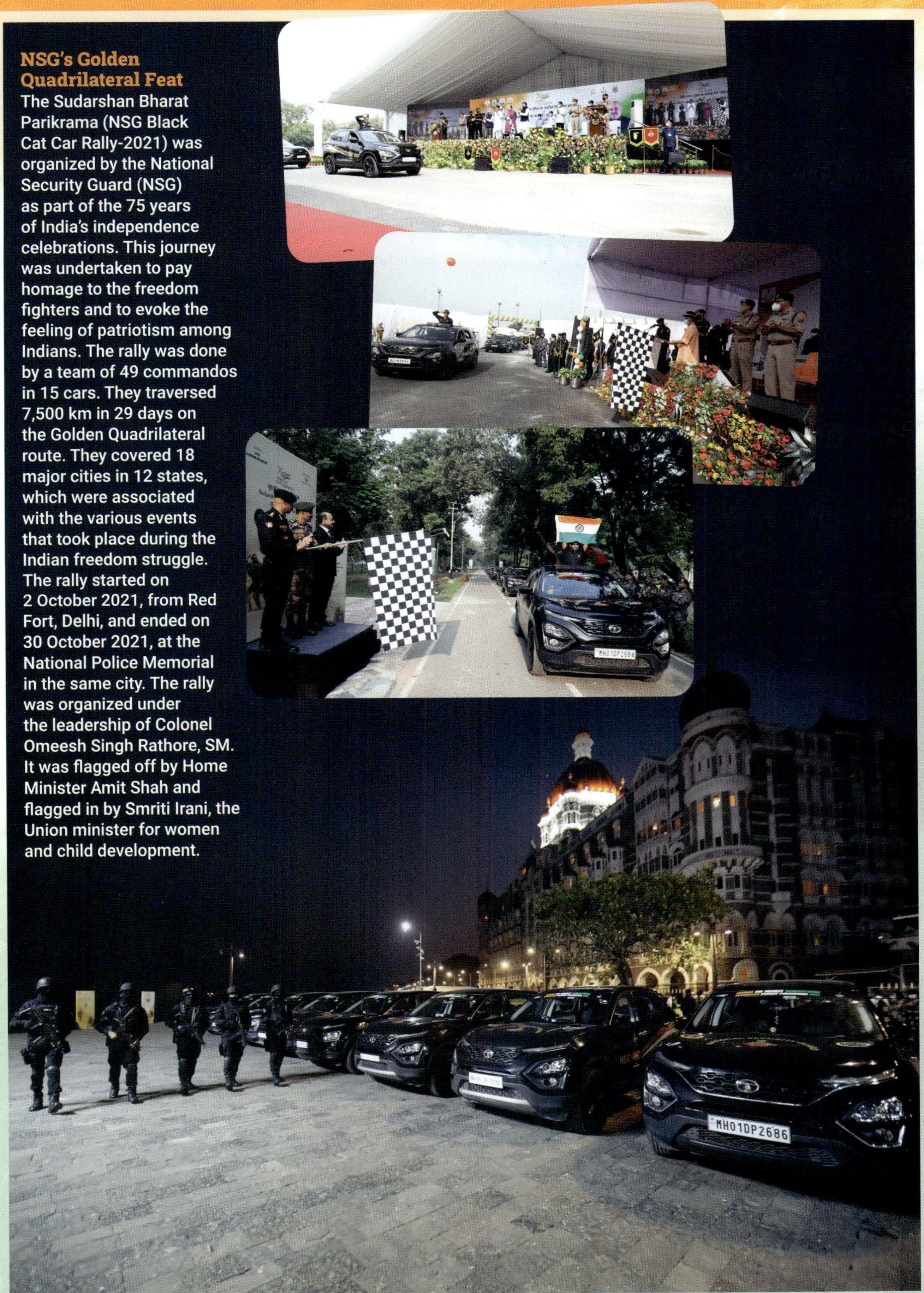

NSG's Golden Quadrilateral Feat

The Sudarshan Bharat Parikrama (NSG Black Cat Car Rally-2021) was organized by the National Security Guard (NSG) as part of the 75 years of India's independence celebrations. This journey was undertaken to pay homage to the freedom fighters and to evoke the feeling of patriotism among Indians. The rally was done by a team of 49 commandos in 15 cars. They traversed 7,500 km in 29 days on the Golden Quadrilateral route. They covered 18 major cities in 12 states, which were associated with the various events that took place during the Indian freedom struggle. The rally started on 2 October 2021, from Red Fort, Delhi, and ended on 30 October 2021, at the National Police Memorial in the same city. The rally was organized under the leadership of Colonel Omeesh Singh Rathore, SM. It was flagged off by Home Minister Amit Shah and flagged in by Smriti Irani, the Union minister for women and child development.

India in Infographics

The statistical story of 75 years of Indian independence is a fascinating one. Here are a few of the highlights depicted in numbers and visuals.

INFANT MORTALITY RATE

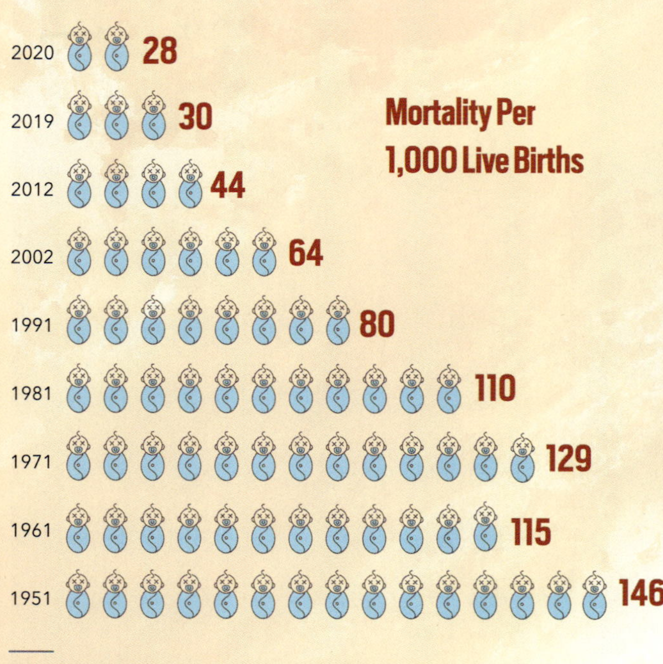

Source: PIB AKAM series, Press Information Bureau, Government of India

GROWTH IN LITERACY RATE

(in Percentage)

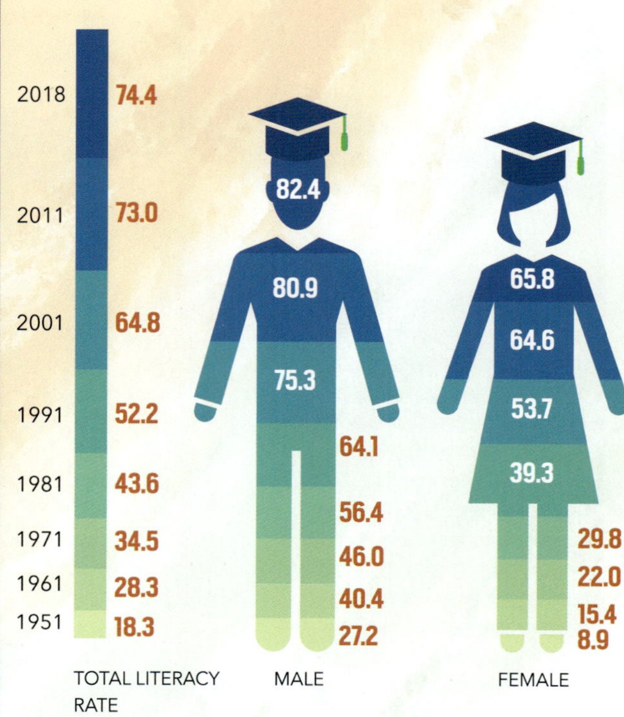

Source: PIB AKAM series, Press Information Bureau, Government of India; {1951–71: Age group 5 and above; 1981–2011: Age group 7 and above: Ministry of Education; 2018: Age group 15 and above: UNESCO: http://uis.unesco.org/country/IN)

HIGHWAYS OF DEVELOPMENT

NH Length (in Kilometres)

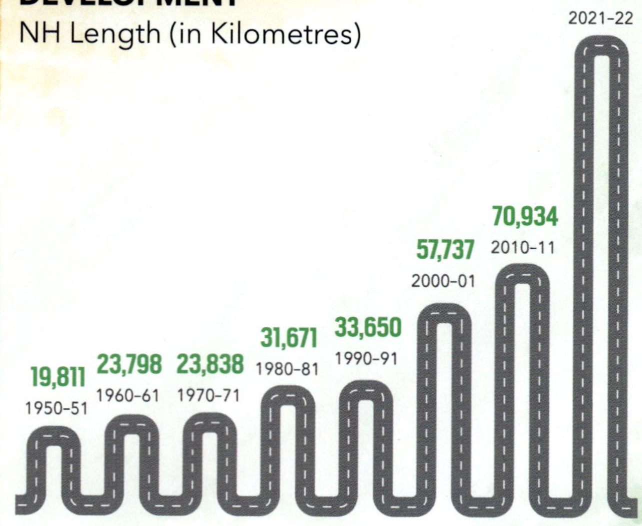

Source: *Annual Report* 2020-21, Ministry of Transport, Government of India

INCREASED FOODGRAIN PRODUCTION

(in Million Tonnes)

Source: PIB AKAM series, Press Information Bureau, Government of India

FOREIGN EXCHANGE RESERVES
(in US$ Billion)

Source: PIB AKAM series, Press Information Bureau, Government of India

GROWTH OF HYDROELECTRICITY GENERATION IN INDIA
(in Gigawatt-hours [GWh])

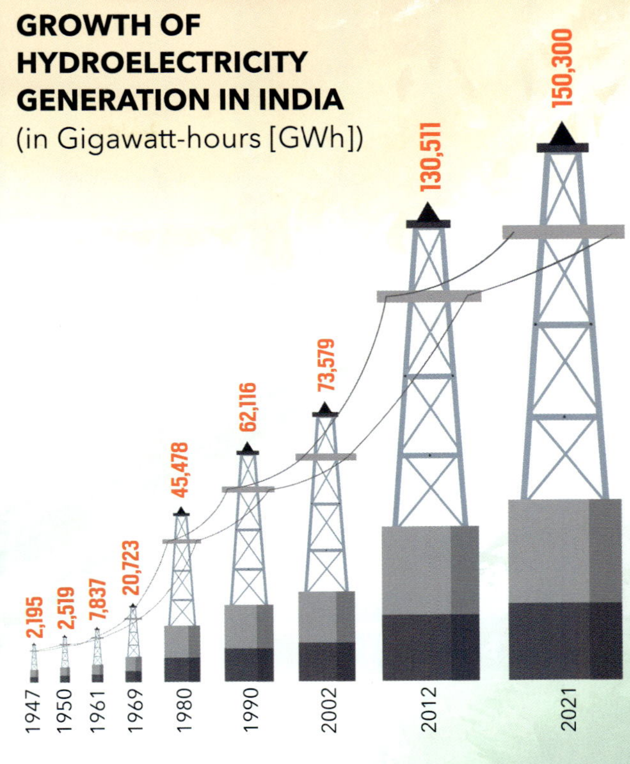

Source: PIB AKAM series, Press Information Bureau, Government of India

GROSS ELECTRICITY GENERATION

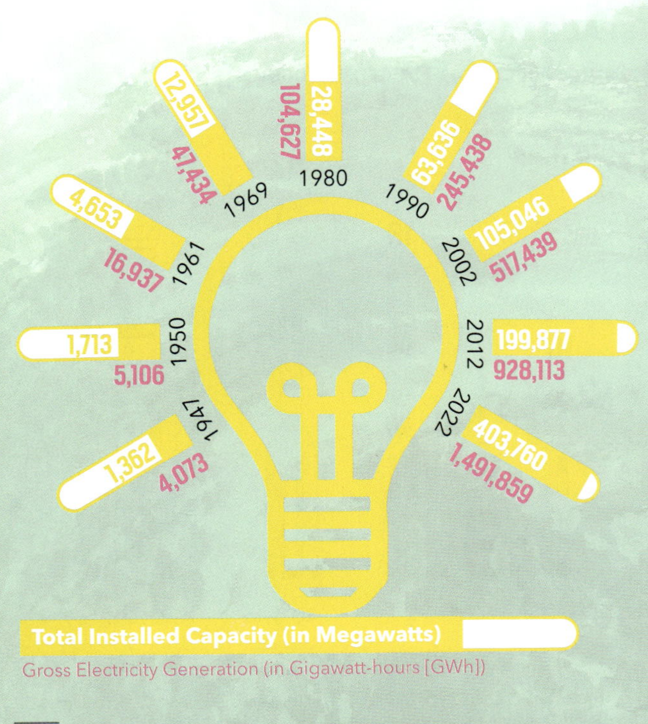

Source: PIB AKAM series, Press Information Bureau, Government of India

POWER GENERATION FROM RENEWABLE RESOURCES
(in Gigawatt-hours [GWh])

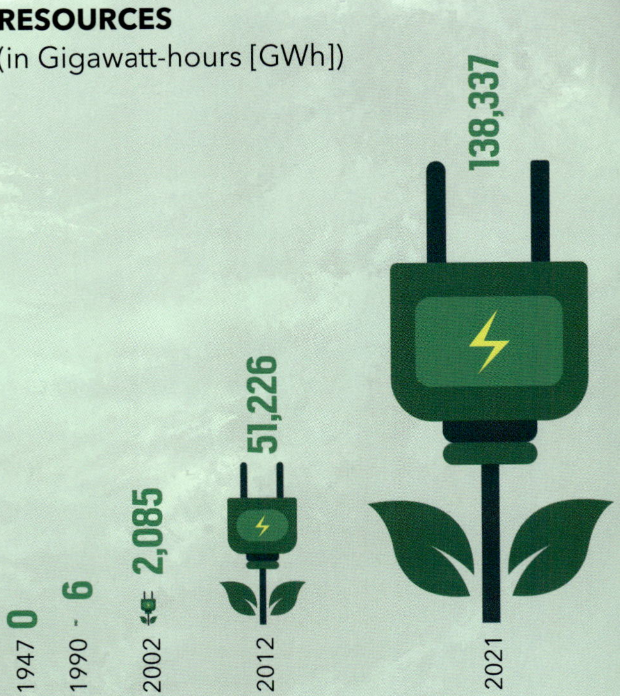

Source: PIB AKAM series, Press Information Bureau, Government of India

EXPORTS FROM INDIA TO THE WORLD

(in US$ Billions)

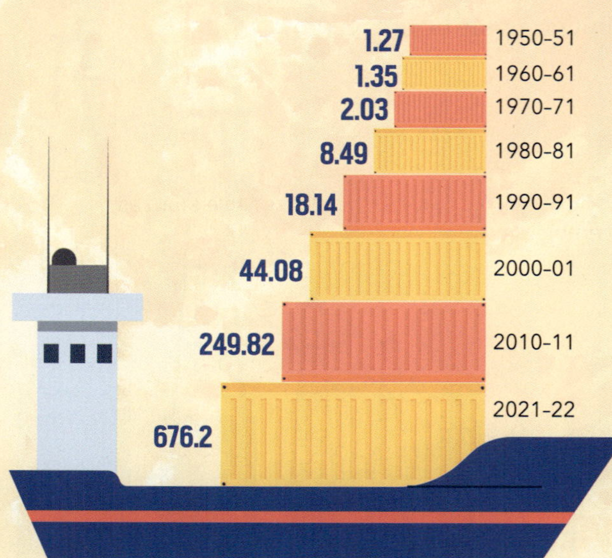

Source: PIB AKAM series, Press Information Bureau, Government of India

UNIFIED PAYMENTS INTERFACE (UPI): DIGITAL PAYMENT LANDSCAPE

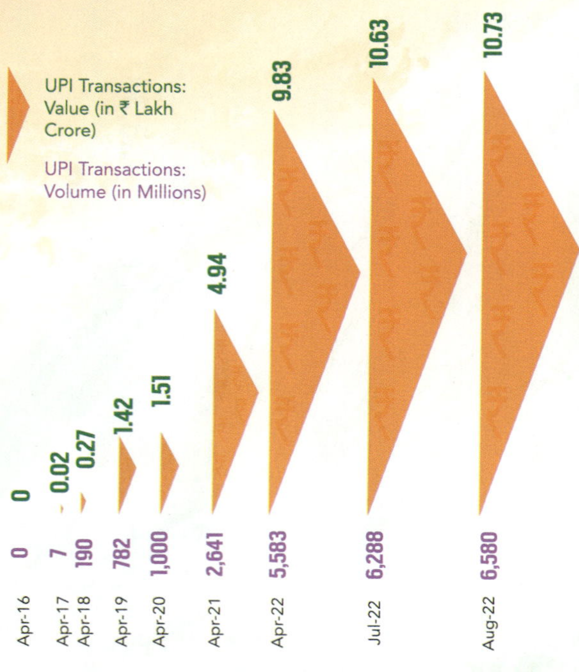

Source: PIB AKAM series, Press Information Bureau, Government of India

HEALTHCARE WORKFORCE

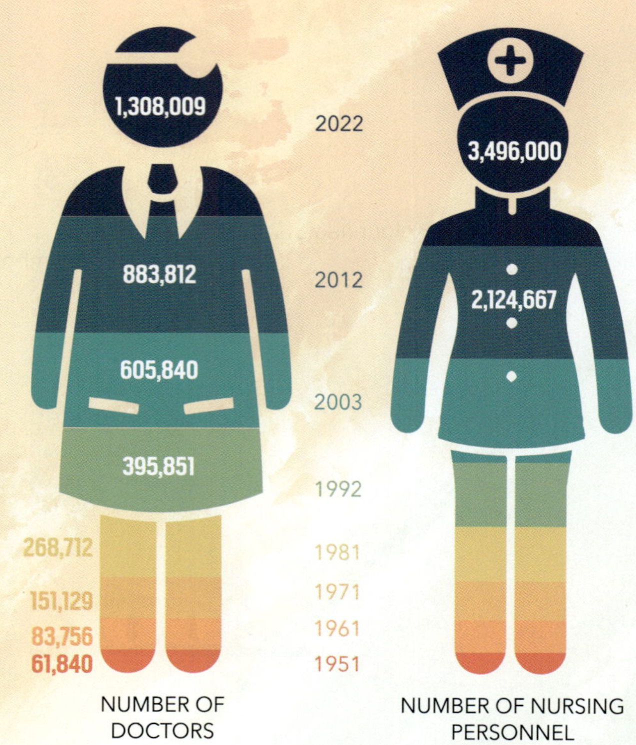

Sources: PIB AKAM series, Press Information Bureau, Government of India

SPACE MISSIONS

(Number of Spacecraft Missions)

1975-85	1986-95	1996-2005	2006-15	2016-22*
10	14	18	34	39

* Note: Data is up to July 2022; Source: PIB AKAM series, Press Information Bureau, Government of India; ISRO: https://www.isro.gov.in/list-of-spacecrafts

Our National Identity

The Government of India lists ten National Identity Elements as symbols intrinsic to Indian identity and heritage. The 75th anniversary of Indian independence gave all Indians the opportunity to recall them with pride.

1 The National Flag

The tricolour flag of India comprises three bands of equal proportion. The saffron or *kesariya* band at the top represents courage and strength, the white band in the middle represents peace and truth, and the green band at the lower end stands for growth, fertility and auspiciousness. The word 'tricolour' (or '*tiranga*') in India is synonymous with the national flag. The blue Dharma Chakra in the middle of the white band has a diameter almost equal to the width of the band and has 24 equally spaced spokes. Its design is similar to the wheel on the abacus of the Sarnath Lion Capital of Ashoka. The ratio of the width of the flag to its length is 2:3. The flag's design was accepted by the Constituent Assembly of India on 22 July 1947.

Indian national flag and state emblem

Originally, the national flag was legally bound to be made of khadi, and the manufacturing process and specifications for it are strictly elucidated by the Bureau of Indian Standards. The Khadi and Village Industries Commission (KVIC), a statutory body formed in April 1957 by the Government of India, holds the right to manufacture the flag, and further allots the right regionally. Since 2009, the Karnataka Khadi Gramodyoga Samyukta Sangha is the only manufacturer of the flag.

The use of the flag is strictly defined in the Flag Code of India and other laws that govern the usage of national symbols and emblems. Under the original code, citizens could not use the flag privately except on nationally significant days such as Independence Day and Republic Day. However, in 2002, subsequent to an appeal from Naveen Jindal, an industrialist and former member of Lower House of the Parliament or the Lok Sabha, the Supreme Court of India directed the Government of India to amend the code to allow common citizens to use the flag. The Union cabinet amended the code to let citizens use the flag in a limited way. The code was amended again in 2005 to expand the use of the flag to include adaptations on certain forms of clothing. The Flag Code lays down the rules regarding the proportions of the flag, the protocol of flying it and its use with other national and non-national flags. On 20 June 2022, an order amending the Flag Code allowed the national flag to be displayed in the open or in the house of a member of public and to be flown both during the day as well as at night.

The National Anthem

'*Jana Gana Mana*', which is the national anthem of India, was originally composed in Bengali by Rabindranath Tagore, a multi-talented Indian polymath, who was a poet, writer, playwright, composer, philosopher, social reformer and painter. It was sung for the first time at the Kolkata session of the Indian National Congress on 27 December 1911. The original song comprised five stanzas, but only the first stanza was considered for the national anthem. On 24 January 1950, the Hindi version of this anthem was adopted by the Constituent Assembly of India. This score was harmonized and orchestrated by English musician, organist and composer Herbert Murrill in collaboration with Norman Richardson. The length of the full version of the national anthem is 52 seconds. A shorter version of the anthem of around 20 seconds is also played on a few occasions.

Rabindranath Tagore

Facsimile of the poet's English translation of *Janaganamana* in his hand.

The musical notations of the national anthem as approved by the Constituent Assembly; Rabindranath Tagore's English translation of the national anthem

3 The National Song

'*Vande Mataram*', the national song of India, was originally composed in Sanskrit by Bankim Chandra Chatterjee, a novelist, poet, essayist, journalist, and government officer in British India. It was also part of the novel *Anandmath*, written by him in 1882.

Above: **Bankim Chandra Chatterjee wrote the national song; *above right*: A rare painting depicting the national song**

The song was an inspiration for front-line Indian leaders and people during the freedom struggle against the British rulers and became a rallying cry in the independence movement. It was sung for the first time in 1896 during a session of the Indian National Congress. Both the song and the book in which it featured were banned by the colonial government. The first two verses of the song were adopted as the national song of India in October 1937 by the Congress Working Committee. On 24 January 1950, the then president Dr Rajendra Prasad declared that the national song would have the same status as the national anthem.

4 The State Emblem

The state emblem was originally adapted from the Lion Capital of Ashoka at Sarnath, around 10 km from Varanasi in Uttar Pradesh. The design consisted of four lions, representing courage and power, mounted back-to-back on an abacus. The abacus was mounted on a bell-shaped lotus and consisted of sculptures of an elephant, a horse, a bull and a lion separated by Dharma Chakras. On 26 January 1950, an altered version of the Lion Capital was adopted as the state emblem. The four lions stand on a short cylindrical base that has four Ashok Chakras, one with each lion bust, and reliefs of four more animals, the guardians of the four directions, in between them – the lion of the north, the horse of the west, the bull of the south and the elephant of the east. In the 2D form, only one Ashok Chakra is visible in the front with the galloping horse to the left and the bull to the right of it. The lotus on the original Lion Capital was replaced by the quote from the Mundaka Upanishad – '*Satyameva Jayate*' in Devanagari script – meaning 'truth alone triumphs'.

5 The National Bird

The peacock, the national bird of India, is a colourful bird with a vibrant fan-shaped crest of feathers and a long neck, along with a spectacular train of tail feathers. In this species, the male is more attractive and colourful compared to the female. The male is blue in colour with a blue-green tail consisting of around 200 feathers. On the other hand, the female is brown in colour and does not have a similar tail. The Indian peacock (which belongs to the peafowl species *Pavo cristatus)* is one of two Asian species; the peafowl of South-East Asia is green.

The peacock, our national bird

6 The National Animal

The Bengal tiger (*Panthera tigris tigris*), which is the national animal of India, is considered a symbol of grace, power, agility and strength. It is an impressive animal with a black and yellow striped fur coat.

Due to poaching, the tiger population declined tremendously and to prevent its extinction, the Indian government launched Project Tiger in 1973. Now there are 27 reserves spanning an area of 37,761 sq. km under this project across the country.

7 The National Flower

The national flower of India, the lotus (*Nelumbo nucifera*), has held an important place in Indian mythology and art. It has been considered sacred and auspicious from ancient times. It represents long life, triumph, honour and good fortune. The lotus design is often used in motifs and patterns in Indian architecture.

8 The National Tree

The Indian banyan tree (*Ficus benghalensis*) is the national tree of India. It has aerial roots and can live for many years. Hence, it is considered immortal and holds an important place in Indian legends and myths. It is a highly venerated tree in India.

Top: The lotus, our national flower; *bottom:* The banyan, our national tree

9 The Currency Symbol

The rupee symbol was first adopted by the government on 15 July 2010. It was designed by Udaya Kumar, who was a postgraduate in design from IIT-Bombay, at that time. His was one of the many entries received by the Ministry of Finance, Government of India, as part of an open competition for Indian nationals. The symbol consists of an amalgam of 'Ra' from Devanagari and the Roman capital letter 'R'. The two stripes drawn across the letter represent the national flag as well as the 'equality' symbol.

The Indian rupee symbol

10 The National Calendar

The national calendar, which is based on the Saka era, was adopted on 22 March 1957 along with the Gregorian calendar. It is used by the Gazette of India, All India Radio, and in calendars and official communications issued by the Government of India. It too consists of 365 days and its usage started officially at 1 Chaitra 1879, Saka Era, or 22 March 1957. The official calendar has Sunday as the first and Saturday as the last day of the week.

The calendar was the result of the efforts of astrophysicist Meghnad Saha, who was the head of the Calendar Reform Committee under the aegis of the Council of Scientific and Industrial Research, after India became an independent country. The challenge before him and the committee members – including mathematicians, astronomers and scholars, such as A.C. Banerjee, K.L. Daftari, J.S. Karandikar, Gorakh Prasad, R.V. Vaidya and N.C. Lahiri – was to arrive at a scientific and accurate calendar that could be adopted uniformly across India. The committee had to take into account the over 30 different local calendars being followed in different regions of the country.

Meghnad Saha

India and the World

India's place in the world is evidenced not only in that it is a member of key international organizations but also that it is a founding member of several. Here is a look at political, economic, cultural and strategic organizations India is part of.

- **AALCO** (Asian-African Legal Consultative Organization). Headquartered in Delhi, India — **1956 Founding Member**
- **ADB** (Asian Development Bank). Headquartered in Manila, Philippines — **1966 Founding Member**
- **AfDB** (African Development Bank). Headquartered in Abidjan, Africa — **1964 Non-regional Member**
- **The Australia Group** — **1985 Member**
- **ASEAN Regional Forum** (The Association of South-East Asian Nations) — **1967 Member**
- **BIMSTEC** (Bay of Bengal Initiative for Multi-Sectoral Technical and Economic Cooperation). Headquartered in Dhaka, Bangladesh — **1997 Member**
- **BIS** (Bank for International Settlements). Headquartered in Basel, Switzerland — **1930 RBI is a Member**
- **BRICS** (Brazil, Russia, India, China and South Africa) — **2006 One of the Leaders**
- **Commonwealth of Nations.** Headquartered in London, United Kingdom — **1931 Member**
- **CERN** (European Organization for Nuclear Research). Headquartered in suburban Geneva, Switzerland — **1954 Associate Member**
- **CP** (Colombo Plan). Headquartered in Colombo, Sri Lanka — **1950 Member**
- **EAS** (East Asia Summit) — **2005 Member**
- **FAO** (Food and Agriculture Organization of the United Nations). Headquartered in Rome, Italy — **1945 Member**
- **G-15** (Group of 15) — **1989 Founding Member**
- **G-20** (Group of 20) — **1999 Member**
- **G-77** (Group of 77) — **1964 Member**
- **IAEA** (International Atomic Energy Agency). Headquartered in Vienna, Austria — **1957 Member**

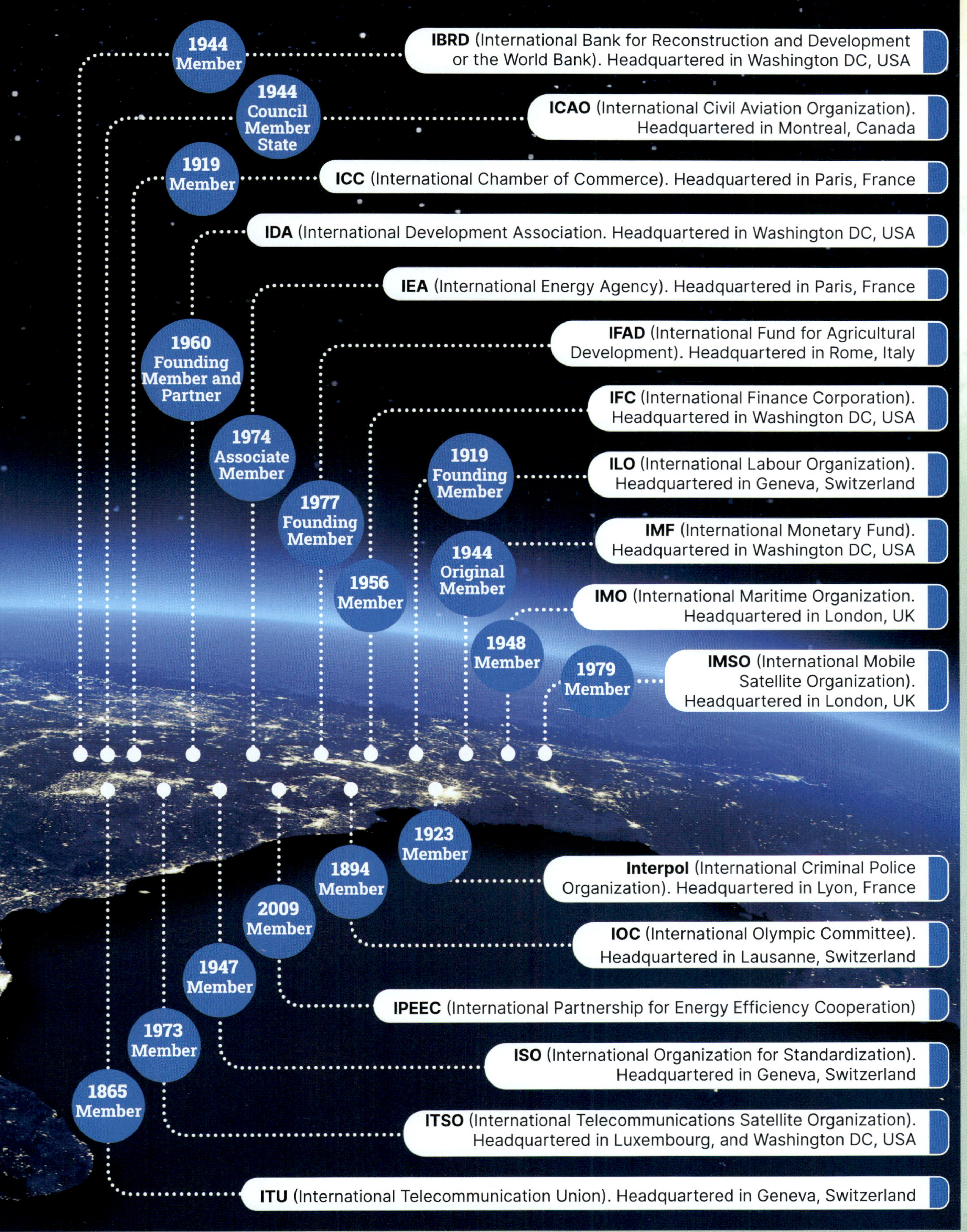
1944 Member
IBRD (International Bank for Reconstruction and Development or the World Bank). Headquartered in Washington DC, USA
1944 Council Member State
ICAO (International Civil Aviation Organization). Headquartered in Montreal, Canada
1919 Member
ICC (International Chamber of Commerce). Headquartered in Paris, France
IDA (International Development Association. Headquartered in Washington DC, USA
IEA (International Energy Agency). Headquartered in Paris, France
1960 Founding Member and Partner
IFAD (International Fund for Agricultural Development). Headquartered in Rome, Italy
1974 Associate Member
IFC (International Finance Corporation). Headquartered in Washington DC, USA
1977 Founding Member
1919 Founding Member
ILO (International Labour Organization). Headquartered in Geneva, Switzerland
1944 Original Member
IMF (International Monetary Fund). Headquartered in Washington DC, USA
1956 Member
IMO (International Maritime Organization. Headquartered in London, UK
1948 Member
1979 Member
IMSO (International Mobile Satellite Organization). Headquartered in London, UK
1923 Member
Interpol (International Criminal Police Organization). Headquartered in Lyon, France
1894 Member
IOC (International Olympic Committee). Headquartered in Lausanne, Switzerland
2009 Member
IPEEC (International Partnership for Energy Efficiency Cooperation)
1947 Member
ISO (International Organization for Standardization). Headquartered in Geneva, Switzerland
1973 Member
ITSO (International Telecommunications Satellite Organization). Headquartered in Luxembourg, and Washington DC, USA
1865 Member
ITU (International Telecommunication Union). Headquartered in Geneva, Switzerland

- **MTCR** (Missile Technology Control Regime) — 1987 Partner
- **NAM** (Non-Aligned Movement) — 1961 Member
- **OPCW** (Organization for the Prohibition of Chemical Weapons). Headquartered in the Hague, Netherlands — 1997 Member of Executive Council
- **PCA** (Permanent Court of Arbitration). Headquartered in the Hague, Netherlands — 1899 Member
- **PIF** (Pacific Islands Forum). Headquartered in Suva, Fiji — 1971 Dialogue Partner
- **SAARC** (South Asian Association for Regional Cooperation). Headquartered in Kathmandu, Nepal — 1985 Founding Partner
- **SACEP** (South Asia Cooperative Environment Programme). Headquartered in Colombo, Sri Lanka — 1982 Member
- **SCO** (Shanghai Cooperation Organization). Headquartered in Beijing, China — 2001 Member
- **UN** (United Nations). Headquartered in New York, USA — 1945 Founding Partner
- **UNAIDS** (United Nations Programme on HIV/AIDS). Headquartered in Geneva, Switzerland — 1944 Member
- **UNESCO** (United Nations Educational, Scientific and Cultural Organization). Headquartered in Paris, France — 1946 Member
- **WHO** (World Health Organization). Headquartered in Geneva, Switzerland — 1948 Member

VISUAL ARTS

studio green
K.E.GNANAVEL RAJA
SURIYA IN & AS
A VENKAT PRABHU SIXER
YUVAN SHANKAR RAJA
RD RAJASEKAR PRAVEEN KL RAJEEVAN GANGAI AMAREN MADAN KARKY
AADNAH ARTS PRODUCTION
EROS INTERNATIONAL WORLDWIDE RELEASE
TRIVANDRUM TALKIES & SOPANAM FILMS RELEASE
EROSNOW
4 SHOWS 29.05.2015
EROS
Badra design

CINEMA

PIONEERS

First film shot in India
Coconut Fair is said to be the first short film shot in India in 1897 and it was made by an unknown foreign photographer. Shortly after, another 'film' made in India, a short dancing scene from the Bengali opera, *The Flower of Persia*, was exhibited at the Star Theatre, Calcutta (now Kolkata, West Bengal) on 9 February 1898.

First films exhibited
The first screening of six short films, by France's famed Lumière Brothers, Louis and Auguste, was held on 7 July 1896. They were: *Entry of Cinematographe*, *Arrival of a Train at la Ciotat Station*, *Sea Bath*, *Workers Leaving the Factory*, *A Demolition* and *Ladies and Soldiers on Wheels*.

First film shot by an Indian
H.S. Bhatavadekar was the first to import a Riley camera from the UK and shoot two short films – *The Wrestlers*, which featured a wrestling match, and *Man and Monkey*, which was about a juggler training his monkeys – both released in November 1899.

First indigenous feature film
Dadasaheb Phalke's silent feature film *Raja Harishchandra* was released at the Coronation Theatre in Bombay (now Mumbai, Maharashtra) on 3 May 1913. It was a fully Indian venture and was shown along with four imported short films, together making up a 90-minute show. It ran for 23 days and was screened again later at multiple venues.

First box-office hit
Dadasaheb Phalke's *Lanka Dahan* (1917), which ran for 23 weeks, was India's first box-office hit. It is on record that the money collected at the ticket counters had to be transported in bullock carts protected by armed guards!

First talkie
Alam Ara, made in Hindustani by Ardeshir Irani and released on 14 March 1931 in Bombay (now Mumbai, Maharashtra), became India's first talkie feature. The first talkie stars were Master Vithal as hero, Zubeida as heroine, Prithviraj Kapoor in a supporting role and W.M. Khan as a singing fakir. The first music directors were Pirojshah Mistry and B. Irani. It was a costume fantasy with seven songs. The film reel was 3,048 m (10,000 ft) long and it ran for seven weeks.

First female actor of the talkies
After silent performances in 36 movies, Zubeida Begum acted in the first Indian talkie *Alam Ara* (1931).

First experiment of colour films
The very first colour venture was by Madan Theatres of Calcutta (now Kolkata, West Bengal) in 1932. Their talkie feature *Bilwamangal* was sent abroad for printing. The Prabhat Company under V. Shantaram tried a colour-processed film, *Sairandhri*, which was sent to Germany for printing. The results of both were unfit for viewing.

First woman film-maker
Fatma Begum was the first woman to produce, direct and script a film in the silent era. She formed Fatma Film Corporation and made *Bulbule Paristan* in 1926.

LANGUAGE

First Indian film in English
Ardeshir Irani's *Noor Jahan*, directed by Ezra Mir in 1931, starring Mazhar Khan, Nayampally, Mubarak and Vimala was given an English version a year later for foreign markets.

First film in multilingual versions
J.B.H. Wadia's *Court Dancer* (*Raj Nartaki*), directed by Madhu Bose and featuring Sadhana Bose and Prithviraj Kapoor, was shot in Hindi, Bengali and English in 1941.

Music scores in most languages
Salil Chowdhury (1925–95), a lyricist, writer, songwriter and music director, mainly composed for Hindi, Bengali and Malayalam films, but reportedly he composed music for films in 13 languages. His repertoire included composing music for Marathi, Tamil, Telugu, Kannada, Gujarati, Odia and Assamese films.

Films edited in most languages/dialects
A. Sreekar Prasad (b. 12 March 1963) from Chennai, Tamil Nadu, has edited films in 17 languages/dialects: English, Hindi, Tamil, Telugu, Malayalam, Kannada, Odia, Assamese, Bengali, Punjabi, Nepali, Marathi, Sinhalese, Karbi, Mishing, Bodo and Pangchenpa.

An advertisement for a Lumière film: first films exhibited

Dadasaheb Phalke: maker of the first indigenous feature film

Ardeshir Irani on the sets of *Alam Ara*: first talkie

Poster for *Around the World*: first film in 70 mm

FIRSTS

First cinemascope films

- Guru Dutt made *Kaagaz Ke Phool* in 1959 in black-and-white Cinemascope.
- Mahesh Kaul made *Pyar Ki Pyaas* in Cinemascope and colour in 1961.

First film in 70 mm

- The first Indian film in 70 mm (using the blowing-up method) was director Pachchi's *Around the World*, starring Raj Kapoor and Rajshri, in 1967. It was in Technicolor and had stereophonic sound.
- G.P. Sippy's multi-starrer blockbuster *Sholay* in 1975 was shot on the 70 mm format in India, along with stereophonic soundtrack, the four channels of which could be connected to amplifiers in cinema theatres. Those not equipped for it were provided flat (35 mm) single-track prints.
- Tarachand Barjatya's *Maine Pyar Kiya* (1989) was made in Cinemascope with a new system of four-track magnetic stereophonic sound. This could be fitted in theatres. Later, mobile equipment was provided for the stereophonic effect in small towns and touring cinemas.

First film serial

Rama Banvas (The Exile of Rama) was made by Patankar Friends and Company, and released on 14 September 1918. It was shown in four parts, each running for a period of a few weeks.

WR First one-actor, one-set film

Sunil Dutt made *Yaadein* in 1964, the first experiment of its kind in the world

The Worldwide Phenomenon of *Ponniyin Selvan*

When *Ponniyin Selvan* was serialized in the weekly magazine *Kalki* (co-founded by the novel's Puthamangalam-born Tamil author, Kalki, aka Ramasamy Aiyer Krishnamurthy) between 1950 and 1954, it created a sensation. People used to rush to neighbourhood bookshops to pick up a copy, there was de facto competition on who could read the latest instalment first and there were feverish discussions on the unfolding plot.

The voluminous novel – which had 293 chapters with more than 2,200 pages in book form – was named after Chola emperor Rajaraja I but had a massive list of interesting characters (both real and fictional) and an intricate plot that kept readers hooked for nearly four years. Published later in five volumes, *Ponniyin Selvan* is surely one of the longest novels in modern India. As a film, *Ponniyin Selvan 1 (PS 1)* was a massive draw for Tamil audiences globally, who flocked to the theatres to watch their favourite classic on screen, and there were reports of extended families – including the elderly – going to watch the film in the first week itself. It is the highest-grossing Tamil film of 2022 and may well become the most successful Tamil film of all time, with only superstar Rajinikanth's *2.0* ahead of it at the time of writing. At a time when the best content in the world can be streamed on your mobile, a well-made historical film like *PS I* brings back audiences to the theatres with its heady mix of national pride, strong plot, amazing action and impressive VFX.

The last few years have seen quite a few big-budget historical films that glorify our medieval and ancient history, which have met with varying degrees of success at the box office. The runaway success of *PS 1* (and the anticipated success of Part 2) may well give this trend a boost.

Film	Language	Period	Status
Ponniyin Selvan I (2022)	Tamil	**10th and 11th century CE:** The early life of Chola King Arulmozhi Varman (later Raja Raja I), who ruled over Tamil Nadu and some other parts of south India	Blockbuster
Samrat Prithviraj (2022)	Hindi	**12th century CE:** The life of Prithviraj Chauhan, who ruled over a kingdom in north India	Flop
Marakkar: Lion of the Arabian Sea (2021)	Malayalam	**16th century CE:** The adventures of admiral Muhammad Ali, who commanded the fleet of the Zamorin of Calicut in Kerala	Flop
Padmaavat (2018)	Hindi	**14th century CE:** The attack of Alauddin Khilji on Chittor, his siege and subsequent capture	Superhit
Mohenjo Daro (2016)	Hindi	**~2000 BCE:** The last days of the Indus Valley Civilization	Flop
Bajirao Mastani (2015)	Hindi	**18th century CE:** The reign of Maratha Peshwa Bajirao I	Superhit

with only one actor (himself) emoting on only one set. In 2005, Kannada film *Shanthi* became the second movie with a single actor to be released.

First adult film

Social Evil, a docudrama, was made by the Social Purity League of Bombay (now Mumbai, Maharashtra) in 1929 to provide information about sex problems. It was also the first sex educational film. It was shown free of cost and was the first film given the label 'For Adults Only'.

First use of surround sound

Khuda Gawah (1992), when screened in big cities, used stereophonic four-track sound with special gadgets fitted into theatre walls and ceilings. This gave the impression of sound surrounding the audience, to give more impact to scenes of fights, horse riding and the Afghan game of *buzkashi*, among others.

First animated film

Directed by R.C. Boral, *On a Moonlit Night* (1934) was the first Indian animated film with a soundtrack.

North–South Crossover Successes (2022)

For decades in India, North was North and South was South and the twain didn't meet! In the 1980s, Tamil superstars – Kamal Haasan and Rajinikanth – saw only moderate success in Hindi cinema and went back. Quite a few male south Indian superstars – Chiranjeevi (*Pratibandh*), Venkatesh (*Anari*) and Nagarjuna (*Shiva*) – had successful debuts in the 1990s but returned to their home industries for a variety of reasons. Of course, female stars – like Sridevi and Jaya Prada – had much greater and sustained success.

This doesn't mean that south India wasn't making an impact in Bollywood. Hindi cinema has successfully remade many south Indian films over the years. Jeetendra had a massive run of south Indian remakes in the 1980s while Amitabh Bachchan and Govinda had quite a few hits that were remakes. This opened a floodgate during 2000–20 when many of Bollywood's top grossers were remakes of south Indian films.

A study by business publication, *Mint*, shows that 28 per cent of the top 50 films of every year between 2000 and 2019 are remakes of some kind – with the lion's share coming from south Indian cinema. And routinely, these remakes earned significantly more than the originals because of the higher catchment area Hindi offers.

Top: *Major*, a Telugu film was dubbed in Hindi as was *RRR* (*above left*) while *K.G.F: Chapter 2* was originally made in Kannada

This trend changed with the success of the two *Baahubalis*. The films were dubbed in Hindi, and Telugu stars like Prabhas and Rana Daggubati were presented to a pan-India audience. It suddenly seemed that unknown faces were no longer a barrier to commercial success. The floodgates that opened created a veritable flood of successes in 2022 – when the Hindi-dubbed versions of Telugu (*RRR, Radhe Shyam, Major*), Kannada (*K.G.F. Chapter 2*) and Tamil (*Vikram*) did good to spectacular business. Barring Kamal Haasan, none of these films featured stars popular (or even known) in the Hindi-speaking markets. And yet, the power of great storytelling and charismatic screen presence made them shine. At the same time, Hindi remakes of south Indian films (*Jersey, Bachchhan Paandey*) did well below expectations.

With easy access to cinemas in different languages on OTT platforms, it seems the Indian audience has gotten over the barrier of 'unknown stars'. So have distributors and exhibitors, who no longer veto films because of language and are keen to make up for the pandemic drought with films of all hues. While this has led to pressure on the Hindi film industry, the Indian moviegoer can look forward to many more entertainment options than before. And in that world, S.S. Rajamouli is as big a draw as Rajkumar Hirani!

South Indian Remakes among the Top 10 Hindi Hits

2009	2010	2011	2012	2014	2018	2019
Wanted	*Housefull*	*Bodyguard*	*Rowdy Rathore*	*Kick*	*Simmba*	*Kabir Singh*
Billu		*Singham*	*Son of Sardaar*	*Jai Ho*	*Baaghi 2*	
				Holiday		

Durga Khote in *Seeta*: first Indian film to win a foreign film award

Poster for *Dilwale Dulhania Le Jayenge*: longest running film

First 3D film

My Dear Kuttichathan (1984), produced by M.C. Punoos and directed by his son, Jijo, was the first Indian 3D film.

First cinema hall

Elphinstone Picture Palace was started by J.F. Madan in Calcutta (now Kolkata, West Bengal) in 1905. It was renamed Minerva and later called Chaplin Cinema. This piece of history was demolished in 2013 by the Kolkata Municipal Corporation (which owned it).

First studio

Khan Bahadur Ardeshir Irani (1886– 1969) started his first studio – Star Films – in 1920.

WR Longest running film

Yash Raj Films' *Dilwale Dulhania Le Jayenge* (*DDLJ*) is still running at Mumbai's Maratha Mandir theatre – twenty-seven years after the film premiered there. The single show at 11:30 a.m. is the result of an arrangement between Yash Raj and the theatre, which agreed to run the film there for (what seems like) eternity. But even before the arrangement, *DDLJ* ran to semi-packed houses for over two decades, making it the longest running film in the world.

First censor boards

- The first film censor boards were set up in Bombay (now Mumbai), Calcutta (now Kolkata) and Madras (now Chennai) in 1920.
- Film censorship was centralized under a central board, the Central Board of Film Certification (CBFC) in Bombay (now Mumbai), Maharashtra, in 1951.

INTERNATIONAL

First Academy Award

Bhanu Athaiya (1929–2020) became the first Indian to win an Academy Award (Oscar) in 1983, for designing the costumes for the acclaimed film *Gandhi* (1982), directed by Sir Richard Attenborough.

First to act in a Hollywood film

The first Indian actor to feature in a role that was credited in a Hollywood movie was Dastagir, who was also known as 'Sabu' in the film world. He hailed from the princely state of Mysore (now Mysuru, Karnataka). He acted in Robert Flaherty's film *Elephant Boy* (1937). His other films included *The Thief of Baghdad* (1940) and *Jungle Book* (1942).

First foreign film award

The film *Seeta* (1934) by East India Films Co., Calcutta (now Kolkata, West Bengal), which was directed by Debaki Bose, was the first film from India to win the gold medal at the Third International Exhibition of Cinematographic Art in Venice, Italy, in 1935.

PERFORMANCE

First woman stunt actor

Nadia, India's legendary woman stunt actor, has been described as 'Zorro, Tarzan and John Wayne rolled into one'. Born Mary Evans, she swung from chandeliers, jumped from moving trains and performed many other incredible stunts that earned her the title of 'Fearless Nadia'. Her best-known film is the 1935 hit, *Hunterwali*.

Most films as a lead

Prem Nazir, born as Abdul Kadar in Chirayinkeezhu, Kerala, played the lead role in as many as 600 films. He starred in Malayalam, Tamil, Kannada and Telugu films, and co-starred in films with at least 85 female actors.

Maximum roles in a single film

- Harish Raj enacted 16 roles in the Kannada film *Shri Sathyanarayana*, which released on 11 March 2016. He essayed the role of the lead character named Sathyanarayana as well as 15 other cameo roles with screen time ranging from one to five minutes for each.
- Priyanka Chopra played 12 roles (one for each sign of the zodiac) in Ashutosh Gowariker's *What's Your Rashee?* (2009).
- Kamal Haasan played 10 different roles in K.S. Ravikumar's *Dasavathaaram* (2008), including one as former US president George W. Bush.

WR Roles in the most numbers of films

- *Women*: Manorama, a popular Tamil heroine of the 1950s and '60s, who later became a character actor, acted in over 1,000 films. Her first film was *Malayitta Mangai* (1958). Her real name was Gopishantha. She received the Padma Shri in 2002.
- *Men*: Brahmanandam Kanneganti, a well-known comedian of Telugu cinema, has received credits for acting in 1,146 films. He achieved this feat over an acting career of more than 30 years and he is still going strong. He received the Padma Shri in 2009.

IT'S A HIT: HIGHEST-GROSSING FILMS*

1940
Zindagi
₹55 lakh

1941
Khazanchi
₹70 lakh

1942
Basant
₹80 lakh

1943
Kismet
₹1 crore

1944
Rattan
₹1 crore

1945
Zeenat
₹70 lakh

1946
Anmol Ghadi
₹1 crore

1947
Jugnu
₹50 lakh

1948
Chandralekha
₹1.55 crore

1949
Barsaat
₹2 crore

1950
Samadhi
₹1.35 crore

1951
Awaara
₹2.3 crore

1952
Aan
₹2.8 crore

1953
Anarkali
₹2.35 crore

1954
Nagin
₹2.9 crore

1955
Pather Panchali
₹10 crore

1956
Jagte Raho
₹4.44 crore

1957
Mother India
₹8 crore

1958
Madhumati
₹4 crore

1959
Char Dil Char Rahen
₹5.27crore

1960
Mughal-e-Azam
₹11 crore

1961
Gunga Jumna
₹11 crore

1962
Bees Saal Baad
₹3 crore

1963
Mere Mehboob
₹6 crore

1964
Sangam
₹8 crore

1965
Waqt
₹6 crore

1966
Phool Aur Patthar
₹17 crore

1967
Humraaz
₹13.33 crore

1968
Ankhen
₹6.5 crore

1969
Aradhana
₹17.85 crore

1970
Mera Naam Joker
₹16.81 crore

1971
Caravan
₹35.3 crore

1972
Seeta Aur Geeta
₹19.53 crore

1973
Bobby
₹30 crore

1974
Roti Kapda Aur Makaan
₹10.5 crore

1975
Sholay
₹58 crore

1976
Barood
₹19.32 crore

*Based on worldwide gross revenue estimates (not adjusted for inflation) from Wikipedia and other sources. Source information may not be exact.

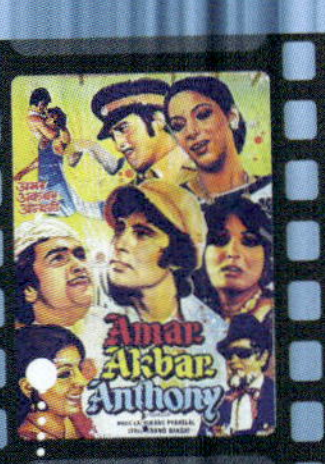

1977
Amar Akbar Anthony
₹15.5 crore

1978
Muqaddar Ka Sikandar
₹26 crore

1979
Suhaag
₹10 crore

1980
Alibaba aur 40 Chor
₹122.11 crore

1981
Kranti
₹20 crore

1982
Disco Dancer
₹100.7 crore

1983
Coolie
₹18 crore

1984
Jagir
₹35.32 crore

1985
Ram Teri Ganga Maili
₹19 crore

1986
Karma
₹14 crore

1987
Hukumat
₹11 crore

1988
Tezaab
₹16 crore

1989
Maine Pyar Kiya
₹28 crore

1990
Dil
₹18 crore

1991
Saajan
₹18 crore

1992
Beta
₹23.5 crore

1993
Aankhen
₹25.25 crore

1994
Hum Aapke Hain Koun..!
₹250 crore

1995
Dilwale Dulhania Le Jayenge
₹200 crore

1996
Raja Hindustani
₹87.5 crore

1997
Dil to Pagal Hai
₹71.87 crore

1998
Kuch Kuch Hota Hai
₹106.74 crore

1999
Hum Saath-Saath Hain
₹81.71 crore

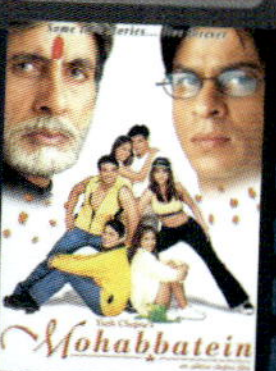

2000
Mohabbatein
₹90.01 crore

2001
Kabhi Khushi Kabhie Gham
₹135.53 crore

2002
Devdas
₹168 crore

2003
Kal Ho Naa Ho
₹86.09 crore

2004
Veer-Zaara
₹97.64 crore

2005
No Entry
₹74.13 crore

2006
Dhoom 2
₹151.39 crore

2007
Om Shanti Om
₹149.87 crore

2008
Ghajini
₹232 crore

2009
3 Idiots
₹459.96 crore

2010
Enthiran
₹289 crore

2011
Bodyguard
₹234 crore

2012
Ek Tha Tiger
₹334.39 crore

2013
Dhoom 3
₹589.2 crore

2014
PK
₹832 crore

2015
Bajrangi Bhaijaan
₹969.06 crore

2016
Dangal
₹2,024 crore

2017
Baahubali 2: The Conclusion
₹1,810 crore

2018
2.0
₹800 crore

2019
War
₹475 crore

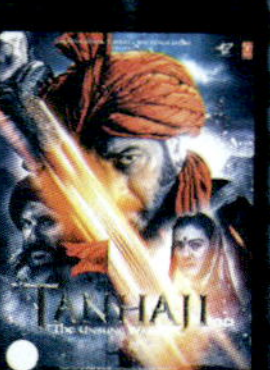

2020
Tanhaji
₹368 crore

2021
Pushpa: The Rise
₹365 crore

2022
K.G.F: Chapter 2
₹1,250 crore

WR Most pairings

Actors Prem Nazir and Sheila paired together in 107 films and hold a world record for the highest number of movies done together. An interesting comparison is with the Hollywood husband-wife pair of Charles Bronson and Jill Ireland, who starred together in 15 films.

Highest-earning actor

Forbes magazine placed Akshay Kumar sixth on its list of the 'World's Highest-Paid Actors of 2020', with estimated earnings of US $48.5 million (₹356.97 crore), making him the country's highest-earning actor. His earnings include remuneration for films (ranging from US $5 to 10 million – around ₹35.58 to 71.17 crore), endorsement deals and appearance fees.

Oldest debut actor in a film

Ninety-three-year-old Chinnakrishnan Kaliyaperumal from Ariyalur, Tamil Nadu, acted as the lead in the Tamil short (20-minute) film, *93* Not Out* (2016), directed by engineer-turned-film-maker Arudra Saravanakumar. It is the story of an old man who, after a pacemaker implant, has the desire to ride a cycle and to buy a book, and how he finally achieves it at the age of ninety-three. The film has won several awards, besides a jury

A stamp commemorating Prem Nazir: most pairings with Sheila

In the Spotlight

S.S. Rajamouli: In the Right Direction

If there's an award for the most successful director in India, Rajamouli's claim for that is getting stronger with each release. His first six releases were all major commercial successes (including *Vikramarkudu*, which was remade into Hindi as *Rowdy Rathore*) but all of those were eclipsed by *Magadheera*, which became the highest-grossing Telugu film of all time. He soon came up with *Eega*, one of the most inventive films about rebirth and revenge. And he made everyone forget everything with the *Baahubali* franchise, a pan-Indian – actually, global – mega hit, which broke every domestic box-office record there was. He then broke the pandemic-induced drought in cinema with *RRR*, a visual spectacle that's so typically him. He now has three movies in the top 10 grossing Indian films, which might become four with his next film!

S.S. Rajamouli

Alia Bhatt

Alia Bhatt: Unstoppable

Trivia hunters would remember Alia Bhatt's debut in her father's film, *Sangharsh*, where she played the kid version of Preity Zinta. Her adult debut – *Student of the Year* – was successful, but nobody was prepared for the roles she followed it up with. *Highway, Udta Punjab, Dear Zindagi* and *Raazi* were all excellent performances, belying the 'silly' off-screen image she got saddled with. In addition to these acclaimed roles, she is also a box-office diva with hit films like *2 States, Humpty Sharma Ki Dulhania, Badrinath Ki Dulhania* and, most recently, *Gangubai Kathiawadi*. After a much-publicized romance and marriage, she has now stepped into international waters with Tom Harper's *Heart of Stone*, co-starring Gal Gadot. All this and she's not even thirty!

Suriya

Suriya: Shining Star of Southern Skies

Saravanan Sivakumar aka Suriya is the star who essentially birthed the 100-crore club of Indian commercial cinema. The first ever film to gross ₹100 crores at the box-office – Aamir Khan-starrer *Ghajini* – was the Hindi remake of Suriya's Tamil superhit. Suriya is in that rare breed of performers who match their box-office clout with critical acclaim. Apart from *Ghajini*, his *Singam* also became a Hindi movie franchise, raking in hundreds of crores (apart from remakes in other languages). His award-winning performances – *Pithamagan, Perazhagan, Varaanam Aayiram* and *Soorarai Pottru* – as well as bold choices (*Jai Bhim*) make him one of the most interesting stars of India.

It's an Anniversary

Angry Young Man: 50 Years of *Zanjeer*

Bollywood legend goes that seven top stars refused to do *Zanjeer*. The story of a short-fuse police officer traumatized by a childhood memory had no scope for songs and dance, no opportunity to showcase histrionics and no romantic or emotional interludes. Writers Salim–Javed were short on experience but not on confidence. They persuaded producer-director Prakash Mehra to make the film with an actor considered a pariah in Bollywood. And the rest, as the cliché goes, is history. Amitabh Bachchan's performance turned heads, dropped jaws and popped eyes. Audiences couldn't get enough of the policeman who threw punches as well as he threw lines, turning him into an overnight superstar, who remained number one for the next decade or two.

Zanjeer was not the biggest hit of 1973, but it was certainly the most influential. It changed the course of Hindi cinema, junking romance and Rajesh Khanna's career, and bringing action centre stage. In the next two-and-a-half decades, this story of a revenge-seeking action hero got remade hundreds of times, making the careers of at least a dozen younger stars.

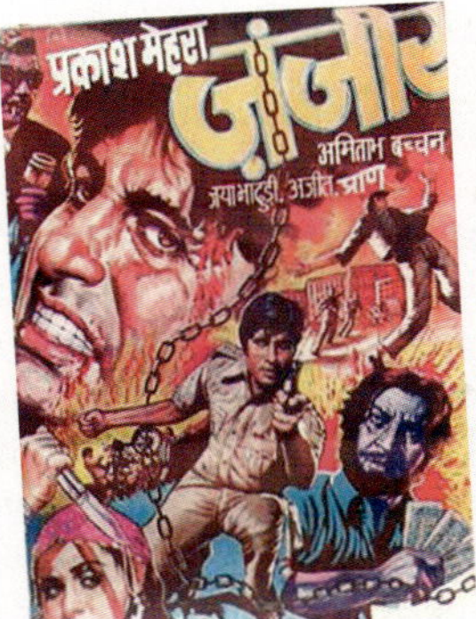

Top: Zanjeer
Bottom: Satya

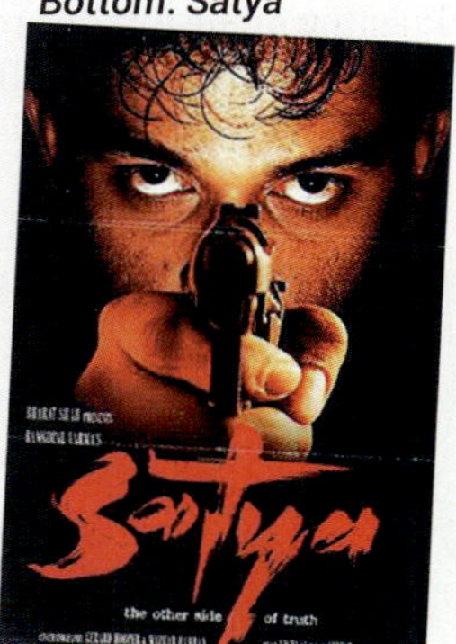

Angry Young Drifter: 25 Years of *Satya*

Zanjeer's Vijay Verma had a childhood trauma that caused his anger. We don't know what triggered *Satya*. In fact, we don't even know where he came from, or anything about him. For the first time, the 'hero' had no reasons for his amoral acts, and he seemed perfectly all right with killing or hurting innocent people. But the film – with its jagged style of film-making, edgy writing and sharp performances – created a cult following, its impact going far beyond its box-office numbers. Ram Gopal Varma's *Satya* kicked off the gangster genre in Bollywood and a slew of similar films followed.

In a year of much bigger hits and a wave of romantic films, *Satya*'s grungy locales, snappy one-liners and swaggering characters brought the underworld right into our drawing rooms. *Satya* blew our minds. Or as they said, '*Goli maar[a] bheje mein...*'

Just as *Zanjeer* energized the careers of its writers, director, and star, so did *Satya*. Anurag Kashyap went from writer to director to cult hero. Debutant editor Apurva Asrani went on to win awards for this and his later films. Acting powerhouses Manoj Bajpayee and Shefali Shah started long, acclaimed careers. And of course, director Ram Gopal Varma started a *Factory* and a *Company*.

The word Bollywood was coined, probably by a film journalist.

mention at the Dadasaheb Phalke film festival 2017, and has been showcased at national and international film festivals.

LENGTH

Films with longest footage

- Vithalbhai Jhaveri's documentary on Mahatma Gandhi, *Mahatma: Life of Gandhi, 1869–1948* (1968), was 5 hrs 30 mins long, and was broken up into many segments for general screening.
- Gemini's *Chandralekha* in 1948, the first big Hindi film from south India, ran for over 3 hrs.
- R.K. Films' productions *Sangam* (1964) and *Mera Naam Joker* (1970) were the first to be run with two intervals.

Most episodic films in a single feature film

BSB Films, a film-making company from Jaipur, Rajasthan, made a Hindi-language film, titled *Prabhu Mahaveer Ki Divyavani*, under their banner. The film features 23 episodic films as part of it, the highest in a single feature film. The film has a total duration of 157 mins and 27 secs. However, the release of the film was delayed due to the COVID-19 pandemic.

WR Shortest film

Pamarthi Sivanaga Rao (b. 28 May 1978) from Vijayawada, Andhra Pradesh, released the shortest film, *The Farmer*, with a total duration of nine seconds. The first three seconds cover the CBFC certificate, making the actual time of the film to be six seconds. The film was released in five theatres on 7 February 2020 under the banner of Siva Arts Creations.

MUSIC

Most songs recorded in a day

In 1993, playback singer Kumar Sanu recorded 28 songs in a single day at the Musicians Studio in the Juhu area in Mumbai, Maharashtra. The session was made for Sterling Records and Cassettes and the chief recordist was Vishram More, who was on the machines for 24 hours.

Most number of songs in a Hindi film

Madan Theatre's film *Indra Sabha*, made in 1932, featured 71 songs. Based on an Urdu play and opera written by Agha Hasan Amanat and first staged in 1853, the 211-minute-long film was made by Jamshedji Framji Madan's company, Madan Theatre.

Most prolific lyricist

Shitala Pande, better known Sameer 'Anjaan', holds the world record for writing lyrics for the most number of songs. Starting in 1983 with the Hindi film *Bekhabar*, he had written lyrics for over 3,500 songs for Hindi and Bhojpuri films by 15 December 2015. He has also written lyrics for music albums. He has done the highest number of films (146) with the music director duo Anand–Milind, writing around 899 songs for them.

MAKERS

Most film-making aspects handled

Narasimha Raju (b. 4 March 1955) from Bengaluru, Karnataka, handled 18 segments of film-making for Kannada film, *The Fire* (2017). He was credited for direction, story, screenplay, dialogues, fight, stunt, direction of cinematography, editing, special effects, grading, DI (digital intermediate), sound, dubbing, voice dubbing, BGM (background music) placing, re-recording, poster design and acting in the film. The 113-minute film participated in the 10th Bengaluru International Film Festival in March 2018.

Sameer 'Anjaan': most prolific lyricist

The Year Music Fell Silent

Lata Mangeshkar (1929–2022): Nobody embodies the phrase 'voice of the nation' for India better than Lata Mangeshkar. Beyond her prodigious talent as a playback singer, she has also been a champion of the music industry (fighting for credits and royalties) and a patriot (being present at significant historical markers of India). She has sung in 36 Indian languages and though the estimates of the number of songs vary, it is likely to be around 10,000. She was awarded not only the highest award of the film industry (Dadasaheb Phalke Award) but also the highest civilian award of India (Bharat Ratna).

Lata Mangeshkar

Bappi Lahiri (1952–2022): Bappi Lahiri, son of two popular Bengali singers, is – somewhat unfairly – mostly referred to as 'Disco King'. While it is true that he ushered in the disco revolution in Bollywood songs, the rest of his repertoire – often based on ragas and Indian melodies – was also very impressive. His popularity peaked in the 1980s with mainly the films of Mithun Chakraborty and Jeetendra. He was also often accused of lifting from Western songs, though life came a full circle for him when he (and the record company Saregama) sued Universal Music Group for lifting portions of his song ('*Thoda resham lagta hai*') in the 2002 song 'Addictive' by American singer Truth Hurts.

Bappi Lahiri

Bhupinder Singh

Bhupinder Singh (1940–2022): If we go beyond Bhupinder the singer, there is Bhupinder the guitarist with an equally impressive career as a musician in the troupes of legendary composers. The magical strumming of '*Chura Liya Hai*' (*Yaadon Ki Baaraat*) and the energetic twang of '*Dum Maaro Dum*' (*Hare Rama Hare Krishna*) were both his. He was, of course, one of the most unusual and soulful voices of the industry and will be forever remembered for his songs in *Mausam*, *Masoom*, *Gharonda*, *Ahista Ahista*, *Bazaar* and many such evocative soundtracks. Beyond cinema, he had a significant career in singing ghazals (often with his wife Mitali), both in concert and on albums.

Krishnakumar Kunnath – KK (1968–2022): When KK passed away – rather sadly and prematurely – videos of his last concert started emerging from phone recordings and it seemed the last song he sang was '*Hum rahein ya na rahein kal*', one of his most popular numbers. Along with '*Yaaron*' (from *Rockford*), this forms a fountain of nostalgia for those who grew up in the 1990s and the first decade of the millennium. Of course, KK's two-decade-old career was studded with super hits from a variety of films, but some songs stood out for their message of hope, friendship and undying love. His songs from *Hum Dil De Chuke Sanam*, *Life...in a Metro*, *Iqbal*, *Woh Lamhe*, *Om Shanti Om* and many others form an impressive discography that will stay for years to come.

Ramoji Film City, Hyderabad: largest film city/ studio

WR Largest film city/studio

Ramoji Film City in Hyderabad, Telangana, spread over a little more than 2,000 acres (810 hectares), is the largest film city/ studio in the world. It has sound stages and permanent sets ranging from railway stations and temples to gardens and residential streets, among others. It is also a tourist attraction because of its unique cinema-like experience.

WR Tallest film cut-out

The world's tallest cut-out – 65.5 m (215 ft) high – advertised a film in Thiruttani town, Tiruvallur District, Tamil Nadu. It featured actor Suriya (in a folded *veshti*, holding a flaming torch) to promote his film *Nandha Gopalan Kumaran (NGK)* in 2019.

WINNING LANGUAGES

Languages in which films have received the most National Film Awards for Best Feature Film between 1953 (the year of the first National Film Awards) and 2022

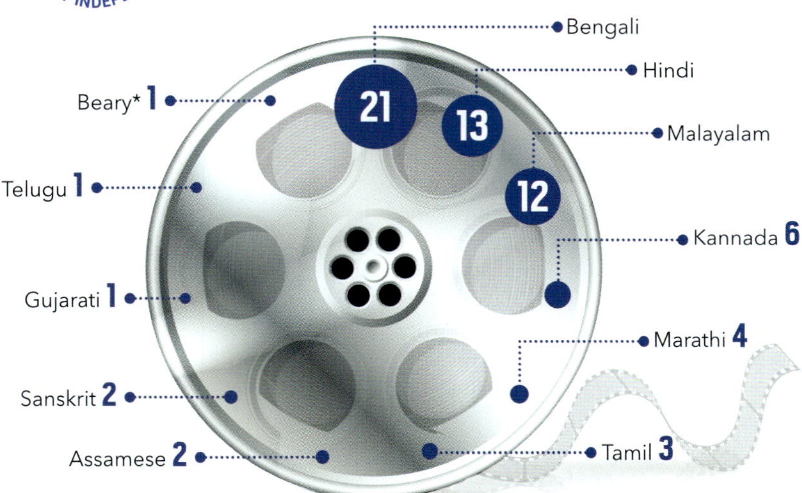

*A language spoken by certain communities in some parts of Karnataka and Kerala. The table above does not take into account two films namely – *Ship of Theseus* (2013) and *Court* (2014) as multiple languages are used in both films. Source: National Film Awards Archive

WR Largest film poster

Global United Media Co. Ltd, in collaboration with Impresario Event Management (I) Ltd, unveiled a 75.28 m (247 ft) long and 63.39 m (208 ft) wide poster of *Baahubali,* to mark the launch of the film's Malayalam audio, at the Sacred Heart College football field in Thevara, Kochi, Kerala, on 27 June 2015. The poster, designed by the director of the movie, S.S. Rajamouli, and made by Sign Maker Digital Solution at Vyttila, Kochi, took 30 hrs to print.

First Indian winner of the Legion d'Honneur

Satyajit Ray is the only Indian film personality to be awarded the Commandeur level of France's highest civilian award, the Legion d'Honneur on 2 February 1989 – one of only two film-makers in the world to have received it. He is also the only Indian film-maker to receive the Magsaysay Award.

Most films produced

Well-known director and producer of Telugu films, Dr D. Ramanaidu holds the record of having produced 110 films (including 11 dubbed films) in six languages over a span of 36 years. He started his career with *Anuragam* in 1963.

Most expensive film produced

Directed by S. Shankar, *2.0* (2018) is a sequel to *Enthiran* (2010). Starring the legendary Rajinikanth and Bollywood star Akshay Kumar in leading roles, the movie was made on an estimated budget of ₹540 crore (5,400 million). It was made in three languages (Tamil, Telugu and Hindi) and two formats – 3D and 2D.

Most tickets booked in advance

BookMyShow, a ticket-booking app, saw a record sale of advance tickets when it sold over a million tickets online in a day. The tickets for Marvel's *Avengers: Endgame* were booked in a manic frenzy as soon as they were available on 22 April 2019. The sale averaged about 18 tickets per second!

Most feature films directed

Dr Dasari Narayana Rao, who completed his 100th directorial venture *Lankeswarudu* (1989) in Telugu, has directed the most films. Among women, Vijaya Nirmala has directed 35 films in Telugu and Tamil.

Highest number of screens

RRR – a period drama about two legendary revolutionaries and their journeys – directed by S.S. Rajamouli, was released worldwide on over 10,200 screens.

Most horror films produced
The seven Ramsay brothers – Kumar, Keshu, Tulsi, Kiran, Shyam, Gangu and Arjun - made more than 30 horror films on low budgets, of which the well-known ones are *Purana Mandir* (1984), *Veerana* (1988) and *Purani Haveli* (1989).

PHOTOGRAPHY

Earliest recorded commercial album
A gilded and bound album of a hundred photographs of Indian buildings, scenery, races, costumes and bazaar incidents was sold for ₹12 in Bombay (now Mumbai, Maharashtra) in 1884. It used to be a popular souvenir among the British.

Earliest commercial studio
Bourne and Shepherd was well known for its studio portraits of the ruling classes, both Indian and British. Its photographers attended royal events, state visits and the imperial durbars of 1877, 1903 and 1911. When India gained Independence, Bourne and Shepherd was bought over by Indian proprietors, who operated under the same name in Calcutta (now Kolkata, West Bengal). The studio was closed down on 20 April 2016 after 176 years of operations.

Earliest book on photography
Pagoda Hallibee written by R.B. Gakley in 1859 was the first book on photography published in India.

First photo exhibition
The first All-India Photographic Exhibition was organized by the Photographic Society of India in Bombay (now Mumbai, Maharashtra) in 1856. The exhibition was inaugurated by the then Governor General of India, Lord Canning.

First use of the daguerreotype
Within a year of its first use in England, the daguerreotype (early photography process using an iodine-sensitized silvered plate and mercury vapour) was used in Calcutta (now Kolkata, West Bengal) in January 1840. They were brought to document India's architecture and landscape.

First commercial photographer
Lala Deen Dayal of Hyderabad, the 'photographer of kings', is India's best-known photographer from the British times. His career began in the mid-1870s and he went on to set up studios in three cities in three different states – Indore (Madhya Pradesh), Bombay (now Mumbai, Maharashtra) and Hyderabad (now in Telangana). He was appointed as the photographer to the viceroy of India in 1885. His lens captured India's rich culture, architecture and landscapes.

First woman photographer
Homai Vyarawalla (1913–2012), born into a priestly family in Navsari, Gujarat, in December 1913, was the first Indian woman photojournalist to document Indian life. Her very first photographs were published in *Bombay Chronicle* in 1936. She and her husband even covered wartime activities for *The Illustrated Weekly of India* and the *Far Eastern Bureau* of the British Information Service. *Life* and *Time* magazines also featured her photographs of the Indian independence movement.

First Kodak Express outlet
Established in 1978, Skylab was the first colour lab in suburban Bombay (now Mumbai), Maharashtra. Initially the lab catered to

Above: Interior Interior of the Chaumhalla Palace in Hyderabad, Telangana, photographed in the 1880s by Lala Deen Dayal; (*inset*): first commercial photographer

The Lalit Kala Akademi awards **40** scholarships every year.

advertising agencies, but gradually the focus shifted to providing a photo colour lab and studio for amateurs and ordinary people.

First personal studio

Maharaja Sawai Man Singh of Jaipur, Rajasthan, was a 19th-century amateur photographer. Thousands of photographic plates of his work were discovered in the 1980s in the storerooms of the City Palace in Jaipur. He recorded the life of the people in his state.

First photo film–manufacturing company

Hindustan Photo Films Manufacturing Co. (HPF), a public sector unit, was set up in 1960 at Ooty (now Udhagamandalam), Tamil Nadu, to make photosensitive materials for the Indian film industry, still photography, and X-ray films for medical and industrial use. It introduced the Indu brand of raw film.

First course in photography

The first photography course began in Elphinstone College, Bombay (now Mumbai, Maharashtra) in 1855. The J.J. School of Art, Bombay, and the Madras School of Art, Madras (now Chennai, Tamil Nadu), began similar courses around the same time.

First photographic society

The Bombay Photographic Society was founded in October 1854 with British Captain Harry J. Barr, as its first president. It had more than 200 people as members, many of them Indian. Divisions in Madras (now Tamil Nadu) and Bengal (now West Bengal) followed in 1856.

Dayanita Singh Brings Home the Hasselblad 2022

Representative image

Dayanita Singh from New Delhi became the first Indian and the first South Asian laureate to receive the Hasselblad Award. She was handed the award on 14 October 2022 in a ceremony held in Gothenburg, Sweden. She won two million Swedish krona, becoming the first to receive the prize since it was upgraded. Awarded annually since 1982, the Hasselblad awards are considered to be one of the most prestigious awards in photography worldwide. She received commendation for her 'mobile museums' (she uses objects that allow for the artwork to be constantly arranged and rearranged) in the official citation for the award.

Oldest extant portrait studio

Sir Victor Sassoon, who was passionate about photography and constructed many public buildings in Bombay (now Mumbai, Maharashtra), set up Hamilton Studios in the E.D. Sassoon Building, which he owned, in 1928. Photography sessions at these studios were held by appointment, and the rich and famous personalities of Bombay were seen coming for quick and glamorous shoots. Currently, the studios are run by Ajita Madhavji and can be found in Ballard Estate.

WR Largest camera museum

The Museo Camera Centre for the Photographic Arts, Gurugram, Haryana, houses more than 2,500 cameras, which is the world's largest collection of vintage and other cameras on display. Inaugurated on 27 September 2019, it is spread over 1672.2 sq. m (18,000 sq. ft) of built-up space and can accommodate up to 200 visitors at a time. It is a collaboration between acclaimed photographer Aditya Arya and the Municipal Corporation of Gurugram.

Largest unit for photo production/ distribution

The Photo Division, Press Information Bureau, under the Ministry of Information and Broadcasting, Government of India, provides photographs to media units, and Central and state government departments. In the year 2020–21, it acquired 51,929 digital images in-house and supplied 376 digital prints.

WR Largest collection of cameras

Dilish Parekh, a photojournalist from Mumbai, Maharashtra, has a collection of 4,425 cameras, some dating back to 1906. It includes brands such as Leica, Nikon, Kodak, Canon, Hasselblad and Royal Mail Postage, and types such as watch, binocular and button cameras. He began the collection in 1977 with 600 cameras gifted by his grandfather.

Most people in a selfie

During Ragam, the annual cultural festival at the National Institute of Technology Calicut (NITC) in Kozhikode, Kerala, actor Sreenath Bhasi clicked a selfie, with a camera mounted on a selfie stick, at the Open Air Theatre on the campus, with 2,151 students on 26 March 2015.

Marathon photography – models

Photographer Vivek Ashok Somani (b. 7 August 1995) from Surat, Gujarat, conducted a marathon photo shoot on 12 May 2019. He clicked 11,076 photographs in 15 hrs 55 mins. Using a Nikon D5300 camera, and a

18–55 mm lens, he photographed 70 models at Future Dance Studio, Surat.

Marathon photography – city/ structures

Hariohm N. Gurjar from Vadodara, Gujarat, set out to document his city's various dimensions at 7:00 a.m. on 14 March 2014. He travelled 95 km in the city, shooting for 13 hrs. He captured 3,555 unduplicated images of people, architecture, markets, monuments and more.

AWARDS AND HONOURS

First Indian fellow of the British Photographic Society

Sir Prodyot Coomar Tagore (1873–1942), a prominent landowner of the time in Calcutta (now Kolkata, West Bengal), was an art collector besides being a keen photographer. He was the first Indian to be elected a Fellow of the British Photographic Society in 1896. He had a studio in his Tagore Castle home and exhibited his works. He was the founder and first president of the Academy of Fine Arts, Calcutta.

First winner of the Wildlife Photographer of the Year title

The Wildlife Photographer of the Year, organized by the Natural History Museum, London, UK, is one of the most famed contests in the world. Rajesh Bedi became the first Indian to win the grand title in 1986 for his photograph of the Asiatic black bear.

First Asian to win the International Photography Awards

Sharad Haksar from Chennai, Tamil Nadu, won one gold, one silver, two bronzes and 21 nominations in the International Photography Awards 2004. India finished fourth behind the USA, the UK and Canada.

First winners of the Pulitzer Prize for feature photography

- Anushree Fadnavis and Adnan Abidi were part of the Reuters team that won in the 'Breaking News Photography' category of the Pulitzer Prize for photography in 2020, for their work on the Hong Kong protests.
- Dar Yasin, Mukhtar Khan and Channi Anand from Associated Press won in the 'Feature Photography' category of the Pulitzer Prize for photography in 2020 for their coverage of Jammu and Kashmir.

WR First permanent photo exhibition in space

Dr Hersh Chadha (b. 27 November 1957) is the first person to organize a permanent photo exhibition in space on the International Space Station (ISS). Five images of different flowers were sent to the ISS on 16 October 2016 with the ISS 49/50 team. The purpose of this was to help the astronauts staying in space for months to remain connected with nature. On 1 March 2017, Dr Chadha was honoured by the Yuri Gagarin Cosmonaut Training Centre, Russia, for this.

WR First winner of the Académie des Beaux-Arts Photography Award – William Klein

Raghu Rai won the first-ever Académie des Beaux-Arts Photography Award – William Klein (Fine Arts Academy award for Photography). He was named the laureate and was awarded the prize at the Palais de l'Institut de France on 30 October 2019. The award carries a prize money of 120,000 euros (approximately ₹10.79 crore). It was instated in honour of William Klein, a celebrated US-born French photographer and film-maker.

41 photo exhibitions were organized by Bureau of Outreach and Communication, Ministry of Information and Broadcasting, Government of India, during 12–17 March 2021.

PAINTING AND CRAFT

FIRSTS

Earliest paintings discovered

Painted pottery, mostly in fragments, excavated at Mohenjo-daro, Chanhu-daro, Harappa and other places in the Indus Valley, are dated to 3000–2250 BCE.

Earliest use of tempera method

The Ajanta Caves are rock-cut Buddhist cave

The Boddhisattva Padmapani with lotus flower – fresco painting at the Ajanta caves: earliest use of tempera

They depict two women who are watching a procession from a balcony.

First Mughal illuminated manuscript

Emperor Humayun engaged Mir Sayyid Ali and a group of painters to paint the '*Dastan-i-Amir*' (the story of Amir Hamza), which featured as many as 1,375 miniatures painted on cotton cloth in the Persian Safavid style.

First painting gallery

Maharaja Ram Singh, a 19th-century king of Jaipur, built a unique hall that was fully displayed with paintings, called the Ram Vilas, in the garden of the Ram Niwas Bagh Palace. The walls of this hall were covered with imitations of several Greek, Roman, Persian and Chinese paintings.

First realist painter

Raja Ravi Varma (1848–1906) from the princely state of Travancore (now in Kerala) painted themes mainly from Indian mythology and legends in the realistic style of the West, making him the first realist painter in the country and the pioneer of a new movement in Indian art. In 1904, the then viceroy Lord Curzon bestowed the Kaisar-i-Hind Gold Medal on him.

First fine arts exhibition

The first fine arts exhibition was held in the Public Library, Calcutta, Bengal (now Kolkata, West Bengal), on 1 February 1831, by the Brush Club, with paintings drawn by foreign artists in India.

First modern art school

The Mechanical Institute was founded by Frederik Corbyn and Tarapada Chakrabarty in Calcutta (now Kolkata, West Bengal) on 2 February 1839. First named 'Society for the Promotion of Industrial Art', it was finally called the School of Industrial Art on 16 August 1854. It held its first exhibition from 22 January to 3 February 1855.

First auction of contemporary Indian paintings abroad

Sotheby's hosted the first ever auction of contemporary Indian paintings in New York, USA, on 12 June 1995. The 38 artists whose works were displayed included Jogen Chowdhury, M.F. Husain, Arpita Singh, Ganesh Pyne, S.H. Raza and Jamini Roy.

First academy for visual arts

The Lalit Kala Akademi, which was established in Delhi in 1954, started its work by organizing national exhibitions of contemporary Indian art. It also gives awards and honours, conducts

Representative image

India Shines at Excellence of Handicraft Awards

Indian handicraft artists won many awards at the International Excellence of Handicraft Awards 2021–22 given by the World Craft Council, an NGO affiliated to UNESCO, in October 2022. Mohammed Arif Khatri was selected for his remarkable work of Bagh Print on a Kota silk stole. Sapna Vedula Dhawla was selected for Godna tussar stole, Pallav Chaudhary for resist-dyed stole, Visalaxmi Ramaswamy for palm-leaf storage basket, Tridib Mohanty for reusable bamboo cutlery, Geetanjali Kasliwal for Bidri stationery accessories, Khatri Abdul Gafur Daud for tree-of-life *rogan* art and Ambika Devi for her Madhubani painting depicting village life during the COVID-19 pandemic.

monuments in Aurangabad, Maharashtra, dating back from the second century BCE to about 650 CE. The paintings in these caves used the tempera method. In this technique the rough mud plaster containing some organic matter like cow dung and animal hair was first pressed on the surface of the rocks and then a coat of fine lime plaster was laid all over it. This layer was allowed to dry thoroughly before applying colour on it. The scenes represented in these caves are mostly from Buddhist texts and events from the Buddha's life.

Earliest rock paintings

The largest and the oldest collection of rock paintings in India is at Bhimbetka, about 46 km from Bhopal, Madhya Pradesh. The paintings, found in more than 700 rock shelters dated to around 30,000 years ago, depict people's everyday lives such as hunting, dancing and decoration of bodies.

Oldest extant murals

Two 1,000-year-old Chola paintings, which were unearthed at the Brihadeeswarar Temple in Thanjavur, Tamil Nadu, are believed to be the oldest existing mural paintings.

1956

The National Crafts Museum was inaugurated. It has 33,000 items acquired over a period of 60 years.

Triennale-India (a global art show) and a Rashtriya Kala Mela (national art fair), where artists from across the country come together to present their work.

First art summit

The first India Art Summit was held at Pragati Maidan, New Delhi, during 22–24 August 2008. The 34 exhibition galleries exhibited over 550 artworks and sold more than half of them. The summit was brought to India by Hanmer MS&L Communications Pvt. Ltd.

First art bank

The Art Bank, set up in 2007 and started by curator Adishwar Puri, primarily for novice collectors apprehensive of making bad choices, now has corporations and government institutions, banks and hospitals as clients. The artists who register benefit by receiving 50 per cent of the rental value of the work.

First cartoon gallery

The Indian Institute of Cartoonists opened its 186 sq. m (2,000 sq. ft) gallery, the Indian Cartoon Gallery, at Midford House, Bangalore (now Bengaluru), Karnataka, on 16 August 2007. It has a seminar hall, a library and a cartoon bibliography from across the world.

First officially recognized female graffiti artist

Kajal Singh from New Delhi, who goes by the moniker 'Dizy', is the first recognized female graffiti artist from India. Her art form includes the use of bright colours and different font styles that instantly pop out. Besides India, she has left her signature in countries like Germany, China, the USA, Russia and Indonesia, among others. She was part of the Indo-German Hip-Hop Urban Art Project (2012), Each One Teach One (2013), 25 Years of the Berlin Wall (2014), Hip-Hop Cultural Exchange (2015) and On The Run Exhibition (2016). She was honoured as the 'First Lady' of graffiti in India by the Ministry of Women and Child Development, Government of India, on 20 January 2018.

First public art district

The Lodhi Art District in New Delhi, inaugurated by the Central Public Works Department on 1 March 2019, is the first public art district in the country. Conceptualized and realized by the St+Art India Foundation, a not-for-profit that works on art projects in open spaces, the artistic transformation of the district began in 2015. With the support of the local community, and civic and cultural bodies, more than 50 artists of 23 nationalities have reimagined the area's facades by creating murals that bring the viewer into a contemporary urban art museum. A total of 56 walls with an area of approximately 16,310 sq. m (175,565 sq. ft) have been painted by the artists. This was followed by the Mahim (East) art district in Mumbai, Maharashtra; the Maqta art district in Hyderabad, Telangana; and the Panjim (Panaji) art district in Goa.

GENERAL

Highest price at an auction for a work of Indian art

Vasudeo S. Gaitonde (1924-2001) was regarded as India's leading abstract painter. On 11 March 2021, a 1961 untitled painting by him was auctioned at the Saffronart Spring Live Auction for ₹39.98 crore (US $5.5 million) – a new record for the highest price achieved for a work of Indian art in an auction worldwide. It broke the painter's earlier record from 2020, when another of his untitled oil-on-canvas made in 1974 was sold for ₹36.8 crore at an auction by Pundole's.

Most National Awards won in a family

Nine members of the Jangid family have won the Master Craftsman Award, the national award for artisans and craft people between 1971 to 2017. Mal Chand Jangid, Richotmal Jangid, Vinod Kumar Jangid, Mahesh Chand Jangid, Sitaram Jangid, Kamlesh Jangid, Pawan Kumar Jangid. Navatmal Jangid and Om Prakash Jangid won these awards.

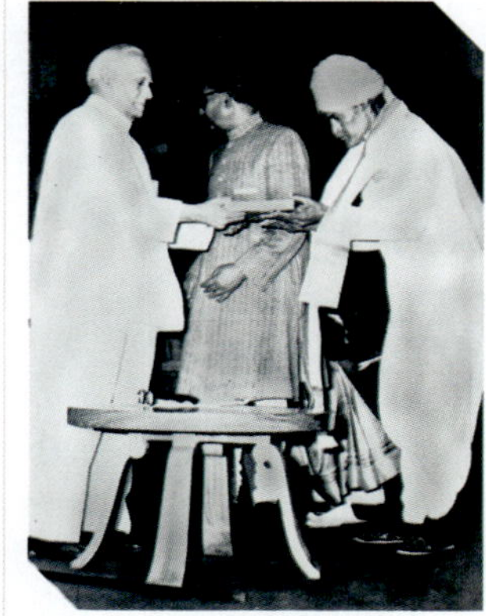

The Jangid family: most National Awards won

LARGEST AND MARATHON ARTWORK

Largest collage – group

Forty-four students and three teachers from Christ University, Bengaluru, Karnataka, created the largest collage on 2 March 2018. The collage, which measured 85.34 m x 9.14 m (280 ft x 30 ft), was made in 2 hrs 12 mins.

Largest quilling artwork – solo

Dr Jiji S. Deepak from Thrissur, Kerala, created a 6.71 m x 3.66 m (22 ft x 12 ft) artwork, using the paper-quilling technique. It took him 45 hrs 10 mins over a period of nine days. The artwork is based on the theme 'Mother Earth'.

Largest drawing – pencils – solo

Megha Harsha (b. 12 July 1992) from Bikaner, Rajasthan, created the largest pencil drawing by an individual. The artwork measured 455.21 sq. m (4,900 sq. ft) and was completed in 86 hours over the course of 17 days from 16 October to 1 November 2019 at Bikaner

The National Gallery of Modern Art, New Delhi, was inaugurated.

Highway no. **52** of Madhubani District, Bihar, has become a tourist spot for the artworks on tree trunks painted by artists to discourage people form cutting trees.

Boys School, Bikaner. The artwork created awareness regarding the United Nations' Sustainable Development Goals (SDGs) related to climate change, safety of women and pollution, among others.

Largest Zentangle Art

Twenty-five students from the NIFT-TEA (Tiruppur Exporters Association) College of Knitwear Fashion, Tiruppur, Tamil Nadu, created the largest Zentangle artwork measuring 185.8 sq. m (2,000 sq. ft), with 'Make in India' as its theme. The students completed the artwork in 34 hrs during 17–18 August 2018.

Largest doodle art – group

Students from the NIFT- TEA College of Knitwear Fashion, Coimbatore, Tamil Nadu, created a doodle artwork measuring 89 sq. m (960 sq. ft), depicting the historical development of the Tiruppur cluster, over 36 hrs during 14–15 July 2016.

Largest mandala artwork – solo

Radha Shankar Narayanan (b. 11 April 1977) from Bengaluru, Karnataka, created a 58.06 sq. m (625 sq. ft) mandala artwork in 89 hrs 20 mins over 12 days at BGS National Public School, Bengaluru. He started his painting on 15 June 2021 and finished on 28 June 2021.

Largest mandala artwork – solo

Largest mandala artwork – group

NIFT-TEA College of Knitwear Fashion in Tiruppur, Tamil Nadu, created a mandala artwork, which was 101.17 sq. m (1,089 sq. ft) in area, in 25 hours over two days in the college premises. The participants began the artwork on 27 February 2021 and finished on 28 February 2021.

Largest wall painting – single wall – solo

NIFT-TEA College of Knitwear Fashion, Tiruppur, Tamil Nadu, created a wall painting measuring 46.82 sq. m (504 sq. ft) in 250 hrs over 25 days in the college premises. The painting was made by R. Sanjay Kumar for the college. He started his painting on 17 June 2020 and finished on 11 July 2020.

WR Largest art competition – multiple venues

Sakal Media Pvt. Ltd organized the largest drawing and painting competition at several locations across Maharashtra and Goa on 16 December 2018. The Sakal Chitrakala Spardha (held annually for the last 33 years) took place at 2,000 locations between 9:00 a.m. to 12:30 p.m., in which 763,264 students from classes I to X participated. The painting centres were schools across the districts of Pune, Satara, Ahmednagar, Nanded, Mumbai, Nagpur, Akola, Jalgaon, Kolhapur, Solapur and Nashik, besides the state of Goa.

Largest sand artwork

Sudarsan Pattnaik (b. 15 April 1977) from Puri, Odisha, created the largest sand artwork, measuring 557.42 sq. m (6,000 sq. ft), at Puri Beach, Odisha, on 24 December 2020, to create awareness about mask usage during the COVID-19 pandemic.

Largest painting – oil paints – solo

Sandeep Sinha (b. 6 January1982), an artist from Pune, Maharashtra, made an oil-on-canvas painting titled 'HiMakhan'. The artwork measures 48.78 sq. m (525.06 sq. ft) and is a single-scene painting of the Himalayas. He began in August 2018 and completed the work by October 2018. His painting was exhibited at the Raja Ravi Varma Art Gallery, Pune. Sinha dedicated this work to acid-attack survivors.

Largest portrait – pencils – solo

Aman Gulati from Lakhimpur, Uttar Pradesh, created the largest pencil portrait, which measured 410.25 sq. m (4,416 sq. ft). in area. The portrait of Mahatma Gandhi was completed on 2 October 2019 to mark Gandhiji's 150th birth anniversary.

Largest portrait – acrylic paints – solo

Rajeev Ranjan (b. 1 March 1977) from Purnea, Bihar, who is popularly known as Rajeev Raj, created a painting of former prime minister Atal Bihari Vajpayee with acrylic paints on canvas. He began painting on 3 December 2018 at 4:43 p.m. and completed the artwork at 11:18 p.m. on 4 December 2018 at the Vidya

Vihar Residential School. He took 31 hrs 17 mins and used 225 pieces of canvas, each 0.762 m x 0.762 m (2.5 ft x 2.5 ft). The artwork covered a total area of 130.6 sq. m (1,406 sq. ft).

Smallest pencil-lead carving

Tribeni Kachari (b. 30 April 1997) from Kamrup, Assam, created the smallest pencil-lead carving of 'India Gate' on a graphite pencil lead. The artwork measures 5 mm (0.196 in.) in length and 3 mm (0.118 in.) in width, and was made on 31 August 2020.

Largest painting – natural colours – solo

Sangeeta Gupta (b. 25 May 1958) from New Delhi, created a painting using natural indigo titled, 'Aadiyogi Shiv – A Journey in Cosmic Indigo'. The artwork measures 169.16 sq. m (1,820.78 sq. ft) and is painted on *khadidar* fabric. She began the artwork on 25 February 2020 and completed it on 4 March 2020 at the Shilpi Sansthan, Rataliya Village, Jaipur, Rajasthan. The artwork was made to create awareness for sustainable living, using natural colours and dyes.

Largest origami artwork – widest – solo

Radhika Chintalapati, an artist from Hyderabad, Telangana, created a butterfly with nine folds in 15 mins at Glendale International School on 21 February 2019.

Marathon sand painting

Neha Umak (b. 22 December 1990) from Thane, Maharashtra, completed 133 pieces of sand painting artwork in 24 hrs 49 mins 19 secs from 9:16 a.m. on 30 June 2019 to 10:05 a.m. on 1 July 2019 at Kundan Talent Academy, Thane. The total break time was 1 hr 37 mins 40 secs. The artworks were a mix of portraits and sceneries.

Marathon pencil-art session

Dinesh K. Gupta (b. 22 May 1978) from Mumbai, Maharashtra, completed 201 drawings in a marathon pencil-art session, starting at noon on 5 April 2019 and ending at noon on 6 April 2019. Using 6B pencils, he sketched famous people, natural sceneries, religious figures and still life on A3 sheets. The event took place at Dr Babasaheb Ambedkar Art Gallery, Kalyan, Maharashtra. The total break time was 1 hr 50 mins.

Marathon portrait making – marker and ink – solo

Srushti Sandeep Ingale (b. 14 March 2000) from Kolhapur, Maharashtra, completed 157 portraits in a marathon marker-and-ink session, starting at 7 a.m. on 20 November 2021 and ending at 8 p.m. on the same day. Using four Montex Mega Tap black ball pens, she sketched portraits of political and sports personalities, amongst others, on A3 sheets. The event took place at Hotel Pearl, Kolhapur, Maharashtra. The total break time was 50 mins.

Marathon painting – acrylic colours – solo

Ramita Bhaduri (b. 27 September 1971) from Nazir Bagan, Kolkata, West Bengal, completed 213 artworks, using acrylic paints in 24 hrs from 4:05 p.m. on 5 June 2018 to 7:35 p.m. on 6 June 2018. The total break time was 3 hrs 30 mins.

Marathon sculpture-making

Ramita Bhaduri (b. 27 September 1971) from Nazir Bagan, Kolkata, West Bengal, completed a marathon sculpture-making session during 29–30 April 2019, using clay and cement. She logged 15 hrs of sculpting and 3 hrs break time (30 mins after every 3 hrs), making 29 sculptures in all. The average dimensions of the sculptures were 30.48 cm x 30.48 cm x 33.02 cm (12 in. x 12 in. x 13 in.) for standing figures, 25.4 cm x 30.48 cm x 38.1 cm (10 in. x 12 in. x 15 in.) for lying down ones and 25.4 cm x 25.4 cm x 30.48 cm (10 in. x 10 in. x 12 in.) for sitting figures.

Smallest pencil-lead carving

Marathon portrait making – marker and ink – solo

BUSINESS AND
ECONOMY

PLANNING

First book on political economy

Written in Sanskrit by Chanakya in the fourth century BCE, the *Arthashastra* is an ancient Indian treatise on statecraft, economic policy and military strategy. It was influential till the 12th century, after which it disappeared. A copy of it was rediscovered in 1905 by R. Shamasastry, a Sanskrit scholar, who published it in 1909. Its first English translation was published in 1915. The *Arthashastra* places the knowledge of economics at the heart of a king's education. Its discussion of taxation and expenditure gave expression to three traditional Indian principles: the taxing power of the state is limited, taxation should not be felt to be heavy or exclusive or discriminatory, and tax increases should be graduated.

Architect of planning

Prashanta Chandra Mahalanobis (1893–1972), an Indian scientist and applied statistician, laid down the framework for the formal foundation of economic planning in India. A member of the first Planning Commission of independent India, Mahalanobis was the first to use statistical tools to forecast, plan, analyse and evaluate social and economic welfare policies and implementation in India.

First budget

The first Indian budget was presented by James Wilson on 18 February 1869 in colonial India. Wilson, who founded *The Economist* magazine, was a finance member of the Council of India, which advised the Indian viceroy at the time.

First Union budget

The first Union budget of independent India was presented by the then finance minister, R.K. Shanmukham Chetty, on 26 November 1947. This was an economic review without any new taxes levied, as the Union budget for 1948–49 was only 95 days away. After this, a budget for a short period was called an 'interim' budget.

First interim budget

An interim budget, to enable government expenditures to continue until the regular budget, was presented first in 1957 by the then finance minister T.T. Krishnamachari.

First Planning Commission

The first Planning Commission was set up in 1951 under the chairmanship of the then prime minister Jawaharlal Nehru, with Gulzari Lal Nanda as the deputy chairman.

First five-year plan

The first five-year plan of free India was launched in 1951, with a total outlay of ₹2,378 crore (23,780 million).

First Union budget papers in Hindi

While introducing the budget for 1955–56, the then finance minister Sir C.D. Deshmukh circulated the Hindi version of the budget speech for the first time. Hindi versions of the Annual Financial Statement and the Explanatory Memorandum were also circulated from then on.

First annual plans

The first annual plans replaced the full five-year plan for an interim period in 1966. These annual plans continued till 1969 and came into force again during 1990–92.

First paperless budget

The Union budget for 2021 was presented on a 'Made-in-India' tablet on 1 February 2021 by Finance Minister Nirmala Sitharaman, doing away with the long-standing tradition of printing the budget papers and also the convention of carrying them in a briefcase. The budget, presented amid the COVID-19 pandemic, was distributed electronically to members of Parliament (MPs).

Only plan to go through four governments

The initial groundwork for the Eighth Five Year Plan (1992–97) was conducted by the Congress (I) government, the approach paper was finalized during National Front rule, the final document was prepared in the Janata Dal (S) regime and the Congress (I) delivered the revised plan in 1992.

WORKFORCE AND HUMAN RESOURCES

Workers on board

Delhi Cloth Mills (DCM) was the first company to recognize labour rights by inducting a workers' representative into its board in 1938.

Earliest public association

The earliest public association in modern India was the Landholders' Society, an association of the landlords of Bengal (now West Bengal), Bihar and Orissa (now Odisha), founded in 1837. It was established to look after the interests of landowners.

Oldest trade unions

- The Madras Labour Union, the first organized trade union, was formed in 1918–19

A stamp honouring P.C. Mahalanobis: first to use statistical tools for social and economic welfare activities

Finance Minister Nirmala Sitharaman: introduced the paperless budget

The Government of India set up the Planning Commission to oversee the gamut of planning, resource allocation, implementation and analysis of the five-year plans.

India Saw the Highest FDI Inflow in 2021

India recorded the highest-ever annual FDI (foreign direct investment) inflow of US $83.57 billion in the financial year (FY) 2021–22, overtaking the previous FY's FDI by US $1.60 billion. India's FDI inflow has witnessed a 23 per cent rise after the COVID-19 outbreak and Russian military intervention in Ukraine. India's FDI inflows have increased by almost 20 times since FY 2003–04 and nearly doubled since FY 2014–15, when it was US $45 billion, showing India's growing status as a preferred country for foreign investments in the manufacturing sector. Karnataka was the state receiving the maximum FDI inflow, while the top FDI inflows were recorded from Singapore (27 per cent) and the USA (18 per cent).

14 banks were nationalized in 1969 to give an impetus to bank lending to agriculture amid big businesses taking away the larger share of the credit flow.

J.R.D. Tata: longest-serving chairperson

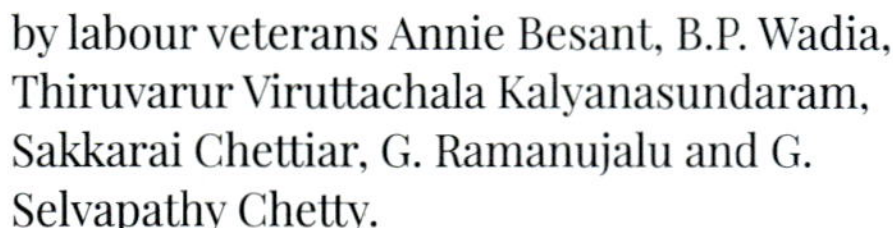

by labour veterans Annie Besant, B.P. Wadia, Thiruvarur Viruttachala Kalyanasundaram, Sakkarai Chettiar, G. Ramanujalu and G. Selvapathy Chetty.

- The All India Trade Union Congress (AITUC), one of the oldest trade unions, set up in 1920, has a history entwined with that of the organized labour movement and the freedom struggle in India.

Oldest banking employees' trade union

The All-India Bank Employees Association (AIBEA), founded on 20 April 1946, is the oldest and largest trade union of bank employees.

Oldest insurance trade union

The All India Insurance Employees Union (AIIEU), established in January 1951, comprised 80 per cent of the nearly 200,000 employees of the Life Insurance Corporation of India (LIC) and the General Insurance Corporation of India (GIC).

First labour strike

The first labour strike in India was that of the palanquin bearers of Calcutta (now Kolkata, West Bengal) in 1827 in pre-Independence India. They refused to wear badges, and demanded fare on the basis of the distance they covered instead of time.

First Labour Day

The International Workers' Day celebrations were first organized by communist leader Singaravelar or Malayapuram Singaravelu Chettiar (1860–1946) in Madras (now Chennai, Tamil Nadu) on 1 May 1923.

First industrial association

The Industrial Association of Western India was formed in 1890 at the annual conference held at Poona (now Pune, Maharashtra).

First all-India farmers' organization

The All-India Kisan Sabha was formed in 1936 in British India. It was the first pan-India organization of farmers.

First labour legislation

- The Industrial Employment (Standing Orders) Act of 1946 was followed by protective regulations, such as the Factories Act and the Minimum Wages Act in 1948.
- The first effort to protect unorganized labour was the Coal Mines Provident Fund and Bonus Schemes Bill introduced in 1948, which became an act in the same year.

First organized strike

In 1877, labourers struck work at the Empress Mills in Nagpur, Maharashtra, following a wage cut. In 1884, as many as 5,000 textile workers of Bombay (now Mumbai, Maharashtra) submitted a petition asking for regular payment of wages, a weekly holiday and a midday recess.

Largest strike

On 26 November 2020, over 250 million (25 crore) workers struck work for 24 hours in a nationwide general strike organized by a joint platform of 10 trade unions.

First legislation for women

The Bombay Maternity Benefit Act was passed in 1929. The Equal Remuneration Act was passed in 1976.

First woman chairperson – public sector undertaking

Laxmi Menon, the chief executive of Hindustan Teleprinters Ltd, became its chairperson and managing director in 1989, thereby becoming the first woman chairperson of a public sector undertaking (PSU) in the country.

Longest-serving chairperson

Jehangir Ratanji Dadabhoy Tata, a recipient of the Bharat Ratna in 1992, held the post of chairman of Tata Sons for 53 years (1938–91).

Largest employer

- In the government-controlled sector, the largest employer is Indian Railways with 1,253,592 regular employees as reported on 31 March 2020.
- In the private sector, Tata Consultancy Services continues to be the largest employer

with 616,171 employees (as reported in July 2022) in 46 countries.

Most students recruited by a company from a single institution

Cognizant Technology Solutions made job offers to 2,500 students from Vellore Institute of Technology's (VIT's) 2022 graduating batch during the campus placement drives held virtually at VIT, Vellore, Tamil Nadu. This is the highest number of job offers given by one company (Cognizant Technology Solutions) to students from a single institution (VIT), surpassing VIT's earlier records of 1,643 (2011 batch), 1,820 (2012 batch), 1911 (2014 batch), and 1,914 (2016 batch) dream job offers.

First LGBTQIA+ job fair

The RISE (Reimagining Inclusion for Social Equity) job fair organized by the Pride Circle on 12 July 2019 in Bengaluru, Karnataka, was the first job fair exclusively for the LGBTQIA+ community. The fair attracted 450 candidates competing for 250 job opportunities in 35 companies. The employers included Goldman Sachs, Uber, Accenture and Intel.

COINS AND CURRENCY

First lead coins

The first lead coins were found in the Deccan, dating back to the reign of Sri Satai (c. 150 BCE). Most Andhra coins were made of lead or bullion (an alloy of gold or silver with a predominant amount of copper or other base metal). They featured Brahmi legends on both sides. The typical devices featured were the elephant, the bow and the Buddhist chaitya.

Earliest gold coins

The Kushanas (130 BCE–185 CE) issued the earliest gold coins in India. They weighed 121 or 123.1 grains (1 grain = 0.068 g approx.) and appear to be based on the auric standard (122.9 grains) of the Romans with whom the Kushanas had regular trade.

Earliest coinage

Ingots of silver, with only three dots as a mark, probably represent the earliest form of coinage on the Indian subcontinent. Following them were heavy silver bars with devices stamped out with a punch on one side of the coin. These two types of coins were in circulation as early as 600 BCE.

Earliest known use of cowries as currency

Cowries were used as legal tender in the Bengal kingdom of Lakhnauti during the reign of Ghiyasuddin Bahadur Shah I (r. 1322–24 CE).

Oldest surviving gold coins

The oldest surviving gold coins are from the reign of Kushana emperor Vima Kadphises (c. 45–78 CE) and they were struck in three denominations – the double stater, the stater or dinara, and the quarter stater. On the obverse of these appears either the king's head or bust, or the king seated cross-legged on a couch, or sitting in a chariot drawn by two horses.

First mint

The East India Company started the first mint in India in 1640 at Fort St. George, Madras (now Chennai, Tamil Nadu). In 1671, the first English mint was installed in Bombay (now Mumbai, Maharashtra) through a letter of patent issued by King Charles II of England, but the first coin was minted there only a few years later in 1678.

First 200-rupee note

The RBI issued the first-ever currency notes in the denomination of ₹200 on 25 August 2017. This currency note, in the Mahatma Gandhi New Series, carries the motif of the Sanchi stupa on the reverse.

Kushana gold coins: earliest surviving gold coins

Representative image

Highest Forex Reserves

India's foreign exchange reserves increased by $8.895 billion to touch a record high of US $642.453 billion in the week ended 3 September 2021, according to Reserve Bank of India (RBI) data. The country's forex reserves rose largely due to an increase in Foreign Currency Assets (FCAs). India's forex reserves cover FCAs, Special Drawing Rights (SDRs), Gold Reserves and the country's reserve position with the International Monetary Fund (IMF). Most of the reserves are usually held in US dollars, given the currency's significant status in the international financial and trading system. After India went past Russia's foreign reserves ($620.8 billion), India's forex reserves were behind only China's (US $3,408 billion), Japan's (US $1,424 billion) and Switzerland's (US $1,087 billion).

The then prime minister Manmohan Singh's government launched the Mahatma Gandhi National Rural Employment Guarantee Scheme in 200 of the most backward districts. The scheme was later applied to all rural districts.

First 2,000-rupee note

The ₹2,000 banknote was released by the Reserve Bank of India (RBI) on 8 November 2016 following the demonetization of ₹1,000 and ₹500 banknotes. In circulation since 10 November 2016, the ₹2,000 banknote is part of the Mahatma Gandhi New Series with a new design featuring Mangalyaan on the reverse. It is the currency note of the highest denomination in active circulation currently.

First coins for the visually impaired

On 7 June 2019, Prime Minister Narendra Modi released a new series of coins, specially conceived to help visually impaired people to identify them, in New Delhi. Designed by the National Institute of Design in Ahmedabad, Gujarat, the series has coins in denominations of ₹1, ₹2, ₹5, ₹10 and ₹20. These coins are characterized by increasing size and weight from lower to higher denominations. The newly included coin of ₹20 was designed as a 12-sided coin with no serrations. The other denominations are circular.

BANKING

First bank

The Bank of Hindostan was established in 1770 by Alexander and Co. of Calcutta (now Kolkata, West Bengal) and survived three economic crises before shutting down in the 1830s.

Punjab National Bank: oldest private bank

A stamp featuring the Standard Chartered Bank, formerly the Chartered Bank: first foreign bank

First government banking agency

The Imperial Bank of India, formed in 1921 by merging the Presidency banks of Bengal, Bombay and Madras, became the State Bank of India (SBI) on 1 July 1955.

Oldest private bank

The Punjab National Bank Ltd, the first private bank wholly owned and run by Indians, opened in 1895.

First regional rural banks

The first regional rural banks (RRB) in India were opened in Moradabad and Gorakhpur in Uttar Pradesh, Bhiwani in Haryana, Jaipur in Rajasthan and Malda in West Bengal on 2 October 1975.

First foreign bank

The Chartered Bank, established in 1853 in Madras (now Chennai, Tamil Nadu), was the earliest foreign bank in India. In 1969, it merged with the Standard Bank in London, UK, and was incorporated as the Standard Chartered Bank.

First cooperative bank

The Greater Bombay Cooperative Bank Ltd was registered on 5 November 1952 under the Bombay State Cooperative Act, with 50 members and an initial capital of ₹21,000.

First bank for housing development

The National Housing Bank (NHB), a subsidiary of the Reserve Bank of India, was established on 9 July 1988.

First Indian bank to open a branch overseas

The Bank of India was the first Indian bank to open a branch outside India in London, UK, in 1946, and also the first to open a branch in Paris, France, in 1974.

First credit card issued by an Indian bank

The Central Bank of India introduced the Central Card in 1980.

First automated teller machine facility

The Hong Kong and Shanghai Banking Corporation (HSBC) started 24-hour banking facilities by installing automated teller machines (ATM) at its main office in Bombay (now Mumbai), Maharashtra, on 4 September 1987.

First floating ATM

The State Bank of India launched a floating ATM installed on a *jhankar* (ferry) plying between Ernakulam and Vypin (one among a group of islands forming part of Kovhi) in Kerala on 9 February 2004. The ship was owned by the Kerala Shipping and Inland Navigation Corporation.

First ATMs on wheels

- In December 2002, the Industrial Credit and Investment Corporation of India (ICICI) Bank introduced an ATM on wheels using vans equipped with ATM machines and parked at four locations in Mumbai suburbs – Vile Parle (East), Juhu, Andheri (West) and Kandivali – for fixed hours. The mobile ATM was connected to the central database of the bank through GPRS (General Packet Radio Service) technology for a fixed number of hours every day.

- The Bank of India was the first government bank to introduce mobile ATMs on 1 January 2003 in Mumbai, Maharashtra.

First Indian bank listed on the New York Stock Exchange

On 22 September 1999, ICICI Bank was listed on the New York Stock Exchange (NYSE), with its American Depository Shares priced at US $9.80. After the Bank of Tokyo-Mitsubishi, it was the second Asian bank to be listed on the NYSE.

First export–import bank

The Government of India set up the Export–Import Bank of India (EXIM Bank) in 1982 as a statutory corporation wholly owned by the Union government, to provide financial assistance to exporters and importers, and to coordinate the operations of export–import institutions.

First indigenous payment card

The National Payments Corporation of India (NPCI) introduced the RuPay debit card in Mumbai, Maharashtra, on 26 March 2012. The Bank of India, the State Bank of India, the Bank of Baroda and the Union Bank of India were among the first set of banks to offer RuPay debit cards to their customers for domestic payments.

First institution for agri loans

On 12 July 1982, the National Bank for Agriculture and Rural Development (NABARD) was established, with its headquarters in Bombay (now Mumbai), Maharashtra, to implement the National Bank for Agricultural and Rural Development Act, 1981. The agricultural credit functions of RBI and refinance functions of the then Agricultural Refinance and Development Cooperation (ARDC) were transferred to NABARD.

First government-owned all-woman bank

Bharatiya Mahila Bank (BMB), India's first government-owned all-woman bank, with the vision of economic empowerment of women, opened its first branch at Nariman Point in Mumbai, Maharashtra, on 19 November 2013. It was incorporated on 5 August 2013 and received a banking licence from the RBI on 25 September 2013. It was merged with the State Bank of India in April 2017.

Bank with most branches

The State Bank of India has 22,219 branches and 62,617 ATMs in India. Outside India, it has 229 branches in 31 countries.

First Indian governor of the Reserve Bank of India

Sir Chintaman Dwarakanath Deshmukh, a member of the Indian Civil Service, was the first Indian governor of the Reserve Bank of India (RBI). His association with the bank commenced in 1939, when he was appointed the government's liaison officer. He was appointed governor of RBI in 1943.

The bank with the largest network

The India Post Payments Bank (IPPB), launched in 2017 with 155,000 access points, became the largest banking network in the country. It is also the bank with the largest rural network, with 110,000 access points.

Largest international bank by number of branches

As reported by the Reserve Bank of India, the Standard Chartered Bank, with the UK as its country of incorporation, leads the list of international banks in India with the highest number of branches, totalling 100.

ICICI Bank: first Indian bank listed on the NYSE

A stamp released on the launch of India Post Payments Bank: bank with the largest network

INDIA AT HER BEST 75 YEARS OF INDEPENDENCE

ANNUAL PER CAPITA INCOME

(in ₹ at Current Prices)

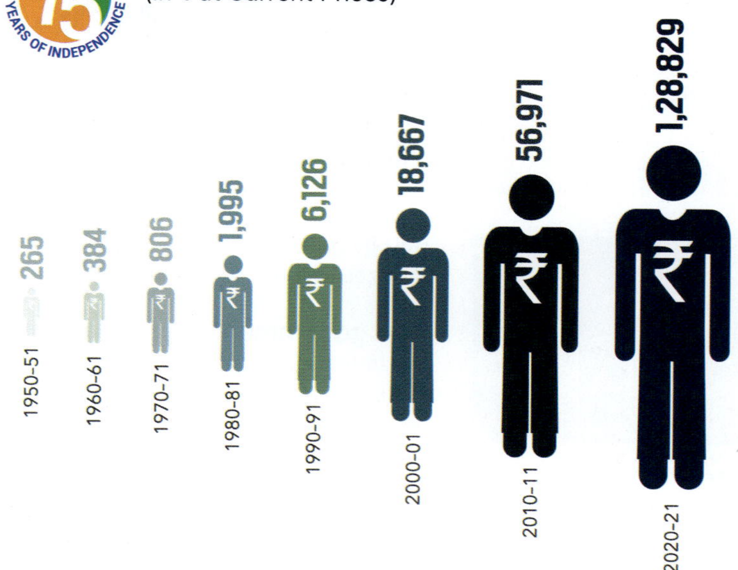

Source: PIB AKAM series, Press Information Bureau, Government of India

Gautam Adani

Gautam Adani: Among the World's Top Three Richest Persons

Sixty-year-old business tycoon Gautam Adani heads the list of India's richest persons with reported wealth of ₹10,94,400 crore (10,994 billion), as per the IIFL Wealth Hurun India Rich List 2022. On 16 September, he surged past Jeff Bezos, founder and executive chairman of Amazon, and French luxury retail baron Bernard Arnault (of LVMH), to become the world's second richest person, according to the *Forbes*'s Real-time Billionaires List. During that day, Adani's wealth had risen to US $155.7 billion, but he lost the position due to a market crash and dropped back to third place with a net worth of US $152.6 billion, giving the no. 2 spot back to Arnault with his family's net worth totalling around US $153.1 billion. Adani, however, remained ahead of Bezos at fourth spot, with a wealth of US $149.7 billion. The list of top 10 billionaires also includes Bill Gates ($105.3 billion), Warren Buffett (US $96.5 billion), Mukesh Ambani (US $91.6 billion) and Google co-founders Larry Page (US $89 billion) and Sergey Brin (US $85.4 billion).

Tata Steel acquired the much larger UK-based company Corus, and Aditya Birla Group's Hindalco Industries Ltd bought out US-based Novelis, starting off the era of huge acquisitions.

State/UT with the most ATMs

Maharashtra ranks first in the country as the state with the highest number of ATMs and WLAs (White Label ATMs) deployed, with 28,024 ATMs as reported in September 2022. Tamil Nadu, with 23,524 ATMs, comes second in the list.

Bank with most foreign offices

The State Bank of India had 80 foreign offices in 36 countries to service the bank's foreign customers, in addition to retail operations (by July 2020). The focus of these offices is India-related business.

First Indian bank with a merchant banking subsidiary

The State Bank of India was the first bank to set up a wholly owned merchant banking subsidiary when it set up SBI Capital Markets Ltd in April 1986.

Biggest bank fraud

On 14 February 2018, Punjab National Bank (PNB), India's second-largest government-owned lender at the time, declared the largest ever bank fraud in India's financial history. It involved fraudulent letters of undertaking worth around ₹11,400 crore (114 billion) issued by PNB at its Brady House branch in Fort, Mumbai, Maharashtra, to overseas branches of other Indian banks. It was allegedly perpetrated by jeweller-designer Nirav Modi and his uncle and alleged partner Mehul Choksi, among others.

First bank with a satellite network

The State Bank of India installed the first satellite network in September 1988, connecting 134 offices in 64 cities. This network facilitated communication by voice, facsimile and message switching via digital electronic exchanges.

First bank to establish a mutual fund

The State Bank of India launched the SBI Mutual Fund in July 1987. Managed by its subsidiary, SBI Capital Markets Ltd, it was established under the amended Banking Regulations Act, 1949, to attract funds from small investors in rural and semi-urban areas.

First woman bank manager

Shanta Kumari became the manager of the Syndicate Bank, Seshadripura, Bangalore (now Bengaluru), Karnataka, in 1962.

First woman to head a foreign bank in India

Naina Lal Kidwai was the first Indian woman to lead a foreign bank (ANZ Grindlays, where she worked from 1982 to 1994) in India. She was also the first Indian woman to graduate from Harvard Business School (1982). Her contribution in the areas of trade and industry earned her the Padma Shri in 2007.

First woman managing director and chief financial officer of World Bank Group

Anshula Kant, born in Roorkee (now in Uttarakhand), was appointed as the managing director (MD) and chief financial officer (CFO) of the World Bank on 12 July 2019. Kant is responsible for managing the International Development Association (which offers concessional loans and grants to the world's poorest developing countries), finance and risk management of the Group. Previously a financial officer of the State Bank of India, Kant became the first woman to become MD and CFO of the international financial institution.

First demonetization

In 1946, ₹1,000 and ₹10,000 currency notes were removed from circulation in the first instance of demonetization. Both notes were then reintroduced in 1954, with the introduction of ₹5,000 and ₹500 notes. In 1978, the then prime minister Morarji Desai took ₹1,000, ₹5,000 and ₹10,000 notes out of circulation. On 8 November 2016, Prime

Minister Narendra Modi declared ₹500 and ₹1,000 notes invalid. Later, new notes of ₹500, ₹200 and ₹2,000 denominations were introduced.

INSURANCE

First general insurance company

Triton Insurance Company Ltd, set up by the British in 1850, was the first general insurance company in India.

First life insurance company

The Oriental Insurance Company, the first life insurance company in India, started in Calcutta (now Kolkata, West Bengal) in 1818, but served only the Europeans in India then.

First Indian life insurance company

The Bombay Mutual Life Assurance Society was the first Indian life insurance company. It started in 1871.

Largest insurance company

The Life Insurance Corporation of India (LIC) was founded on 1 September 1956. It grew into what is now the biggest public sector insurance company in the country and leads in the insurance sector. It has a total life fund of ₹31,14,496.05 crore (31,144.96 billion), with ₹2.19 crore (21.9 million) new policies, thus garnering 75.9 per cent of the market share in terms of policies and 68.74 per cent of the market share in terms of first-year premiums (financial year 2019–20).

FINANCIAL INSTRUMENTS

First domestic mutual fund

The Unit Trust of India's (UTI) scheme launched in 1964 was the first domestic mutual fund in the country.

First offshore mutual fund

Unit Trust of India (UTI) and Merrill Lynch promoted the ₹75 million India Fund in 1986.

First rating agency

Crisil, formed in 1988, was the first rating agency in India. It was set up jointly by the LIC, lClCl, GIC and various banks.

First automatic exchange and screen-based trading

The automated Over the Counter Exchange of India (OTCEI), set up in 1992 in Bombay (now Mumbai), Maharashtra, was the ideal avenue for small- and medium-sized companies with an issued capital ranging from ₹30 lakhs (3 million) to ₹25 crore (250 million).

LIC India: largest insurance company

This exchange failed to live up to its promise and the National Stock Exchange (NSE) came into being in November 1994. It started the first screen-based trading system, in which a network of computers is linked to a central computer located in the stock exchange.

First global depository receipts issue

Reliance Industries Ltd issued global depository receipts worth US $150 million in March 1992.

Tata Iron and Steel Company Ltd (now Tata Steel Ltd): first issued secured promissory notes

First woman president of a stock exchange

Forty-five-year-old Omana Abraham became the first woman president of a stock exchange in India, when she was nominated the president of the Cochin Stock Exchange in Kochi, Kerala, in 1991.

First secured promissory notes

Tata Iron and Steel Company Ltd (TISCO), now Tata Steel Ltd, issued secured promissory notes in June 1992.

First PSU to go public

Indian Petrochemicals Corporation Ltd (IPCL)

LIC's Mega Listing

Life Insurance Corporation of India (LIC), the country's largest life insurer with a market share of 64.1 per cent in terms of premiums at the time, filed for an initial public offering (IPO) in February 2022. There are currently 24 life insurance companies in India, with LIC being the only public player. The Government of India had 100 per cent stake in the insurer and planned to sell 5 per cent of it. LIC's listing was part of the Central government's privatization programme to replenish the public coffers emptied during the COVID-19 pandemic and to create funds to initiate new infrastructure. Up to 10 per cent of shares on offer were for policyholders.

Representative image

On the day of its much-anticipated mega listing in the Indian stock exchanges on 17 May 2022, LIC reduced its IPO size to 3.5 per cent from 5 per cent due to uncertain market conditions. A qualified institutional buyer (QIB) segment was subscribed 1.07 times. The non-institutional investors (NII) section was subscribed 1.24 times. The retail category was subscribed 1.60 times. The employee section was subscribed 3.80 times and the policyholder segment was subscribed 5.07 times. Overall, the IPO was subscribed 1.90 times.

Even after the reduced size of about ₹20,557 crore, LIC's IPO was the biggest initial public offering ever in the country. So far, the amount mobilized from the IPO of Paytm in 2021 was the largest ever at ₹18,300 crore, followed by Coal India (2010) at nearly ₹15,500 crore and Reliance Power (2008) at ₹11,700 crore.

The NSE: stock exchange with the highest turnover

went public on 16 November 1992, with a ₹320 crore (3.2 billion) equity issue.

Highest price for stock exchange membership

A broking card for the Bombay Stock Exchange was auctioned for ₹41 million (₹4.1 crore) to Jardine Fleming Asia, which later shut down. Before that, Baring Securities India Ltd had paid ₹3 crore (30 million) for one in 1995.

India's first depository

The National Securities Depository Limited (NSDL) was jointly promoted by the IDBI, UTI and NSE, and it started operations in August 1996. C.B. Bhave was the first managing director of the NSDL. In September 2016, when the depository completed 20 years of operations, it had 15 million demat accounts.

First woman director of the Bombay Stock Exchange

Forty-year-old Deena Mehta became the first woman director of the Bombay Stock Exchange (BSE), elected by securing 382 of 413 votes in March 1997. This was the first time in 122 years that the BSE elected a woman to its board.

First private sector mutual fund

Shyam Kothari, head of the H.C. Kothari group of companies, floated the Kothari Pioneer Bluechip Fund in November 1993.

First sectoral fund

The first sector mutual fund by the name of CanExpo was offered by Canara Bank during February–March 1994 as the first emerging industry fund.

Largest mutual fund

HDFC Asset Management Company Ltd is the largest mutual fund company in India, with assets worth ₹450376.22 crore under its management, as reported in December 2021.

FINANCIAL INSTITUTIONS

Oldest stock exchange

The Bombay Stock Exchange (BSE) was born under the shade of a giant banyan tree way back on 9 July 1875. Indian brokers doing business in stocks and shares decided to form an association in Bombay (now Mumbai, Maharashtra) to protect the interests of Indian share brokers and stockbrokers. It was also Asia's first stock exchange.

Stock exchange with most listed companies

The BSE, with 4,817 listed companies, is the

FROM THE ARCHIVES

India's business and economic history has many fascinating nuggets that showcase its varied and complex past. Here are a few of them...

State Bank of India: Oldest Bank in Operation

The State Bank of India, with a heritage of 200 years, descended from the oldest banks on the subcontinent. The story began when the three presidency banks of colonial India – the Bank of Bengal (established on 2 June 1806), the Bank of Bombay (incorporated on 15 April 1840), and the Bank of Madras (incorporated on 1 July 1843) – were reorganized and merged into a single banking entity, the Imperial Bank of India, on 27 January 1921, This bank was 80 per cent privately owned and 20 per cent by the state.

Initially, it acted as the central bank for British India, carrying out banking functions for the government and other banking institutions, including overseas functions, and managing the rupee debt before the Reserve Bank of India (RBI) was formed in 1935. Many of its responsibilities were taken over by the RBI, after which the Imperial Bank of India remained mainly a commercial bank. Amid the post-Independence effort to bring funds into sectors like agriculture and give rural India the benefits of a banking system, the Imperial Bank was nationalized and established as the State Bank of India on 1 July 1955, through an Act of the Parliament of India. At that time, the bank reportedly had 480 branches and sub-offices, as well as three local head offices; slightly more than a quarter of the resources of the Indian banking industry was under its control and command.

Top: the logo of the Imperial Bank of India; *middle*: the SBI headquarters in Mumbai, Maharashtra; *bottom*: a stamp featuring the creation of the State Bank of India

LIC of India: Largest Life Insurer

When India became independent, there were many different types of insurers – Indian and foreign – operating in the subcontinent. On 19 January 1956, the Government of India issued an ordinance to nationalize 154 Indian insurers, 16 non-Indian insurers and 75 provident societies (a total of 245). They were merged to create the mammoth state-owned Life Insurance Corporation of India. On 19 June 1956, the Life Insurance Corporation (LIC) Act was passed, and on 1 September, LIC was formed with an initial capital of ₹5 crore. With the mandate to provide the benefits of life insurance more equally and widely, especially in rural regions, it began with five zonal offices, 33 divisional offices and 212 branch offices. Headquartered in Mumbai, this largest of Indian insurance companies (on premiums), became the first Indian insurance company to be listed on the stock exchange when it went public in May 2022.

First Union Budget

The budget was first introduced in India on 7 April 1860, two years after the transfer of Indian administration from the East India Company to the British Crown. During the transfer of power from the British Crown to free India, Liaquat Ali Khan, member of the interim government, presented the budget of 1947–48. After Independence, India's first finance minister, R.K. Shanmukham Chetty, presented the first budget of independent India on 26 November 1947.

The Union budget was conventionally presented at 5 p.m. on the last working day of February following the British practice. However, in 1999, the then finance minister Yashwant Sinha changed the timing of the budget presentation to 11 a.m. In 2017, the then finance minister Arun Jaitley presented the budget on 1 February. In that year, the railway budget, presented separately until then, was merged in the Union budget. Amid the COVID-19 pandemic the budget for 2021–22 became paperless, marking a milestone.

R.K. Shanmukham Chetty: presenter of first Union budget; *below:* The Union budget was traditionally carried in a briefcase

Premchand Roychand

The BSE: First Stock Exchange

A group of stockbrokers first gathered in the 1850s under a banyan tree in front of the Town Hall in present-day Mumbai, and then under the banyans at today's Mahatma Gandhi Road. In 1874, they formed the Native Share and Stock Brokers Association, with cotton and bullion trader Premchand Roychand as the founder of the exchange. In 1930, their building near Horniman Circle became the Bombay Stock Exchange (BSE), and the street became 'Dalal Street' ('broker street'). Now known as BSE Ltd, it was then Asia's first exchange. On 31 August 1957, the BSE was the first stock exchange to be recognized by the Government of India under the Securities Contracts Regulation Act. The name of its current building, built in the late 1970s, was changed from BSE Towers to Phiroze Jeejeebhoy Towers after Sir Phiroze, chairman of the BSE from 1966 until 1980.

The iconic 29-story building of the BSE

The Government Mint, Kolkata: Oldest Mint in Operation

Among the four current government mints in India – in Kolkata, Mumbai, Hyderabad and Noida – the one in Kolkata is the oldest, though it has changed both location and name. It was first established as the Calcutta Mint in 1757 in colonial India and was located in a building where the GPO (General Post Office) is housed today. It used to produce coins under the mint name Murshidabad. On 19 August 1757, the first rupee coin was minted by the East India Company. The second Calcutta Mint was set up in 1790 with more modern machines from England and situated at the site of the Gillet Ship Building Establishment. Its coins still bore the name Murshidabad.

A gold mohur minted at the Calcutta Mint

The third Calcutta Mint was founded in March 1824 in a Parthenon-style building on Strand Road. From 1 August 1829 until 1835, its coins continued to bear the mint name Murshidabad. Called the 'Old Silver Mint', this mint, along with the 'Copper Mint' in its annexe (from 1860 onwards) reportedly produced 300,000 and 600,000 coins per day in bronze, silver and gold, along with medals and decorations (which continues to the present day). This mint was shut down in 1952 and declared a heritage building.

A new building for the mint was started at Taratala, near Alipore, in the late 1930s but was completed only in the early 1950s, due to the Second World War. This Alipore Mint, the current Government Mint, was opened on 19 March 1952 for domestic coinage, coins for other nations, medals, official decorations and badges.

largest exchange going by the number of listed companies on the exchange.

Stock exchange with highest turnover

The National Stock Exchange is the stock exchange with the highest turnover, with an average daily turnover of ₹48,022 crore (480.22 billion) for October 2022.

Stock exchange with highest membership

With a total of 1,406 members across different segments of financial markets, the NSE had the highest number of members in a stock exchange (2021).

WR Stock exchange with highest volume of derivative contracts

The NSE maintained its position as the world's largest derivatives exchange for a second consecutive year in 2020. It reported a trading volume of 8.85 billion contracts in 2020.

Highest BSE sensitive index level

The BSE sensitive index touched an all-time intra-day high of 62245 on 19 October 2021, the highest ever level since it was formed in 1979.

State/UT with the highest contribution to equity trading

Maharashtra leads among states in its contribution to equity trading, with 12,673,663 investors in 2020.

POWER AND ENERGY

First builder of the steam engine

Goluk Chandra, who was a blacksmith in Titigur (now Titagarh), near Barrackpore in West Bengal, indigenously built a steam engine to pump groundwater, without any European help, in 1828.

First steam-powered plant

The Calcutta Electric Supply Company (CESC) set up a steam-powered plant in 1899 at Emambagh Lane near Prinsep Ghat in Calcutta (now Kolkata, West Bengal), marking the start of thermal power generation in India.

First commercial use of electricity

Electricity was first introduced commercially on 10 November 1897 at Sidrapong Hydroelectric Power Station in Darjeeling, West Bengal.

First electrification

Calcutta (now Kolkata, West Bengal) was the first city in India to go electric when it received current in 1899 when the first thermal power plant of the Calcutta Electric Supply Corporation Ltd was commissioned.

Largest private sector thermal power station

The 4,620 MW Mundra Thermal Power Station at Mundra in the Kachchh District of

Rakesh Jhunjhunwala

Rakesh Jhunjhunwala: 'The Big Bull of Dalal Street'

Most recently in the news for launching Akasa Air, India's newest airlines of which he was founder, ace investor Rakesh Jhunjhunwala (5 July 1960–14 August 2022) passed away in Mumbai in August 2022 due to multiple health issues.

An alumnus of Sydenham College, Mumbai, and a chartered accountant by profession, Jhunjhunwala began investing in stocks around 1985 with a base capital of ₹5,000. Over the next 30 years he went from strength to strength, becoming one of the most well-known and profit-churning stock bearers in the country. Beginning with his first big profitable investment in 1986 in Tata Tea, by 2017 his portfolio had reportedly grown to over ₹15,000 crore and included stocks of companies such as Titan, Rallis India, Escorts, Canara Bank and Tata Motors, among others. His individualistic and risk-taking trading style earned him the monikers of 'The Big Bull of Dalal Street' and 'India's Warren Buffet'.

In July 2020, according to *Forbes*'s Real-time Billionaires Index, Jhunjhunwala was listed among the top 500 richest billionaires in the world and the 36th richest man in India. He was also the chairman of Aptech Limited and Hungama Digital Media Entertainment, and on the boards of Viceroy Hotels, Provogue India, Concord Biotech and Geojit Financial Services, among others. He also owned an asset management firm called Rare Enterprises.

Calcutta (now Kolkata, West Bengal): first city to be electrified

A stamp commemorating the Tata Power Company Ltd: first private sector power company

Gujarat is the largest privately operating thermal power plant in India, with nine generating units. It is a coal-based power plant, owned and operated by Adani Power.

Largest power supplier

The National Thermal Power Corporation (NTPC) Ltd, set up in 1975, is the country's largest power company. Currently, it has an installed capacity of 70,254 MW (including joint ventures). NTPC's own stations include 23 coal-based, seven gas-based, one hydroelectric, one wind, 18 solar and one small hydroelectric plant. Under joint ventures, the company has nine coal based, four gas-based, eight hydroelectricity-based and five renewable energy projects.

First private sector power company

Tata Power Company Ltd (TPCL) was the first private sector power company to start operations in 1910 in Bombay (now Mumbai, Maharashtra).

First state electricity board

On 1 May 1955, the West Bengal State Electricity Board was the first electricity board in the country to become operational.

Tarapur Atomic Power Project, Palghar, Maharashtra: first nuclear power plant

First nuclear power plant

The Tarapur Atomic Power Station in Palghar, Maharashtra, with an installed capacity of 380 MW, was commissioned in 1969. It had two boiling-water reactor units of 210 MW each, fuelled by enriched uranium. It was built by Bechtel Corporation and General Electric Company, USA, under an agreement between the Government of India, the USA and the International Atomic Energy Agency.

First heavy water plant

The first heavy water plant was set up at Nangal in the Rupnagar District of Punjab in 1962. Heavy water or deuterium oxide was the basic fuel used by first-generation nuclear power plants.

First indigenous atomic power plant

Madras Atomic Power Station (MAPS) at Kalpakkam near Chennai, Tamil Nadu, was India's first fully indigenously built nuclear power station under the Indira Gandhi Centre for Atomic Research (IGCAR). Each of its two units generates 220 MW of electricity. The first indigenous 40 MW Fast Breeder Test Reactor (FBTR) was commissioned in August 1985 here.

First hydropower station

Sidrapong Hydroelectric Power Station in the foothills of Arya Tea Estate near Darjeeling, West Bengal, is the oldest hydroelectric power plant in India. It was commissioned on 10 November 1897 with a capacity of 2 x 65 kW. This was increased in phases as per rising demands to reach 1,000 kW (1 MW) by 1916.

First solar-powered thermal plant

The country's first 50 MW solar-powered thermal power plant, developed by Chhattisgarh-based Godawari Green Energy Ltd (GGEL) in Nokh Village in Jaisalmer District, Rajasthan, went operational in 2013.

Launch of green fuel

On 1 April 2017, Bharat Stage-IV (BS-IV grade) fuel was officially launched across the country to keep carbon emissions in check.

Largest thermal power plant

Vindhyachal Super Thermal Power Station in Singrauli District, Madhya Pradesh, with an installed capacity of 4,760 MW, is ranked as the biggest thermal power plant in the country. It is a coal-based power plant, owned and operated by NTPC Ltd.

Largest grid-connected rooftop solar plant

The country's largest grid-connected rooftop solar plant, with a capacity of 7.52 MW, started operations in May 2016 at the Dera Beas in Amritsar District, Punjab.

Longest natural gas pipeline

- The HVJ (Hazira–Vijaipur–Jagdishpur) gas pipeline, owned by Gas Authority of India Ltd (GAIL) and laid during 1986–89, is 2,300 km long.
- Indian Oil Corporation (IOC), Bharat Petroleum Co. Ltd (BPCL) and Hindustan Petroleum Corporation Ltd (HPCL) announced

a joint venture in June 2019 to lay the world's longest (2,757 km) LPG pipeline from Kandla in Gujarat to Gorakhpur in Uttar Pradesh, at a cost of ₹10,000 crore (100 billion).

First oil well

- Oil was first located at Borbil (later Digboi) in Assam in 1890, but systematic drilling for oil had begun in Upper Assam in 1866 and oil was struck at Makum near Margherita at a depth of 36 m (118 ft) on 26 March 1867.
- The first offshore well was sunk in the Bombay High oilfield in 1974.

First pipeline

The Guwahati–Siliguri petroleum product pipeline (between Assam and West Bengal) was commissioned by the Indian Oil Corporation in 1965.

First refinery

The Assam Railways and Trading Co. built a small refinery at Margherita in present-day Tinsukia District, Assam, in 1893 to refine oil from Makum and Digboi areas.

WR Oldest running refinery

The Digboi Refinery, under the Indian Oil Corporation, started in 1899 in Assam, is the world's oldest running refinery.

Tamil Nadu: state with the highest installed capacity of renewable power

First company to market LPG

The first company to market liquefied petroleum gas (LPG) in India was BPCL in 1955. Now BPCL reaches around 25 million households with 2,137 LPG distributors across the country.

State with highest installed capacity of renewable power

Tamil Nadu has surpassed Karnataka with the highest installed capacity of grid-connected renewable power. As of 31 January 2022, Tamil Nadu's total installed renewable capacity stood

Crypto Budget: Digital Currency Coming Up

Representative image

In the wake of increasing demand for private cryptocurrencies such as bitcoin, Union finance minister Nirmala Sitharaman announced the government's plan to introduce a digital rupee in her 2022–23 budget speech, saying that the digital currency or digital rupee will be introduced by the Reserve Bank of India (RBI) using blockchain and other related technologies.

Reportedly, the RBI digital currency or the digital rupee was planned to be issued starting from the 2022–23 fiscal year. The RBI digital currency will be held in a digital wallet, under the supervision of the central bank, so that it can be tracked easily. Those interested may be given the option of converting their deposits in banks into the new RBI digital rupee.

The finance minister put forward that the introduction of the central bank digital currency will give a massive boost to the economy. For those apprehensive of investing in private cryptocurrencies because of the perceived or real risks involved, the RBI digital currency will offer a safer option. For the RBI, the costs of creating and distributing the digital currency will be almost nil unlike the costs normally incurred in printing and distribution of physical currency. The digital rupee will also be in line with the mission of a digital India. As the RBI will monitor digital currency, incidents of corruption and fraud are also expected to reduce.

The finance minister also announced the tax parameters for digital currency, including the rule that income earned from the transfer of virtual digital assets would be taxed at a rate of 30 per cent.

Bharat Coking Coal Ltd, a subsidiary of Coal India Ltd: largest coal producing company

at 15,914 MW as compared to Karnataka's total clean energy capacity of 15,795 MW.

First private branded LPG

Reliance Gas was launched in 1998 by Reliance Petroleum Ltd in collaboration with the local LPG bottlers for the packaging of the product.

MINING

 Largest coal-producing company

Coal India Limited (CIL), a government-owned coal-mining corporate headquartered in Kolkata, West Bengal, came into being in November 1975 when the Government of India took over private coal mines. It is now the single largest coal producer in the world. Operating through 84 mining areas, it has seven wholly owned coal-producing subsidiaries, as well as a mine planning and consultancy company, across eight states in India. Coal India Ltd (CIL) and its subsidiaries accounted for 596.221 million tonnes during 2020–21, while its production during 2021–22 was 622.634 MT (provisional).

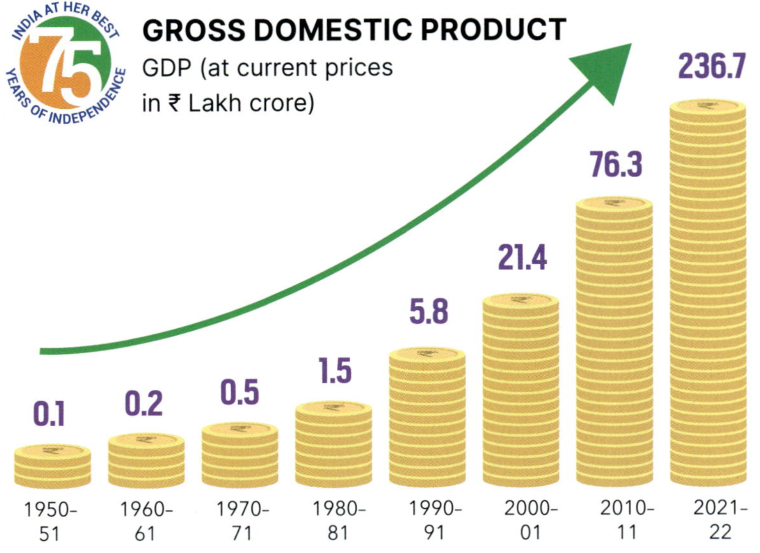

Source: PIB AKAM series, Press Information Bureau, Government of India

State/UT with the most mines

There are 1,303 reporting mines in the country as recorded in 2019–20. Among these, Madhya Pradesh leads in the number of reporting mines (excluding atomic and fuel minerals) with 220 mines, followed by Gujarat (167), Karnataka (140), Odisha (129), Andhra Pradesh (123), Chhattisgarh (92), Telangana (92), Rajasthan (84) and Maharashtra (67). In terms of the value of mineral production, Odisha leads with ₹32,841 crore (328.41 billion), followed by Rajasthan (₹22,776 crore/227.76 billion)) and Andhra Pradesh (₹17,906 crore/179.06 billion).

Oldest gold mine

India's oldest gold mine was located in Kolar, Karnataka. The production here in the mid-1970s was 3,000 kg a year, but was on a decline ever since, and the mines were closed in 2001. The three mines collectively, viz., Champion, Mysore and Nandydroog, at the Kolar goldfields, made it one of the largest and deepest gold mine areas of the world and the only recognized gold mine in the country, known for gold mining for over a century.

First coal mining

The first tonne of coal was struck in Raniganj Coalfield in 1775 by Suetonius Grant Heatly, the then collector of the East India Company for Palamu and Hazaribagh, in present-day Jharkhand. Records have shown that John Summer and Grant Heatly jointly obtained a licence from the then British Governor General Warren Hastings in 1774 to exploit what they then called 'Panchet coal'. They were later joined by another Englishman called Redfern.

Only diamond mines

India's only diamond mines are at Panna in Madhya Pradesh and are administered by the government-owned National Mineral Development Corporation (NMDC).

INDUSTRIES AND COMPANIES

First factory

The first factory in India, which was a dye-manufacturing unit, was set up by the East India Company with the permission of the then Mughal emperor Jahangir in Surat in 1609, marking the beginning of colonialism.

First commercial production of iron and steel

- In 1830, a unit was set up at Porto Novo (now Parangipettai) in Cuddalore District, Tamil Nadu, to produce iron, but it failed.
- In 1853, the East India Iron Company set up two blast furnaces in South Arcot and Coimbatore districts, Tamil Nadu. These closed in 1858.
- In 1875, the Barakar Iron Works, Kulti, Bengal, produced pig iron.
- Steel production began in 1892 at the Metal and Steel Factory at Cossipore (now Kashipur, West Bengal), moving to Ichapore (now Ishapur, West Bengal) in 1905.

First cigarette company

Imperial Tobacco Company (ITC) was established in Calcutta (now Kolkata, West Bengal) in 1910.

First rubber estate and company

The first rubber company, called Malankara Rubber and Produce Company, was started in 1910 by P. John on a 70-acre (28.3-hectare) estate in Thodupuzha, Idukki District, Kerala.

Representative image

India's first international Bullion Exchange

Prime Minister Narendra Modi inaugurated India's first international bullion exchange, the India International Bullion Exchange (IIBX) at Gujarat's GIFT (Gujarat International Finance Tec-City) in Gandhinagar on 29 July 2022. This exchange is the third such exchange in the world.

India's first bullion exchange will sell physical gold and silver. The jewellers registered as trading partners with the exchange, with a minimum net worth of ₹25 crore as a prerequisite, will be able to buy and sell gold and silver in the exchange. Jewellers abroad will also be able to do the same, following certain conditions, after registering with the International Financial Services Centre Association (IFSCA).

First ice-cream company

Joy Ice Creams Pvt. Ltd, which was founded by L.C. Java, was the first company to manufacture and market ice cream. In 1948, Java bought a homogenizer and pasteurizer, and set up a small business that became India's first ice-cream company.

First tea company

- Tea seeds were first imported into India from China in 1774. In 1837, the East India Company set up the first tea estate at Chabua, Dibrugarh District, Assam.
- The Alubari Tea Company, established in 1856 in Darjeeling (now in West Bengal) under the Kurseong and Darjeeling Tea Company, first commercialized tea.

First tyre company

The Dunlop Rubber Company (India) Ltd was established on 19 August 1926, with its registered office in Bombay (now Mumbai, Maharashtra) and an authorized share capital of ₹5 million (50 lakh).

Oldest engineering company

Jessop & Company Ltd, the oldest engineering company in the country, was established in 1788 by two engineers from Britain – Henry and George Jessop.

First scooter manufacturing company

Lambretta, the first scooter introduced by Automobile Products of India (API), was manufactured in 1956.

First cotton textile mill

Though the British had established a cotton textile mill in 1817, the first truly Indian textile mill was set up in July 1854 in Bombay (now Mumbai, Maharashtra), by Cawasji N. Davar. It was called the Bombay Spinning and Weaving Company.

First foreign collaboration

Carr, Tagore and Company was the first Indo-British collaboration under the Charter Act of 1833. There were four partners: W. Carr, Dwarakanath Tagore, D.M. Gordon and William Prinsep. It closed down in 1847.

Oldest jute mill

Wellington Jute Mill in Rishra, near Serampore (now Srirampur, West Bengal), was established by George Auckland in 1855 as the Rishra Twine and Yarn Mills Ltd, with machinery bought from John Kerr of the Douglas Foundry, the leading manufacturers of flax and manufacturing machines in Dundee, Scotland. The mill had an output of eight tonnes a day. It shut down in 1868 and resumed as Calcutta Jute Mills, which later became Wellington Jute Mills. It is now under AI Champdany Industries Ltd.

First champagne manufacturer

In 1987, its very first year, Shyam Chougule's

The Indian economy has expanded just short of 6 times in less than two decades.

Taj Mahal Palace Hotel, Mumbai, Maharashtra: first five-star hotel

The Maruti 800 and the surging demand for it indicated the clear rise of a new Indian middle class.

Champagne India, a subsidiary of Indage in Narayangaon, Pune District, Maharashtra, with a 42-acre (17 hectare) vineyard, entered the export market. Champagne Indage Ltd, as it was renamed after being restructured, was the market leader in wines then, with a production of about 100,000 cases a year.

First five-star hotel

The Taj Mahal Hotel in Mumbai, Maharashtra, said to have been built back to front, was founded by Jamshetji Nusserwanji Tata in 1904. The story goes that in those days there were very few hotels that permitted entry to Indians and Tata himself had been denied admission to Pyrke's Apollo Hotel, close to the present-day Taj Mahal Hotel. This motivated Tata to build the hotel.

First plastic factories

A plastic factory was established in 1926 at Jessore, now in Bangladesh. It manufactured combs, soapboxes, ashtrays and other articles from imported celluloid sheets and rods. In 1933, two units for compression moulding were started with machinery that was imported from Germany. The first thermosetting plastic produced in India, starting in 1946, was phenol formaldehyde.

First car to be exported

Hindustan Motors Ltd's Ambassador was the first car to be exported in 1975–76 to Guyana in South America.

First retail chain for computers

Computer Point launched the country's first retail chain for computers and computer accessories by establishing the first showroom in Bombay (now Mumbai), Maharashtra, on 31 December 1984. It also had stores in other cities, like New Delhi.

First car factory

In 1928, General Motors had commenced the assembly of cars and trucks in Bombay (now Mumbai, Maharashtra) while using imported components. The first indigenous car manufacturing company was the Birlas' Hindustan Motors, which was established at Uttarpara near Calcutta (now Kolkata, West Bengal). The first Indian car, 'Hindustan 10', rolled off the assembly line in 1948.

First power loom

The first power loom for jute cloth was started in 1958 by Henderson and Company, agents of Borneo Jute Company, in present-day Baranagar, Kolkata, in West Bengal. On becoming a limited company, it was named the Baranagore Jute Manufacturing Company and had 512 looms at its peak.

WR Fastest growing tech-hub

Bengaluru, Karnataka, was declared the fastest growing tech-hub in the world, based on data analysed for the years 2016–20. The research by London and Partners, UK, released on 14 January 2021, revealed that there was a 5.4 per cent increase in investment during the specified period. Bengaluru was followed by London, Munich, Berlin, Paris and Mumbai.

First batch of microchips

The first microchips first rolled out of Semiconductor Ltd, located in Chandigarh, in March 1984.

WR India leads in the export of measles vaccines

Ninety per cent of measles vaccines in the world are supplied by India, which also supplies 65 per cent of DPT and BCG vaccines in the world.

Bengaluru, Karnataka: fastest growing tech-hub

ECONOMY AND GENERAL

Largest slum

Dharavi in Mumbai, Maharashtra, is the country's largest slum with an estimated population of between 300,000 and a million, and spread over 500 acres (202 hectares).

WR Largest share of youth

The share of India's youth in the total population, the highest in the world, is 34.8 per cent (as per the 2011 census) or 42.2 crore (422 million). The National Youth Policy defines 'youth' as persons between 15 and 29 years.

State/UT with the best performance in alleviating poverty

At the end of 2020–21, Tamil Nadu, with a score of 86, topped the chart of states/UTs on the Sustainable Development Goals (SDG) India Index for the no-poverty goal.

State/UT with the lowest score on the poverty scorecard

Bihar, with a score of 28, was the lowest-scoring state on SDG India Index's no-poverty scorecard at the end of 2020–21.

Lowest level the rupee touched

The rupee touched an all-time low of 83 against the US dollar on forex outflows on 19 October 2022.

First infrastructural index

The Government of India launched a City Liveability Index on 23 June 2017 to measure the quality of life in 116 major cities, based on a set of 79 parameters, such as the availability of roads, education, healthcare, mobility, employment opportunities, emergency response, grievance redressal, pollution, availability of open and green spaces, cultural and entertainment opportunities and so on.

First winner of the Nobel Prize in Economics

- Dr Amartya Kumar Sen (b. 3 November 1933) received the Nobel Prize in economic sciences in 1998, becoming the first Indian and Asian to do so. Born in Santiniketan, West Bengal, he is considered to be a pioneer of welfare economics.
- On 14 October 2019, Indian-origin economist Abhijit Vinayak Banerjee shared the 2019 Nobel Prize in economic sciences with his co-researchers – his wife Esther Duflo, and Michael Kremer – for their work on alleviating global poverty.

India Is the World's Fifth Largest Economy

In September 2022, according to the projections from the International Monetary Fund, India overtook the UK to become the world's fifth largest economy. Just a decade ago, India's GDP was the 11th highest in the world, but now it is behind only that of the USA, China, Japan and Germany. This coincides with the UK economy being beleaguered by rapid inflation, political turmoil, a cost-of-living crisis and the long shadow of Brexit.

Representative image

The size of the Indian economy in nominal cash terms in the quarter through March 2022 was US $854.7 billion while for the UK it was US $816 billion. Looking ahead, the IMF forecasts this as the new status quo, with India expected to leap further ahead of the UK up to 2027. Surpassing one of the biggest economies in the world, especially one that ruled over the Indian subcontinent for two centuries, is an achievement to be proud of. However, economists have pointed out that other parameters, such as the low GDP per capita, the human development index and universal health coverage, among others, need to be kept in mind for a balanced perspective in future.

Equity market

The total market capitalization of the Indian market, based on the companies listed on the Bombay Stock Exchange (BSE), was ₹28,542,454.84 crore (285.4245 trillion) on 25 November 2022.*

RETAIL

Highest number of stores opened in a single day

On 29 October 2018, the Chinese electronics company Xiaomi opened 500 retail stores, called Mi Stores, in rural regions of India, thereby setting a record for the most number of stores opened in a single day. These stores are on the lines of the larger 'Mi Home' stores in metropolitan cities.

First virtual mall

The Digital Mall of Asia is a virtual e-commerce platform, an amalgamation of digital space and real estate, making it the first virtual mall in the country. The mall is open in Delhi, Noida, Pune, Ahmedabad, Bengaluru, Chennai, Gurugram, Hyderabad, Jaipur, Lucknow and Mumbai. Each location has a

Dr Amartya Kumar Sen: first Indian winner of the Nobel Prize in economics

* The total number of companies excludes real estate investment trusts REITs), exchange-traded funds (ETFs), infrastructure investment trusts (InVITs) and differential voting rights (DVRs).

Representative image

The Rupee Plummets

The Indian rupee fell to a record low of 83 against the US dollar in October 2022. A resurgent dollar has been strengthening consistently. India imports many of its commodities, purchasing them in US dollars. If the rupee continues to depreciate, the Current Account Deficit (CAD) will continue to rise, pushing inflation in the economy and overall price rise, especially due to expensive and large-scale import of raw materials like crude oil, which form the end consumption products like petrol and diesel. The weakening rupee causes not only increased domestic fuel costs but also transportation costs, further adding to price rise in commodities.

BOMBAY  COURIER.

VOL. XXVI.] SATURDAY, NOVEMBER, 23, 1816. [NUMBER 1265.

His Majesty's Naval Yard.

Eduljee Cursetjee, WILL SELL

Bombay Theatre.

THE HEIR AT LAW.

ADVERTISEMENT.

ALGEBRA OF THE HINDUS.

Hindoostanee PHILOLOGY &c.

WORCESTER CHINA BOWL Lost.

Baxter & Co.

FOR SALE

Eduljee Cursetjee, WILL SELL.

Bombay Courier: first to carry an advertisement in an Indian language

different digital interface and e-shops can be bought or acquired on rent. The mall works 24 hours a day, seven days a week.

Biggest business deal

In August 2018, Walmart Inc., a US multinational retail corporation, announced the deal agreements that made it the largest shareholder in the Flipkart Group, an e-commerce company founded by Sachin Bansal and Binny Bansal in 2007, and based in Bengaluru, Karnataka. Walmart bought roughly 77 per cent stake in the e-retailer for around US $16 billion (approx. ₹1,000 billion then). This was India's largest acquisition and also the world's biggest purchase of an e-commerce company.

ADVERTISING

First patented brand

Horlicks, the first patented brand in the country, was launched in the last decade of the 19th century. In the 1940s, Hindustan Thompson Associates (HTA), an advertising agency, which is now J. Walter Thompson India (JWT), coined the 'Balanced Nourishment' concept for the malt-based beverage to make Horlicks more relevant to India.

First known 'advertisements'

- Advertising in India began with the first printed newspaper, called *Hicky's Bengal Gazette* and printed from the 1780s onwards in Calcutta (now Kolkata, West Bengal). The advertisements consisted of a series of simple messages 'classified' into different categories for easy reference of readers, or they were lists of the latest merchandise from England.
- The first true advertisement was printed in Marathi in the *Bombay Courier* in 1802.

First multinational advertising agencies

- Alliance Advertising was set up during the First World War (1914–18), and other foreign (American) agencies such as L.A. Stronach and D.J. Keymer followed later.
- The first fully multinational agency in the country was Hindustan Thompson Associates (now JWT) in 1926.

First full-service Indian advertising agency

In 1934, Venkatrao Sista opened Sista Advertising and Publicity Services in Bombay (now Mumbai, Maharashtra) as the first Indian agency offering creative work and space selling in the media. Sista, who came to Mumbai as a stenographer of the Great Indian Peninsular Railway, will always be

Largest LED display screen on water

associated with Khatau Voiles, popularized by his agency's campaign.

First ad association

On 21 September 1945, the Advertising Agencies Association of India (AAAI) was registered as a society in Calcutta (now Kolkata, West Bengal). In 1961, its headquarters moved to Bombay (now Mumbai).

First ad agency abroad

Interads, a Delhi-based ad agency, was the first Indian advertising agency to open a foreign branch in Moscow, Russia, in 1962.

First Indianized foreign brand

Lux toilet soap, sold as the 'favourite beauty soap of film stars', signed on Hindi cinema actor Leela Chitnis as its first Indian model in 1941, in order to Indianize the brand.

First commercials on radio

The first commercial came on Vividh Bharati in 1967.

First ads on TV

The first product to be advertised on TV was Gwalior Suitings in an advertisement that appeared in January 1976.

First colour TV ad

An advertisement made for Bombay Dyeing was the first colour TV ad in 1982, the year that colour TV came to India.

Longest sustained advertising campaign

The Amul 'utterly butterly' topical ad series is the longest sustained campaign, with its tongue-in-cheek, pithy comments on current affairs. The first ad featuring the now iconic 'Amul girl' appeared in March 1966. Started by Sylvester da Cunha in 1966 and run by da Cunha Communications, Mumbai, Maharashtra, the Amul Butter campaign has continued for more than 50 years.

Largest hoarding

A hoarding of Mumbai-based Global Advertisers was installed in Bandra in Mumbai, Maharashtra, on 24 January 2014. It measured 1,560.77 sq. m (16,800 sq. ft) by area, making it the largest in India. The 42.67 m wide and 36.58 m high (140 ft by 120 ft) front-lit hoarding overlooked the Western Express Highway, the Bandra Kala Nagar Junction and other important vantage points. It was visible from a distance of 3 km.

Largest LED display screen – on water (aboard a ship/boat/vessel)

On 21 March 2021, Zen Media Ltd LLP, a digital-first Make-in-India start-up, launched Broadcoasters, LED screens on waters in India, used as an advertising platform on a ship. The vessel *My Blue Papillon*, in the waters near the Bandra-Worli Sealink, carried a screen measuring 20 m (65.61 ft) x 5 m (16.40 ft) – with a total area of 100 sq. m (1076.39 sq. ft). The LED screen was powered with a display of 10,000 NITs (Network Interface Taps) with auto-sensors to adjust picture brightness as per daylight.

Firsts at the Cannes Lions

In 1996, the advertising fraternity bagged three awards at the International Advertising Festival in Cannes, France.

Most awards at the Cannes Lions

In 2017, India won 40 metals including a Grand Prix award.

Start-ups begin to go public. These included EaseMyTrip, Nazara, Zomato, CarTrade, Freshworks, Nykaa, Fino, Policybazaar, Paytm, RateGain and MapMyIndia. Zomato's strong listing in July welcomed a new period for start-ups.

PERFORMING ARTS

DANCE

Earliest scriptural mention of dancers

The first known textual mention of dancers can be traced back to the Rig Veda (composed between c. 1500 and 1200 BCE), which has references to mythical apsaras (divine dancers) in the story of the celestial dancer Urvashi and the mortal king Pururava.

Earliest known treatise on the performing arts

The *Natyashastra,* said to be the work of Bharata Muni, is dated variously between the second and third centuries BCE and the fourth and fifth centuries CE. It is the earliest known treatise on the performing arts. The *Natyashastra* has 37 chapters with 5,569 slokas. It is the basis of classical Indian dance, music and drama, and is often referred to as the fifth Veda.

Earliest evidence of formalized dancing

The statuette of a dancing girl from Mohenjo-daro in the Indus Valley that dates to 2500 BCE, is the earliest evidence of formal dance.

Earliest sculptures of Odissi

Sculptures depicting dancers in the Jain cave temples of Khandagiri and Udayagiri, such as the Machapuri and Hathigumpha caves (second century BCE) in present-day Odisha, show the existence of a dance form in the region, in which the dance of the *mahari*s (devadasis) formed a ritual during worship in temples. Hundreds of figures depicting dance movements are carved on the walls of the Parashurameshwara, Kapileshwara, Brahmeshwara, Mukteshwara, Rajarani and Lingaraj Temples in Bhubaneswar, Puri and Konark in Odisha, displaying the complete complex vocabulary of Odissi.

Earliest text to mention Odissi

Odissi has been traced to a dance form that prevailed in present-day Odisha and Bihar in ancient times in a region referred to as Odhra-Magadha in the *Natyashastra.* The dance was performed by devadasis (female temple dancers) called *mahari*s and male temple acolytes called *gotipua*s. It is also mentioned in Maheswar Mahapatra's *Abhinaya Chandrika* (15th–16th century CE). This dance form, which includes the *tandava* style and the *lasya* style, has its own repertoire, costumes, music and grammar.

Oldest surviving dance drama form

Mudiyettu from Kerala, now incorporated in Kathakali, is the oldest extant dance drama form, traced back to the ninth century CE.

Gita Govinda: the inspiration for Krishnanattam, the first known dance drama form

First known dance drama form

In the early 17th century, Manaveda Raja, Zamorin of Calicut (now Kozhikode), Kerala, was inspired by Jayadeva's *Gita Govinda* to compose the *Krishna Geeti* in Sanskrit. He set it to a new dance drama form known as Krishnanattam – 'the dance of Krishna'. It combined ancient theatre traditions such as Kutiyattam, ritual performances like Theyyam and folk dances like Kaikottikali.

First modern translation of the *Natyashastra*

In 1950, Manmohan Ghosh translated the *Natyashastra* into English for the Asiatic Society. This was the first successful attempt at translating the definitive text on Indian performing arts.

First English periodical on Carnatic music and dance

Sruti, a periodical on music, first published in October 1983 in Madras (now Chennai), Tamil Nadu, by P.N. Sundaresan and edited by N. Pattabhiraman, gained 30,000 readers in its very first year. It was the first known English periodical on Carnatic music and dance.

First revivalist dance school

The Kerala Kalamandalam in Trichur (now Thrissur, Kerala) was founded in 1930 by the

The Pratibha Sangam competition, a global competition for performers around the world in Indian classical music and dance, was started by the Indian Council of Cultural Relations (ICCR).

poet Vallathol Narayana Menon to re-establish Kathakali as a major regional theatre art and to revive Mohiniattam, a classical dance form from Kerala. These art forms flourished briefly under Maharaja Swathi Thirunal in the 19th century and then languished, until they were revived by Vallathol Narayana Menon.

First dance schools

- Santiniketan, which was founded in 1901 in Bolpur, Birbhum District, Bengal (now West Bengal) by Rabindranath Tagore, had a department of dance to which he invited gurus from regions as far-flung as Manipur and Kerala to live on the campus and teach their dance forms to students. Santiniketan, which later evolved into the Visva-Bharati University, now has an institute of dance, drama and music, called the Sangit Bhavan.
- Kalakshetra, a premier school for classical dance, was established in 1936 at Adyar, Madras (now Chennai), Tamil Nadu, by Indian classical dancer Rukmini Devi Arundale. Initially called the International Academy of Arts, it was renamed Kalakshetra on the suggestion of Sanskrit and Tamil scholar Pandit P.S. Subrahmanya Sastri. Its first dance production was titled *Kutrala Kuravanji*.

First classical dance to be revived

Odissi was rediscovered by dancer Indrani Rehman, who then popularized it abroad in the early 1940s, though it was recognized as a classical dance form only from the 1960s.

First modern work on dance

The book titled *Classical Indian Dance in Literature and the Arts* by scholar Dr Kapila Vatsyayan, published in 1968 by the country's premier institution of dance and music, the Sangeet Natak Akademi, was the first definitive modern work on dance, written in English. Dr Vatsyayan received the Sangeet Natak Akademi fellowship in 1970.

First national dance seminar

The Sangeet Natak Akademi held the first national seminar on dance from 30 March to 7 April 1958. Dr P.V. Rajammar was the Akademi's chairman then. The seminar's inaugural dance was performed by leading Kathak exponent Pandit Shambhu Maharaj.

First campaign for revival of Bharatanatyam

E. Krishna Iyer, a lawyer based in Madras (now Chennai, Tamil Nadu), was the first to fight the anti-nautch campaigns of the 1920s by learning the dance form Bharatanatyam in 1926 from the famous Natesa Iyer from Melattur, Kerala. For six years, he lectured and wrote for his cause, and presented devadasis in public performances outside of temples. Finally, it was with T. Balasaraswati's dance performance at the All-India Music Conference in Varanasi, Uttar Pradesh, in 1935, that the dance became accepted as a respectable art form.

First Kuchipudi dance couple to receive the Padma Shri

Raja and Radha Reddy were the first couple to receive the Padma Shri award, for a single cause, individually and together, in 1984. Widely travelled, they were responsible for popularizing the Kuchipudi form of dance in India and abroad. They also won the Padma Bhushan in 2000.

First woman to perform Chhau

Sonal Mansingh, the well-known exponent of Kuchipudi, was the first woman to learn the Chhau dance form. It is a semi-classical dance with martial, tribal and folk origins, and is found in three styles drawing their names from the region where they are traditionally performed.

First Sangeet Natak Akademi award winners for dance

T. Balasaraswati and Shambhu Maharaj won the first Sangeet Natak Akademi awards for dance in 1955 for their contribution to Bharatanatyam and Kathak respectively. The awards were instituted in 1952 to honour performing artistes.

First Sangeet Natak Akademi award for creative dance

Dance pioneer Uday Shankar was the first to be honoured by the Sangeet Natak Akademi

India's Last Living Sadir Dancer Receives Padma Shri

R. Muthukannammal (*left*)

R. Muthukannammal from Viralimalai, Tamil Nadu, is one of the last remaining women who identify with the devadasi tradition. She is a seventh-generation Sadir performer and a custodian of the art form that was later popularized as Bharatanatyam. Following a now controversial custom, devadasis were women artistes who dedicated themselves to temple establishments. In 2018, she was a recipient of the Dakshina Chitra Virudhu, an annual award given by the Madras Craft Foundation and the Friends of Dakshina Chitra, and she was also awarded the Padma Shri 2022 for her contribution to the dance form.

with an award for creative dance in 1960. Two years later, he received the Sangeet Natak Akademi fellowship. In 1971, Uday Shankar became the first modern dancer to receive the Padma Vibhushan.

First Kuchipudi solo

Vedantam Lakshminarayana Sastri (1886–1956) performed the first solo recital in the traditional dance drama form of Kuchipudi. He learnt the dance form from Sri Vempati Venkatanarayana. He also introduced the popular *tarangam* into the form, during which the dancers have to balance themselves on the edges of a thali.

First ballet film

Classical–folk fusion guru Uday Shankar's film *Kalpana,* which was released in 1948, used the ballet form for a major part of its narration, making it the country's first ballet film.

First known Kathak teacher

Pandit Birju Maharaj (1938–2022) is the first known Kathak teacher. Born in Lucknow, Uttar Pradesh, to Shri Achhan Maharaj, a Kathak exponent, he was the popular face of the dance form globally. He was invited to teach Kathak at the age of 13 at Sangeet Bharati, and later at the Bharatiya Kala Kendra, New Delhi. He received the Sangeet Natak Akademi award in 1966 and the Padma Vibhushan in 1986.

First dance theatre form recognized by UNESCO: Kutiyattam

Kutiyattam, a traditional Sanskrit performing art form originating in Kerala, is recognized by UNESCO as a 'Masterpiece of the Oral and Intangible Heritage of Humanity'. It is considered to be at least 2,000 years old and the oldest living theatre tradition globally. UNESCO usually considers only monuments and heritage sites, and this was the first art form recognized for its exceptional value. Mizhavu, a large percussion instrument, is the primary musical instrument that accompanies Kutiyattam. Considered to be sacred, Kutiyattam was traditionally performed only in temple theatres, called *koothambalam*.

First to win an international dance competition

Madame Menaka (1899–1947), whose real name was Leila Sokhey, was the first Indian to win an international dance competition, at the Berlin Dance Olympiad in July 1936. A pioneering choreographer and dancer, she set up a dance company in Bombay (now Mumbai, Maharashtra), to produce dance dramas on Indian themes. Her troupe, which featured on two days, performed Menaka's original ballet, *Deva Vijaya Nritya*, and won the first three individual prizes, along with the first prize in the competition.

First celebrity dance competition

Ten famous television couples participated in the first ever celebrity dance competition, *Nach Baliye*, on TV channel Star One. The show premiered on 11 October 2005. The judges were choreographer Saroj Khan, film-maker Farhan Akhtar and VJ-and-model Malaika Arora Khan. TV stars Sachin and Supriya Pilgaonkar were the first winners of the contest.

First Indian–European fusion

Versatile dancer Uday Shankar (1900–77), who was born in Udaipur, Rajasthan, is known as the father of modern dance in India. He combined European theatrical dance techniques with the classical and folk dance forms of India. Uday Shankar danced with Anna Pavlova, the Russian ballerina, during the 1920s and created *Hindu Wedding* as well as the duet *Radha and Krishna*, which was included in Pavlova's performance *Oriental Impressions*. In 1971, he was awarded the Padma Vibhushan, the second highest civilian award in India.

WR Thickest make-up

The *chutti*, used in Kathakali, is a three dimensional mask-like attachment made of rice paste and paper, which may extend to 15 cm (6 in.) from the face. It is the thickest make-up used in any dance form in the world.

WR Performance at the highest altitude

Shruti Gupta (b. 15 August 1987) from Solan, Himachal Pradesh, performed Kathak in freezing conditions at an altitude of 5,602 m (18,379 ft), at Khardung La, Ladakh, on 27 October 2016. The 20-minute performance, attended by Indian Army and Indo-Tibetan Border Police (ITBP) officers, was dedicated to the armed forces.

Oldest recipient of President's Award

Asan Chandu Panikkar (1873–1969), a pioneer of 20th-century Kathakali, received the President's Award in 1958 at 84 years. He danced at the award ceremony, in front of the then prime minister Jawaharlal Nehru and the then president Dr Rajendra Prasad.

Only extant pre-Vedic dances

Bhutam and Theyyam are ritual dances of Karnataka and Kerala respectively. The dancers represent local gods and ancestral spirits, based on a pre-Vedic belief system.

Madame Menaka: first to win an international dance competition

Thanjavur (or T.) Balasaraswati, a Bharatanatyam dancer from Tamil Nadu, was the first woman dancer to receive the Padma Vibhushan.

Birju Maharaj: a Synonym of Kathak

Birju Maharaj

Birjmohan Nath Mishra Maharaj, widely known as Birju Maharaj, was a Kathak maestro who died on 17 January 2022 at the age of eighty-three. His death was a deeply felt loss to the cultural world. He belonged to a well-known Kathak *gharana* and began performing the dance form as a child alongside his father. However, owing to the early demise of his father, Birju Maharaj was forced to start working at the age of 13 as a dance teacher. He migrated from his hometown Lucknow to Delhi. His fame grew slowly and steadily over the years, and he came to be known for his rhythmic fluid movements, footwork and use of expressions, so much so that his name began to embody Kathak. The etymology of the word Kathak goes back to '*katha*' (story) and Birju Maharaj did not shy away from using the dance form to comment on social issues. He was awarded the Padma Vibhushan in 1986 for his craft. He was also an accomplished classical singer and played many instruments like the tabla, the violin and the *naal*. He taught generations of Kathak students at the Bhartiya Kala Kendra and the Kathak Kendra in New Delhi.

6 artists won a Padma Award for dance in 2022.

Only pan-Indian dance text
Jayadeva's Sanskrit book of verse, the *Gita Govinda* (12th century CE), has been choreographed in all major Indian dance styles. It is sung in both Hindustani and Carnatic modes, and has been translated into many European languages.

Only dance form varied in three states
Chhau, the classical folk dance with martial overtones, has three versions based on the regions it is performed in – as Seraikela Chhau in Jharkhand (masked), Mayurbhanj Chhau in Odisha and Purulia Chhau in West Bengal.

Only dance drama performed by women alone
Kuravanji, a form of musical play popular at the beginning of the 18th century, was meant only for devadasis and was performed at the annual festivals of some temples in Tamil Nadu.

Only Asthana Nartaki
In 1978, Bharatanatyam exponent Yamini Krishnamurthy was awarded the title of 'Asthana Nartaki', meaning 'resident dancer' of Lord Venkateswara Temple, Tirupati, Andhra Pradesh.

Only classical dancer with an artificial foot
Accomplished Bharatanatyam dancer Sudha Chandran, who lost a leg in a car crash in 1981, resumed her dancing career with a prosthetic Jaipur Foot in 1984. She was rehabilitated by Dr P.K. Sethi of the Sawai Man Singh Hospital in Jaipur, Rajasthan.

Only Persianized classical dance
Kathak is a classical dance form that derives its name from the female professional storytellers or *kathikas* who recited verses from the Ramayana and the Mahabharata, along with explanatory gestures, appropriate choreography and music, as part of a system of ritualistic worship. This dance form, with its fast and intricate movements, attracted the attention of the Mughal rulers. Over time, the dance form split into two main schools: 'Temple Kathak', with its emphasis on *bhava* (or emotion), and a court dance or 'Darbari Kathak', with its focus on rhythmic display.

Largest Charadakuthi Kolkali ensemble*
Shenoy Smaraka Government Higher Secondary School and Mahadeva Gramam Kolkali Sangham, under the leadership of Gurukal K. Sivakumar, organized the largest Charadakuthi Kolkali performance with 212 participants at the school in Kannur, Kerala, on 29 December 2019. It lasted for 20 mins. The inner circle was made up of 42 participants while 64 were in the middle circle, and the outer circle had 106 participants.

Largest Margamkali ensemble*
Syro Malabar Cultural Association–Kuwait organized the largest Margamkali performance with 870 participants on 7 February 2020 at the Amateur Athletic Stadium, Kaifan, Kuwait. The performance lasted for 26 mins 30 secs. Margamkali, an Indian group dance that traces its roots to Kerala, is practised by the Saint Thomas Christians, a community of Syrian Christians from Kerala.

Largest arts festival
Soorya Festival, organized annually by the Soorya Stage and Film Society, Thiruvananthapuram, Kerala, is the largest of its kind in India, both in terms of membership and the number of activities. The festival is held across 111 days between September and

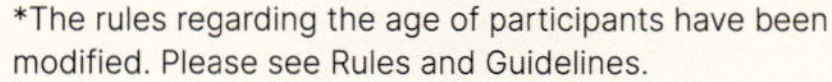
*The rules regarding the age of participants have been modified. Please see Rules and Guidelines.

INDIA AT HER BEST 75 YEARS OF INDEPENDENCE

CLASSICAL DANCE FORMS OF INDIA

Indian classical dance forms have complex histories, detailed structures and incredible uniqueness. The Sangeet Natak Akademi recognizes eight classical dance forms.

Bharatanatyam: originated in Tamil Nadu

Manipuri: originated in Manipur

Sattriya: originated in Assam

Kathak: originated in Uttar Pradesh

Odissi: originated in Odisha

Kuchipudi: originated in Andhra Pradesh

Kathakali: originated in Kerala

Mohiniattam: originated in Kerala

January each year. The 30,000-plus members of Soorya Society, founded in 1978, conduct around 200 programmes annually.

WR Largest Bharatanatyam ensemble

The Department of Tourism, Government of Tamil Nadu, organized the largest Bharatanatyam ensemble with 10,176 dancers on 8 February 2020. The event, 'Sathir 10000', which based the dance on the famous Tamil text *Thirukkural*, was held at S.I.V.E.T College in Chennai, Tamil Nadu.

Marathon performance of Ottanthullal

Jaimon V.J. (b. 10 February 1974) from Kottayam, Kerala, performed a non-stop marathon session of Ottanthullal, a dance drama form, depicting 10 stories in 12 hrs from 5:00 a.m. to 6:45 p.m. on 12 May 2019 at the Karippadavathu Temple, Uzhavoor, Kerala. The break time was 1 hr 45 mins.

MUSIC

First raga

The first raga is believed to be the Carnatic Mayamalavagowla (equivalent to the Hindustani raga Bhairavi) that Purandara Dasa (c. 1484–c. 1565), the bhakti poet and musician, also known as Adi Guru, used as the teaching scale. Called Adi Raga, it is said to have emanated from Lord Shiva.

Earliest ballad singing

Both Vedic and epic literature mentions minstrels singing *akhyanas* (texts narrated by professional storytellers), sung to the veena, in the *marga* style of singing. While the Vedas mentions both instrumental music and *akhyana* recitation in yagnas, the Ramayana (400 BCE to 200 CE) also has several references to the singing of ballads.

Earliest form of classical song

The Dhrupad, originally called Dhruvapada, was the prevailing mode of music until medieval times. While this form traces its roots to the *Natyashastra*, it was developed by Swami Haridas and the legendary singer Tansen in the 15th century.

Only multilingual classical songs

Manipravalam *kritis* are songs in the Carnatic tradition in which two or even three languages are used and the lines sung alternately in these languages, which include Tamil and Sanskrit.

Earliest Prakrit (popular) songs

The *Natyashastra* mentions *dhruvas*, i.e., songs of five different kinds that were an integral part of drama. These songs indicate the context, place and people in a scene. *Dhruvas* were originally in Prakrit and were mostly sung by a choir.

Earliest reference to musical performances

The grammarian Panini (c. fourth century BCE) in his comments on *nritya* (dancing) mentions composers of sutras on dancing. The *Pali Pitaka* (c. 300 BCE) mentions two disciples of Gautama Buddha attending one such recital.

First medieval treatise on music

The Chalukyan king, Someshvara III, who ruled in the Karnataka region in the 12th century CE, wrote the *Manasollasa*, an encyclopaedic work in Sanskrit on a variety of topics, including music, with 2,500 verses dedicated to the topic. The music section, one of the largest sections in the book, is considered the earliest treatise on music. Other well-known works on music from the period are the *Sangitaratnakara* by Sarangadeva, chief accountant of King Soddhala (r. 1210–1247 CE) of the Yadava dynasty, and a Jain work, *Sangita Samaya Sara*, by Parsvadeva (c. 13th century).

Earliest form of music

The Rig Veda has references to *saman* hymns, the earliest form of music in India. *Saman* singing is also mentioned in the *Brahmanas* as well as the Upanishads, and features as a part of spiritual observances and exercises.

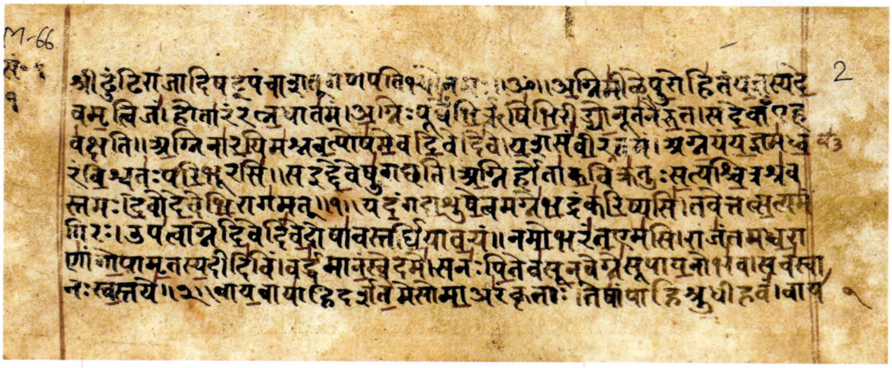

Earliest musical notes

The Sama Veda, which is believed to date to c. 1200–1000 BCE, mentions seven musical notes in *saman* singing, viz., Krushta, Prathama, Dvitiya, Tritiya, Chaturtha, Mandra/Panchama and Antya/Atisvara.

Earliest mention of raga

The term 'raga' in its modern connotation

Kathakali is said to be a combination of 5 arts: music, literature, painting, acting and dance.

Rig Veda: mentions the earliest form of music

The Sangeet Natak Akademi, based in New Delhi, was founded in this year.

appears first in the classical Sanskrit text *Brihaddeshi* by Matanga (c. eighth century CE). It is described as 'a combination of tones which, with beautiful illuminating graces, pleases people'.

First to standardize music

Purandara Dasa (1484–1564) is revered as Sangeet Pitamaha ('grandfather of music'). He standardized Carnatic music for teaching, besides classifying 35 types of tala. He pioneered a musical notation system that is still being used.

Early treatises on Carnatic music

- Rama Amatya, a royal composer at the court of King Ramaraja of Vijayanagar, gave the first detailed exposition of the Carnatic system of music in his text titled *Swaramela Kalanidhi*, around 1550 BCE. He described the first collection of ragas.
- The *Ragavibodha*, an important work on Carnatic music, was written by Somanatha, a famous scholar and poet, in 1609. It is written in masterly couplets in the Arya metre.
- Another work of the same period, the *Chaturdandi Prakashika* by Pandit Venkatamakhi gives the basis of the present-day Carnatic system of music and its raga classification.

Maharaja Swathi Thirunal: one of the earliest royal composers

Most prolific composer

Purandara Dasa (1484–1564), the philosopher-saint and bhakti poet, is credited with as many as 475,000 compositions.

Earliest royal composers of ragas

- Maharaja Swathi Thirunal (r. 1813–46), the ruler of the erstwhile princely state of Travancore (now in Kerala), created more than 400 classical compositions in both the Carnatic and Hindustani modes.
- The 25th maharaja of Mysore (now Mysuru), Karnataka, Jayachamaraja Wodeyar, who ruled from 1940 to 1950, was a 20th-century scholar, patron of arts, philosopher and an accomplished pianist. He composed 94 songs under his signature Sri Vidya and invented many new ragas.

The trinity of Carnatic music

The three prolific 18th-century composers – Thyagaraja, Muthuswamy Dikshitar and Syama Sastri – are known as the Trinity of Carnatic music as the music system is based centrally on compositions attributed to them. The compositions of Syama Sastri are known for their intricate rhythmic patterns, those of Thyagaraja for the blend of emotion and melody, and those of Dikshitar for their depiction of melodic beauty and variety.

A stamp honouring Ramanuja Iyengar: first codifier of the Carnatic concert format

First codifier of Carnatic concert format

Ariyakudi Ramanuja Iyengar (1890–1967) was the architect of modern concert Carnatic music. He pioneered the transition of the Carnatic concert from temples and courts to modern concert halls, codifying and adapting its format, order and duration. He introduced the largest number of compositions from the trinity of Thyagaraja, Muthuswamy Dikshitar and Syama Sastri to the concert repertoire, new *pallavis* (opening phrase of a song), the order of *tukkadas* (composition played towards the end of a Carnatic concert), and *padams* (other songs) that follow the main item of *ragam-thanam-pallavi*.

First fusion melody

The 14th century saw the introduction of Persian models into Indian music. Amir Khusrau (1253–1325), the famous singer at the court of Alauddin Khilji (r. 1296–1316) introduced the qawwali mode of singing, a mixture of Persian and Indian music. He also introduced the sitar, a modification of the veena.

Oldest gharana

The Gwalior gharana was founded in the 16th century by Nathan Khan Pir Bakhsh.

Oldest *sabha* for dance and music

- Sri Parthasarathy Swami Sabha at Triplicane, Madras (now Chennai, Tamil Nadu), was established in 1900.
- The Bangalore Gayana Sabha, Bangalore (now Bengaluru), Karnataka, set up on 5 August 1905, is the second oldest private cultural organization with programmes in dance and music.

Oldest south Indian stringed instrument

The *yazh*, a seven-stringed lute is mentioned in Tamil Sangam literature (first to fourth century CE), making it the oldest south Indian stringed instrument known.

Oldest known percussion instrument

The *ghatam* or mud pot, still in vogue in Carnatic concerts, is mentioned in the Ramayana. It was used in folk music for centuries and later elevated to concert status by maestro Palani Krishna Iyer (1876–1908). This tradition continued with maestros such as Kodandarama Iyer and T.H. 'Vikku' Vinayakram, who popularized it.

Oldest musical instrument

A lithophone (stone chimes comparable to a xylophone), around 3,000–4,000 years old, was identified by German archaeologists in Sankarjang Village in Angul District, Odisha. All the 20 similar-shaped polished basalt stones found possibly formed fragments of a lithophone, with excellent acoustic quality, as the edges were ground thin to achieve a specific pitch.

First mention of the drum

The *Mahajanaka Jataka* (c. second century BCE) mentions the drum, along with horns, gongs and cymbals. Two ancient Tamil books – *Purananuru* and *Pattupattu* (c. 100–200 CE) – mention the drum as occupying a position of great honour in the musical tradition of India.

Earliest musical instruments

Drums came into being during the Vedic period. The earliest drums included the *dundubhi* and *adambara*, ordinary drums; *bhumi dundubhi*, an earth drum made by digging a hole in the ground and covering it with hide; and *vanaspati*, a wooden drum. Early stringed instruments included the *skanda veena* and *karkari*, ordinary lutes; *vana*, a lute with a hundred strings; and the veena (similar to the present-day one). Wind instruments included the *tunava*, a wooden flute; the *nadi*, a reed flute; and *bakura*, whose shape is unknown.

First three-in-one classical instrument

The *mridanga veenai*, a stand-up instrument that is framed in wood and played sitting on a chair, was invented by Audanoor P. Haridass, who demonstrated it on 23 September 1984 at the Purasawalkam Arts Academy, Madras (now Chennai), Tamil Nadu. Played with bamboo sticks, it not only reproduces the sounds of percussion and strings, but also simulates the sound of cymbals used in *natuvangam* (rhythmic sound play) and the tinkle of *gajjai* (ankle bells).

Earliest use of the Carnatic veena

Govinda Dikshitar modified the Saraswati veena into the Carnatic veena to enable the playing of all ragas. He was a minister of King Raghunatha Naik of Thanjavur (r. 1614–32 CE), Tamil Nadu.

First Indian performer at the Royal Albert Hall

The first Indian singer to perform at the iconic venue, the Royal Albert Hall, in London, UK, was Bollywood playback singer Lata Mangeshkar, who gave a performance at the venue in 1974. Other Indians who have also performed here included sitar players Pandit Ravi Shankar and Anoushka Shankar, flautist Hariprasad Chaurasia and singer Shreya Ghoshal, among others.

A lithophone

First recorded song

Sashi Mukhi of Classic Theatre in Calcutta (now Kolkata, West Bengal) recorded the first song '*Kanha Jeevan Dhan*' in 1902, from the play *Srikrishna* on a 22.86 cm (9 in.), one-sided disc made by the Gramophone and Typewriter Ltd.

First gramophone record

Indian music was first produced on a gramophone record in 1898 at the Beliaghata factory of the Gramophone and Typewriter Ltd. In July 1908, the production of disc records was started at the Sealdah factory located on Beliaghata Road, Calcutta (now Kolkata), West Bengal. In 1928, the Sealdah factory was closed and building work commenced at the new factory on Jessore Road, Dum Dum, Calcutta.

First singer to be recorded on gramophone

Gauhar Jaan (1873–1930) was selected to sing when Fred Ginsberg introduced the gramophone in India with the first disc being cut in Calcutta (now Kolkata, West Bengal), in 1902. She was paid ₹3,000 for the recording session.

First gramophone company

On 7 July 1901, J. Watson Harrod opened a branch of the Gramophone Company Ltd at Calcutta (now Kolkata), West Bengal, which was further developed by T.W. Gainsberg. In 1908, the first factory to process and press records, was set up in Beliaghata, Calcutta.

Only gramophone museum

Discs and Machines – Sunny's Gramophone

The first Hindi rap album *Thanda Thanda Pani* by Baba (Harjeet Singh) Sehgal had a then record sale of 30,000 copies.

A harp

Museum and Records' Archive in Kottayam, Kerala, is a unique repository of around 110,000 records and more than 260 gramophones. Owner Sunny Matthew has been collecting them for the last 32 years and opened the museum to public on 25 January 2015. A copy of the first recorded song in India is also on display here. The museum may be visited by appointment.

First voices recorded on gramophone

The voices of Dr Harnamdas and Ahmed were recorded by the Gramophone Company in 1899 in London, UK. They sang songs based on the Ramayana and recited the *aayat*s of the Quran for the recordings.

First electronic instruments

- The first electronic tala aid called talometer was invented by M.G. Raj Narayan of Bangalore (now Bengaluru), Karnataka, in June 1978. It helps musicians to get a precise, unerring and continuous course of cycles in all the talas.
- The first electronic tanpura was also developed by M.G. Raj Narayan in December 1979. This innovative box-like device had knobs for fine tuning. Nine years after this, he developed the first electronic tabla, designed to produce the actual sounds of a tabla as played in a live performance.

First duo to introduce *jugalbandi*

Pandit Ravi Shankar and Ustad Ali Akbar Khan formed the first musical duo to introduce instrumental duets popularly known as *jugalbandi*. Shankar and Khan performed the *jugalbandi* for the first time at the debut performance of the former in 1939, with Shankar playing the sitar and Khan playing the sarod. The duo was also among the first to popularize Indian classical music abroad.

First harp player

Meagan Pandian from Mumbai, Maharashtra, is the first harp player from India and the first Indian harpist to participate in A.R. Rahman's concerts. She received the 'Young Musician of the Year' award from the Olga and Jules Craen Foundation in 2014.

First use of *shehnai* in Hindustani classical music

The *shehnai*, like the *sundari* and *surnayi*, was originally a folk instrument that was played on festive occasions. It was Bharat Ratna Ustad Bismillah Khan (1916–2006) who brought it into the realm of classical music, on par with other classical instruments.

First woman instrumentalist

Renowned sarod player Sharan Rani Backliwal (1929–2008) was a leading exponent of Hindustani instrumental music and the first female instrumentalist to give a public recital, in the 1930s. She trained under sarod maestros Baba Allauddin Khan and Ustad Ali Akbar Khan. Popularly known as Sarod Rani, she was given the Sahitya Kala Parishad award and the Sangeet Natak Akademi award for classical Hindustani instrumental music in 1974. She received the Padma Shri in 1968.

First woman *nadaswaram* player

Madurai M.S. Ponnuthayi from Madurai, Tamil Nadu, was the first professional woman player of the *nadaswaram*, long considered a male bastion. Born into a family of musicians, she was introduced to the instrument by her father. After receiving training under Natesa Pillai, she gave her first performance at the age of nine in the 1940s.

First woman *shehnai* player

Bageswari Gamar was crowned 'Shehnai Queen' at Chandigarh in 1983, the year she made her debut. A disciple of Ustad Bismillah Khan, she recorded a *jugalbandi* with the maestro, besides releasing solo cassettes. She represented India at the Bharat Mahotsav in Russia in 1988.

First woman *ghatam* player

Sukanya Ramgopal (b. 13 June 1957) from Bangalore (now Bengaluru), Karnataka, became the first woman to play the *ghatam* in the Carnatic music tradition. Born in Mayiladuthurai, Tamil Nadu, she began training in the instrument at the age of 12 years, under the guidance of T.R. Harihara Sharma and later under T.H. 'Vikku'

Ilaiyaraaja, a musician, composer, arranger, conductor, orchestrator, instrumentalist, lyricist and singer, became the first Indian to compose a Western classical symphony.

Vinayakram. Among many of her innovations are the 'Ghata Tarang', a melody created out of six *ghatams*, and the 'Sthree Taal Tarang', an all-woman percussion ensemble, experiments that have taken her to stages across India and abroad. She received the Sangeet Natak Akademi Award in 2014.

First female professional saxophone players

Sisters M.S. Lavanya and M.S. Subbalaxmi from Chennai, Tamil Nadu, have given a new dimension to Carnatic music by playing ragas on the saxophone. Daughters of mridangam exponent M.R. Sainath, the duo, called the 'Saxophone Sisters', learnt the instrument from Padma Shri Dr Kadri Gopinath. They have performed at venues such as the Soorya Festival in Thiruvananthapuram, Kerala, the Sri Thyagaraja Festival at Thiruvaiyaru, Tamil Nadu, and the Malleswaram Sangeetha Sabha, Bengaluru, Karnataka. They have also performed at the 'One City One World Festival' in Nottingham and the Bath International Music Festival in the UK.

First to perform at the UN

M.S. Subbulakshmi (1916– 2004) was the first Indian to perform at the United Nations (UN) in a concert at the UN General Assembly on UN Day, 23 October 1966. She received the Padma Bhushan in 1954, the Padma Vibhushan in 1975, and became the first musician to be awarded the Bharat Ratna in 1998. Subbulakshmi was also the first Indian musician to receive the Ramon Magsaysay Award for Public Service in 1974.

First foreign concert tour by a woman instrumentalist

According to a report in *Amrita Bazar Patrika*, dated 11 September 1912, Satyabala Devi, an 18-year-old Bengali girl, had gone to America in the summer of 1911 to play the veena. The article stated that she was the first Indian woman to have gone abroad to perform in an instrumental music concert and it was declared a great success.

First music school

Pandit Vishnu Digambar Paluskar (1872–1931) set up the Gandharva Mahavidyalaya – India's first known music school – in Lahore (now in Pakistan) on 5 May 1901. It was run on public donations and funds raised by his concerts. Another branch was opened in Bombay (now Mumbai), Maharashtra, by Pandit Vishnu Digambar Paluskar in September 1908, and Pandit Vinayakrao Patwardhan started a branch in Poona (now Pune), Maharashtra, on 8 May 1932. Later, the Lahore school was shifted to Bombay after Independence in 1947.

First to perform at an international jazz festival

Brahma Naad, a jazz band, became the first Indian band to perform at the Festival International de Jazz de Montreal in Montreal, Canada, in 2010. The band, which was founded by Louiz Banks, India's best-known jazz performer, had his son Gino on drums, Tony Lakatos on saxophone, Joe Alvares as the lead vocalist, Shelden D'Silva on bass, Bala Bhaskaran on the Carnatic violin and Sameera Koppikar as the Indian vocalist. The band played a fusion of Indian classical music and jazz.

WR Most recorded artiste

Asha Bhosle is the most recorded artiste in the history of music. Having begun her career in 1948 with the Hindi film *Chunariya*, she had recorded 11,000 solo, duet and chorus songs by 2011. In a career spanning more than six decades, she has sung in over 20 Indian and foreign languages. She received the Dadasaheb Phalke Award in 2000 and the Padma Vibhushan in 2008. She was also the first Indian singer to be nominated for the Grammy Awards.

T- series owns rights to over 35,000 audio titles and 2,000 video titles, approximately 24,000 hours of music.

Most recorded artiste: Asha Bhosle

First set of records

Renowned businessman H. Bose's Talking Machine Hall, a recording shop in Calcutta (now Kolkata), West Bengal, released the first set of phonograph records on 19 March 1906. The set featured eight songs by Rabindranath Tagore and four by D.L. Roy.

First recorded music

In the 1930s, an organization called Shining

Star Society recorded sets of discs with mythological themes. A mix of music and dialogue, the sets ran into several records. A 10-disc *Ramayana* by Saraswati Stores was very popular, followed by other drama sets: *Tukaram* (four discs), *Purandara Dasa* (five discs), *Siruthondar* (three discs) and *Thirugnana Sambandhar* (four discs). Their recording was supervised by the Katcheri set pioneer, Thuraiyur Rajagopala Sharma.

First compact disc

Pankaj Udhas's album titled *Shagufta* was the first to be formally released in a compact disc (CD) format by Music India in December 1987.

First fusion album

Violinist Yehudi Menuhin and sitar maestro Pandit Ravi Shankar collaborated on a double album called *West Meets East,* which was released in Britain in January 1967, where both played Western and Indian classical pieces alternately.

Carvaan: first portable digital audio player

WR First portable digital audio player

Carvaan, by Saregama India Ltd, is the world's first portable digital audio player with over 5,000 inbuilt songs. The songs are categorized based on singers, lyricists, music composers and moods. Using a jog dial, music stations can be selected, from Kishore Kumar classics and R.D. Burman's hits to timeless love songs and soulful Sufi tracks. Carvaan can function as an FM radio, and also has Bluetooth and USB features.

Resul Pookutty: first Asian to win the Golden Reel Award

First Asian to win the Golden Reel Award

Resul Pookutty was the first Asian to win the 63rd American Motion Picture Sound Editor's Golden Reel Award in 2016 for best sound for the documentary *India's Daughter.* A sound designer, editor and mixer who works in Hollywood and Indian cinema, he also won the Academy Award (Oscar) in 2009 for best sound mixing for the movie *Slumdog Millionaire,* along with Richard Pryke and Ian Tapp. He was awarded the Padma Shri in 2010 and the National Film Award for best audiography in the same year.

First all-woman Hindustani–Carnatic music band

Tabla soloist Anuradha Pal from Mumbai, Maharashtra, founded Stree Shakti, the first all-woman Hindustani–Carnatic music band, in 1996. It performed in India as well as other countries, including at international festivals such as BBC Music Live and Rhythm Sticks.

Grammy Award for the Best World Music Album

Music composer and tabla player Sandeep Das won a Grammy Award for the Best World Music Album in 2017 for his collaboration with Yo-Yo Ma and The Silk Road Ensemble on the album *Sing Me Home*.

Only Indian to win both an Oscar and a Grammy Award

Composer and singer A.R. Rahman won two Grammys following his Oscar wins for the soundtrack of Danny Boyle's *Slumdog Millionair*e, becoming the first Indian to win an individual Grammy. He won the first Grammy in the Best Compilation Soundtrack for a Motion Picture category. The second was for the song '*Jai Ho*' in the Best Motion Picture Song category for the same in 2009.

First Grammy Award–winning Indian percussionist

T.H. 'Vikku' Vinayakram was the first Indian percussionist to win the Grammy Award in 1991. He won it for his participation in *Planet Drum* by Mickey Hart. Vinayakram, well-known for playing the *ghatam* and popularizing Carnatic music, was honoured with the Padma Shri in 2002 and with the Padma Bhushan in 2014. He also won the Sangeet Natak Akademi fellowship in 2012.

First Indo-jazz (fusion) albums

Indo-jazz came into its own in India in the 1970s with Shakti, a group formed by jazz guitarist John McLaughlin, along with L. Shankar on the electric double violin (which he invented), Zakir Hussain on tabla and T.H. 'Vikku' Vinayakram on the *ghatam*.

First whistling LP

An album of Carnatic and Hindustani ragas entirely whistled by Siva Prasad from Hyderabad (now in Telangana) was released on 15 June 1985.

First Indian band on MTV

Rana Banerjee and Sanjoy Sengupta's band, Extinct, was the first Indian group to be featured on MTV Asia, in September 1993.

First all-girl pop music band

Channel [V], through a nationwide hunt from 12 January 2001 across 10 cities, handpicked five girls – Pratichi Mohapatra, Mahua Kamat, Neha Bhasin, Anoushka Manchanda and Seema – to constitute India's first customized all-girl band, Viva. It disbanded in 2003.

First female rapper
Taran Kaur Dhillon (b. 29 July 1979) aka Hard Kaur was the first female rapper of Indian origin. A British citizen of Indian origin, she topped the UK charts with her song, '*Ek Glassy*' in 2007. Her first solo album *Supawoman*, released the same year, had 11 tracks. She marked her Bollywood debut with the title track (which she co-wrote) of the film *Johnny Gaddaar* (2007).

First differently abled DJ
Varun Khullar aka DJ Aamish from New Delhi is the first differently abled professional disc jockey (DJ) in India. He began his career in May 2017 and is currently a resident DJ with Kitty Su, New Delhi, a part of Lalit Group and Hotels. He has performed at festivals like Time Out 72 and Greeshma Utsav.

India's only music director couple
Samir and Mana Raval from Ahmedabad, Gujarat, are India's first and only music director couple, having composed music for more than 100 songs in 35 feature films in Gujarati and Hindi. Having started with music direction for *Teenagers Gang*, a Gujarati film, in 2013, the couple continues to compose music for Hindi and other films, and TV serials and jingles.

First virtual music festival
Sunburn Home Festival, a two-day virtual music festival, was organized from 11 to 12 July 2020. The festival featured a line-up of international stars such as Bassjackers, Vini Vici and Ummet Ozcan, among others. The highlight of the event was the application of extended reality (XR) technology offering a mixed reality and holistic environment, also used for the first time.

Longest *ravanhatha*
Praveen Singh Rathore along with Shiv Pal Ram, Sugana Ram and Manwari from Jodhpur, Rajasthan, made the longest *ravanhatha*, a folk string instrument of Rajasthan. The *ravanhatha*, measuring 224 cm (7 ft 4.19 in.), was made in two weeks at Bhakrasani, Jodhpur, using bamboo, mango wood, goat leather, bull horn, iron, cotton threads, plastic threads, *baval* (babul) wood, *ghungroo* (bells) and fabric.

WR Longest innings as a conductor
Western music maestro Zubin Mehta (b. 29 April 1936) from Bombay (now Mumbai), Maharashtra, spent over 13 years as the music director and principal conductor of the New York Philharmonic Orchestra from 1978 to 1991. Currently, he is the music director of the Israel Philharmonic Orchestra.

Why Work from Home When You Can Work from a Music Museum?
The Indian Music Experience Museum (IME) at JP Nagar, Bengaluru, Karnataka, provided a work-from-museum service from April to August 2022. The pandemic prompted work from home (WFH) to become the norm. This initiative of work from museum (WFM) by the IME Museum offered people a new environment to work remotely. An area close to the open-air café was provided as a workspace for professionals. There were also indoor spaces and a couple of cubicles available for the same. People had the option to engage with the music museum and its green surrounding during their breaks. There were numerous exhibit galleries that one could visit and listen to music in different languages. The café had a capacity of 15–20 people, and charging spots and Internet were also offered at a service charge of ₹250 per day. People could also sign up for weekly, biweekly or monthly packages.

Marathon flute performance
Ananthakrishnan S.R., a flautist from Thiruvananthapuram, Kerala, played the flute for 33 hrs 36 mins, from 6:30 a.m. on 13 July to 6:30 p.m. on 14 July 2017 in Thrissur, Kerala, with a total break time of 2 hrs 24 mins.

WR Marathon qawwali performance
Haji Mohammad Idris and Mohammad Ilyas, known as the Qutbi brothers of Dargah Hazrat Qutbuddin, performed Sufi qawwali for 12 hrs. They began at 9:00 p.m. on 12 November 2016 and ended at 9:00 a.m. on 13 November 2016 at the Sangeet Natak Akademi in Delhi. Sixteen singers accompanied them.

Marathon duet singing
Venkatesh and Sangeetha Rajeshkumar from Chennai, Tamil Nadu, sang duets together for 28 hours at the Akshaya Mahalakshmi Mahal, Chennai, Tamil Nadu, during 28–29 January 2017. They sang 342 Tamil film songs from around 4:00 a.m. on 28 January and ended by

Singer Ila Arun's *Banjaran* is said to be the country's first folk album.

5 **ragas, the fountainhead of all others – Shree, Deepak, Hindol, Megh and Bhairavi – are said to have emanated from Lord Shiva's *panchamukhas*.**

12:30 p.m. the next day. The total break time was 4 hrs 30 mins.

Marathon Carnatic vocal performance

Sajna Sudheer (b. 1 August 1984) from Thiruvananthapuram, Kerala, performed a marathon Carnatic vocal recital for 37 hrs 50 mins at the Ganesham Natakakalari of Soorya Stage and Film Society. She began her performance at 3:15 a.m. on 21 January 2019 and ended at 9:15 p.m. on 22 January 2019, with a total break time of 4 hrs 10 mins.

Most people playing the harmonica together

Hindustan Petroleum Corporation Ltd, as part of its mega festival – Yuvantage BLITZ during 6–7 January 2019 – set a record for most people playing the harmonica simultaneously. The music was played by 457 of the company's employees on their harmonicas for 6 mins 17 secs on 6 January 2019 at Ramoji Film City, Hyderabad, Telangana.

Largest folk artiste gathering

Ranga Samsthana organized the largest folk artiste gathering in an event called the – 'Kannada Geet Mala', with 1,112 *bhavageethe* singers singing together at the Samsa Open Air Theatre, Bengaluru, Karnataka, on 10 January 2017. The performance was led by Bandlahalli Vijayakumar, a folk artiste and *bhavageethe* virtuoso from Bengaluru.

Most events in a day

Pernod Ricard India Pvt. Ltd organized 104 musical events on a single day – 29 November 2019. These events were held in different venues across 27 cities in the country, including Delhi, Mumbai, Pune, Chennai, Visakhapatnam and Chandigarh, among others. Titled 'Play for a Cause', this campaign raised awareness on issues such as pollution, nature, plastic use, and meals for the underprivileged. Bands and artistes including Perfect Strangers (Bengaluru), Parikrama (Gurugram), Ankur Tiwari and the Ghalat Family (Mumbai), Cherry Singh (Chandigarh) and Usha Uthup (Kolkata), among others, performed at these events.

Parikrama: one of the bands that performed during 'Play for a Cause': most events in a day

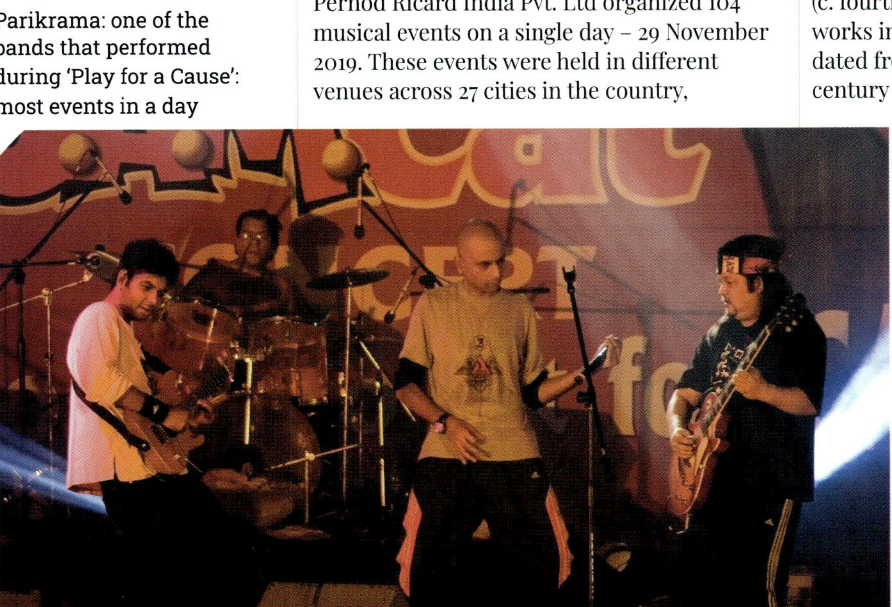

THEATRE

Oldest extant play

Palm-leaf fragments belonging to the Kushana period (around first century CE) feature a nine-act Buddhist play by Ashvaghosha, the court poet of King Kanishka, titled *Sariputra-Prakarana*. It follows all the rules for drama laid down in the *Natyashastra.*

Oldest cave theatre

The cave theatres at Sita Bengra and Jogimara in the Surguja District of Chhattisgarh are estimated to be around 3,000 years old. Sita Bengra, which pre-dates the Lomas Rishi caves of the Mauryan period (322–187 BCE), was chiefly used for dance and drama.

Early dramatic references

There are references to drama, dancing, music and acting in the Ramayana, the Mahabharata and the Puranas. Buddhist and Jain texts mention that monks were forbidden to watch dramatic performances. Panini (c. fourth century BCE) mentions dramatic works in his *Ashtadhyayi*. Patanjali (variously dated from second century BCE to the fourth century CE), describes the conditions of dramatic performers. Kautilya also refers to music, dance and drama in the *Arthashastra*.

Earliest plays

- Patanjali mentions plays such as *Kamavadha*, *Balibandhan* and *Sariputra-Prakarana* in his text *Mahabhashya* (c. third century BCE).
- Bharata also mentions plays such as *Devasura Sangrama*, *Amrita Manthana* and *Tripuradaha* in his *Natyashastra.*
- *Uparupakas* (secondary dramas) are found in the Rig Veda in the form of dialogue hymns. The most famous one tells the story of Pururava and Urvashi. Eighteen such *uparupakas* are mentioned in the *Sahitya Darpana*, a book on rhetoric and dramaturgy from the

14th century, authored by Pandit Vishwanath Kaviraj. These plays pre-date even the *Natyashastra. Uparupakas* were probably enacted before the public on royal occasions and temple festivals.

Early political plays
Mrichchhakatika by Shudraka (dated between third and fifth century CE) and Vishakhadatta's *Mudrarakshasa* (dated between late fourth and eighth century CE), both depict clashes between different powers, political intrigue, espionage and counter-espionage. They are considered to be the first plays with political themes.

Origins of social theatre
The folk theatre form of Bhavai in Gujarat is said to have been introduced in the early 15th century by Asaita Thakar, a brahmin of the Andichya clan. Legend goes that Asaita, after being ostracized for saving a lower-caste girl from dacoits, composed playlets attacking social injustice and the caste system.

Earliest playwright
Bhasa (third to fourth century CE) of the Chola era in south India is believed to be the earliest playwright. Well-known plays by him include *Abhisheka*, *Swapnavasavadattam* and *Pratimanatakam*.

Earliest street plays
Therukoothu, a theatre form originating during 200 BCE–200 CE in ancient Tamilakam, literally means 'street play'. It was performed on streets on an improvised stage with very few props and hardly any special costumes. Themes were taken from the epics. Therukoothu as well as other forms of street plays like Pallu, Kuravanji and Nandi Natakam are still performed in south India.

Oldest children's theatre
Children's Little Theatre, the oldest children's theatre in the country, was founded in Calcutta (now Kolkata), West Bengal, by Samar Chatterjee (1908–86) in May 1951. It included dance, drama, music and puppetry.

First modern Indian plays (translations)
Gerasim Lebedev, a Russian adventurer, founded the first European-style proscenium drama theatre in Calcutta (now Kolkata, West Bengal), in 1795, helped by local intellectuals. Along with his Bengali tutor, Goloknath Das, he presented the plays *The Disguise* and *Love Is the Best Doctor* on 7 November 1795. These English comedies, translated into Bengali, were the first urban theatrical performances.

First foreign translation of a Sanskrit play
Poet Kalidasa's *Abhijnana Shakuntalam* was translated into German in 1791 by revolutionary Georg Forster and into English by Anglo-Welsh philologist Sir William Jones in 1795.

First protest play
Nil Darpan, a play in Bengali about the plight of indigo farmers, was written by Dinabandhu Mitra in 1860. The play was banned by the British authorities.

Marathon *nukkad natak* performance
The Mayaar Group of the Bhopal School of Social Sciences in Bhopal, Madhya Pradesh, organized a street-play marathon to celebrate Mahatma Gandhi's 150th birth anniversary. A record was set with a team of 17 members performing 151 street plays from 5:00 a.m. on 3 March 2019 to 3:56 a.m. on 4 March

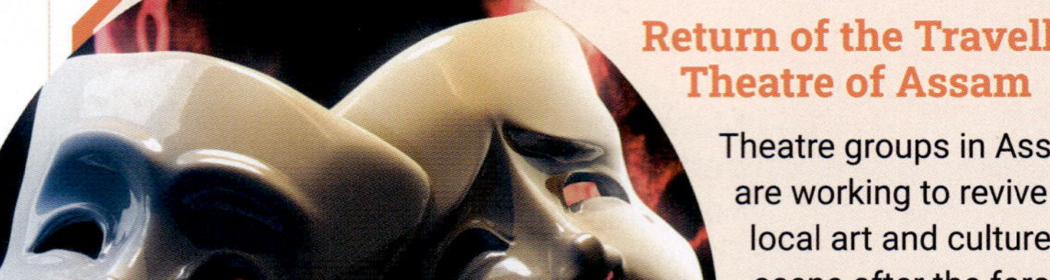

Representative image

Return of the Travelling Theatre of Assam

Theatre groups in Assam are working to revive the local art and culture scene after the forced hiatus due to COVID-19. Before the pandemic, around 50 theatre groups constituted the travelling theatre movement with nearly 150 people. They would travel all through the state, starting from September and ending in April. After nearly two years of the gap, seven roving theatre companies are back to performing for crowds in 2022. The groups travel with directors, actors, dancers, singers and technicians along with all the stage infrastructure. They perform three shows at one location before moving on to the next. The response to this revival has been great as travelling theatre has always been a big part of local entertainment in Assam. The Awahan Theatre is among the well-known theatre groups to have resumed performances. A key feature of Awahan Theatre's performances is the diverse themes they cover. They do not restrict their performances to depicting stories from only the Indian subcontinent but cover classical Greek tragedies, Shakespearean tales and turning-point subjects such as the attack on the World Trade Center in the USA in 2001.

Mahendravarman Pallava, a king of 7th century CE, was known to be a good player of the *parivadini* veena.

2019 at different locations in the city. The performance time added up to 21 hrs 34 mins, with a break time of 2 hrs 26 mins. The plays conveyed the importance of the Swachh Bharat Mission of the Government of India.

First dramatic club

The first dramatic club was the Parsi Natak Mandali established in 1853 in Bombay (now Mumbai), Maharashtra. They performed their first play *Roostum Zabooli and Sohrab* that year, followed by *King Afrasiab and Rustom Pehlvan* and *Padshah Faredun*. Other Parsi theatre clubs were the Elphinstone, established in 1860, and the Victoria, established in 1867. These drama clubs inspired Gujarati theatre.

First public theatre hall

The Star Theatre in Calcutta (now Kolkata), West Bengal, was inaugurated on 21 July 1883 with the play *Daksha Yajna*. Among the first to produce plays here was acclaimed playwright, novelist, theatre director and actor Girish Chandra Ghosh. The theatre shifted to its present site on Bidhan Sarani in 1888 and now mainly functions as a cinema hall with plays also being staged.

Star Theatre, Kolkata: first public theatre hall

First commercial theatre

The first commercial Parsi theatre, started by Pestonji Framji in 1870, was the first aimed at commercialized mass entertainment, while dealing with social problems. Though based in Bombay (now Mumbai), Maharashtra, the theatre company travelled widely all over north India.

First and only play on Broadway and West End

The Ramayana by Gopal Sharman, enacted in a one-woman tour de force by Jalabala Vaidya, was played at the Barbizon Plaza Theatre, Manhattan, New York, in February 1975. The play was also performed at other venues, such as the Smithsonian Institution, Washington DC, and the United Nations headquarters, New York, USA, and Sedler's Wells Theatre, London, UK.

First full-fledged opera

The Fakir of Benares, an Indo-French opera was staged at the Siri Fort Auditorium, New Delhi, on 27 February 2002. The opera was directed by Muzaffar Ali while his wife Meera Ali designed the costumes.

First Marathi musical

Shakuntala was staged as a Sangeet play on 31 October 1880 by Balwant Pandurang 'Annasaheb' Kirloskar and his Kirloskar Natak Mandali. Written in Marathi, it featured simple songs. This format was followed by Marathi stage in the musical drama genre called Sangeet plays. It attracted giants like Bal Gandharva (Narayanrao Rajahansa) and Keshavrao Bhonsle.

First opera in English by an Indian

Well-known author Vikram Seth's *Arion and the Dolphin*, which premiered in the UK in June 1994, was the first opera written in English by an Indian. Commissioned by the English National Opera, it was performed at the 964-seat drill shed of HMS *Drake*, a high-security naval base. The opera was directed by Rebecca Meitlis.

Only national institute for theatre training

The National School of Drama (NSD), set up by the Sangeet Natak Akademi in 1959, became autonomous in 1975.

Play performed in most languages – single day

Yugpurush – Mahatma's Mahatma, a two-hour play based on the relationship between Mahatma Gandhi and his spiritual guide, Shrimad Rajchandra-ji, was performed in five languages, viz., English, Hindi, Bengali, Gujarati and Tamil, on 11 August 2017. It was organized by the Shrimad Rajchandra Mission in Dharampur, Valsad District, Gujarat, as one of the 808 performances for the 150th birth anniversary celebrations of Shrimad Rajchandra-ji.

WR Most theatrical performances

The Gujarati stage actor Pransukhlal Nayak (1910–89) had 22,455 theatrical performances to his credit by December 1986. He had played 241 roles in stage productions in a career he started at the age of nine.

WR Longest play*

The Mayaar Group of the Bhopal School of Social Sciences, Bhopal, Madhya Pradesh, organized the longest play, titled *Katha-e-Hind: The Journey of India*, which lasted for 48 hrs 29 mins 6 secs. Sixty artistes performed from 12:47 p.m. on 29 February 2020 to 1:16 p.m. on 2 March 2020. The play depicted the history of India from the Harappan civilization right up to the country's independence.

Asia's biggest theatre festival

Bharat Rang Mahotsav, the annual theatre festival of the National School of Drama (NSD), is the biggest theatre festival in Asia. Established in 1999, the Bharat Rang Mahotsav includes theatre groups from around the world. The 20th edition of the Bharat Rang Mahotsav concluded in February 2019 and featured 111 national and international acts including folk theatre, plays by groups invited for this, and plays by NSD students.

Most performances as a personality – stage and screen

Deepak Madhukant Antani (b. 20 August 1964) from Ahmedabad, Gujarat, is a professional actor who has performed the most times as Mahatma Gandhi on screen and stage. His maiden venture enacting the role of the Mahatma was on 20 June 2000 in *Sardar Patel*, a play written by him for Sardar Vallabhbhai Patel's 125th birth anniversary celebrations. As a Gandhi lookalike he has performed in one advertisement, two feature films, 21 short films, one TV serial, 190 stage plays, three documentaries, four voice-overs and a 200 km *padyatra* completed in nine days.

Most performances as a character – (mythological) stage

V.S. Narayanan (b. 20 November 1943) from Bombay (now Mumbai), Maharashtra, has been performing the role of Hanuman for the annual Ramnavami festival held by the Mulund Bhajana Samaj, Mumbai, since 1967. He has performed each year for 53 years.

Most media elements used in a live act

ITANT, a creative media and events business based in Pune, Maharashtra, organized a multimedia show, with six elements, titled *Main Hoon NDA*, on 29 November 2019 from 7:05 p.m. to 8:00 p.m. The show used lights, sounds, laser, video, pyrotechnics and 3D mapping, along with live acts. The show was pre-programmed and played on one-touch synchronization on the Sudan Block, the administrative building of the National Defence Academy, Khadakwasla, Pune.

Longest-serving director of the NSD

Ebrahim Alkazi (1925–2020) was appointed as the second director of the National School of Drama (NSD) in 1962 and served till 1977.

First recipient of the Kalidas Samman (theatre)

Shombhu Mitra (1915– 1997) from Kolkata, West Bengal, was the first recipient of the Kalidas Samman for his contribution to Bengali theatre.

Badal Sircar (1925 –2011) from Kolkata, West Bengal, introduced a new form of political theatre called the 'third' theatre and formed the first known Indian theatre group called 'Satabdi'.

Main Hoon NDA: most media elements used in a live act

*The rules regarding the age group of participants have been changed. Please see Rules and Guidelines.

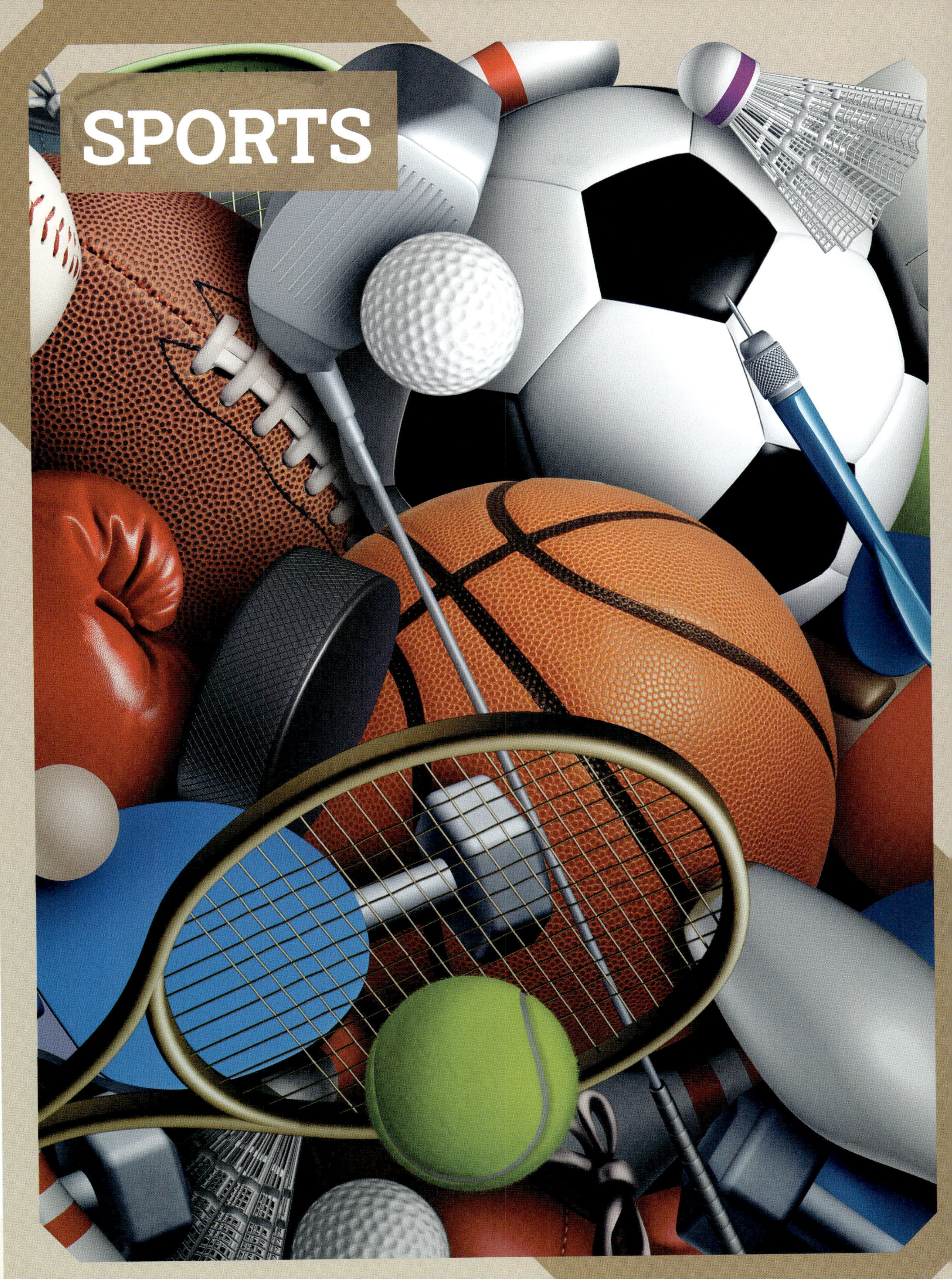
SPORTS

GENERAL

First Indian president of the International Cricket Council

Jagmohan Dalmiya became the first Indian president of the International Cricket Council (ICC) in 1997 and served till 2000.

First Indian chairman of the ICC

N. Srinivasan was the first ICC chairman from India (2014–15).

First Indian independent chairman of the ICC

Shashank Manohar was the first independent chairman of the International Cricket Council in 2016 and he was re-elected for another two years.

First Indian president of the World Squash Federation

Indian squash administrator Narayana Ramachandran was president of the World Squash Federation (WSF) for two terms, from 2008 to 2016.

First Indian president of the International Kabaddi Federation

Sports administrator Janardan Singh Gehlot was the founder president of the International Kabaddi Federation from 1985 to 2013, and then life president from May 2013.

First Indian on the Federation Internationale de Football Association (FIFA) executive panel

Praful Patel, president, All India Football Federation, and senior vice president, Asian Football Confederation, was the first Indian to be elected to the FIFA Executive Council in April 2019.

First Indian to become a FIFA World Cup match commissioner

Former All India Football Federation president Priya Ranjan Dasmunsi was the match commissioner in a FIFA World Cup 2006 game, a group stage match between Australia and Croatia.

First Indian woman to be a member of International Olympic Committee's (IOC) Athletes' Commission

In October 2016, badminton player Saina Nehwal was appointed a member of the IOC's Athletes' Commission.

First sportsman to be nominated to the Rajya Sabha

Wrestler Dara Singh was the first sportsman to be nominated to the Rajya Sabha, the Upper House of the Indian Parliament, in 2003. He was the world champion of a kind of exhibition wrestling.

First sportsperson to be awarded the Padma Shri

Triple Olympian gold medallist Balbir Singh (senior) (1924–2020) became the first sportsperson to be awarded the Padma Shri in 1957. The versatile centre forward played a key role in India's victories in the Olympics in 1948 in London, in 1952 in Helsinki and in 1956 in Melbourne.

First woman sportsperson to receive the Padma Vibhushan

Boxer M.C. Mary Kom was honoured with the Padma Vibhushan in 2020. She is the fourth sportsperson in the country to receive the award after chess wizard Viswanathan Anand, mountaineer Edmund Hillary (posthumous) and cricket icon Sachin Tendulkar, who all received the award in 2008.

First sportsperson to receive an honorary doctorate degree

- *Man:* The Lakshmibai Institute of Physical Education, Gwalior, Madhya Pradesh, conferred an honorary doctorate degree on former shooter Raja Randhir Singh on 8 September 2000. He represented India in six Olympic Games in Tokyo (1964), Mexico City (1968), Munich (1972), Montreal (1976), Moscow (1980) and Los Angeles (1984).
- *Woman:* Kannur University, Kannur, Kerala, conferred an honorary doctorate degree on ace athlete P.T. Usha on 1 November 2000 for her contribution to athletics.

Saina Nehwal: first Indian woman to become a member of IOC's Athletes' Commission

The country's highest sporting honour, the Rajiv Gandhi Khel Ratna, was renamed after hockey legend Major Dhyan Chand by Prime Minister Modi. The award was launched in 1992.

She represented India in four Olympic Games, five Asian Games and five Asian Championships. She also won the most medals ever by an Indian athlete at the Jakarta Asian Championships in 1985, with five gold medals and a bronze medal.

First sportsman and coach to receive an honorary doctorate degree

The Indian Institute of Technology, Kanpur, Uttar Pradesh, bestowed an honorary doctorate degree on former badminton sports star and chief Indian coach Pullela Gopichand on 28 June 2019 in recognition of his contribution to badminton. The second Indian to win the All England Open Badminton Championships in 2001, he switched to coaching and launched his academy in Hyderabad, Telangana, in 2008.

First woman to head a state cricket association

Rupa Gurunath became the first woman president of the Tamil Nadu Cricket Association (TNCA), a BCCI State Association, on 27 September 2019 and was to be in office for a term of three years.

First book on India's football journey

The first comprehensive book on football in India, *Barefoot to Boots: The Many Lives of Indian Football*, covering the sport from 1888 to 2017, was written by sportswriter and broadcaster Novy Kapadia in 2018. The first book on Indian football was *Stories from Indian Football* by Jaydeep Basu in 2003.

First sports magazine

Bengal Sporting was first published in 1837 and edited by British journalist Joachim Hayward Stocqueler.

First sweep in the Asian Para Games

At the 2018 Asian Para Games, Indian para athletes occupied all three positions in high jump when Sharad Kumar (1.90 m), Varun Bhati (1.82 m) and Thangavelu Mariyappa (1.67 m) got the gold, silver and bronze medals respectively, in the T-42/63 category (lower limb deficiency, leg length difference, impaired muscle power and impaired range of movement).

First Indian woman to participate in the World Transplant Games

Reena Raju (b. 4 December 1982) from Bengaluru, Karnataka, was the flag bearer in the opening ceremony at the World Transplant Games 2017 in Malaga, Spain. She represented India in the 100 m sprint and badminton mixed doubles. She was the first Indian to undergo a repeat heart transplant on 22 October 2017 at Frontier Lifeline Hospital, Chennai, for cardiac allograft vasculopathy.

First recipient of the Olympic Order (Gold)

The Olympic Order (Gold), the highest award of the Olympic movement, is given for distinguished contribution to the movement. Former Indian prime minister Indira Gandhi was its first recipient in 1983. The Olympic Order is also awarded in silver and bronze categories.

First international rugby 15s win

The Indian women's rugby team scripted history by clinching their first ever international 15s victory against a higher ranked Singapore for a bronze medal in the Asian women's Division 1Rugby 15s Championship 2019.

First to win a world title in motorsport

Aishwarya Pissay from Bengaluru, Karnataka, became the first Indian to win a world title in motorsport. She won the Federation Internationale de Motocyclisme (FIM) Bajas World Cup (women's category) with 65 points on 13 August 2019 in Varpalota, Hungary. She won the first round in Dubai, UAE, was placed third in Portugal, fifth in Spain and fourth in Hungary.

First fencer to qualify for the Olympics

C.A. Bhavani Devi became the first Indian fencer to qualify for the 2020 Tokyo Olympics on 14 March 2021 at the Women's Sabre World Cup in Budapest, Hungary. Chennai-based Devi secured her slot through the Asia/Oceania Zone of the Adjusted Official Ranking (AOR).

Best performance in the Asian Games

India participated in the 2018 Asian Games in Jakarta and Palembang, Indonesia (from 18 August to 2 September) and had the best ever haul with 69 medals, including 15 gold, 24 silver and 30 bronze medals from 465 events. After 67 years, since the inaugural edition of the Games in Delhi in 1951, India matched its best haul of 15 golds.

Best performance in the Asian Para Games

Indian para athletes won 72 medals in the 2018 Asian Para Games in Jakarta, Indonesia, bagging 15 golds, 24 silvers and 33 bronzes.

Best performance in the South Asian Games

India bagged 174 gold, 93 silver and 45 bronze medals in the 13th South Asian Games 2019 in Kathmandu, Nepal.

Best performance in the Commonwealth Games

India's best performance by number of medals was in the 2010 CWG held in New Delhi, when India won 101 medals in all.

Best performance in the Olympic Games

India capped off its best-ever performance in the 2020 Tokyo Olympics with a haul of seven medals, including a gold (athletics), two silver and four bronze medals.

Most national awards

- *Woman:* Six-time world champion M.C. Mary Kom was the recipient of the Arjuna Award in 2003, the Rajiv Gandhi Khel Ratna Award in 2008–09, the Padma Shri in 2006, the Padma Bhushan in 2013 and the Padma Vibhushan in 2020.
- *Man:* The second Indian to win the All England Open Badminton Championships in 2001, Pullela Gopichand was the recipient of the Arjuna Award in 1999, the Rajiv Gandhi Khel Ratna Award in 2000–01, the Dronacharya Award in 2009, the Padma Shri in 2005 and the Padma Bhushan in 2014.

Youngest Commonwealth Games captain

Seventeen-year-old Prachi Tehlan was the youngest captain representing India in netball at the 2010 Commonwealth Games, New Delhi.

Youngest to receive the Padma Bhushan

Badminton player P.V. Sindhu, at 24 years, became the youngest sportsperson to receive the Padma Bhushan in 2020. Sindhu is the third badminton player to be awarded the honour after Pullela Gopichand received it in 2014 and Saina Nehwal in 2016.

M.C. Mary Kom: sportswoman to receive the most national awards

Pullela Gopichand: sportsman (and coach) to receive the most national awards

Best Performance in the Olympics

INDIA AT HER BEST 75 YEARS OF INDEPENDENCE

The nation sent its largest-ever contingent of 126 players to the 2020 Tokyo Olympics Games. The 2020 Summer Olympics were the most successful Games for India since its first regular Olympics appearance in 1920, with Indian Olympians winning seven medals (one gold, two silver and four bronze medals) and Paralympians winning 19 medals across disciplines. Neeraj Chopra won gold in the men's javelin throw with his best throw of 87.58 m); Saikhom Mirabai Chanu lifted 202 kg to become the second Indian to win a gold in weightlifting after Karnam Malleswari; Ravi Kumar Dahiya became the fifth Indian wrestler after K.D. Jadhav, Sushil Kumar, Yogeshwar Dutt and Sakshi Malik to reach the podium, followed by Bajrang Punia; P.V. Sindhu became a double medallist at the Olympics; Lovlina Borgohain became only the third Indian boxer with an Olympic medal; and the men's hockey team won a medal after 41 years, in a thrilling 5-4 victory against Germany in the bronze medal play-off.

SUMMER OLYMPICS MEDAL TALLY

Medal	Winners	Sport	Event	Date
1 Gold	Neeraj Chopra	Athletics	Men's javelin throw	7 August
2 Silver	Saikhom Mirabai Chanu	Weightlifting	Women's 49 kg	24 July
2 Silver	Ravi Kumar Dahiya	Wrestling	Men's freestyle 57 kg	5 August
3 Bronze	P. V. Sindhu	Badminton	Women's singles	1 August
3 Bronze	Lovlina Borgohain	Boxing	Women's welterweight	4 August
3 Bronze	Men's national field hockey team Dilpreet Singh, Rupinder Pal Singh, Surender Kumar, Manpreet Singh (C), Hardik Singh, Gurjant Singh, Simranjeet Singh, Mandeep Singh, Harmanpreet Singh, Lalit Upadhyay, P.R. Sreejesh, Sumit, Nilakanta Sharma, Shamsher Singh, Varun Kumar, Birendra Lakra, Amit Rohidas, Vivek Prasad	Field hockey	Men's tournament	5 August
3 Bronze	Bajrang Punia	Wrestling	Men's freestyle 65 kg	7 August

COMMONWEALTH GAMES 2022

The 2022 Commonwealth Games took place in Birmingham, UK, between 28 July and 8 August 2022. Nearly 200 Indian athletes competed in the event, winning 61 medals: 22 golds, 16 silvers and 23 bronzes, out of which eight medals were won in athletics. It was India's 18th appearance at the Commonwealth Games and its fifth best yet in terms of the number of medals.

Year	1934	1938	1954	1958	1970	1974	1978	1982	1990	1994	1998	2002	2006	2010	2014	2018	2022
Venue	London, UK	Sydney, Australia	Vancouver, Canada	Cardiff, UK	Edinburgh, UK	Christ Church, New Zealand	Edmonton, Canada	Brisbane, Australia	Auckland, New Zealand	Victoria, Canada	Kuala-Lumpur, Malaysia	Manchester, UK	Melbourne, Australia	New Delhi, India	Glasgow, UK	Gold Coast, Australia	Birmingham, UK
Gold	0	0	0	2	5	4	5	5	13	6	7	30	22	39	15	26	22
Silver	0	0	0	1	3	8	5	3	8	12	10	22	17	26	30	20	16
Bronze	1	0	0	0	4	3	5	8	11	7	8	17	10	36	19	20	23
Total	1	0	0	3	12	15	15	16	32	25	25	69	49	101	64	66	61

TOP TEN MEDALS TALLY

Commonwealth Games 2022: Overall Medal Tally

Rank	Country	Gold	Silver	Bronze	Total
1	Australia	67	57	54	178
2	England	57	66	53	176
3	Canada	26	32	34	92
4	India	22	16	23	61
5	New Zealand	20	12	17	49
6	Scotland	13	11	27	51
7	Nigeria	12	9	14	35
8	Wales	8	6	14	28
9	South Africa	7	9	11	27
10	Malaysia	8	8	8	24

INDIAN MEDALS

Athletics

Athletes	Event	Medal	Date
Eldhose Paul	Men's Triple Jump	GOLD	7 August
Abdulla Aboobacker	Men's Triple Jump	SILVER	7 August
Avinash Sable	Men's 3000 m Steeplechase	SILVER	6 August
Priyanka Goswami	Women's 10 km Race Walk	SILVER	6 August
Murali Sreeshankar	Men's Long Jump	SILVER	4 August
Tejaswin Shankar	Men's High Jump	BRONZE	3 August
Annu Rani	Women's Javelin Throw	BRONZE	7 August
Sandeep Kumar	Men's 10 km Race Walk	BRONZE	7 August

Badminton

Athletes	Event	Medal	Date
P.V. Sindhu	Women's Singles	GOLD	8 August
Lakshya Sen	Men's Singles	GOLD	8 August
Satwiksairaj Rankireddy and Chirag Shetty	Men's Doubles	GOLD	8 August
K. Srikanth, Satwiksairaj Rankireddy, B. Sumeeth Reddy, Lakshya Sen, Chirag Shetty, Treesa Jolly, Aakarshi Kashyap, Ashwini Ponnappa, Gayatri Gopichand, P.V. Sindhu	Mixed Team	SILVER	2 August
Treesa Jolly and Gayatri Gopichand	Women's Doubles	BRONZE	7 August
K. Srikanth	Men's Singles	BRONZE	7 August

Boxing

Athletes	Event	Medal	Date
Nikhat Zareen	Women's 50 kg	GOLD	7 August
Nitu Ghanghas	Women's 48 kg	GOLD	7 August
Amit Panghal	Men's 51 kg	GOLD	7 August
Sagar Ahlawat	Men's +92 kg	SILVER	7 August
Rohit Tokas	Men's 67 kg	BRONZE	6 August
Jaismine Lamboriya	Women's 60 kg	BRONZE	6 August
Mohammed Hussamuddin	Men's 57 kg	BRONZE	6 August

Hockey

Athletes	Event	Medal	Date
Manpreet Singh, Harmanpreet Singh, Jarmanpreet Singh, Abhishake Nain, Surender Kumar, Hardik Singh, Gurjant Singh, Mandeep Singh, Krishan Bahadur Pathak, Lalit Kumar Upadhyay, P.R. Sreejesh, Nilakanta Sharma, Shamsher Singh, Varun Kumar, Akashdeep Singh, Amit Rohidas, Jigraj Singh, Vivek Sagar Prasad	Men's Hockey	SILVER	8 August
Savita Punia, Gurjit Kaur, Deep Grace Ekka, Monika, Sonika, Sharmila Devi, Nikki Pradhan, Rajani Etimarpu, Sangita Kumari, Nisha, Vandana Katariya, Udita, Lalremsiami, Jyoti, Navneet Kaur, Sushila Chanu Pukhrambam, Salima Tete, Neha Goyal	Women's Hockey	BRONZE	7 August

Table Tennis and Para Table Tennis

Athletes	Event	Medal	Date
A. Sharath Kamal and Sreeja Akula	Mixed Doubles	GOLD	7 August
A. Sharath Kamal, G. Sathiyan Harmeet Desai, Sanil Shetty	Men's Team	GOLD	2 August
Bhavina Patel (para)	Women's Singles Classes 3-5	GOLD	6 August
A. Sharath Kamal	Men's Singles	GOLD	8 August
A. Sharath Kamal and G. Sathiyan	Men's Doubles	SILVER	7 August
G. Sathiyan	Men's Singles	BRONZE	8 August
Sonal Patel (para)	Women's Singles Classes 3-5	BRONZE	6 August

Cricket

Athletes	Event	Medal	Date
Harmanpreet Kaur, Smriti Mandhana, Taniya Bhatia, Yastika Bhatia, Harleen Deol, Rajeshwari Gayakwad, Sabbineni Meghana, Sneh Rana, Jemimah Rodrigues, Deepti Sharma, Meghna Singh, Renuka Singh Thakur, Pooja Vastrakar, Shafali Verma, Radha Yadav	Cricket T20	SILVER	7 August

Judo

Athletes	Event	Medal	Date
Shushila Devi Likmabam	Women's 48 kg	SILVER	1 August
Tulika Maan	Women's +78 kg	SILVER	3 August
Vijay Kumar Yadav	Men's 60 kg	BRONZE	August

Lawn Bowls

Athletes	Event	Medal	Date
Lovely Choubey, Rupa Rani Tirkey, Naynmoni Saikia, Pinki	Women's Fours	GOLD	2 August
Chandan Kumar Singh, Dinesh Kumar, Navneet Singh, Sunil Bahadur	Men's Fours	SILVER	6 August

Para Powerlifting

Athletes	Event	Medal	Date
Sudhir	Men's Heavyweight	GOLD	4 August

Squash

Athletes	Event	Medal	Date
Saurav Ghosal	Men's Singles	BRONZE	
Dipika Pallikal Karthik and Saurav Ghosal	Mixed Doubles	BRONZE	7 August

Para Weightlifting

Athletes	Event	Medal	Date
Saikhom Mirabai Chanu	Women's 49 kg	GOLD	30 July
Jeremy Lalrinnunga	Men's 67 kg	GOLD	31 July
Achinta Sheuli	Men's 73 kg	GOLD	31 July
Sanket Sargar	Men's 55 kg	SILVER	30 July
Bindyarani Devi	Women's 55 kg	SILVER	30 July
Vikas Thakur	Men's 96 kg	SILVER	2 August
Gururaja Poojary	Men's 61 kg	BRONZE	30 July
Harjinder Kaur	Women's 71 kg	BRONZE	1 August
Lovepreet Singh	Men's 109 kg	BRONZE	3 August
Gurdeep Singh	Men's 109+ kg	BRONZE	3 August

Weightlifting

Athletes	Event	Medal	Date
Saikhom Mirabai Chanu	Women's 49 kg	GOLD	30 July
Jeremy Lalrinnunga	Men's 67 kg	GOLD	31 July
Achinta Sheuli	Men's 73 kg	GOLD	31 July
Sanket Sargar	Men's 55 kg	SILVER	30 July
Bindyarani Devi	Women's 55 kg	SILVER	30 July
Vikas Thakur	Men's 96 kg	SILVER	2 August
Gururaja Poojary	Men's 61 kg	BRONZE	30 July
Harjinder Kaur	Women's 71 kg	BRONZE	1 August
Lovepreet Singh	Men's 109 kg	BRONZE	3 August
Gurdeep Singh	Men's 109+ kg	BRONZE	3 August

Wrestling

Athletes	Event	Medal	Date
Bajrang Punia	Men's 65 kg	GOLD	5 August
Sakshi Malik	Women's 62 kg	GOLD	5 August
Deepak Punia	Men's 86 kg	GOLD	5 August
Ravi Kumar Dahiya	Men's 57 kg	GOLD	6 August
Vinesh Phogat	Women's 53 kg	GOLD	6 August
Naveen Kumar	Men's 74 kg	GOLD	6 August
Anshu Malik	Women's 57 kg	SILVER	5 August
Divya Kakran	Women's 68 kg	BRONZE	5 August
Mohit Grewal	Men's 125 kg	BRONZE	5 August
Pooja Gehlot	Women's 50 kg	BRONZE	5 August
Pooja Sihag	Women's 76 kg	BRONZE	5 August
Deepak Nehra	Men's 97 kg	BRONZE	5 August

MEDAL COUNT

COMMONWEALTH GAMES, BIRMINGHAM 2022: MEDAL TALLY BY SPORT

Sport	Gold	Silver	Bronze	Total
Wrestling	6	1	5	12
Weightlifting	3	3	4	10
Athletics	1	4	3	8
Boxing	3	1	3	7
Table Tennis	4	1	2	7
Badminton	3	1	2	6
Judo (W)	0	2	1	3
Lawn Ball	1	1	0	2
Hockey	0	1	1	2
Squash	0	0	2	2
Powerlifting	1	0	0	1
Cricket T-20 (W)	0	1	0	1
Total	22	16	23	61

INDIA'S BEST 5 PERFORMANCES IN THE COMMONWEALTH GAMES

Year	Gold	Silver	Bronze	Total	Place
2010	39	26	36	101	New Delhi, India
2002	30	22	17	69	Manchester, UK
2018	26	20	20	66	Gold Coast, Australia
2014	15	30	19	64	Glasgow, UK
2022	22	16	23	61	Birmingham, UK

Members of the Commonwealth Games contingent with Prime Minister Narendra Modi

ATHLETICS

INTERNATIONAL

First Indian elected to the International Association of Athletics Federations (IAAF) Council
Adille J. Sumariwalla was elected to the IAAF (now World Athletics) Council at the IAAF Congress in 2015.

First Olympic marathoner
Phadeppa Dareppa Chaugule represented India in the 1920 Antwerp Olympic Games. He finished 19th in 2 hrs 50 mins 45.2 secs.

First women at the Olympics
Mary D'Souza and Nilima Ghose participated in the 1952 Helsinki Olympics. They were both eliminated in the heats of the 100 m and 200 m races, and 80 m and 100 m hurdles, respectively.

First woman captain
Shiny Wilson captained the Indian athletes' contingent at the 1992 Olympic Games in Barcelona, Spain.

First international medal in a marathon – women
Asha Agarwal won the Hong Kong Marathon on 27 January 1985. She later won the Asian track and field gold at Jakarta, Indonesia, in 1985, and the Trinidad Marathon in 1986.

First World Championship medal
Anju Bobby George won a bronze in long jump at the 2003 World Championship in Paris, France, in August, with a leap of 6.70 m. She surpassed this at the 2004 Olympics in Athens, Greece, finishing sixth with 6.83 m.

First double gold at the Asian Games
Seven Indian athletes have won at least two golds each in a single Asian Games event:

- Lavy Pinto: 100 m and 200 m races in Delhi (1951).
- Parduman Singh Brar: Shot put and discus throw in Manila, Philippines (1954).
- Milkha Singh: 200 m and 400 m in Tokyo, Japan (1958), and the 400 m and 4 x 400 m relay races in Jakarta, Indonesia (1962).
- Hari Chand: 5,000 m and 10,000 m races in Bangkok, Thailand (1978).
- P.T. Usha: Four golds and one silver in Seoul, South Korea (1986).
- Jyotirmoyee Sikdar: Two golds (800 m and 1,500 m) in Bangkok, Thailand (1998).
- Ashwini Chidananda Akkunji: Women's 400 m hurdles and 4 x 400 m relay race in Guangzhou, China (2010).

First Asian Games medals –women
In the 1951 Asian Games in Delhi, Roshan Mistry won the silver in the 100 m race, while Mary D'Souza (200 m) won a bronze. The women's 4 x 100 m relay team of Nilima Ghose, Stephie D'Souza, Mary D'Souza and Roshan Mistry also won a silver.

First Asian Games gold – men – individual
Ranjit Singh won a gold in the 800 m marathon on 8 March 1951 at Delhi, clocking 1 hr 59 mins 3 secs. Indian men won 10 golds in this edition of the Asian Games.

First Asian Games gold – women – individual
Kamaljeet Sandhu won the 400 m race in 57.3 secs at the Asian Games in Bangkok, Thailand, in 1970.

Only Asian Games gold medal in marathon
Chhota Singh won a gold in the men's marathon in 1951 in Delhi with a timing of 2 hrs 42 mins 58 secs 6 microseconds.

First gold medal – women – team
Christine Brown, Stephie D'Souza, Violet Peters and Mary D'Souza won the gold in the 4 x100 m relay, clocking 49.5 secs at the second Asian Games in Manila, Philippines, in 1954.

First to win three golds successively in the Asian Games
Manjeet Kaur was the first Indian to win three consecutive gold medals in the women's 4 x 400 m relay race in the Asian Games (2002, 2006 and 2010).

First gold at World Athletics final
Anju Bobby George was upgraded to a gold medal, India's first, in January 2014 after Tatyana Kotova of Russia was disqualified for her long-jump win in the World Athletics Championships in Monte Carlo in September 2005, following a failed retest for doping.

First gold at the World Universiade
Dutee Chand, the current national champion in the women's 100 m race, became the first Indian to win the gold at the World Universiade, Naples, Italy, in the 100 m race with a timing of 11.32 secs on 10 July 2019. She is also the first Indian to win a gold in the 100 m race at a global championship. She also won a silver in the 100 m race at the 2018 Asian Games in Jakarta.

For the first time in a global multi-sport events there were more women's events **(136)** than men's **(134)** in the Birmingham Commonwealth Games 2022.

Dutee Chand: first gold at the World Universiade

NATIONAL SPORTS AWARDS 2021

ATHLETICS

Arjuna Award
Arpinder Singh; Yogesh Kathuniya, Nishad Kumar, Praveen Kumar and Sharad Kumar (para athletics)

Dronacharya Award
Radhakrishnan Nair P.; T.P. Ouseph (Lifetime)

Major Dhyan Chand Khel Ratna
Neeraj Chopra; Sumit Antil (para athletics)

First gold medal in throws at the Commonwealth Games – men – individual

- This feat was achieved by the 6 ft 9 in. tall Vikas Gowda in discus throw. Gowda won this event in 2014 in Glasgow, Scotland, with a throw of 63.64 m.
- Neeraj Chopra hurled the javelin to a distance of 86.47 m in 2018 in Gold Coast, Australia, to win the gold medal.

First individual gold medal in track events at the IAAF World U-20 Championships

Hima Das won the gold in the400 m race in the IAAF (now World Athletics) World U-20 Championships in Tampere, Finland, on 12 July 2018 with a timing of 51.46 secs. She holds the current Indian national record in 400 m with a timing of 50.79 secs set at the 2018 Asian Games in Jakarta, Indonesia.

First clean sweep in a major international meet

Krishna Poonia, Harwant Kaur and Seema Antil bagged the gold, silver and bronze medals respectively in the women's discus throw in the 2010 Commonwealth Games in New Delhi.

Krishna Poonia: part of the first clean sweep in an international meet

First medal in the Commonwealth Games – women

Anju Bobby George won the bronze medal in long jump with a best of 6.49 m at the 2002 Commonwealth Games in Manchester, UK, followed by Neelam J. Singh, who won a silver in the women's discus throw.

Bahadur Singh Chouhan: triple honours in shot put and longest career

First athlete to win a medal at the IAAF Continental Cup

Arpinder Singh, the 2018 Asian Games gold medallist in triple jump, was the first Indian to win a medal in the IAAF Continental Cup. He won a bronze medal in triple jump with a distance of 16.59 m.

First Indian to win gold at the IAAF World U-20 Championships

Neeraj Chopra, by clinching the gold on 23 July 2016 at the IAAF (now World Athletics) World U-20 championships in Bydgoszcz, Poland, with a winning javelin throw of 86.48 m, became the first Indian to win a gold medal at any event in the championships and the first Indian to set a junior world record in athletics. In 2018, he became the second Indian after the legendary runner Milkha Singh to win both Commonwealth and Asian Games gold medals in the same year, breaking the national record on both occasions. At 20 years, he was the youngest ever flagbearer of the Indian contingent at the 2018 Jakarta Asian Games.

First Commonwealth Games gold medal – women

The first Commonwealth Games gold medal for women came when Krishna Poonia won the discus throw (61.51 m), while the quartet of Sini Jose, Mandeep Kaur, Manjeet Kaur and Ashwini Chidananda Akkunji won the women's 4 x 400 m relay (3 mins 27.77 secs) at the 2010 New Delhi Games.

Gold medal in Commonwealth and Asian Games

Milkha Singh won gold in the 440 yards (the quarter-mile dash) race at the 1958 British Empire and Commonwealth Games in Cardiff, Wales, with a timing of 46.6 secs. He also won the 400 m races back-to-back in the Asian Games in Tokyo, Japan (1958), in 47.0 secs, and Jakarta, Indonesia (1962), in 46.9 secs. He was the first Indian to win individual gold medals in both the Asian Games and the Commonwealth Games. He was also the first Indian athlete to win a gold medal in the Commonwealth Games.

Triple excellence in shot put

Former shot putter Bahadur Singh Chouhan is the only Indian to receive the Arjuna Award, the Dronacharya Award as well as the Padma Shri. Between 1973 and 1985 he won three gold, two silver and three bronze medals at the Asian Games and Asian Championships.

First to receive IAAF Veteran Pin

Indian track and field legend P.T. Usha was presented the Veteran Pin by the World Athletics governing body – IAAF (now World Athletics), on 24 September 2019.

First to win a gold medal in triple jump in the Commonwealth Games

Eldhose Paul became the first Indian to win a gold medal in the men's triple jump at the Commonwealth Games 2022, recording a massive 17.03 m.

First World U-20 Athletics Championships twin medals

Quarter-miler Rupal Chaudhary is the first Indian to win twin medals in a single edition of the 2022 World U-20 Athletics Championships. She won silver in 4x400 m relay silver and a bronze medal in the women's 400 m.

First medal in race walk – women
Priyanka Goswami is the first Indian woman to win the silver medal in the women's 10,000 m race walk at the 2022 Commonwealth Games. It is India's second medal in the race walk at the Commonwealth Games after Harminder Singh's bronze in the 20 km event in the 2010 Commonwealth Games.

First high jump medal in the Commonwealth Games
Tejaswin Shankar, the 2015 Commonwealth Youth Games gold medallist in high jump, became the first Indian to win a medal – a bronze – in high jump with a jump of 2.22 m at the 2022 Commonwealth Games.

First javelin throw medal in the Commonwealth Games – women
Annu Rani, a javelin thrower, is the first Indian woman to win a medal, a bronze, in the 2022 Commonwealth Games in Birmingham, UK.

Oldest gold medallist
Bhagwani Devi, at 94 years, won a gold medal in the 100m sprint at the World Masters Athletics Championship on 11 July 2022 in Tampere, Finland.

Most appearances in marathons
Sunita Godara has completed 85 half- and 69 full marathons in 24 different countries. Starting with the Rath Marathon in 1984, she finished first in 25 marathons, second in 12 and third in 14 of them. She has won 25 gold medals in half-marathons.

Most individual golds in the Asian Games
Two sportspersons have won four gold medals each at the Asian Games:
- Milkha Singh won four golds in two Asian Games in 1958 and 1962.
- P.T. Usha won four golds in the 1986 Asian Games at Seoul, South Korea, in the 200 m, 400 m, 400 m hurdles and the 4 x 400 m relay, and the silver in the 100 m race. In the1982 Asian Games she won silver in the 100 mand 200 m races.

Best performance in the Asian Youth Athletics Championships
India clinched six gold, eleven silver and three bronze medals in the 2022 Asian Youth Athletics Championships, held in in Kuwait between 13 and 16 October 2022, topping the medal tally.

Best performances in the Olympics
Milkha Singh and P.T. Usha finished fourth in the 400 m and the 400 m hurdles in the 1960 Rome and the 1984 Los Angeles Olympic Games respectively.

Best Commonwealth performance
India won 12 medals – two golds, three silvers and seven bronzes – during the 19th Commonwealth Games in New Delhi in 2010.

Best performance in the Asian Athletics Championships
India clinched five gold, one silver and three bronze medals in the 2017 Asian Athletics Championships in Bhubaneswar, Odisha, to top the medal tally for the first time in the championships.

Longest career – men
Bahadur Singh Chouhan who represented India in the inaugural Asian Track and Field (ATF) meet in 1971, also participated in the ninth one at Delhi in 1989. He won gold medals in shot put in the Asian Games in 1978 and 1982, and a silver medal in 1974.

Longest career – women
- P.T. Usha represented India from 1980 to 1998 in four Olympic Games, five Asian Games and five ATF meets.
- Shiny Wilson represented India 72 times in international meets from 1981 to 1995. She won the 800 m in her last major meet – the ATF meet in 1995 in Jakarta, Indonesia.

First title in the Commonwealth Fencing Championship
Chennai-born fencer C.A. Bhavani Devi made history in November 2018 by becoming the first Indian to win the gold medal at the Commonwealth Championship. The 42nd ranked Indian fencer and the first ever Indian fencer to have qualified for an Olympics (Tokyo 2020) Bhavani Devi defeated second-seeded Australian Veronika Vasleva 15-10 in the senior women's sabre individual category final in London, UK, in the Commonwealth Championship in August 2022.

PARA ATHLETICS

First participation in the Paralympics
In 1968, India made its Paralympics debut at the Tel Aviv Games. India did not participate in the first two Games, in 1960 and 1964. India

Milkha Singh: sportsman with the most individual golds in the Asian Games

NATIONAL SPORTS AWARDS 2021

FENCING

Arjuna Award
Bhavani Devi

Iconic Indian athlete Anju Bobby George was bestowed with the Woman of the Year Award on 1 December 2021 by World Athletics (WA) for grooming talent in the country and advocating gender equality.

Sumit Antil: best javelin throw – para athletics

NATIONAL SPORTS AWARDS 2022

ATHLETICS

Arjuna Award
Seema Punia, Eldhose Paul, Avinash Mukund Sable

Dhyan Chand Award*
Ashwini Akkunji C.; Nir Bahadur Gurung (para athletics)

completed again in 1972 and then consistently from the 1984 New York Games in the USA to Tokyo 2020 in Japan.

First triple medal in the Paralympics
India's Joginder Singh Bedi had won three medals – a silver each in javelin and shot put, and a bronze in the discus throw – at the 1984 Paralympics in Stoke Mandeville and New York, USA.

First Paralympics gold – women
Deepa Malik became the first Indian woman to win a medal at the Paralympics by bagging a silver medal in shot put in the 2016 Paralympic Games. She also won gold in the F-53/54 javelin event at the para-athletic Grand Prix held in Dubai in 2018.

First gold in javelin
Sumit Antil won the gold medal in the men's javelin throw F64 category at the 2020 Summer Paralympics in Tokyo, Japan. He holds the current world record, having thrown 68.55 m in the Paralympics final.

Best performance in the World Para Athletics Championships
India won two gold, two silver and five bronze medals (a total of nine) at the World Para Athletics Championships 2019 held in Dubai.

Best throw – discus F-36 (para athletics) – men
Yogesh Kathuniya smashed the world record in men's discus F-36, when he threw 45.18 m to win the gold medal in the World Para Athletics Grand Prix in Berlin, Germany, on 1 July 2018.

First bronze medal at the World Para Athletics Championships
Varun Kumar Bhati won the bronze medal in the men's T-42 category high jump and Karan Jyoti Dalal settled for bronze in the discus throw F-55 at the World Para Athletics Championships in London in 2017.

First para athlete to get the Rajiv Gandhi Khel Ratna Award – women
Deepa Malik was the first woman para athlete to receive the Rajiv Gandhi Khel Ratna Award in 2019.

Best javelin throw – men
Sumit Antil's world record javelin throw of 68.55 m in the F64 category came at the 2020 Tokyo Olympics. He threw the spear to a record distance of 68.62 m in the Open National Para Athletics Championships.

First ever IAS officer to win a silver medal
Suhas Yathiraj, a 2007 Indian Administrative Services (IAS) officer of Uttar Pradesh cadre bagged the silver medal in the men's SL4 category at the Tokyo 2020 Paralympics.

NATIONAL GAMES

Fastest 100 m hurdles – women
In the women's-only 100 m hurdles, Jyothi Yarraji became the first Indian woman to finish the race with a sub-13 timing, as she clocked 12.82 seconds at the 61st National Open Athletics Championships in Bengaluru on in October 2022.

Highest pole vault
- *Women*: At the 36th National Games Rosy Meena Paulraj cleared a height of 4.20 m to break the eight-year-old record of 4.15 m held by V. S. Surekha in the women's pole vault in the National Games 2022. A week later, she rewrote her own record by vaulting 4.21 m on 15 October 2022 at the National Open Athletics Championships 2022 in Bengaluru.
- *Men*: At the 36th National Games, held between 29 September and 12 October 2022, Siva Subramani (5.31 m) eclipsed his own record of 5.30 m in the men's pole vault, set four years back.

Fastest race walk
Ram Baboo clocked 2.36.34 to break the previous national record in the men's 35 km race walk (2.40.16) by nearly four minutes in the 36th National Games in 2022.

Longest triple jump – women
On 13 June 2022, Aishwarya Babu made a record in the triple jump among women at the 2022 National Inter-State Athletics Championships in Chennai, Tamil Nadu, leaping 14.14 m and breaking the national

P.T. Usha: Ace Athlete

P.T. Usha

Former athlete P.T. Usha was nominated as a Rajya Sabha member on July 2022 by former president Ram Nath Kovind. She wrote Indian sporting history with her outstanding performance in the Asian Championships of 1985 in Kuwait, where she won gold medals in 100 m, 200 m and 400 m events (setting Asian records in all three). She also won the gold medals in the 200 m, 400 m, 4 x 400 m relay and the 400 m hurdles, and the silver in the 100 m event in the 1986 Asian Games in Seoul, Currently, she coaches and mentors young, upcoming athletes.

* Dhyan Chand Award for Lifetime Achievement in Sports and Games

Neeraj Chopra: Going the Distance

At 17 years of age, Neeraj Chopra won the gold medal in javelin throw on 23 July 2016 at the IAAF World U-20 championships in Bydgoszcz, Poland, becoming the first Indian to win a gold medal at any event in the championships and the first ever Indian to set a junior world record in athletics.

This was just the beginning for the youngster from a village near Panipat, Haryana, who began his athletics career in 2011 at the district level and broke the national record in 2013. In 2018, he became the second Indian after the legendary runner Milkha Singh to win the Commonwealth and Asian Games gold medals in the same years. He was the youngest ever flag-bearer of the Indian contingent at the 2018 Jakarta Asian Games. He became the first Indian track and field athlete to win a gold medal in the 2020 Tokyo Olympics. He also made history at World Athletics Championships, held in Oregon in 2022, to win a silver medal. This is only the second medal for India at the World Athletics Championships after long-jumper Anju Bobby George's bronze in 2003.

NATIONAL SPORTS AWARDS 2021

ARCHERY

Arjuna Award

Harvinder Singh (para archery)

record of 14.11 m set by Mayookha Johny set at the Asian Championships in Japan in 2011.

Youngest athletics champion

Henry Rebello won the triple jump at Bangalore (now Bengaluru), Karnataka, in 1946 when he was only 17 years old. He set a record of 50 ft 2 in. at the 1948 National Games, which was surpassed only after a gap of 23 years by Mohinder Singh in 1971.

Oldest gold medallist

Rambai, at 105 years, won gold in the 100 m race at the National Open Masters Athletics Championships on 21 June 2022 in Vadodara, Gujarat.

ARCHERY

First Junior World Championships title – men

Palton Hansda won the World Junior Archery Championships (compound – men's) in 2006 at Merida in Mexico.

Deepika Kumari: first to win back-to-back titles in recurve

First to win back-to-back titles

Deepika Kumari became the first Indian archer to win titles back-to-back when she won the cadet individual recurve title in 2009 at Ogden in Utah, USA, and the junior individual recurve gold in 2011 at Legnica, Poland.

First individual international medal

Shyam Lal won a bronze in the 50 m event at the fifth Asia Cup championship in Calcutta (now Kolkata), West Bengal, in January 1988. He represented India in the 1988 Seoul Olympics in South Korea.

First Archery World Cup team gold – women

Rimil Buriuly, Bombayla Devi Laishram and Deepika Kumari toppled Olympic champions South Korea 219–215 to win the first back-to-back World Cup titles at the Archery World Cup (stage 4) at Wroclaw, Poland, on 25 August 2013, after winning the first medal at the World Cup (stage 3) in Medellin, Colombia, in July.

First international gold

In October 1989, India took the gold in the team event at the Asian Archery Championships in Beijing, China, with 1,850 points, while reigning Olympic champion South Korea stood second with 1,842 points. The Indian team comprised Limba Ram, Shyam Lal and Skalzang Dorje.

NATIONAL SPORTS AWARDS 2022

ARCHERY

Dronacharya Award

Jiwanjot Singh Teja

First international gold – individual

Jayanta Talukdar won an individual gold medal at the Federation Internationale de Tir a l'Arc (FITA) Meteksan World Cup, in 2006 in Merida, Mexico.

First international gold – women

Dola Banerjee outclassed Tatyana Dorkhova of Ukraine 102–96 in the women's recurve final at the 18th Golden Arrow Grand Prix Championship 2005 at Antalya, Turkey.

First medal in the Asian Championships – men

Limba Ram became the first Indian archer to win an Asian Archery Championships medal in 1988.

First Olympics representation – men

The Indian national archery team, with Shyam Lal, Limba Ram and Sanjeeva Singh, participated in the individual and team archery events at the Olympics in 1988 at Seoul, South Korea.

First Olympics representation – women

Dola Banerjee, Reena Kumari and Sumangala Sharma were the first women to represent India in archery at the 2004 Olympic Games in Athens, Greece.

First Indian compound archery women's team to be ranked world no. 1

The Indian compound archery women's team of Jyothi Surekha Vennam, P. Lily Chanu, Trisha Deb, Muskan Kirar, Divya Dhayal and Madhumita was the first ever team from India to be ranked world no. 1 in 2018.

First gold medal in a World Cup

Dola Banerjee from West Bengal is the only Indian archer to win gold in a World Cup final, in the women's individual recurve event at the World Cup in Dubai, UAE, in November 2007.

First World Cup compound title – men – individual

Abhishek Verma won an archery World Cup (stage 3) event at Wroclaw, Poland, on 15 August 2015.

First World Cup compound title – men – team

The men's compound archery team of Abhishek Verma, Chinna Raju Srither and Amarjeet Singh bagged the World Cup (stage 1) on 20 May 2017 in Shanghai, China, scoring 226–221 against Colombia.

First World Championship medal

The Indian men's archery team won a silver

medal, behind Korea, at the 43rd World Outdoor Target Archery Championship 2005 in Madrid, Spain. The recurve team comprised Tarundeep Rai, Gautam Singh Sardar, Jayanta Talukdar and Robin Hansda.

First gold medal in the Asian Para Games

Harvinder Singh won India's maiden archery gold in the Asian Para Games 2018 in the men's individual recurve. He outplayed China's Zhao Lixue 6–0 in the W2/ST category.

First compound para medal

Indian compound mixed pair of Shyam Sundar Swami and Jyoti Bullyan made history with a silver at the World Archery Para Championships 2022 in Dubai.

First silver at the Youth Olympics

Fifteen-year-old Akash Malik from Haryana became India's first archery silver medallist at the Youth Olympic Games 2018 in Buenos Aires, Argentina, on 17 October 2018.

Most medals in the World Championship

India won a silver and two bronzes in the World Archery Championships during 10–15 June 2019 at 's-Hertogenbosch, Netherlands. The men's team of Tarundeep Rai, Atanu Das and Pravin Yadav won silver. The women's compound team of Jyothi Surekha Vennam, Muskan Kaur and Raj Kaur won the bronzes.

Most medals in the Asian Championship

Indian recurve archers won one gold, four silver and two bronze medals at the 2021 Asian Archery Championships in Dhaka (Bangladesh). In the Asian Championships in 2019 too, in Bangkok, Thailand, during 22–28 November 2019, India had won seven medals: one gold, two silver and four bronze medals.

Most medals in a World Cup

India won one gold, two silver and two bronze medals in the Archery World Cup (stage 4) at Wroclaw, Poland, in August 2014. The team of Deepika Kumari, Bombayla Devi Laishram and Laxmirani Majhi won the gold in the women's recurve team event. The men's recurve team, with Tarundeep Rai, Jayanta Talukdar and Atanu Das, won a silver medal. Abhishek Verma and Purvasha Shende clinched the silver in the compound mixed pair event. Deepika Kumari bagged two bronze medals in the women's recurve individual event and in the mixed team event with partner Jayanta Talukdar.

Most medals in the Commonwealth Games

The Indian team won three gold, a silver and four bronze medals in archery at the 2010 Commonwealth Games in Delhi.

Most gold medals at the World Cup by an individual

India won three gold medals in the Archery World Cup (stage 3) 2021 in Paris, France: the individual gold – Deepika Kumari; the mixed team event – Deepika Kumari with her husband Atanu Das; and the women's team event trio of Deepika Kumari, Komalika Bari and Ankita Bhakat.

Only siblings to represent India in archery at the Olympics

Archers Dola Banerjee and Rahul Banerjee are the only brother-and-sister pair to represent India at the Olympics.

Only Indian couple to represent India at the Olympic Games

Atanu Das and Deepika Kumari are the only Indian archer couple to represent India at the Olympic Games 2020. They had got married in June 2019 amid the pandemic.

Hat-trick of bronzes – men

Atanu Das bagged three bronze medals in the 2019 Asian Archery Championships in Bangkok, Thailand. He clinched the men's recurve individual bronze, the recurve mixed team bronze (with Deepika Kumari), and the third bronze with Tarundeep Rai and Jayanta Talukdar in the team recurve event.

Two medals in World Cup Stage 3

Jyothi Surekha Vennam claimed two medals in the World Cup (Stage 3) in Paris in June 2022. When she was four years old, she crossed the River Krishna in 3 hrs, 20 mins and 6 secs to cover 5 km three times across, entering the *Limca Book of Records*.* Starting with two bronze medals in the World Youth Archery Championships in 2013, she went on to win 10 medals in the Asian Archery Championships, nine medals in the World

Jyothi Surekha Vennam: two medals in World Cup (Stage 3)

Bombayla Devi Laishram: part of most medals in a World Cup

Archers Dola Banerjee and Rahul Banerjee: the only siblings to represent India at the Olympics

* *LBR* rules for minors differed at the time.

Archer Abhishek Verma received the Arjuna Award in 2014

Abhishek Verma Bags 50 International Medals in Compound Archery

The duo of Abhishek Verma and Jyothi Surekha Vennam gave a fine performance to win the compound mixed team bronze medal in the World Games in Birmingham, USA, on 9 July 2022. The top-ranked Indian team, comprising Verma and Vennam, defeated New Zealand 156-155 before losing to Colombia 159-157 in the semi-finals. With this, Verma reached a personal milestone of bagging his 50th international medal. He also became the only Indian compound archer to win medals at all top-level events, including the World Championships, the World Games, the World Cup final, the World Cup stages, the Asian Games and the Asian Championships.

Satwiksairaj Rankireddy: first doubles medallist in the Olympic Games

Chirag Shetty: first doubles medallist in the Olympic Games

Cup and six medals in the World Archery Championships. She has nearly 100 medals in national and international competitions.

Three gold medals in the World Cup

Deepika Kumari won three gold medals in the World Cup (stage 3) in Paris in 2021. India took the top honour in the women's team, mixed team and women's individual events.

Two individual golds in the World Cup

Abhishek Verma won the compound men's individual gold in Paris 2021 after the one in Wroclaw, Poland, in 2015.

PARALYMPICS

First archery medal in Paralympics

Harvinder Singh clinched India's first-ever archery at the 2020 Paralympics. He won the bronze medal in the men's singles recurve archery at the 2020 Summer Paralympics in Tokyo, Japan.

BADMINTON

INTERNATIONAL OLYMPIC GAMES

First medallist

Saina Nehwal became the first Indian medallist, winning a bronze medal in London, UK, in 2012.

First silver medallist

P.V. Sindhu finished runner-up in Rio de Janeiro, Brazil, in 2016.

First two-time medallist

P.V. Sindhu remains the only two-time medallist with the silver medal in Rio de Janeiro, Brazil (2016), and the bronze medal in Tokyo, Japan (2020).

WORLD CHAMPIONSHIP

First individual medallist – men – singles

Prakash Padukone claimed the men's singles bronze medal in Copenhagen, Denmark, in 1983.

First individual medallist – women – singles

P.V. Sindhu received the women's singles bronze medal in Guangzhou, China, in 2013.

First doubles medallists – women

Jwala Gutta and Ashwini Ponnappa became the first Indian bronze medallists in women's doubles in London, UK, in 2011.

First doubles medallists – men

Satwiksairaj Rankireddy and Chirag Shetty finished with a bronze in the men's doubles in Tokyo, Japan, in 2022.

First silver medallist – men – singles

K. Srikanth finished runner-up in thje men's singles in the 2021 edition at Huelva.

First silver medallist – women – singles

Saina Nehwal finished runner-up in the women's singles in Jakarta in 2015.

First two-time silver medallist – women - singles

P.V. Sindhu finished runner-up in women's singles in Glasgow (2017) and Nanjing (2019).

First world champion

P.V. Sindhu claimed the honour by winning the women's singles in 2019.

Highest number of medals

P.V. Sindhu has five medals – a gold, two silver and two bronze medals – from the premier championship.

Two medals from one edition – women

P.V. Sindhu, with the silver medal, and Saina Nehwal, with the bronze, were on the podium of the women's singles at Glasgow in 2017.

Two medals from one edition – men

K. Srikanth, with the silver medal, and Lakshya Sen, with the bronze, made it to the podium in Huelva, Spain, in 2021.

ASIAN GAMES

First medal – men – team
The men's team comprising Prakash Padukone, Dinesh Khanna, Davinder Ahuja, Partho Ganguli and Raman Ghosh won a bronze medal in Tehran in 1974.

First medal – women – team
The women's team comprising Ami Ghia, Madhumita Goswami, Amita Kulkarni, Hufrish Nariman, Kanwal Thakur Singh and Vandana Chiplunkar claimed a bronze medal in New Delhi in 1982.

First to win a medal – men – singles
Syed Modi claimed a bronze in New Delhi in 1982.

First to win a medal – women – singles
Saina Nehwal received a women's singles bronze in Jakarta-Palembang in 2018.

First to win a medal – mixed – doubles
Leroy D'Sa and Kanwal Thakur Singh received a bronze medal in New Delhi in 1982.

First to win a medal – men – doubles
Leroy D'Sa and Pradeep Gandhe claimed a bronze medal in New Delhi in 1982.

Multiple medal–winner in a single edition
Leroy D'Sa received three bronze medals – for the men's team, the doubles and the mixed doubles – in New Delhi in 1982.

Two medallists in a single event
P.V. Sindhu (silver) and Saina Nehwal (bronze) made it to the podium in the women's singles in Jakarta-Palembang in 2018.

COMMONWEALTH GAMES

First medallist – men – singles
Dinesh Khanna claimed a bronze medal in 1966 in the British Empire and Commonwealth Games. (In 1978, these Games were rechristened as the Commonwealth Games).

First medallist – women – singles
Aparna Popat received a bronze medal in women's singles in Manchester in 2002.

First medallists – men – team
The team comprising P. Gopichand, Abhinn Shyam Gupta, George Thomas, Jaseel P. Ismail, Marcos Bristow, Nikhil Kanetkar and Vincent Lobo claimed a silver medal in Kuala Lumpur in 1998.

First medallist – women – doubles
Ami Ghia and Kanwal Thakur Singh claimed a bronze in Edmonton in 1978.

First medallists – women – team
The team comprising Manjusha Kanwar, P.V. V. Lakshmi, Madhumita Bisht, Aparna Popat, Archana Deodhar, K. Neelima Chowdhary and C. Deepthi won a bronze medal in Kuala Lumpur in 1998.

First gold medallist – mixed – team
The team comprising K. Srikanth, Saina Nehwal, P.V. Sindhu, H. S. Prannoy, Ashwini Ponnappa, Sikki Reddy, Ruthvika Shivani, Chirag Shetty, Satwiksairaj Rankireddy and Pranaav Chopra won the title in Gold Coast in 2018.

First silver medallist – mixed – team
The team comprising Saina Nehwal, P. Kashyap, Jwala Gutta, Ashwini Ponnappa, Chetan Anand, Aditi Mutatkar, Sanave Thomas, Rupesh Kumar, Aparna Balan and V. Diju finished runner-up in Delhi in 2010.

First bronze medallist – mixed – team
The team comprising Anup Sridhar, Aparna Popat, Chetan Anand, Jwala Gutta, Shruti Kurien, Saina Nehwal, Trupti Murgunde, V. Diju, Sanave Thomas and Rupesh Kumar claimed the bronze in Melbourne in 2006.

First gold medallist – men – singles
Prakash Padukone won the men's singles title in Edmonton in 1978.

First gold medallist – women - singles
Saina Nehwal won in New Delhi in 2010.

First gold medallists – women – doubles
Jwala Gutta and Ashwini Ponnappa won gold in Delhi in 2010.

First gold medallists – men – doubles
Chirag Shetty and Satwiksairaj Rankireddy won the title in Birmingham in 2022.

NATIONAL SPORTS AWARDS 2021

BADMINTON

Arjuna Award
Suhash Yathiraj (para badminton)

Major Dhyan Chand Khel Ratna
Krishna Nagar and Pramod Bhagat (para badminton)

H.S. Prannoy: part of the first gold medal–winning mixed team in the Commonwealth Games

Most gold medals from one edition
India won three gold medals – from men's singles (Lakshya Sen), women's singles (P.V. Sindhu) and men's doubles (Chirag Shetty and Satwiksairaj Rankireddy) – in Birmingham, UK, in 2022.

Most medals from one edition
India won six medals – women's singles gold (Saina Nehwal), mixed team gold, men's singles silver (K. Srikanth), women's singles silver (P.V. Sindhu), men's doubles silver (Chirag Shetty and Satwiksairaj Rankireddy) and women's doubles bronze (Ashwini Ponnappa and N. Sikki Reddy) – in Gold Coast, Australia, in 2018.

ASIAN CHAMPIONSHIP

First gold medal from Asian championship
Dinesh Khanna won the men's singles gold medal in Lucknow in 1965.

First bronze medal – men – singles
Suresh Goel claimed a men's singles bronze in Lucknow in 1965.

First medal – women – singles
Meena Shah claimed a women's singles bronze in Lucknow in 1965.

First medal – men – doubles
Dipu Ghosh and Raman Ghosh received a bronze at Jakarta in 1971.

First silver medal – men – doubles
Prakash Padukone and Syed Modi received the silver medal in Peking in 1978.

First medal – mixed – doubles
Owen Roncon-Sarojini Apte and A.I. Sheikh-Achala Karnik received bronze medals in Lucknow in 1965.

First medal – women – doubles
Jwala Gutta and Ashwini Ponnappa received a bronze medal in Gimcheon in 2014.

WORLD JUNIOR CHAMPIONSHIP

First medallist – girls – singles
Saina Nehwal received a silver medal in the girls' singles in Incheon, South Korea, in 2006.

First gold medallist – girls – singles
Saina Nehwal won the girls' singles in Pune in 2008.

First medallist – boys – singles
R.M.V. Gurusaidutt claimed a bronze medal in the boys' singles in Pune in 2008.

First silver medallist – boys – singles
Siril Verma received a silver medal in the boys' singles in Lima, Peru, in 2015.

BWF SUPER SERIES MASTERS FINALS/ BWF WORLD TOUR FINALS

First medallist – women – singles
Saina Nehwal received a bronze in Kota Kinabalu, Sabah, Malaysia in 2008.

First medallist – men – singles
K. Srikanth received a bronze medal in Dubai in 2014.

First gold medallist – women – singles
P.V. Sindhu won the title in Guangzhou, China, in 2018 when the event was rechristened as BWF World Tour Finals.

First silver medallists – mixed – doubles
V. Diju and Jwala Gutta finished runner-up in the mixed doubles in Johor Bahru, Malaysia, in 2009.

First silver medallist – women – singles
Saina Nehwal received a silver in Liuzhou, China, in 2011.

Highest world ranking – women – singles
Saina Nehwal became the world no. 1 in the women's singles in April 2015.

Highest world ranking – men – singles
K. Srikanth became the world no. 1 in the men's singles in April 2018.

NATIONAL SPORTS AWARDS 2022

BADMINTON

Arjuna Award
Lakshya Sen, H.S. Prannoy; Manasi Girishchandra Joshi and Tarun Dhillon (para badminton); Jerlin Anika J. (deaf badminton)

P.V. Sindhu: first gold medal in the BWF World Tour Finals

Highest world rankings – mixed – doubles
Jwala Gutta and V. Diju were ranked world no. 6 in August 2010.

Highest world ranking – women – doubles
Jwala Gutta and Ashwini Ponnappa were ranked world no. 10 in August 2015.

Highest world ranking – men – doubles
Chirag Shetty and Satwiksairaj Rankireddy were ranked world no. 7 in November 2019.

OTHER INTERNATIONAL COMPETITIONS

First medal in the Thomas Cup – men – team championship
India defeated 14-time champion Indonesia at the Thomas Cup 3-0 to win the prestigious title in 2022 for the first time ever, with World Championships medallist Lakshya Sen, K. Srikanth and the current world no. 8 doubles duo of Chirag Shetty and Satwiksairaj Rankireddy.

First winner of the World Cup – men – singles
Prakash Padukone won in Kuala Lumpur, Malaysia, in 1981.

K. Srikanth: highest world ranking – men – singles

First winner at the All England Championship
Prakash Padukone won in London in 1980.

First finalist at the All England – men – singles
Prakash Nath reached the men's singles final in 1947 in London.

Two semi-finalists at the All England
Prakash Nath and Davinder Mohan reached the men's singles semi-finals in 1947. Interestingly, the two players chose not to

First medal in the Thomas Cup – men – team championship

Badminton: National Awards

Arjuna Award: Nandu Natekar (1961); Meena Shah (1962); Dinesh Khanna (1965); Suresh Goel (1967); Dipu Ghosh (1969); Damayanti Tambe (1970); Shobha Moorthy (1971); Prakash Padukone (1972); Raman Ghosh (1974); Davinder Ahuja (1975); Ami Ghia (1976); Kanwal Thakur Singh (1977–78); Syed Modi (1980-81); Madhumita Goswami-Bisht (1982); Partho Ganguli (1982); P. Gopichand (1999); George Thomas (2000); Abhinn Shyam Gupta (2004); Aparna Popat (2005); Chetan Anand (2006); Anup Sridhar (2007); Saina Nehwal (2009); Jwala Gutta (2011); P. Kashyap (2012); Ashwini Ponnappa (2012); P.V. Sindhu (2013); V. Diju (2014); K. Srikanth (2015); N. Sikki Reddy (2018); B. Sai Praneeth (2019); Satwiksairaj Rankireddy (2020); Chirag Shetty (2020); Lakshya Sen (2021); and H.S. Prannoy (2021).

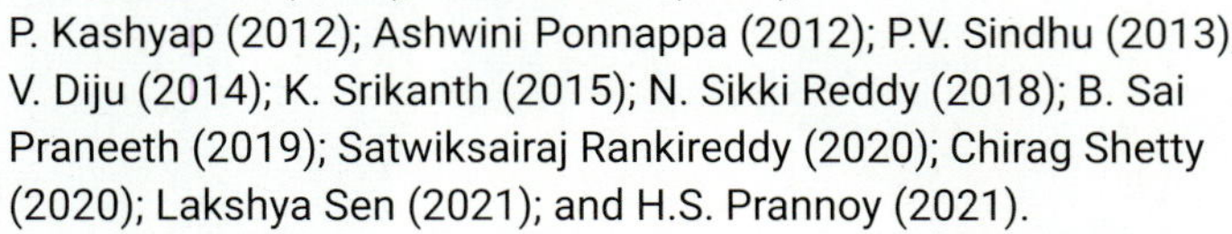

Nandu Natekar

Dhyan Chand Award: Pradeep Gandhe (2020) and Trupti Murgunde (2020).

Dronacharya Award: S.M. Arif (2000); P. Gopichand (2009); Gangula Prasad (2017); and Vimal Kumar (2019).

Khel Ratna: P. Gopi Chand (2001); Saina Nehwal (2010); and P.V. Sindhu (2016).

Padma Bhushan: P. Gopichand (2014); Saina Nehwal (2016); and P.V. Sindhu (2021).

Prakash Padukone

Padma Shri: Prakash Padukone (1982); P. Gopichand (2005); Madhumita Goswami-Bisht (2006); Saina Nehwal (2010); S.M. Arif (2012); P.V. Sindhu (2015); and K. Srikanth (2018).

play each other. They tossed a coin, Prakash Nath called it right and advanced to the final.

First medal in the Uber Cup – women's – team

India claimed its first bronze medal in New Delhi in 2014.

Jwala Gutta (*right*): most titles in Nationals – doubles – women

Most titles – women

Saina Nehwal won 10 titles in the BWF Superseries from 15 appearances in the final.

Most titles – men

K. Srikanth won six titles in the BWF Superseries in seven appearances in the final.

PARALYMPICS

First gold medallist– men – singles

Pramod Bhagat became the first gold medallist after winning the men's singles in the SL3 category in the 2020 Tokyo Paralympics.

First silver medallist – men – singles

Suhas Yathiraj became the first silver medallist in men's singles in the SL4 category in Tokyo in 2020.

First bronze medallist – men – singles

Manoj Sarkar became the first bronze medallist in the men's singles SL3 category in Tokyo in 2020.

DOMESTIC: NATIONALS

First National champions

Vijay Madgavkar (men's singles in 1934); T. P. Boland (women's singles in 1935),; D. Minas–V. Minas (men's doubles in 1934); T. P. Boland–Cameron (women's doubles in 1935); and N. Knight–I. Brydges (mixed doubles in 1936).

Most titles – men – singles

Prakash Padukone holds a unique record of winning all his nine singles titles in a row from 1971 to 1979.

Most titles – women – singles

Aparna Popat matched Prakash's record by winning her nine singles titles on the trot from 1997 to 2005.

Most titles – men – doubles

Rupesh Kumar was part of the men's doubles title winning pair for nine successive years between 2002 and 2010. Rupesh partnered Markose Bristow in 2002 and 2003, and thereafter joined hands with Sanave Thomas.

Most titles – women – doubles

Jwala Gutta formed part of the title-winning combination 10 times between 2000 and 2013. She won with Shruti Kurien in 2000 and again from 2002 to 2008. She paired with Ashwini Ponnappa in 2009 and 2013.

Most titles – mixed – doubles

Madhumita Goswami-Bisht won the mixed doubles title 12 times with five different partners. She won in 1981, 1986-88 (with Sanat Mishra); In 1989-1990 (with Harjeet Singh); in 1994-97 (with Vinod Kumar); in 2000 (with Vincent Lobo); and 2001 (with Markose Bristow).

Most versatile and successful player in the Nationals
Madhumita Goswami-Bisht, in an international career spanning almost a quarter of a century from 1978, won eight National women singles, nine women's doubles and 12 mixed doubles titles.

First badminton gold – Paralympics
Pramod Bhagat of Odisha won India's first ever Paralympics Gold in badminton. (Badminton made its debut at the 2020 Tokyo Olympics). He clinched Gold in men's singles badminton (SLB) event.

BASKETBALL

First appearance in the Asian Games
India took part in the first Asian Games at New Delhi in 1951, under the captaincy of Ranbir Chand. In its best performance at the Games to date, the team came fourth.

First India-born player in the NBA
Satnam Singh Bhamara set a milestone in the history of Indian basketball when he was drafted into the National Basketball Association (NBA), the premier professional basketball league in the USA, in June 2015. Selected by the Dallas Mavericks, he played his Summer League debut match against the New Orleans Pelicans, scoring four points for his team, on 11 July 2015.

First and only sisters representing the country
Prashanti, Pratima, Priyanka and Divya Singh, four sisters from Varanasi, Uttar Pradesh, have all played basketball for India.

Longest sequence of Nationals titles
- Services won the men's national title 26 years in a row from 1957 to 1982.
- Railways won the women's title 17 years in a row from 1986 to 2002.

Most appearances in the Asian Games – women
Prashanti Singh is the only woman basketball player to represent the Indian team in two Asian Games, in 2010 and 2014. She also represented the national team in the 2006 CWG. She has won 22 medals in national championships and federation events.

Best win
Indian basketball's biggest win was at the 2014 FIBA Asia Cup, held in Wuhan, Hubei, China, with the win against home favourites and most successful Asian team China by 7 points.

Vijender Singh: first Olympic medal winner and most successive professional wins

BOXING

Oldest existing boxing association
The Maharashtra Amateur Boxing Association was formed in 1924.

First Olympic appearance
India entered a boxing team in seven divisions for the first time at the 1948 London Olympics but could not reach the quarter-finals.

First Olympic medal – men
Vijender Singh won a bronze medal (middleweight) in the 2008 Beijing Olympics.

First Olympic medal – women
Six-time women's world champion M.C. Mary Kom won a bronze medal (51 kg) in the 2012 London Olympics. Lovlina Borgohain (69 kg) became the second Indian woman to win a bronze medal at Tokyo 2020 after losing to Turkey's Busenaz Surmeneli 0-5 in the semi-finals.

First medal in the World Boxing Championships – men
- Amit Panghal was the first Indian male boxer to win a silver medal in the World Boxing Championship 2019. Seven Indian have won World Championships medals until now: Amit Panghal (2019, silver), Vijender Singh (2009, bronze), Vikas Krishan (2011, bronze), Shiv Thapa (2015, bronze) Gaurav

Amit Panghal: first male boxer to win a silver in the World Boxing Championships

NATIONAL SPORTS AWARDS 2021

BOXING

Arjuna Award
Simranjit Kaur

Major Dhyan Chand Khel Ratna
Lovlina Borgohain

Dhyan Chand Award (Lifetime)
Lekha K.C.

Dronacharya Award
Sandhya Gurung

(2017, bronze), Manish Kaushik (2019, bronze) and Akash Kumar (2021, bronze)

- Parveen Kumar won a bronze medal in the lightweight category in the World Junior Championship in Budapest, Hungary, in November 2000.

First World Boxing Championships medal – women

- M.C. Mary Kom from Manipur bagged a silver medal in the 48 kg category in the USA in December 2001.
- Manju Rani became the second Indian to enter the World Boxing Championships final and won the silver at Ulan-Ude, Russia, in 2019.

First medal at the World Cup – men

Zoramthanga defeated teammate Dharmender Yadav 17–4 on points to win the light flyweight bronze on 17 November 1990 in Bombay (now Mumbai), Maharashtra.

First Asian Games medal – men

Hari Singh won the silver in the middleweight category at the 1958 Manila Games in the Philippines. Sunder Rao and Ranganathan won the bronze in the lightweight and the welterweight categories respectively.

First Asian Games gold – men

Padam Bahadur Mal won the gold medal in the lightweight category in 1962 in the Asian Games held in Jakarta, Indonesia.

First Commonwealth Games gold

Mohammed Ali Qamar won the gold medal in the lightweight category, defeating Darren Langley 27–25 at the Commonwealth Games in Manchester, UK, in 2002.

First medal in the World Championship – senior – men

Vijender Singh won a bronze medal in the 2009 Milan World Cup in Italy.

First male boxer to win the APB Best Boxing trophy

Asian Games gold medallist Vikas Krishan was awarded the APB Best Boxing trophy at AIBA's 70th anniversary in Montreux, Switzerland, 2016.

First boxer in the AIBA athletes commission

In November 2019, veteran Indian boxer Laishram Sarita Devi was elected unopposed to the AIBA's first ever athletes commission to represent the Asian bloc. She is an eight-time Asian Championship medallist, with five being gold medals.

First Indian woman boxer to receive AIBA Legends award

M.C. Mary Kom received the AIBA Legends Award at AIBA's 70th anniversary gala in Montreux, Switzerland, in 2016.

First National Championship

The very first National Boxing Championship in the country, organized by the Indian Amateur Boxing Federation, was held in Bombay (now Mumbai), Maharashtra, from 18 to 22 March 1950.

WR Most World Championship titles – women

M.C. Mary Kom is the first female pugilist to win the World Championship crown six times (2002, 2005, 2006, 2008, 2010 and 2018). She also won the most world titles (five) in a row between 2002 and 2010. Others to have won gold medals in the World Championships are Sarita Devi (2006) , Jenny R. Lalremliani, (2006), Lakha K.C. (2006) and Nikhat Zareen (2022).

Most golds in an international meet

India won 10 gold and two silver medals at the 1995 South Asian Games (SAG; formerly SAF) in Chennai, Tamil Nadu. This achievement is second only to South Korea's haul of all 12 gold medals in the 1986 Seoul Asian Games.

Most international titles

- Heavyweight boxer Kaur Singh won gold at four major international events: the q980 Asian Boxing Championship (Bombay, now Mumbai, Maharashtra) and 1982 (Seoul, South Korea), the 1982 Delhi Asian Games and the 1982 King's Cup in Bangkok, Thailand.
- Super heavyweight boxer Rajkumar Sangwan also won four golds: at the 1991 Asian Invitational Championship in Bangkok, Thailand; the 1993 China Invitational Championship in Beijing, China; the 1993 South Asian Federation (SAF) Games at Dhaka, Bangladesh; and the 1994 Asian Boxing Championship at Tehran, Iran.

Most Asian Games golds

Hawa Singh (heavyweight) won two golds at the 1966 and 1970 Asian Games, both held in Bangkok, Thailand.

Most medals in the Asian Championship – women

M.C. Mary Kom (46 kg), L. Sarita Devi (54 kg), Jenny R. Lalremliani (63 kg) and Jyotsna (80 kg and 86 kg) won two golds each at the 2003 and the 2005 Asian Women's Boxing Championship, in Hisar, Haryana, and Kaohsiung, Taiwan, respectively.

NATIONAL SPORTS AWARDS 2022

BOXING

Arjuna Award
Amit Panghal,
Nikhat Zareen

Dronacharya Award
Mohammad Ali Qamar

Most Commonwealth Championship gold medals

India won six gold medals and the overall title at the Commonwealth Championship in New Delhi in March 2010. Amandeep Singh (49 kg), Suranjoy Singh (52 kg), Jai Bhagwan (60 kg), Vijender Singh (75 kg), Dinesh Kumar (81 kg) and Paramjeet Samota (+91 kg) won a gold medal each.

Nikhat Zareen: part of the best performance at the Asian Championship

Most medals in the World Cup – men

The Indian team won a silver and a bronze medal, and the sixth position overall, in the AIBA Boxing World Cup in October 2019 in Yekaterinburg, Russia.

Most medals in the World Boxing Championships

In October 2019, M.C. Mary Kom became the first boxer in the world (male or female) to win eight World Championship medals (six gold, a silver and a bronze).

Most successive professional wins

Vijender Singh demolished former Commonwealth champion Charles Adamu to claim his 12th straight win in November 2019. The winning streak ended when he was defeated by Russian opponent, Artysh Lopsan, in Goa in March 2021.

Most medals at the Youth Boxing Championships

The Indian team won five gold, two silver and five bronze medals at the Youth Boxing Championship in November 2019 in Ulaanbaatar, Mongolia.

Best performance in the World Boxing Championships – women

India won four gold, one silver and three bronze medals in the fourth World Women's Boxing Championship 2006 in New Delhi. M.C. Mary Kom (46 kg), L. Sarita Devi (52 kg), Jenny R. Lalremliani (63 kg) and Lekha K.C. (75 kg) won gold medals. N. Usha (57 kg) won a silver. The bronze winners were Chhotu Loura (50 kg), Aruna Mishra (60 kg) and Renu (82 kg).

Best performance in the Asian Games

India won two gold, three silver and four bronze medals in the 2010 Asian Games, its best haul at an Asian Games. The gold medallists were Vikas Krishan (60 kg) and Vijender Singh (75 kg). Silver medals were won by V. Santosh Kumar (64 kg), Dinesh Kumar (81 kg) and Manpreet Singh (91 kg). The bronze went to Suranjoy Singh (52 kg), Paramjeet Samota (+91 kg), M.C. Mary Kom (51 kg) and Kavita Goyal (75 kg).

Best performance at the Asian Championship

Indian boxers won two gold, four silver and seven bronze medals in Bangkok, Thailand, in April 2019 to finish at the third position with 13 medals. Pooja Rani (81 kg) and Amit Panghal (52 kg) won gold medals; Deepak Singh (49 kg), Kavinder Singh Bisht (56 kg), Ashish Kumar (75 kg) and Simranjit Kaur (64 kg) won silvers; Nikhat Zareen (51 kg), Manisha Moun (54 kg), Sonia Chahal (57 kg), L. Sarita Devi (60 kg), Shiva Thapa (60 kg), Ashish (69 kg) and Satish Kumar (+91 kg) won bronze medals.

M.C. Mary Kom: most medals in the World Championships

Asian Games gold medallist Dingko Singh, who motivated a generation of Indian boxers with his win in Bangladesh in 1998, passed away on 10 June 2022.

Best performance in Asian Games – women
India won a gold and two bronze medals at the 2014 Incheon Asian Games in South Korea. M.C. Mary Kom won the gold in the women's flyweight (51 kg) event. L. Sarita Devi (lightweight, 60 kg) and Pooja Rani (middleweight, 75 kg) won bronze medals.

Best performance in the World Youth Women's Boxing Championship
Seven Indian women boxers clinched gold medals in their respective weight categories in the AIBA Youth World Boxing Championships in Kielce, Poland, in August 2021. They were Gitika (48 kg), Naorem Babyrojisana Chanu (51 kg), Poonam (57 kg), Vinka (60 kg), Arundhati Choudhary (69 kg), T. Sanamacha Chanu (75 kg) and Alfiya Pathan (+81 kg).

Best performance at the Commonwealth Games
At the 2018 CWG in Gold Coast, Australia, India won three gold, three silver and three bronze medals. M.C. Mary Kom in women's lightweight (48 kg), Gaurav Solanki in flyweight (52 kg) and Vikas Krishan in middleweight (75 kg) won gold medals. Amit Panghal in light flyweight (49 kg), Manish Kaushik in lightweight (60 kg) and Satish Kumar in superweight (+91 kg) won silver medals. Mohammed Hussamuddin in bantamweight (56 kg), Manoj Kumar in welterweight (69 kg) and Naman Talwar in heavyweight (91 kg) won bronze medals.

World no. 1
- In 2009, AIBA announced Vijender Singh as the top-ranked boxer in the annual middleweight category.
- In January 2019, M.C. Mary Kom (48 kg category) was the top ranked boxer in the AIBA World Ranking (women)

Best youth boxer – men
Sachin Siwach was named Asian Boxing Confederation's Best Youth Boxer of 2017.

Pravin Thipsay: first winner of the Commonwealth title

CHESS

GENERAL

World Champions
So far, 36 Indians have won 55 world titles. They are: Viswanathan Anand (World 2000, 2007, 2008, 2010, 2012 and Junior, 1987); P. Harikrishna (U-10, 1996 and junior 2004); K. Humpy (girls' U-10, 1997, girls' U-12, 1998, girls' U-14, 2000 and junior 2001); Aarthie Ramaswamy (U-18, 1999); Deep Sengupta (U-12, 2000); D. Harika (girls' U-14, 2004, girls' U-18, 2006, and junior girls', 2008); N. Srinath (U-12, 2005); Sahaj Grover (U-10, 2005); Girish A. Koushik (U-8, 2006); Ivana Furtado (girls' U-8, 2006 and 2007); C.H. Mohineesh (U-10, 2006); Ch. Sahajasri (U-10, 2006); Abhijeet Gupta (junior, 2008); Sayantan Das (U-12, 2008); Vidit Gujarathi (U-14, 2008); Padmini Rout (girls' U-14, 2008); B. Adhiban (U-16, 2008); Sowmya Swaminathan (junior girls', 2009); M. Karthikeyan (U-12, 2011, U-16, 2013); M. Mahalakshmi (girls' U-14, 2012 and girls' U-18, 2015); R. Vaishali (girls' U-12, 2012 and girls' U-14, 2015); N. Priyanka (U-10, 2012); Saina Salonika (girls' U-10, 2013; R. Praggnanandhaa (U-8, 2013 and U-10, 2015); Divya Deshmukh (girls' U-10, 2014, and girls' U-14, 2017)); Nihal Sarin (U-10, 2014, and U-18 (online), 2020); Bharath Subramanium (U-8, 2015); Rakshitta Ravi (girls' U-10, 2015); Aakanksha Hagawane (girls' U-16, 2016); D. Jishitha (girls U-14, 2017); D. Gukesh (U-12, 2019 and U-14 (online), 2020); B. Savitha Shri (girls' U-12, 2019); A. Charvi (girls' U-8, 2022), Shubhi Gupta (girls' U-12. 2022); A. R. Ilamparthi (U-14, 2022); and Pranav Anand (U-18, 2022).

Most times world champion
Viswanathan Anand has won the World Chess Championship five times (2000, 2007, 2008, 2010 and 2012).

Oldest to regain the world rapid title
Viswanathan Anand, at 48, became the oldest world champion in the rapid format (25-minute time format) in Riyadh in December 2017. He regained the title won in 2003. Two days later, he also became the oldest medallist in the blitz format (five-minute time format) by claiming the bronze medal.

Commonwealth champions
Twelve Indians have won the Commonwealth title. They are: Pravin Thipsay (1985), D.V. Prasad (1986), P. Mithrakanth (1996), Atanu Lahiri (1999), K. Sasikiran (2000), P. Harikrishna (2001), Dibyendu Barua (2003), R.B. Ramesh (2007), R.R. Laxman (2010), M.R. Lalith Babu (2012), Abhijeet Gupta (2013, 2015, 2016, 2017 and 2019) and P. Karthikeyan (2018).

Most successful Commonwealth champion
Abhijeet Gupta is the only player to win the title five times, including three times in a row from 2015 to 2017.

Asian champions – men
Five men – K. Sasikiran (2003), Surya Shekhar Ganguly (2009), P. Harikrishna (2011), Parimarjan Negi (2012) and S.P. Sethuraman (2016) – have been crowned Asian champions.

Asian champions – women
Seven Indian women have won the title on nine occasions – Rohini Khadilkar (1981 and 1983), Anupama Gokhale (1985 and 1987), Bhagyashree Thipsay (1991), K. Humpy (2003), Tania Sachdev (2007), D. Harika (2011), Bhakti Kulkarni (2016) and Padmini Rout (2018).

Asian junior champions – boys
V. Ravi Kumar (1978); Viswanathan Anand (1984 and 85); Abhijit Kunte (1997); Tejas Bakre (1998); K. Sasikiran (1999); P. Harikrishna (2000); Deepan Chakravarthy (2002); P. Magesh Chandran (2003); S. Arun Prasad (2004); P. Karthikeyan (2007); Aswin Jayaram (2008 and 2009); M. Shyam Sundar (2010 and 2011); N. Srinath (2012, 2013 and 2014); and Aravindh Chithambaram (2016).

Asian junior champions – girls
Anupama Abhyankar (1985); Saheli Dhar (1993); K. Humpy (2000); M. Kasturi (2001); Tania Sachdev (2002); Y. Pratibha (2003); Mary Ann Gomes (2006, 2007, 2008); Padmini Rout (2009); Bhakti Kulkarni (2011); and Ivana Furtado (2012 and 2017).

Board Prize with a 'perfect' score
Viswanathan Anand scored seven points from seven rounds to win the top Board Prize in the Asian Team Championship in 1989.

Domination in Advanced Chess
Viswanathan Anand won a hat-trick of titles in 1999, 2000 and 2001 in Leon, Spain. IIn 2000 and 2001 he beat Alexei Shirov of Spain in the final to win the tournament. In Advanced Chess, players have the benefit of using database searches on their computers before making a move.

Four successive Asian Junior titles
Indians twice won the title for four years in a row. The Indian boys won from 1997 to 2000 and again from 2007 to 2010.

Golden sweep – Asian Youth Championship
India won 18 medals, including all eight gold medals at stake, in the Asian Youth Championship in 2006. Sweety Patel (girls' U-8), Sahajasri (Girls U-10), Padmini Rout (girls' U-12), Bhakti Kulkarni (girls' U-14), Prince Bajaj (boys' U-8), G.V. Sai Krishna (boys' U-10), Vidit Gujarati (boys' U-12) and S. Nitin (boys' U-14) were the gold medal winners.

Grandmasters of India
The list of Indian grandmasters now stands at 75. They are: 1. Viswanathan Anand (1987); 2. Dibyendu Barua (1991); 3. Pravin Thipsay (1997); 4. Abhijit Kunte (2000); 5. K. Sasikiran (2000); 6. P. Harikrishna (2001); 7. Koneru Humpy (2001); 8. Surya Shekhar Ganguly (2002); 9. Sandipan Chanda (2003); 10. R.B. Ramesh (2004); 11. Tejas Bakre (2004); 12. P. Magesh Chandran; (2006); 13. Neeloptal Das (2006); 14. Deepan Chakravarthy (2006); 15. Parimarjan Negi (2006); 16. G.N. Gopal (2007); 17. Abhijeet Gupta (2008); 18. S. Arun Prasad (2008); 19. S. Kidambi (2009); 20. R.R. Laxman (2009); 21. Sriram Jha (2010); 22. Deep Sengupta (2010); 23. B. Adhiban (2010); 24. S.P. Sethuraman (2011); 25. D. Harika (2011); 26. M.R. Lalith Babu (2012); 27. Vaibhav Suri (2012); 28. M.R. Venkatesh (2012); 29. Sahaj Grover (2012); 30. Vidit Gujarathi (2012); 31. M. Shyam Sundar (2012); 32. Akshayraj Kore (2013); 33. Vishnu Prasanna (2013); 34. Saptarshi Roy Choudhury (2013); 35. Debashis Das (2013); 36. Ankit Rajpara (2014); 37. Aravindh Chithambaram (2015); 38. Murali Karthikeyan (2015); 39. Ashwin Jayaram (2015); 40. Swapnil Dhopade (2015); 41. S.L. Narayanan (2015); 42. Shardul Gagare (2015); 43. Diptayan Ghosh (2016); 44. K. Priyadarshan (2016); 45. Aryan Chopra (2016); 46. N. Srinath (2017); 47. Himanshu Sharma (2017); 48. Anurag Mhamal (2017); 49. Abhimanyu Puranik (2017); 50. M.S. Thej Kumar (2017); 51. Saptarshi Roy (2018) and 52. R. Praggnanandhaa (2018); 53. Nihal Sarin (2018); 54. Arjun Erigaisi (2018); 55. Karthik Venkatraman (2018); 56. Harsha Bharathakoti (2018); 57. P. Karthikeyan (2018); 58. G.A. Stany (2018); 59. N. R. Vishakh (2019); 60. D. Gukesh (2019); 61. P. Iniyan (2019); 62. Swayams Mishra (2019); 63. Girish Koushik (2019); 64. Prithu Gupta (2019); |65. Raunak Sadhwani (2019); 66. G. Akash (2020); 67. Leon Mendonca (2021); 68. Arjun Kalyan (2021); 69. Harshit Raja (2021); 70. Raja Rithvik (2021); 71. Sankalp Gupta (2021); 72. Mithrabha Guha (2021); 73. Bharath Subramaniyam (2022); 74. Rahul Srivatshav (2022); and 75. V. Pranav (2022).

Grand Slam victories
In chess, the tournaments in Wijk Aan Zee, Linares and Dortmund were considered the equivalent of the Grand Slam in golf. Anand

NATIONAL SPORTS AWARDS 2021

CHESS

Dhyan Chand Award (Lifetime)
Abhijeet Kunte

Viswanathan Anand: first Grandmaster

won at Wijk Aan Zee five times, and at Linares and Dortmund, both three times.

Master of the rapid game

Anand was considered master of the rapid version of the game. In 2004, Anand reinforced the impression by winning the rapid section of the Melody Ambers tournament, and events in Mainz, Sao Paulo, Bastia and Tallinn (Estonia). Anand has been victorious in the Chess Classic of Mainz and the Corsica Masters in Bastia five times each.

Medal sweep at Asian Junior Championship

India swept all the six medals at stake in the Asian Junior Championship in Colombo in 2003. The medal winners were:

- *Boys*: P. Magesh Chandran (gold), S. Poobesh Anand (silver) and Prathamesh Mokal (bronze)
- *Girls*: Y. Pratibha (gold), J.E. Kavitha (silver) and Saheli Nath (bronze).

India repeated the feat in December 2007. P. Karthikeyan (gold), Aswin Jayaram (silver) and Shyam Sundar (bronze) won medals in the open section. Among the girls were Mary Ann Gomes (gold), Padmini Rout (gold) and Kiran Manisha Mohanty (gold).

Mir Sultan Khan: first international recognition

Success in Advance Chess tournament

Viswanathan Anand has the distinction of claiming a hat-trick of titles in the Advanced Chess tournament in Leon, Spain. He won in 1999, 2000 and 2001.

World Railways champion

Indian Railways won the World Railway championship in Piest'any, Slovakia, in November 2005. The members of the victorious team that scored 37.5 points from a maximum of 42 were P.D.S. Girinath, Vikramaditya Kamble, Suvrajit Saha, Saptarshi Roy Chowdhury, Nassir Wajih, K. Ratnakaran and Gurpreet Pal Singh.

Dibyendu Barua: first Olympiad gold

FIRST

First 2-medal win in the Chess Olympiad

Abhijeet Gupta (silver) and Tania Sachdev (bronze) helped India win two medals for the first time in a Chess Olympiad in Istanbul in September 2012.

First Asian Junior title

V. Ravi Kumar won the Asian Junior title in 1978.

First Asian Junior title twice

Viswanathan Anand was the first Indian to win the Asian Junior title in 1984 and 1985.

First Asian Sub-junior Champion

Tejas Bakre won the title in 1998.

First GM norm

Pravin Thipsay was the first to achieve GM norm in the 1985 Commonwealth championship in London.

First GM norm in National Championship

P. Konguvel was the first Indian to date to gain a nine-game norm from the National 'A' Championship at New Delhi in June 2001.

First Grandmaster (GM)

Viswanathan Anand became India's first GM on 28 December 1987 at the Sakthi Finance Grandmaster tournament in Coimbatore.

First International Master (IM) – men

Manuel Aaron of Tamil Nadu became an International Master in 1961. 30 (b).

First International Master (IM) - women

S. Vijayalakshmi got the International Master's title in Sept 2000.

First Olympiad gold

Dibyendu Barua won the gold on the second board of the Olympiad in Novi Sad (erstwhile Yugoslavia) in 1990.

First Olympiad gold on top board

D. Gukesh won the gold on top board in Mahabalipuram in 2022.

First Olympiad medal

Rafiq Khan won a silver medal in the 1980 Olympiad.

First time when India won medals in both sections of Olympiad

India won bronze medals in Open and women sections of the Olympiad in Mahabalipuram in 2022.

First medal in the Chess Olympiad

India won its maiden medal from the Tromso Chess Olympiad in 2014 in Norway. In the open section, India was represented by Parimarjan Negi,

K, Sasikiran, S.P. Sethuraman, B. Adhiban and M.R. Lalith Babu claimed the bronze medal, ahead of traditional powerhouses like Russia, Armenia and Ukraine.

First international recognition
Mir Sultan Khan, born in 1905 in village Mittha, Punjab, received international recognition at a time when there was no system of Elo ratings. In 1928, he won the all-India title scoring 8.5 out of 9 points at the British Championship. He won again in 1932 and 1933. He also defeated world champion Jose Casablanca of Cuba at the Hastings tournament. Considered among the 10 best players in the world then, he returned to India in 1933 but played little chess. He died in Sargodha, Pakistan on 25 May 1966.

First medal in Asian Games
K Humpy won the gold in the Doha Asian Games in 2006.

First team medal in Asian Games
The trio of K. Sasikiran, P. Harikrishna and K. Humpy won the mixed team gold in Doha in 2006.

First to win the Asian Junior girls' title thrice
Mary Ann Gomes won the title in 2006 (New Delhi), 2007 (Mumbai) and 2008 (Chennai).

First WGM norm
Bhagyashree Thipsay was the first to achieve a Woman Grand Master (WGM) norm in 1986 in the Lloyds Bank Master's tournament when she was twenty-one.

First WIM
Jayshree Khadilkar became a WIM (Woman International Master) in 1978.

First woman to lead a team in the open section
K. Humpy led India 'B' in the open section of the Asian Team Championship at Jodhpur in 2003.

Two World Cups
Viswanathan Anand is the first person in the world to successfully defend the men's World Cup title. He did so at Hyderabad in October 2002.

First World Junior title
Viswanathan Anand was 17 years 225 days when he won the title on 2 August 1987 at Baguio city in the Philippines. P. Harikrishna (2004) and Abhijeet Gupta (2008) are the other junior title winners.

First World Sub-junior medal
Viswanathan Anand claimed a bronze after sharing the second place in the 1984.

WR First country to win both World Junior titles in a single edition
India became the first country to win both the World Junior titles in a single edition in 2008 when Abhijeet Gupta and D. Harika won the open and girls' sections respectively in the World Junior Chess Championship in Gazientep. Parimarjan Negi claimed the silver to give India a rare 1-2 finish in the open section.

MOSTS

Highest cheque
Viswanathan Anand won €1.20 million for retaining the World Chess title in Sofia, Bulgaria, in May 2010. This is the biggest cheque received by an Indian sportsperson.

Most International age group titles (in a single year)
Tejas Bakre won three gold medals in eight months in 1998: the Asian Junior at Rasht (Iran) in May, the World Youth Games championship in Moscow in July and the Asian Sub-Junior in Mumbai in December.

Most medals
Indians won 21 medals – seven gold, seven silver and seven bronze – in the Asian Youth Championship held in New Delhi in 2005. This was the biggest haul by India in a continental competition.

Most National titles (in a season)
P. Harikrishna won five National titles in 1997–98 season – the 1997 National Sub-juniors held in January 1998 at Aurangabad, the U-12 in Ahmedabad, the U-18 in Bikaner, the U-14 rapid chess title in Guntur and the 1998 National Sub-junior at Aurangabad.

Most National titles
- *Men*: Manuel Aaron won nine National titles, five of them in a row from 1969-74.
- *Women*: S. Vijayalakshmi has claimed the National title six times, including five times in a row from May 2002.

Most titles in a year
Viswanathan Anand won a string of eight titles in the year 2000. Starting with the World Blitz Cup, he won the Wydra International at Haifa, the Advanced Chess title in Leon, the Giants Classic in Frankfurt, the Dortmund International (joint winner), the World

P. Harikrishna: most National titles (in a season)

NATIONAL SPORTS AWARDS 2022
CHESS
Arjuna Award
Bhakti Pradip Kulkarni,
R. Praggnanandhaa

Cup in Shenyang, China, and the Corsica Masters in France, finishing with the World Championship title in December 2000.

R. Praggnanandhaa: youngest International Master

City to host most Commonwealth Championships

New Delhi hosted the Commonwealth championship six times between 2007 and 2019.

Most participants in an International Open

As many as 2,810 entries were received across three sections of the 17th Delhi International Open held in January 2019.

Most prize money offered in an International Open

The 2019 Delhi International Open offered ₹1.01 crore as prize money across three sections.

FASTEST

Fastest to achieve norms

P. Harikrishna achieved three norms – his IM norm in the Asian Championship in Udaipur, the Goodricke tournament in Kolkata and the Commonwealth Championship in Sangli – in less than two months in 2000.

D. Gukesh: youngest Grandmaster

YOUNGEST

Youngest to achieve an IM norm

R. Praggnanandhaa became the youngest Indian to make an IM norm. At 10 years, six months, he gained the distinction in Cannes (France) in February 2016.

K. Humpy: youngest Grandmaster – female

Youngest International Master

R. Praggnanandhaa, at the age of 10 years and nine months, became the youngest International Master in chess history in May 2017 by making his third and final IM norm at Bhubaneswar. His earlier two norms had come in Cannes and Moscow.

Youngest Grandmaster

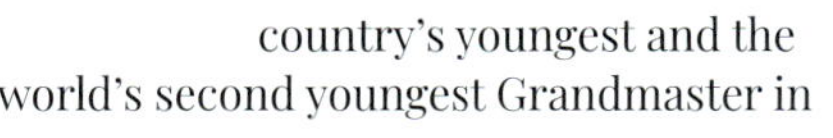

D. Gukesh became the country's youngest and the world's second youngest Grandmaster in January 2019 at the age of 12 years, seven months and 17 days.

Youngest Grandmaster – female

K. Humpy is the youngest female to become a GM at 15 years 58 days.

Youngest Indian in the World Cup and the Chess Olympiad

D. Harika played in the World Cup at 11 years and nine months in Hyderabad 2002. She also became the youngest to play for India in the Chess Olympiad after her undefeated performance in Mallorca, Spain, in 2004.

Youngest international title winners

Sanskruti Wankhede and Vallabh Kavi were the winners of the Asian Schools' chess (U-5) girls' and boys' titles respectively, in New Delhi in 2011.

Youngest National champion

Sixteen-year-old G. Akash became the youngest National champion in 2012.

Youngest National Junior champion

Abhijeet Gupta of Bhilwara became the youngest National Junior champion at Nagpur in 2002. He won the U-19 event at the age of 13 years 10 days.

Youngest to beat a GM

Hetul Shah (9) defeated Kazakh Nurlan Ibrayev in the first round of the Parsvnath International Open chess tournament in New Delhi on 11 January 2009, to become the youngest Indian to beat a Grandmaster. He broke the record of Parimarjan Negi who had achieved the feat at the age of eleven.

Youngest to qualify for the National Championship

- Dibyendu Barua, then 12, remains the youngest to qualify for the National championship in 1978.
- D. Harika holds the unique record of being the youngest girl to qualify for the men's National championship in 2004 as well as for tthe women's National championship in 2001.

Youngest to win the Commonwealth title

P. Harikrishna, then fifteen, won the gold in London in 2001 after a three-way tie with two British players.

Youngest to win the World Junior title

P. Harikrishna won the World junior title in Kochi in November 2004 when he was 18 years 204 days old.

Youngest WIM
K. Humpy became the youngest Woman International Master (WIM) in Asia at 12 years, three months, four days.

Youngest winner of Asian Junior (U-20) title
M Kasturi, then 14 years old, won the Asian Junior title in Teheran in 2001.

Youngest world champion in any sport
Ivana Furtado claimed the World Girls' U-8 crown at the age of seven years and 226 at Batumi, Georgia on 29 October 2006.

BEST

Best achievement
• *Men*: Viswanathan Anand's rating of 2817 in March 2011 is the highest recorded by an Indian.
• *Woen*: Among women, Koneru Humpy's rating of 2623 in July 2009 is the highest.

Best performance (Category 21)
Viswanathan Anand beat a field of seven super Grandmasters at Madrid between Feb 21 and March 10, 1998. The Category 21 tournament attracted seven of the top nine GMs of the world. Anand beat Alexey Shirov, Peter Svidler, Vassily Ivanchuk, Vaselin Topalov 1.5-0.5; lost to Gary Kasparov 0.5-1.5 and drew 1-1 with Vladimir Kramnik.

Best performance in Asian Team Championship
Indian men won the gold and women won the silver medal at Esfahan, Iran in 2006.

Highest title
K. Humpy won the World Junior Girls (U-20) Championship in August 2001 at 14 years.

ONLY

First/only winner of Asian Junior and Sub-junior titles
Tejas Bakre won the Asian Junior and Asian Sub-junior titles at the same time, in 1998.

Only Asian to win at Wijk Aan Zee
Viswanathan Anand is the only Asian to win the Hoogovens Chess Tournament (Corus tournament since 2000) at Wijk Aan Zee in 1989, though jointly with three others. He won the title again in 1998, jointly with Vladimir Kramnik, and outright in 2003, 2004 and 2006.

Only Chess Oscar award winner
Viswanathan Anand is the only Indian to receive the Chess Oscar (founded in 1967) by the Russian chess magazine *64 - Chess Review*. He has claimed the Chess Oscar six times (in 1997, 1998, 2003, 2004, 2007 and 2008).

Only Indian to reach the final of World Championship
K. Humpy reached the final of Championship 2011 where China's Hou Yifan won 5.5-2.5 with two games to spare in their 10-game title-match.

Only Indian to win against computers
Viswanathan Anand simultaneously played six computers and won 4-2, in the Aegon Man versus Computer Chess Event in 1997.

Only Indian to win rapid/ blindfold event
Viswanathan Anand won the first-of-its-kind Melody Amber Blindfold and Rapid chess event in 1994, 1997, 2003 and jointly in 2006.

Only semi-finalist of World Championship and World Cup
K. Humpy reached the semi-finals of the World Championship in Elista in 2004 and the World Cup held at Hyderabad in 2002.

Only Indian with three World Championship bronze medals
D. Harika claimed three successive bronze medals from the Women's World Championship in 2012, 2015 and 2017.

WR Only girl to win the National U-12 – open section
K. Humpy won the U-12 title in Ahmedabad in 1999.

INDIA AT HER BEST 75 YEARS OF INDEPENDENCE

Chess: National Awards

Arjuna Award: Manuel Aaron (1961); Rohini Khadilkar (1980); Dibyendu Barua (1983); Pravin Thipsay (1984); Viswanathan Anand (1985); D.V. Prasad and Bhagyashree Thipsay (1987); Anupma Gokhale (1990); S. Vijayalakshmi (2000); K. Sasikiran (2002); K. Humpy (2003); Surya Shekhar Ganguly (2005); P. Harikrishna (2006); D. Harika (2007); Tania Sachdev (2009); Parimarjan Negi (2010); and Abhijeet Gupta (2013).

Rajiv Gandhi Khel Ratna: Viswanathan Anand (1991–92).

Dronacharya Award: Raghunandan Gokhale (1986); K. Ashok (2006).

Padma Shri: Anupama Abhyankar (1986), Viswanathan Anand and Bhagyashree Thipsay ((1987); D. Harika (2019).

Padma Bhushan: Viswanathan Anand (2001).

Padma Vibhushan: 2007 Viswanathan Anand

CRICKET

WOMEN'S CRICKET

GENERAL

Mithali Raj: most career runs in women's international cricket

Jhulan Goswami: most career wickets across formats

Youngest to debut across all formats

Shafali Verma became the youngest Indian cricketer to make her debut across all three formats of the game when she played her first One-Day International (ODI) on 27 June 2021, against England in the UK, when she was 17 years and 150 days old. She made her Test debut on 16 June 2021 in Bristol, UK, against England. Her T20I debut came at the age of 15 against South Africa in September 2019 in Surat, Gujarat. She is also the youngest woman ever to play an ODI, and the first Indian and fourth woman to score a half-century in both innings on a Test debut.

WR Most career runs in women's international cricket

Mithali Raj has scored 10,868 runs in her international career, with 669 runs in Tests, 7,805 in ODIs and 2,364 in T20Is.

Longest career

Mithali Raj's cricketing career spans more than 23 years.

Most career wickets across formats

Jhulan Goswami, with 355 wickets in 284 matches, has the most wickets across formats.

TESTS

Most career dismissals by a wicketkeeper

Anju Jain has the most career dismissals by a wicketkeeper with 23 dismissals from 1995 to 2003, including 15 caught and eight stumped.

Biggest victory margin

India won by an innings and 34 runs while playing against South Africa in Mysuru, Karnataka, on 16 November 2014.

Narrowest victory margin

India won by 5 wickets against West Indies in Patna, Bihar, on 17 November 1976, and then against England at Taunton, UK, on 1 September 2006.

Lowest total

The lowest total ever was 65 runs for 10 wickets in 46 overs against the West Indies at Jammu, Jammu and Kashmir, on 29 November 1976.

Highest total

The highest total by the women's Test cricket team is 467 in 177.1 overs versus England at Taunton, UK, on 17 August 2002.

First and only double century

Mithali Raj scored 214 runs in 407 balls, against England at Taunton, UK, on 16 August 2002. She also has the best batting average of 51.00 in 10 matches.

Most runs

Sandhya Agarwal has 1,110 runs in 13 matches. She also holds the record for the most centuries, with four in 13 Tests and 23 innings.

Most balls delivered

Former Indian player and left-arm spinner Diana Edulji is the only woman to deliver more than 5,000 balls (5,248) in Test matches.

Most wickets in a Test

Right-arm pacer Jhulan Goswami took 10 wickets in the match against England at Taunton, UK, on 1 September 2006.

Most career wickets in Tests

The record for most wickets in a Test career belongs to Diana Edulji, with 63 wickets taken from 1976 to 1991.

Best bowling average

Jhulan Goswami, with an average of 17.36 with 44 wickets in 12 matches, has an unmatched bowling average in women's Test cricket in India.

Best bowling – innings

Neetu David's eight wickets for 53 runs in the India versus England match at Jamshedpur, Jharkhand, on 27 November 1995, makes her the only bowler in women's Test cricket to have claimed eight wickets in an innings.

Most career catches by a fielder

Sudha Shah has taken 21 catches in as many matches, an Indian record for a fielding position.

ONE-DAY INTERNATIONALS

Highest partnership

Deepti Sharma and Poonam Raut made a 320-run stand for the first wicket at the India versus Ireland match at Potchefstroom, South Africa, on 15 May 2017.

Highest individual score
Deepti Sharma was 188 not out at the India versus Ireland match at Potchefstroom, South Africa, on 15 May 2017.

Best bowling average – minimum 50 wickets
Neetu David holds the record with an average of 16.34 (141 wickets in 97 matches).

Clean sweep victories in a bilateral series
The Indian team won all five matches in a bilateral series twice – against England in January 2002, and then against West Indies during February–March 2004.

Century on debut
Mithali Raj scored a century on her debut with 114 runs (not out) versus Ireland at Milton Keynes, UK, on 26 June 1999.

WR Most runs scored
Mithali Raj has scored 7,805 runs in 232 matches. She is the only woman cricketer to score more than 7,000 runs.

Most career dismissals by a wicketkeeper
Anju Jain has 81 dismissals to her credit, including 30 caught and 51 stumped.

Most career catches by a fielder
Jhulan Goswami has notched up 69 catches in 204 matches.

WR Most career stumpings by a wicketkeeper
Anju Jain holds a world record with 51 stumpings across her career.

T20 INTERNATIONALS

Largest victory margin
- The largest victory margin in terms of runs is 142 runs versus Malaysia on 3 June 2018 at the Kinrara Academy Oval, Kuala Lumpur, Malaysia.
- In terms of wickets, the largest victory margin has been by 10 wickets against the Australian team on 29 January 2016 at Melbourne, Australia.

Highest partnership
Shafali Verma and Smriti Mandhana put on a 143-run stand for the first wicket versus West Indies at the Darren Sammy National Cricket Stadium, Saint Lucia, on 9 November 2019.

Narrowest margin of victory
- By runs, the narrowest margin was 3 runs on two occasions. The first was against the West Indies at North Sound, Antigua, on 19 February 2012, and the second was against New Zealand in Melbourne, Australia, on 27 February 2020.
- By wickets, India's narrowest margin has been against New Zealand, of 3 wickets at Aldershot, England, on 27 June 2011.

Most career runs
Harmanpreet Kaur has scored 2,694 in 137 matches with a batting average of 27.48.

Highest team total
India's highest team total was 198 for 4 wickets in the third match versus England at Brabourne Stadium in Mumbai, Maharashtra, in the Tri-Nation Women's T20I Series in March 2018.

Lowest team total
India scored only 62 runs in 18.2 overs versus Australia at Billericay, Essex, UK, on 23 June 2011.

Most career wickets
Poonam Yadav has notched up 98 wickets in 72 matches.

Best bowling average (minimum qualification of 30 matches)
Poonam Raut has a record bowling average of 9.66.

Best bowling
Jhulan Goswami took 5 wickets for 11 runs in a T20I match against Australia at Visakhapatnam, Andhra Pradesh, on 23 March 2012.

Most career dismissals by a wicketkeeper
Tania Bhatia has 67 dismissals (23 caught and 44 stumped) in 50 matches.

Harmanpreet Kaur: most career runs in T20 Internationals

Poonam Yadav: most career wickets in T20 Internationals

Level Paying Field
On 27 October 2022, the Board of Control for Cricket in India (BCCI) took a big step by announcing their 'pay equity policy', saying that its centrally contracted men and women players would get the same match fees. It is a significant move towards bringing gender pay parity in the country. According to the policy, women players will now get 15 lakh rupees per Test match, six lakh rupees for a One-Day International and three lakh rupees for a T20 International. Till now, they were paid ₹one lakh rupees for a white-ball match and four lakh rupees for a Test. India has become only the second country in international cricket, after New Zealand, to implement equal pay in cricket.

Most career catches by a fielder
Harmanpreet Kaur holds the record of 53 catches in 137 matches, the highest number of career catches.

MEN'S CRICKET

GENERAL

Player with the most IPL titles
Rohit Sharma has earned the most IPL titles, totalling six: one with the Deccan Chargers, Hyderabad (2009) and five with the Mumbai Indians (2013, 2015, 2017, 2019 and 2020).

TESTS

First victory
India, captained by Vijay Hazare, defeated England by an innings and 8 runs on 10 February 1952 at Madras (now Chennai), Tamil Nadu. The victory came in the fifth match of a five-match series and India managed to draw the series 1–1.

First to reach 10,000 runs
Indian cricket legend Sunil Gavaskar first went past the 10,000 mark in 125 matches, reaching 10,122 Test runs in his last series against Pakistan in 1987.

Highest team innings score
The highest innings score was 759 runs for 7 wickets against England at Chennai, Tamil Nadu, in 2016.

Sachin Tendulkar: most career runs and most individual centuries

Highest score on debut (series)
Legendary batsman Sunil Gavaskar scored 774 runs in his very first Test series against West Indies in 1971, a record that remains unbroken.

WR **Most consecutive wins at home (series)**
India recorded their 15th consecutive Test series wins at home when they beat Sri Lanka in a two-match series in March 2022, beating Australia to the top spot in the longest winning streak by any team.

Most career wickets
Anil Kumble holds the record with 619 wickets in his Test career spanning from 1990 to 2008.

Most wickets in a debut series
In the India–England Test series from 5 February to 8 March 2021, Axar Patel took 27 wickets in the four-match series. He holds the record jointly with Dilip Doshi, who took the same number of wickets during a six-match home series against Australia in 1979.

WR **Most career runs**
Sachin Tendulkar's total of 15,921 runs is an unbroken world record for the most career runs in men's Test cricket.

WR **Most individual centuries**
Sachin Tendulkar scored 51 centuries – three versus West Indies in 19 Tests, 11 versus Australia in 35 Tests, two versus Pakistan in 18 Tests, seven versus England in 28 Tests, four in 22 Tests versus New Zealand, nine in 25 Tests versus Sri Lanka, seven in 25 Tests versus South Africa, five in seven Tests versus Bangladesh and three in nine Tests versus Zimbabwe.

Most runs in an over
Jasprit Bumrah scored 35 runs (not out) in an over off England Stuart Broad at Edgbaston, Birmingham in May 2022. He hit two fours off the first two deliveries, followed by a wide ball, then a six, followed by a no ball, and the next three balls were hit for fours. The penultimate ball went for a six and he scored a single off the last ball.

WR **Most sixes in a series**
Rohit Sharma scored 17 sixes in the Test series against South Africa on 20 October 2019 in Ranchi, Jharkhand.

Highest run chase
India's run chase of 406 runs for 4 wickets against West Indies in Port-of-Spain, Trinidad, in 1976 is its highest successful chase to date.

Highest individual score in a day
Virender Sehwag, in his knock of 293 against Sri Lanka in Mumbai, Maharashtra, during 2009–10, made 284 runs on the second day of the Test match – the highest individual score in a single day to date.

Highest individual innings
Virender Sehwag's 319 against South Africa in

Chennai, Tamil Nadu, in 2008 is the highest individual score in a Test match.

Fastest Indian opener to score 1,000 runs

Right-handed batsman Rohit Sharma achieved this landmark in his 17th innings as the Indian opener against England on 5 March 2021.

Lowest team innings score

India recorded an all-time low of 36 runs against Australia in Adelaide in December 2020. It is the fifth lowest in the world.

WR Highest run aggregate

Sachin Tendulkar's score of 15,921 runs from 1989 to 2013 in 200 Tests is a world record. This score, from 329 innings, amounts to an average of 53.78.

WR Most 1,000+ runs in a calendar year

Sachin Tendulkar has scored more than 1,000 runs in a calendar year on six occasions. He made 1,000 runs in 12 Tests in 1997; 1,088 runs in 10 Tests in 1999; 1,003 runs in 10 Tests in 2001; 1,392 runs in 16 Tests in 2002; 1,063 runs in 13 Tests in 2008; and 1,562 runs in 11 Tests in 2010.

WR Highest century partnerships

Rahul Dravid has been part of the most three figure partnerships, on 88 occasions; thrice for the first wicket, 34 times for the second, 26 times for the third, eight times for the fourth, 12 times for the fifth, thrice for the sixth and twice for the eighth wicket. He partnered with Sachin Tendulkar in 100-plus stands in a world record 20 times and with V.V.S. Laxman 12 times. Dravid's highest stand was with Virender Sehwag in a 410-run stand against Pakistan at Lahore in 2006. Dravid and Tendulkar have added 6,920 partnership runs, the most by any pair in history.

Highest individual innings

Rohit Sharma scored 118 versus Sri Lanka in Indore, Madhya Pradesh, in 2017.

Wicket off first ball on debut

Nilesh Kulkarni is the first and only Indian, and the 15th in the world, to capture a wicket off the very first ball on debut, when he bowled out Marvan Atapattu of Sri Lanka in Colombo, Sri Lanka, in 1997.

Wicket off first ball in a match

Syed Abid Ali took the wicket of Roy Fredricks off the very first ball in Port-of- Spain, Trinidad, against the West Indies in 1971. Kapil

Virat Kohli: Winner All the Way

The former men's national cricket team captain who repeatedly puts up record-making performances, Virat Kohli has many achievements to his credit:

- **First cricketer to win all the three major ICC awards:** Sir Garfield Sobers Trophy for Cricketer of the Year, Test Player of the Year and the ICC Men's ODI Player of the Year in 2018.
- **Only player to touch an average of 50+ across formats:** 54.46 (Test), 58.20 (ODI) and 52.65 (T20I).
- **10 centuries across all formats in a year (2017):** These are the most by a captain, surpassing the record of former Aussie skipper Ricky Ponting and former South Africa captain Graeme Smith, who had nine each.
- **First Indian captain to win a Test series in Australia:** In 2018–19, India won the four-match series 2–1. Virat led India to a record eight consecutive Test series wins.

WR **Six double centuries as skipper:** In December 2017, Kohli overtook former West Indies captain Brian Lara (Kohli took only 48 innings to make the double tons, while Lara took 85).

Fastest cricketer to score 23,000 international runs in 490 innings.

TESTS

- **Most wins as captain:** India has won in 40 Test matches out of 68 under Kohli's captaincy. In his seven-year stint as India's Test captain, those 40 wins also made Kohli the fourth most successful captain in Test history, behind only Graeme Smith, Ricky Ponting and Steve Waugh.
- After the India–England Test series from 5 February to 8 March 2021, Kohli joined former India skipper M.S. Dhoni, having notched up the most number of matches as India's captain in Test cricket, totalling 60.

ONE-DAY INTERNATIONALS

- **First to score a century on World Cup debut:** India versus Bangladesh, 2011 World Cup at Mirpur, Bangladesh, on 21 February 2011.
- **Best batting average:** 57.68 in 262 matches. (minimum criteria is 100 matches)
- **Fastest century:** 100 not out in 52 balls against Australia at Jaipur, Rajasthan, on 16 October 2013.

WR Fastest to score 12,000 runs: Kohli achieved this in his 242nd innings beating Sachin Tendulkar's record of 12,000 runs in 300 innings.

- **Fastest to score 43 centuries:** He achieved this in his 230th innings.
- Won the ICC Men's ODI Player of the Decade award in 2020.
- Won the Sir Garfield Sobers Award for Male Cricketer of the Decade in 2020.

T20 INTERNATIONALS

- **Only player to take a wicket on 0th ball:** Virat Kohli dismissed England's Kevin Pietersen with a wide ball (his first in T20I) in 2011, stumped by Dhoni.

WR First cricketer to reach 4,000 runs: Virat Kohli became the first player ever to breach the 4,000 run mark in the T20 International format. He achieved this during his World Cup match against England on 10 November 2022 at the Adelaide Oval in Australia.

Dev emulated him twice by dismissing Mohsin Khan at Jalandhar, Punjab, against Pakistan during 1983–84, and Jimmy Cook at Durban versus South Africa in 1992–93.

Best bowling figures on Test debut

Narendra Hirwani took 16 wickets for 136 runs against West Indies at Madras (now Chennai), Tamil Nadu, during 1987–88.

Best bowling in an innings

Anil Kumble took 10 wickets for 74 runs against Pakistan at Delhi in one innings during 1998–99. He became the second bowler after England's Jim Laker to do so, and is now joined by Ajaz Patel of New Zealand.

WR Best bowling in a match

Narendra Hirwani took 16 wickets for 136 runs versus West Indies at Madras (now Chennai), Tamil Nadu, during 1987–88.

WR Most catches in an innings

The world record of five catches is held by four individuals (along with eight foreign players): Yajurvindra Singh (versus England at Bengaluru, Karnataka, in 1977); Mohammad Azharuddin (versus Pakistan at Karachi, Pakistan, in 1989); K. Srikkanth (versus Australia at Perth, Australia, in 1992); and Ajinkya Rahane (versus Sri Lanka at Galle, Sri Lanka, in 2015).

Dismissing all 11 batsmen in a match

S. Venkataraghavan dismissed all 11 batsmen in the Delhi Test against New Zealand in 1964–65. His final tally was 12 for 152. He became the second bowler after England's Jim Laker and one among only six bowlers in the world to do this.

WR Most dismissals by a wicketkeeper in a match

Rishabh Pant shares the world record with England's Jack Russell (versus South Africa, 1995) and South Africa's A.B. de Villiers (versus Pakistan, 2013), with 11 dismissals in Adelaide, versus Australia, in December 2018.

Most career dismissals by a wicketkeeper

M.S. Dhoni has dismissed 294 batsmen (caught 256 and stumped 38) in 90 Tests.

Most dismissals by a wicketkeeper in an innings

The record for dismissals is six, shared by four players: Syed Kirmani, who caught five and stumped one against New Zealand at Christchurch, New Zealand, in 1975–76; M.S. Dhoni, who caught six against New Zealand at Wellington, New Zealand, in 2008–09; Wriddhiman Saha, with five caught and one stumped against West Indies at North Sound, Antigua, in 2016; and Rishabh Pant, with six caught in Adelaide in December 2018 versus Australia.

WR Most catches in a match

With eight catches in the match against Sri Lanka at Galle, Sri Lanka, in 2015 (three in the first innings and five in the second), Ajinkya Rahane holds the world record for most catches in a match.

Most dismissals by a wicketkeeper in a series

N.S. Tamhane holds the record with 19 dismissals in five Tests against Pakistan in the 1954–55 series.

Wicketkeeper with the fastest 100 dismissals

Risabh Pant reached the milestone of 100 dismissals in only 26 matches, with 92 catches and 8 stumpings. He achieved it in the first Test against South Africa at SuperSport Park, Centurion, in December 2021.

WR Highest score and fastest 100 on debut

Shikhar Dhawan scored 187 runs in 174 balls (33 fours, two sixes) in his Test debut against Australia at Mohali, Punjab, in 2013. Dhawan reached his 100 in just 85 balls – the fastest by a debutant (where full figures are available).

ONE-DAY INTERNATIONALS

Highest team total

The Indian men's cricket team scored 418 runs for 5 wickets in 50 overs against West Indies at Indore, Madhya Pradesh, on 9 December 2011.

Highest run chase

The Indian team's score of 362 runs for 1 wicket, chasing Australia's 359 runs for 5 wickets in Jaipur, Rajasthan, on 16 October 2013, was the highest run chase.

Highest score on debut

K.L. Rahul scored an unbeaten 100 against Zimbabwe at Harare, Zimbabwe, on 11 June 2016 – the only Indian to make an ODI century on debut.

WR Fastest 50 runs on debut

Krunal Pandya became the fastest-scoring debutant to post a half-century in an ODI match in just 26 balls, finishing at 58 not out in 31 balls on 23 March 2021 at the

NATIONAL SPORTS AWARDS 2021

CRICKET

Arjuna Award
Shikhar Dhawan

Dronacharya Award (Lifetime)
Sarkar Talwar

Major Dhyan Chand Khel Ratna
Mithali Raj

NATIONAL SPORTS AWARDS 2022

CRICKET

Dronacharya Award (Lifetime)
Dinesh Jawahar Lad

Maharashtra Cricket Association Stadium in Pune, Maharashtra, against England. He became the 15th Indian to score over 50 runs on an ODI debut.

First bowler to take more than three wickets on debut

Prasidh Krishna is the only bowler to take four wickets in an ODI debut. He finished 4/54 in his debut ODI on 23 March 2021, against England, at the Maharashtra Cricket Association Stadium in Pune.

Most centuries scored in a decade –

Virat Kohli is the batsman who has notched up the most centuries in a decade (2010–20) with 42 centuries.

First to score 100 centuries in international cricket

Sachin Tendulkar was the first to score 100 international centuries (51 Test and 49 ODI hundreds). He scored his 100th century at the fourth ODI of the Asia Cup versus Bangladesh on 16 March 2012.

Suryakumar Yadav: Brilliance off the Bat

Suryakumar Yadav has been in exceptional form in T20Is in 2022. He is the highest run-getter with 1,164 runs in 31 games this year, averaging 46.56 and striking at 187.43. Amidst India's gloomy World Cup campaign in Australia, it was Yadav's performance that stood out for its sparkling brilliance. He notched up 239 runs in six innings at a strike rate of 189.68, often overshadowing the likes of Virat Kohli and Rohit Sharma. Yadav continued his tremendous form on a short tour of New Zealand where he got another ton in the T20I format, becoming only the second Indian to score two tons in a single calendar year (besides his captain Rohit Sharma). Australian player Glenn Maxwell acknowledged Yadav's genius, saying that he 'makes everyone else look so much worse'. Overall, if the year 2022 can be remembered for one cricketer's extraordinary show, then it is this 32-year-old Mumbaikar's.

Lowest team total

India scored only 54 runs in 26.3 overs against Sri Lanka at Sharjah, UAE, on 29 October 2000.

WR Most ODI century partnerships

Sourav Ganguly and Sachin Tendulkar have 26 century-plus stands as a pair.

Most career wickets

Anil Kumble holds the record with 337 wickets.

WR Most runs in all World Cups

Sachin Tendulkar scored 2,278 runs in 45 World Cup matches from 1992 to 2011. He also holds the world record for the most centuries in World Cups, with six in 45 World Cup matches; this was equalled by Rohit Sharma in 17 matches.

WR Most centuries

Sachin Tendulkar has scored 49 centuries in 463 ODI matches.

WR Most career Man of the Match awards

Sachin Tendulkar has won 62 Man of the Match awards in his career. He won the first Man of the Match award in the 1992 World Cup, against Pakistan.

Most career catches

Mohammad Azharuddin took 156 catches in ODIs.

Most player of the series awards

In the India–England Test series during February–March 2021, R. Ashwin became the first Indian with more than 30 (he took 32) wickets and a century in a four-match Test series, and only the fifth player in the world to do so. He also became the first Indian to take 30 or more wickets in a Test series twice. Ashwin's nine Player of the Series awards in Test cricket are the most won by an Indian, just behind Sri Lankan player Muttiah Muralitharan (11) in this format.

WR Most total career runs

Sachin Tendulkar has made a total of 18,426 runs (including 49 centuries) in his ODI career spanning 463 matches.

Highest individual innings

Rohit Sharma's 264 runs versus Sri Lanka on 13 November 2014 at Kolkata, West Bengal.

Most sixes in an innings

Rohit Sharma's 16 sixes in his total of 209 runs against Australia in Bengaluru, Karnataka, on 2 November 2013. This record, at the world

AN EVENTFUL INNINGS

Indian cricket has such a long, vast and brilliant history, studded with amazing performances at the international level and legendary cricketers who are part of cricket folklore, that it's impossible to encapsulate it in a small space. Here are a few highlights from the past decades:

1930s: Under the name of the 'All-India' cricket team, the Indian cricket team toured England for the first time in 1932. The team's captain was the maharaja of Porbandar Natwarsinhji Bhavsinhji. It was the national team's second tour of England following one way back in 1911. India had just then been granted the status of a Full Member of the ICC in 1932, the sixth nation to do so, and they played their inaugural Test match at Lord's on 25 June against England (the 1983 World Cup was also won on this same red-letter date!).

In this Test, England won by 158 runs after scoring 259 and 275/8 down in the two innings while India were bowled out for 189 and 187. India played 37 matches on the tour, including 26 first-class fixtures. The Indian team won nine first-class matches, drew nine and lost eight. Because of the relentless playing schedule from the first match on 29 April to the last one on 10 September, it is reported that the team experienced injuries. The shining light of India's team effort was the right-handed batsman and cricketing legend C.K. Nayudu, who played in all the first-class matches, scoring 1,618 runs at an average of 40.45, including five centuries and a highest score of 162.

The 'All-India' team that toured England in 1932 after India became a Full Member of the ICC

1940s: The notable international event for the Indian national team in this decade was their first ever tour to Australia. Here, they got the chance to play against the then world's greatest batsman, Don Bradman. In 1948, in domestic cricket, right-handed batsman B.B. Nimbalkar made the record first-class score of 443 not out for Maharashtra versus Kathiawar in the Ranji Trophy, and assisted in establishing the world record–making partnership of 455 for the second wicket. That mammoth innings is still the fourth highest in first-class cricket! And at that point, Nimbalkar came agonisingly close to breaking Bradman's highest ever unbeaten 452.

1950s: From 1932, India had to wait until 1952 for its first Test victory. India won by an innings and 8 runs in Madras (now Chennai) against a strong England attack. Vinoo Mankad's 12 wickets in the match, and Polly Umrigar and Pankaj Roy's tons for India were the highlights for the hosts.

A stamp featuring legendary cricketer Vinoo Mankad

1960s: Internationally, India did not achieve anything extraordinary, but in domestic cricket the emergence of Bombay (now Mumbai) as an undisputed force changed the course of Indian cricket forever. As part of 15 consecutive victories in the Ranji Trophy (from 1958–59 to 1972–73), Bombay won the title in all 10 seasons of the period. The finest players from this decade – Farokh Engineer, Dilip Sardesai, Ajit Wadekar and Sunil Gavaskar – went on to become the great achievers in Indian cricket.

1970s: This decade saw India's first-ever back-to-back overseas Test series wins in West Indies and England in 1971 under the captaincy of Ajit Wadekar.

1980s: In the third ODI World Cup in 1983 in England and Wales, India defeated the mighty West Indians who were aiming for their third consecutive World Cup win. This is heralded as the best moment of Indian cricket, one which changed the landscape of cricket forever. This victory, recalled again and again over the years, became the abiding ambition and dream of the Indian team and of all Indians. In this decade, India also co-hosted the World Cup in 1987 (with Pakistan), which was the first one played outside England.

The 1983 World Cup–winning team with the then president and prime minister of India

1990s: Even though as a team India did not shine, the debuts of Sachin Tendulkar and Anil Kumble during the England tour of 1990 had a deep impact on Indian cricket. While Tendulkar went on to became the finest of his era with 100 international hundreds, Kumble became a legendary figure with 619 Test wickets, which was then the third in the all-time best list after Australian bowler Shane Warne and Sri Lankan bowler Muttiah Muralitharan.

2000s: The highlight of this decade was India's triumph over Australia by 2-1 in an iconic Test series. V.V.S. Laxman's 281 in Kolkata and Harbhajan Singh's haul of 32 wickets in that series is written in golden letters. However, the abiding memory of the decade will be that of winning the inaugural 2007 T20 World Cup under the leadership of M.S. Dhoni in South Africa.

2010s: The brilliant moment of this decade was the unforgettable victory in the ODI World Cup at home in 2011, again under the leadership of M.S. Dhoni.

Winners of the 2011 ODI World Cup

2020s: India registered its first ever series win in Australia when Virat Kohli led the team that defeated Australia by a margin of 2-1.

level, was broken by England's Eoin Morgan who hit 17 sixes against Afghanistan during the 2019 World Cup.

Best strike rate

Hardik Pandya has achieved a record strike rate of 115.59 across 66 matches.

Best bowling

Stuart Binny took 6 wickets for 4 runs against Bangladesh at Mirpur, Bangladesh, on 17 June 2014.

Winning four ODI Man of the Match awards in a row

Sourav Ganguly is the only player to have won four consecutive Man of the Match awards in ODIs, a record made against Pakistan at Toronto, Canada, in 1997.

Most centuries in a single World Cup

Rohit Sharma notched up five centuries in the 2019 World Cup, breaking Kumara Sangakkara's previous record.

First wins in the World Cup and ICC World Twenty20

India won its first World Cup under the captaincy of Kapil Dev in 1983 and its second World Cup under the leadership of M.S. Dhoni in 2011, thus becoming the third nation after West Indies and Australia to win the World Cup more than once. Dhoni also led India to its first ICC World Twenty20 win in its inaugural 2007 edition.

Unique 100

Shikhar Dhawan scored a century in his 100th ODI, a first-of-a-kind feat in Indian cricket.

WR

Most career catches

Rahul Dravid holds the record for most career catches, with 210 catches in 164 matches (including one catch for the ICC World XI): 47 versus Australia, 30 versus England, 26 versus West Indies, 21 versus

Rahul Dravid: most career catches in ODIs

South Africa, 21 versus Zimbabwe; 19 versus Pakistan; 17 versus New Zealand; 16 versus Sri Lanka; and 13 versus Bangladesh.

T20 INTERNATIONALS

Highest team total
The highest team total is 260 for 5, for India versus Sri Lanka in Indore, Madhya Pradesh, on 22 December 2017.

Lowest team total
India scored 74 runs in 17.3 overs against Australia at Melbourne on 1 February 2008.

Highest run chase
The Indian team made 211 runs for 4 wickets on 12 December 2009, chasing Sri Lanka's 206 runs for 7 wickets, at Mohali, Punjab.

Most career wickets
Bhuvneshwar Kumar has the most T20I career wickets with 90 in 86 matches.

Best bowling average (minimum 10 wickets)
L. Balaji's bowling average of 12.10 is the best on record for T20I matches.

Best individual bowling
Deepak Chahar took 6 wickets for 7 runs while playing against Bangladesh at Nagpur, Maharashtra, on 10 November 2019.

Most career dismissals as a wicketkeeper
M.S. Dhoni holds the record of most career dismissals, with 91 dismissals in 98 matches, including 57 caught and 34 stumped.

WR

Best batting average (minimum 50 matches)
Virat Kohli has the best batting average of 52.73 in 115 matches.

Most runs in T20
Virat Kohli has 4,008 runs in 115 matches.

Fastest to 50
Yuvraj Singh's 50 runs in 12 balls against England in Durban, South Africa, on 19 September 2007, is the fastest half-century in T20Is.

Only captain to win all three ICC trophies
M.S. Dhoni is the only captain to lead his team to victory in all the three major ICC tournaments: the World T20 in 2007, the Cricket World Cup in 2011 and the Champions Trophy in 2013.

CUE SPORTS

DOMESTIC

First National Championship – billiards
The first National Championship was held in 1931 in Calcutta (now Kolkata), West Bengal, with only eight entries. M.M. Beg won the title.

First National Championship – snooker
The first National Snooker Championship was held in 1939 in Calcutta (now Kolkata, West Bengal). P.K. Deb won the title.

First billiards and snooker hat-trick
Geet Sethi achieved a hat-trick of three consecutive National Championship titles in billiards and snooker from 1985 to 1987. He also won the national titles for both sports in 1988.

Most national titles – billiards and snooker
Pankaj Advani has won the national titles for both billiards and snooker a record 32 times.

Highest break – snooker
Geet Sethi had the maximum possible break of 147 against Latif Nazarali at the 54th National Championship in Guntur, Andhra Pradesh, in 1988.

INTERNATIONAL

First world snooker champion
Om B. Agarwal won the IBSF World Snooker Championship at Dublin, Ireland, in 1984.

First world billiards team title
India 'B' won a gold while India 'A' bagged a silver in the inaugural World Billiards Team Championship in Glasgow, Scotland, in August 2014. The winning team, with Pankaj Advani, Rupesh Shah, Devender Joshi and Ashok Shandilya, beat India 'A' 5–4.

First World Games snooker title
Aditya Mehta won the Quadrennial World Games snooker gold at Cali, Colombia, in July 2013.

First win at the World Ladies Billiards and Snooker Championship
Chitra Magimairaj and Varsha Sanjeev won the senior gold medal and the U-21 gold medal respectively at the World Ladies Billiards and Snooker (WLBS) Championship in Leeds, UK, in April 2016.

First World Ladies Billiards and Snooker Association title

R. Umadevi won her maiden, and India's first, World Ladies Billiards and Snooker Association title, beating the then world no. 13, Eva Palmius, 2–0 in the final at Cambridge, England, in April 2012.

First snooker team World Cup title

Pankaj Advani and Manan Chandra won the inaugural International Billiards and Snooker Federation (IBSF) Snooker Team World Cup in 2018 in Doha, Qatar.

First world champion on debut

Geet Sethi became world champion on debut when he beat legendary billiards player Bob Marshall, fifty years his senior, to win the 25th World Amateur Billiards Championship in 1985 in Delhi. He was also the first unseeded player to become world champion.

Geet Sethi: first world champion on debut

Pankaj Advani: most world titles in billiards and snooker

First Asian Games title

Billiards was introduced at the 1998 Bangkok Asian Games. India won two golds, a silver and a bronze. Ashok Shandilya won the gold, beating the world champion Geet Sethi 5–4. In the doubles, Ashok Shandilya and Geet Sethi won a gold, beating Devendra Joshi and Balachandra Bhaskar, who won the bronze.

First Asian snooker title

Yasin Merchant beat Udon Khaimuk of Thailand by eight frames in New Delhi on 15 July 1989 to win the Asian Confederation of Billiard Sports (ACBS) Championship.

Best performance at the Asian Billiards Sports Championship

India won a gold, a silver and three bronze medals in the inaugural Asian Billiards Sports Championship at Al Fujairah, UAE, held from 24 September to 2 October 2016. Siddharth Parikh (billiards 100-up) won the gold medal and Vidya Pillai won the silver (6-red, women). The bronze medallists were Sourav Kothari (billiards 100-up), Kamal Chawla (6-red, men), Amee Kamani and Arantxa Sanchis (6-red, women), Manan Chandra, Sundeep Gulati and Ishpreet Singh Chadha (team snooker).

Most billiards gold medals in the Asian Games

Pankaj Advani won two gold medals in the 2006 Doha Asian Games and in the 2010 Asian Games at Guangzhou, China.

Most world titles – billiards and snooker

Pankaj Advani has the world champion titles for both billiards as well as snooker a record 24 times. Pankaj Advani claimed at least one International Billiard and Snooker Federation world title every calendar year.

Best performance in the Asian Games – snooker

At the 2010 Asian Games held in Guangzhou, China, the Indian team won a silver, while Aditya Mehta (individual) and Alok Kumar (8-ball pool) won bronze medals.

Highest break in the World Billiards Championship

Geet Sethi had a break of 1,276 over two sessions in 80 mins against Bob Close of England in the quarter-final of the World Professional Championship in Mumbai, Maharashtra, on 1 October 1992.

Highest break under three-pot rule – billiards

Michael Ferreira scored 630 against

S.B. Agrawal at the World Championship in Delhi in 1981, a world record for the highest break under the three-pot rule.

Most billiards grand doubles
Pankaj Advani has won four world doubles in billiards (time and points format) in 2005, 2008, 2014 and 2018.

World 6-red title
Laxman Rawat won the 6-red title versus Muhammad Asif of Pakistan in Mandalay, Myanmar, on 20 September 2019.

Most Asian titles
Pankaj Advani – 24-time snooker and billiards world champion – retained the Asian snooker title by defeating former champion Amir Sarkhosh of Iran. Advani had won the title in 2019 before the 2020 edition got scrapped due to COVID-19. Advani's tally of Asian titles across both snooker and billiards stand at 13, including two Asian Games gold medals in 2006 and 2010.

Most competitive 147 breaks in snooker
Aditya Mehta became the first Indian to make 147 maximum breaks in 2014 at the Paul Hunter Classic snooker tournament.

Youngest world champion – snooker
Pankaj Advani was 18 years old when he won the amateur World Snooker Championship title in October 2003.

Youngest to win the World Professional title
Pankaj Advani was 24 years old when he won the World Professional Billiards title at the Northern Snooker Centre, Leeds, England, on 6 September 2009. He outclassed 41-year-old Mike Russell, who has won the World Professional Billiards title a record nine times.

Two titles in 6-red snooker
Pankaj Advani was the world's first player to hold both world and continental titles in 6 red snooker at the same time. He is also the only player to win world titles in both 15-red and 6-red snooker.

Oldest woman champion – billiards
Kamala Devi Chandrababu from Tamil Nadu beat Judy Walia from Karnataka 109–63, 65–112, 53–76, 98–72, 95–74 in the 1995 National Championship at Bangalore (now Bengaluru), Karnataka. At 63 years, it was her fourth championship and the second national title after 1991.

FOOTBALL

GENERAL

Oldest football tournament
The Durand Football Tournament is the third oldest tournament in the world and the oldest in Asia and India. Started by British diplomat and civil servant Sir Henry Mortimer Durand in 1888 for the British troops in India, it was held in Simla (now Shimla, Himachal Pradesh). In 1940, the tournament was moved to New Delhi. The latest edition, the 131st in the history of the tournament, was held from 16 August to 18 September 2022, with Bengaluru FC winning the tournament.

First Indian team to win the Durand Cup
Mohammedan Sporting won the Durand Cup in 1940 when it was first moved to Delhi and the final played at Irwin Amphitheatre (now Dhyan Chand National Stadium). Mohammedan Sporting beat Royal Warwickshire Regiment 2–1 in the final.

Most wins at the Durand Cup
Mohun Bagan has won the Durand Cup 16 times and finished runner-up 11 times. East Bengal has won 16 times and been runner-up 10 times.

Most individual goals at the Durand Cup
Mohammed Habib scored 12 goals for East Bengal in seven matches (both the semi-finals and the final were replayed) in the 1972 Durand tournament.

First football academy
The Tata Football Academy (TFA) was started at Jamshedpur, Jharkhand, in 1986 with Mohammed Habib and Ranjan Chowdhury as coaches, and Subimal 'Chuni' Goswami as technical director. It has produced over 100 junior and senior international players for India. It was followed by the Williamson Magor Football Academy in Assam and the Chandigarh Football Academy that started in the 1990s.

First Indian to be national coach of a foreign country
Syed Nayeemuddin was appointed national coach of Bangladesh in July 2007. He was also the first Indian to coach a club side abroad – the Brothers Union of Bangladesh in 2004. In India, he won 33 trophies with Mohammedan Sporting, East Bengal and Mohun Bagan. As national coach, he led India to victory in the 1987 South Asian Federation (SAF) Games in

NATIONAL SPORTS AWARDS 2021

FOOTBALL

Major Dhyan Chand Khel Ratna
Sunil Chhetri

Calcutta (now Kolkata), West Bengal, the 1997 Kathmandu South Asian Football Federation (SAFF) Championship in Nepal and the 2005 Karachi SAFF Championship in Pakistan.

First Olympic referee

Komaleeswaran Sankar became an Olympic referee when he was selected for the football tournament of the 2000 Sydney Olympics, one among the four match officials chosen from Asia. Sankar, who became a referee in 1988 and a national referee in 1994, retired in 2007 at the age of forty-five, as mandated by FIFA rules.

First World Cup referee

Komaleeswaran Sankar was the first World Cup referee from India when he was chosen to officiate at the 2002 World Cup in South Korea and Japan. His first match was a Group G league match between Mexico and Croatia on 3 June 2002. He officiated in three matches.

Mohammedan Sporting in action in a match

First international tournament win by a club

- Mohammedan Sporting won the Aga Khan Gold Cup in Dhaka (then Pakistan, now Bangladesh) on 11 October 1960, defeating Makassar XI, Indonesia 4–1 in the final.
- East Bengal, coached by Subhas Bhowmick, won the LG ASEAN Club Cup Championship on 26 July 2003 in Jakarta, Indonesia, beating BEC Tero Sasana of Thailand in the final 3–1.

First Indian club to enter the Asian Football Confederation Cup final

- Bengaluru FC was the first Indian club to enter the final of Asia's prestigious club competition, the Asian Football Confederation (AFC) Cup, in October 2016. They lost the final match against Iraq Air Force 0–1 in Doha, Qatar, on 5 November 2016.
- Dempo SC (Goa) was the first club to enter the semi-finals of the Cup in September 2008.

First hat-trick in Mohun Bagan versus East Bengal match

On 13 July 1997, Bhaichung Bhutia scored a hat-trick for East Bengal versus Mohun Bagan in the KBL Federation Cup semi-final, in which East Bengal won 4–1.

First professional coach

Amal Dutta, India's first professional coach, started his career in 1963, coaching East Bengal. He also coached the other two big Kolkata clubs: Mohun Bagan and Mohammedan Sporting (Dhaka).

First foreign coach

English professional footballer Harry Wright was appointed coach of the Indian football team in 1963. He held the position till 1964, leading India to one of its best performances – a runner-up position at the 1964 Asian Football Confederation (AFC) Cup.

First Indian club to win a major trophy

The first win in a major domestic tournament was by Mohun Bagan of Calcutta (now Kolkata, West Bengal), who beat East Yorkshire Regiment of Ghaziabad 2–1 in the Indian Football Association (IFA) Shield tournament final at the Calcutta Football Club Ground on 29 July 1911.

First in English professional club

- Mohammed Salim from Calcutta (now Kolkata, West Bengal), was the first from the Indian subcontinent to play for a European club, Celtic FC, in 1936.
- Bhaichung Bhutia was the first Indian footballer to join an English club when he signed a contract to represent second division outfit, Bury FC, from 1999 to 2002.
- Aditi Chauhan was the first Indian woman to play in the English league football on 16 August 2015, as a goalkeeper for West Ham United. She attended Loughborough University, completing an MSc in sports management and represented their football team from 2014–15. Chauhan joined Gokulam Kerala FC for the 2019–20 Indian women's league.

First hat-trick in Indian football

Norman Pritchard scored a hat-trick for St Xavier's College, Calcutta (now Kolkata, West Bengal), against Sovabazar Club in the 1889 Trades Cup.

First tiebreaker

- The first tiebreaker in a final came when Mohammedan Sporting won the tie 3–1 against Mohun Bagan at the 1983 Peerless Trophy final at Calcutta (now Kolkata, West Bengal).

- The first tiebreaker match occurred in a third round match of the Durand Tournament played on 17 February 1972 at Delhi. Mohun Bagan beat Indian Navy 5–3.

First woman player to sign a contract with a foreign club

Ngangom Bala Devi made history when she signed a contract with Scottish Giant Rangers FC, a professional football club in Glasgow, UK. She donned a no. 10 jersey for the club and created yet another record on 6 December 2020 when she scored the final goal against Motherwell Women in the Scottish Women's Premier League, becoming the first Indian woman to score in a professional European Club.

Most matches officiated

S.S. Hakim officiated in 33 international matches and was a referee in the final of every major domestic tournament including three Nehru Cups. He represented India in the 1960 Rome Olympics and was the team's assistant coach for the 1982 Delhi Asiad. He is the only individual to have played football, coached the national team and functioned as an international referee.

Most appearances as coach in the Olympics

S.A. Rahim (1909–63) from Hyderabad (then in Andhra Pradesh) was the coach of the Indian football team in three consecutive Olympic Games in 1952 (Helsinki), 1956 (Melbourne) and 1960 (Rome).

Most appearances as coach in the Nehru Cup

Syed Nayeemuddin coached the Indian team in the Nehru Cup on four occasions – in 1987 at Kozhikode, Kerala; in 1988 at Siliguri, West Bengal; in 1989 at Margao, Goa; and in 1997 at Kochi, Kerala.

Most successful coach at the Asian Games

- S.A. Rahim led as coach on five successful occasions – twice at the Asian Games (1951 and 1962), and thrice at the Quadrangular Tournament (1953, 1954 and 1955).
- The foreign coach with the best record is Bob Houghton of the UK with three trophies: the Nehru Cup (2007 and 2009) and the AFC Challenge Cup in 2008.

Most successful Indian coaches in domestic tournaments

P.K. Banerjee led domestic teams to 53 trophies, Amal Dutta to 35 and Syed Nayeemuddin to 33 of them.

Left: Sunil Chhetri

Sunil Chhetri: Eternal Talisman

Sunil Chhetri is part of Indian football history as the all-time top scorer for the national team. But his contribution to Indian football cannot be limited to his goal-scoring abilities. He is truly a big-match player, undoubtedly one of country's greatest ever. The significance of many of Sunil Chhetri's goals often gets buried under the enormity of his haul of 84 international goals in 129 caps, making him one of the all-time highest scorers in international football.

For instance, without his crucial strike against Myanmar in the semi-finals of the AFC Challenge Cup in 2008, India would have found it difficult to qualify for the 2011 Asian Cup. In the final, he did even better. That header along with the first of his three hat-tricks in international football, against Tajikistan in the final on 13 August 2008, is perhaps the most important goal in the national team's 21st century history, as India qualified for the elite AFC Asian Cup after 27 years and for only the third time (after 1964 and 1984).

India needed 20 years to make it to their first two AFC Asian Cup appearances but played their next two in the space of eight years (2011 and 2019). It had more to do with Chhetri's brilliance in front of goal than any drastic improvement in the overall standard of the national team.

If his hat-trick in 2008 fetched a ticket to Qatar for the AFC Asian Cup's 2011 edition, his right-footed jab in added time from inside the box in Yangon's Thuwanna YTC Stadium initiated the process for the 2019 edition. India went to the UAE-hosted tournament after winning four of their six third-round qualifying games, with Chhetri netting four of the 11 goals scored by the country. His match-deciding strikes against Myanmar (1-0), which gave India their first away win in Yangon since 1953, and Kyrgyzstan (1-0) fetched six points and provided the momentum that ultimately pulled them through a tricky qualifying group.

Only the second Indian with 100 caps, after Bhaichung Bhutia, Chhetri capped off his century of appearances with a brace against Kenya in the Intercontinental Cup in 2018.

His commitment towards the national team over 17 years has seen him only speaking through his boot, as exemplified by four goals out of India's eight in the 2023 AFC Asian Cup final round qualifiers, pulling the team to successive appearances in the continental event. On the strength of those goals (two versus Cambodia in the 2-0 victory, one versus Afghanistan in the 2-1 win, one versus Hong Kong in 4-0 triumph), he is now poised to become the first Indian to feature in three Asian Cup campaigns.

Most individual goals in an international club match

Bhaichung Bhutia scored six goals, a double hat-trick, for East Bengal against Army FC of the Philippines in the LG ASEAN Cup in Jakarta, Indonesia, on 16 July 2003.

Longest sequence of wins

Mohun Bagan won 42 consecutive matches in the 1994 season till they lost to Dempo SC (Goa) in the Scissors Cup final in November 1994.

Only Indian coach to gain success with a foreign club

In his eight-year stint in Bangladesh, Syed Nayeemuddin helped his club, Brothers Union of Bangladesh, win three trophies.

Best record against foreign clubs

East Bengal has the best record against foreign clubs: played 239 matches (both exhibition and tournaments), won 97, drawn 40 and lost 102. They scored 343 goals and conceded 348.

Fastest goal

Midfielder Dipankar Roy scored a goal in 9.33 seconds after kick-off for Bengal versus Karnataka in the 2000 Santosh Trophy held in Thrissur, Kerala.

SANTOSH TROPHY RECORDS

Most wins in Santosh Trophy

The National inter-state championships for the Santosh Trophy started in 1941. The football trophy was instituted in the name of Maharaja of Santosh, the former president of IFA, the parent body of Bengal football. Bengal won the title 32 times and finished runners-up on 14 occasions. Punjab have won eight times, Kerala seven times, Services six times and Goa five times. Bengal hold the record of winning the trophy six times in a row from 1993-98 and five times in a row from 1975 to 1979.

Most individual goals in the final match

Playing for Bengal, Mohammed Habib scored five goals in the 6-1 win over Services in Nowgong in 1969.

Most individual goals in a single edition

Playing for Punjab, Inder Singh scored 23 goals in the 1974 edition in Jalandhar.

Highest number of goals by an individual in a single match

- Burma (now Myanmar) striker Fred Pagsley, while playing for Bengal, scored seven goals against Rajputana in Mumbai in 1945.
- Punjab's Inder Singh scored seven goals against Gujarat in Jalandhar in 1974.

Biggest margin of victory

Bengal beat Tripura 18-0 in Jalandhar in 1974; Punjab beat Gujarat 17-0 in Jalandhar in 1974; Kerala beat Andaman and Nicobar Islands 17-0 in Siliguri in 2014.

All-time top scorers

Inder Singh (Punjab) has 45 goals. Mohmmed Habib and Shyam Thapa (both Bengal) have 34 and 31 goals to their credit.

Success for different teams

Peter Thangaraj won the Santosh Trophy for three different teams – Services (1960), Bengal (1962) and Railways (1966).

INDIAN SUPER LEAGUE (ISL)

Maximum titles

ATK (now ATK Mohun Bagan) has won three titles in 2014, 2016 and 2019-20 season.

Biggest margin of victory

FC Goa defeated Mumbai City FC 7-0 in Margao, Goa, in 2015.

Most goals scored in a match

A total of 11 goals were scored when Odisha FC defeated SC East Bengal 6-5 in the 2020-21 season.

Most goals scored by a team

FC Goa has scored 267 goals, followed by Chennaiyin FC's 199 goals.

Most wins by a team

FC Goa have won 62 matches, followed by Mumbai City FC, who have won 61 matches.

Most individual goals by a foreign footballer

- Punjab's Nigerian footballer Bartholomew Ogbeche has played four seasons in ISL for NorthEast United, Kerala Blasters, Mumbai City FC and Hyderabad FC, scoring a total of 53 goals.
- Punjab's Spanish striker Ferran Corominas, who played for FC Goa starting July 2017, has record 48 goals to his credit for one club.

Most individual goals by an Indian footballer

- Sunil Chhetri has played in all editions of the Indian Super League since 2014, scoring 51 goals. He played for Mumbai City FC and Bengaluru FC.
- Jeje Lalpekhlua, while playing for Chennaiyin FC and SC East Bengal, has 24 goals.

NATIONAL SPORTS AWARDS 2022

FOOTBALL

Dronacharya Award (Lifetime)

Bimal Prafulla Ghosh

Hat-trick records

A total of 31 hat-tricks have been scored. Brazilian Andre Mortiz, while playing for Mumbai City FC against FC Pune City, scored the competition's first hat-trick in October 2014. Canadian Iain Hume (ATK and Kerala Blasters) and Nigerian Bartholomew Ogbeche have scored three hat-trick each in the ISL. Sunil Chhetri (Mumbai City FC and Bengaluru FC) has two hat-tricks to his credit.

DOMESTIC EVENTS

First to win three National Football League titles

Mohun Bagan has won three National Football League (NFL) titles: in 1997–98, 1999– 2000 and 2001–02. East Bengal emulated this when they won their third NFL crown in 2003–04. Their earlier wins were in 2000–01 and 2002–03.

Most individual goals in a match in NFL

- Bhaichung Bhutia scored the most goals in an NFL match when he scored five goals playing for JCT against Mahindra in the first NFL in 1997. JCT won the match 6–1.
- In the fourth NFL, Francis Silveira of Churchill Brothers scored four goals in a match against Dempo SC (Goa) for a 5–0 win.

Most goals by a club in the NFL/ Indian League (I-League)

East Bengal has scored 690 goals in 460 matches. Other teams to score are Churchill Brothers with 664 goals in 406 matches and Mohun Bagan with 619 goals in 446 matches.

Most individual goals in a match in the I-League

The most goals by a player in an I-League match are seven by Ranti Martins for Dempo SC (Goa) in their 14–0 win versus Air India in Margao, Goa, on 30 May 2011.

Most individual hat-tricks in the NFL and I-League

Nigerian striker Odafa Onyeka Okolie has scored 14 hat-tricks: nine for Churchill Brothers; four for Mohun Bagan; and one for Sporting Clube de Goa.

Biggest victory margin in I-League

- Dempo SC (Goa) beat Air India 14–0 on 30 May 2011.
- The next best is Prayag United's 10–1 rout of United Sikkim Football Club on 10 November 2012 in the sixth I-League.

Top Indian scorers in ISL: 2014–18/19

Sunil Chhetri: 30 goals;
Jeje Lalpekhlua: 23 goals.

Top Indian scorers in NFL: 1997–2007

Bhaichung Bhutia: 78 goals;
R.C. Prakash: 49 goals.

I-League winners in 2020–21: Gokulam Kerala FC

Indian Senior National Men's Team

In this century, India got one of the most memorable victories against United Arab Emirates on 8 April 2001 in a pre–World Cup tie in Bengaluru by 1-0, under the leadership of Bhaichung Bhutia. He became India's captain in 2000, with his last engagement as captain in the 2011 Asian Cup final round.

First International match
With seven barefoot players, India entered the 1948 Olympics under captain Talimeren Ao from Bengal but lost to France 1–2. Sarangapani Raman scored the lone goal. Since then, India has played eight matches in four Olympic Games – 1948, 1952, 1956 and 1960 – won one, drawn one, lost six; scored 10 and conceded 27 goals. After 1960, India has been eliminated in the pre-Olympic stage.

Best performance in Olympics
India is the first Asian country to reach the semi-finals of the Olympics. In 1956, in the Melbourne Olympics, captained by Samar Banerjee, India reached the semi-finals and finished fourth.

Only win in Olympics
On 1 December 1956, India beat hosts Australia 4-2 to register their only win in Olympics.

Indian football players at the 1956 Olympic Games: best performance at the Olympics

Best performance at the Olympics
India became the first Asian nation to reach the semi-finals of an Olympic football event, beating Australia 4-2 at the 1956 Melbourne Games. India took the lead against Yugoslavia but lost 1-4. In the play-off for the bronze, India lost 0-3 to Bulgaria, ending at fourth position. Samar 'Badru' Banerjee was India's captain and S.A. Rahim was the coach.

Overall Olympics performance
India played in four consecutive Olympics: in 1948 London, 1952 Helsinki, 1956 Melbourne and 1960 Rome. They did not qualify for the Games thereafter.

Subimal "Chuni' Goswami

Biggest margin of victory
In the 1963 pre-Olympics, India won 7–0 against Ceylon (now Sri Lanka) at Bangalore (now Bengaluru), Karnataka, and later 7–0 against Bangladesh in the Aga Khan Tournament at Dhaka, Bangladesh, in 1977.

Biggest margin of victory at the Asian Games
India beat Hong Kong 5–2 at the 1958 Asiad in Tokyo, Japan, in its biggest margin of victory at the Asian Games. Mohammad Rahmatullah scored two goals while Subimal 'Chuni' Goswami, D. Damodaran and T. Balaram scored a goal each. India scored three goals in extra time, the first time India played extra time in an international match.

Biggest defeat at the Asian Games
India lost 1–7 to China in 1974 at Tehran in Iran. Magan Singh scored the lone goal.

Best performance at pre–World Cup
With three wins, two draws and one defeat (0–1 versus UAE in an away match in Al Ain), India's performance in the 2001 World Cup qualifiers has been the best yet. It is also the only series of matches where the Indian team scored more goals (11) than they conceded (5).

Biggest margin of victory at pre–World Cup
India beat Brunei 5–0 at Bangalore (now Bengaluru, Karnataka) in a Group 8 qualifier on 20 May 2001. Jules Alberto, I.M. Vijayan, Bhaichung Bhutia, Jo Paul Ancheri and Abdul Hakeem scored for India.

Worst defeat at pre–World Cup
India lost 0–7 to South Korea at Seoul, South Korea, in the 1993 World Cup qualifiers.

India's longest unbeaten run in a year
In 2017, India remained unbeaten in nine matches, three away games and six at home:

Memorable Performances

Gold medals in the Asian Games

India won the gold medal twice in football in the Asian Games.

- In the inaugural Asian Games on 1951 in New Delhi, India beat Iran 1-0 on 10 March 1951 in the final, to win the gold.
- In 1962 Jakarta Asian Games, India beat South Korea 2-1 in the final on 4 September 1962, to win their second gold medal.

Bronze medal in the Asian Games

India won the Asian Games bronze medal in 1970 Bangkok Asian Games. India beat Japan 1-0 on 19 December 1970, in the match for the third place.

Bristol Cup champions

India won the Bristol Freedom Cup in 1998 in Colombo. In the final on 21 November 1998 in Colombo, India beat hosts Sri Lanka 3-2 in the final.

LG Cup triumph

India won the LG Cup in Vietnam in 2002. In the final in Ho Chi Minh City on 10 August 2002, India beat hosts Vietnam 3-2.

Runners-up in the Asian Cup

India finished runners-up the only time in Asian Cup in 1964. In the round robin final rounds played between 26 May and 3 June 1964 in Tel Aviv, India finished runners-up in the four-team group behind hosts Israel.

Joint winners in the Asian Youth Championships

India won the Asian Youth Championships for the Under-20 boys in 1974 jointly with Iran. In the final on 30 April 1974 in Bangkok, India drew with Iran 2-2 and were declared joint winners.

Pesta Sukan joint winners

India won the Pesta Sukan tournament jointly with South Vietnam in 1971. In the final on 28 August 1971, India drew with South Vietnam goalless and shared the title.

Nehru Cup wins

On 29 August 2007, India beat Syria 1-0 in the final to win the Nehru Cup for the first time. India's second triumph in Nehru Cup came on 31 August 2009, defeating Syria in the tiebreaker. On 2 September 2012, India beat Cameroon in tiebreaker to win the Nehru Cup for the third time. On all three occasions, the tournament was played in New Delhi.

AFC Challenge Cup victory

India won the 2008 AFC Challenge Cup in New Delhi to qualify for the 2011 Asian Cup final rounds. In the final on 13 August 2008, India beat Tajikistan 4-1.

- 1–0 versus Myanmar; 1–0 versus the Kyrgyz Republic; 2–0 versus Macau; 4–1 versus Macau; and 2–2 versus Myanmar (all Asian Cup qualifiers).
- 3–2 versus Cambodia; 2-0 versus Nepal; 2-1 versus Mauritius; and 1-1 versus St Kitts and Nevis (all friendly matches).

Worst defeats

In international tournaments, India's worst defeats have been 1-10 to Yugoslavia at the 1952 Helsinki Olympics and 1–9 to Burma (now Myanmar) in the 1971 Merdeka Tournament in Kuala Lumpur, Malaysia.

Individual Records

Maximum caps earned (top five)

Sunil Chhetri (131 matches), Bhaichung Bhutia (107), IM Vijayan (88), Shabbir Ali (81) and Mahesh Gawli (79) have played the maximum number of matches for India.

Neville D'Souza: only hat-trick at the Olympics

Maximum goals scored (top five)

Sunil Chhetri (84), Bhaichung Bhutia (42), I.M. Vijayan (39), Shabbir Ali (30) and P.K. Banerjee (26) have scored the maximum goals for India.

Hat-trick in Olympics

Neville D'Souza is the only Indian to score a hat-trick in Olympics. He scored three goals in India's 4-2 win over Australia on 1 December 1956.

Fastest international goal

I.M. Vijayan scored against Bhutan within 12 seconds after kick-off in a Group A league match played on 28 September 1999 at the SAF Games at Kathmandu, Nepal.

Most goals in the Asian Games

P.K. Banerjee scored the highest number of individual goals for India in the Asian Games, He scored six goals – one in 1958, four in 1962 and one in 1966.

Hat-trick on debut

K. Appalaraju scored a hat-trick in his first international appearance against Ceylon (now Sri Lanka) on 22 December 1963 in the pre-Olympics.

Maximum hat-tricks

Sunil Chhetri is the only Indian to score three hat-tricks in international matches. Chhetri's three hat-tricks came against Tajikistan (13 August 2008, AFC Challenge Cup, New Delhi), against Vietnam (10 October 2010, Friendly, Pune) and against Chinese Taipei (1 June 2018) in the Hero International Cup, Mumbai).

Back to back hat-tricks

K. Appalaraju and I.M. Vijayan scored back-to-back hat-tricks in international matches. Appalaraju scored against Ceylon (now Sri Lanka) on 22 December 1963 in the pre-Olympics in Colombo and against Ceylon (now Sri Lanka) on 29 December 1963 in the pre-Olympics in Bengaluru. I.M. Vijayan scored against Pakistan in Kathmandu on 26 September 1999 in the SAF Games and against Bhutan on 28 September 1999 in the SAF Games in Kathmandu.

Most successful captain

Bhaichung Bhutia has five tournament wins to his credit as captain: the LG Cup in Vietnam (2002), the SAFF Cup in Karachi, Pakistan (2005), the Nehru Cup in Delhi (2007 and 2009), and the AFC Challenge Cup in Hyderabad and Delhi in 2008. He is also the second highest international scorer, with 42 goals in 107 matches.

Youngest match winner at the Nehru Cup

Bhaichung Bhutia was 19 years old when he scored a goal to beat Uzbekistan 1-0 in 1995 at Calcutta (now Kolkata), West Bengal.

Bhaichung Bhutia: most successful captain (*extreme left*), at the Nehru Cup, 2007

In Remembrance

Ahmed Hussain (1932–16 April 2021)
Ahmed Hussain made his debut against Bulgaria on 7 December and went on to make 11 appearances for India. He had represented the national team in the 1956 Melbourne Olympics, where India finished fourth, and followed that up with a fourth-place finish in the 1958 Asian Games in Tokyo. He had also played for Mohammedan Sporting in club football, and created history when his side became the first Indian team to win the Aga Khan Gold Cup in Dhaka in 1960.

Fortunato Franco (2 May 1937–10 May 2021)
A brilliant midfielder, Franco was an integral part of India's Asian Games gold medal–winning team in the 1962 Asian Games in Jakarta, where India beat South Korea 2-1 in the final. Besides, he was a member of the Indian team in the 1960 Rome Olympics, the team which finished second in the 1964 Asian Cup, the team that was the runner-up in the 1964 Merdeka Cup in Kuala Lumpur and the national team that finished third in the Merdeka Cup in 1965. He represented India 26 times, making his international debut against Pakistan in the Asian Cup Qualifiers in Ernakulam in December 1959.

S.S. Hakim (23 June 1939–22 August 2021)
Popularly referred to as 'Hakim Saab', he was part of the Indian squad in the 1960 Rome Olympics. He was also a FIFA referee and supervised many matches in the Asian Cup 1988 at Doha. Son of legendary coach S.A. Rahim, he excelled as a coach too. Hakim was a former assistant coach of the Indian national team and coached Mahindra United, Salgaocar SC, Hindustan FC and Bengal Mumbai Club. He was conferred with the Dhyan Chand Lifetime Achievement Award in 2017.

S.S. Hakim

O. Chandrasekhar (10 July 1935–August 24, 2021)
A defender, Chandrasekhar was part of the Indian football team that took part in the 1960 Olympic Games in Rome. He was a member of the gold medal–winning side at the 1962 Asian Games in Jakarta and the team that finished runner-up at the AFC Asian Cup in 1964. He has a total of 25 caps to his name and also played in the Asian Cup Qualifiers in 1959, where he made his international debut, and Merdeka Cup in 1961, among other tournaments.

Sanat Sett (1930–24 December 2021)
An acrobatic goalkeeper during his playing days, Sett made his international debut for India against Japan in the 1954 Asian Games. He represented India in z 11 international matches. He was part of the national squad that won the Quadrangular Cup in 1953, 1954 and 1955.

Subhas Bhowmick (2 October 1950–22 January 2022)
An Asian Games bronze medal–winner (1970), Bhowmick made his international debut for India on 30 July 1970 in the Merdeka Cup against Formosa. He represented India in 24 International matches and scored nine goals in the process – including a hat-trick against Philippines in the Merdeka Cup in 1971 – a match that India won 5-1. He was a triumphant member of the Indian national team that finished joint winner at the Pesta Sukan Cup against South Vietnam in Singapore (1971), and won a bronze medal in the Merdeka Cup in 1970. He was also a member of the Indian team that toured the USSR in 1971.

Surajit Sengupta (30 August 1951–17 February 2022)
An exceptionally skilful winger, Sengupta, who made his international debut on 24 July 1974 against Thailand in the Merdeka Cup in Kuala Lumpur, went on to represent India in 17 international matches, and scored one goal against Kuwait in the 1978 Asian Games. Over the years, he represented India in the Asian Games in 1974 and 1978, the Merdeka Cup in 1974, the President's Cup in 1977 in Seoul, and International Friendlies against the UAE and Bahrain in 1979.

Samar 'Badru' Banerjee (30 January 1930–20 August 2022)
The former India forward had captained the national team to a historic fourth-place finish in the 1956 Melbourne Olympic Games, which also included a famous 4-2 victory against hosts Australia in the quarter-finals. Banerjee played a total of nine matches for India, scoring three goals.

Top foreign scorers in NFL: 1997–2007

Yusif Yakubu: 78 goals;
José R. Baretto: 62 goals.

Top Indian scorers in I-League: 2007–2017

Sunil Chhetri: 69 goals;
Jeje Lalpekhlua: 39 goals.

Top foreign scorers in I-League: 2007–2017

Ranti Martins: 169 goals;
Odafa Onyeka Okolie: 160 goals.

Only club to win both I-League and ISL titles

Bengaluru FC is the only club to win both I-League and ISL titles. They won the seventh I-League in 2014 and the ninth I-League in 2016. On 17 March 2019 they won the ISL title, beating FC Goa 1–0 in the final in Mumbai. Bengaluru FC joined the ISL in 2017.

GOLF

GENERAL

Sponsorship bonanza

Golf offered the most prize money in any individual event on the domestic circuit. The prize fund offered in 2010 was ₹8.80 crore spread over 29 tournaments.

Indian Open winners

Nine Indians have won this prestigious title spread over 13 times. They are: P.G. Sethi, Kolkata, 1965; Ali Sher, Delhi, 1991 and 1993; Feroze Ali, Kolkata, 1998; Arjun Atwal, Kolkata, 1999; Jyoti Randhawa, Gurugram, 2000; Vijay Kumar, Delhi, 2002; Jyothi Randhawa, Delhi, 2006 and 2007; C. Muniyappa, Gurugram, 2009; Anirban Lahiri, Delhi, 2015; S.S.P. Chawrasia, Delhi, 2016 and Gurugram, 2017.

Indian men winning international tournaments

So far, 25 Indians have won 88 international titles on various tours. Jeev Milkha Singh heads the list with 13 victories, followed by Gaganjeet Bhullar (11), Arjun Atwal (10) and Jyoti Randhawa (9).

Most Indian tournaments on the Asian Tour

In 2002, for the first time, three tournaments – the Royal Challenge Indian Open, the Hero Honda Masters and the Honda-SIEL tournament figured on the Asian Professional Golf Association Tour.

Indian Open record

Jyoti Randhawa won the Indian Open in October 2007 at the Delhi Golf Club course for the third time and equalled the record of Australia's Peter Thomson.

Indians at the Majors

So far, eight Indians – Anirban Lahiri (17 times); Jeev Milkha Singh (14 times); Jyoti Randhawa, Arjun Atwal, Shiv Kapur, Shubhankar Sharma (5 each); Gaganjeet Bhullar and Gaurav Ghei (1 each) – have made 52 appearances at the Majors.

Indians topping the Asian Tour Order of Merit

Jeev Milkha Singh won the Asian Tour Order of Merit in 2006 and 2008. Jyoti Randhawa (2002), Arjun Atwal (2003), Anirban Lahiri (2015) and Shubhankar Sharma (2018) are the other Indians to top the Order of Merit.

'Rookie' on a rampage

The Rookie Golfer of the Year award was introduced in 1997–98 on the domestic tour. Till date, S. Chikkarangappa remains the most successful 'rookie' on the Tour. He won ₹32,65,313 and finished second to Rashid Khan on the 2013 Order of Merit.

FIRST

First international recognition

India was invited to the 1969 World Cup qualifying event at Singapore. Ruda Valji and Shadi Lal represented India.

First International event in India

India's flagship event – the Indian Open – was launched in 1964 at the Delhi Golf Club. Five-time British Open champion Peter Thomson (Australia) was the winner. In 1970, the Indian Open became part of the Asian Golf Circuit and thereby attracted many overseas challengers including winners of the Majors.

• *First Indian winner of the Indian Open*: P.G. Billoo won the event in 1965 Indian Open as an amateur at the par-73 Royal Calcutta Golf Course by a seven-stroke margin.

First Olympians

Anirban Lahiri, S.S.P. Chawrasia and Aditi Ashok represented the country in the 2016 Rio Olympics in Brazil.

First to win all three National titles

Arjuna Award–winner Amit Luthra is the first Indian to have won all three National titles: the Junior National (1979), the men's National (1993, 1994) and the Senior Nationals (2015, 2016).

Ali Sher: Indian Open winner in 1991 and 1993

Arjun Atwal: First to gain qualification for the PGA Tour

First victory in Nomura Cup

India's first major victory in an international team event came in the 1973 Nomura Cup at Jakarta where the squad of Raj Kumar Pitamber, P.G. Sethi, Vikramjit Singh and Lakshman Singh was crowned Asia-Pacific Golf champions.

First sweep of gold medals in the Asian Games

Golf was introduced in the Asian Games in 1982. Besides the team gold, India won the individual gold and silver medals through champion Lakshman Singh and runner-up Rajiv Mohta. Two other members of the gold-winning team were Amit Luthra and Rishi Narain.

First to gain qualification for the PGA Tour

Arjun Atwal became the first Indian to gain qualification for the full US Tour after making it through the Q-school for the year 2004.

First to qualify for the British Open

Gaurav Ghei was the first Indian to qualify for the premier event in 1997.

First to play in the US Open

Jeev Milkha Singh was the first to play the US Open in 2002.

First to play the Masters at Augusta

Jeev Milkha Singh was the first to play the Masters at Augusta in 2007.

First to play the PGA Championship

Arjun Atwal was the first to play the PGA Championship in 2005.

First European–Asian Tour win

Arjun Atwal is the first Asian to win two co-sanctioned titles on the Tour. He won the Caltex Singapore Open in February 2002 and the Carlsberg Malaysian Open in February 2003. Both these events enjoy joint sanction of the European and Asian PGA Tours.

S.S.P. Chawrasia: one of the first Olympians

Jeev Milkha Singh: first to qualify for a Major

First participation in World Cup

Arjun Atwal and Jyoti Randhawa formed the first Indian team to take part in the World Cup in 2005.

First to play in three WGC events in a year

Jyoti Randhawa became the first Indian to play in three events in the World Golf Championship (WGC) series in 2005.

First to play in a Major

Jeev Milkha Singh became the first Indian to qualify for a Major when he made it to the 2002 US Open in July.

First to gain a full 'card' on PGA Tour

Arjun Atwal became the first Indian to gain a full card (exemption from playing qualifying rounds) after his stupendous showing in the 2005 season.

First to qualify for European PGA Tour

Jeev Milkha Singh was the first to qualify for the European Tour for the 1998 season.

First to make the 'cut' in a Major
Jeev Milkha Singh became the first Indian to make the 'cut' of a Major championship playing all four rounds of the 2002 US Open.

First to win on the Japanese PGA Tour
Jyoti Randhawa won the Suntory Open in 2003.

First win on PGA Tour
Arjun Atwal won the 2010 Wyndham Championship.

First win on the European Tour
Arjun Atwal won the 2002 Singapore Masters.

First win on the European Tour in Europe
Jeev Milkha Singh won the Volvo Masters in Spain in October 2006.

First team to qualify for World championship
The Indian team of Gaurav Ghei and Digvijay Singh qualified for the 2003 World Golf Championship held at Kiawah Island, USA, after finishing joint-second in the Nations Cup.

First to win the Ladies Indian Open
Aditi Ashok became the first to win the Ladies Indian Open in November 2016.

First to secure her card (playing rights) winner on the Ladies European Tour
By winning the Lalla Aicha Tour School, Aditi Ashok secured the Ladies European Tour card for 2016 season. She also became the youngest to win the title.

Frist woman to qualify for the Olympic Games
Aditi Ashok is the first woman to qualify in golf for the Olympic Games in Rio in 2016. She attained her best finish – fourth – in the 2020 Tokyo Olympics.

First to win on the Ladies European Tour (LET)
Aditi Ashok is the first to win a title on the Ladies European Tour by claiming the 2016 Ladies Indian Open.

First to represent the country in four multi-discipline Games
Aditi Ashok has participated in the 2013 Asian Youth Games, the 2014 Youth Olympic Games, the 2014 Asian Games, and the 2016 and 2020 Olympic Games.

First to win LET title outside India
Aditi Ashok won the 2016 Qatar Ladies Open.

Best finish on the LET Order of Merit
Aditi Ashok finished second on the 2016 LET Order of Merit and also won the 'Rookie of the Year" award.

First to qualify for the Ladies PGA Tour
Aditi Ashok gained the playing rights for the 2017 LPGA Tour via the LPGA Final Qualifying School.

MOSTS

Highest prize money (women)
Aditi Ashok collected US $60,000 in becoming the first to win the Ladies Indian Open title in November 2016.

Highest prize money earner in a domestic season
Rashid Khan won two events from 14 tournament appearances in the 2019 season and collected ₹66,27,650 as prize money.

Tournament with highest prize money
The ₹1.50 crore McLeod Russel Tour Championship in 2014 became the first domestic tournament to offer such high prize money in any individual domestic sport.

Most birdies
Jyoti Randhawa broke the course record at Shanghai with a seven-under par 65 that included eight birdies at the Volvo China Open Golf tournament in 2000. He finished in a tied fourth place.

Most lucrative season
During the 2017–18 PGAI Tour, 97 golfers earned over ₹1 lakh, including 79 over ₹2 lakh, 67 over ₹3 lakh, 51 over ₹5 lakh, 29 over ₹10 lakh, 19 over ₹15 lakh, 13 over ₹20 lakh and six players over ₹25 lakh during the season.

Most international titles
Jeev Milkha Singh has won 14 tour titles spread over three tours – four on the European Tour, six on the Asian Tour and four on the Japanese Tour.

Aditi Ashok: first to win the Ladies Indian Open

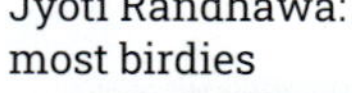
Jyoti Randhawa: most birdies

Most titles on the Asian Tour

Jyoti Randhawa has won eight titles: the 1998 Hero Honda Masters, the 1999 Hero Honda Masters, the 2000 Indian Open, the 2000 Singapore Open, the 2004 Volvo Masters of Asia, the 2006 Indian Open, the 2007 Indian Open and the 2009 Thailand Open.

Most titles in an Indian Tour season

Mukesh Kumar won six titles during the 2004-05 season.

Most career prize money from the domestic Professional Golf Tour of India (PGTI)

Shamim Khan has earned ₹4,38,03,143 from 265 tournament appearances.

Quickest to reach the million mark in prize money

Ashok Kumar won ₹1,00,10,334 in the 2004-05 season of the Indian Tour after just nine events.

Anirban Lahiri: best finish in a Major

Five titles in a season twice on the Indian Tour

Ashok Kumar won five titles in 2004 and repeated the feat in 2007.

BEST

Best finish in a Major

Anirban Lahiri finished tied-fifth in the 2016 PGA Championship

Best finish in the European Tour Order of Merit

Jeev Milkha Singh finished 12th on the 2008 European Tour Order of Merit.

Best Indian performance on the PGA Tour

In the ongoing 2022 season, Anirban Lahiri has already earned $3,084,598 – the highest by an Indian on the PGA Tour – from 24 events. His best came in the Players Championship where he finished runner-up, earning a $2.18 million pay cheque.

Best world ranking

Jeev Milkha Singh was placed 28th in the World ranking list in 2009.

Best performance based on prize money received

Arjun Atwal became the first Indian to win a title on the PGA Tour by claiming the honours in the Wyndham Championship in August 2010. The first qualifier to win the title in 24 years on the PGA Tour, Atwal collected $918,000 – the highest ever by an Indian golfer.

LOWEST

Lowest winning score on the European Tour

Arjun Atwal's scored title-winning 24-under 260 in the Carlsberg Malaysian Open in February 2003.

Least putts on the European Tour

Jeev Milkha Singh needed just 94 putts for four rounds of the 2001 Desert Classic. Jeev fell one short of the world record of 93, which stands in the name of Kenny Knox from the USA since 1990.

Lowest winning score on the Asian Tour

Jeev Milkha Singh scored 26 under par in the Philip Morris Championship in Seoul, when he won the four-round tournament on the Asian Tour. This is the lowest score by an Indian in winning an international title.

Lowest winning score on the Indian Tour

Mukesh Kumar fired 30-under 250 to win the DDA Open tournament at the Qutub Golf Course in New Delhi in April 2005.

Lowest round on the Indian Tour

Mukesh Kumar carded 11- under 59 in the third round of the DDA Open tournament at the Qutub Golf Course, New Delhi, in April 2005.

ONLY

Only team title in the USA

Former Test cricketer Kapil Dev led India to the TAG Heuer Invitational Golf title in Boston in Sept 2004. The team comprising Kapil Dev, Rakesh Rao, Nikhil Dewan and Rohit Duggal shot seven 65-under to win ahead of China, Indonesia, South Africa and two teams from North America, among others.

Only Indian to win four European Tour events in India

S.S.P. Chawrasia's all four European Tour titles have come in India: the 2008 Emaar MGF Indian Masters, New Delhi, the 2011 Avantha Masters, Gurugram, the 2016 Indian Open, New Delhi and the 2017 Indian Open, Gurugram.

Only Indian to win four titles on Japanese Tour

Jeev Milkha Singh has won four titles on the Japanese Tour: the 2006 Casio World Open, the 2006 Golf Nippon Series JT Cup, the 2008 Nagashima Shigeo Invitational Sega Sammy Cup and the 2008 Golf Nippon Series JT Cup.

Only Indian to win two European Tour titles in a year
Anirban Lahiri won the Malaysian Open and the Indian Open – both co-sanctioned events on the European Tour – in 2015.

Quickest to win two European Tour titles
Shubhankar Sharma won two European Tour titles in the space of 55 days. He won the Joburg Open in December 2017 and Maybank Championship in February 2018.

GENERAL

Oldest club
The Royal Kolkata Golf Club founded in 1829 is the oldest club outside Britain. The Kolkata Ladies Golf Club was established in 1891.

Highest golf course
The Yak Golf Club is located at an altitude of 13,025 ft at Kupup, Sikkim.

First international success in the U-10 category
Tanya Wadhwa of Delhi finished third in an U-10 International Golf tournament in San Diego, USA in July 2001.

YOUNGEST

Youngest hole-in-one
Viraat Badhwar (b August 28, 1995) was all of 6 years 11 months and 19 days when he scored a hole-in-one at the sixth hole (par 3 at 155 yards) using a 3 wood at the Peacock Course, Delhi Golf Club on 17 August 2002.

Youngest to win two back-to-back international titles
Shubham Juglan won the IMG Academy golf championship in San Deigo and the International Golf Academy titles in Vegas – both for children aged 9–10 – in successive weeks in 2015.

Youngest to win European Tour title
Shubhankar Sharma, at 21 months and four months, won the Joburg Open to become the youngest Indian winner on the European Tour.

Youngest to win Asian Tour Order of Merit
Shubhankar Sharma became the youngest to win the Asian Tour Order of Merit in December 2018.

Youngest winner on the domestic PGTI Tour
Playing only his second pro event, amateur Karandeep Kochar became the youngest winner on the PGTI Tour by beating the field in the 2016 Players Championship in Kolkata. Kochar, at 17 years and five months, broke Shubhankar Sharma's record of 17 years and eight months set in 2014.

Golf: National Award Winners
Asian Games: India won the team gold in 1982 and the individual men's gold medal twice, both in Bangkok in 1966 and 2002.

Padma Shri: Jeev Milkha Singh (2007).**Arjuna Award:** P.G. Sethi (1961); A.S. Malik (1963); R.K. Pitambar (1967); Anjali Desai (1972); Vikramjit Singh (1973); S.K. Jamshed (1975); Sita Rawlley (1977); Lakshman Singh (1982); Nonita Lall Qureshi (1987); Ali Sher (1991); Amit Luthra (1996); Jeev Milkha Singh (1999); Shiv Kapur (2002); Jyoti Randhawa (2004); Arjun Atwal (2007); Gaganjeet Bhullar (2013); Anirban Lahiri (2014); S.S.P. Chawrasia (2017). 2019 Shubhankar Sharma, 2020 Aditi Ashok.

Oldest to get hole-in-one
Lt Gen Ajit Singh at the grand old age of 90 achieved his first hole-in-one on 18 October 2005 at the Delhi Golf Club on the 9th hole (par 3; 160 yards).

Longest hole-in-one
Amit Luthra scored a hole-in-one at the second hole of Delhi Golf Club (par 4 at 258 yards) using a 5-iron on 16 March 1998.

GYMNASTICS

DOMESTIC

First National Championship
The first National Gymnastics Championship was held in 1952 in Madras (now Chennai, Tamil Nadu) where Khushi Ram emerged as the all-round individual champion and Punjab won the team championship.

First National Rhythmic Gymnastics event – women
The first National Rhythmic Gymnastics Championships held in 1989 at Kottayam, Kerala, had an event for women, where Neelamjit Kaur won the rhythmic gymnastics title. She won it again in 1990 at Udaipur, Rajasthan, and in 1991 at Delhi.

Most individual titles in the Nationals
- Kalpana Debnath from Madhya Pradesh won the all-round individual title four years in a row from 1976–77 to 1979–80.
- Rajesh Kumar from Chandigarh won the

Dilip Tirkey: First Olympian to head Indian hockey

Harmanpreet Singh: FIH Hockey 'best player of the year' winner, 2021

Savita Punia: FIH Hockey 'best goalkeeper' award winner, 2021

all-round individual title four times in a row between 1990–91 and 1994–95.

Most successive titles – team

Services won the team National Championship six times in a row between 1954–55 and 1961–62. They won it again six times in a row between 1963–64 and 1971–72. (The tournament was not held for some years in between.)

INTERNATIONAL

First World Cup medal

Aruna Reddy, then 22 years old, from Hyderabad, Telangana, became the first Indian gymnast to win a medal at the Gymnastics World Cup when she won a bronze in vault in Melbourne, Australia, with a score of 13.649 points on 24 February 2018.

First Olympic appearance

Khushi Ram and Vir Singh were the first gymnasts to represent India at the Olympics, in 1952 at Helsinki.

First appearance in the World Championship

Daljit Inder Singh, Manjit Singh and Vithal Karande participated in the 1970 World Championship held at Ljubljana (in present-day Slovenia).

First appearance in the Commonwealth Games

Manjit Singh, B.S. Nandi and N.B. Bhosle represented India at the 1978 Edmonton Commonwealth Games in Canada.

First medal in the Commonwealth Games – men

Ashish Kumar won the first ever medals (and a rare two at that) in gymnastics: a bronze in the individual floor exercise (score: 14.475) and a silver in the vault (with 15.312 points) at the 2010 Commonwealth Games, New Delhi.

First medal in the Asian Games – men

With a score of 14.925, Ashish Kumar won a bronze in the floor exercise at the 2010 Guangzhou Asian Games in China, which was India's first and only medal in gymnastics at the Asian Games.

First medal in the Asian Championship

Ashish Kumar won a bronze medal in the floor exercise at the third Senior Asian Gymnastics Championship at Pandit Deen Dayal Upadhyay Indoor Stadium, Surat, Gujarat, on 2 August 2006.

Most Olympic representations

Anantram Dogra is the only gymnast who has represented India in two Olympic Games – in Melbourne in 1956 and in Tokyo in 1964. He was also selected for the 1960 Rome Olympic Games, but the Indian Army team was called back due to an emergency.

HOCKEY

GENERAL

First Indian to head the International Hockey Federation

Dr Narinder Dhruv Batra was the first non-European president of the FIH. He was elected twice to the prestigious post, first in 2016 and re-elected in 2022.

First Olympian to head Indian hockey

Dilip Tirkey from Odisha, who had participated in three Olympic Games (in 1996 in Atlanta, USA; in 2000 in Sydney, Australia; and in 2004 in Athens, Greece), was unanimously elected president of Hockey India on 23 September 2022.

Most Arjuna Awards for any sport in a year

Normally, two or three hockey players (both men and women collectively) used to get the Government of India's top sporting award. However, with the success of Indian men's team at the Tokyo Olympics, all the 16 members (except the duo of goalkeeper P.R. Sreejesh and captain Manpreet Singh, who have already received the award earlier), were awarded the honour. P.R. Sreejesh and Manpreet Singh were given the Khel Ratna award.

Most FIH Hockey Star Awards

Indian players and coaches swept all the annual FIH Hockey Star Awards in 2021. The winners include Player of the Year: Harmanpreet Singh (men) and Gurjit Kaur (women); Best Goalkeeper: P.R. Sreejesh (men) and Savita Punia (women); Best Rising Star Vivek Sagar Prasad (men) and Sharmila Devi (women); Best Coach: Graham Reid (national men's team coach) and Sjoerd Marijne (national women's team coach).

DOMESTIC

Oldest tournament – men

The Beighton Cup was started in Calcutta (now Kolkata, West Bengal) in 1895 and is considered to be the oldest tournament. Presented by T.D. Beighton, the legal remembrancer of the then Government of Bengal, the Cup was held initially in the form of local matches, evolving into a regular tournament. Its latest edition was held in December 2016, with Indian Oil defeating Bharat Petroleum 5–3.

Oldest tournament -- women

First National Championship that was in 1947 in the then Bombay is the oldest domestic tournament for women.

First National Championship – men

The first National Championship, then known as the Inter-Provincial Championship, was staged in 1928 at Kolkata (then Calcutta). India became a member of the International Hockey Federation in 1927 and thus became eligible to participate in the 1928 Olympics. The Calcutta edition was held to select the team for participation in the 1928 Olympic Games in Amsterdam.

First National Championship – women

Various attempts were made to start a National Championship. However, these efforts did not bear any results, after an edition was initially held. Subsequently, when the Bombay Inter-Provincial Hockey Association started in 1947, it got the much elusive consensus of all the states and thus a legacy was born.

First Domestic League – men

The Premier Hockey League (2005).

First Domestic League – women

The Khelo India Women Hockey League for U-21 (2021)

Most wins in the National Championship – men

Indian Railways has won 25 times.

Most wins in the National Championship – women

Indian Railways has won 30 times.

INTERNATIONAL HOCKEY

First international appearance - men

In 1926, the Indian Army team went to New Zealand to play 21 matches. They won 18, drew two and lost one match. They scored 192 and conceded 24 goals.

First major success by a foreign coach

Australian Terry Walsh was India's coach at the time of the gold medal win at the 2014 Incheon Asian Games in South Korea. In the final, India drew with Pakistan 1–1 but won 4–2 in the penalty shoot-out.

An international hockey match in progress

First women professional players

Penalty corner expert Jasjeet Kaur Handa and Subhadra Pradhan played for HC Den Bosch club in the Dutch League in 2007.

First medal and most successful team in the Olympics

The Indian hockey team won its first Olympic medal in 1928, under the captaincy of Jaipal Singh Munda. From 1928 to 1956, the team was unbeaten, winning six gold medals. Since then, India has been adding medals to its Olympic tally, and currently, with a total of eight gold, one silver and two bronze medals, it is the single most successful team at the Olympic Games.

First foreign coach

- *Men*: Gerard Rach from Germany, India's first foreign coach, was with the team at the 2004 Athens Olympics, and till January 2005.
- *Women*: Herman Kruis from the Netherlands was the first foreign coach for the women's hockey team, and was in charge of the Asia Cup in Hong Kong in September 2007.

First Commonwealth Games success – women

At the 2002 Commonwealth Games in Manchester, UK, the Indian women's hockey team won the gold medal, defeating England 3–2. The team was led by Suraj Lata Devi.

First Asia Cup win – women

Coached by M.K. Kaushik, the Indian women's hockey team won the Asia Cup for the first time, beating Japan 1–0 in the final at the National Stadium (now Dhyan Chand National Stadium), New Delhi, in February 2004.

First Junior Asia Cup win

India won the fifth Junior Asia Cup in Karachi, Pakistan, in March 2004, beating the hosts 5–2.

NATIONAL SPORTS AWARDS 2021

HOCKEY

Arjuna Award
Monika, Vandana Katariya, Dilpreet Singh, Harman Preet Singh, Rupinder Pal Singh, Surender Kumar, Amit Rohidas, Birendra Lakra, Sumit, Nilakanta Sharma, Hardik Singh, Vivek Sagar Prasad, Gurjant Singh, Mandeep Singh, Shamsher Singh, Lalit Kumar Upadhyay, Varun Kumar, Simranjeet Singh

Dhyan Chand Award
Davinder Singh Garcha

Dronacharya Award
Pritam Siwach; Harpal Singh (Lifetime)

Major Dhyan Chand Khel Ratna
P.R. Sreejesh, Manpreet Singh

The gold medal–winning team at the 1936 Berlin Olympics

Dhyan Chand: 33 goals in three Olympics

The Indian hockey team in the 1932 Olympics: biggest victory margin

Tushar Khandekar scored a memorable hat-trick in the final.

Inaugural FIH Hockey 5s Championship win

The International Hockey Federation (FIH) introduced a new tournament in 2022. India, led by Gurinder Singh, won, by defeating Poland (4-3) in the final on 7 June 2022 in Geneva, Switzerland.

First Asian Men's Hockey Champions Trophy win - Men

India won the inaugural edition of the tournament held in Ordos City, China, during August–September 2011, by defeating Pakistan 4–2 in the final via penalty strokes.

First Asian Women's Hockey Champions Trophy win - Women

India, led by Deepika Thakur, won the Asian Women's Champions trophy held in Singapore in 2016, beating China in the final on shoot out.

WR Most Olympic goals – individual

Dhyan Chand scored 33 goals in three Olympics – 10 in 1928, 12 in 1932 and 11 in 1936.

WR Most goals in the Olympics – team

India scored 43 goals in six matches at Moscow in 1980, a record for the most goals in an Olympics. In the 1936 Berlin and 1956 Melbourne Olympics, India notched up 38 goals in five matches. It did not concede a single goal in 1928 and 1956.

WR Most medals in the Olympics

The world record for the most medals in hockey at the Olympics is held by Leslie Claudius and Udham Singh, who were in four medal-winning teams – with three golds and one silver. Claudius was in the team that won the gold in 1948, 1952 and 1956, and silver in 1960, while Singh played for the gold-winning team in 1952, 1956 and 1964, and the silver-winning team in 1960.

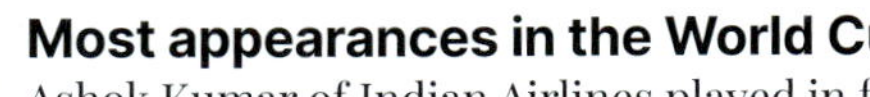

Most appearances in the World Cup

Ashok Kumar of Indian Airlines played in four World Cups from 1971 to 1978, a record for the most appearances at the World Cup.

Most appearance in the Women's World Cup

Deepika Thakur is the only Indian woman hockey player to appear in three World Cups (2006, 2010, 2018). India did not qualify for the 2014 edition.

Most capped player

Dilip Tirkey is the most capped player in India (412).

Playing for teams with most Olympic golds

The record for playing for teams winning the most Olympic golds – three each – is held by seven Indians: Richard Allen and Dhyan Chand (1928–36); Balbir Singh, R.S. Gentle, Leslie Claudius and R. Francis (1948–56); and Udham Singh (1952, 1956, 1964).

Most goals in a World Cup

In the fifth World Cup in Bombay (now Mumbai), Maharashtra, during 1981–82, India scored 29 goals in seven matches, winning five and losing two.

WR Biggest victory margin in the Olympics

India created a world record for the biggest victory margin at the Olympics when they beat the USA 24–1 on 11 August 1932 at Los Angeles, USA.

Best performance in the World Cup – men

India, led by Ajitpal Singh, beat Pakistan 2–1 in the final of the third World Cup at Kuala Lumpur, Malaysia, in 1975, displaying its best performance at the World Cup.

Best performance in the World Cup – women

India, led by Ajinder Kaur, finished fourth in 1974.

Hockey: A Gender-Balanced Sport

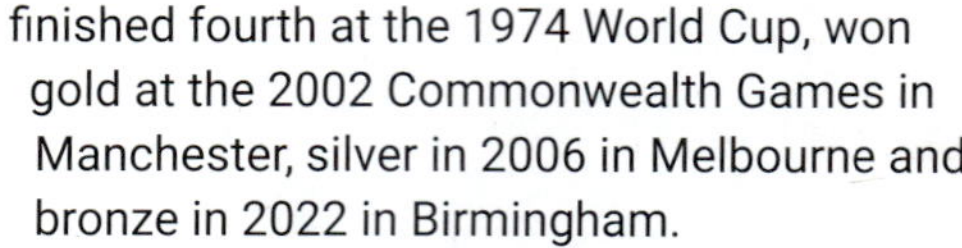

In independent India, hockey kept the sporting fire burning as it had in the colonial times. Led by Kishan Lal, hockey gave the free nation its first gold at the 1948 London Olympics, beating past masters Great Britain 4-0 in the final. Three more gold medals (1952, 1956 and 1980), a silver (1960) and three bronze medals (1968, 1972 and 2020) followed.

Overall, Indian hockey's Olympic record – eight gold, a silver and three bronze medals – making for a total of 12 medals, is a world record for the sport. Thankfully, this unique contribution doesn't stop with the Olympics.

Indian hockey's performance in all the tournaments that came into being since 1947 was also formidable.

Hockey held its first World Cup in 1971 in Barcelona where India won a bronze. They went one better in 1973 in Amsterdam, finishing with a silver before wresting the title in 1975 in Kuala Lumpur.

Hockey in the Asian Games was introduced in its third edition (1958 in New Delhi). Since then, the Indian men's team won medals at every edition except once (2006 in Doha, Qatar) for an envious record of three gold, nine silver and three bronze medals.

The tradition continued in other continental tournaments: Asia Cup (three golds – 2003, 2007 and 2016; five silver and two bronze medals) and Asian Champions Trophy (three golds, a silver and a bronze).

Since hockey was introduced at the Commonwealth Games in 1998, the men's team has won silver three times (2010, 2014 and 2022).

Not to be left behind, Indian women's hockey, despite getting fewer platforms and less support, finished fourth at the 1974 World Cup, won gold at the 2002 Commonwealth Games in Manchester, silver in 2006 in Melbourne and bronze in 2022 in Birmingham.

They qualified for all Asian Games editions since the introduction of hockey at the 1982 Games in New Delhi where they won their only gold medal, and also picked two silver and three bronze medals in the years to come.

Out of 10 appearances in the Asia Cup, they won medals seven times (two golds – in New Delhi, 2004 and in Kakamigahara, 2017 – two silvers and three bronzes). Their Asian Champions Trophy record is a gold (Singapore, 2016), two silvers and a bronze out of six appearances.

The women's hockey team came into renewed focus when they defeated three-time champions Australia in the 2020 Tokyo Olympics' quarter-finals. They went down to Argentina 1-2 in the semi-finals and to Britain 3-4 in the bronze medal match but not before the nation woke up to their indomitable spirit.

Indian men's hockey, despite increasing competition amid escalating costs, performed well to qualify for all Olympics (except once – Beijing 2008) since Amsterdam 1928, World Cups, Asian Games and Asia Cups.

In both Asian events, India won medals in all editions except once. It's a creditable feat given the fact that in other team sports like football and volleyball, India most often fails to qualify even for the Asian Games.

Significantly, Indian hockey maintained a healthy tradition in gender parity insofar as qualification for major tournaments, winning medals, eliciting popular support and administrators are concerned. Two women administrators – Vidya Stokes and Mariamma Koshy – headed the unified hockey federations. With the successful conduct of the hockey world's most popular and highly commercial venture, the Hockey India League, India made path-breaking contribution to the collective welfare of global hockey. Fittingly, an Indian, Dr Narinder Dhruv Batra, rose to become the first non-European president of the Federation Internationale de Hockey (FIH) for two spells.

V for victory: hockey celebrates an equitable spirit

The Indian hockey team at the 1928 Olympic Games: best goalkeeping in the Olympics

NATIONAL SPORTS AWARDS 2022

HOCKEY

Arjuna Award
Deep Grace Ekka

Dhyan Chand Award (Lifetime)
Dharamvir Singh

Best performance in the Commonwealth Games

Hockey was first introduced in the Commonwealth Games in 1998. India's best performances at the Commonwealth Games include three silver medals (in 2010 in New Delhi 2010, in 2014 in Glasgow and in 2022 in Birmingham).

Best performance on a foreign tour

Dhyan Chand, who led the team to New Zealand in 1935, played 48 matches and won them all. India scored 584 goals and conceded 40 goals. Dhyan Chand alone scored 201 goals, his brother Roop Singh scored 187 and F.C. Wells scored 112 goals.

Best performances in the Champions Trophy

India reached the final in the 2016 Champions Trophy in London, UK, and the 2018 Champions Trophy in Breda, Netherlands. In both, India lost 1–3 to Australia in the penalty shoot-out. The traditional tournament has not being held after 2018.

Biggest victory margin in the Asian Games – men

India's biggest victory margin at the Asian Games was 26–0 versus Hong Kong in the League phase of the 2018 Jakarta Asian Games in Indonesia.

Biggest victory margin in the Asian Games – women

India's biggest victory margin at the Asiad n Games came in the League phase of the 2018 Bangkok Asian Games when it beat Kazakhstan 21–0 on 21 August 2018.

Best recovery in the Men's Hockey Champions Trophy

- The Indian team rallied from 0–3 at Amstelveen, Netherlands, to beat Pakistan 5–4 in 1982.
- India trailed West Germany 1–5 in 1985 at Perth, but in the last seven minutes levelled at 5–5. Centre half Joaquim Carvalho scored an equalizing penalty stroke.

Biggest win in the Asia Cup finals

India beat South Korea 7–2 in the final of the 2007 Asia Cup in Chennai, Tamil Nadu, on 19 September 2007.

Biggest win over Pakistan

India's 7–1 win over Pakistan on 17 June 2017 in the World Hockey League semi-final in London, UK, is their biggest victory margin over their arch-rivals.

Best goalkeeping in the Olympics

Richard J. Allen did not concede a single goal in the five matches in the 1928 Olympics. He let in only two goals in 1932 and one in five games in 1936, conceding only three goals in three successive Olympics – a rare feat.

Highest goal scorer at the World Cup

Defender Rajender Singh, who played a solitary World Cup, scored all 12 goals in the 1981–82 tournament in Bombay (now Mumbai), Maharashtra, making him the highest goal scorer at the World Cup.

Highest goal scorer in the Asia Cup

Centre forward Sheikh Mohammed Nayeem scored 11 goals in the second Asia Cup in Dhaka, Bangladesh, in 1985.

Highest goal scorer and double hat-trick in the Youth Asia Cup

Defender Jugraj Singh scored 14 goals, including a double hat-trick, in the Youth Asia Cup in Malaysia in June 2001.

Fastest goal

Ajit Singh scored within 15 seconds of the start of the League match against Argentina in the 1976 Montreal Olympics – the fastest goal on artificial turf.

Only captain in successive Olympics

Pargat Singh was the captain first at Barcelona in 1992 and then in 1996 at the Atlanta Olympics in the USA, but India did not win a medal at either Games.

Only goalkeeper in three finals

Goalkeeper Shankar Laxman played in three Olympic finals – in 1956 in Melbourne, in 1960 in Rome and in 1964 in Tokyo.

Only double hat-trick in the Olympics

Mohammed Shahid scored seven goals,

In Remembrance

Maharaj Krishan Kaushik (2 May 1955–8 May 2022)
M.K. Kaushik, a right-winger, was employed with Mumbai-based Tata Hockey Club and represented the same city in the National Championship 12 times from 1975 onwards. He made his international debut in 1974 in the young Indian team that visited Afghanistan. His career peaked at the 1980 Moscow Olympics, where the Indian team won a gold after a gap of 16 years and he struck one of India's four goals in the final against Spain (4-3). He also played in the 1981–82 World Cup and the Asia Cup (1982). Later, under his coaching, the Indian men's team won their second Asian Games gold (1998, Bangkok) after a gap of 32 years, the first women's Asia Cup medal (a bronze; 1993, Hiroshima) and then a gold (2004, New Delhi). He received the Arjuna (1998) and Dronacharya (2002) awards and headed the National Hockey Academy.

Charanjit Singh (20 November 1928–27 January 2022)
Charanjit Singh represented Punjab Police, as the centre half, playing a vital role in their winning many major tournaments. With him, India won gold at the first major tournament for the country, the Munich Hockey Festival (1959). He played in the 1960 Rome Olympics (silver), where for the first time India lost the title. Under his leadership, India regained the gold at the 1964 Tokyo Olympics, winning all the matches on the way to the podium. He was also part of the title-winning Indian teams of Ahmedabad International (1962) and Lyons Cup (1964).

Elvera Britto (15 June 1940–27 April 2022)
A pioneer of Indian women's hockey and only the second woman hockey player to be decorated with the Arjuna Award (1965), Elvera – and her sisters Priscilla, Rita and Mae – represented Mysore State in the domestic circuit. With them, the state won the National Championship for a record eight times on the trot. Elvera, as midfielder and captain, won the home and away Series against Sri Lanka in the mid-60s. Later, besides heading the Karnataka Women's Hockey Federation, she was a national selector and government nominee for hockey.

Varinder Singh (16 May 1947–22 June 2022)
This legendary midfielder won the hearts of connoisseurs of the game early on, and the Indian Railways quickly got him in their hockey team. He went on to win the Olympic bronze (1972) in his international debut. He was India's hero in the 1975 World Cup, having already won silver in the previous edition (1973). He also figured in two Asian Games (silver at 1974, Tehran and 1978, Bangkok) along with another World Cup (1978, Buenos Aires) and an Olympics (1976, Montreal), besides many invitational tournaments.

Varinder Singh

including a double hat-trick, against Thailand (11–0) on 24 September 1986 in the Seoul Olympics in South Korea.

Only hat-trick in succession
At the 1952 Helsinki Olympics, centre forward Balbir Singh scored three goals in the semi-final against Great Britain and netted five, including a hat-trick, against the Netherlands in the final.

Only hat-trick in xthe Olympics – women
Vandana Katariya scored a hat-trick against South Africa on 31 July 2021 in the 2020 Tokyo Olympics in Japan.

Youngest to win a gold in the Olympics
Cinnadorai Desamuthu was the youngest player to be in a gold-winning team, aged 19 years and 272 days, when India won in the 1952 Helsinki Olympics.

Oldest players in the Olympics
- Udham Singh (b. 1928) was 36 when he played in the 1964 Tokyo Olympics. Prithipal Singh (b. 1932) was also 36 when he was joint captain of the Indian team at the 1968 Mexico Olympics.

KABADDI

First Nationals
- The first kabaddi Nationals for men were held in 1951 in Maharashtra. The host state won the title.
- The first Nationals in kabaddi for women were held in 1955 in Calcutta (now Kolkata), West Bengal. Maharashtra won here too.
- The first championships for junior boys and girls were held in 1974 and 1976 respectively at Asansol, West Bengal.

First demonstration in the Olympics
Kabaddi and other indigenous games were the demonstration games in the 1936 Olympic Games held in Berlin, Germany.

NATIONAL SPORTS AWARDS 2021

KABADDI

Arjuna Award
Sandeep Narwal

Dhyan Chand Award
Vikas Kumar

Dronacharya Award (Lifetime)
Ashan Kumar

NATIONAL SPORTS AWARDS 2022
KABADDI
Arjuna Award
Sakshi Kumari
Dhyan Chand Award (Lifetime)
B.C. Suresh

First appearance of kabaddi in the Asian Games

Kabaddi was played for the first time in the 11th Asian Games in 1990 in Beijing, China. Pakistan, Japan, China, Nepal, Bangladesh and India participated, with India winning the gold medal.

First demonstration at the Asian Games

Kabaddi was an exhibition sport at the 1982 Asian Games held in New Delhi.

First Asian Championship

The first Asian Championship for men was held at Calcutta (now Kolkata), West Bengal, in 1980, in which teams from Bangladesh, Nepal and India played. India won the gold medal.

First Pro Kabaddi League

The first Pro Kabaddi League was held in 2014 with eight teams participating. Sixty games were played, with the Jaipur Pink Panthers winning the inaugural title, defeating U-Mamba 35–24.

First team to win three consecutive Pro Kabaddi titles

Patna Pirates won three consecutive Pro Kabaddi League titles in 2016–17.

First participation in the Asian Junior Championship

The championship was held for the first time at Faridabad, Haryana, in January 2000, with teams from Bangladesh, Nepal, Sri Lanka and Thailand. India won the gold.

NATIONAL SPORTS AWARDS 2022
WUSHU
Arjuna Award
Parveen Kumar

Most World Cup wins – men

The Indian team has won all three Kabaddi World Cups, organized by the International Kabaddi Federation, in 2004, 2007 and 2016, beating Iran in the finals of all three.

Most Asian Games titles – men

Kabaddi was introduced in the Asian Games in 1990 in Beijing, China, and was open only to men at that time. The Indian team has since won the Asian Games gold seven times – in 1990, 1994, 1998, 2002, 2006, 2010 and 2014.

Most World and Asian Championship medals – women

Sarala Shetty of Bank Sports Board is the only Indian to win the Asian Kabaddi Championship eight times. Captain of the Indian team on eight occasions, she has also won three World Championship medals.

Most Asian Games titles – women

Kabaddi first made an appearance as a competitive sport for women in the 2010 Guangzhou Asian Games in China, 20 years after it was introduced for men. The Indian team won gold in 2010 and 2014, but got a silver in the 2018 Asian Games in Jakarta, Indonesia, losing to Iran in the final.

Most expensive non-cricket player

Raider Monu Goyat from Haryana became India's most expensive non-cricket sportsperson when Haryana Steelers bought him at ₹1.51 crore (15.1 million) for season 6 of the Pro Kabaddi League 2018.

LUGE

WR Youngest luge Olympian

India's single representative at luge in the Winter Olympics, Shiva Keshavan from Manali, Himachal Pradesh, was the youngest luge Olympian in history, when he participated in the 1998 Nagano Olympics in Japan at the age of 16 years. Keshavan holds the record of participating in six winter Olympics: 1998 Nagano, Japan; 2002 Salt Lake City, USA; 2006 Turin, Italy; 2010 Vancouver, Canada; 2014 Sochi, Russia; and 2018 Pyeongchang, South Korea. He won the Asian Luge Championships in 2011, 2012, 2016 and 2017. He set a new Asian speed record of 134.3 kmph in 2011.

MARTIAL ARTS

WUSHU

First world wushu champion – men

Praveen Kumar of the Indian Army became t he first Indian to win the gold medal on 23 October 2019 in the Sanda 48 kg category of the 15th World Wushu Championship.

First world wushu champion – women

In 2017, Pooja Kadian became the first Indian to be crowned World Champion in the women's 75 kg Sanda category.

JUDO

First National Championship

The first National Championship was held in Hyderabad in 1965. Till 1981, it was held every two years.

Youngest champion

Sandeep Bayala was 15 years old when he won the Nationals at Srinagar in 1982.

First international medal

India, represented by Sandeep Bayala (below

65 kg), Cawas Billimoria (below 95 kg), Shyam Singh Gurjar (+95 kg) and Bannu Singh (open), won four bronze medals in the 1986 Asian Games in Seoul.

Most wins in the Nationals
Sandeep Bayala of Delhi Police has won 11 titles successively during 1982–93.

First judoka to win a world title
Sixteen-year-old Linthoi Chanambam clinched a historic gold medal at the World Cadet Championship on 22 August 2022. She won the title across age groups.

First medal in the Asian Games – women
Poonam Chopra won a silver medal in the 56 kg weight category at the 1994 Hiroshima Games in Japan.

First medal in the Asian Championship – women
Poonam Chopra won a bronze medal in 56 kg weight category at the Asian Championship in 1993 in Macau, China.

India's first participation in the Asian Games
India participated in judo at the Seoul Asian Games in 1986.

Oldest competitor
Banu Singh was 39 years old when he represented India at the Seoul Games in 1986. He won a bronze in the open category.

Best performance in the Commonwealth Games
India won two silver and two bronze medals in 2018 at Gold Coast in Australia,

Most silver medals in the Commonwealth Games – women
Judoka Shushila Devi Likmabam won two silver medals in the women's 48 kg category, the first in Glasgow in 2014 and the second in Birmingham in 2022.

Most international appearances by a couple
Narendra Singh represented India in the 1992 Olympics in Barcelona and the 1996 Olympics in Atlanta; two Asian Games: Beijing, 1990, and Hiroshima, 1994; and the Asian Championships (1991–1995). He won gold medals at the South Asian Championships, Commonwealth Championships and other international tournaments. His wife Sunita Thakur appeared in two Asian Games (Beijing, 1990 and Hiroshima, 1994) and one Olympic Games (Atlanta, 1996) and one Commonwealth Games (Auckland, 1990), among other international competitions.

POWERLIFTING

Most medals in one edition of the Asian Championship
V.S.N.L. Renuka won four golds in the 48 kg category in squat, bench, deadlift and overall lift of 310 kg at the Asian Powerlifting Championship in Zarafshan, Uzbekistan, in 2000.

Most Commonwealth Championship golds – individual
Sampa Guha won four gold medals in the first Commonwealth Championship in Newcastle, UK, in September 2005.

Most medals in Asian Championship
In the biggest haul at the Asian Championship to date, Indian powerlifters won 49 medals (22 gold, 19 silver and eight bronze medals), besides the Women's Team Championship and overall medals (men and women), at the 18th Asian Senior, Junior, Sub-junior and Masters (men and women) Championship 2006 at Taebaek City, Korea.

Best performance in the World Championship
India won all three medals in the World Championship in Akita, Japan, in November 2000. N. Anbu (52 kg) won gold in the deadlift and an overall silver, while Jentry Francis (56 kg) won the bronze medal.

Shushila Devi Likmabam: most silver medals in judo in the Commonwealth Games – women

A ppowerlifting bench press competition in progress

Best performance in the Asian Junior Championship

At the Asian Junior Championship, Indian boys won the team trophy with four gold, four silver and two bronze medals at New Delhi in May 2001. In the same championship, Indian girls also won the team trophy with three gold medals, two silver medals and two bronze medals.

Best performance in the Commonwealth Championship – men

India bagged a total of five gold, three silver and four bronze medals, and were declared runner-up in the team event in the second Commonwealth Championship at Christchurch, New Zealand, held from 6 to 9 December 2007.

Best performance in the Asian Sub-junior Championship

The Indian boys' team won the team trophy with five gold and two silver medals at the inaugural Asian Sub-junior Championship held at New Delhi in May 2001. In the same championship, the Indian girls' team bagged four gold and two silver medals.

Back-to-back Olympia Pro-Powerlifting wins

Mukesh Singh Gehlot from Delhi is the only Indian to win an individual medal in successive IPL Olympia Pro-Powerlifting. He won the gold on his debut in IPL Olympia Pro-Powerlifting 2017 in the 100 kg open category and a bronze in Las Vegas, USA, in 2018.

First medal in powerlifting in the Asian Para Games

Farman Basha won India's first medal – a bronze – in the 48 kg category at the inaugural Asian Para Games held in Guangzhou, China, in December 2010.

First medal in the Commonwealth games in para powerlifting

Sakina Khatun won the bronze medal in the lightweight category at the 2014 Commonwealth Para Games held in Glasgow, UK.

First gold in para powerlifting

Sudhir Lath claimed the gold medal in the men's heavyweight para powerlifting event at the 2022 Commonwealth Games in Birmingham. The 27-year-old, who has an impairment due to polio, lifted 212 kg.

SHOOTING

World champion with a world record

Rudrankksh Patil became the world champion in men's air rifle in the World Championship in Cairo, Egypt, in October 2022. He had shot a world record 633.9 in the first stage of qualification. The 18-year-old Rudrankksh beat Danilo Dennis Solazzo of Italy 17-13 for the gold. He beat two Chinese shooters, including the reigning world and Olympic champion Yang Haoran. He became the second Indian to become world champion in air rifle after Abhinav Bindra in 2006. Rudrankksh also led the Indian team to the gold later, along with Arjun Babuta and Kiran Jadhav, as the trio beat China 16-10.

First skeet gold in the World Cup

Olympian Mairaj Ahmad Khan became the first Indian to win a skeet gold in a World Cup in Changwon, Korea, in July 2022. The 46-year-old Mairaj beat Kin Minsu of Korea 37-36 for the gold. Khan shot 119 in qualification and had to win a shoot-off with four others for the last two slots in the second stage. Mairaj had lost the shoot-off for the gold in the World Cup in Rio de Janeiro in 2016, and won the silver.

First Asian Games medals

- *Men:* India's Asian Games medal haul started with Dr Karni Singh winning silver in the trap event in 1974 at Tehran, Iran.
- *Women:* Soma Dutta won a silver in the individual rifle 3-position event and a bronze medal in air rifle at the 1986 Seoul Games, South Korea.

First Olympic finalist

Anjali Vedpathak-Bhagwat of the Central Industrial Security Force (CISF), Mumbai, Maharashtra, reached the air rifle final in the 2000 Sydney Olympics. She finished eighth with 493.1 points.

First World Championship medal

India's first World Championship medal came

Three Shooters Win Olympic Quota for the 2024 Paris Olympic Games

Bhowneesh Mendiratta (trap), Rudrankksh Patil (air rifle) and Swapnil Kusale (rifle 3-position) have won the Olympic quota in the World Championships in shooting, for the Paris Olympic Games in 2024. Bhowneesh won it in the shotgun World Championship in Osijek, Croatia, while the other two won in the World Championship in Cairo, Egypt.

when Dr Karni Singh from Bikaner, Rajasthan, won a silver medal in the trap event in Cairo, Egypt, in 1962. The gold medal in the event was bagged by Vladimir Zimenko of the USSR.

First ever individual Olympic gold medal

Abhinav Bindra won India's first individual Olympic gold medal by claiming the honour in the men's air rifle event on 11 August 2008 in Beijing, China.

First World Championship gold

- Ace shooter Abhinav Bindra won India's first gold medal in a World Championship in air rifle at Zagreb, Croatia, on 24 July 2006.
- Manavjit Singh Sandhu won the first shotgun gold medal in a World Championship by beating 124 shooters to the title in the trap event at Zagreb, Croatia, two days after Bindra's effort.

First Asian Games gold

- Randhir Singh won gold in the trap event in the 1978 Games in Bangkok, Thailand, and a bronze in 1982.
- Jaspal Rana won the men's individual 25 m centre-fire pistol event in the 1994 Hiroshima Asian Games with 588 points, a new Asian record then. It was the only individual gold medal for India that year and the first Asian Games gold in that event.

First Commonwealth Games gold

- *Men:* Ashok Pandit won the gold in the free pistol event in Auckland, New Zealand, in 1990.
- *Women:* Roopa Unnikrishnan clinched the gold in the rifle prone event in the 1998 Commonwealth Games in Kuala Lumpur, Malaysia. In the 1994 Games in Victoria, Australia, Unnikrishnan won two medals – a silver in the small-bore rifle 3-position and a bronze in the pairs with Kuheli Ganguly.

First woman to win a gold in the Asian Games

Rahi Sarnobat became the first Indian woman to win a gold in the Asian Games (25 m pistol event) in 2018 at Jakarta, Indonesia.

First World Cup silver and gold medals

Anjali Vedpathak-Bhagwat won the gold in the air rifle event in the World Cup at Milan, Italy, in 2003. She had earlier won the silver in Munich, Germany, in 2002.

First World Cup pistol medal

Sonia Rai from Himachal Pradesh won the bronze in the women's air pistol in the World Cup at Resende, Brazil, on 28 April 2006. She shot a 482.2, after 384/400 in the qualification phase.

WR Gold in the World Cup

Saurabh Chaudhary won the gold medal in the 10 m air pistol event in the World Cup at Munich, Germany, in May 2019. He shot a 246.3 to break his own world record of 245.5 set in the World Championship. He won gold medals in the 2018 Youth Olympics in Buenos Aires, Argentina, and in the 2018 Asian Games in Jakarta, Indonesia.

First gold in the Asian Championship

Dr Karni Singh won an individual gold in the trap event in 1971 in Seoul, South Korea. This was India's first gold in the Asian Championship.

First medal haul in the Asian Championship

India won two gold, one silver and two bronze medals in Jakarta, Indonesia, in 1983, in its first haul in the Asian Championship. Ashok Pandit and Mohinder Lal won the gold in the centre-fire pistol team event with a world record.

First mixed air pistol gold medal in the World Cup – team

Heena Sidhu and Jitu Rai won the gold in the

Rahi Sarnobat: first woman to win a gold in the Asian Games

Saurabh Chaudhary: gold medal in the World Cup

Junior Gold Medals in the 2022 World Championship

Esha Singh

- Esha Singh won three gold medals in the World Championship in Cairo, Egypt, in October 2022. She won the junior women's 25 m sports pistol gold. She also won the junior women's air pistol team gold along with Shikha Narwal and Varsha Singh. She won the junior mixed team gold medal in air pistol with Samrat Rana.
- Ramita Jindal won the junior women's air rifle gold medal, and the team gold medal along with Nancy and Tilottama Sen.
- Payal Khatri and Adarsh Singh won the rapid fire pistol mixed team junior gold medal.
- Arya Vansh Tyagi, Shardul Vihan and Shapath Bharadwaj won the trap team junior men's gold medal in the shotgun World Championship in Osijek, Croatia.
- Sagar Dangi, Samrat Rana and Varun Tomar won the men's 10 m air pistol junior team gold medal.
- Karthik Sabari Raj, Vidit Jain and Divyansh Singh Panwar won the junior men's air rifle team gold medal.
- Vijayveer Sidhu (men's standard pistol junior) and Divanshi (women's free pistol junior) won the gold medal in non-Olympic events in the World Championship in Cairo, Egypt.

NATIONAL SPORTS AWARDS 2021

SHOOTING

Arjuna Award
Abhishek Verma; Singhraj Adhana (para shooting)

Major Dhyan Chand Khel Ratna
Avani Lekhara and Manish Narwal (para shooting)

Dronacharya Award:
Jai Prakash Nautiyal (para shooting)

Manu Bhaker: first to win two World Cup gold medals

Jaspal Rana: most career golds at the South Asian Games

mixed air pistol team event in the World Cup in Delhi in 2017, when it was officially made a medal event.

First team gold in the Asian Clay Championship

Mansher Singh, Moraad Ali Khan and Manavjit Singh won India's first team gold at the Asian Clay Shooting Championship at Chengdu, China, in July 1995 with a tally of 357/375, equalling Kuwait's Asian record at the 1994 Hiroshima Asian Games in Japan.

First Nationals

The first shooting national tournament was held in Delhi from 9 to 16 November in 1952.

First to win two golds in a World Cup

Manu Bhaker, then 16 years old, from Jhajjar, Haryana, won the 10 m air pistol gold medal and partnered with Om Prakash Mitharval for the 10 m air pistol mixed team gold in the 2018 World Cup in Mexico.

First ever Olympic medal in shooting

Rajyavardhan Singh Rathore won the silver medal in double-trap shooting, behind Ahmed Al Maktoum of the UAE, in the 2004 Athens Olympics in Greece. Rathore made his maiden Olympic appearance in the 2004 Olympic Games in Athens, Greece, merely about six years after he had taken up the sport. A year before, he had won the gold medal in the 2003 World Cup in Sydney, Australia.

WR World record in skeet in the Asian Championship

Angad Vir Singh Bajwa shot a perfect 60 out of 60 to win the gold medal in the men's skeet final in the Asian Championship held in Kuwait in November 2018.

Most individual medals in the Asian Shooting Championship

Ronak Pandit won seven gold medals and a silver medal in the junior pistol events of the Asian Championship in Kuala Lumpur, Malaysia, in 2004.

WR World record at the Asian Championship

Suma Shirur shot a perfect 400 out of 400 to win the gold- medal in the women's air rifle in the Asian Championship at Kuala Lumpur, Malaysia, in February 2004. She shares the record with eight others.

Most career golds at the South Asian Games

Jaspal Rana won 23 golds and a silver in three editions of the SAF Games (now South Asian Games). He won eight golds each at Madras (now Chennai), Tamil Nadu, in 1995 and at Kathmandu, Nepal, in 1999; and seven golds and a silver at Islamabad, Pakistan, in 2004.

Best haul in the Asian Clay Shooting Championship

The best performance in the Asian Clay Shooting Championship was five gold medals in Bangkok, Thailand, in September 2005.

Best haul in the World Championship

- The Indian team won 34 medals including 12 gold medals in the World Championship for rifle and pistol in Cairo, Egypt, in 2022. It is the best ever performance by India in a World Championship and India finished second in the medals table behind China.
- In 2018, India had won 27 medals in the World Championship in Changwon, Korea, finishing third behind China and Korea.

Best haul in the World Cup

The Indian team topped the medals table with a record total of 30 medals in the World Cup in Delhi in March 2021, with 10 gold, eight silver and four bronze medals. The USA came a distant second with four gold, three silver and a bronze medal. Yashaswini Singh Deswal (women's air pistol), Aishwary Pratap Singh Tomar (men's rifle 3-position) and Chinki Yadav (women's sports pistol) won the individual gold medals.

Back-to-back gold medals in the Junior World Cups

Elavenil Valarivan (b. 2 August 1999) won gold medals in air rifle in the 2018 Junior World Cups in Sydney, Australia, and Suhl, Germany. She also won the mixed air rifle team gold with Divyansh Singh Panwar in the Junior World Cup in Suhl, with a junior world record of 498.6 in the final.

Best Asian Games haul

Indian shooters won three gold, five silver and six bronze medals in the Asian Games at Doha, Qatar, in 2006, for their best haul of 14 medals in an edition of the Asian Games. India had won only 17 medals in all the previous editions put together.

Best performance at the World Cup on debut

Shahzar Rizvi created a world record at the ISSF World Cup when he scored 242.3 points in the final of the 10 m air pistol event on 3 March 2018 at Guadalajara, Mexico. In his debut performance at the World Cup, Rizvi won the gold medal beating the reigning Olympic champion Christian Reitz of Germany.

Best haul in the Junior World Championship

The Indian juniors topped the medal standings in the Junior World Championship in LIma, Peru, in October 2021, with a total of 31 medals, including 12 gold and 13 silver medals. Manu Bhaker (women's air pistol), Naamya Kapoor (women's sports pistol), Aishwary Pratap Singh Tomar (men's rifle 3-position), Vijayveer Sidhu (men's standard pistol), Rhythm Sangwan (women's standard pistol) and Arjun Singh Cheema (men's free pistol) won the individual gold medals.

Best haul in the Commonwealth Games

Indian shooters bagged 27 medals in the 2006 Commonwealth Games in Melbourne, Australia, with 16 gold, seven silver and four bronze medals. Gagan Narang bagged four gold medals (a feat he repeated in the 2010 Commonwealth Games, New Delhi), while Vijay Kumar and Omkar Singh bagged three gold medals each.

WR Double world record

• Ronjan Sodhi gained the unique distinction of equalling both the qualifying and final world records in double trap while winning the gold in the World Cup in Belgrade, Serbia, in 2008. He shot 147 in the qualifying phase and ended with 194.

• Gagan Narang won the World Cup final gold medal in men's air rifle with two world records in Bangkok, Thailand, in November 2008.

Best haul in the Olympics

India's win of two medals in the 2012 London Olympics was the best in terms of numbers. Gagan Narang won the bronze medal in the air rifle and Vijay Kumar won the silver in the rapid fire pistol.

Youngest to win a Junior World Championship gold – men

In 2017, Anish Bhanwala (b. 26 September 2002) became the youngest Indian shooter to win a Junior World Championship gold medal in standard pistol.

Youngest to win a World Cup gold – women

At Guadalajara, Mexico, in March 2018, Manu Bhaker (b. 18 February 2002) was the youngest to win a gold medal in the women's air pistol, and the air pistol mixed gold with Om Prakash Mitharval. She also clinched the gold medals in the Junior World Cups in Sydney, Australia, and Suhl, Germany in 2018. She also won the air pistol gold, ahead of compatriot and former world record holder Heena Sidhu, in the 2018 Commonwealth Games in Gold Coast, Australia.

Most medals in a World Cup

India topped the medals table in the 2019 World Cup in Rio de Janeiro, Brazil, with five gold, two silver and two bronze medals.

Most medals in a Junior World Cup

India topped the medals table in the 2018 Suhl World Cup in Germany with 26 medals: 15 gold, two silver and nine bronze medals. This bettered the country's share of 22 out of 66 medals in the 2017 Sydney World Cup in Australia, when it won nine gold, five silver and eight bronze medals, to be placed second behind China (25).

Most medals in four consecutive World Cups

India has topped the medals table in four consecutive World Cups in rifle and pistol events. India topped the table in the 2018 Munich World Cup (with five gold medals and one silver medal), the 2019 New Delhi World Cup (with three golds), the 2019 Beijing World Cup (with three golds and a silver) and the 2019 Rio de Janeiro World Cup (with five golds, two silver and two bronze medals).

SQUASH

First professionals

In the early 1990s, the first pros were Arjun Singh (men) and Misha Grewal. The latter became a professional in 1993, and played the women's professional circuit in Asia, Europe and the USA. Her best rankings were second in Asia and 27th in the world.

First champion

Rajkumar Narpat Singh won the first squash Nationals in 1953 and made a hat-trick, holding the title for two more years.

First junior and senior Nationals title

Anil Nayyar won both the junior and senior titles in the Nationals in 1964, when he was 18 years old.

First junior world no. 1

Saurav Ghosal was the first Indian to be ranked junior world no. 1 when he won the British Junior Open in 2004.

First individual medals in the Asian Championships

• Bhuvaneshwari Kumari won the bronze in the 1990 and 1992 Asian Championships.

• Misha Grewal won a silver in the Asian Championship in 1996 at Amman, Jordan.

Ronjan Sodhi: double world record in double trap

NATIONAL SPORTS AWARDS 2022

SHOOTING

Arjuna Award
Elavenil Valarivan, Omprakash Mitharval

Dronacharya Award
Suma Siddharth Shirur (para shooting)

First silver in the Asian Junior Championship

The Indian girls' squad bagged a silver medal in the Asian Junior Championship in Chennai, Tamil Nadu, in February 2003. They lost 0–3 to Malaysia in the final.

First to win world ranking titles

In August 2003, Ritwik Bhattacharya became the first Indian to win back-to-back international Professional Squash Association (PSA) world ranking tournaments in New Zealand when he won the North Island Championship and the Royal Oak Open titles. In 2005, he annexed two more titles – the Esportiu Rocafort Squash Open in Barcelona, Spain, and the Rochester ProAm Squash Championship in New York, USA. He has won four international squash titles.

First international success – women

Joshna Chinappa became the first Indian woman to claim a Women's International Squash Players Association (WISPA) title, defeating Malaysia's Low Wee Wern 11–8, 11–5, 11–3 in the NSC Super Satellite (no. 3) Squash Tournament final at National Squash Centre, Kuala Lumpur, Malaysia, in November 2008.

Dipika Pallikal: member of the team that won the first Commonwealth Games gold

First Commonwealth Games gold

India bagged its first gold medal when Dipika Pallikal and Joshna Chinappa defeated Laura Massaro and Jenny Duncalf of England 11–6, 11–8 to win the women's doubles event in the Commonwealth Games in Glasgow, UK, in 2014.

First to win the Asian junior title – girls

Joshna Chinappa was the first to win the Asian junior title (U-19) in 2003. Later, Dipika Pallikal also won the title in July 2010.

First doubles champions in the Nationals

In the first National Doubles Squash Championship held in Chennai, Tamil Nadu, in 2004, Joshna Chinappa and Dipika Pallikal, representing Tamil Nadu, won the women's title and Saurav Ghosal and Harinder Pal Singh Sandhu, also representing Tamil Nadu, won the men's title.

Best performance in the World Championships

Saurav Ghosal was the first Indian to reach the quarter-finals of the World Championships in Manchester, UK, in October 2013. Though he lost to world no. 1 Ramy Ashour in the match, this is India's best performance to date at the World Championships.

Best in the Asian Games

For the first time, India won the men's team event gold medal in the 2014 Incheon Asian Games in South Korea, beating Malaysia 2–0. Saurav Ghosal, Harinder Pal Singh Sandhu and Mahesh Mangaonkar represented India in this event. The women's team of Dipika Pallikal, Joshna Chinappa and Anaka Alankamony won the silver medal, losing to Malaysia 0–2 in the 2014 Asian Games team event final.

Most titles in a row in the Nationals – women

Bhuvaneshwari Kumari was the women's national champion 16 times in a row from 1977 to 1992, a record that remains unbeaten. Her first national triumph was in 1977 at 16 years.

Most National titles won

Joshna Chinappa won 18 national titles, the most yet by an Indian.

Most titles in a row in the Nationals – men

Major K.S. Jain and Brigadier R.K. Manchanda hold the men's record for the highest number of titles won in the Nationals, with six wins in a row. Jain won the title from 1958 to 1963, while Manchanda was the champion from 1978 to 1983.

Best performance in the World Team Championships

The Indian men's team, led by Saurav Ghosal, made a second successive appearance among the top eight in the World Team Championships in June 2013. The women's team also reached the quarter-finals in 2012. This is India's best performance in the World Team Championships.

Best performance in the Asian Juniors

Anaka Alankamony from Chennai, Tamil Nadu, became the youngest winner of the Asian Junior title (U-19) at 16 years when she beat Tsz-Wing Tong of Hong Kong 6–11, 11–8, 10–12, 11–7, 11–7 at Amman, Jordan, in June 2011. India enjoyed triple success in this event: Ramit Tandon (U-19 boys' and Saumya Karki (U-17 girls') won silver medals in India's largest haul at the event.

Oldest champion

Brigadier R.K. Manchanda was 37 years old when he won the Nationals title in 1983, thus becoming the oldest national champion in squash. He also became the oldest finalist in 1987 when he was 41 years old. He reached the final in the Nationals a record 11 times, as did Anil Nayyar. Manchanda won six of the 11 finals in which he competed.

Youngest national champion – women

Joshna Chinappa became the youngest national women's champion at 14 years in 2001.

Youngest to represent India

Saurav Ghosal and Joshna Chinappa were the youngest to represent India in an international event. Ghosal was 16 years old and Chinappa was 15 when they played for India in the 2002 Asian Games in Busan, South Korea.

Youngest champion – men

Adrian Ezra and Ritwik Bhattacharya were both 17 when they won the senior national singles title in 1989 and 1997 respectively, making them the youngest national squash champions to date.

Highest rankings

- Saurav Ghosal is the first Indian to break into the top 10 in the Professional Squash Association (PSA) world rankings. He was ranked 10th with 6,455 points in April 2019.
- Joshna Chinappa is the highest ranked Indian woman in the 27th position with 2,345 points (*at the time of going to press*).
- In 2012, Dipika Pallikal and, in 2016, Chinappa were placed 10th in the world rankings.

SWIMMING

First swimmer in the Olympics

D.D. Mulji of Bengal was the first Indian swimmer in the Olympics, taking part in the 1928 Amsterdam Olympics. Indian women participated in the Olympics for the first time at the 1952 Helsinki Olympics, with Dolly Nazir and Arati Saha representing India.

First women to participate in the Asian Games

Kumari Rima Dutta participated in the fifth Asian Games in Bangkok, Thailand, in 1966.

First swimmers in the Asian Games

Nine Indian swimmers participated in the inaugural Asian Games in 1951: Sachin Nag, Bimal Chandra, Issar Mansoor, Santosh Bhattacharjee, Kanti Shaw, Protip Mitra, Shambu Shaw, J.J. Naigamwalla and Bhubaneswar Pandey. The first Indian women to participate in Asian Games were Kumari Rima Dutta in the fifth Asian Games held at Bangkok in 1966.

First water polo team in the Asian Games

- In 1951, the Indian water polo team first participated in Asian Games and won a gold medal. The team members were Ganesh Dass (captain), G. Rattansey, D. Daver, Isaac Mansoor, Jhair Ahir, Rober Dean and Kanti Shaw.
- The Indian water polo team participated in Asian Games in 1970 in Bangkok and won the silver medal. The team included Pijus Mitra (Captain), Samir Kapadia, Tarun Goswami, Abdul Mutlib, Ashok Biswas, Bharat Merchant, Chand Ram, Umed Singh, Avinash Sarang, Pattabhi Raman and Deep Narayan Singh.

First diver in the Asian Games

Three Indian divers participated in the first Asian Games in 1951: K.P. Thakkar, Ashu Dutta and T.T. Dand. Thakkar of Maharashtra won gold medals in the high-board and springboard events, while Dand won a bronze in high-board diving.

Saurav Ghosal: led the best performance in the World Team Championships in squash

NATIONAL SPORTS AWARDS 2021
SWIMMING
Dronacharya Award (Lifetime)
Tapan Kumar Panigraphi

NATIONAL SPORTS AWARDS 2022
SWIMMING
Arjuna Award
Swapnil Sanjay Patil (para swimming)

Aquatics: Arjuna Award Winners

Year	Name	Category
1961	Jam. Bajarangi Prasad	Diving
1966	Rima Datta	Swimming
1967	Arun Shaw	Swimming
1969	Baidyanath Nath	Long-distance Swimming (adventure sports)
1971	Bhanwar Singh	Diving
1973	D. (Tingoo) Khatau	Swimming
1974	Avinash B.Sarang	Long-distance swimming (adventure sports)
1974	Manjari Bhargava	Diving
1975	M.S. Rana	Swimming
1975	Smita Desai	Swimming
1982	Persis Madan	Swimming
1983	Anita Sood	Swimming
1984	Khajan Singh Tokas	Swimming
1985	Taranath Narain Shenoy	Long-distance swimming (adventure sports)
1986	Aart Pradhan	Long-distance swimming (adventure sports)
1988	Wilson Cherian	Swimming
1990	Bula Choudhury	Swimming
1996	V. Kutraleeswaran	Long-distance swimming (adventure sports)
1998	Bhanu Sachdeva	Swimming
1999	Nisha Millet	Swimming
2000	Sebastian Xavier	Swimming
2000	J. Abhijith	Swimming
2005	Shikha Tandon	Swimming
2010	Rehan Jahangir Poncha	Swimming
2011	Virdhawal Vikram Khade	Swimming
2011	Prasantha Karmakar	Para swimming
2012	Sandeep Sejwal	Swimming
2014	Sharath Gayakwad	Para swimming
2020	Suyash Narayan Jadhav	Para swimming

INDIA AT HER BEST 75 YEARS OF INDEPENDENCE

Shikha Tandon: first to win a medal in the Asian Indoor Games

Sandeep Sejwal: among the first to reach a Commonwealth Games final

First Asian Games gold

India won its first Asian Games gold when Sachin Nag clocked 1 min 4.7 secs to win the 100 m freestyle in the 1951 Asian Games in Delhi. In the same Asian Games he won two bronze medals as well. He represented India in two Olympics: in 1948 in London and in 1952 in Helsinki.

First to participate in the the Commonwealth Games

- Divers Dum Bahadur and Vasant Gadge were the first to represent India in the aquatics events at the 1978 Commonwealth Games in Edmonton, Canada.
- In 1982, for the first time, Indian swimmers participated in the Commonwealth Games at Brisbane, Australia. The team members were Wilson Cherian, Khazan Singh Tokas, T. Thoiba Singh, Sanjeev Chakraborty, Persis Madaan, Geeta Anand and Giselle Bharucha.

First to qualify for two Olympic events

Shikha Tandon of Bengaluru, Karnataka, qualified for the 50 m and 100 m freestyle events in the 2004 Athens Olympics, but did not win.

First to reach a Commonwealth Games final

During the 2010 Commonwealth Games in New Delhi, two Indian men – Virdhawal Khade and Sandeep Sejwal – reached the finals in their best events. Khade was placed seventh in the 50 m butterfly, while Sejwal came eighth in the 50 m breaststroke.

First relay team in a the Commonwealth Games final

The quartet of Virdhawal Khade, Anshul Kothari, Arjun Jayaprakash and Aaron D'Souza qualified for the 4 x 100 m freestyle relay final at the 2010 Commonwealth Games in New Delhi. They clocked 3 mins 27.14 secs to better their qualifying timing, but only finished sixth.

First National Championship

The first National Championship was held in Mumbai, Maharashtra, in 1945.

First to win a medal in the Asian Indoor Games

Shikha Tandon won a bronze in the 100 m backstroke event at the Asian Indoor Games in Bangkok, Thailand, in November 2005.

First 200 m freestyle – under 2 mins

J. Abhijit of Karnataka clocked 1 min 58.68 secs at the 1997 National Games, becoming the first Indian swimmer to swim

200 m freestyle in under 2 mins. Virdhawal Khade of Maharashtra, who clocked 1 min 49.86 secs, holds the record.

First 100 m freestyle – under 1 min.

- The first Indian swimmer to swim under 1 min. in the 100 m freestyle category was Basakha Singh, clocking 59.75 secs in 1971.
- The best performance is by Virdhawal Khade, who clocked 49.47 secs in October 2008. Among women, Shikha Tandon of Karnataka holds the record, with 58.91 secs in 2003.

First para swimmer to win bronze at the Commonwealth Games

Prasanta Karmakar was the first Indian para swimmer to claim a bronze medal in the 50 m freestyle in the S-9 category at the 2010 Commonwealth Games in New Delhi.

First visually impaired swimmer to win a gold

Kanchanmala Pande won gold in the 200 m medley event in the S-11 category on 8 December 2017 at the World Para-swimming Championship in Berlin.

First Indian para swimmer to win gold in the Para Asian games

Jadhav Suyash Narayan won the gold medal in men's 50 m butterfly S7 (6 –7) category at the Para Asian Games held at Jakarta, Indonesia, in 2018. He clocked 32.71 secs.

First Indian para swimmer to qualify for the Paralympic Games

Sharath Gayakwad was the first Indian para swimmer to qualify for the 2012 London Paralympic Games. He secured the ninth position. He also has a bronze at the 2010 Asian Para Games.

First swimmer to make Olympic 'A' cut 200 m butterfly – men

On 26 June 2021, Sajan Prakash became the first-ever Indian swimmer to breach the 'A' Olympic qualification time by clocking 1:56:38 secs in the men's 200 m butterfly event at the Sette Colli Trophy in Rome. He made the Tokyo Games 'A' standard, set at 1:56:48 secs, by 0.10 seconds at the FINA-accredited Olympic qualifier. Earlier, he was the only Indian male swimmer who represented India in the 2016 Rio Olympics and was the only one to qualify with B timings for Rio.

First swimmer to make Olympic 'A' cut – 100 m backstroke – men

Srihari Nataraj became the second Indian swimmer to qualify for the 2020 Tokyo Olympics after FINA approved his 'A' standard qualification time in men's 100 m backstroke time trial at the Sette Colli Trophy in Rome. He clocked 53.77 secs in time trial.

Aquatics: National Award Winners

Dronacharya Award: Nihar Ameen (2015); S. Pradeep Kumar (2016); Tapan Kumar Panigrahi (2021).

Padma Shri: Arati Saha (1960)– the first sportswoman to be awarded this honour); Mihir Kumar Sen (1967), Taranath Narayan Shenoy (1990); Bula Choudhury (2008).

Dhayanchand Award: Sushil Kohli (2011); Khatau P. Thakkar (2014); Sachin Nag 2020 (posthumous).

Bula Choudhury

Participation in two consecutive Olympic Games

Sachin Nag represented India in the 1948 London Olympics and the 1952 Helsinki Olympics. Sajan Prakash represented India at Rio in 2016 and Tokyo Olympics (in 2021).

Participation in two consecutive Paralympics

Suyash Narayan Jadhav represented the country at Rio in 2016 and the 2020 Tokyo Paralympics (in 2021).

Dr Meenakshi Pahuja was the first swimmer to win the Nari Shakti Puraskar.

TABLE TENNIS

GENERAL

Most National singles titles in a row

A. Sharath Kamal among men and Indu Puri among women have won most National singles titles in a row. Kamal won the title five times between 2006 and 2010. Indu was champion six times between 1980 and 1985.

A. Sharath Kamal: most National singles titles in a row

Junior/ Senior titles in a year

Four girls have won both titles in one calendar

year – Rinku Gupta Acharya (Madhya Pradesh) in 1988; Mantu Ghosh (Bengal) in 1991; Kasturi Chakraborty (Bengal) in 1998 and Poulomi Ghatak (Bengal) in 1998-99.

No games conceded

Farokh Khodaiji was the first to achieve this feat, winning the men's singles title in 1967 in Guwahati, followed by Kaity Chargeman in the women's singles in Kolkata in 1970 and Chetan Baboor in the men's singles in 1999.

Mouma Das: first woman to play in two Olympic Games

FIRST

First gold medallist in the Asian Championship

Gool Nasikwala won the singles, doubles and mixed doubles gold medals in the 1952 Asian Championship in Singapore.

First Indian to reach World championship quarter-finals

Krishna Nagaraj reached the men's singles quarter-finals in the 1956 World Championship in Tokyo, Japan.

First doubles pair in World championship quarter-finals

Mouma Das and Manika Batra became the first to reach the women doubles quarter-finals in the 2017 World Table Tennis Championship.

First woman to play in two Olympics

Mouma Das became the first woman player to qualify for two Olympic Games (2004, Athens and 2016, Rio).

Manika Batra: first Commonwealth Games singles winner (women)

Youngest to qualify for the Olympic Games

Manika Batra became the youngest to play Olympic Games in Rio (2016) at the age of 21 years and two months.

First to be a medallist in five successive Commonwealth Games

A. Sharath Kamal is the only player to win Commonwealth Games medals in five successive editions – 2006, Melbourne; 2010, New Delhi; 2014, Glasgow; 2018, Gold Coast; and 2022, Birmingham.

First Commonwealth Games winner – men – singles

A. Sharath Kamal won the men's singles gold at Melbourne in 2006. He regained the medal in Birmingham in 2022.

First Commonwealth Games winner – women – singles

Manika Batra won the women's singles gold at Gold Coast in 2018.

First Commonwealth Games gold – men – team

The Indian men's team won the first Commonwealth Games table tennis gold medal in Melbourne in 2006.

First to regain Commonwealth Games gold – men – team

A. Sharath Kamal was the only member of the Indian team that won the men's team gold in 2006 and again in 2022.

First Commonwealth Games gold – women – team

India's women team won the first Commonwealth Games team gold medal in Gold Coast in 2018.

First Commonwealth Games gold medal – mixed doubles

A. Sharath Kamal and Sreeja Akula won the mixed doubles gold in Birmingham in 2022.

First Commonwealth Championship team title – men

India won the Commonwealth men's team title in Kuala Lumpur in 2004.

First Commonwealth Games gold – men – doubles

A. Sharath Kamal and Subhajit Saha won the men's doubles gold in New Delhi in October 2010.

First Commonwealth Games medal – women – doubles
Poulomi Ghatak and Mouma Das claimed the bronze in the women's doubles in New Delhi in October 2010.

First ITTF Pro-Tour title
A. Sharath Kamal won the Egypt Open to become the first Indian to win an ITTF Pro-Tour event in July 2010.

First time when six Indian men and three women broke into the top 100 in world rankings
G. Sathiyan (ranked 49th), Sharath Kamal (51st) Soumyajit Ghosh (58th), Harmeet Desai (60th), Sanil Shetty (68th) and A. Amalraj (87th) were in the top 100 of world rankings in January 2018. At the same time, Manika Batra (62nd), Mouma Das (74th) and Madhurika Patkar (81st) also made the grade.

First Indian to be ranked world no. 1 in U-18
Manav Thakkar became the first Indian to be ranked world no. 1 in the boys' U-18 category in February 2018.

First medal in Asian juniors
India won the bronze medal in the 2006 Asian Junior Championship at Kitakyushu, Japan, by reaching the semi-finals of the girls' event.

First National champion
- M. Ayub won the men's singles title in Calcutta (now Kolkata) in 1938.
- P. Lima won the women's singles in Bombay (now Mumbai) in 1939.

First professional
Chetan Baboor played as a professional with Enig Club in Kalmar, Sweden, from 1998.

First team medal in the World Junior Championship
The Indian boys' team, comprising Soumyajit Ghosh, Harmeet Desai and G. Sathiyan, won India's first ever bronze medal in the 2011 Junior Championship held in in Bahrain.

First title-triumph in the ITTF Junior tour
Harmeet Desai defeated Soumyajit Ghosh in the 2011 Austrian Open junior boys' final to become the first Indian to win a title on the ITTF (International Table Tennis Federation) Junior Tour.

First international league
The first edition of the Ultimate Table Tennis (UTT) was held in July 2017 in Chennai, New Delhi and Mumbai. Six teams took part the event and Falcons Club won the title by beating Shaze Challengers 14-9 in the final.

Poulomi Ghatak: first Commonwealth Games doubles medal with Mouma Das – women

First Indian in the ITTF's Umpires and Referees Committee
Neelakanta Ganeshan was the first Indian inducted as a member of International Table Tennis Federation's Umpires and Referees Committee (URC) in June 2017.

MOST

Most medals from the Commonwealth Games
Indians won eight medals, including three golds, in the 2018 edition of the Games in Gold Coast. India claimed gold medals in the men's team, women's team and women's singles (Manika Batra); silver medals in the men's doubles (A. Sharath Kamal and G. Sathiyan) and the women's doubles (Manika Batra and Mouma Das); and bronze medals in the men's singles (A. Sharath Kamal), men's doubles (Harmeet Desai and Sanil Shetty) and mixed doubles (Manika Batra and G. Sathiyan).

Most Commonwealth Games medals won by an individual player in a single edition
- *Men*: A. Sharath Kamal won four medals in the 2022 Commonwealth Games in Birmingham, UK.
- *Women*: Manika Batra won four medals in the 2018 Commonwealth Games in Gold Coast.

Most medals from Commonwealth-level competitions
Mouma Das has claimed 19 medals in both team and individual events of the Commonwealth Games and Commonwealth championships between 2001 and 2018.

NATIONAL SPORTS AWARDS 2021

TABLE TENNIS

Arjuna Award
Bhavina Patel (para table tennis)

Dronacharya Award
Subramanian Raman

G. Sathiyan: highest world ranking reached among Indian players – men

Most World Championship appearances

Mouma Das has played in 16 editions of World Championship since 1997.

Longest mixed doubles reign

Farokh Khodaiji and Kaity Khodaiji of Mumbai won the Susan Barna Cup five years in a row during 1967-71. They had earlier won the title in 1965.

Most state representations at the Nationals

N. Ravichandran represented five different units, including four states in the National Championships: Tamil Nadu, Punjab, Goa and Puducherry apart from the Central Revenue Sports Board at National-level tournaments.

Most appearances in the National Championship

S. Ramaswamy, who first played the Nationals in Allahabad in 1976, appeared in 30 successive National Championships until February 2006.

Most gold medals in the South Asian Federation (SAF) Games

A. Sharath Kamal won four gold medals – men's team event, men's singles, doubles and mixed doubles – in Colombo in August 2006.

Most National titles – singles

- A. Sharath Kamal has won 10 National singles titles in the men's singles section. Sharath broke Kamlesh Mehta's record of eight singles titles in 2019.
- Indu Puri won the ladies singles title eight times — 1972, 1975 and from 1979-84.

Most team titles – men/women

Bombay won the team title for the Barna Bellack Cup 16 times. Maharashtra won the team title for the Corbillion Cup 14 times. The championship was first introduced in 1946 at Madras (now Chennai) where Bombay (now Mumbai) won the title and remained unbeaten till 1952.

Most participants in a tournament

An unprecedented 4,104 entries were received across 17 categories in the first Indian Table Tennis Marathon 2019 held between 1 and 5 May 2019 at the Table Tennis Federation TT Hall, Sant Sujan Singh Ji International School, Swaroop Nagar, New Delhi. A record 4,102 matches were played.

YOUNGEST

Youngest to win the National title

Mantu Ghosh was 16 when she won the title at Jaipur in 1990-91.

Highest world ranking

- *Men*: G. Sathiyan attained his career-high world ranking of 24 as of 1 May 2019.
- *Women*: Manika Batra reached her career-best world ranking of 38 as of 3 May 2022.

BEST

Best team performance in the World Championship

India finished 10th – its best finish till date – in the men's team events of the 1959 World Championship in Dortmund (Germany). In 2018, India produced its second-best performance and took the 13th place.

Best Indian performance (individual): beating three top-20 players in one event

A. Sharath Kamal defeated three players from the world's top 20 list in the Asian Cup held in Jaipur in March 2015. They included world no. 8 Chuang Chih-Yuan (Chinese Taipei), world no. 15 Gao Ning (Singapore) and world no. 16 Joo Sae Hyuk (Korea).

Best performances in the Commonwealth Games – doubles

A. Sharath Kamal holds the distinction of winning the men's doubles medal in four successive Commonwealth Games. He partnered Subhajit Saha to win the gold in the 2010 Commonwealth Games in New Delhi. In 2014, he joined hands with Anthony Amalraj

NATIONAL SPORTS AWARDS 2022

TABLE TENNIS

Arjuna Award
Sreeja Akula

Major Dhyan Chand Khel Ratna
A. Sharath Kamal

Table Tennis: National Award Winners

INDIA AT HER BEST 75 YEARS OF INDEPENDENCE

Rajiv Gandhi Khel Ratna: Manika Batra (2020).

Arjuna Award: J.C. Vohra (1961); Gautam Diwan (1965); Usha Sundararaj (1966); F.R. Khodaiji (1967); Mir Kasim Ali (1969); G. Jagannath (1970); K.F. Khodaiji (1971); Niraj Bajaj (1973); Shailaja Salokhe (1976); Indu Puri (1979); Manjit Dua (1980); V. Chandrashekhar (1982); Kamlesh Mehta (1985); Monalisa Baruah (1987); Niyati Shah (1989); M.S. Walia (1990); Chetan Baboor (1997); S. Raman (1998); Mantu Ghosh (2002); A. Sharath Kamal (2004); Soumyadeep Roy (2005); Subhajit Saha (2006); Poulomi Ghatak (2009); Mouma Das (2013); Soumyajit Ghosh (2016); Anthony Amalraj (2017); G. Sathiyan and Manika Batra (2018); Harmeet Desai (2019); and Madhurika Patkar (2020).

Padma Shri: A. Sharath Kamal (2019).

to claim the silver in the men's doubles in Glasgow. In 2018, he and G. Sathiyan settled for a silver medal in Gold Coast and again in 2022 in Birmingham.

Best doubles performance in the Commonwealth Championship
Chetan Baboor and S. Raman won two successive Commonwealth Championship titles in 1997 and 2000.

Second division titles in World championship
Indian men and women won the second division titles in the 2016 World Championship in Kuala Lumpur on5 March 5 2016. In the final, Indian men beat Brazil 3-2 and the women defeated Luxemburg 3-1.

TENNIS

GENERAL

Best women's singles result
Karman Kaur Thandi's singles title in the US $60,000 ITF women's tournament in Saguenay, Canada, with a 3-6, 6-4, 6-3 victory over Katherine Sebov (Canada) in the final in October 2022 was a big breakthrough for Indian women's tennis. It was the biggest singles title for an Indian woman since Sania Mirza won the $75,000 tournament in Dubai in 2010. The biggest title ever by an Indian woman was Mirza winning the US $140,000 WTA event in Hyderabad in 2005. The 24-year-old Karman became no. 1 in India with a rank of 217.

BILLIE JEAN KING (FEDERATION) CUP

First world play-offs qualifying team
Earlier known as the Fed Cup, the Billie Jean King Cup is a team event for women's tennis players who represent their country in singles and doubles matches. The Indian Fed Cup team created history by progressing to the play-offs for the first time ever in March 2020, defeating Indonesia in the Asia-Oceania Group I event in Dubai, and finishing second behind China. They lost the world group play-off tie against Latvia. The team comprised Ankita Raina, Rutuja Bhosale, Zeel Desai, Karman Kaur Thandi and Sania Mirza.

ASIAN GAMES

First gold – men – doubles
Leander Paes and Gaurav Natekar won the gold medal in the Hiroshima Asian Games, held in 1994 in Japan – making this the country's first doubles gold medal at the Asian Games. They won by defeating the South Korean duo of Chang Eui-jong and Kim Chi-wan.

First singles gold
Somdev Devvarman won the gold medal at the 2010 Guangzhou Asiad in China, defeating Denis Istomin of Uzbekistan 6–1, 6–2.

First gold medallist – doubles – mixed
India got its first mixed doubles gold at the Asian Games when the team, with Leander Paes and Sania Mirza, won the gold in the Doha Asian Games in Qatar in 2006. They defeated the Japanese pair of Satoshi Iwabuchi and Akiko Morigami 7–5, 5–7, 6–2.

Karman Kaur Thandi: best women's singles result

DAVIS CUP

Most successful player – doubles
Leander Paes became the most successful doubles player in the history of the Davis Cup with a record 45th victory in March 2020, when he and his partner Rohan Bopanna won India's Davis Cup match against Croatia in the do-or-die round of the World Group Qualifiers.

First appearance
India played in the Davis Cup for the first time in 1921 against France in Paris and won 4–1. The Indian team comprised S.M. Jacob, Mohammed Sleem, A.A. Fyzee and L.S. Dean.

Best Davis Cup record in Asia
Though India has never yet won the Davis Cup, they have managed to reach the finals three times (in 1966, 1974 and 1987). Japan is the only other Asian nation to have figured in the Davis Cup finals (once in 1921).

Most appearances
Leander Paes holds the record of playing the most Davis Cup matches – 128 in 58 ties (as of

Ankita Raina: part of the qualifying team for the Billie Jean King Cup world play-offs

Sania Mirza: first Wimbledon junior girls' doubles title

March 2020). His win/loss records are 48/22 in singles and 45/13 in doubles.

Junior Davis Cup regional champs

The Indian under-16 team of Rushil Khosla, Bushan Haobam and Debasis Sahoo under the captaincy of Sajid Lodi won the Asia-Oceania Junior Davis Cup title in Delhi, to make the World Group along with Japan and Australia in 2022. In the World group played in Turkey, India, represented by Rushil Khosla, Kriish Tyagi and Vansh Nandal, finished 14th among 16 countries.

GRAND SLAM TOURNAMENTS

WIMBLEDON

First to play at Wimbledon

Sardar Nihal Singh was the first Indian to play at Wimbledon in 1908. He lost in the first round to Briton Herbert Wilson Fox, who beat him 11–9, 6–2, 6–4.

First junior boys' title

Ramanathan Krishnan won the first junior boy's Wimbledon title in 1954, defeating Ashley Cooper of Australia 6–2, 7–5. Twenty-five years later, Ramanathan's son Ramesh Krishnan won the same title in 1979, creating a unique father-and-son record. Both were recipients of the Padma Shri in 1962 and 1998 respectively. Ramanathan Krishnan was also awarded the Padma Bhushan in 1967.

Mahesh Bhupathi (*right*): first US Open doubles title, with Max Mirnyi

First seeded at Wimbledon

Dilip Bose was the first seeded Indian player, at no. 15, in Wimbledon singles in 1950. He was a product of the Calcutta South Club (now in Kolkata, West Bengal), one of Asia's oldest tennis clubs.

First men's title – doubles

The dominant Indian tennis pair of Leander Paes and Mahesh Bhupathi, then popularly known as Lee-Hesh, won India's first men's doubles title at Wimbledon in 1999, defeating Paul Haarhuis (the Netherlands) and Jared Palmer (USA) 6–7, 6–3, 6–4, 7–6.

First title – doubles – mixed

Leander Paes was the first Indian to win a mixed doubles title when he won it with Lisa Raymond (USA) in 1999. They defeated the pair of Anna Kournikova (Russia) and Jonas Björkman (Sweden) 6–4, 3–6, 6–3. Paes was awarded the Padma Shri in 2001.

First junior girls' title – doubles

Sania Mirza and her Russian partner Alisa Kleybanova won the junior girls' doubles title in 2003.

First Indian woman at Wimbledon

Jenny Sandison was the first woman to represent India in tennis at Wimbledon, way back in 1929. However, she lost in the first round to French player Simone Barbier 6–2, 6–3.

FRENCH OPEN

First title – doubles – mixed

Mahesh Bhupathi and his Japanese partner Rika Hiraki won the French Open title in 1997, defeating the American team of Lisa Raymond and Patrick Galbraith 6–4, 6–1. With this Bhupathi became the first Indian to win a Senior Grand Slam title.

First and only junior champion

Ramesh Krishnan won the juniors title in 1979, the first and only Indian to achieve this feat, and was ranked the world's no. 1 junior player. He became India's Davis Cup captain in 2007.

First all-Indian title – mixed doubles

Mahesh Bhupathi and Sania Mirza won India's first ever all-Indian mixed doubles title in 2012, defeating Klaudia Jans-Ignacik (Poland) and Santiago González (Mexico) 7–6 (7–3), 6–1.

First all-Indian men's title – doubles

Leander Paes and Mahesh Bhupathi won India's first men's doubles title in 1999. The pair defeated Goran Ivanisevic (Croatia) and Jeff Tarango (USA) 6–2, 7–5.

US OPEN

First title – doubles

Mahesh Bhupathi and his partner Max Mirnyi of Belarus won the US Open doubles title in 2002, defeating the Czech pair of Jiri Novak and Radek Stepanek 6–3, 3–6, 6–4.

First title – doubles – women

Sania Mirza was the first Indian to win a women's doubles title in 2015 at the US Open in New York, with Swiss player Martina Hingis. The pair defeated Casey Dellacqua (Australia) and Yaroslava Shvedova (Kazakhstan) 6–3, 6–3.

First title – doubles – mixed

Mahesh Bhupathi, with his Japanese partner Ai Sugiyama, won the mixed doubles US Open title in 1999, the first Indian to win a mixed doubles title here. The pair defeated Kimberly Po and Donald Johnson of the USA 6–4, 6–4.

First and only junior boys' title

Leander Paes is the first and only Indian to win the junior boy's crown at the US Open in 1991. He beat Karim Alami (Morocco).

AUSTRALIAN OPEN

First men's title – doubles

Leander Paes became the first Indian to win a men's doubles title at the Australian Open, along with Radek Stepanek (Czech Republic) in 2012. They defeated Bob Bryan and Mike Bryan of the USA 7–6 (7–1), 6–2.

First title – doubles – mixed

Leander Paes, with Martina Navratilova of the USA, won the mixed doubles title in 2003, becoming the first Indian to do so. They defeated Eleni Daniilidou (Greece) and Todd Woodbridge (Australia) 6–4, 7–5.

First all-Indian title – doubles – mixed

Mahesh Bhupathi and Sania Mirza won India's first all-Indian mixed doubles Australian Open title in 2009, defeating the pair of Nathalie Dechy (France) and Andy Ram (Israel) 6–3, 6–1.

First junior boys' champion

Yuki Bhambri defeated Alexandros-Ferdinandos Georgoudas of Greece 6–3, 6– to win the Junior Boys' Championship in 2009.

NATIONALS

First Nationals – grass court

The first tennis Nationals were held in 1946 at the Calcutta South Club lawns in Calcutta (now Kolkata, West Bengal). Sumant Misra beat Manmohan Lal in the final, becoming the first national champion. Khanum Singh (née Haji) was the first women's national champion.

Most Nationals titles

Ramanathan Krishnan won eight grass-court titles in 1953, 1956, 1958 to 1960 and 1962 to 1964.

WEIGHTLIFTING

First medals in the World Championships

Kunjarani Devi from Manipur bagged three silvers at Manchester, UK, in 1989 in India's debut performance at the World Championships. The Indian squad won seven medals in all at the event. Shyamala Shetty and Chhaya Adak won silver medals for individual lifts, while Lalita Polley claimed two bronze medals.

First gold in the Commonwealth Games – men

E. Karunakaran won gold in the flyweight class in the 1978 Edmonton Games in Canada.

First Junior weightlifting gold

Harshada Sharad Garud became the first Indian boy or girl to win a World Junior Weightlifting Championship by lifting a total of 153 kg (clean and jerk 83 kg + snatch 70 kg)

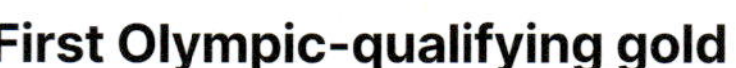

First Olympic-qualifying gold

Saikhom Mirabai Chanu won the gold medal in the women's 49 kg category at the EGAT Cup International Weightlifting Championship, an Olympic qualifying event in Chiang Mai, Thailand, on 7 February 2019. She lifted 82 kg in snatch and 110 kg in clean and jerk to total 192 kg, and took gold on her return to international competition after a nine-month lay-off due to an injury. She had won the gold medal on her last appearance in 2018 at the Gold Coast Commonwealth Games in Australia.

First back-to-back gold medals

Khumukcham Sanjita Chanu made history for the second time when she bagged the gold medal in the women's 53 kg weightlifting event at the 2018 Commonwealth Games at Gold Coast, Australia. Her first gold was at the 2014 Commonwealth Games in the 48 kg category.

First silver medal at the Olympic Games

Saikhom Mirabai Chanu scripted a remarkable performance by winning a silver in the 2020 Olympic Games held in Tokyo, Japan, on day one. With an 87 kg lift in snatch and a 115 kg lift in the clean and jerk section, Chanu finished with a total of 202 kg.

First Asian Games medals – women

Women's weightlifting was introduced in the 1990 Beijing Asian Games in China, where India won two silvers: Bharati Singh (82 kg category) and Jyotsna Dutta (+82 kg); and two

Leander Paes: first and only Wimbledon junior boys' title

NATIONAL SPORTS AWARDS 2021
TENNIS
Arjuna Award
Ankita Raina

Saikhom Mirabai Chanu: first silver medal at the Olympic Games

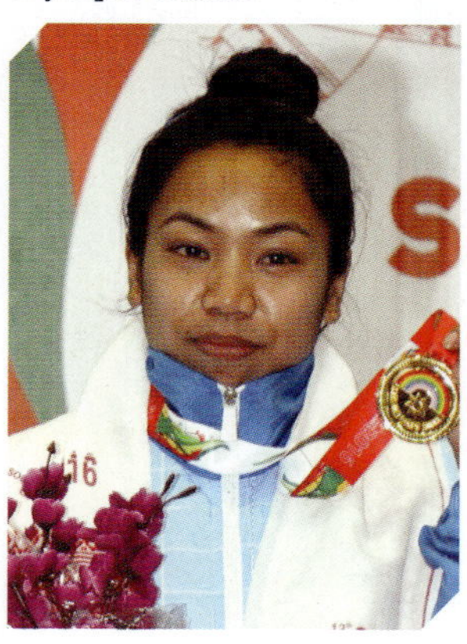

bronzes: Kunjarani Devi (44 kg) and Chhaya Adak (52 kg).

First Asian Games medal

Kamineni Eswara Rao won the silver in the 90 kg category in the 1951 Asian Games held in New Delhi. He was also adjudged the 'Strongest Man of India' at the 1954 Senior Nationals.

First gold medal at the Youth Olympic Games

Jeremy Lalrinnunga became the first Indian to win a gold medal at the Youth Olympics Games 2018 held in Buenos Aires, Argentina.

WR Clean and jerk at the Asian Weightlifting Championships

Saikhom Mirabai Chanu set a new world record in the women's 49 kg clean and jerk with a lift of 119 kg on 17 April 2022 at the Asian Weightlifting Championships in Tashkent, Uzbekistan.

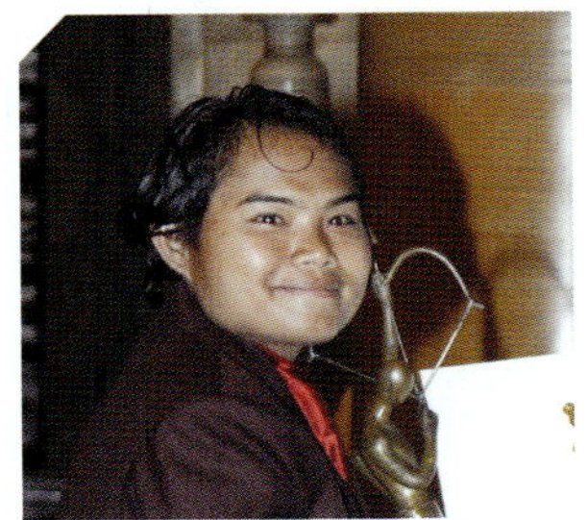

Yumnam Renu Bala Chanu: most medals in the Commonwealth Games

Most medals in the Commonwealth Games – women

Yumnam Renu Bala Chanu has won two golds in the Commonwealth Games. Her first came in the women's 58 kg category in Melbourne in 2006. She repeated this in the 2010 Delhi Commonwealth Games in the same category.

Best performance at an Asian meet

India's weightlifters bagged five gold medals and a bronze at Busan, South Korea, in July 1995. Karnam Malleswari won three gold medals, and Kunjarani Devi claimed two gold medals and the overall title. Arun Murugesan won a bronze in snatch in the 54 kg category for men.

Most medals in world and Asian meets

Kunjarani Devi, who holds the record for the highest number of world and Asian meet medals, won 55 medals overall – 21 in six World Championships and the remaining in the Asian Games, and the Asian and Commonwealth Championships.

Most national titles

Balbir Singh Bhatia won 15 national and all-India titles.

Most medals in the Commonwealth Games

India won five gold, two silver and two bronze medals at the 2018 Gold Coast Commonwealth Games, the most at the Commonwealth Games in weightlifting. Saikhom Mirabai Chanu made a record-breaking performance in the clean and jerk event in the 48 kg category. Khumukcham Sanjita Chanu (53 kg) set a Commonwealth Games record in snatch and Punam Yadav won a gold in the 69 kg category. In the men's section, Sathish Sivalingam (77 kg) and Ragala Venkat Rahul (85 kg) won gold medals too. P. Gururaja (56 kg) and Pradeep Singh (105 kg) won silvers, and Vikas Thakur (94 kg) and Deepak Lather (69 kg) won bronzes.

Most gold medals in World Championships

Karnam Malleswari won the gold in the World Championships twice – in 1994 (Istanbul, Turkey) and 1995 (Guangzhou, China).

Oldest national champion

Alok Nath Ghosh won the National Championship title in 1974 at 40 years. He had won the first national title in 1958 in Cuttack, Odisha. His first title was for Services and the last one was for the Railways.

Youngest Commonwealth Games medal winner

Eighteen-year-old Deepak Lather (69 kg) from Haryana became the youngest Indian weightlifter to win a medal at the 2018 Commonwealth Games in Glasgow, UK, by clinching a bronze medal.

Youngest National champion

P.K. Mahanand from Hyderabad won the All-India Championship at Calcutta (now Kolkata), West Bengal, in 1955 at the age of eighteen.

WRESTLING

First woman at the Olympics

Geeta Phogat from Bhiwani, Haryana, was the first Indian woman wrestler to compete at the Olympics during the 2012 London Games. However, she did not advance to the quarter-finals.

First at the Olympics

U. Zaw Weik (75 kg), the first to represent India at the Olympics, was placed 15th in the 1936 Olympics in Berlin, Germany.

First Olympics medal – men

Khashaba Dadasaheb Jadhav from Satara, Maharashtra, won a bronze in the bantamweight category (57 kg) in the 1952 Helsinki Olympics.

First Olympic medal – women

Sakshi Malik created history as the first Indian woman to win an Olympic medal, a bronze,

NATIONAL SPORTS AWARDS 2022
WEIGHTLIFTING
Arjuna Award
Vikas Thakur

for wrestling, in the women's freestyle 58 kg category in the Rio Olympics in Brazil on 17 August 2016.

First winner of both Olympic and World Championship medals

Sushil Kumar is the first Indian to win medals at both the Olympics and the World Championships. He won a bronze at the 2008 Beijing Olympics in the 66 kg freestyle category and a silver medal in the same category at the 2012 London Olympics. He also won a gold in the same category at the Moscow World Championship in Russia in 2010.

First medal at the World Championship – men

India's first medal in the World Championship was a bronze in the freestyle category ((67 kg) won by Udey Chand from Hisar, Haryana, in the 1961 World Championships at Yokohama, Japan. He participated in three Olympics: at Rome, Italy, in 1960; at Tokyo, Japan, in 1964; and at Mexico City, Mexico, in 1968.

First Indian woman to win a silver medal at the World Championship

Anshu Malik (57 kg) became the first Indian female wrestler to win a silver medal at the 2021 World Championship in Oslo.

First woman triple winner – World Championships, Asian Games and Commonwealth Games

Vinesh Phogat became the first Indian woman to win medals at the World Championships, Asian Games and Commonwealth Games. While she won bronze at the 2019 World Championships in the 53 kg freestyle and a bronze at the 2014 Incheon Asian Games in the 48 kg category, she was also the first Indian woman to win a gold medal in the 2018 Asian Games in Jakarta and Palembang, Indonesia, in the 50 kg category. She won three consecutive Commonwealth crowns at Glasgow in 2014, Gold Coast in 2018 and Birmingham in 2022.

First medal at the World Championships – women

Alka Tomar of the Noida College of Physical Education won a bronze in the women's 59 kg class at the Senior World Wrestling Championship in Guangzhou, China, during September–October 2006. She was the first Indian woman wrestler to win a World Championship medal after a gap of 39 years.

First World Championship gold medallist

Sushil Kumar from Delhi was the first Indian to win a World Championship gold medal in the 66 kg freestyle category in Moscow, Russia, in 2010.

First medal in the Commonwealth Games

- Rashid Anwar won a bronze medal at the 1934 Commonwealth Games held in London, UK, in the 74 kg category. This was the country's first medal won in the Commonwealth Games.
- Lila Ram won the first gold medal in the 1958 Games at Cardiff, Wales, in the heavyweight (100 kg) category.

First medal in the Asian Games

Vinesh Phogat, competing in the 50 kg freestyle category, bagged India its first gold medal in wrestling in the Asian Games in 2018 in Jakarta, Indonesia. She is the first Indian woman to win a gold medal in wrestling and to win back-to back Asian Games medals, having won a bronze in 48 kg in Incheon, South Korea, in 2014.

First and only Indian woman wrestler to win the Laureus World Sports Award

Vinesh Phogat is the first and only Indian wrestler to be awarded the Laureus World Sports Award 2019 in the comeback-of-the-year category. Phogat not only returned from her injury but also won the gold medal in both the 2018 Commonwealth Games at Gold Coast, Australia, and the 2018 Asian Games in Jakarta and Palembang, Indonesia.

First to win gold in U-20 World Championships – women

Antim Panghal became the first to win gold in the U-20 World Championships on 10 September 2022 in Sofia, Bulgaria.

First Asian Games gold – men

Gold medals were won by Maruti Mane in 90 kg freestyle, Malwa Singh in 52 kg Greco Roman and Ganpat Andalkar in 100 kg Greco-Roman section at the 1962 Asian Games in Jakarta, Indonesia.

First Asian Championships gold medal – women

Navjot Kaur from Punjab became the first Indian woman to win the gold at the Senior Asian Wrestling Championships on 2 March 2018 at Bishkek, Kyrgyzstan. She beat Japan's Miya Imai 9–1 to win in the women's 65 kg category.

First Coach of the Year award

Late Yashvir Singh was the first Indian coach to be recognized as the Coach of the Year in

Sakshi Malik: first Olympic medal

NATIONAL SPORTS AWARDS 2021

WRESTLING

Arjuna Award:
Deepak Punia

Dhyan Chand Award (Lifetime)
Sajjan Singh

Major Dhyan Chand Khel Ratna Award
Ravi Kumar

NATIONAL SPORTS AWARDS 2022

WRESTLING

Arjuna Award
Anshu Malik, Sarita Mor

Dronacharya Award
Sujeet Maan; Raj Singh (Lifetime)

2010 by the Federation Internationale des Luttes Associées (FILA), the then apex body that governed wrestling.

First Junior Wrestler of the Year award

Deepak Punia (86 kg freestyle) became the first Indian wrestler to receive the Junior Wrestler of the Year title in 2019 from the UWW.

First Junior World Champion

- The first gold medallists at the Junior World Championship were Ramesh Kumar (69 kg) and Palwinder Singh Cheema (130 kg) in 2001.
- Deepak Punia became India's junior world champion after 18 years, winning the gold medal at Tallinn, Estonia, on 14 August 2019. He defeated Russia's Alik Shebzukov in the 86 kg men's freestyle category.

First gold in Greco-Roman wrestling

- Pappu Yadav was the first grappler to win a gold medal in the 48 kg Greco-Roman category at the 1993 Asian Wrestling Championships held in Ulaanbaatar, Mongolia.
- On 19 February 2020, Sunil Kumar (87 kg) won a gold in Greco-Roman wrestling in the Asian Championships, which came 27 years after the first gold in 1993.

First gold medal in the Asian Games

- The first Indian to win a gold medal in the Asian Games was Kartar Singh in the 1986 Seoul Asiad in South Korea in the 100 kg category.
- Yogeshwar Dutt became the first Indian in 28 years to win a gold in the 2014 Incheon Asian Games in the 65 kg freestyle.

First Indian couple to win silver medals

Sakshi Malik (65 kg) and Satyawart Kadian (97 kg) became the first Indian wrestler couple to win silver medals in the 2020 Asian Championships in New Delhi.

First medals in Greco-Roman Championships – Under-17

- Vinod Kumar (1980) and Pappu Yadav (1990) bagged the U-17 world title.
- Suraj Vashisht (55 kg) won it again after 32 years in July 2022 in Rome.

Ranked as world no. 1

In March 2021, the UWW announced Bajrang Punia (65 kg) and Vinesh Phogat (53 kg) as top-ranked wrestlers.

Back-to-back World Championship medals

Sajan Bhanwal became the first Indian to win back-to-back medals in the World Championship in the 77 kg category in the Greco-Roman style. He won a silver on 20 August 2019 in Trnava, Slovakia, and a bronze at the Tampere World Championship, Finland, in 2017.

Best performance in the Asian Championship

India won a record haul of 20 medals (five gold, six silver and nine bronze) across formats and genders in the 2020 Asian Championships. The gold medallists were: Sunil Kumar (87 kg Greco-Roman [GR]); Pinki (55 kg women's freestyle [WFS]); Sarita Mor (59 kg WFS); Divya Kakran (68 kg WFS); and Ravi K. Dahiya (57 kg men's freestyle [MFS]). The silver medals were won by Nirmala Devi (50 kg WFS); Sakshi Malik (65 kg WFS); Bajrang Punia (65 kg MFS); Gourav Baliyan (79 kg MFS); Satyawart Kadian (97 kg MFS); and Jitender (74 kg MFS). The bronze went to Arjun Halakurki (57 kg GR); Ashu (67 kg GR); Adity Kundu (72 kg GR); Hardeep (97 kg GR); Vinesh Phogat (53 kg WFS);Anshu Malik (67 kg WFS); Gursharan Preet Kaur (72 kg WFS); Rahul Aware (61 kg MFS); and Deepak Punia (86 kg MFS).

Best performance at the Commonwealth Games – men

At the Commonwealth Games in 2010 in Delhi, the Indian men's team won seven gold, three silver and three bronze medals in freestyle and the Greco-Roman style. The gold medals were won by Yogeshwar Dutt (60 kg); Sushil Kumar (66 kg); and Narsingh Panch Yadav (74 kg), all in freestyle wrestling; and Rajender Kumar (55 kg); Ravinder Singh (60 kg); Sanjay Kumar (74 kg); and Anil Kumar (96 kg), all in Greco-Roman wrestling. The silver medals were won by Anuj Kumar (84 kg) and Joginder Kumar (120 kg) in freestyle, and Manoj Kumar (84 kg) in the Greco-Roman style. The bronze medals were bagged by Anil Kumar (55 kg in freestyle); and Sunil Kumar (66 kg) and Dharmender Dalal (120 kg), both in the Greco-Roman style. These wrestlers made history by winning 10 gold medals (in both freestyle and Greco-Roman categories), the highest by any country in the Commonwealth Games.

Best performance in the Greco-Roman event of the Asian Championships

India's best performance in the Greco-Roman category was at the 2020 Asian Championships in New Delhi where Indian grapplers won one gold and four bronze medals. Sunil Kumar (87 kg) won the gold medal while Arjun Halakurki (55 kg), Ashu (67 kg), Aditya Kundu (72 kg) and Hardeep (97 kg) won the bronzes.

Best performance at the World Championship

India has a record haul of five medals at the 2019 World Championship held at Nur-Sultan, Kazakhstan. Deepak Punia won a silver in the 86 kg category. Bronze medals were won by Bajrang Punia (65 kg), Rahul Aware (61 kg), Ravi Dahiya (61 kg) and Vinesh Phogat (women, 53 kg).

Best performance in the Commonwealth Games – women

Women's wrestling was introduced in the 2010 Delhi Commonwealth Games, where India bagged three gold medals, two silver medals and one bronze medal in freestyle. Geeta Phogat (55 kg), Alka Tomar (59 kg) and Anita Sheoran (67 kg) won gold medals. The silver medals were won by Nirmala Devi (48 kg) and Babita Phogat (51 kg). Suman Kundu (63 kg) won the bronze medal.

Most consecutive Commonwealth Games titles – women

Vinesh Phogat became the first to win three consecutive Commonwealth Games crowns at Glasgow, UK, in 2014; Gold Coast Australia in 2018; and Birmingham, UK, in 2022.

Most medals in the Asian Games – men

Kartar Singh won the gold at Bangkok, Thailand, in 1978, a silver in 1982 at Delhi and another gold at the 1986 Seoul Asian Games in South Korea. He competed in the 90 kg category in 1978 and 1982, and in 100 kg in 1986 (all in freestyle).

Most medals in the Commonwealth Championships

The Indian contingent, with 42 wrestlers, bagged 40 medals – 15 gold, 20 silver and five bronze – in the 2011 Commonwealth Championships in Melbourne, Australia.

Most individual medals in the Commonwealth Championships – men

Sushil Kumar won the title five times between 2003 and 2017. He won the gold medal in 2003 (London, UK), 2005 (Cape Town, South Africa), 2007 (London, UK), 2009 (Jalandhar, India) and 2017 (Johannesburg, South Africa).

Most individual medals in the World Championship

Bajrang Punia won the World Championship medal three times between 2013 and 2019. He won the bronze medal in the 60 kg category in 2013, a silver in the 65 kg category in 2018 and a bronze in 2019.

Most gold medals in the Asian Championship

Sushil Kumar won the title in 2003, 2008 and 2010. Thereafter Ravi Kumar Dahiya won triple gold in Asian Championship titles in 2020, 2021 and 2022.

Most medals in the Asian Championship

Between 2013 and 2022, Bajrang Punia won a record eight medals in the 60 kg to 65 kg categories. He won bronze in 60 kg (2013, New Delhi), silver in 61 kg (2014, Astana, Kazakhstan), gold in 65 kg (2017, New Delhi), bronze in 65 kg (2018, Bishkek, Kyrgyzstan), gold in 65 kg (2019, Xian, China) and silver in 65 kg (2020, New Delhi; 2021, Almaty, Kazakhstan; 2022, Ulaanbaatar, Mongolia).

Most gold medals in the Commonwealth Games – men

Sushil Kumar of the Indian Railways and an alumnus of the Noida College of Physical Education, Noida, Uttar Pradesh, won India's first ever men's triple gold in the Commonwealth Games (2010, Delhi; 2014, Glasgow, UK; and 2018, Gold Coast, Australia).

Most medals at the Asian Girls Championship (U-15)

Indian girl wrestlers won seven medals in the Asian Girls Championships (U-15) in November 2018 in Fujimi, Japan. The gold medallists were: Pooja Rani (33 kg), Komal (36 Kg) and Sweety (43 kg). Silver medals were won by: Pinki (39 kg), Antim Panghal (46 kg) and Bhagyashreee Fand (58 kg). Pratibha Janghu (54 kg) won the bronze.

Youngest champion in the Asian Games

Malwa Singh won the gold medal in the Greco-Roman style in the light flyweight category at the 1962 Asian Games in Jakarta, Indonesia, at the age of 14 years, thus creating history by becoming the youngest wrestling champion from India.

Youngest gold medallist at the Commonwealth Games

Ved Prakash was 14 years old when he won the gold medal in the light flyweight class at the 1970 Commonwealth Games in Edinburgh, UK.

Vinesh Phogat: most consecutive Commonwealth Games titles

Bajrang Punia: most medals in the World Championship and Asian Championship

ADVENTURE

AERO SPORTS

First jump from a microlight

Wing Commander U.K. Palat skydived from a powered hang-glider piloted by Captain K.A. Vasan from 8,000 ft at 7:40 a.m. on 18 October 1999 in Bangalore (now Bengaluru), Karnataka.

First woman skydiver

Rachel Thomas (b. 9 August 1955) from Chittaranjan, West Bengal, was the first Indian woman to skydive, from 2,133.6 m (7,000 ft) over the North Pole on 20 April 2002, to commemorate 150 years of the Indian Railways. An employee of the Indian Railways, Thomas was also the first woman to represent the country in a skydiving competition in 1987. She was honoured with the Padma Shri in 2005.

First international paramotor medallist

Appasaheb Bhimraj Dhus (b. 26 December 1970) from Maharashtra, is the first Indian to win international medals in paramotor games. He won a gold medal in the Pure Economy Task category of the World Paramotor Championship Test Event at Lopburi, Thailand, held from 28 April to 7 May 2017. In the same event, Captain Prafulla Raj Singh won a silver medal in the Pure Navigation Task category.

First Indian woman to skydive over seven continents

Shital Mahajan (b. 19 September 1982) from Pune, Maharashtra, completed 705 skydives across seven continents during 2017–18, adding to her skydive at Skydiver Empuriabrava in Spain (Europe) in 2014. She skydived at Skydive Go Fly at Boituva in Brazil (South America); Skydive Utti in Sky Dance Skydiving Center, USA (North America); Sydney Skydivers in Sydney (Australia); Patriot Hill, Antarctica (Antarctica); Skydive Pretoria, Johannesburg, South Africa (Africa) and Skydive Pattaya, Thailand (Asia), taking the total to seven continents.

First differently abled skydiver in Asia

Major Devender Pal Singh (b. 13 September 1973) from Gurugram, Haryana, is the first differently abled skydiver in Asia. A war-injured amputee veteran, Major Singh skydived from an altitude of 2,743.2 m (9,000 ft) on 28 March 2019 at the military cantonment in Nashik, Maharashtra.

First paraglide from a high cliff

Anand Munje (b. 7 November 1956) from Kitty Hawk Ground School, Pune, Maharashtra, launched a flight from the 1,646 m (5,400 ft) high Kalsubai Peak, part of the Western Ghats in Maharashtra, on 25 February 1997. The flight covered 4 km in 11 mins.

First aerial world circumnavigation in a single-engine plane

Ravinder K. Bansal (b. 26 February 1949) from Clarence, New York, USA, undertook an aerial circumnavigation in a Cessna 400 and flew solo, covering 36 cities over 20,959 nautical miles. He started from Buffalo, New York, USA, on 4 July 2017 and returned on 20 August 2017. The expedition was undertaken to raise funds for the Rotary Ambala Cancer and General Hospital.

First to paraglide with a prosthetic leg

Lieutenant Colonel Dharamdatt Goel (b. 14 August 1976) from Pune, Maharashtra, successfully performed solo paragliding on 19 October 2013 at Al-Hilal, Himachal Pradesh, thereby becoming the first Indian with a prosthetic leg to paraglide. He performed the paraglider flight from an altitude of 2,400 m (7,874 ft) and for 25 mins.

First visually impaired person to paraglide

Divyanshu Ganatra, who lost his eyesight due to glaucoma at 19 years, performed a solo paraglider flight over Kamshet near Pune, Maharashtra, on 30 April 2014. The flight up to 213.36 m (700 ft) lasted 1 min. 30 seconds.

First at the Mantar Paragliding XC Open Championship

Prakash Chand Thakur won the first prize at the Mantar Paragliding XC Open Championship, organized from 18 to 24 July 2017 by the Asian Continental Paragliding Association in Mantar, Indonesia.

First balloon bungee jump

Major M.K. Yadav jumped from a hot-air balloon, which was at a height of 3,310.73 m (10,862 ft) on 18 August 1995 over Leh, Ladakh.

First BASE jump

- *Men*: Lieutenant Colonel Satyendra Verma (b. 24 August 1969), then an officer of the Indian Army from the Corps of Signals, carried out a BASE jump from the 137.16 m (450 ft) high deck of the Pitampura TV Tower, New Delhi, on 29 October 2010. This feat was part of the centenary celebrations of the Corps of Signals and the silver jubilee of the Army Adventure Wing.
- *Women*: Archana Sardana (b. 1 April 1972) from

Wings India 2022, Asia's largest civil aviation event, saw the participation of 125 exhibitors, 3,253 business visitors and 52,345 general visitors.

Visakhapatnam, Andhra Pradesh, is India's first female BASE jumper. She performed 25 BASE jumps off a 122 m (400 ft) high bridge above a canyon in Utah, USA, on 13 July 2010.

First Asian triple amputee to complete a bungee jump

Tinkesh Kaushik (b. 21 June 1993) from Jhajjar, Haryana, became the first Asian triple amputee to bungee from the world's highest canyon swing. He performed the jump from a height of 160 m (525 ft) on 25 November 2018 at The Last Resort, Kathmandu, Nepal.

First to complete a BASE jump during day and night

Mayank Nagpal (b. 21 September 1983) from New Delhi became the first Indian to complete a BASE (Building, Antenna, Span and Earth) jump from all four platforms, during both day and night. For the World BASE number, he jumped from Perrine Bridge, USA (5 September 2014), a cliff called Crooked Stick in Idaho, USA (11 September 2014), a mobile antenna in Gua Damai Xtreme Park, Malaysia (6 October 2015), and an under-construction building in Delhi, India (31 December 2016). For the Night BASE number he jumped from Perrine Bridge, USA (7 September 2014), an antenna in Idaho, USA (on 8 September 2014), an under-construction building in Delhi (26 June 2017) and Gua Damai Cliff, Malaysia (28 September 2018).

Vijay Kumar Deverkhyani: highest zipline by a differently abled person

Highest hot-air balloon take-off

Indradhanush, the hot-air balloon of the Ballooning Club of India, piloted by the then club president, Vishwa Bandhu Gupta, along with pilot R.K. Wason, took off from the Kushok Bakula Rimpochee Airport (3,310.7 m/10,862 ft) in Leh, Ladakh, on 29 September 1988 in Leh, Ladakh.

Highest skydive landing team

Highest flight

Megha Jain (b. 21 September 1988) from New Delhi made the highest flight in an MiG-29 fighter jet, touching 18,400 m (60,367 ft 5 in.) at a top speed of 1,850 km/hr over Sokol Airbase in Nizhny Novgorod, Russia, on 16 February 2017.

Highest bungee jump – woman

Sudhalakshmi Thanigai Arasu (b. 2 July 1965) performed a 220 m (721 ft 9 in.) high bungee jump on 13 August 2010 at Diga Verzasca, Switzerland.

Highest and longest wingsuit flight

Lieutenant Colonel Satyendra Verma (b. 24 August 1969), a retired Indian Army officer, on 31 March 2018, jumped from 5,913.12 m (19,400 ft) using a hot-air balloon platform at Phalodi, Rajasthan. He flew in his wingsuit for 4 mins, covering 10 km across the Jodhpur desert in this time.

Highest zipline by a differently abled person

Vijay Kumar Devarkhyani (b. 13 March 1989) from Delhi zipped across Tower 1 and Tower 3 at a height of 473 ft for a distance of 250 ft at 9:58 p.m. on 19 May 2013 at the 40th level of Crown Regency Hotel and Tower, Philippines.

Highest skydive landing

Warrant Officer Anshu Kumar Tiwari (b. 3 February 1978) and Wing Commander Gajendra Yadava from the Indian Air Force jumped off an aircraft and landed at Khardungla Pass, 5,481 m (17,982 ft) above the mean sea level on 8 October 2020.

Highest BASE jump

Mayank Nagpal (b. 21 September 1983) from New Delhi, performed the highest BASE jump from the 3,080 m (10,105 ft) high point of Eiger Mountain in the Bernese Alps in Switzerland on 24 July 2019.

Lowest BASE jump

Lieutenant Commander Mahesh V. Birajdar from the Indian Navy performed the lowest BASE jump from a 116 m (380 ft 6 in.) high span over a river in the Solang Valley, Himachal Pradesh, on 30 January 2011.

Longest motor glider flight

Captain Surendra Prasad Sinha (b. 26 July

1968), director, Flying Operations, Civil Aviation Department, Government of Jharkhand, flew a Sinus 912 VT-GEE two-seater aircraft for 1,098.24 km in eight flying hours, making it the longest motor glider flight in the country. Along with his co-pilot Captain Anil Gill, he took off from Karnal in Haryana on 13 March 2014 and reached Ranchi, Jharkhand, the next day.

Longest cross-country microlight expedition

The Cross India Air Expedition 2011, organized by the Indian Air Force, covered 7,600 km in 80 hrs 15 mins over 19 days. Wing Commander Akhilesh Chauhan piloted the two-seater microlight, while Squadron Leader Asha Vashisht, Squadron Leader N.D. Gholba and Sergeant M.P. Singh joined him as co-pilots at different stages of the journey. The flight took off from Air Force Station, Hindon, Ghaziabad, Uttar Pradesh, on 8 February 2011, proceeded to Udhampur, Jammu and Kashmir, and traversed the length of the country, flying over Delhi, Jodhpur (Rajasthan), Vadodara (Gujarat), Pune (Maharashtra), Bangalore (now Bengaluru, Karnataka), Sulur (Tamil Nadu) and Thiruvananthapuram (Kerala), returning to Hindon by the same route on 27 February 2011.

Longest paramotor expedition

The Indian Air Force paramotor team, with Wing Commander M.P.S. Solanki as their leader, conducted a circumnavigation-of-India expedition called 'Pradakshina', covering 10,041.7 km in 53 days from 3 February to 26 March 2016. Flagged off from the air force station in Kalaikunda, West Bengal, the team flew along the periphery of the country before returning to Kalaikunda. They followed a clockwise route along the eastern and western coasts and the north-western and eastern regions, covering an average of 218.3 km per day.

Longest harness hang-glider flight

Havildar Sanjeev Kumar from the Indian Army Hang Gliding Team, completed the longest harness hang-glider flight from Suratgarh to Barmer, Rajasthan, on 12 December 2018. He covered 465.33 km on Fox hang-gliders powered by a Mosquito NRG harness. He covered the distance in 8 hrs 43 mins.

Most podium finishes in FAI F3M Championship

Harshil Virendra Mane (b. 3 March 1999) from Pune, Maharashtra, has six international podium finishes in the FAI F3M category championship of aeromodelling, the highest number by an Indian. He is also the first aeromodeller representing India in international championships including the World Cups conducted by the Federation Aeronautique Internationale (FAI).

Most skydiving jumps

Rajkumar Balakrishnan (b. 1 April 1977) from Theni, Tamil Nadu, started making skydiving jumps in February 2006 and completed his 10,000th jump on 23 March 2018.

Most hours logged in free fall

Rajkumar Balakrishnan (b. 1 April 1977) from Theni, Tamil Nadu, has logged a total of 84 hours in free fall while skydiving, up to 6 July 2018.

Oldest woman skydiver

Usha Arun Mahajan (b. 20 November 1945) from Pune, Maharashtra, successfully performed a tandem skydive from an altitude of 13,500 ft on 1 October 2017 in Pennsylvania, USA at the age of 71 years 10 months 11 days.

Microlight aircraft flight

First: Flying at a cruising speed of 56 km/hr on a 90 kg tricycle-shaped aircraft, Lieutenant Anil Kumar Yadav covered 3,000 km from Jaisalmer, Rajasthan, to Calcutta (now Kolkata), West Bengal, in 31 days from 21 September 1994.
Fastest: Squadron Leader B.K. Das flew a microlight aircraft from Jaisalmer, Rajasthan, to Dibrugarh, Assam, covering 3,250 km during 1–23 February 1999.

Most microlight expeditions

Mountain Eagles, the Indian Army microlight formation flying team, based at Army Adventure Nodal Centre (Microlight and Powered Hang-Gliding), Mhow, Madhya Pradesh, conducted three expeditions in 13 months from February 2015. The first, with seven aircraft, covered 1,800 km in 10 flying days between 13 and 26 February 2015. In the second one, commemorating the golden jubilee of the India–Pakistan war in 1965, three microlights covered 3,050 km in 10 flying days from 5 to 14 September 2015. The third one, at the 15th reunion of the Corps of Signals, was from 9 to 17 February 2016, with six aircraft covering 1,500 km in nine flying days. The core team remained the same in all three expeditions.

Daring dives

Wing Commander Gajanand Yadava of the Indian Air Force (IAF) created four national records in the field of wingsuit skydive jumping in 2019 in Agra, Uttar Pradesh:
1. First wingsuit skydive jump from high-speed aircraft (An-32);

Usha Arun Mahajan: oldest woman skydiver (*right*)

The Royal Aero Club of India and Burma Ltd (now Aero Club of India) was founded.

Press conference held to announce India's first aero-sports policy

First National Air Sports Policy

Keeping in mind the vision of India as one of the top countries in sports by 2030, the National Air Sports Policy 2022 was launched by Jyotiraditya M. Scindia, the Union minister for civil aviation. It was drafted to ensure the establishment of good infrastructure, equipment, services and instructors for aero sport enthusiasts. It focuses on developing an air-sports ecosystem that is affordable, accessible, safe and sustainable as well as enjoyable to the citizens of the country. It encompasses 11 air sports such as aerobatics, air-racing, aero modelling, paragliding, para motoring, hang-gliding, skydiving, ballooning and parachuting, among others. As per the policy, a four-tier governance structure will be established, which includes the Air Sports Federation of India (ASFI) as the main governing body, national associations for different individual sports or a set of sports, regional- or state- and UT-level bodies of the aforementioned associations and, finally, district-level associations. To ensure safety, penalties, fines and levies have been put in place for those who flout the safety requirements.

2. Highest wingsuit jump from an altitude of 7,437.12 m (24,400 ft);
3. First to do a night wingsuit jump from 2,438.40 m (8,000 ft); and
4. The only jumper to undertake high-altitude night-time wingsuit jump from 3,657.60 m (12,000 ft), where he opened the chute at 914.40 m (3,000 ft) after doing wingsuit flying for 2,743.2 m (9,000 ft).

Part of the IAF's skydiving team Akashganga and a parachute jump instructor, Wing Commander Yadava has taken more than 2,900 jumps till date and was awarded the Tenzing Norgay National Adventure Award 2019 in the air adventure category.

ROAD EXPEDITIONS

FOUR-WHEELER

First all-India expedition – group

Arun Kumar Basra and Kamaljit Singh Virdi from Rapid Action India completed an all-India car expedition in their Fiat Padmini, covering 15,179 km in 19 days 19 hrs 5 mins. They were flagged off from Delhi on 5 January 1998 and returned on 25 January 1998.

First Four Corners of India expedition – solo

Dr S.S. Chaudhari (b. 7 March 1962) from Jalgaon, Maharashtra, completed a solo drive connecting the four corners of India, covering 13,834 km in 26 days 22 hrs 15 mins. Driving a Maruti SX4 car, he set out from Kanniyakumari, Tamil Nadu, on 30 October 2014. He reached Tezu, Lohit District, Arunachal Pradesh, on 8 November 2014; Leh, Ladakh, on 16 November 2014; Koteshwar, Kachchh District, Gujarat, on 22 November 2014; and concluded the expedition at Kanniyakumari on 26 November 2014.

First North–South India round expedition – solo

Suresh Joseph (b. 14 May 1958) from Tamil Nadu is the first person to complete the trailblazing North–South expedition India round trip and, in the process, breaking the record of the fastest North–South solo expedition in 2012. He started his expedition from Kanniyakumari, Tamil Nadu, on 2 July 2012 and reached Leh, Ladakh, on 7 July 2012, covering 3,811 km in 129 hrs 30 mins. Four days later, he was back on the trip, taking off from Leh on 11 July 2012. He reached Kanniyakumari on 15 July 2012. He drove a Maruti Swift car for the journey.

First trans-Himalayan expedition – solo

Suresh Joseph (b. 14 May 1958) from Tamil Nadu set out in a Ford Endeavour to create a new record for a trans-Himalayan solo trip, which he accomplished in 18 days 13 hrs 15 mins. Starting his journey from Jammu in Jammu and Kashmir on 21 August 2015, he reached Tezu in Arunachal Pradesh on 8 September 2015. Joseph covered 5,845 km across nine Indian states, Nepal and Bhutan, and crossed altitudes of up to 2,554.2 m (8,380 ft).

First West–East India round expedition – solo

Daljit Singh Matharoo (b. 29 September 1986) completed a solo West–East–West India expedition, covering 7,715 km in 217 hrs 25 mins. He broke the record for the fastest solo East–West India expedition by covering 3,832 km in 94 hrs 44 mins. He started in his Maruti Zen car from Koteshwar, Kachchh District, Gujarat, on 27 April 2018, and reached Tezu, Arunachal Pradesh, on 1 May 2018. He started back on 1 May 2018 and reached Koteshwar on 6 May 2018.

Fastest East–West India expedition – group

Apurba Kumar Deka (b. 27 March 1975), Animesh Deka (b. 15 January 1982) and Md Zillur Rahman (b. 2 December 1975) from Guwahati, Assam, completed the fastest East–West India expedition from Tezu, Arunachal Pradesh, to Koteshwar, Gujarat, covering 3,771.4 km in 70 hrs 52 mins. The team drove a Renault Duster car, starting their journey on 27 October 2015 and ending the expedition on 30 October 2015.

Fastest East–West India expedition by a differently abled person – solo

Eric Paul (b. 14 January 1988), a wheelchair-bound paraplegic from Rohini, New Delhi, completed the East–West India solo expedition in a hand-controlled Maruti Swift, covering 3,697 km in 4 days 18 hrs 55 mins. He started from Tezu, Arunachal Pradesh, on 30 November 2017 at 4:13 a.m., reaching Koteshwar, Gujarat, at 11:43 p.m. on 4 December 2017.

Fastest Four Corners of India expedition – solo

Suresh Joseph (b. 14 May 1958) from Tamil Nadu successfully completed the four corners of India tour (Kanniyakumari, Tamil Nadu; Koteshwar, Gujarat; Leh, Ladakh; and Tezu, Arunachal Pradesh), covering 13,214 km in 403 hrs. Driving a Mahindra XUV500, he started his expedition on 7 May 2015 and ended it on 12 June 2015.

Longest journey within a country – solo

Shashi Kapila (b. 3 November 1942) from New Delhi completed the longest journey in a Honda Mobilio car, covering 8,227 km in 105 hrs 15 mins. He started from Delhi at 6:00 a.m. on 12 November 2016 and reached back at 12:28 p.m. on 22 November 2016. The farthest location he travelled to was Kanniyakumari.

Longest journey within a country – group

A two-member team of Sagar Thakar (b. 30 June 1982) and Kanak Barsadia (b. 14 February 1984) from Surat, Gujarat, completed the longest journey in a Maruti Swift Dzire car, covering 60,830 km in 82 days. They set off from Bardoli, Gujarat, on 20 March 2017 and reached back on 12 June 2017.

Longest distance travelled across countries – solo

Hitendra Sharma (b. 11 January 1978) from Gwalior, Madhya Pradesh, successfully undertook a solo expedition by road, covering 30,195 km across 11 Asian countries in a Honda Amaze car in 92 days. Starting from Gwalior in Madhya Pradesh, India, on 10 February 2017, he reached Bangladesh, driving through India, Myanmar, Thailand, Laos, Vietnam, Cambodia, Malaysia, Singapore, Bhutan and Nepal, and returned to India on 21 May 2017.

Nitin Gadkari at an event

Green Expressways – the Road to Sustainability

In an attempt to promote sustainable living in India, Road Transport Minister Nitin Gadkari, introduced a plan to construct 26 solar-powered green expressways in India by 2024, in a speech at the Rajya Sabha. Not only will these highways have facilities for charging heavy-duty trucks and buses, but will also have solar- and wind-powered toll booths. A system of overhead power lines will be developed to support the charging of vehicles. Apart from being environment friendly, these highways will also help generate new jobs and businesses, and boost economic activities. It will also reduce travel time tremendously. All in all, it will be a positive step for the country on its journey to sustainable living.

TWO-WHEELER (MOTORCYCLE)*

UP TO 150 CC

First trans-Himalayan expedition – solo

Rajeev Kumar Mondal from Burdwan, West Bengal, successfully completed a solo two-wheeler expedition along the trans-Himalayan route covering 7,120 km in 303 hrs 58 mins of travel time. Kick-starting the expedition on a 150 cc Hero Honda Achiever from Guwahati, Assam on 5 May 2013, he first went to Arunachal Pradesh and then, passing through Bhutan, West Bengal, Nepal, Uttarakhand and Himachal Pradesh, reached Srinagar in Jammu and Kashmir on 12 July 2013. He crossed 22 passes including Khardung La at 5,602 m (18,380 ft).

151–450 CC

Fastest East–West India expedition – solo

Dr S.T. Thomas (b. 8 January 1987) from Tamil

A cash prize of ₹15,00,000 were given to all recipients of the Tenzing Norgay National Adventure Award in 2021.

* Records for expeditions on two-wheelers (motorcycles) may be categorized according to engine capacity: up to 150 cc, 151–450 cc and over 451 cc.

Fastest North–South expedition – four-wheeler group

Sameer A.S. (b. 14 December 1986), Noufal K.N. (b. 30 May 1985) and Bibin Krishnan (b. 20 April 1984) from Kerala set a record for the fastest North–South India group expedition, covering 3,870 km in 49 hrs 34 mins. The trio started from Leh, Ladakh, at 7:05 a.m. on 1 September 2021, reaching Kanniyakumari, Tamil Nadu, at 8:39 a.m. on 3 September 2021.

Fastest North–South expedition – four-wheeler – solo

Dhruveer Singh Gandhi (b. 6 March 1985) from Mumbai, Maharashtra, completed the North–South expedition, covering a distance of 3,819.17 km in 56 hrs 20 mins. He started his expedition at 4:45 a.m. on 10 September 2021 from the Deputy Commissioner GST Division, Srinagar, and concluded it at 1:05 p.m. on 12 September 2021 at the Deputy Superintendent of Police's office in Kanniyakumari.

Dhruveer Singh Gandhi

Nadu covered 3,729 km from Tezu, Arunachal Pradesh, to Koteshwar, Gujarat, in 68 hrs 18 mins to set a new record in the East–West India two-wheeler expedition category. He started his journey on his Honda CBR 250R bike on 20 March 2016 and concluded the expedition on 23 March 2016.

First North–South India round expedition by a differently abled person – solo

Vadivel Baluchamy (b. 14 June 1990), an amputee from Madurai, Tamil Nadu, completed the first North–South solo round expedition by a differently abled person, covering 9,136 km in 576 hrs 23 mins. He started on a Royal Enfield Classic 350 bike from Kanniyakumari on 30 August 2018 at 4:25 p.m. and travelled to Leh, Ladakh. He returned to Kanniyakumari on 22 September at 8:18 p.m.

Fastest Four Corners of India expedition – solo

Vishvesh Dhirendrakumar Mehta (b. 10 June 1980) from Jamnagar, Gujarat, completed the fastest solo expedition connecting the four corners of India, covering 11,217 km in 313 hrs 51 mins. Riding a Royal Enfield Classic 350, he set out from Koteshwar, Gujarat, on 21 May 2019 and returned to Koteshwar (covering Kanniyakumari, Tamil Nadu; Leh, Ladakh; and Tezu, Arunachal Pradesh) on 8 June 2019. His break time was 113 hrs.

Fastest North–South India expedition – solo

Sridhar Ramulu Chidumalla (b. 2 January 1978) from Mumbai, Maharashtra, completed the fastest North–South solo expedition on a Royal Enfield motorcycle, covering 3,849 km in 74 hrs 45 mins. He started from Leh, Ladakh, on 25 June 2018 and reached Kanniyakumari, Tamil Nadu, on 28 June 2018.

Fastest GQ expedition by a differently abled person – solo

Vadivel Baluchamy (b. 14 June 1990), an amputee, completed the fastest Golden Quadrilateral (GQ) expedition by a differently abled person, covering 6,723 km in 14 days 9 hrs 30 mins. He started on a Royal Enfield Classic 350 bike from Chennai, Tamil Nadu, on 25 September 2017 and travelled to Kolkata, Delhi and Mumbai, returning to Chennai on 9 October 2017.

Longest journey within the country – solo

Krishanu Kona (b. 27 September 1991) from Delhi travelled 50,338 km on his motorcycle in 224 days to set the record for the longest motorcycle journey in India. He started on a Bajaj Pulsar NS200 bike on 30 August 2015 from Delhi and returned on 9 April 2016.

Longest distance covered within the country by a differently abled person – solo

Mahinder Singh Raghuwanshi (b. 2 October 1987), an amputee with 70 per cent disability, and a prosthetic limb, covered 5,331.5 km on an Enfield Bullet 350 bike in 17 days. He started from his hometown Mhow, Madhya Pradesh, on 3 June 2016, and went up to Khardung La (5,359 m/17,582 ft) in Leh, Ladakh, returning to Mhow on 19 June 2016.

OVER 451 CC

Fastest All-India expedition – solo

Prashant Kumar (b. 14 July 1987) from Bengaluru, Karnataka, completed the all-India expedition on 7 November 2019 on his Triumph Tiger XCA 800 bike, covering 16,305 km in 23 days 9 hrs 46 mins. He started from Hyderabad, Telangana, on 15 October 2019 and returned on 7 November 2019, travelling through the then 29 states and five Union Territories.

Fastest GQ expedition – solo

Souvig Sarkar (b. 22 October 1986) from Mumbai, Maharashtra, completed the GQ solo motorcycling expedition, covering 5,962.09 km in 87 hrs 42 mins on a Triumph Street Triple RS motorcycle, between 18 and 22 October 2019.

GENERAL

First to cross Umling La pass – solo

Pallavi Fauzdar (b. 20 December 1979) from Delhi was the first to cross Umling La pass on 4 August 2017 at 3:16 p.m. It is the highest motorable pass in the world, situated at an altitude of 5,882.64 m (19,300 ft) above sea level. On her expedition, she even named the Bonni La pass, situated at an altitude of 5,083 m (16,677 ft), which was unnamed before.

Largest rally (less than 100 km) by woman riders – multiple venues

The largest two-wheeler rally by only women riders was organized by the Akhil Bharatiya Terapanth Mahila Mandal on 8 March 2020, International Women's Day. As many as 6,205 women rode distances ranging from 1.5 to 10 km at locations like Udaipur, Ahmedabad, Balotra, Surat and Delhi, among others. The rally was held as part of their 'I Respect' campaign to emphasize the need for women to respect one another for their choices.

The Redditch company partnered with Madras Motors in India to form 'Enfield India'.

Feats on Wheels

Most people in a human pyramid on two motorcycles – fastest

The Army Service Corps 'Tornadoes' formed a human pyramid on two motorcycles with 17 personnel on 9 November 2020 at Air Force Station, Yelahanka, Karnataka. They began riding at 9:10 a.m. and covered a distance of 1 km in 46.26 secs, setting a new record.

Most people in a human pyramid on five motorcycles – fastest

The Army Service Corps 'Tornadoes' formed a human pyramid on five motorcycles with 44 personnel on 9 November 2020 at Air Force Station, Yelahanka, Karnataka. They began riding at 9:30 a.m. and covered a distance of 1 km in 53.30 secs, setting a new record.

Most people in a human pyramid on seven motorcycles – fastest

The Army Service Corps 'Tornadoes' formed a human pyramid on seven motorcycles with 39 personnel on 9 November 2020 at Air Force Station, Yelahanka, Karnataka. They began riding at 9:40 a.m. and covered a distance of 1.2 km in 1 min. 11 secs, setting a new record.

Longest ramp jump over people

Captain Dishant Kataria (b. 25 September 1993), captain of the Daredevils team, jumped on a ramp covering a distance of 61.04 ft on an unmodified Hero Xpulse 200 cc motorcycle over 65 people lying down. This was performed on 10 November 2020 at Gouri Shankar Parade Ground, 1 Military Training Regiment, 1 Signal Training Centre, Jabalpur, Madhya Pradesh.

TWO-WHEELER (BICYCLE)

GEARED

Fastest North–South expedition – geared – solo

Nimesh Mansukhbhai Jivrajani (b. 11 February 1980) from Bhavnagar, Gujarat, completed a solo North–South India expedition on a geared bicycle, covering 3,400 km in 14 days 16 hrs 15 mins. He started from Jammu, Jammu and Kashmir, at 5:40 a.m. on 24 December 2018 and reached Kanniyakumari, Tamil Nadu, at 10:00 p.m. on 7 January 2019.

Fastest East–West expedition – geared – solo

Naresh Kumar Rajendran (b. 3 June 1992) from Vellore, Tamil Nadu, completed the fastest East–West solo expedition in a geared bicycle by covering 3,613 km in 10 days 8 hrs 57 mins. He started from Tezu, Arunachal Pradesh, at 4:00 a.m. on 5 December 2018 and ended at Koteshwar, Gujarat, at 12:57 p.m. on 15 December 2018.

Fastest GQ expedition – geared bicycle – solo

Bharat Pannu (b. 8 May 1983) from Bengaluru, Karnataka, completed the GQ solo expedition, covering a distance of 5,938.2 km in 14 days 23 hrs 52 mins on his geared bicycle. He started his expedition at 12:08 a.m. on 16 October 2020 from India Gate, New Delhi and concluded it at 12:20 a.m. on 31 October 2020 at Indian Gate, New Delhi.

Longest distance covered within the country – geared – solo

Karan Singh Jagawat (b. 1 March 1948) covered a distance of 20,948 km on his geared cycle in 178 days. He started his journey on 23 April 2017 from Jaipur, Rajasthan, and returned to Jaipur on 18 October 2017. He travelled through Koteshwar, Gujarat; Tezu, Arunachal Pradesh; Khardung La, Ladakh; and Kanniyakumari, Tamil Nadu.

GEARLESS

Fastest North–South expedition – gearless – solo

Saurabh Bharat Zagade (b. 28 October 1996) from Pune, Maharashtra, completed a solo North–South India expedition on a gearless bicycle, covering a distance of 3,440 km in 14 days 7 hrs. He started the expedition from Dharmal, Jammu and Kashmir, at 6:25 a.m. on 15 April 2019 and reached Kanniyakumari, Tamil Nadu, at 1:25 p.m. on 29 April 2019.

Fastest North–South expedition – gearless – group

Ashwani Kumar Singh (b. 14 August 1995) from Deoria, Uttar Pradesh, and Akash Yadav (b. 1 February 1990) from Azamgarh, Uttar Pradesh, completed the fastest North–South India tour by cycle, covering 4,197 km in 14 days 15 hrs 37 mins. The duo started from Leh, Ladakh, on 13 June 2016 and reached Kanniyakumari, Tamil Nadu, on 27 June 2016.

GENERAL

Largest bicycling marathon

Organized by Vodafone India, the second edition of the Vodafone Cycling Marathon held in Bengaluru, Karnataka, on 1 March 2015, attracted 6,123 cyclists. The event was held under four different categories: Champion Race (60 km), Passion Race (40 km), Green Ride (20 km) and Fashion Ride (5 km). It was conducted under the aegis of the Cycle Federation of India, supported by Bengaluru City Traffic Police. Around 5,000 cyclists took part in the first edition of this marathon.

Oldest Super Randonneuse

Ela Ghose (b. 8 April 1961) successfully completed 4 brevets organized by Noida Randonneurs and Delhi Randonneurs (a part of Audax India Randonneurs) under the aegis of Audax Club Parisien of France, and earned the title of Super Randonneuse in the 2018–19 season. A randonneuring event is called a randonnée or brevet, and a rider who has completed a 200 km event is called a randonneur. The Super Randonneur/Randonneuse title is awarded on the completion of a series of 4 brevets within a single (cycling) year, i.e., November 2018–October 2019. The 4 brevets cover 200 km (completed within 13.5 hrs), 300 km (completed within 20 hrs), 400 km (completed within 27 hrs) and 600 km (completed within 40 hrs).

The first Brevet de Randonneur Mondiaux in India was conducted in January 2010.

Bharat Pannu: fastest GQ expedition – geared bicycle – solo

44 awards were presented as part of the National Sports and Adventure Awards 2022.

First tandem bicycling

Ashok N. Bhanushali (b. 21 May 1974) from Mumbai, Maharashtra, and Dr Meera Velankar (b. 11 December 1975) from Bengaluru, Karnataka, completed India's first 300 km brevet ride on a tandem bicycle. The feat was part of an event organized by Surat Randonneurs on 10 July 2016. The duo started the ride from M.T.B. College, Surat, Gujarat, and covered a distance of 309 km in 17 hrs 36 mins.

Longest tandem bicycling – women

Sheetal Bambulkar (b. 27 October 1978) from Mumbai, Maharashtra, and Dr Meera Velankar (b. 11 December 1975) from Bengaluru, Karnataka, completed a tandem cycling brevet ride of 206 km in 12 hrs 27 mins in Vadodara, Gujarat, on 20 December 2015.

Fastest Asian to cycle across the world

Vedangi Kulkarni (b. 1998) from Pune, Maharashtra, became the fastest Asian to cycle across the world. She started her expedition from Perth, Australia, in July 2018 and reached Kolkata, West Bengal, on 23 December 2018. She crossed 29,000 km in 159 days, pedalling up to 300 km every day. She covered 14 countries including New Zealand, Canada, Iceland, Portugal, Spain, France, Belgium, Germany, Denmark, Sweden, Finland and Russia, and endured temperatures ranging between –20°C and 37°C.

All-India tour on a mono-wheeler

Subrata Chakraborty (b. 5 November 1976) from Kolkata, West Bengal, completed an all-India solo expedition on a monocycle, covering 10,500 km in 256 days. He started his journey from Raj Bhavan, Kolkata, on 8 September 2000 and returned to Kolkata on 21 May 2001. He passed through 17 states of the country, viz., West Bengal, Odisha, Andhra Pradesh, Tamil Nadu, Kerala, Karnataka, Goa, Maharashtra, Gujarat, Rajasthan, Haryana, Delhi, Uttar Pradesh, Madhya Pradesh, Bihar, Assam and Arunachal Pradesh.

Most consecutive cycling expeditions – 100 km

Gurpreet Singh (b. 28 June 1972) from Jalandhar, Punjab, cycled at least 100 kms consecutively for 300 days from 19 May 2020 to 14 March 2021 with geared Merida Sculptura 400 and Trek – FX2 bicycles in Jalandhar, Punjab.

WATER SPORTS

First sail down the River Ganga

Captain P.P. Sabharwal and Captain S.N. Dubey completed the first sail down the River Ganga in a racing craft from Chandi Ghat at Haridwar, Uttarakhand, to Kolkata, West Bengal, from 26 to 28 July 1960. The total distance they covered was 1,931.23 km.

First circumnavigation of the globe – group

On 28 September 1985, ten sappers, led by Colonel T.P.S. Chowdhury, set off on INS *Trishna*, for a 55,000 km sail in an 11.3 m (37 ft) long, 10.5 tonne fibreglass yacht. They sailed from Mumbai, Maharashtra, to Maldives and Mauritius, and then to St Helena Island. Crossing the Equator for the second time, they sailed into the Port of Belem in Brazil, then through the Panama Canal towards the Galapagos Islands, the Polynesian Islands and Bali, reaching Mumbai on 10 January 1987.

First circumnavigation of the globe by a differently abled sailor

ajor Ashok Kumar Singh, a permanent member of the INS *Trishna* crew and winner of the National Adventure Award in 1994, went around the globe in 1985. It was the longest journey undertaken by a differently abled person.

First sailing expedition on the River Brahmaputra and longest on any Indian river

Sixty NCC cadets of Assam undertook a 220 km long sailing expedition on the capricious River Brahmaputra in three whaler boats of the NCC naval units, with safety and support vessels provided by the Indian Army Eastern Command. The maiden expedition named 'Lachit-1' was flagged off at Biswanath Chariali, Assam, and flagged in at Pandu Port, Guwahati, on 16 October 2019.

First circumnavigation – woman – solo

On 15 October 1988, Ujwala Rai became not only the first Indian woman, but also the first Asian one, to sail around the world after a 17-month voyage in *Jaykus III*, a 9.75 m (32 ft) Vancouver-class sailboat.

First circumnavigation – man – solo

Commander Dilip Donde of the Indian Navy completed a solo circumnavigation of the globe in 276 days. He covered 21,600 nautical miles sailing on INSV *Mhadei*, a 17 m (56 ft) long sailing boat fitted with high-tech navigation and communication equipment. He embarked on the voyage on 19 August 2009. On return, his boat touched base at Sunk Rock Lighthouse at Mumbai harbour on 22 May 2010. The expedition was part of the Indian Navy's 'Sagar Parikrama' project.

First expedition on the River Beas

A team of 13 people from Atal Bihari Vajpayee Institute of Mountaineering and Allied Sports (ABVIMAS), Manali, Himachal Pradesh, was the first to raft across the length of the River Beas from 23 to 26 October 2019. Led by Colonel Neeraj Rana, the director of ABVIMAS, the 230 km long rafting expedition was undertaken with two rafts and three kayaks from Manali to Dehra Gopipur Bridge at Pong Dam.

First rafting event in the country

The Indo-USA Upper Ganga Rafting Expedition in 1984 was the first rafting expedition in India led by American Ken Warren and Avinash Kohli. The expedition rafted sections of the Rivers Bhagirathi and Alaknanda till Devprayag, and the River Ganga from Devprayag to Rishikesh in Uttarakhand.

First catamaran sailing expedition

A team of sailors from the Artillery Water Sports Association, Hyderabad, Telangana, completed the Sarvatra Sailing Expedition, a 1,364 km long marine voyage along the eastern coast of India. The longest such expedition in the country, it was launched from Marina Beach, Chennai, Tamil Nadu, on 18 December 2011 and culminated at Gopalpur, Odisha, on 3 January 2012. They also set records of sailing 153 km non-stop in a day on 21 December 2011 and of 15 hours of non-stop sailing on 31 December 2011.

First sailing expedition around the Indian peninsula

Alok Kumar Yadav (b. 20 June 1984) from EME Sailing Association completed the first sailing expedition around the Indian peninsula. He started from Haldia, West Bengal, along the east coast on 21 October 2018 and reached Porbandar, Gujarat, on the west coast on 1 December 2018. He covered a distance of 4,597 nautical miles in 41 days.

First deep-bounce dive

Commodore Vimal Kumar of the Indian Navy was the first person to dive to a depth of 160 m in a diving bell in the Black Sea in 1970. He explored the bottom of the sea for about 10 mins. After surfacing, he underwent a decompression schedule for 10 hrs.

First saturation dive

Commodore Vimal Kumar of the Indian Navy conducted the first saturation dive in May 1985 in a decompression chamber, using a mix of helium and oxygen, on INHS *Ashvini* in Mumbai, Maharashtra. Pratap Singh and T. Vinod Rao were pressurized to a depth of 67 m (219 ft 10 in.) on 16 May 1985 and stayed in saturation for six days.

First canoeing expedition

Sheo Shankar Gope and Ravindra Kumar Bhuyan were team leaders of a canoeing expedition that started from Kolkata, West Bengal, on 6 July 1991. They paddled upstream on the Ganga and sailed a distance of 2,000 km, touching Bhagalpur, Mokama, Patna, Allahabad (now Prayagraj) and Etawah, reaching Delhi on 25 September 1991.

First backstroke swimming across the Strait of Gibraltar without neoprene

Tejesh Vishnu Parsekar (b. 30 May 1990) from Mumbai, Maharashtra, became the first Indian and second in the world (since 1928) to successfully complete backstroke swimming across the Strait of Gibraltar from Isla de Tarifa, Spain, to Perejil Island near Morocco on 16 August 2010. He was the first in the world to complete it without neoprene (protective suit). He covered 19. 4 km in 5 hrs 21 mins.

WR Youngest in the world and first Asian to complete the Ocean's Seven challenge

Rohan Dattatrey More (b. 30 October 1985) from Pune, Maharashtra, at the age of 32, became the world's youngest swimmer to complete the Ocean's Seven challenge on 9 February 2018 when he swam across the Cook Strait between North and South Islands of New Zealand in 8 hrs 37 mins. He is the first Asian swimmer and the ninth in the world to complete the difficult open-water swimming challenge that includes the English Channel, the North Channel, the Molokai Channel, the

Water sports centre, Bilaspur, Himachal Pradesh

Water Sports Centre Inaugurated

A unique and first of its kind water sports centre was inaugurated by Anurag Singh Thakur, the Union minister of youth affairs and sports in October 2022 in Koldam Barmana, Bilaspur, Himachal Pradesh. It was jointly initiated by the National Thermal Power Corporation (NTPC) and Sports Authority of India (SAI). It not only houses state-of-the-art equipment but also offers training and hostel facilities to both girls and boys. The centre is dedicated to water sports such as rowing, canoeing and kayaking, and will train 40 players chosen to compete in these sports.

Bhakti Sharma: first and youngest Asian woman to swim in Antarctic waters

Till date there have been **27** recipients of the Tenzing Norgay Adventure Award in Water adventure.

Catalina Channel, the Tsugaru Channel, the Strait of Gibraltar and the Cook Strait.

WR Youngest in the world and first Asian to swim across the Cook Strait

Rohan Dattatrey More (b. 30 October 1985) of Pune, Maharashtra, became the world's youngest swimmer to swim across the Cook Strait between the North and South Islands of New Zealand in 8 hrs 37 mins on 9 February 2018. He is the first Asian swimmer and the ninth in the world to complete the difficult Ocean Seven open-water swimming challenge that includes the English Channel, North Channel, Molokai Channel, Catalina Channel, Tsugaru Channel, the Strait of Gibraltar and the Cook Strait.

WR First and youngest Asian woman to swim in Antarctic waters

Bhakti Sharma (b. 30 November 1989) from Udaipur, Rajasthan, is the first Asian woman and the youngest in the world to set a record in open swimming in Antarctic waters. She swam 2.3 km in 41 hrs 14 mins, in temperatures of around 1°C, breaking the record of L. Cox (USA) and L. Pugh (Britain). She was awarded the Tenzing Norgay National Adventure Award in 2010.

First Asian woman to swim across the seven seas

Bula Chowdhury (b. 2 January 1970) from West Bengal was the first Asian woman to swim across seven seas: the Arctic Ocean, the North Atlantic Ocean, the South Atlantic Ocean, the Indian Ocean, the North Pacific Ocean, the South Pacific Ocean and the Antarctic Ocean. She crossed the English Channel twice in 1989 and 1999, and in 2005 she became the first woman to swim across sea channels off five continents. She received the Arjuna Award in 1990 and the Padma Shri in 2008.

First to swim from mainland to Anacapa Island

Prabhat Raju Koli (b. 27 July 1999) from Mumbai, Maharashtra, successfully swam from Hollywood Beach, Oxnard, to Anacapa Island in 6 hrs 22 mins 17 secs on 10 July 2019. The route was 20 km long in open sea.

First woman to cross the English Channel – solo

Arati Saha (b. 24 September 1940) from West Bengal became the first Indian woman to cross the English Channel on 29 September 1959. She swam from Cape Gris Nez, France, to Sandgate, England, in 16 hrs 20 mins.

First to swim the English Channel thrice – solo

- *Men*: Taranath Narayan Shenoy (b. 1958) from Maharashtra became the first person to cross the English Channel thrice in 1985. Deaf and nearly blind, he had previously swum across the channel in 1983 and 1984.
- *Women*: Rashmi Sharma (b. 1988) from Kolkata, West Bengal, became the first woman to cross the English Channel thrice in 2009. She had previously swum across the channel in 2006 and 2007.

WR King of Gibraltar

B. R. Ghadge of Mumbai Police, Maharashtra, crossed the shark-infested and freezing Strait of Gibraltar (Spain–Morocco) four times. He was conferred the title 'King of Gibraltar' by the Gibraltar Strait Association in August 2002 as he completed the fourth feat in 6 hrs 10 mins on 2 August 2002. He was the first Indian to cross the 26 km long Toroneos Gulf, Greece, in 10 hrs 43 mins on 20 July 2002.

First to complete the Triple Crown

Taranath Narayan Shenoy (b. 1958) from Maharashtra became the world's second swimmer and the first Indian to complete the Triple Crown of Open Water Swimming when he crossed the 32.2 km long Catalina Channel (or San Pedro Channel, separating Santa Catalina Island from the southern California mainland, USA) on 25 August 1987. Deaf and nearly blind, he had previously swum the 20 Bridges Swim (a 45.9 km circumnavigation of Manhattan Island, New York City, USA) on 9 August 1987 and the English Channel on 18 August 1983.

First to complete the Round-Trip Angel Island marathon

Shubham Dhananjay Vanmali (b. 20 December 1995) from Mumbai, Maharashtra, was the first Indian to complete the Round-Trip Angel Island marathon swimming. He completed the 16.1 km marathon swim in 10 hrs in San Francisco, USA, on 24 May 2018. He is also the youngest male swimmer and 12th in the world to complete this challenging bay-water swim marathon.

First woman to swim the Strait of Gibraltar

Aarti Pradhan from Maharashtra became the first Indian woman to swim the Strait of Gibraltar in 1988. She covered the distance of 22.2 km in 7 hrs 17 mins from Isla de Tarifa, Spain, to Morocco. She received the Arjuna Award in 1988.

First surfing and stand-up paddle competition

The Surfing Federation of India, with the Kerala Tourism Department, organized Spice Coast Open, India's first official national surfing and stand-up paddle (SUP) competition at Kovalam Beach, Kerala, from 3 to 5 May 2013. The three-day event had more than 100 participants in surfing contests under five categories and SUP races under two.

Most stand-up paddle-boarding

Kumaran M. (b. 2 March 1981) from Chennai, Tamil Nadu, had completed stand-up paddle-boarding on 19 different waterbodies, including 17 in India and one each in Sri Lanka and Malaysia, as on 30 June 2016.

Most rivers rafted in a month

National Institute of Mountaineering and Allied Sports (NIMAS), Dirang, Arunachal Pradesh, conducted an expedition with seven members, namely, Colonel Sarfaraz Singh, Nb Sub Jadhav Laxman Vishnu, Hav Loushambam Labango Singh, Hav Darshan Singh, LNk Patil Suraj Ravindra, LNk Himmat Singh, and Mr Tosap Rime and rafted seven rivers in one month. They rafted on Kamseng, Dibang, Nao Dhiling, Lohit, Subhansri, Siyom and Siyan in Arunachal Pradesh from 23 November 2020 to 23 December 2020, covering a total distance of 720.21 kms.

Longest stand-up paddle-boarding – group

Sri Krishnan (b. 31 July 1991) and Siddharth C. (b. 6 July 1992) from Chennai, Tamil Nadu, accomplished the longest stand-up paddle-boarding in the open sea, covering 31 km in the Bay of Bengal on 15 April 2016. They started at Kovalam Beach, Kerala, and paddled to reach Marina Beach, Tamil Nadu, covering the distance in 6 hrs 27 mins.

Longest social campaign through an adventure sport

The National Mission for Clean Ganga, operated under the Department of Water Resources, River Development and Ganga Rejuvenation, Ministry of Jal Shakti, Government of India, organized the Ganga Aamantran Abhiyaan – a river-rafting and kayaking expedition on the River Ganga, conducted between 10 October and 12 November 2019 with a team of nine members. The expedition started from Devprayag and culminated at Ganga Sagar after covering 2,500 km. They spread the message of water conservation and river rejuvenation.

Longest kayaking – solo

Kaustubh Kisan Khade (b. 17 January 1987) from Mumbai, Maharashtra, completed the west coast expedition from Dwarka, Gujarat, to Kanniyakumari, Tamil Nadu, from 17 November 2016 to 7 February 2017. He paddled 1,845 km in 83 days.

Longest kayaking – group

Tarun K. Roy and Brij Mohan Bisht from New Delhi completed the Himalaya-to-Ocean Ganga Expedition from Rishikesh, Uttarakhand, to Ganga Sagar Island in the Bay of Bengal from 5 January to 19 March 2003. They paddled 2,443 km in 74 days.

Longest open-sea swimming by a paraplegic

M.S.A. Shaikh (b. 17 July 1986) from Mumbai, Maharashtra, a paraplegic with 100 per cent disability due to a spinal cord injury, participated in open-sea swimming from Sinquerim to Baga and back to Candolim Beach, Goa, on 8 April 2017 at the UMOJA #BeachFest 2017. He completed the 8 km swim in 4 hrs 4 mins.

WR Long-distance swimming by a paraplegic woman

Deepa Malik (b. 30 September 1970) is an Indian athlete from New Delhi. She swam against the current in the River Yamuna at Allahabad (now Prayagraj), Uttar Pradesh, covering a distance of 1 km in 35 mins 36 secs on 15 June 2008. She received the Khel Ratna in 2019.

Deepa Malik: long-distance swimming by a paraplegic woman

WR Longest white-water rafting expedition

Aqua Scullers, the nine-member rafting team of the Indian Air Force, completed the longest white-water rafting expedition on the River Ganga, covering over 3,000 km from Gangotri in Uttarakhand to Ganga Sagar in West Bengal in 16 days from 19 October to 4 November 2013. The first such expedition undertaken by the Indian Air Force, it included the Himalayan portion of the river from Gangotri (3,049 m/10,003 ft) to Haridwar (295 m/968 ft), a very challenging white-water stretches with Grade IV–V rapids.

Marathon windsurfing

Rahul Rastogi from Hyderabad, Telangana, was the first Asian to windsurf 400 km from

Kavaratti, Lakshadweep, to Kozhikode, Kerala. He started on 22 April 1988 and completed the marathon three days later. His average windsurfing timing was 14 hrs a day.

Non-stop rafting expedition

Eight members of the Bihar Adventure Foundation, led by Sanjay Kumar Dutta, set off on a non-stop rafting expedition on the River Ganga. They began from Haridwar, Uttarakhand, on 29 October 1991 and covered 2,400 km in 621 hrs, ending at Calcutta (now Kolkata), West Bengal, on 24 November 1991.

Yachting at the highest altitude

Captain Gautama Dutta from Mumbai, Maharashtra, carted his laser boat to an altitude of 5,460 m (17,913 ft) at Devtal Lake, Uttarakhand, and yachted there on 18 September 1993.

INSV *Mhadei* crew: fastest to complete the Cape2Rio race; (*third from right*) Captain Atool Sinha, skipper

Swimming at the highest altitude

Petty officer R.L. Sharma and leading seaman Dhani Ram swam a distance of 4,746 m (15,571 ft) across the breadth of Kedartal, a glacial lake at an altitude of 4,750 m (15,584 ft) in Uttarakhand, on 25 September 1995.

Oldest to cross English Channel

Srikaanth Viswanathan (b. 15 July 1972) from Bengaluru, Karnataka, crossed the English Channel on 21 July 2018, at the age of 46, becoming the oldest Indian to do so. He started swimming at 5:00 a.m. and completed the crossing at 7:07 p.m., crossing the channel in 14 hrs 7 mins.

Oldest to complete the Triple Crown

Srikaanth Viswanathan (b. 15 July 1972) from Bengaluru, Karnataka, at the age of 47, completed the 20 Bridges Swim in New York City, USA, in 8 hrs 7 mins on 31 August 2019, becoming the oldest Indian to complete the Triple Crown of Open Water Swimming. He had previously swum across the English Channel (14 hrs 7 mins) on 21 July 2018 and the Catalina Channel (13 hrs 4 mins) on 16 August 2019.

Open-water swimmer Shivam Dhananjay Vanmali won the Tenzing Norgay National Adventure Award 2021 for Water Adventure.

Fastest Asian swimmer to cross Gibraltar Strait

Shubham Dhananjay Vanmali (b. 20 December 1995) from Mumbai, Maharashtra, became the fastest Asian swimmer to cross the Strait of Gibraltar, completing 16.7 km from Isla de Tarifa in Spain to Point Cires in Morocco in 3 hrs 16 mins on 14 August 2014. Earlier, Vanmali had also swum the English Channel (England–France), crossing the channel in 12 hrs 42 mins on 4 August 2014 and the 35 km long stretch from Dharamtar to the Gateway of India in Mumbai, Maharashtra, in 8 hrs 1 min. 17 secs on 21 January 2014.

Fastest to swim across the English Channel

Anita Sood from Maharashtra remains the fastest Indian to swim the Great English Channel. She swam in the year 1987 with the time 8 hrs 15 mins (England to France).

Fastest to complete Cape2Rio race

Indian Navy's Captain Atool Sinha (b. 1 August 1968) from Pune, Maharashtra, skippered INSV *Mhadei* in the Trans-Atlantic Intercontinental Cape2Rio Race 2017 and completed the race in a record time of 20 days 19 hrs 27 minutes. The crew began the race on 1 January 2017 at 12:00 p.m. and finished the race on 22 January 2017 at 7:27 a.m., covering a distance of 3,800 nautical miles (7,038 km). The boat had six crew members including the skipper.

Deepest underwater cycling – ocean – solo

Nishant K. Patel (b. 15 February 1982) from Mumbai, Maharashtra, successfully attempted underwater cycling at a depth of 32.7 m (107 ft 3 in.) on 25 October 2016. He covered a distance of 100 m in 6 mins 47 secs in the Bay of Bengal off Puducherry coast. He used a Firefox Vortex 20 cycle and tied weights of 5 kg in the front and 2 kg in the back of the cycle to avoid floating. He had a 12-litre (200 bar) air tank attached for breathing support.

MARATHONS

First to complete Grand-to-Grand Ultramarathon

Arpita Maitra (b. 31 October 1978) from Kolkata, West Bengal, became the first Indian to successfully complete the Grand-to-Grand Ultra (G2G) marathon, a gruelling week-long foot race from the Grand Canyon to the Grand Staircase in the USA, in which she covered the 273 km route in 76 hrs 21 mins 43 secs in six stages from 22 to 28 September 2013.

First 4 Deserts Grand Slam winner

Atul Patki (b. 8 November 1965), a US citizen of Indian origin, completed the 4 Deserts Ultramarathons Series on 8 November 2014. He became the first Indian to complete all four 250 km events in one calendar year.

WR First to complete all Six World Marathons

Siddhartha Ghosh (b. 21 February 1975) from Kolkata, West Bengal, was the first person to complete all Six World Marathons in one calendar year during 2013. He is also the first recipient of the Six Star World Marathon certificate and has received the Six Star World Marathon certificate five times consecutively from 2012 to 2016. The World Marathon Majors consist of six races annually across cities and are accredited by the International Association of Athletics Federations.

First to complete the 7 Emirates Run

M.A. Shaikh (b. 29 September 1974) from Mumbai, Maharashtra, became the first Indian to successfully complete the 7 Emirates Run, an ultramarathon across all seven emirates of the United Arab Emirates (UAE). He covered a distance of 575 km in 12 days from 21 November to 2 December 2014.

First to complete the GQ run

Michelle Kakade (b. 9 October 1968), a long-distance runner from Pune, Maharashtra, became the first person to cover the Golden Quadrilateral (GQ) on foot. The GQ is a highway network connecting Mumbai, Delhi, Kolkata and Chennai. She covered 5,968.4 km in 193 days, 1 hr 9 mins from 21 October 2015 to 1 May 2016.

First to complete the World Marathon Challenge – full marathon

Aditya Raj (b. 22 June 1983) from Gurugram, Haryana, became the first Indian to complete the World Marathon Challenge in 2020, in which runners travel across the globe, completing seven marathons (each 42.2 km) in seven days on seven continents. Starting on 6 February 2020 in Novo, Antarctica, Raj travelled to Cape Town in Africa, Perth in Australia, Dubai in Asia, Madrid in Europe and Brazil in South America, finishing his seventh marathon in Miami, North America, on 12 February 2020. His total running time was 36 hours 47 minutes 36 seconds.

First Ultraman triathlete

Arunaabh Shah (b. 11 August 1990) from Delhi completed the Ultraman Triathlon (a 10 km swim, 421.1 km of cycling and an 84.3 km run) in Australia on 16 May 2016. He is the first Indian to do so in Ultraman's 33-year-long history.

First Ironman triathlon

The first Indian Ironman triathlon was held in Goa with over 1,000 participants on 20 October 2019. Considered the most prestigious endurance triathlon event worldwide, the race included 1.9 km of swimming, 90 km of cycling and 21.1 km of running, which were all done sequentially in a single day. Bishworjit Singh Saikhom from Pune, Maharashtra, completed the triathlon in 4 hrs 42 mins 44 seconds, securing the first place.

A Run for Independence

INDIA AT HER BEST 75 YEARS OF INDEPENDENCE

A marathon was organised by the Border Security Force (BSF) to mark the occasion of 75 years of Indian independence in October 2022. The theme of the marathon was 'Dillan Di Daud Seema Prahari De Naal' which loosely translates to 'heart-to-heart with the border population'. It had participants from the Army and the CAPF along with police personnel and the general public. The participants had to choose from three categories – a full marathon of 42 km, a half-marathon of 21 km and a 10 km run. This marathon was recognized by the Athletics Federation of India. The full marathon was flagged off from the Golden Gate in Amritsar, Punjab; the half-marathon from the War Memorial in New Delhi; and the 10 km run from the village Lahori Mal in Attari, Punjab. All marathons culminated at the Attari–Wagah joint check post. As many as 2,294 people participated in different categories of this event. This event evoked the spirit of patriotism among the participants and raised awareness of the border management task done by the BSF in difficult environments.

Representative image

First differently abled Ironman

Praveen Kumar (b. 17 July 1985) from New Delhi became India's first differently abled Ironman on 17 November 2018 in the Ironman event organized in Langkawi, Malaysia. He completed a 3.86 km long swim in 1 hr 36 mins 7 secs, 180 km of cycling in 7 hrs 49 mins 50 secs and a 42 km long run in 5 hrs 40 mins 55 secs. Kumar is a battle-casualty soldier who was injured during the terrorist attack in Mumbai, Maharashtra, in November 2008.

First to finish the Ultraman World Championship

Gaurav Makkar (b. 26 November 1979) from Gurugram, Haryana, became the first Indian to finish the Ultraman World Championship. The championship is a three-day, 515 km multi-sport race held annually in Hawaii, USA.

A marathon run is for a distance of 42.19 km, a half-marathon is for a distance of 21.09 km and ultramarathons are all runs beyond a marathon distance.

He completed a 10 km swim (in 4 hrs 24 mins), a 421 km bicycle ride (in 16 hrs 20 mins) and an 84 km run (in 8 hrs 56 mins) during 23–25 November 2018. He also completed the Ultraman Florida 2018 during 16–18 February 2018, thereby completing two Ultraman races, the most by an individual in a year.

Longest cross-country run

Long-distance runner Raj Vadgama (b. 18 June 1967) from Mumbai, Maharashtra, successfully undertook 'Bharathon 10,000', a unique run across 70 cities in 17 states of India to spread the message of unity. He covered a distance of 9,902 km from 15 August 2014 to 26 January 2015, making it the first and longest such self-supported cross-country run. He ran 60 km a day for 165 days.

Abhishek Singh Pandher: most consecutive half-marathon distance runs

Longest relay race

As part of its golden jubilee celebrations, while also paying tribute to former president A.P.J. Abdul Kalam, the Border Security Force (BSF) Sector Headquarters in West Bengal organized the BSF Golden Jubilee Baton Relay Race 2015. The event saw 1,785 BSF jawans in commando uniform cover a distance of 174.2 km in relay format in 8 hrs 55 mins 36 secs on 24 August 2015.

Longest distance covered while running – single day

Ullas Narayana from Bengaluru, Karnataka, ran 250.3 km in 24 hours on 1 December 2018, becoming the first to cover this distance in a day. He completed the non-stop run at the 2018 International Association of Ultra Running (IAU) 24-Hour Asia and Oceania Championships in Taipei, Taiwan.

Pragnya Mohan won the gold medal at the 36th National Games Individual Triathlon Event with a timing of 1:07:32.

Most half-marathons in a year

Vijay Boddupalli (b. 1 September 1988) from Chennai, Tamil Nadu, completed 17 half-marathons, the most by an individual in a year, from 1 June 2017 to 31 May 2018. The 17th half-marathon was completed at the H2O Run on 22 April 2018. The half-marathons were conducted across seven states in India.

Most full marathons in a year

Sivabalan Pandian (b. 21 September 1958) from Mumbai, Maharashtra, completed 114 full marathons, the most by an individual in a year, from 6 January to 31 December 2019. These full marathons were conducted at venues both within India and abroad. The count also includes 14 ultramarathons.

Most ultramarathons in a year

Sivabalan Pandian (b. 21 September 1958) from Mumbai, Maharashtra, has run and completed 18 ultramarathons in a year from 16 June 2018 to 23 December 2018.

Most half-marathons by an individual

Adil S. Nargolwala (b. 31 August 1969) from Gurugram, Haryana, completed his 164th half-marathon, the most by an individual, at the Ironman Virtual Club 5 (70.3 (miles/113 km) race on 1 May 2020. These half-marathons were conducted at venues both in India and abroad, and included road as well as trail events. He had also completed at least one marathon in each of the seven continents by 15 January 2019.

Most consecutive half-marathon distance runs

Abhishek Singh Pandher (b. 27 September 1977) from Ahmedabad, Gujarat, completed 685 half-marathon distance (21.09 km) runs in 685 days from 15 July 2020 to 30 May 2022. The runs were conducted in Gujarat and Madhya Pradesh.

Most half-marathons organized in a single day – multiple venues

The Indian Air Force organized half-marathons simultaneously across 100 air force stations as part of the centenary celebrations of the Marshal of the Indian Air Force Arjan Singh on 14 April 2019. The marathon began at 5:30 a.m. and concluded at 9:30 a.m., and saw the participation of 12,600 air force officers. The marathon distance was 21 km and it was conducted in three age categories: below 35 years; between 35 and 45 years; and 45 years and above. Marshal of the Indian Air Force Arjan Singh was the first and only officer of the Indian Air Force to hold a five-star rank.

Most triathlons completed in a year

Adil S. Nargolwala (b. 31 August 1969) from Gurugram, Haryana, completed the most triathlon races in a year in 2019. He completed the Triathlon Sprint at the Delhi International Triathlon 2019, the Triathlon Olympics at the New Delhi Triathlon Championship, the Ironman 70.3 (miles/113 km) in Kazakhstan, the Ironman in Sweden and the Ultraman India Race conducted in Delhi-NCR.

Most visually impaired athletes completing marathons

Six visually impaired athletes –Nandeesh J., Sunita N.D., Renuka Rajput, Kavya Ramesh, Ajay and Mala Kolkar – ran a full marathon in 7 hrs 21 mins on 21 October 2018 at Sree Kanteerava Outdoor Stadium, Bengaluru, Karnataka. Helped by guide runners, the students, who were from the Samarthanam Trust for the Disabled, Bengaluru, Karnataka, were led by their coach, Bhumika Patel.

WR Oldest marathoner

Fauja Singh (b. 1 April 1911) of Indian origin, residing in the UK, is the world's oldest marathon runner. He completed the London Marathon, covering a distance of 42.16 km in 6 hrs 2 mins on 22 April 2012. His marathon record, for age 90-plus, was 5 hrs 40 mins at the Toronto Waterfront Marathon held in Canada in 2013.

Only Asian to complete Ironman triathlons in six continents

Kaustubh Radkar has completed the Ironman triathlon in six continents between March 2014 and November 2016, and is the only Asian to do so. He has completed 25 Ironman triathlons since he ran his first triathlon in 2008.

Fastest at Badwater Ultramarathon

Brij Mohan Sharma (b. 1 January 1974) of the Indian Navy, from Mumbai, Maharashtra, is the fastest Indian at the Badwater Ultramarathon, one of the world's toughest foot races, held in California, USA, from 18 to 20 July 2016. He completed the 217 km run in 40 hrs 47 mins.

MOUNTAIN ADVENTURES

First club

The Himalayan Club was founded in February 1928 in the room of Field Marshal Sir William Birdwood, then commander-in-chief of the British Indian Army.

First mountaineering institute

The first Himalayan Mountaineering Institute at Darjeeling, West Bengal, was formed in 1954 by the then prime minister Jawaharlal Nehru, along with Major Nandu Jayal of the Corps of Engineers of the Indian Army, who was the first director.

First mountaineering expedition

In 1951, Gurdial Guru Singh from Dehradun, Uttarakhand, led an expedition to the 7,120 m (23,360 ft) high Trishul 1 Peak in the Garhwal Himalayas, Uttarakhand.

First to walk the Siachen Glacier

Siachen Glacier, lying along India's border with China, is about 700 sq. km in area and situated at an altitude touching 5,753 m (18,875 ft) above the mean sea level. Under Indian Army protection since 1984, it is the highest battlefield in the world. In 1984, Captain (now Colonel) Ashok Pratap Tanwar became the first person to cover the entire glacier on foot. Appointed as the official photographer of a military formation, he walked the length and breadth of the 76 km long and 3–5 km broad glacier.

First to complete the Seven Summit challenge

Mastan Babu Malli (3 September 1974–24 March 2015) was an Indian mountaineer best known for his 2006 world-record-setting feat of climbing each continent's highest peak in the shortest period at the time – a total of 172 days – with the first climb on 19 January 2006 and the seventh on 10 July 2006. This feat made him the fastest Seven Summiteer in the world by 2006, and the first Indian and South Asian to climb the Seven Summits.

Nanda Devi

Most Himalayan summits

Sange Sherpa from Darjeeling, West Bengal, has six summits to his credit, which include Mt Everest thrice, Aqtash in 1993, Jaloni in 1994 and Nanda Devi in 2000. He is the only person in the world to climb Mt Everest from three faces: from South Col in 1992, North Col in 1996 and Kangshung face in 1999. He received the National Adventure Award in 1998.

First to summit the Volcanic Seven and youngest to climb both the Seven Summits and Volcanic Seven summits

At 34 years, Satyarup Siddhanta (b. 29 April 1983) from Bengaluru, Karnataka, completed the Volcanic Seven Summits (Messner list) on 15 December 2017 becoming the first Indian to do so. The Volcanic Seven Summits include Mt Kilimanjaro (5,895 m/19,341 ft – Africa), Mt Ojos del Salado (6,893 m/22,615 ft – South America), Mt Elbrus (5,642 m/18,510 ft – Europe), Mt Damavand (5,628 m/18,465 ft – Asia), Mt Giluwe (4,367 m/14,327 ft Australasia),

Mt Pico de Orizaba (5,610 m/18,406 ft – North America) and Mt Sidley (4,181–4,285 m/ 13,717–14,058 ft – Antarctica). He also completed the Seven Summits challenge in on 15 January 2019, becoming the youngest Indian to climb both the Volcanic Seven Summits and Seven Summits.

Oldest to climb the Seven Summits

Ankur Bahl (b. 25 January 1961) from Haryana, at 57 years, became the oldest to complete the Messner list of the Seven Summit challenge in 2018, which involves the summiting of the highest mountains in each continent, which include Mt Kilimanjaro (5,895 m/19,341 ft – Africa), Mt Elbrus (5,642 m/18,510 ft – Europe), Mt Denali/McKinley (6,194 m/20,322 ft – North America), Mt Aconcagua (6,961 m/22,838 ft – South America), Mt Everest (8,848.86 m/ 29,031 ft 8 in. – Asia), Mt Kosciuszko (2,228 m/7,310 ft – Australia) and Mt Vinson (4,897 m/16,066 – Antarctica).

First woman to scale Mt Everest

Bachendri Pal (b. 24 May 1954) became the first Indian woman to reach the summit of Mt Everest in 1984.

First Indian to Summit the Three Highest Peaks of South America

Vikas Shukla (b. 6 December 1989) from Bhusawal, Maharashtra, is the first Indian to summit the three highest peaks of South America. He scaled Mt Aconcagua (6,961 m/ 22,838 ft) on 16 February 2019; Mt Pissis (6,793 m/22,287 ft) on 24 February 2019; and Mt Ojos del Salado (6,893 m/22,615 ft) on 1 March 2019.

First to summit Mt Everest without supplemental oxygen

Phu Dorjee was the first to summit Mt Everest (then measured at 8,848m/29,028 ft) without supplemental oxygen on 9 May 1984 through the South-east Ridge route. He was part of the third Everest expedition led by Captain M.S. Kohli in 1965. Dorjee died in 1987 on the Kangchenjunga Expedition of the Assam Rifles.

First to summit four unscaled peaks above 6,000 m

A team of eight mountaineers from the Nehru Institute of Mountaineering, in collaboration with Uttarakhand Tourism Development Board, summited four unscaled and unnamed peaks in the Gangotri region of the Garhwal Himalayas in 8 days between 9 October and 16 October 2018. The team, led by Colonel Amit Bisht, SM, scaled peaks 6,566 m (21,542 ft), 6,557 m (21,512 ft), 6,126 m (20,098 ft) and 6,086 m (19,967 ft) high.

Mountaineer Naina Dhakad won the Tenzing Norgay National Adventure Award 2021 for Land Adventure.

Oldest to scale Mt Everest

- *Men*: S.C. Negi (b. 8 March 1950), additional deputy inspector general of the Border Security Force, became the oldest to scale Mt Everest on 24 May 2006 at the age of 56 years.
- *Women*: Sangeeta Sindhi (b. 9 February 1965) from Gurugram, Haryana, became the oldest Indian woman to summit Mt Everest on 19 May 2018 at the age of 53 years.

Fastest scaling of Mt Everest

Kazi Sherpa climbed Mt Everest in 20 hrs 24 mins in 1998, breaking the earlier record of 22 hrs 29 mins.

Fastest to scale most 8,000 m peaks

Baljeet Kaur became the first Indian to summit four out of the 14 peaks of 8,000 metres in less than a month. The 27-year-old from Solan, Himachal Pradesh, started her journey by summitting Mt Annapurna I (8,091 m) on 28 April 2022 and Mt Kanchenjunga (8,586 m) on 12 May 2022 and became the first Indian woman to summit these peaks in less than two weeks. She continued her journey two weeks later and summitted Everest (8,849 m) on 21 May 2022 and Mt Lhotse (8,517 m) on 22 May 2022, the first and fourth highest mountains in the world respectively.

TREKKING

First women's team to complete Snowman Trek

A team of 11 women led by iconic Indian mountaineer Bachendri Pal successfully completed the Snowman Trek in Bhutan, considered one of the toughest in the world. Starting at Paro Valley on 4 June 2011, the trek was completed at Sephu Village on 27 June 2011. It involved crossing 11 high mountain passes and other difficult terrain. This expedition was sponsored by the Tata Steel Adventure Foundation in Jamshedpur, Jharkhand.

Oldest trekker

Gopal Vasudev Lele (b. 8 March 1932) from Pune, Maharashtra, then 81 years of age, made a week-long trek to Rupin Pass (4,680 m/15,354 ft) in Himachal Pradesh from 21 to 28 September 2013. He completed a 70-degree climb. Lele had completed 20 treks since 1972.

Fastest Everest Base Camp trek by a differently abled person

Mahinder Singh Raghuwanshi (b. 2 October 1987) completed the longest trekking in Nepal, with a prosthetic leg, to the Everest Base Camp from an altitude of 2,859.9 m to 5,642.7 m

(9,383 ft to 18,513 ft). He started his trek on 28 April 2018 and ended it on 11 May 2018, covering 150 km in 14 days. He started his trek from Lukla, Nepal, and covered Kala Patthar (5,550 m/18,209 ft), Cho La (5,368 m/ 17,612 ft), Gokyo (4,790 m/15,715 ft), Renjo La (5,360 m/17,585 ft) and Everest Base Camp (5,364 m/17,598 ft). He was accompanied by a friend and a guide.

Longest desert trek – group

The 22nd battalion of the Mahar Regiment, part of the Golden Katar Division of the Indian Army, successfully completed the 'Golden Katar Desert Trek 2017–18'. A ten-member team of soldiers trekked 700 km through the Thar Desert, Rajasthan, in 21 days from 22 December 2017 to 12 January 2018. The arduous journey on foot through the Great Indian Desert began from Bakhasar, Barmer District, and concluded in Gajjewala, Bikaner District, Rajasthan.

THE POLES

First at the Arctic

Sharat Kumar Roy (1897–1962) was the first to reach the Arctic as a member of the Rawson-Macmillan Arctic Expedition in 1927.

First at Antarctica

Meher Moos (b. 1944) from Maharashtra was the first woman to set foot on the icy continent of Antarctica way back in 1976, long before any of the scientific expeditions went there.

First to reach North Pole by surface

Dr M.R. Shetty from Bangalore (now Bengaluru), Karnataka, reached the North Pole by surface on 5 August 2001 with a 100-strong team, by *Yamal*, a nuclear-powered ice-breaking ship, starting from Longyearbyen, Svalbard's administrative centre in Norway, on 1 August 2001.

First organization to reach 'three' poles

Indian Navy teams have been to three poles: Mt Everest, the vertical pole, in 2004; the Geographic South Pole in 2006; and the North Pole in 2008. Commander Satyabrata Dam and two POMAs (petty officer medical assistants) Vikas Kumar and Rakesh Kumar were the first to reach all three poles.

First at the Geographic South Pole

On 17 January 1989, Colonel J.K. Bajaj became the first Indian to reach the Geographic South Pole at 22:15 hrs (GMT). He was the only Indian in this 11-member international expedition that skied over 1,200 km in 50 days to the Geographic South Pole. The five-nation expedition was organized by Mountain Travel, USA, and the International Adventure Network, Canada.

First route recce to the South Pole

Major Anand Swaroop and Captain R.R. Bhat of the Corps of Engineers of the Indian Army were the first to recce the route from the Maitri base, Antarctica, to the Polar/Antarctic Plateau in 2000.

First to ski to the North Pole

Ajeet Bajaj is the first Indian to ski to the North Pole and complete the polar trilogy, which entails skiing to the North Pole and South Pole, and crossing the Greenland Ice Sheet. He started his ski expedition to the North Pole from the Russian Arctic Polar Research Station called Barneo and reached the North Pole on 26 April 2006, along with three other skiers.

Longest stay in Antarctica

Shaik Mastan (b. 12 February 1968) from Gudavalli Village, Guntur District, Andhra Pradesh, had the longest uninterrupted stay of 490 days in Antarctica at the Indian Antarctic research station, Bharati, from 16 November 2011 to 19 March 2013. He was a member of the 35th Indian expedition to Antarctica.

Representative image

Trekking Banned in Kangra District

The district of Kangra, Himachal Pradesh, has several mountain passes that are used by *gaddi* shepherds to cross to the other side. However, as the weather is extremely unpredictable and is often accompanied by mist and high-velocity winds, these passes become a hotspot for tragedies. In view of the tragedies that occurred in Kinnaur and Lahaul-Spiti, the deputy commissioner of the Kangra district has banned trekking above 3,000 m to ensure public safety. Several lapses on the part of the trekkers led to causalities or being stranded in horrible weather conditions, which made the government take this step.

The average temperature during summer at the North Pole is 0 degree Celsius and at the South Pole is -28.2 degrees Celsius.

STATES AND UNION TERRITORIES

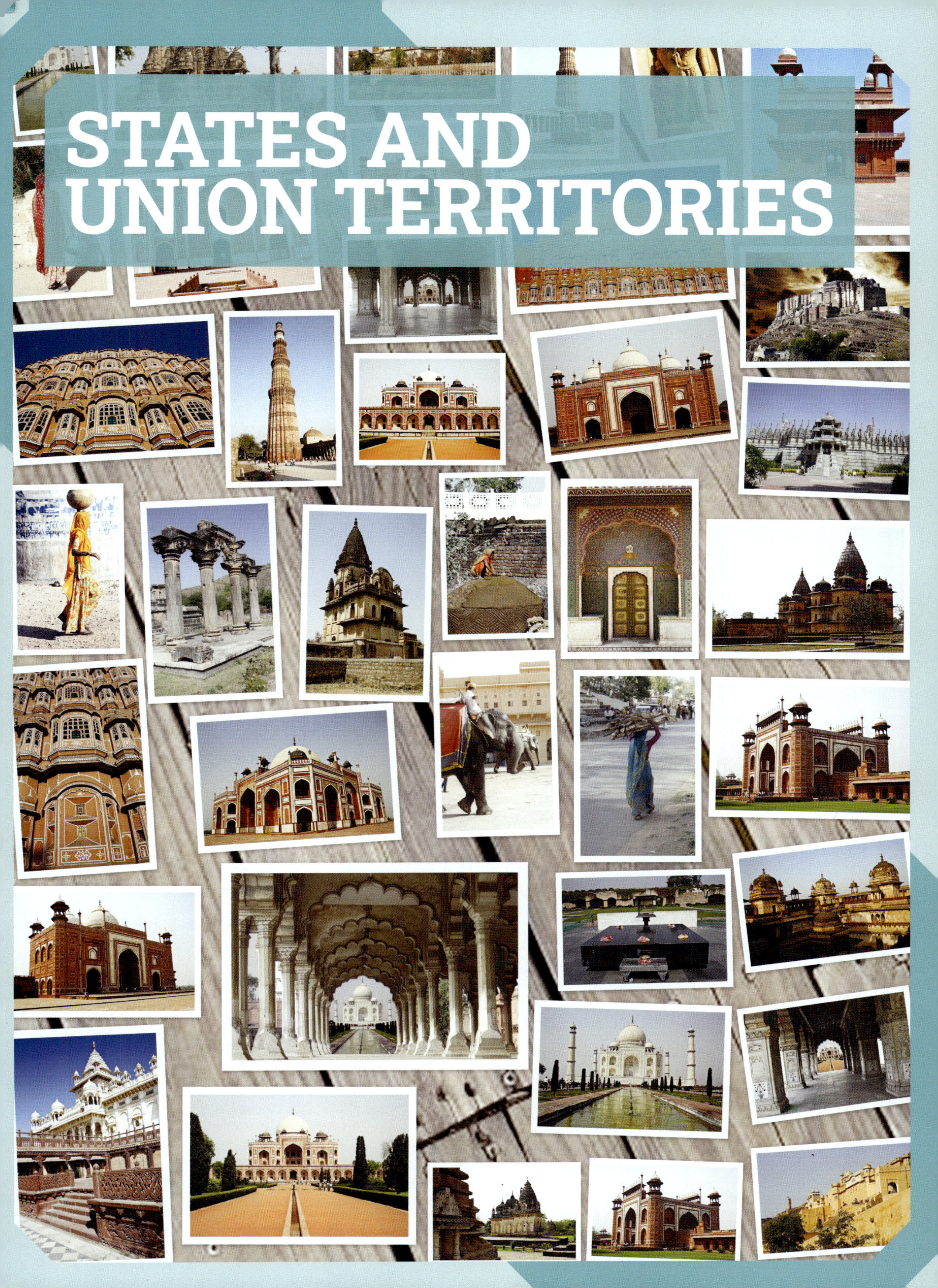

STATES AND UNION TERRITORIES

India is a Union of states with a parliamentary system of government. It has 28 states and eight Union Territories. Here is a ready reckoner for each.

STATES

ANDHRA PRADESH

- **Area:** 160,205 sq. km
- **Capital:** Amaravati
- **Population:** 49.67 million
- **FDI Equity Inflow***: ₹4,056.89
- **Main Language:** Telugu
- **Literacy Rate:** 67 per cent
- **Higher Education:** Universities: 41; Colleges: 2,750
- **Constitution/Assembly:** Bicameral. Legislative council: 58; Legislative assembly: 175
- **Governor:** Biswa Bhusan Harichandan
- **Chief Minister:** Y.S. Jagan Mohan Reddy
- **Agriculture:** NFSA Ranking**: 3; major crops: Rice, cotton, maize and tobacco. The state is the largest producer of mangoes in India.
- **Minerals:** Bauxite, copper ore, manganese, coal and limestone
- **Industries:** Textiles, shipbuilding, aquaculture, cement, automobile and auto components
- **Roads:** National highways: 8,207 km; No. of National highways: 54
- **Railway Route Length:** 3,965 km
- **Airports:** International: 1; Domestic: 4; Visakhapatnam also has a bustling port.
- **Art/Culture:** Kuchipudi, a dance-drama style, has a long history in the region. Folk theatre forms such as Yakshagana, Burra Katha and Veethi Bhagavatamu, and *kalamkari* fabrics are specialities of this state.
- **Nature Reserves:** National parks: 3; Wildlife sanctuaries: 13
- **Tourism:** The Tirumala–Tirupati Temple, Orvakal Rock Garden, Talakona Falls, Kondaveedu Fort and Borra Caves
- **State Symbols:** bird: Rose-ringed parakeet (*Psittacula krameri*); flower: Jasmine (*Jasminum* spp.); tree: Neem (*Azadirachta indica*); animal: Blackbuck (*Antilope cervicapra*)
- **Do Not Miss!** The INS *Kursura*, after being decommissioned, was turned into a submarine museum at Visakhapatnam. This unique museum is open to public to see the weaponry and machinery used on submarines.
- **Swachh Survekshan Ranking***:** 7>
- **UNESCO Heritage (Intangible cultural, historical or other sites):** None
- **Sustainable Development Index Score****:** 72
- **Smart Cities:** 4
- **Air Pollution Index:** 99 (Satisfactory)

Talakona Falls, Tirupati District, Andhra Pradesh

ARUNACHAL PRADESH

- **Area:** 83,743 sq. km
- **Capital:** Itanagar
- **Population:** 1.25 million
- **FDI Equity Inflow:** ₹40.94
- **Main Languages:** Hindi, Assamese, Bengali, Nepalese, Nisi, Dafla
- **Literacy Rate:** 65.4 per cent
- **Higher Education:** Universities: 10; Colleges: 39
- **Constitution/Assembly:** Unicameral. Legislative assembly: 60
- **Governor:** Brigadier Dr B.D. Mishra (Retd)
- **Chief Minister:** Pema Khandu
- **Agriculture:** NFSA Ranking: 28; major crops: Rice, potato, tea, apple and pineapple
- **Minerals:** Coal, limestone, dolomites, graphite, lead, quartzite, petroleum, natural gas
- **Industries:** Petrochemicals, textiles and handicrafts
- **Roads:** National highways: 2,537 km; No. of National highways: 13
- **Railway Route Length:** 12 km
- **Airports:** Domestic: 2
- **Art/Culture:** Carpet making, wood carving and Apatani tribal dance

* Foreign Direct Investment in ₹Crores; from October 2019 to June 2022.
**Comprehensive country-level index; Chandigarh and Puducherry not listed in the country-level index due to variation in the scoring criteria. Separate ranks and scores generated for these UTs in all categories.

Representative image

Medicine from the Sky

Arunachal Pradesh launched its first drone-based healthcare services on 15 August 2022. The launch took place from Seppa to Chayang Tajo in East Kameng District. This pilot project will be developed further to provide not just healthcare but also assistance in agriculture and disaster management. The World Economic Forum (WEF) was involved in the development of this project, and financial and technical support was lent by SAMRIDH Healthcare Blended Financial Facility, an initiative supported by the United States Agency for International Development (USAID). The project was executed by Redwing Labs, a Bengaluru-based start-up, and implemented by IPE Global.

- **Nature Reserves:** National parks: 2; Wildlife sanctuaries: 13
- **Tourism:** Tawang Monastery, Parashuram Kund, Malinathan and Itanagar
- **State Symbols:** bird: Hornbill (*Buceros bicornis*); flower: Foxtail orchid (*Rynchostylis retusa*); tree: Hollong (*Dipterocarpus macrocarpus*); animal: Mithun (*Bos frontalis*)
- **Do Not Miss!** The eco-friendly Ziro Festival of Music in Ziro Valley brings together music and nature.
- **Swachh Survekshan Ranking:** 13<
- **UNESCO Heritage (Intangible cultural, historical or other sites):** None
- **Sustainable Development Index Score:** 60
- **Smart Cities:** 2
- **Air Pollution Index:** Not applicable†

ASSAM

- **Area:** 78,438 sq. km
- **Capital:** Dispur
- **Population:** 31.20 million
- **FDI Equity Inflow:** ₹147.67
- **Main Languages:** Assamese and Bengali
- **Literacy Rate:** 72.2 per cent
- **Higher Education:** Universities: 26; Colleges: 558
- **Constitution/Assembly:** Unicameral. Legislative assembly: 126
- **Governor:** Prof. Jagdish Mukhi
- **Chief Minister:** Himanta Biswa Sarma
- **Agriculture:** NFSA Ranking: 27; major crops: Rice, jute, tea, cotton, sugar cane and maize
- **Minerals:** Coal, silica sand, limestone, china clay, iron ore and granite, petroleum and natural gas
- **Industries:** Tea, cement, textiles, sericulture and oil refining
- **Roads:** National highways: 4,077 km; No. of National highways: 38
- **Railway Route Length:** 2,519 km
- **Airports:** International: 1; Domestic: 5
- **Art/Culture:** Crafts include handloom, sericulture, and bamboo and cane items. Muga silk is produced only here in the world.
- **Nature Reserves:** National parks: 5; Wildlife sanctuaries: 18
- **Tourism:** Kamakhya Temple, Navagraha Temple, Manas National Park and Tiger Reserve and, Kaziranga National Park, Hajo and Sualkuchi
- **State Symbols:** bird: White-winged wood duck (*Asarcornis scutulata*); flower: Foxtail orchid (*Rynchostylis retusa*); tree: Hollong (*Dipterocarpus macrocarpus*); animal: One-horned rhinoceros (*Rhinoceros unicornis*)
- **Do Not Miss!** Majuli, the world's largest river island and the Kaziranga National Park, which is home to the famed Indian one-horned rhinoceros
- **Swachh Survekshan Ranking:** 9<
- **UNESCO Heritage (Intangible cultural, historical or other sites):** Kaziranga National Park and Manas Wildlife Sanctuary
- **Sustainable Development Index Score:** 57
- **Smart City:** 1
- **Air Pollution Index:** 67 (Satisfactory)

Golden langur at Manas National Park, Assam

***2022 Rankings; > = States with more than 100 Urban Local Bodies (ULBs); < = States with fewer than 100 ULBs; Only 13 states are ranked. Union Territories are not ranked.
****SDI score scale: Achiever: 100; Front Runner: 65–99; Performer: 50–64; Aspirant: 0–49

BIHAR

- **Area:** 94,163 sq. km
- **Capital:** Patna
- **Population:** 104.09 million
- **FDI Equity Inflow:** ₹1,257.20
- **Main Language:** Hindi
- **Literacy Rate:** 61.8 per cent
- **Higher Education:** Universities: 35; Colleges: 874
- **Constitution/Assembly:** Bicameral. Legislative council: 75; Legislative assembly: 243
- **Governor:** Phagu Chauhan
- **Chief Minister:** Nitish Kumar
- **Agriculture:** NFSA Ranking: 8; major crops: Rice, wheat, lentils, sugar cane and jute
- **Minerals:** Steatite, pyrites, quartzite, mica and limestone
- **Industries:** Food and beverages, plastic and rubber, tobacco, textiles, leather and dairy
- **Roads:** National highways: 5,940 km; No. of National highways: 54
- **Railway Route Length:** 3,803 km
- **Airports:** International: 1; Domestic: 1
- **Art/Culture:** Chhat, a festival of sun worship; Madhubani art, a traditional painting made with vegetable dyes
- **Nature Reserves:** National park: 1; Wildlife sanctuaries: 12
- **Tourism:** Rajgir, Nalanda, Bodhgaya, Patna (ancient city of Pataliputra) and Madhubani
- **State Symbols:** bird: House sparrow (*Passer domesticus*); flower: Kachnar (*Phanera variegata*); tree: Peepul (*Ficus religiosa*); animal: Gaur (*Bos gaurus*)
- **Do Not Miss!** The annual Sonepur Cattle Fair held during November–December is the largest cattle fair in Asia.
- **Swachh Survekshan Ranking:** 11>
- **UNESCO Heritage (Intangible cultural, historical or other sites):** The Mahabodhi Temple complex at Bodhgaya and the archaeological site of Nalanda Mahavihara, southeast of Patna
- **Sustainable Development Index Score:** 52
- **Smart Cities:** 4
- **Air Pollution Index:** 88 (Satisfactory)

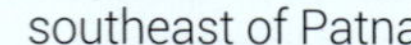

From Bottles to Bangles

The Bihar government announced a programme to facilitate rural women in making glass bangles out of impounded liquor bottles. The Prohibition Department of the state has sanctioned ₹1 crore for the setting up of bangle-making factories. JEEVIKA, a pre-existing initiative of the Bihar government that works towards alleviating poverty is funded by the World Bank, and women from this group are already being trained to make these bangles. The first unit will be set up in Patna. Bottles with the capacity to hold nearly 13.87 lakh litres of liquor were seized in Bihar from January to May in 2022. The trained women will be provided with the powdered glass of liquor bottles along with the other raw materials required to create the bangles. This move is being applauded for its waste recycling aspect while also creating a livelihood for numerous women.

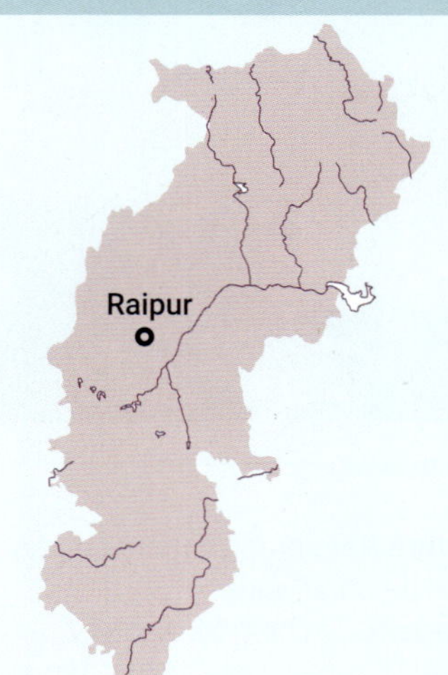

CHHATTISGARH

- **Area:** 135,194 sq. km
- **Capital:** Raipur
- **Population:** 25.54 million
- **FDI Equity Inflow:** ₹7.53
- **Main Language:** Hindi
- **Literacy Rate:** 70.3 per cent
- **Higher Education:** Universities: 28; Colleges: 810
- **Constitution/Assembly:** Unicameral. Legislative assembly: 91
- **Governor:** Anusuiya Uikey
- **Chief Minister:** Bhupesh Baghel
- **Agriculture:** NFSA Ranking:22; major crops: Rice, maize, wheat, niger seed (*ramtil*), groundnut and pulses. The state has one of the biggest collections of rice germ plasm.
- **Minerals:** Coal, iron ore, limestone, bauxite and dolomite
- **Industries:** Cement, mining, steel, aluminium and electricity
- **Roads:** National highways: 3,620 km; No. of National highways: 20
- **Railway Route Length:** 1,170 km
- **Airport:** Domestic: 3
- **Art/Culture:** Bamboo art, bell metal (*dhokra*), Kosa silk, wrought iron and terracotta statues
- **Nature Reserves:** National parks: 3; Wildlife sanctuaries: 11
- **Tourism:** Bastar, Chitrakote Falls, Danteshwari Temple, Kutumsar Cave, Tirathgarh Falls and Kanger Ghati National Park

[†] Does not have an Air Quality Index station; Air pollution Index (as per the most crowded station of the capital city of the state/UT; Last updated on 15 September 2022.

Danteshwari Temple, Durg, Chhattisgarh

- **State Symbols:** bird: Hill mynah (*Gracula religiosa*); tree: Sal (*Shorea robusta*); animal: Wild buffalo (*Bubalis bubalis*)
- **Do Not Miss!** The Chitrakote Falls: 29.2 m (96 ft) high waterfalls of the River Indravati, popularly called the 'Niagara Falls of India'
- **Swachh Survekshan Ranking:** 1
- **UNESCO Heritage (Intangible cultural, or historical, or other sites):** None
- **Sustainable Development Index Score:** 61
- **Smart Cities:** 3
- **Air Pollution index:** 60 (Satisfactory)

GOA

- **Area:** 3,702 sq. km
- **Capital:** Panaji
- **Population:** 1.45 million
- **FDI Equity Inflow:** ₹866.39
- **Main Language:** Konkani
- **Literacy Rate:** 88.7 per cent
- **Higher Education:** Universities: 3; Colleges: 58
- **Constitution/Assembly:** Unicameral. Legislative assembly: 40
- **Governor:** P.S. Sreedharan Pillai
- **Chief Minister:** Pramod Sawant
- **Agriculture:** NFSA Ranking: 25; major crops: Rice, coconut and cashew nut
- **Minerals:** Iron ore, manganese ore, bauxite and laterite stones
- **Industries:** Agriculture, mining, tourism and hospitality
- **Roads:** National highways: 299 km; No. of National highways: 6
- **Railway Route Length:** 69 km
- **Airport:** International: 1
- **Art/Culture:** Woodcarving, bamboo, seashell and brass crafts, papier mâché and wooden lacquered ware
- **Nature Reserves:** National park: 1; Wildlife sanctuaries: 6
- **Tourism:** Baga, Anjuna, Palolem and Miramar beaches, Basilica of Bom Jesus and Se Cathedral churches in Old Goa, Fort Aguada and Chapora Fort
- **State Symbols:** bird: Ruby-throated yellow bulbul (*Pycnonotus gularis*); flower: Red jasmine (*Jasminum beesianum*); tree: Matti (*Terminalia elliptica*); animal: Gaur (*Bos gaurus*)
- **Do Not Miss!** The 310 m (1,017 ft) high Dudhsagar Falls on the River Mandovi, overlooking a small railway track section on the Madgaon–Belagavi route
- **Swachh Survekshan Ranking:** 2<
- **UNESCO Heritage (Intangible cultural, historical or other sites):** Churches and Convents of Goa, and the Western Ghats (shared)
- **Sustainable Development Index Score:** 72
- **Smart City:** 1
- **Air pollution index:** Not applicable†

Palolem Beach, Goa

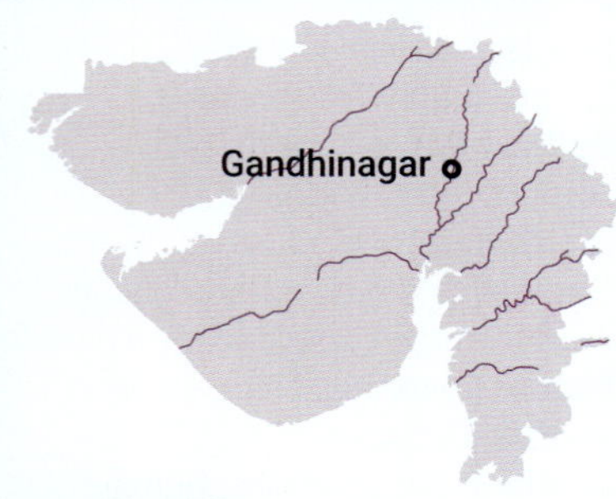

GUJARAT

- **Area:** 196,024 sq. km
- **Capital:** Gandhinagar
- **Population:** 60.38 million
- **FDI Equity Inflow:** ₹2,26,658.54
- **Main Language:** Gujarati
- **Literacy Rate:** 78.03 per cent
- **Higher Education:** Universities: 76; Colleges: 2,275
- **Constitution/Assembly:** Unicameral. Legislative assembly: 182
- **Governor:** Acharya Devvrat
- **Chief Minister:** Bhupendra Patel
- **Agriculture:** NFSA Ranking: 4; major crops: Cotton, rice, jowar, maize, tobacco and groundnut
- **Minerals:** Lignite, bauxite, manganese, silica and limestone
- **Industries:** Petroleum, diamond, cement, agriculture and textiles. Gujarat is the largest producer of denim in India.
- **Roads:** National highways: 7,885 km; No. of National highways: 43
- **Railway Route Length:** 5,327 km
- **Airports:** International: 2; Domestic: 7
- **Art/Culture:** Needlework and Kachchhi embroidery, pottery, Patola weaves and furnishings. Ahmedabad hosts the annual International Kite Festival.
- **Nature Reserves:** National parks: 4; Wildlife sanctuaries: 23
- **Tourism:** Gir Forest National Park/ Wildlife Sanctuary, Lakshmi Vilas Palace, Dwarka, Somnath Temple, Sabarmati Ashram and Marine National Park, Patan
- **State Symbols:** bird: Greater flamingo (*Phoenicopterus roseus*); flower: Marigold (*Tagetes* spp.); tree: Banyan(*Ficus benghalensis*); animal: Asiatic lion (*Panthera leo persica*)
- **Do Not Miss!** The white sands and salty marshes of Kachchh, nestled between the Arabian Sea and the Thar Desert
- **Swachh Survekshan Ranking:** 6>
- **UNESCO Heritage (Intangible cultural, historical or other sites):** Champaner–Pavagadh Archaeological Park, the historic city of Ahmedabad, Western Ghats (shared), Rani Ki Vav (step well) at Patan, and Dholavira (a Harappan city)
- **Sustainable Development Index Score:** 69
- **Smart Cities:** 6
- **Air Pollution Index:** 105 (Moderate)

Representative image

Modhera Lights up with Solar Power

Modhera, a village in the Mehsana District of Gujarat, was declared the first 24 x 7 solar-powered village in India on 9 October 2022 by Prime Minister Narendra Modi. A ground-mounted solar power plant and 1,300 rooftop solar panel systems of 1 kW each on homes and government buildings have been set up to generate electricity. The famed Sun Temple in Modhera will also get heritage lighting and 3D projections that run on solar power. Besides, the first grid-connected mega-watt hour-scale battery energy storage system (BESS) here will ensure power supply after sunset with the huge advantages of reducing the carbon footprint and being non-polluting. The project investment was ₹80.66 crore in two phases by both the state and Central governments. Modhera is also the first village to have an solar-based electric charging station. Cleaner energy generation and renewable resources all the way!

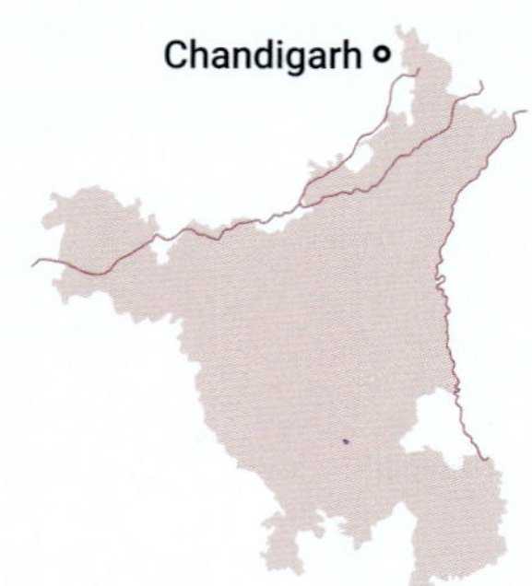

HARYANA

- **Area:** 44,212 sq. km
- **Capital:** Chandigarh
- **Population:** 25.35 million
- **FDI Equity Inflow:** ₹46,917.77
- **Main Language:** Hindi
- **Literacy Rate:** 75.6 per cent
- **Higher Education:** Universities: 53; Colleges: 1,087
- **Constitution/Assembly:** Unicameral. Legislative assembly: 90

Morni Hills, Haryana

- **Governor:** Bandaru Dattatreya
- **Chief Minister:** Manohar Lal Khattar
- **Agriculture:** NFSA Ranking: 20; major crops: Wheat, rice, sugar cane, cotton, oilseeds, pulses, mustard and maize
- **Minerals:** Baryte, slate, copper ore, marble, limestone and quartz
- **Industries:** Textiles, agriculture, manufacturing of automobiles and auto components, and information technology
- **Roads:** National highways: 3,259 km; No. of National highways: 39
- **Railway Route Length:** 1,703 km
- **Airports:** Domestic: 2
- **Art/Culture:** Traditionally rich in folklore, it is the backdrop of the Mahabharata by Vedavyasa. Saangh (folk theatre) and shisha embroidery are also popular.
- **Nature Reserves:** National parks: 2; Wildlife sanctuaries: 7
- **Tourism:** Surajkund, Damdama Lake, Kurukshetra and Morni Hills
- **State Symbols:** bird: Black francolin (*Francolinus francolinus*); flower: Lotus (*Nelumbo nucifera*); tree: Peepul (*Ficus religiosa*); animal: Blackbuck (*Antilope cervicapra*)
- **Do Not Miss!** The National Cactus and Succulent Botanical Garden and Research Centre at Panchkula has more than 3,500 species of endangered and rare cacti. It is considered the biggest such garden in Asia and organizes an annual cactus show in the month of March.
- **Swachh Survekshan Ranking:** 5<
- **UNESCO Heritage (Intangible cultural, historical or other sites):** None
- **Sustainable Development Index Score:** 67
- **Smart Cities:** 2
- **Air pollution index:** 143 (Moderate)

HIMACHAL PRADESH

- **Area:** 55,673 sq. km
- **Capital:** Shimla
- **Population:** 6.86 million
- **FDI Equity Inflow:** ₹1,254.81
- **Main Languages:** Hindi and Pahari
- **Literacy Rate:** 82.8 per cent
- **Higher Education:** Universities: 27; Colleges: 344
- **Constitution/Assembly:** Unicameral. Legislative assembly: 68
- **Governor:** Rajendra Vishwanath Arlekar
- **Chief Minister:** Jai Ram Thakur
- **Agriculture:** NFSA Ranking: 11; major crops: Rice, wheat, maize, pulses and sugar cane
- **Minerals:** Antimony, gypsum, manganese, limestone, baryte, rock salt and silica sand
- **Industries:** Agriculture, food and beverages, cement, pharmaceuticals and hydroelectricity
- **Roads:** National highways: 2,607 km; No. of National highways: 19
- **Railway Route Length:** 312 km
- **Airports:** Domestic: 3
- **Art/Culture:** Folk plays such as Swang, Banthra and Bhagtu, and the ancient architecture across Kullu and Kinnaur districts
- **Nature Reserves:** National parks: 5; Wildlife sanctuaries: 28
- **Tourism:** Shimla, Manali, Lahaul and Spiti, Baspa Valley, Seraj and Tirthan
- **State Symbols:** bird: Western tragopan (*Tragopan melanocephalus*); flower: Pink rhododendron (*Rhododendron campanulatum*); tree: Deodar (*Cedrus deodara*); animal: Snow leopard (*Uncia uncia*)
- **Do Not Miss!** Chandra Tal or the 'lake of the moon', a high-altitude glacial lake situated at more than 4,267 m (14,000 ft) above the mean sea level in Lahaul and Spiti District
- **Swachh Survekshan Ranking:** 4<
- **UNESCO Heritage (Intangible cultural, or historical, or other sites):** Kalka–Shimla Railway (part of Mountain Railways of India) and Great Himalayan National Park conservation area
- **Sustainable Development Index Score:** 74
- **Smart Cities:** 2
- **Air Pollution Index:** 124 (Moderate)

Kalka–Shimla Railway (part of Mountain Railways of India)

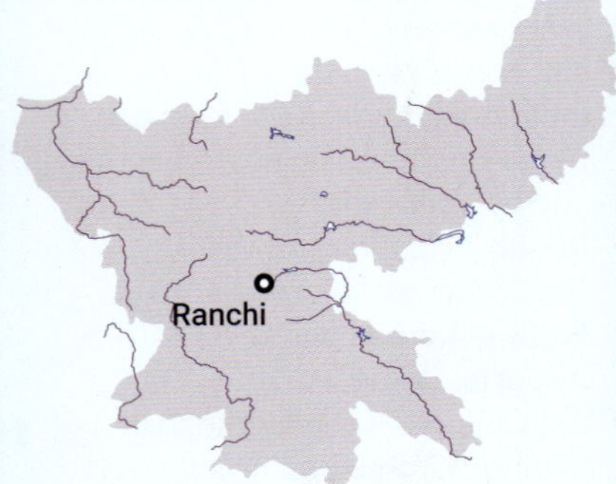

JHARKHAND

- **Area:** 79,714 sq. km
- **Capital:** Ranchi
- **Population:** 32.98 million
- **FDI Equity Inflow:** ₹19,290.45
- **Main Language:** Hindi, Santhali
- **Literacy Rate:** 66.4 per cent
- **Higher Education:** Universities: 32; Colleges: 323
- **Constitution/Assembly:** Unicameral. Legislative assembly: 81
- **Governor:** Ramesh Bais
- **Chief Minister:** Hemant Soren
- **Agriculture:** NFSA Ranking: 12; major crops: Rice, millet, maize, wheat, pulses, gram and mustard
- **Minerals:** Coal, iron ore, limestone, copper ore, bauxite, pyrite and china clay
- **Industries:** Locomotives, cement, steel, aluminium, mining and quarrying, and sericulture
- **Roads:** National highways: 3,430 km; No. of National highways: 31
- **Railway Route Length:** 2,573 km
- **Airport:** Domestic: 3
- **Art/Culture:** Santhali dance, wood and bamboo work, Paitkar paintings, tribal ornaments and stone carving
- **Nature Reserves:** National park: 1; Wildlife sanctuaries: 11
- **Tourism:** Ichagarh Bird Sanctuary, Topchanchi Lake, Palna Dam, Dassam Falls, Chachro Crocodile Breeding Centre, Jawaharlal Nehru Zoological Garden, Sir Dorabji Tata Park, and Surya Mandir
- **State Symbols:** bird: Koel (*Eudynamys scolopaceus*); flower: Palash (*Butea monosperma*); tree: Sal (*Shorea robusta*); animal: Indian elephant (*Elephas maximus indicus*)
- **Do Not Miss!** Experience the Paitkar art form of Amadubi Village, East Singhbhum District: the artists paint on soiled or used papers, and on scrolls made from leaves and bark, applying vermilion and natural dyes with needles or the hairs of a goat.
- **Swachh Survekshan Ranking:** 2<
- **UNESCO Heritage (Intangible cultural, historical or other sites):** Chhau dance (shared)
- **Sustainable Development Index Score:** 56
- **Smart City:** 1
- **Air Pollution Index:** Not applicable†

Sir Dorabji Tata Park, Jamshedpur, Jharkhand

Bengaluru

KARNATAKA

- **Area:** 191,791 sq. km
- **Capital:** Bengaluru
- **Population:** 61.10 million
- **FDI Equity Inflow:** ₹2,72,908.46
- **Main Language:** Kannada
- **Literacy Rate:** 75.4 per cent
- **Higher Education:** Universities: 69; Colleges: 4,047
- **Constitution/Assembly:** Bicameral. Legislative council: 75; Legislative assembly: 224
- **Governor:** Thaawar Chand Gehlot
- **Chief Minister:** Basavaraj Bommai
- **Agriculture:** NFSA Ranking: 9; major crops: Rice, ragi, sorghum, pulses, pearl millet and pigeon pea
- **Minerals:** Iron ore, magnesite, dunite, chromite, limestone and china clay
- **Industries:** Automobile, cement, agro-industries, aerospace, information technology, biotech and heavy engineering
- **Roads:** National highways: 7,656 km; No. of National highways: 45
- **Railway** Route Length: 3,572 km
- **Airports:** International: 2; Domestic: 6
- **Art/Culture:** Dance forms like Veeragase, Dollu Kunitha and Kamsale Nrutya, and Yakshagana folk theatre
- **Nature Reserves:** National parks: 5; Wildlife sanctuaries: 35
- **Tourism:** Hampi, Kodagu, Bengaluru, Mysuru, Gokarna and Murudeshwar
- **State Symbols:** bird: Indian roller (*Coracias indica*); flower: Lotus (*Nelumbo nucifera*); tree: Sandalwood (*Santalum album*); animal: Indian elephant (*Elephas maximus indicus*)
- **Do Not Miss!** The 643 sq. km Nagarhole National Park, which flanks the River Kabini, is a wildlife reserve that houses many species including tigers and elephants. This protected region includes Bandipur National Park.
- **Swachh Survekshan Ranking:** 12>
- **UNESCO Heritage (Intangible cultural, historical or other sites):**

Anegundi: A Village Older than Hampi

A temple on wheels in Anegundi

Anegundi, close to the UNESCO World Heritage Site Hampi, was previously known as Kishkindha and served as the capital of the Vijayanagara dynasty before it shifted to Hampi. When the king of Vijayanagara lost his kingdom to British rule, he, along with his family, sought refuge in Anegundi. Anegundi has been in Hampi's shadow as a tourist attraction, yet now it is slowly gaining traction. It has also started becoming known as the birthplace of Lord Hanuman. The Huchappayan Matha Temple, the Ranganatha Temple and old ruins of the Aramane Palace are a few of the heritage sites worth visiting there. It is located on one of the oldest plateaus on Earth, estimated to be around 3,000 million years old, and remains of Neolithic civilizations have been excavated in its surrounding areas as well.

Western Ghats (shared), Group of Monuments at Hampi and Group of Monuments at Pattadakal
- **Sustainable Development Index Score:** 72
- **Smart Cities:** 7
- **Air Pollution Index:** 84 (Satisfactory)

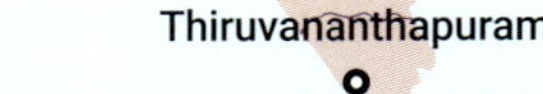

KERALA

- **Area:** 38,863 sq. km
- **Capital:** Thiruvananthapuram
- **Population:** 33.39 million
- **FDI Equity Inflow:** ₹4,806.38
- **Main Language:** Malayalam
- **Literacy Rate:** 94 per cent
- **Higher Education:** Universities: 23; Colleges: 1,417
- **Constitution/Assembly:** Unicameral. Legislative assembly: 141
- **Governor:** Arif Mohammed Khan
- **Chief Minister:** Pinarayi Vijayan
- **Agriculture:** NFSA Ranking: 13; major crops: Natural rubber, pepper, cardamom, nutmeg, cinnamon, coffee and tea
- **Minerals:** China clay (kaolin), limestone, lime shell, silica sand, bauxite and graphite
- **Industries:** Handlooms and textiles, information technology, manufacturing of electronics, tourism and hospitality, agro-based industries and tea production
- **Roads:** National highways: 1,782 km; No. of National highways: 11
- **Railway Route Length:** 1,047 km
- **Airports:** International: 4
- **Art/Culture:** Classical dance forms like Kathakali, Kutiyattam and Mohiniattam. *Kalamezhuthu* and *kolamezhuthu* (kolam) are popular floor decoration art forms.
- **Nature Reserves:** National parks: 6; Wildlife sanctuaries: 18
- **Tourism:** Shree Padmanabhaswamy Temple in Thiruvananthapuram, Munnar, Kochi, Jatayu Bird Sculpture, Paradesi Jewish Synagogue, houseboats and backwaters
- **State Symbols:** bird: Great hornbill (*Buceros bicornis*); flower: Kanikonna (*Cassia fistula*); tree: Coconut (*Cocos nucifera*); animal: Indian elephant (*Elephas maximus indicus*)
- **Do Not Miss!** Boat races are among the grandest traditions of the state. People throng these events to watch snake-shaped boats go head to head to the beat of old boat songs.
- **Swachh Survekshan Ranking:** 6<
- **UNESCO Heritage (Intangible cultural, or historical, or other sites):** Western Ghats (shared), Kutiyattam (Sanskrit theatre) and Mudiyettu
- **Sustainable Development Index Score:** 75
- **Smart Cities:** 1
- **Air Pollution Index:** 64 (Satisfactory)

Houseboat in the backwaters, Kerala

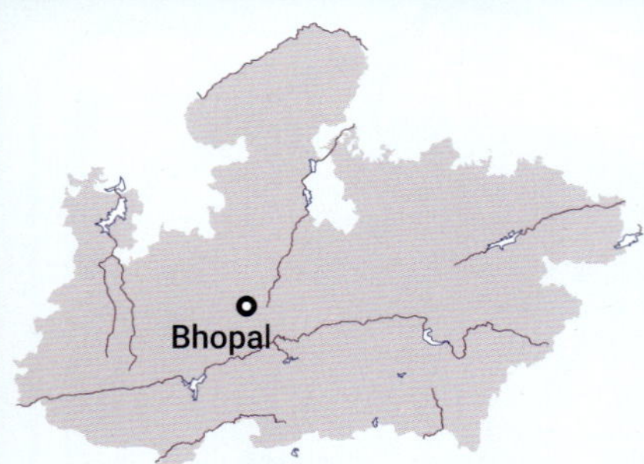

MADHYA PRADESH

- **Area:** 308,245 sq. km
- **Capital:** Bhopal
- **Population:** 72.62 million
- **FDI Equity Inflow:** ₹3,786.52
- **Main Language:** Hindi
- **Literacy Rate:** 69.3 per cent
- **Higher Education:** Universities: 66; Colleges: 2,411
- **Constitution/Assembly:** Unicameral. Legislative assembly: 230
- **Governor:** Mangubhai Chhaganbhai Patel
- **Chief Minister:** Shivraj Singh Chouhan
- **Agriculture:** NFSA Ranking: 7; major crops: Rice, wheat, jowar, maize, pulses, cotton and sugar cane
- **Minerals:** Diamonds, dolomites, bauxite, coal, limestone and copper
- **Industries:** Automobiles, cement, tourism, electronics and optical fibre, telecommunications and information technology
- **Roads:** National highways: 8,911 km; No. of National highways: 46
- **Railway Route Length:** 5,140 km
- **Airports:** International: 1; Domestic: 6
- **Art/Culture:** 'Lokranjan', an annual dance festival at Khajuraho, organized by the state tourism department and Adivasi Lok Kala Academy is a platform to present a number of popular folk and tribal dance forms.
- **Nature Reserves:** National parks: 11; Wildlife sanctuaries: 24
- **Tourism:** Gwalior, Jabalpur, Orchha, Raisen and Bhimbetka
- **State Symbols:** bird: Indian paradise flycatcher (*Terpsiphone paradisi*); flower: Madonna lily (*Lilium candidum*); tree: Banyan (*Ficus benghalensis*); animal: Swamp deer or barasingha (*Cervus duvaceli*)
- **Do Not Miss!** A ride on the hot-air balloons in Pench National Park over the vast fields encompassed by the River Pench
- **Swachh Survekshan Ranking:** 1>
- **UNESCO Heritage (Intangible cultural, historical or other sites):** Khajuraho Group of Monuments, rock shelters of Bhimbetka, Kumbh Mela (shared) at Ujjain and Buddhist monuments at Sanchi
- **Sustainable Development Index Score:** 62
- **Smart Cities:** 7
- **Air Pollution Index:** 91 (Satisfactory)

Rock shelters, Bhimbetka, Madhya Pradesh

MAHARASHTRA

- **Area:** 307,713 sq. km
- **Capital:** Mumbai and Nagpur (Winter)
- **Population:** 112.37 million
- **FDI Equity Inflow:** ₹3,29,291.70
- **Main Language:** Marathi
- **Literacy Rate:** 82.3 per cent
- **Higher Education:** Universities: 65; Colleges: 4,494
- **Constitution Assembly:** Bicameral. Legislative council: 78; Legislative assembly: 288
- **Governor:** Bhagat Singh Koshyari
- **Chief Minister:** Eknath Shinde
- **Agriculture:** NFSA Ranking: 16; major crops: Rice, jowar, bajra, moong, tur and gram
- **Minerals:** Coal, limestone, manganese, iron ore, bauxite, silica sand and sea sand
- **Industries:** Food products, breweries, tobacco and related products, textile products, cinema, printing and publishing, cement, rubber and plastic
- **Roads:** National highways: 18,317 km; No. of National highways: 102
- **Railway** Route Length: 5,823 km
- **Airports:** International: 3; Domestic: 10
- **Art/Culture:** Festivals such as Ganesh Chaturthi and Gudi Padwa. *Mashru* and *himroo* fabrics are part of the woven art forms.
- **Nature Reserves:** National parks: 6; Wildlife sanctuaries: 48
- **Tourism:** Mumbai, Ajanta, Ellora, Elephanta, Mahabaleshwar, Matheran and Panchgani
- **State Symbols:** bird: Yellow-footed green pigeon (*Treron phoenicoptera*); flower: Jarul (*Lagerstroemia speciosa*); tree: Mango (*Mangifera indica*); animal: Indian giant squirrel (*Ratufa indica*)

Ganesh Chaturthi celebrations in Mumbai, Maharashtra

- **Do Not Miss!** Taraporewala Aquarium in Mumbai, India's oldest aquarium, houses a multitude of freshwater and marine fishes.
- **Swachh Survekshan Ranking:** 3>
- **UNESCO Heritage (Intangible cultural, historical or other sites):** Ajanta, Ellora and Elephanta caves, Chhatrapati Shivaji Maharaj Terminus, Western Ghats (shared), Kumbh Mela (shared) at Nashik, and the Victorian and Art Deco ensembles of Mumbai
- **Sustainable Development Index Score:** 70
- **Smart Cities:** 9
- **Air Pollution Index:** 101 (Moderate)

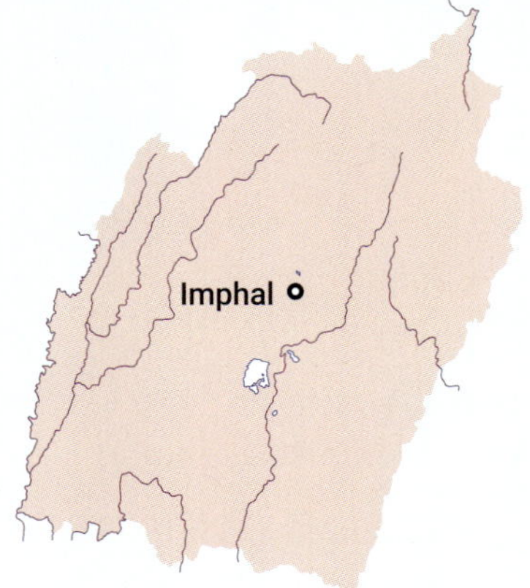

MANIPUR

- **Area:** 22,327 sq. km
- **Capital:** Imphal
- **Population:** 2.85 million
- **FDI Equity Inflow:** Not applicable
- **Main Languages:** Manipuri, Tangkhul
- **Literacy Rate:** 76.9 per cent
- **Higher Education:** Universities: 8; Colleges: 102
- **Constitution/Assembly:** Unicameral. Legislative assembly: 60
- **Governor:** La. Ganesan
- **Chief Minister:** N. Biren Singh
- **Agriculture:** NFSA Ranking: 32; major crops: Potato, mustard, sugar cane, tobacco, rice, maize and pulses
- **Minerals:** Chromite, limestone and serpentinite, china clay, idocrase and rock salt
- **Industries:** Handloom, agriculture and tourism
- **Roads:** National highways: 1,840 km; No. of National highways: 11
- **Railway Route Length:** 13 km
- **Airport:** International: 1
- **Art/Culture:** Cane and bamboo basketry, pottery, and Manipuri dance
- **Nature Reserves:** National parks: 2; Wildlife sanctuaries: 7
- **Tourism:** Shree Govindajee Temple, Moirang, Khwairamband Bazaar (Ima Keithel, entirely a women's market), Nupi Lan (Women's War) Memorial Complex and Khonghampat Orchidarium
- **State Symbols:** bird: Nongyeen (*Syrmaticus humiae*); flower: Siroi/shirui lily (*Lilium mackliniae*); tree: Uningthou (*Phoebe hainesiana*); animal: Sangai deer (*Rucervus eldii eldii*)
- **Do Not Miss!** Loktak Lake, which is known for ***phumdi***, a floating mass of vegetation, soil and organic matter that has solidified over time (people can even build houses on it), and the habitat of Sangai deer
- **Swachh Survekshan Ranking:** 7<
- **UNESCO Heritage (Intangible cultural, historical or other sites):** Sankirtana, ritual singing, drumming and dancing
- **Sustainable Development Index Score:** 64
- **Smart City:** 1
- **Air Pollution Index:** 92 (Satisfactory)

INDIA AT HER BEST 75 YEARS OF INDEPENDENCE

Manipur's First Freight Train in 75 Years

The first freight train rolled out from Rani Gaidinliu railway station in Tamenglong District to Khongsang railway station in Imphal East District, marking its entry in the Indian Railway network. The train came with 52 BOBNYL wagons on 27 January 2022. This milestone will boost the socio-economic development of the state by providing faster and reliable transportation. A month later, on 14 March 2022, a passenger train engine reached the Khongshang railway station, covering 62 km from Jiribam via Rani Gaidinliu and Thingou stations.

Manipur cityscape

Representative image

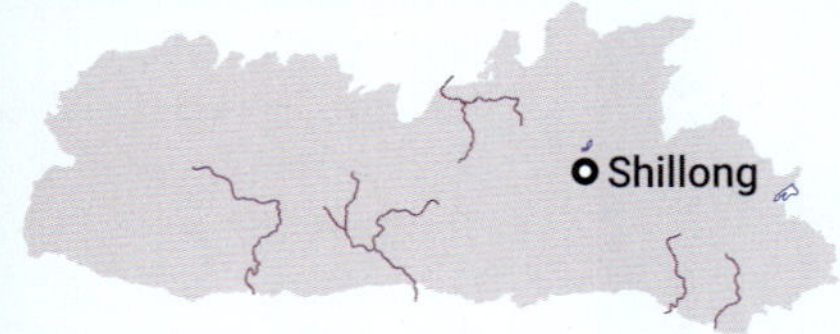

MEGHALAYA

- **Area:** 22,429 sq. km
- **Capital:** Shillong
- **Population:** 2.97 million
- **FDI Equity Inflow:** ₹8.16
- **Main Languages:** Khasi, Pnar, Garo, Bengali, Assamese and English
- **Literacy Rate:** 74.4 per cent
- **Higher Education:** Universities: 10; Colleges: 67
- **Constitution/Assembly:** Unicameral. Legislative assembly: 60
- **Governor:** Brigadier (Dr) B.D. Mishra (Retd)
- **Chief Minister:** Conrad Kongkal Sangma
- **Agriculture:** NFSA Ranking: 33; major crops: Rice, maize, oranges (Khasi mandarin), pineapple, plums and peaches
- **Minerals:** Limestone, coal, clay (lithomargic), granite, copper ore, silica sand, sillimanite and quartz
- **Industries:** Agriculture and food processing, horticulture, tourism, hydroelectricity, handlooms, cement, handicrafts and sericulture
- **Roads:** National highways: 1,156 km; No. of National highways: 5
- **Railway Route Length:** 9 km
- **Airport:** Domestic: 1
- **Art/Culture:** Behdienkhlam is the most important festival; Phawar is a form of Khasi music.
- **Nature Reserves:** National parks: 2; Wildlife sanctuaries: 4
- **Tourism:** Sohra, Shillong, Mawsynram, Mawlynnong, Nohwet, River Umngot, Garo Hills, East Khasi Hills, Mawsmai Falls and Cave
- **State Symbols:** bird: Hill mynah (*Gracula religiosa*); flower: Lady's slipper orchid (*Paphiopedilum insigne*); tree: White teak (*Gmelina arborea*); animal: Clouded leopard (*Neofelis nebulosa*)
- **Do Not Miss!** The Nohkalikai Falls, the highest plunge waterfall in India, falling from 340 m (1,115 ft)
- **Swachh Survekshan Ranking:** 14<
- **UNESCO Heritage (Intangible cultural, historical or other sites):** None
- **Sustainable Development Index Score:** 60
- **Smart City:** 1
- **Air Pollution Index:** 25 (Good)

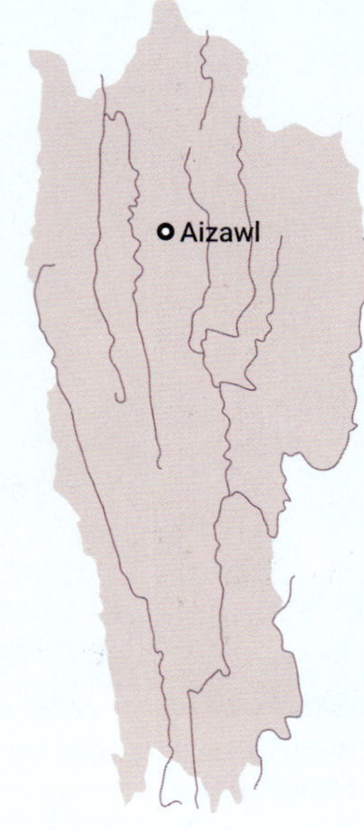

MIZORAM

- **Area:** 21,087 sq. km
- **Capital:** Aizawl
- **Population:** 1.092 million
- **FDI Equity Inflow:** Not applicable
- **Main Languages:** Mizo and English
- **Literacy Rate:** 91.3 per cent
- **Higher Education:** Universities: 3; Colleges: 35
- **Constitution/Assembly:** Unicameral. Legislative assembly: 40
- **Governor:** Dr Kambhampati Hari Babu

River Umngot, Meghalaya

Hume's pheasant: the state bird of Mizoram

- **Chief Minister:** Pu Zoramthanga
- **Agriculture:** NFSA Ranking: 26; major crops: Maize, rice, sugar cane, tapioca, ginger and cotton
- **Minerals:** Sandstone, clay, lignite and pyrite
- **Industries:** Bamboo, sericulture, tourism, agro-products and agro-processing industries
- **Roads:** National highways: 1,423 km; No. of National highways: 9
- **Railway Route Length:** 2 km
- **Airport:** Domestic: 1
- **Art/Culture:** Often called the 'songbird of the East', Mizoram resonates with vibrant music, songs and beautiful energetic dances. Among the different folk dances, Cheraw, performed using bamboo poles, is popular.
- **Nature Reserves:** National parks: 2; Wildlife sanctuaries: 9
- **Tourism:** Hmuifang, Phawngpui (the Blue Mountain), Reiek, Palak Lake, Tuirihiau Waterfalls and Tamdil
- **State Symbols:** bird: Hume's pheasant (*Syrmaticus humiae*); flower: Red vanda (*Renanthera imschootiana*); tree: Indian rose chestnut (*Mesua ferrea*); animal: Saza/serow (*Capricornis thar*)
- **Do Not Miss!** The Mizo Heritage Museum in the capital city
- **Swachh Survekshan Ranking:** 11<
- **UNESCO Heritage (Intangible cultural, historical or other sites):** None
- **Sustainable Development Index Score:** 68
- **Smart City:** 1
- **Air Pollution Index:** 19 (Good)

NAGALAND

- **Area:** 16,579 sq. km
- **Capital:** Kohima
- **Population:** 1.98 million
- **FDI Equity Inflow:** ₹0.105
- **Main Languages:** English and Nagamese
- **Literacy Rate:** 79.6 per cent
- **Higher Education:** Universities: 5; Colleges: 67
- **Constitution /Assembly:** Unicameral. Legislative assembly: 60
- **Governor:** Prof. Jagdish Mukhi
- **Chief Minister:** Neiphiu Rio
- **Agriculture:** NFSA Ranking: 23; major crop: Rice
- **Minerals:** Coal, limestone, nickel, cobalt, copper, dunite, petroleum and natural gas
- **Industries:** Bamboo processing, agro-based and forest-based industries, food processing, mining, horticulture, tourism, sericulture, handloom and handicrafts
- **Roads:** National highways: 1,670 km; No. of National highways: 12
- **Railway Route Length:** 11 km
- **Airport:** Domestic: 1
- **Art/Culture:** The state is linguistically rich with each tribe having its own language. The tribes also celebrate festivals all the year round, earning the state its popular title, 'The Land of Festivals'.
- **Nature Reserves:** National park: 1; Wildlife sanctuaries: 4
- **Tourism:** Kohima (including the War Cemetery), Khonoma, Dimapur, Mokokchung, Diezephe craft village, Kachari ruins, Diphupar and Chumukedima village
- **State Symbols:** bird: Blyth's tragopan (*Tragopan blythii*); flower: Rhododendron (*Rhododendron arboreum*); tree: Alder (*Alnus nepalensis*); animal: Mithun (*Bos frontalis*)
- **Do Not Miss!** The Hornbill festival, conceived by the state's tourism department and held in the first week of December, is an annual event where all tribes come together to celebrate, exhibit and sell their traditional wares, food and crafts.
- **Swachh Survekshan Ranking:** 12<
- **UNESCO Heritage (Intangible cultural, historical or other sites):** None
- **Sustainable Development Index Score:** 61
- **Smart City:** 1
- **Air Pollution Index:** Not applicable[†]

Rhododendron: the state flower of Nagaland

River Island Gets a Bank

In August 2021, Kud Gunderpur river island in Sambalpur District in Odisha gained access to a banking network. The Utkal Grameen Bank opened a customer service point under the state-run project, Odisha Livelihood Mission, supported by the district administration of Sambalpur. This welcome development after 75 years of Independence became possible after the island finally got connected to the mainland via a bridge in February 2020. Located 35 km from Sambalpur town, Kud Gunderpur is surrounded by the River Mahanadi, making it difficult to access. The opening of the bank will help in the financial inclusion of the around 5,000 residents of the island, and address their banking and credit needs.

ODISHA

- **Area:** 155,707 sq. km
- **Capital:** Bhubaneswar
- **Population:** 41.97 million
- **FDI Equity Inflow:** ₹971.39
- **Main Language:** Odia
- **Literacy Rate:** 72.9 per cent
- **Higher Education:** Universities: 32; Colleges: 1,087
- **Constitution/Assembly:** Unicameral. Legislative assembly: 147
- **Governor:** Prof. Ganeshi Lal
- **Chief Minister:** Naveen Patnaik
- **Agriculture:** NFSA Ranking: 1; major crops: Rice, pulses, oilseeds, jute, coconut, tea, cotton and rubber
- **Minerals:** Iron ore, manganese, coal, bauxite, dolomite and limestone
- **Industries:** Thermal power, aluminium, steel, petrochemicals, hydel power, cement and tourism
- **Roads:** National highways: 5,897 km; No. of National highways: 32
- **Railway Route Length:** 2,703 km
- **Airports:** International: 1; Domestic: 2
- **Art/Culture:** Talapatra Chitras, an ancient craft – etchings and paintings on palm leaf
- **Nature Reserves:** National parks: 2; Wildlife sanctuaries: 19
- **Tourism:** Puri, Konark, Cuttack, Chandaneswar, Gopalpur, Udayagiri and Khandagiri. Chilika Lake is the largest brackish-water lake in Asia.
- **State Symbols:** bird: Indian roller (*Coracias benghalensis*); flower: Ashoka (*Saraca asoca*); tree: Fig (*Ficus carica*); animal: Sambar deer (*Rusa unicolor*)
- **Swachh Survekshan Ranking:** 9>
- **UNESCO Heritage (Intangible cultural, historical or other sites):** The Sun Temple at Konark and Chhau dance (shared)
- **Sustainable Development Index Score:** 61
- **Smart Cities:** 2
- **Air Pollution Index:** 48 (Good)

Sun Temple in Konark, Odisha

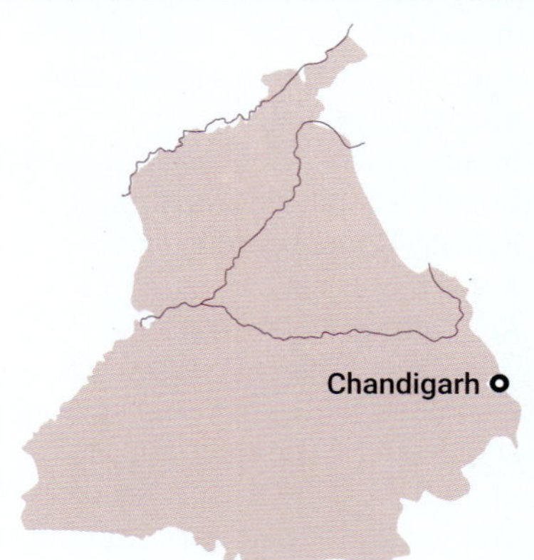

PUNJAB

- **Area:** 50,362 sq. km
- **Capital:** Chandigarh
- **Population:** 27.74 million
- **FDI Equity Inflow:** ₹6,444.88
- **Main Language:** Punjabi
- **Literacy Rate:** 75.8 per cent
- **Higher Education:** Universities: 32; Colleges: 1,079
- **Constitution/Assembly:** Unicameral. Legislative assembly: 117
- **Governor:** Banwarilal Purohit
- **Chief Minister:** Bhagwant Singh Mann
- **Agriculture:** NFSA Ranking: 19; major crops: Wheat, rice, cotton, sugar cane, yellow mustard, maize, barley and fruits
- **Minerals:** Quartz, silica sand, quartzite and sulphur
- **Industries:** Dairy, agriculture,

Wagah Border, Punjab

logistics, handloom and handicraft, food and beverages, real estate and information technology
- **Roads:** National highways: 4,105 km; No. of National highways: 37
- **Railway Route Length:** 2,265 km
- **Airports:** International: 1; Domestic: 5
- **Art/Culture:** Gatka, Kikli, Jaago, Dhamal, Sammi, Dankara, Julli, Luddi, Jhumar, Giddha and Bhangra are popular folk dance forms.
- **Nature Reserves:** National parks: None; Wildlife sanctuaries: 13
- **Tourism:** Golden Temple, Jallianwala Bagh and the Wagah border in Amritsar, Bhakra Dam, Qila Androon, Moti Bagh Palace and Chhatbir Zoo in Patiala
- **State Symbols:** bird: Northern goshawk (*Accipiter gentilis*); flower: Gladiolus (*Gladiolus grandiflorus*); tree: Sheesham (*Dalbergia sissoo*); animal: Blackbuck (*Antilope cervicapra*)
- **Do Not Miss!** Punjabi cuisine: *sarson da saag* with *makke di* roti is famous all over the country.
- **Swachh Survekshan Ranking:** 5>
- **UNESCO Heritage (Intangible cultural, historical or other sites):** Traditional craft of making utensils using copper and brass among the Thathera community of Jandiala
- **Sustainable Development Index Score:** 68
- **Smart Cities:** 3
- **Air Pollution Index:** 103 (Moderate)

RAJASTHAN

- **Area:** 342,239 sq. km
- **Capital:** Jaipur
- **Population:** 68.548 million
- **FDI Equity Inflow:** ₹11,724.58
- **Main Languages:** Hindi and Rajasthani
- **Literacy Rate:** 66.1 per cent
- **Higher Education:** Universities: 89; Colleges: 3,380
- **Constitution/Assembly:** Unicameral. Legislative assembly: 200
- **Governor:** Kalraj Mishra
- **Chief Minister:** Ashok Gehlot
- **Agriculture:** NFSA Ranking: 18; major crops: Wheat, rice, jowar, bajra, maize, pulses, small millets and mustard
- **Minerals:** Lead, zinc, silver, soapstone, gypsum, limestone, ball clay and jasper
- **Industries:** Mineral processing, tourism and hospitality, agriculture, handicrafts, chemicals, cement and textiles
- **Roads:** National highways: 10,477 km; No. of National highways: 51
- **Railway Route Length:** 6,019 km
- **Airports:** International: 1; Domestic: 5
- **Art/Culture:** Ghoomar, Gair, Chari, Terathali and Kalbelia dance forms, and Kathputli theatre are famous.
- **Nature Reserves:** National parks: 5; Wildlife sanctuaries: 25
- **Tourism:** Jaipur, Jodhpur, Udaipur, Bikaner, Mount Abu (Sirohi) and Ranthambore National Park (Tiger Reserve) in Sawai Madhopur
- **State Symbols:** bird: Indian bustard (*Ardeotis nigriceps*); flower: Rohida (*Tecomella undulata*); tree: Khejri (*Prosopis cineraria*); animal: Camel (*Camelus dromedarius*) and Chinkara (*Gazella bennettii*)
- **Do Not Miss!** Golden sand dunes in the Thar Desert
- **Swachh Survekshan Ranking:** 8>
- **UNESCO Heritage (Intangible cultural, historical or other sites):** Hill forts, Jaipur city, Jantar Mantar, Keoladeo Ghana National Park, Kalbelia folk songs and dances
- **Sustainable Development Index Score:** 60
- **Smart Cities:** 4
- **Air Pollution Index:** 156 (Moderate)

City Palace of Udaipur, Rajasthan

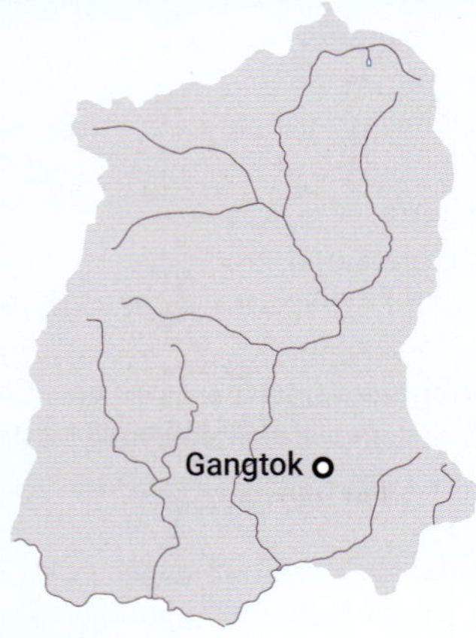

SIKKIM

- **Area:** 7,096 sq. km
- **Capital:** Gangtok
- **Population:** 0.61 million
- **FDI Equity Inflow:** Not applicable
- **Main Languages:** English; Bhutia, Lepcha and other local languages
- **Literacy Rate:** 81.4 per cent
- **Higher Education:** Universities: 8; Colleges: 22
- **Constitution/Assembly:** Unicameral. Legislative assembly: 32
- **Governor:** Ganga Prasad
- **Chief Minister:** Prem Singh Tamang
- **Agriculture:** NFSA Ranking: 15; major crops: Oranges, large cardamom, ginger, turmeric, cherry, pepper and baby corn
- **Minerals:** Copper, lead, zinc, silver, dolomite, quartzite and talc/steatite/soapstone
- **Industries:** Tourism, agriculture, floriculture, agro-processing, hydroelectric power, tea, electronics and pharmaceuticals
- **Road:** National highways: 709 km; No. of National highways: 8
- **Railway Route Length:** None
- **Airport:** Domestic: 1
- **Art/Culture:** Singhi Chham masked/costumed dance is performed on ceremonial and festive occasions. Thangka art, displaying elaborate hand painting on scrolls also flourishes in the region.
- **Nature Reserves:** National park: 1; Wildlife sanctuaries: 7
- **Tourism:** Gangtok, Pelling, Zuluk, Nathu La and Tsomgo Lake
- **State Symbols:** bird: Blood pheasant (*Ithaginis cruentus*); flower: Noble dendrobium (*Dendrobium nobile*); tree: Rhododendron (*Rhododendron arboreum*); animal: Red panda (*Ailurus fulgens*)
- **Do Not Miss!** Gurudongmar Lake, at more than 5,182 m (17,000 ft) above the mean sea level, is the second highest glacial lake in India.
- **Swachh Survekshan Ranking:** 8<
- **UNESCO Heritage (Intangible cultural, historical or other sites):** Khangchendzonga (Kangchenjunga) National Park
- **Sustainable Development Index Score:** 71
- **Smart Cities:** 2
- **Air Pollution Index:** Not applicable[†]

Red panda: the state animal of Sikkim

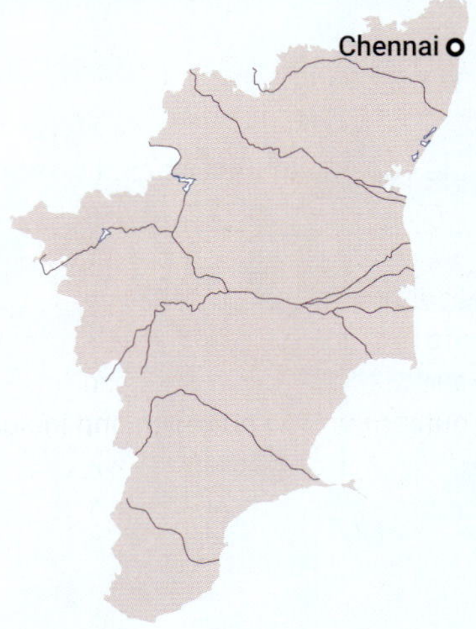

TAMIL NADU

- **Area:** 130,058 sq. km
- **Capital:** Chennai
- **Population:** 72.14 million
- **FDI Equity Inflow:** ₹52,675.88
- **Main Language:** Tamil
- **Literacy Rate:** 80.1 per cent
- **Higher Education:** Universities: 59; Colleges: 2,610
- **Constitution/Assembly:** Unicameral. Legislative assembly: 234
- **Governor:** R.N. Ravi
- **Chief Minister:** M.K. Stalin
- **Agriculture:** NFSA Ranking: 10; major crops: Rice, millets, pulses, sugar cane, cotton, sunflower, coconut and cashew nuts
- **Minerals:** Granite, lignite, graphite, bauxite, magnesite and limestone
- **Industries:** Textiles, heavy commercial vehicles, engineering, information technology, leather tanning industries, cement, electronic hardware and tourism
- **Roads:** National highways: 6,858 km; No. of National highways: 50
- **Railway Route Length:** 4,033 km
- **Airports:** International: 4; Domestic: 2
- **Art/Culture:** Pongal is the harvest festival celebrated by farmers in January. Bharatanatyam is a classical dance from the state. At the Natyanjali Dance Festival, the temple city of Chidambaram pays special tribute to Lord Nataraja.
- **Nature Reserves:** National parks: 5; Wildlife sanctuaries: 30
- **Tourism:** Chennai, Mamallapuram, Chidambaram, Thanjavur, Madurai, Srirangam, Kanniyakumari and Rameswaram

IIT Madras: First Rank in NIRF 2022

Entry gate of IIT, Madras

Tamil Nadu emerged as the leading state with 18 institutions in the Top 100 of the National Institution Rankings Framework (NIRF) 2022 (Overall). The NIRF rankings are given out by the Ministry of Education, Government of India, based on a methodology to rank educational institutions. In the overall category, the institutions are ranked on four parameters including teaching; learning and resources; research and professional practice; graduation outcomes; and outreach and inclusivity. The Indian Institute of Madras, Chennai, topped the list with a score of 87.59. Out of the 18 institutes, seven institutes are located in Chennai. Maharashtra was a close second with 12 institutions, followed by Uttar Pradesh with eight institutions in the list.

- **State Symbols:** bird: Emerald dove (*Chalcophaps indica*); flower: Gloriosa lily (*Kandhal*) (*Gloriosa superba*); tree: Palm tree (*Borassus flabellifer*); animal: Nilgiri tahr (*Nilgiritragus hylocrius*)
- **Do Not Miss!** The Nilgiri Mountain Railway at Udhagamandalam (part of Mountain Railways of India).
- **Swachh Survekshan Ranking:** 13>
- **UNESCO Heritage (Intangible cultural, historical or other sites):** The Great Living Chola Temples, Nilgiri Railway (part of Mountain Railways of India), Group of Monuments at Mamallapuram and the Western Ghats (shared)
- **Sustainable Development Index Score:** 74
- **Smart Cities:** 11
- **Air Pollution Index:** 165 (Moderate)

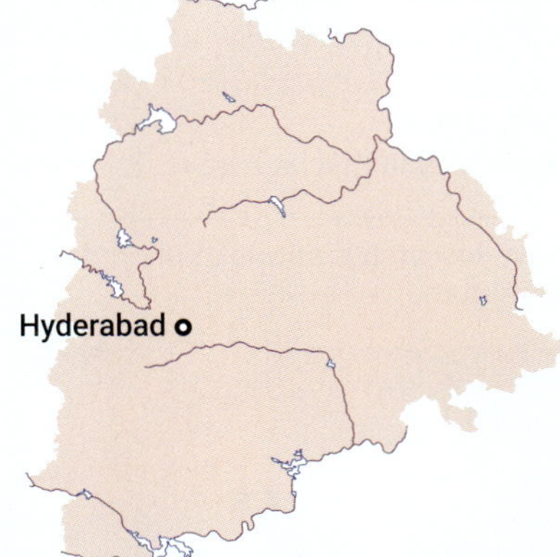

TELANGANA

- **Area:** 112,077 sq. km
- **Capital:** Hyderabad
- **Population:** 35.04 million
- **FDI Equity Inflow:** ₹29,690.12
- **Main Language:** Telugu
- **Literacy Rate:** 66.5 per cent
- **Higher Education:** Universities: 24; Colleges: 2,071
- **Constitution/Assembly:** Bicameral. Legislative council: 40; Legislative assembly: 119
- **Governor:** Dr Tamilisai Soundararajan
- **Chief Minister:** K. Chandrashekar Rao
- **Agriculture:** NFSA Ranking: 14; major crops: Rice, jowar, bajra, maize, sunflower, pulses and groundnut
- **Minerals:** Manganese, iron ore, limestone, coal, quartz and dolomite
- **Industries:** Information technology, pharmaceuticals, tourism, textiles, cement, mining
- **Roads:** National highways: 4,926 km; No. of National highways: 30
- **Railway Route Length:** 1,871 km
- **Airport:** International: 1; Domestic: 2
- **Art/Culture:** Perini Sivatandavam or the 'dance of warriors'; traditions of storytelling such as Golla Suddulu, Oggu Kathalu and Gotralu
- **Nature Reserves:** National parks: 3; Wildlife sanctuaries: 9
- **Tourism:** Hyderabad, Warangal, Alampur, Adilabad and Nalgonda
- **State Symbols:** bird: Palapitta (*Coracias indica*); flower: Tangedu Puvvu (*Senna auriculata*); tree: Jammi Chettu (*Prosopis cineraria*); animal: Jinka (*Axis axis*)
- **Do Not Miss!** The famous Salar Jung Museum in Hyderabad
- **Swachh Survekshan Ranking:** 4>
- **UNESCO Heritage (Intangible cultural, historical or other sites):** Kakatiya Rudreshwara (Ramappa) Temple
- **Sustainable Development Index Score:** 69
- **Smart Cities:** 2
- **Air Pollution Index:** 106 (Moderate)

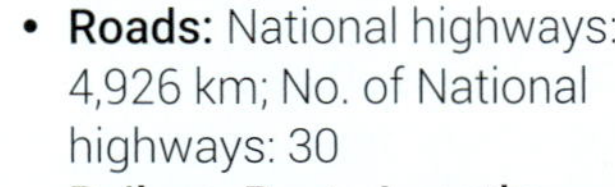

Kakatiya Rudreshwara (Ramappa) Temple, Nandi Mandapam, Mulugu, Telangana

TRIPURA

- **Area:** 10,492 sq. km
- **Capital:** Agartala
- **Population:** 3.67 million
- **FDI Equity Inflow:** ₹4.20
- **Main Languages:** Bengali, Kokborok and English
- **Literacy Rate:** 87.2 per cent
- **Higher Education:** Universities: 4; Colleges: 53
- **Constitution/Assembly:** Unicameral. Legislative assembly: 60
- **Governor:** Satyadeo Narain Arya
- **Chief Minister:** Dr Manik Saha
- **Agriculture:** NFSA Ranking: 5; major crops: Pineapple, orange, cashew nut, jackfruit, coconut, tea, rice and rubber
- **Minerals:** Natural gas, glass sands, fireclay, shale and silica sand
- **Industries:** Natural gas, food processing, rubber, tea, bamboo, handloom and handicrafts, sericulture and tourism
- **Roads:** National highways: 854 km; No. of National highways: 6
- **Railway Route Length:** 265 km
- **Airport:** Domestic: 1
- **Art/Culture:** Hoza Giri dance of the Reang tribesmen, Garia tribal dance, Dhamail dance and musical duels (Kabi Gaan)
- **Nature Reserves:** National parks: 2; Wildlife sanctuaries: 4
- **Tourism:** Ujjayanta Palace, Kunjaban Palace, Lake Palace, Unakoti near Kailashahar, Tripura Sundari/ Tripureswari Temple in Udaipur, Dumboor Lake, Rudrasagar, Amarsagar, Jagannath Dighi and Kalyan Sagar
- **State Symbols:** bird: Green imperial pigeon (*Ducula aenea*); flower: Indian rose chestnut (*Mesua ferrea*); tree: Agarwood (*Aquilaria malaccensis*); animal: Phayre's leaf monkey (*Trachypithecus phayrei*)
- **Do Not Miss!** The Poush Sankranti Fair held every year in January at Tirthamukh to mark the beginning of the sun's northern course
- **Swachh Survekshan Ranking:** 1>
- **UNESCO Heritage (Intangible cultural, historical or other sites):** None
- **Sustainable Development Index Score:** 65
- **Smart City:** 1
- **Air Pollution Index:** 38 (Good)

Green imperial pigeon: the state bird of Tripura

UTTARAKHAND

- **Area:** 53,483 sq. km
- **Capital:** Dehradun (temporary); and Gairsain (summer)
- **Population:** 10.08 million
- **FDI Equity Inflow:** ₹939.66
- **Main Languages:** Hindi, Garhwali and Kumaoni
- **Literacy Rate:** 78.8 per cent
- **Higher Education:** Universities: 36; Colleges: 454
- **Constitution/Assembly:** Unicameral. Legislative assembly: 70
- **Governor:** Lt Gen. Gurmit Singh (Retd)
- **Chief Minister:** Pushkar Singh Dhami
- **Agriculture:** NFSA Ranking: 24; major crops: Rice, wheat, soyabean, groundnuts, coarse cereals and pulses
- **Minerals:** Limestone, marble, rock phosphate, dolomite, magnesite and gypsum
- **Industries:** Hydroelectricity, tourism and hospitality, automobile components, agro-based industries and textiles
- **Roads:** National highways: 3,449 km;

Forest Research Institute in Dehradun, Uttarakhand

Carnivorous Plant Found in Uttarakhand

A carnivorous plant found at a staggering altitude of 4,800 ft (1,463 m) in Mandal, Chamoli District, Uttarakhand, made news in September 2021. Documented by *Japanese Botany*, a century-old journal, the plant was last spotted in Meghalaya 37 years ago in 1986. With a distinct bladder-like structure to trap prey, the plant thrives on tadpoles, mosquito larvae and protozoa. Mostly found in fresh water and wet soil, the plant is very rare and highly susceptible to biotic pressure and climate change.

No. of National highways: 24
- **Railway Route Length:** 346 km
- **Airports:** Domestic: 3
- **Art/Culture:** Several fairs and festivals celebrated by tribes such as the Bhotias (Shaukas), Tharus, Buxas and Jaunsaris
- **Nature Reserves:** National parks: 6; Wildlife sanctuaries: 7
- **Tourism:** Dehradun, Mussoorie, Jageshwar, Baijnath, Sat Tal, Bhimtal, Harshil, Dhanaulti and Dayara meadow
- **State Symbols:** bird: Himalayan monal (*Lophophorus impejanus*); flower: Brahma kamal (*Saussurea obvallata*); tree: Burans (*Rhododendron arboreum*); animal: Alpine musk deer (*Moschus chrysogaster*)
- **Do Not Miss!** Maha Ganga aarti or the worship of the River Ganga at Triveni Ghat in Rishikesh or Har Ki Pauri in Haridwar
- **Swachh Survekshan Ranking:** 3<
- **UNESCO Heritage (Intangible cultural, historical or other sites):** Nanda Devi and Valley of Flowers National Parks, Ramman– ritual theatre of the Garhwal and Kumbh Mela (shared) in Haridwar
- **Sustainable Development Index Score:** 72
- **Smart City:** 1
- **Air Pollution Index:** 90 (Satisfactory)

UTTAR PRADESH

- **Area:** 243,286 sq. km
- **Capital:** Lucknow
- **Population:** 199.81 million
- **FDI Equity Inflow:** ₹7,357.07
- **Main Languages:** Hindi and Urdu
- **Literacy Rate:** 67.7 per cent
- **Higher** Education: Universities: 81; Colleges: 7,788
- **Constitution/Assembly:** Bicameral. Legislative council: 100; Legislative assembly: 403
- **Governor:** Anandiben Patel
- **Chief Minister:** Yogi Adityanath
- **Agriculture:** NFSA Ranking: 2; major crops: Rice, millet, sugar cane, wheat, maize, mustard and pulses
- **Minerals:** Dolomite, bauxite and glass sand, sandstone, *maurang*
- **Industries:** Information technology, agro-processing, tourism, mineral-based industries, textiles, handloom and handicrafts, food processing and sports goods
- **Roads:** National highways: 12,245 km; No. of National highways: 87
- **Railway Route Length:** 8,799 km
- **Airports:** International: 2; Domestic: 5
- **Art/Culture:** Chikankari – traditional, delicate hand embroidery on chiffon, muslin, organza, organdie and silk
- **Nature Reserves:** National park: 1; Wildlife sanctuaries: 26
- **Tourism:** Mathura, Vrindavan, Kanpur, Prayagraj, Varanasi, Agra and Ayodhya
- **State Symbols:** bird: Sarus crane (*Grus antigone*); flower: Palash (*Butea monosperma*); tree: Ashoka (*Saraca asoca*); animal: Barasingha (*Rucervus duvaucelii*)
- **Do Not Miss!** Varanasi, located on the banks of the River Ganga, is a holy city for Hindus.
- **Swachh Survekshan Ranking:** 10>
- **UNESCO Heritage (Intangible cultural, historical or other sites):** Taj Mahal, Fatehpur Sikri and Agra Fort, and Kumbh Mela (shared) in Prayagraj
- **Sustainable Development Index Score:** 60
- **Smart Cities:** 10
- **Air Pollution Index:** 83 (Satisfactory)

Imambara in Lucknow, Uttar Pradesh

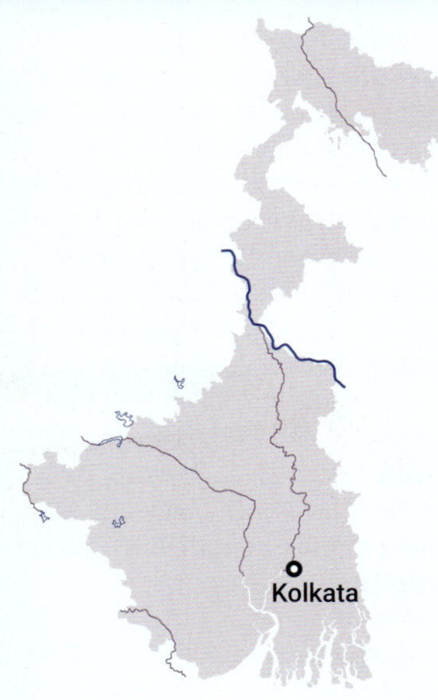

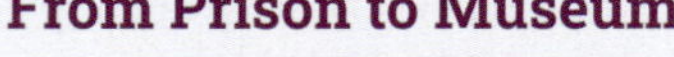

From Prison to Museum

On 21 September 2022, the Alipore Independence Museum in Kolkata was inaugurated by Chief Minister Mamata Banerjee after it was converted from the historic Alipore Prison. The 116-year-old correction home was functional till 2019, after which all its inmates were shifted to Baruipur Central Correctional Home near Kolkata. Now a museum, the building consists of solitary cells marked with their most famous inmates during the freedom struggle. There is a Nehru Cell in which Jawaharlal Nehru was held for 80 days because of his involvement in the Civil Disobedience Movement. Revolutionary freedom fighters like Netaji Subhas Chandra Bose, Jatindra Mohan Sengupta, Bidhan Chandra Roy and C.R. Das were also held at this prison. Other than the cells of freedom fighters, the museum has also preserved the gallows, and the cells of death-row convicts which highlight the brutality of the system. Anantahari Mitra, Promod Ranjan Chowdhury, Ramkrishna Biswas and many others were hanged on those very gallows between 1926 and 1934.

WEST BENGAL

- **Area:** 88,752 sq. km
- **Capital:** Kolkata
- **Population:** 91.28 million
- **FDI Equity Inflow:** ₹7,791.22
- **Main Language:** Bengali
- **Literacy Rate:** 76.3 per cent
- **Higher Education:** Universities: 47; Colleges: 1,411
- **Constitution/Assembly:** Unicameral. Legislative assembly: 294
- **Governor:** Dr C.V. Ananda Bose
- **Chief Minister:** Mamata Banerjee
- **Agriculture:** NFSA Ranking: 17; major crops: Jute, rice, tea, maize and sugar cane
- **Minerals:** China clay resources, dolomite, coal and fireclay
- **Industries:** Electronics and information technology, iron and steel, metallurgy, engineering, textiles, leather products and aquaculture
- **Roads:** National highways: 3,675 km; No. of National highways: 34
- **Railway Route Length:** 4,212 km
- **Airports:** International: 2; Domestic: 5
- **Art/Culture:** Baul singing is an ancient tradition, besides Patachitra art, dhokra metal casting, Bankura terracotta horses and Kantha embroidery.
- **Nature Reserves:** National parks: 6; Wildlife sanctuaries: 16
- **Tourism:** Darjeeling, Santiniketan, Digha, Shankarpur, Kolkata, Purulia, Howrah and Dakshineswar
- **State Symbols:** bird: White-throated kingfisher (*Halcyon smyrnensis*); flower: Night-flowering jasmine (*Nyctanthes arbortristis*); tree: Chhatim tree (*Alstonia scholaris*); animal: Fishing cat (*Prionailurus viverrinus*)
- **Do Not Miss!** A ride on the city tram and India's first metro rail. Kolkata is considered to be the only city in India with all modes of transportation – land, water and air.
- **Swachh Survekshan Ranking:** 28
- **UNESCO Heritage (Intangible cultural, historical or other sites):** Darjeeling Himalayan Railway (part of Mountain Railways of India), Chhau dance (shared), Sundarbans National Park and Durga Puja
- **Sustainable Development Index Score:** Unavailable
- **Smart City:** 1
- **Air Pollution Index:** 118 (Moderate)

Tea estate in Darjeeling, West Bengal

UNION TERRITORIES

ANDAMAN AND NICOBAR ISLANDS

- **Area:** 8,249 sq. km
- **Capital:** Port Blair
- **Population:** 0.43 million
- **FDI Equity Inflow:** Not applicable
- **Main Languages:** Hindi, English, Nicobarese, Bengali, Tamil, Malayalam, Telugu
- **Literacy Rate:** 86.6 per cent
- **Higher Education:** Universities: None; Colleges: 8

- **Constitution/ Assembly:** The Union Territory is governed by the Central government. A lieutenant governor appointed by the president of India presides over the territory.
- **Lt Governor:** Admiral Devendra Kumar Joshi (Retd)
- **Agriculture:** NFSA Ranking: 31; major crops: Rice, coconut, areca nut, pulses and oilseeds
- **Minerals:** Subeconomic concentrations
- **Industries:** Small-scale village and handicraft industries, fish processing, production of polythene bags, steel furniture, mild steel barrels, aluminium doors and windows
- **Roads:** National highways: 331 km; No. of National Highways: 1
- **Railway Route Length:** None
- **Airport:** International: 1
- **Art/Culture:** The indigenous peoples of the islands belong to four major tribes: The Great Andamanese, the Onge, the Jarawa and the Sentinelese. They are tribes of hunter-gatherers.
- **Nature Reserves:** National parks: 6; Wildlife sanctuaries: 96
- **Tourism:** Cellular Jail, National Memorial, Marine Museum, Water Sports Complex, Mahatma Gandhi Marine National Park, islands such as Ross, Viper, Havelock and Neil

Port Blair

- **Official Symbols:** bird: Andaman wood pigeon (*Columba palumboides*); flower: Andaman pyinma (*Lagerstroemia hypoleuca*); tree: Andaman padauk (*Pterocarpus dalbergioides*); animal: Dugong or sea cow (*Dugong dugon*)
- **Do Not Miss!** The glass-bottomed boat ride at Jolly Buoy Island
- **Swachh Survekshan Ranking:** Not applicable
- **UNESCO Heritage (Intangible cultural, historical or other sites):** None
- **Sustainable Development Index Score:** 67
- **Smart City:** 1
- **Air Pollution Index:** Not applicable†

Scuba divers in Havelock, Andaman and Nicobar Islands

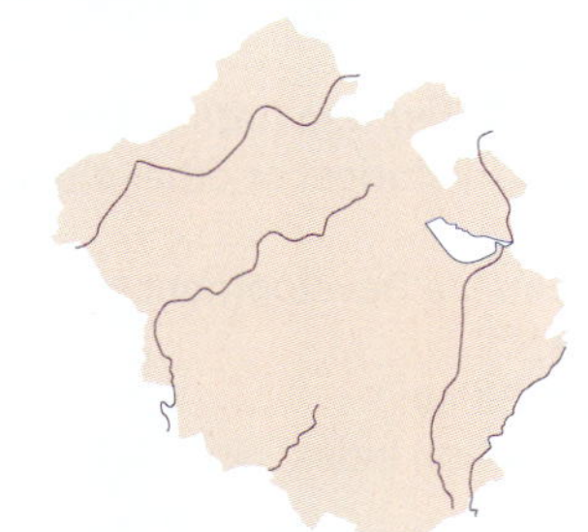

CHANDIGARH

- **Area:** 114 sq. km
- **Population:** 1.05 million
  FDI Equity Inflow: ₹498.29
- **Main Languages:** Hindi, Punjabi and English
- **Literacy Rate:** 86 per cent
- **Higher Education:** Universities: 3; Colleges: 25
- **Constitution/Assembly:** It has only one parliamentary constituency.
- **Administrator:** Banwarilal Purohit
- **Agriculture:** NFSA Ranking: Not applicable; major crops: Rice, wheat and maize

Indian grey mongoose: the state animal of Chandigarh

- **Minerals:** None
- **Industries:** Light engineering industry, industrial fasteners, electrical/electronic items, machine tools, pharmaceuticals, plastic goods, sanitary fittings, steel/ wooden furniture and food products
- **Roads:** National highways: 15 km; No. of National Highways: 1
- **Railway Route Length:** 16 km
- **Airport:** International: 1
- **Art/Culture:** Chandigarh shares the cultural aspects of both Haryana and Punjab, and hosts cultural festivals annually, such as the Festival of Gardens and the Annual Chandigarh Carnival.
- **Nature Reserves:** National parks: None; Wildlife sanctuaries: 2
- **Tourism:** Sukhna Lake, Rock Garden, International Dolls Museum and Sector-17 Plaza
- **Official Symbols:** bird: Indian grey hornbill (*Ocyceros birostris*); flower: Dhak (*Butea monosperma*); tree: Mango (*Mangifera indica*); animal: Grey mongoose (*Herpestes edwardsii*)
- **Do Not Miss!** Chandigarh War Memorial, which is located in a bougainvillea garden
- **Swachh Survekshan Ranking:** Not applicable
- **UNESCO Heritage (Intangible cultural, historical or other sites):** The architectural work of Le Corbusier
- **Sustainable Development Index Score:** 79
- **Smart** City: 1
- **Air Pollution Index:** 50 (Good)

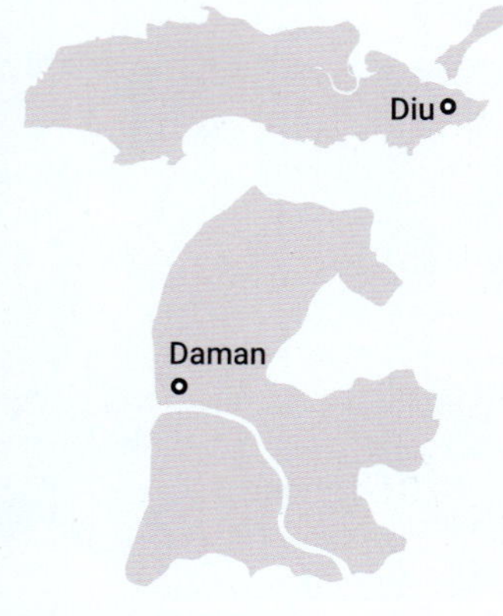

Fort Diu, Dadra and Nagar Haveli and Daman and Diu

DADRA AND NAGAR HAVELI AND DAMAN AND DIU

- **Area:** 603 sq. km
- **Capital:** Daman
- **Population:** 0.58 million
- **FDI Equity Inflow:** ₹1,102.07
- **Main Languages:** Gujarati and Hindi
- **Literacy Rate:** 81.67 per cent (average of the two)
- **Higher Education:** Universities: None; Colleges: 18
- **Constitution/Assembly:** The territory has only one parliamentary constituency.
- **Administrator:** Praful Patel
- **Agriculture:** NFSA Ranking: 6; major crops: Rice, bajra, mangoes and sapota (*Manilkara zapota*)
- **Minerals:** Limestone (marginal)
- **Industries:** Textiles and yarns, plastic, rubber, chemical material production and metal-based units
- **Roads:** National highways: 59 km; No. of National highways: 4
- **Railway** Route Length: None
- **Airports:** Domestic: 1
- **Art/Culture:** Tribal festivals such as Kanseri festival, Divaso festival, Garba festival, folk-dance festival and Vagh Baras
- **Nature Reserves:** National parks: None; Wildlife sanctuaries: 2
- **Tourism:** Tadkeshwar Mahadev Mandir at Valsad, Deer Park at Khanvel, Dudhni Lake, Forts of Moti Daman and Nani Daman, Basilica of Bom Jesus, Fort Diu, Dadra, and Hirwa Van Garden at Silvassa
- **Official Symbols:** Not designated
- **Do Not Miss!** The Tribal Museum in Silvassa is a tribute to and an effort to safeguard and depict the rich legacy of tribal culture and society in its untouched form. The museum also showcases puppets and dolls depicting a unique way of life.
- **Swachh Survekshan Ranking:** Not applicable
- **UNESCO Heritage (Intangible cultural, historical or other sites):** None
- **Sustainable Development Index Score:** 62
- **Smart Cities:** 2
- **Air Pollution Index:** Not applicable†

NATIONAL CAPITAL TERRITORY OF DELHI

- **Area:** 1,483 sq. km
- **Population:** 16.75 million
- **FDI Equity Inflow:** ₹1,47,961.97
- **Main Languages:** Hindi, Punjabi, Urdu and English
- **Literacy Rate:** 86.2 per cent
- **Higher Education:** Universities: 28; Colleges: 179
- **Constitution/Assembly:** Unicameral. Legislative assembly: 70
- **Lt Governor:** Vinai Kumar Saxena
- **Chief Minister:** Arvind Kejriwal
- **Agriculture:** NFSA Ranking: 21; major crops: Wheat, bajra, jowar, gram and maize
- **Minerals:** Kaolin, fireclay, silica sand and quartzite
- **Industries:** Manufacturing light engineering machines and automobile parts, sports goods, bicycles, footwear, textiles and leather goods
- **Roads:** National highways: 157 km; No. of National highways: 13
- **Railway Route Length:** 184 km
- **Airport:** International: 1
- **Art/Culture:** The Delhi Tourism and Transportation Development Corporation organizes events such as the Roshanara Festival, Shalimar Festival, Qutub Festival, Winter Carnival, Garden Tourism Festival, Jahan-e-Khusrau Festival and Mango Festival every year.
- **Nature Reserves:** National parks: None; Wildlife sanctuary: 1
- **Tourism:** Rashtrapati Bhavan, Lal Qila (Red Fort), Jama Masjid, Qutub Minar, India Gate, Humayun's Tomb, National Museum and Lotus Temple
- **Official Symbols:** bird: House sparrow (*Passer domesticus*); flower: Alfalafa (*Medicago sativa*); tree: Gulmohar (*Delonix regia*) animal: Nilgai (*Boselaphus tragocamelus*)
- **Do Not Miss!** The Sulabh International Museum of Toilets in Mahavir Enclave is the only such museum in the world.
- **Swachh Survekshan Ranking:** Not applicable
- **UNESCO Heritage (Intangible cultural, historical or other sites):** Humayun's Tomb, Qutub Minar complex and Red Fort complex
- **Sustainable Development Index Score:** 68
- **Smart City:** 1
- **Air Pollution Index:** 91(Satisfactory)

The University of Delhi: A 75-Year Snapshot

The University of Delhi has gone through a substantial transformation in the last 75 years. It predates Indian independence and in fact celebrated its 100 years since inception on 16 January 2022. Before Independence, there were only four colleges in Delhi – Zakir Husain Delhi College (then known as The Delhi College, founded in 1792), St Stephen's College (1881), Hindu College (1899), and Ramjas College (1917), which were later affiliated to the university, and a reported total of 750 students. It was after Partition that colleges like Hansraj College, SGTB Khalsa College, Deshbandhu College and Kirori Mal College were established to accommodate the displaced students. Today, the university has 91 colleges and 70,000 seats in its academic year. Of these colleges, 22 are for women, while the rest are co-educational. More than four lakh students competed for a seat in the university in 2022. There are 16 faculties and 86 departments now compared to only two faculties and eight departments before Independence.

Srinagar (summer)

Jammu (winter)

JAMMU AND KASHMIR

- **Area:** 42,241 sq. km
- **Capital:** Srinagar (summer); Jammu (winter)
- **Population:** 12.5 million
- **FDI Equity Inflow:** ₹5.92
- **Main Languages:** Urdu, Kashmiri and Dogri
- **Literacy Rate:** 67.2 per cent (before the division)
- **Higher Education:** Universities: 15; Colleges: 316
- **Constitution/Assembly:** Unicameral. Legislative assembly: to be announced
- **Lt Governor:** Manoj Sinha
- **Agriculture:** NFSA Ranking: 30; major crops: Apples, rice, wheat, saffron and cumin
- **Minerals:** Limestone, chromite, bauxite, coal and lignite
- **Industries:** Machinery, sericulture, horticulture and handicrafts
- **Roads:** National highways: 1,752 km; No. of National highways: 11
- **Railway Route Length:** 298 km
- **Airports:** International: 1; Domestic: 1
- **Art/Culture:** Woodcarving, papier mâché, hand embroidery, carpet weaving, and musical traditions employing the rabab and the santoor
- **Nature Reserves:** National parks: 4; Wildlife sanctuaries: 14
- **Tourism:** Kashmir Valley, Dal Lake, Gulmarg, Pahalgam and Shri Vaishno Devi shrine
- **Official Symbols:** bird: Black-necked crane (*Grus nigricollis*); flower: Lotus (*Nelumbo nicifera*); tree: Chinar tree (*Planatus orientalis*); animal: Hangul (*Cervus elaphus hanglu*)
- **Do not miss!** Carved walnut wood is a local speciality. Walnut trees locally called 'doon kul' are traditionally cut only on maturation after hundreds of years.
- **Swachh Survekshan Ranking:** Not Applicable
- **UNESCO Heritage (Intangible cultural, or historical, or other sites):** None
- **Sustainable Development Index Score:** 66
- **Smart Cities:** 2
- **Air Pollution Index:** 53 (Satisfactory)

Intricate carving on walnut wood, Jammu and Kashmir

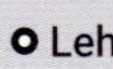

LADAKH

- **Area:** 59,146 sq. km
- **Capital:** Leh, Kargil (joint capital)
- **Population:** 0.27 million
- **FDI Equity Inflow:** ₹1.19
- **Main Languages:** Ladakhi (Bhoti), Tibetan, Urdu and Hindi
- **Literacy Rate:** (Leh) 62 per cent
- **Higher Education:** Universities: 1; Colleges: 5
- **Constitution/Assembly:** The territory is represented by a single constituency in the Parliament.
- **Lt Governor:** Radha Krishna Mathur
- **Agriculture:** NFSA Ranking: 34; major crops: Wheat, barley, pulses, fruits, oilseeds
- **Minerals:** Borax, potash, sulphur and pyrite
- **Industries:** Tourism, mountaineering and agriculture
- **Roads:** National highways: 806 km; No. of National highways: 3
- **Railway Route Length:** None
- **Airport:** Domestic: 1
- **Art/Culture:** Woodcarving, papier mâché and thangka art
- **Nature Reserves:** National park: 1; Wildlife sanctuaries: 2
- **Tourism:** Leh, Pangong Tso, Nubra Valley, Shanti Stupa, Alchi Monastery and Thikse Monastery
- **Official Symbols:** bird: Black-necked crane (*Grus nigricollis*); animal: Snow leopard (*Panthera uncia*)
- **Do Not Miss!** The Indian Astronomical Observatory at Hanle is one of the world's highest sites for optical, infrared and gamma-ray telescopes.
- **Swachh Survekshan Ranking:** Not Applicable
- **UNESCO Heritage (Intangible cultural, historical or other sites):** Buddhist chanting of Ladakh: recitation of sacred Buddhist texts in the trans-Himalayan Ladakh region.
- **Sustainable Development Index Score:** 66
- **Smart Cities:** None
- **Air Pollution Index:** Not applicable†

India's First 'Night Sky Sanctuary' in Ladakh

India's first 'Night Sky Sanctuary' is all set to come up in Ladakh by the end of 2022. This dark sky reserve refers to an area where a distinct nocturnal environment is present along with starry nights, undisturbed by light pollution. Hanle was selected for the project as it is located amid Ladakh's cold desert region, and has clear sky and dry weather conditions throughout the year. This reserve will have low human activity and become one of the highest sites for optical, infrared and gamma-ray telescopes. The location of this reserve will be around 4,500 m (14,764 ft) above sea level in the Changthang Wildlife Sanctuary. While tourists will be permitted in the reserve, it will be ensured that tourism is conducted while being cognisant of the environment. The project is expected to boost astro-tourism in the country.

Changthang Plateau, Ladakh

LAKSHADWEEP

Kavaratti

- **Area:** 32 sq. km
- **Capital:** Kavaratti
- **Population:** 0.064 million
- **FDI Equity Inflow:** Not applicable
- **Main Languages:** Malayalam, Jeseri (Dweep Bhasha) and Mahal
- **Literacy Rate:** 91.8 per cent
- **Higher Education:** Universities: None; Colleges: None
- **Constitution/Assembly:** It is represented by one constituency in the Parliament.
- **Administrator:** Praful Patel
- **Agriculture:** NFSA Ranking: 29; major crop: Coconut
- **Minerals:** Limestone/lime shell
- **Industries:** Coconut fibre extraction and conversion into fibre products, coir fibre factories and tourism
- **Roads:** Not recorded
- **Railway Route Length:** None
- **Airport:** Domestic: 1
- **Art/Culture:** Kolkali and Parichakali are the two popular folk-art forms, and Lava is the most popular local dance form.
- **Nature Reserves:** National parks: None; Wildlife sanctuary: 1
- **Tourism:** Agatti, Bangaram, Kalpeni, Kadmat, Kavaratti and Minicoy
- **Official Symbols:** bird: Noddy tern (*Anous stolidus*); flower: Neelakurinji (*Strobilanthes kuntheiana*); tree: Breadfruit (*Artocarpus altilis*); animal: Butterfly fish (*Chaetodon falcula*)
- **Do Not Miss!** An open-sea dive at Minicoy Island.
- **Swachh Survekshan Ranking:** Not applicable
- **UNESCO Heritage (Intangible cultural, historical or other sites):** None

A stunning seascape, Lakshadweep

- **Sustainable Development Index Score:** 63
- **Smart City:** 1
- **Air Pollution Index:** Not applicable†

PUDUCHERRY

- **Area:** 294 sq. km
- **Capital:** Puducherry
- **Population:** 1.24 million
- **FDI Equity Inflow:** ₹463.08
- **Main Languages:** Tamil, Telugu, Malayalam, English and French
- **Literacy Rate:** 85.8 per cent
- **Higher Education:** Universities: 4; Colleges: 79
- **Constitution/Assembly:** Unicameral. Legislative assembly: 33
- **Lt Governor:** Dr Tamilisai Soundararajan
- **Chief Minister:** N. Rangaswamy
- **Agriculture:** NFSA Ranking: Not applicable; major crops: Rice, pulses, coconut, areca nut and spices
- **Minerals:** Limestone, kaolin and lignite
- **Industries:** Food and beverages, pharmaceuticals, mechanical and chemical industries
- **Roads:** National highways: 64 km; No. of National highways: 2
- **Railway Route Length:** 22 km
- **Airport/Port:** Domestic: 1
- **Art/Culture:** Korai mats and handmade Bommai dolls made of terracotta, papier mâché and plaster
- **Nature Reserves:** National parks: None; Wildlife sanctuary: 1
- **Tourism:** Backwaters, rivers, Auroville, beaches and other areas developed as sustainable eco-tourist facilities.
- **Official Symbols:** bird: Koel (*Eudynamys scolopaceus*); flower: Cannonball (*Couroupita guianensis*); tree: Bael (*Aegle marmelos*); animal: Indian palm squirrel (*Funambulus palmarum*)
- **Do Not Miss!** A guided tour on vintage bicycles through the classical French colonies and traditional Tamil settlements.
- **Swachh Survekshan Ranking:** Not applicable
- **UNESCO Heritage (Intangible cultural, historical or other sites):** None
- **Sustainable Development Index Score:** 68
- **Smart City:** 1
- **Air Pollution Index:** 50 (Good)

Matrimandir in Auroville, Puducherry

IMAGE COPYRIGHT INFORMATION

NOTE: CCA-SA refers to the Creative Commons Attribution-Share Alike Wikimedia Commons/International Wikimedia Commons licences; Public Domain/PD: All public domain photographs have been sourced from: Wikimedia Commons/Public Domain; PIB: Press Information Bureau; GODL: Government Open Data Licence – India; GoI: Government of India.

All clipart for trivia boxes: flaticon.com

PRELIMS I – XVI

Title page: by courtesy of the record holder; **vi**: **top**: Vijaya Ghose: by courtesy of Ela Ghose; **bottom**: Thomas Abraham and Vijaya Ghose: by courtesy of Thomas Abraham; **vii**: **top and bottom**: by courtesy of Thomas Abraham; **viii**: Novy Kapadia: by courtesy of Jonathan Page; **ix**: Novy Kapadia with Sunil Chhetri: Mohammed Shafiq; **x – xvi**: **contents**: images have been credited under the respective chapters below.

HUMAN STORY 1–48

Images are by the courtesy of record holders; **1–2**: **background**: Shutterstock.com; **23**: **background**: Karolina Grabowska/ Pexels.com; **27**: **background**: Tim Mossholder/Pexels.com; **28–29**: **background**: Pixabay/Pexels.com; **41**: **background**: Karolina Grabowska/Pexels.com; **42–43**: **background**: Tim Mossholder/Pexels.com; **45**: **background**: Karolina Grabowska/Pexels.com; **47**: **background**: Karolina Grabowska/ Pexels.com.

STRUCTURES 49–74

Opener pic, 49: Pikoso.kz/Shutterstock.com; **50**: **top right**: Rakhigarhi Burial: by courtesy of Vasant Shinde; **bottom**: Lothal dockyard: Darshan Kumar/Shutterstock.com; **51**: Sanchi stupa: Deepesh Paliwal/Shutterstock.com; **52**: Dashashwamedh Ghat: niladrilovesphotography/Shutterstock.com; **53**: Arjuna's Penance: 265466417/Shutterstock.com; **54**: Reclining Buddha statue: Debjit Chakraborty/Shutterstock.com; **55**: Taj Mahal: Stockbym ST/Shutterstock.com; **56–57**: **background**: Martand Sun Temple: Naresh Sharma/Shutterstock.com; **58**: Vishnu Dashavatara Temple: mdsharma/Shutterstock.com; **59**: Se Cathedral: CRS PHOTO/Shutterstock.com; **60**: **from top, clockwise**: Muthumalai Murugan: ELAMARAN ELAA PHOTOGRAPHY/ Shutterstock.com; Statue of Equality: NARSIMHULU VANARASI/Shutterstock.com; Statue of Unity: Sagittarius Pro/Shutterstock.com; **61**: **from top, clockwise**: Tathagata Tsal: Sudip Bhar/Shutterstock.com; Dhyana Buddha: reddees/ Shutterstock.com; Padmasambhava: saiko3p/ Shutterstock.com; Thiruvalluvar: VIKRAM SK/Shutterstock.com; **62**: Brihadeeswarar Temple: gnanistock/Shutterstock.com; **63**: **top**: Global Vipassana Pagoda: saiko3p/Shutterstock.com; **bottom**: Jatayu Earth Center: Libin Kallada Photography/ Shutterstock.com; **64**: Adiyogi Lord Shiva statue: travel sojourns/ Shutterstock.com; **66**: Indira Gandhi Canal: Maninder.dsw/ Shutterstock.com; **67**: Thalassery Lighthouse: Shutterstock.com; **68–69**: Rashtrapati Bhavan: AlexAnton/Shutterstock.com; **70**: New Parliament Building National Emblem: by courtesy of PIB; **71**: **background**: Chandigarh Rock Garden: shalender/ Shutterstock.com; **72–73**: Noida Demolition: PradeepGaurs/ Shutterstock.com; **74**: Green Buildings: Sunset Paper/ Shutterstock.com.

AGRICULTURE 75–88

Opener pic, 75: pakpoomkh/Shutterstock.com; **76**: Farmers in paddy field: Noppadon stocker/Shutterstock; **77**: William Carey: PD/Unknown Author; **78**: Tuber Crops Research Institute: by courtesy of Indian Council of Agricultural Research portal, Ministry of Agriculture and Farmers' Welfare; **79**: ICICI Bank: mrinalpal/Shutterstock.com; **81**: **top**: Plant: Kannika Taenkhum/ Shutterstock.com; **bottom**: ash gourd: by courtesy of the record holder; **82**: *Bhut jolokia*: Swapan Photography/Shutterstock; **83**: Milk churning: Olja Reven/Shutterstock.com; **84**: **from top, clockwise; Grains**: Rice: KITSANANAN/Shutterstock.com; Wheat: Kovaleva_Ka/Shutterstock; Pulses: deepak bishnoi/ Shutterstock.com; **Oilseeds**: Groundnuts: Dzha33/Shutterstock. com; Rapeseed: 1392360443/Shutterstock.com; **Commercial Crops**: Sugarcane: anny ta/Shutterstock.com; Tea and Coffee: DENIS ESAULOV 1987/Shutterstock.com; Potato: Chatham172/ Shutterstock.com; Vegetables: Vallabh Soni/Shutterstock. com; Fruits: Abhi photo studio/Shutterstock.com; **85**: **from top, clockwise**: **Livestock**: Buffalo: k86/Shutterstock.com; Camels: OlegD/Shutterstock.com; Sheep: Jojobearz/Shutterstock.com; Goat: **mteicnler**/Shutterstock.com; Cows: Aleksandar Todorovic/ Shutterstock.com; Chicken: Olhastock/Shutterstock.com; **Dairy Products**: Eggs and Meat: Supattra Luasook/Shutterstock.com; **86**: Milk cans: clickedbynishant/Shutterstock.com; **87**: Dr Ramesh Raliya: by courtesy of Dr Ramesh Raliya; **88**: **top**: Neem: Swapan Photography/Shutterstock.com; **bottom**: Tractors: Rinku Dua/ Shutterstock.com.

GOVERNMENT 89–106

Opener pic, 89: Priyank Pamkar/Shutterstock.com; **90**: **top right**: Dom Francisco de Almeida: PD/Unknown; **middle**: soldiery of Tantia Tope: PD/Unknown; **91**: National Flags: Rawpixel.com/ Shutterstock.com; **92**: Sukumar Sen: GODL – India/India Post; **93**: President Droupadi Murmu: GODL – India/President's Secretariat; **94–95**: **background**: Parliament House: Dzha33/ Shutterstock.com; **96**: **top right**: L.K. Advani: PD/US State Department; **middle**: Dr S. Radhakrishnan: PD/Cecil W. Stoughton; **bottom**: Aadhaar: WESTOCK PRODUCTIONS/Shutterstock.com; **97**: **top left**: Dr Rajendra Prasad: CCA-SA 2.0/ Archives New Zealand from New Zealand; **middle**: V.V. Giri: GODL – India/India Post; **bottom left**: Sardar Vallabhbhai Patel: PD/Government of India work; **98**: **top right**: Srinagar: Mazur Travel/Shutterstock.com; **bottom right**: Dr S. Muthulakshmi Reddy: PD/Unknown; **100**: Babu Jagjivan Ram: GODL – India/India Post; **101**: Kerala Government Secretariat: Manu M. Nair/Shutterstock.com; **102**: **top right**: Pema Khandu: GODL – India/Ministry of Home Affairs; **middle**: Vijay Lakshmi Pandit: PD/Unknown; **104**: S. Subramania Iyer: PD/ Unknown; **105**: myScheme: screenshot of website; **106**: Calcutta High Court: PD/Samual Borne.

DEFENCE 107–132

Opener pic, 107: IR Photos/Shutterstock.com; **108**: **top**: General Bipin Rawat: GODL – India/Integrated Defence Staff; **bottom**: Major Somnath Sharma:GODL – India/India Post; **109**: **top**: Army Uniform: GODL – India/Whiteknight_AI; **bottom**: Oldest Infantry: PD/Alfred Crowdy Lovett (1862–1919); **110**: Vijayanta: Matyas Rehak/Shutterstock.com; **111**: Women Colonels: Sonu Mehta/ Hindustan Times; **112**: **from top, clockwise**: F-INSAS; Nipun; Thermal Imager: by courtesy of PIB; **113**: **top**: AERV: GODL – India/ Government of India; **bottom**: Agni-V: GODL – India/Ministry of

Defence; **114**: **top**: Brigadier S.V. Saraswati: by courtesy of PIB; **bottom**: National War Memorial: by courtesy of PIB; **115**: **top**: Killer Squadron: by courtesy of PIB; **116**: Guard of Honour: GODL – India/Indian Navy; **117**: **top**: Armed Forces: SumanBhaumik/Shutterstock.com; **bottom**: INS *Chakra*: CCA_SA 4.0/Krishna Chaitanya Velaga; **118–119**: **background**: INS *Vikrant*: GODL – India; **inset**: Cochin Shipyard: GODL – India; **120**: **background**: Pexels/Pixabay; **insets, from top, clockwise**: Navy Ensign: PD; **121**: INS *Talwar*: PD/Mass Communication Specialist 3rd Class Cheyenne Geletka; **122**: **top**: INS *Sarvekshak*: GODL – India/Ministry of Defence; **bottom**: GRSE: GODL – India/Indian Navy; **123**: Vice Admiral Arun Prakash: PD/U.S. Navy; **124**: Air Marshal Subroto Mukherjee: PD/Solomon; **125**: Chetak Tribute: by courtesy of PIB; **126**: Flying Officer Nirmal Jit Singh Sekhon; GODL – India/India Post; **127**: **top**: Vampire Jet: PD/Pseudopanax; **bottom**: Tejas: GODL – India/Ministry of Defence; **128**: **from top, clockwise**: HAL Tejas: GODL – India/Ministry of Defence; Jaguar: PD/U.S. Navy photo by Mass Communication Specialist 2nd Class Jarod Hodge; MiG-29: GNU Free Documentation License 1.2/Aktug Ates; MiG-21: GODL–India/Indian Air Force; Dassault Rafale: EdictGov-India/ Indian Air Force; Dassault Mirage 2000: PD/SRA GREG L. DAVIS, USAF; Sukhoi 30Mk-I: PD/ 1st Lt. George Tobias; **129**: **top to bottom**: Ilyushin Il-76: PD/TSgt Shane A. Cuomo; McDonnel Douglas: PD/U.S. Air Force by Jet Fabara; Antonov: GNU Free Documentation License/Paul Spijkers; HAL Kiran: EdictGov-India/Ministry of Defence (India); **130**: Rudram-1: GODL – India/Defence Decode; **131**: **top and middle**: Rajnath Singh: by courtesy of PIB; **132**: Indian Coast Guard: GODL – India/Indian Navy.

THE NATURAL WORLD 133–154

Opener pic, 133: Sourabh Bharti/Shutterstock.com; **134**: **top**: Kangchenjunga: Tara Shankar Snai/Shutterstock.com; **bottom**: Lonar crater: Padmanabh Choudhury/Shutterstock.com; **135**: Barren Island: NASA/PD; **136**: Dolphin: Sergey Uryadnikov/Shutterstock.com; **137**: **top**: Gibbon: Anuradha Marwah/Shutterstock.com; **bottom**: Titanosaurus: PD/ДиБгд ; **138**: Himalayan wolf: Suman_Ghosh/Shutterstock.com; **bottom**: Vulture: Fabio Nodari/Shutterstock.com; **139**: **top**: Black-necked crane: pallav pranjal sarma/Shutterstock.com; **middle**: Butterfly: Shubhrojyoti/Shutterstock.com; **140–141**: **background**: Cheetah: Roel Roelofs/Pixabay; **insets**, **top and bottom**: Kuno National Park: by courtesy of PIB; **142**: **top**: Balerion forest gecko: Saunak Pal; **bottom**: Chameleon: Azay photography/Shutterstock.com; **143**: **top**: Gharial: Vladislav T. Jirousek/Shutterstock.com; **bottom**: Mugger: gnanistock/Shutterstock.com; **144**: **top**: Kaziranga National Park: Mousam Ray/Shutterstock.com; **middle**: Manas Wildlife Sanctuary: Akkil Suvarna/Shutterstock.com; **bottom**: Sundarbans National Park: Arabindu Sardar/Shutterstock.com; **145**: **top**: Valley of Flowers National Parks: Brinda Tailor/Shutterstock.com; **middle**: Keoladeo National Park: Sunil_Sharma_ab/Shutterstock.com; **bottom**: Western Ghats: dilurakesh/Shutterstock.com; **146**: **top**: King cobra: tb-photography/Shutterstock.com; **middle**: Leatherback sea turtle: catalinaug/Shutterstock.com; **147**: **top**: Whale shark: Jan Finsterbusch/Shutterstock.com; **bottom**: Banyan tree: saiko3p/Shutterstock.com; **148**: **top**: Corpse flower: gkgegk/Pixabay; **middle**: Jackfruit: Siva prasad/Pixabay; **149**: **top**: White tiger: Y Shots/Shutterstock.com; **middle**: Dugong: vkilikov/Shutterstock.com; **150**: **top**: Elephants: Mogens Trolle/Shutterstock.com; **middle**: Bamboo species: by courtesy of the record holder; **151**: **top**: Great Indian bustard: Thomas Hardwicke/PD; **bottom**: Longest tapioca plant: by courtesy of the record holder; **152**: Orchids: by courtesy of Ashis Kumar Roy; **154**: Indore: bodom/Shutterstock.com.

TRANSPORT 155–172

Opener pic, 155: Shutterstock.com; **156**: Kempegowda Airport: Hari Santhosh/Shutterstock.com; **157**: *Swati*: CCO 1.0 Universal Public Domain Dedication/Jane's Encyclopedia of Aviation; **158**: Leh Airport: Rangeecha/Shutterstock.com; **159**: Akasa Air: Exploring_frog/Shutterstock.com; **160**: Air India Maharajah: PhotographerIncognito/Shutterstock.com; **161**: Deccan Queen: Dinesh Hukmani/Shutterstock.com; **162**: Train: Deepak Bobby/Shutterstock.com; **164**: **from top, clockwise**: Kolkata Metro: Every Shutter Counts/Shutterstock.com; Mumbai Metro: Tukaram.Karve/Shutterstock.com; Namma (Bengaluru) Metro: CCO 1.0 Universal Public Domain Dedication/Fly2Blue; Kochi Metro: Basil45667/Shutterstock.com; Jaipur Metro: Umesh Gogna/Shutterstock.com; Chennai Metro: Gulpa/Shutterstock.com; Delhi Metro: joyfull/Shutterstock.com; Lucknow Metro: PradeepGaurs/Shutterstock.com; **165**: Hauz Khas Station: by courtesy of Yusra Adeeb; **167**: Charging Station: PradeepGaurs/Shutterstock.com; **170–171**: Mundra Port: Ungureanu Catalina Oana/Shutterstock.com.

MEDICAL SCIENCES 173–188

Opener pic, 173: AshTproductions/Shutterstock.com; **174**: Ayushman Bharat Pradhan Mantri Jan Arogya Yojana stamp: GODL – India/Post of India; **175**: **top**: Family planning stamp: Boris15/Shutterstock.com; **bottom**: Tata Memorial Centre: GODL – India/India Post; **176**: P.D. Hinduja National Hospital: RAMNIKLAL MODI/Shutterstock.com; **177**: **background**: Big Data for the Brain: Shutterstock.com; **178**: **top**: The Serum Institute of India: MudaCom/Shutterstock.com; **bottom**: Dr Jacob Chandy: PD/Unknown; **179**: Autism Spectrum Disorder: Shutterstock.com; **180**: **top**: Sandfly: PD/CDC/Frank Collins; **bottom**: Dr N. Gopinath: Wikimedia Commons/Fair Use; **181**: Dr Kewal Kishan Talwar: GODL – India/ President's Secretariat; **182**: **top**: AIIMS Delhi: mrinalpal/Shutterstock.com; **bottom**: AIIMS Rishikesh: staff personal; **183**: **top**: AIIMS Jodhpur: by courtesy of Dr Tanya Batra; **bottom**: AIIMS Bhopal: Paulose NK/Shutterstock.com; **184**: Dr P. Venugopal: GODL – India/Prime Minister's Office; **185**: COVID-19 Vaccine: siam.pukkato/Shutterstock.com; **186**: Cancer cells: Lightspring/Shutterstock.com; **188**: Pharmaceutical: cortex-film/Shutterstock.com.

SCIENCE AND TECHNOLOGY 189–210

Opener pic, 189: ktsdesign/Shutterstock.com; **191**: **top**: D.R. Kaprekar: Wikimedia Commons/Fair Use/Author Unknown; **bottom**: Neelkantha Bhanu Prakash: CCA-SA 4.0/Bhanuprakash13; **192**: KIRAN: AshTproductions/Shutterstock.com; **193**: Osmania University: Nagesh12/Shutterstock.com; **194**: **top**: Jagdish Chandra Bose: suprabhat/Shutterstock.com; **bottom**: Atomic Research Centre: PD/Sobarwiki; **195**: **top**: Satyendra Nath Bose: PD/India; **bottom**: Anna Mani: Fair Use/Historic Image; **196**: **background**: WikiImages/Pixabay; **inset**, **bottom**: ESA/Hubble; **197**: **top**: ARIES: by courtesy of Aryabhatta Research Institute of Observational Sciences (ARIES); **bottom**: Presidency College: PD/Francis Frith; **198**: **top**: Biotechnology: Chokniti Khongchum/Pixabay; **middle**: Shanti Swaroop Bhatnagar: GODL – India/India Post; **199**: **top**: Uttarakhand Observatory: WikiImages/Pixabay; **bottom**: Dr. D.N. Wadia: GODL – India/India Post; **200**: **top**: Iron ore deposits: Shutterstock.com; **middle**: Dr S.Z. Qasim: PD/niyogibooksindia; **201**: **top**: R.S. Paroda: by courtesy of PIB; **middle**: Rama Brahma Sanyal: PD/India; **bottom**: Dr. Kamaljit Bawa: CCA-SA 4.0/The

Royal Society; **202**: Hollierth Electronic Computer at the National Museum of Computing: CCA-SA 4.0 International/user:geni - https://commons.wikimedia.org/wiki/File:Hollerith_Electronic_Computer_National_Museum_of_Computing_.JPG; **203**: Private Sector Space: GODL/ISRO; **204**: Cartosat-3: GODL/ISRO; **205**: **background**: Pexels/Pixabay; **inset**: Aryabhatta Satellite: PD-USA/ISRO; **206–207**: **background**: Pexels/Pixabay; **insets, from top, clockwise**: Cartosat-1: PD; Megha Tropiques spacecraft: GODL – India/ISRO; Astrosat-1: GODL – India/ISRO; **208**: Chandrayaan-1: GODL/ISRO; **209**: Gaganyaan: GODL/ISRO; **210**: GSAT-II: GODL/ISRO.

EDUCATION 211–230

Opener pic, 211: SIHASAKPRACHUM/Shutterstock.com; **212**: Artificial Intelligence: AlesiaKan/Shutterstock.com; **213**: Kendriya Vidyalaya Sangathan headquarters: PD/Chawla. mohali; **214**: **top**: Corridor of Presidency University: PD/Taritwan Pal; **bottom**: University of Allahabad: PD/Abhijeet Vardhan; **215**: **top**: Bethune School building: PD/Unknown; **bottom**: Calcutta Medical College: PD/Dwaipayanc; **216**: University of Delhi: PD/ Seek1; **217**: Test Sheet: Constantine Pankin/Shutterstock.com; **218**: NDA Khadakwasla: GODL – India/Indian Navy; **219**: Kamala Sohonie: Wikimedia Commons/Fair Use/ http:/ / www.ias.ac.in/ womeninscience/ kamala.html; **220**: **from top, clockwise**: Artefact: Scarabaeus/Shutterstock.com; Indian Museum: Bhaven Jani/ Shutterstock.com; Victoria Memorial Hall: Ktkrypton/Shutterstock. com; **221**: **top**: National Gallery of Modern Art in New Delhi: TK Kurikawa/Shutterstock.com; **middle**: National Gallery of Modern Art in Mumbai: AnilD/Shutterstock.com; **bottom**: Salar Jung Museum: Kittu's/Shutterstock.com; **222–223**: **from top, clockwise**: Sir Jamsetjee Jejeebhoy: PD/George Chinnery; University of Calcutta: PD/Francis Frith; National Library: Biswajit.Dutta.Photo/ Shutterstock.com; **224**: Anna Centenary Library: johntallboy/ Shutterstock.com; **225**: **top**: Rail Transport Museum: Sun_Shine/ Shutterstock.com; **bottom**: Partition Museum: WandererAbhi/ Shutterstock.com; **226–227**: Heritage Transport Museum: singh_ lens/Shutterstock.com; **228**: **top**: School children: CRS PHOTO/ Shutterstock.com; **bottom**: Fanattic Sports Museum: Hindustan Times; **229**: Science City Kolkata: saiko3p/Shutterstock.com; **230**: Arna Jharna: by courtesy of Arna Jharna Museum/Rupayan Sansthan, Rajasthan Institute of Folklore, Jodhpur.

MEDIA AND COMMUNICATIONS 231–250

Opener pic, 231: Shutterstock.com; **232**: PTI: Funstock/ Shutterstock.com; **233**: IIMC: Hindustan Times; **234**: UP Magazine Stall: PradeepGaurs/Shutterstock.com; **235**: Gobind Behari Lal: PD – India; **236**: AIR: Bhaven Jani/Shutterstock.com; **237**: Microphone Radio: Shutterstock.com; **239**: **top**: NDTV: monticello/Shutterstock.com; **middle**: Aaj Tak: Postmodern Studio/ Shutterstock.com; **240**: **top**: Broadcast Seva Portal: by courtesy of PIB; **bottom**: Pigeon Post: Shutterstock.com; **242**: Gandhi Stamps: saptuletail/Shutterstock.com; **244–245**: **background**: Hikkim Post Office: by courtesy of Department of Posts, GoI; **insets, from top, clockwise**: Kolkata Post Office: Abir Roy Barman/Shutterstock. com; Dakshin Gangotri: tristan tan/Shutterstock.com; Mumbai Post Office: Snehal Jeevan Paikar/Shutterstock.com; Hikkim Post Office: by courtesy of Department of Posts, GoI; Floating Post Office: Sandhya Mandal/Shutterstock.com; **246**: **top**: Golden Letter Box: Haryana Circle. Ambala, Department of Posts, Government of India; **bottom**: Philatelic Museum: Bhaven Jani/Shutterstock.com; **247**: Dak Karamyogi: by courtesy of PIB; **248**: BSNL: mrinalpal/ Shutterstock.com; **249**: **top**: 5G Services: by courtesy of PIB; **bottom**: Hotmail: Piotr Swat/Shutterstock.com; **250**: Android OS: quietbits/Shutterstock.com.

LITERATURE 251–260

Opener pic, 251: Nicole Ashley Rahayu Densmoor/Pexels.com; **252**: *Tomb of Sand* cover: by courtesy of Penguin Random House India; **253**: Shakespeare's folio: Andreas Praefcke/PD; **254**: The Bhagavadgita: Wesleyan Mission Press, Bangalore/PD; **255**: College Street: Sirada Wichitaphornkun/Shutterstock.com; **256**: Sweets: Shutterstock.com; **257**: **from top**: *Turn a Blind Eye* cover: by courtesy of Pan Macmillan India; *Do Epic Shit* cover: by courtesy of Juggernaut Books; *My Life in Full* cover: by courtesy of Hachette India; *A Touch of Eternity* cover: by courtesy of Penguin Random House India; *They Found What?/They Made What?* cover: by courtesy of Hachette India; *The Christmas Pig* cover: by courtesy of Hachette India; *Favourite stories from Hindu Myths* cover: by courtesy of Juggernaut Books; **258**: **clockwise from top**: Benyamin: by courtesy of Juggernaut Books; M. Mukundan: by courtesy of Westland Books; *Delhi: A Soliloquy* cover: by courtesy of Westland Books; *India, Empire and First World War Culture* cover: by courtesy of Cambridge University Press; Santanu Das: by courtesy of Santanu Das; Manu Joseph: by courtesy of Rohit Chawla; Dinyar Patel: Hindustan Times; **259**: **top**: Nayantara Sehgal: PD – India; **middle**: Amrita Pritam: Amarjit Chandan Collection/ PD – India; **bottom**: G. Sankara Kurup: GODL/India Post; **260**: **left**: Jhumpa Lahiri: Andrea Raffin/Shutterstock.com; **right**: Banned books: Shutterstock.com.

INDIA AT HER BEST: 75 YEARS OF INDEPENDENCE 261–274

Opener pic, 261: **background**: ArtEver/Shutterstock.com; **262**: **left**: Commemorative stamps: by courtesy of Department of Posts/GoI; **right**: PM Modi: by courtesy of PIB; **263**: **from top, clockwise**: Make-in-India drones: Hindustan Times; Space Kidz India: by courtesy of Space Kidz India; PM Sangrahalaya: by courtesy of PIB; **264**: A 'flag' march: Hindustan Times; **265**: **all photographs**: National Security Guard; **269**: **from top, clockwise**: National flag: ARAVIND TEKI/Shutterstock.com; Tagore: PD/India; Tagore's English translation: PD/United States; Musical notations: PD/India; **270**: **from top, clockwise**: Bankim Chandra Chatterjee: PD/Sibnath Sastri; Painting: PD/India; Peacock: Manan Nimawat/Shutterstock.com; Tiger: PhotocechCZ/Shutterstock. com; **271**: **top**: lotus: Doikanoy/Shutterstock.com; **middle**: banyan tree: saiko3p/Shutterstock.com; **bottom left**: Indian rupee: Nila Newsom/Shutterstock.com; **bottom right**: Meghnad Saha: PD; **272–274**: **background**: ixpert/Shutterstock.com.

VISUAL ARTS 275–292

Opener pic, 275: AjayTvm/Shutterstock.com; **276**: **top**: Lumière film advertisement: Henri Brispot/PD; **middle**: Dadasaheb Phalke: Palaviprabhu/PD – India; **bottom**: Ardeshir Irani: PD – India and USA; **277**: **top**: *Around the World* poster: Theo's little bot/Fair use; **middle**: *Ponniyin Selvan I* poster: Kailash29792/Fair use; **278**: **top**: *Major* poster: Sush150/Fair Use; **middle left**: *RRR* poster: Ab207/ Fair Use; **middle right**: *K.G.F. Chapter 2* poster: Deluxe Vegan/Fair Use; **279**: **top**: Durga Khote: Shruti Swamy/ PD – India; **middle**: *Dilwale Dulhania Le Jayenge* poster: Kailash29792/Fair use;

280: **background**: Pixabay; **Insets, left**: *Anmol Ghadi* poster: Theo's little bot/Fair use; **middle**: *Mother India* poster: Theo's little bot/Fair use/PD – India and USA; **right**: *Mera Naam Joker* poster: Theo's little bot/Fair use; **281**: **background**: Pixabay; **insets, from top, clockwise**: *Amar Akbar Anthony* poster: DatBot/Fair Use; *Coolie* poster: Theo's little bot/Fair use; *Mohabbatein* poster: Begoon/ Fair use; *Enthiran* poster: Kailash29792/Fair use; *Tanhaji* poster: Sush150/Fair Use; *Alibaba aur 40 Chor* poster: Theo's little bot/ Fair use; **282**: **top**: Prem Nazir: GODL – India/India Post; **middle**: S.S. Rajamouli: GODL – India/Vice President's Secretariat; **bottom left**: Alia Bhatt: Suhail Suri/Shutterstock.com; **bottom right**: Suriya: GODL – India/Ministry of Information and Broadcasting;
283: **top**: *Zanjeer* poster: Theo's little bot/Fair use; **middle**: *Satya* poster: Ronjones/Fair Use; **284**: **from top**: Sameer 'Anjaan': CCA 3.0 Unported/Bollywood Hungama – http://www.bollywoodhungama.com/moviemicro/images/id/54349/type/view/imageid/1143848/category/parties; Lata Mangeshkar: CCA 3.0 Unported/Bollywood Hungama – http://www.bollywoodhungama.com/more/photos/view/stills/parties-and-events/id/1781920; Bappi Lahiri: CCA 3.0 Unported/Bollywood Hungama – http://www.bollywoodhungama.com/news/parties-and-events/celebs-grace-musical-concert-rehmatein-3/celebs-grace-musical-concert-rehmatein-3-15/ Bollywood Hungama; Bhupinder Singh: CCA 3.0 Unported/ Bollywood Hungama – http://www.bollywoodhungama.com/more/photos/view/stills/parties-and-events/id/1710890;
285: Ramoji Film City: Ritu Manoj Jethani/Shutterstock.com;
286: **top**: Chaumhalla Palace: Lala Deen Dayal/PD; **bottom**: Lala Deen Dayal: Lala Deen Dayal/PD; **287**: Camera: Krizek Vaclav/ Shutterstock.com; **288**: Ajanta Caves: Shutterstock.com;
289: Handicraft: Shutterstock.com; **290**: Jangid family: by courtesy of the record holder; **291**: Mandala: by courtesy of the record holder; **292**: **top**: pencil carving: by courtesy of the record holder; **bottom**: Marathon portrait: by courtesy of the record holder.

BUSINESS AND ECONOMY 293–312

Opener pic, 293: Deacons docs/Shutterstock.com; **294**: **top**: P.C. Mahalanobis: GODL – India/India Post, Government of India;| **middle**: Nirmala Sitharaman: by courtesy of PIB; **295**: **top**: FDI inflow: bsd studio/Shutterstock.com; **bottom**: J.R.D. Tata: PD/ http:/ / photodivision.gov.in/ IntroPhotodetails.asp?thisPage= 953 -; **296**: **top**: Kushana gold coins: Wikimedia Commons-CC0/Cleveland Museum of Art; **bottom**: Forex Reserves: metamorworks/Shutterstock.com; **297**: **middle**: Punjab National Bank: PhotographerIncognito/Shutterstock.com; **bottom**: Standard Chartered Bank: GODL – India/India Post; **298**: **top**: ICICI Bank: mrinalpal/Shutterstock.com; **middle**: Post Payments Bank: GODL – India/India Post; **299**: Gautam Adani: Wikimedia Commons/ Creative Commons Attribution 3.0 Unported license/free for use; **300**: **top**: LIC: mrinalpal/Shutterstock.com; **middle**: TATA Steel: Arnav Pratap Singh/Shutterstock.com; **301**: **top**: LIC documents: Nisha Dutta/Shutterstock.com; **bottom**: NSE: PD; **302**: **top**: Imperial Bank of India logo: PD –India; **middle**: SBI headquarters: CC0 1.0 Universal Public Domain Dedication/Digamber –https://www.pexels.com/photo/mumbai-state-bank-of-india-building-330601/; **bottom**: SBI stamp: GODL – India/India Post, GoI; **303**: **top**: R.K. Shanmukham Chetty: PD; **middle right**: Union budget: by courtesy of PIB; **middle left**: Premchand Roychand: PD; **bottom**: BSE: CCA-SA 3.0/BSE India; **sidebar**: Gold mohur: National Numismatic Collection, National Museum of American History.; **304**: **top**: Rakesh Jhunjhunwala: PD; **bottom**: Calcutta: PD/Clyde Waddell - http:/ / www.library.upenn.edu/ collections/ sasia/ calcutta1947; **305**: **top**: TATA stamp: GODL – India/India Post; **bottom**: Tarapur Atomic Plant: GODL – India/Department of Atomic Energy; **306**: **top**: Tamil Nadu: SreeSince91/Shutterstock.com; **bottom**: Crypto Budget: Irina Anosova/Shutterstock.com; **307**: Bharat Coking Coal Ltd.: mrinalpal/Shutterstock.com; **308**: Bullion exchange: istara/Pixabay; **309**: **top**: Taj Mahal Hotel: sushmaghadge/Pixabay/Shutterstock.com; **bottom**: Bengaluru: Noppasin Wongchum/Shutterstock.com; **310**: **top**: India GDP: Bhaskar dhapu 3/Shutterstock.com; **bottom**: Amartya Kumar Sen: GODL – India (cropped); **311**: **top**: Rupee plummets: Blackboard/Shutterstock.com; **bottom**: Bombay Courier: PD/Asiatic Society of Mumbai; **312**: LED Display screen: by courtesy of the record holder.

PERFORMING ARTS 313–330

Opener pic, 313: Don Mammoser/Shutterstock.com;
314: **top**: *Gita Govinda*: Nous/PD; **middle**: *Gita Govinda*: Hiart/PD;
315: R. Muthukannammal: by courtesy of PIB; **316**: Madame Meneka: PD–India; **317**: Birju Maharaj: reddees/Shutterstock.com;
318: **from top, clockwise**: Bharatnatyam: JN STUDIO/ Shutterstock.com; Manipuri: silentwings_M_ Ghosh/Shutterstock.com; Kathak: JN STUDIO/Shutterstock.com; Sattriya: JN STUDIO/Shutterstock.com; **319**: **from top, clockwise**: Odissi: Shutterstock.com; Kuchipudi: Aminami/PD; Mohinattam: Storm Is Me/Shutterstock.com; Kathakali: Shutterstock.com; **320**: Rig veda: CCA-SA 4.0 International/Ms Sarah Welch; **321**: **top**: Maharaja Swathi Thirunal: Stephen Crening/PD; **bottom**: Ramanuja Iyengar: SUDARSHAN BHATLA/Shutterstock.com; **322**: Lithophone: Shutterstock.com; **323**: Harp: Shutterstock.com; **324**: Asha Bhosle: Feroze Edassery/Shutterstock.com; **325**: **top**: Digital audio player: Suryanshu Awasthi/Shutterstock.com; **bottom**: Resul Pookutty: Hindustan Times; **326**: Indian Music Experience Museum: by courtesy of IME museum; **327**: Parikrama band: Girish Menon/ Shutterstock.com; **328**: Traveling theatre: Shutterstock.com;
329: Star Theatre: CRS PHOTO/Shutterstock.com; **330**: NDA: by courtesy of the record holder.

SPORTS 331–410

Opener pic, 331: Lightspring/Shutterstock; **332**: Saina Nehwal: GODL – India/Ministry of Youth Affairs and Sports; **334**: **top**: M.C. Mary Kom: GODL – India/croppeden; **middle**: Pullela Gopichand: GODL – India; **337**: Commonwealth Games members: by courtesy of PIB; **338**: Dutee Chand: Wikimedia Commons/CC BY SA 4.0/ from the 22nd Asian Games in Odisha. 2017 Asian Athletics Championships. 6 to 9 July 2017 at the Kalinga Stadium in Bhubaneswar, Odisha Government; **339**: **middle**: Krishna Poonia: GODL – India/Ministry of Youth Affairs and Sports; **bottom**: Bahadur Singh Chouhan: PD/Unknown author; **340**: Milkha Singh: GODL – India/Vice President's Secretariat; **341**: **top**: Sumit Antil: GODL – India/President's Secretariat; **bottom**: P.T. Usha: GODL – India/Ministry of Youth Affairs and Sports; **342**: **background**: Neeraj Chopra: Hindustan Times; **343**: Deepika Kumari: GODL – India/ President's Secretariat; **344**: **top**: Jyothi Surekha Vennam: GODL – India/President's Secretariat; **middle**: Bombayla Devi Laishram: GODL – India/Ministry of Youth Affairs and Sports; **bottom**: Archers Dola Banerjee and Rahul Banerjee: Hindustan Times; **345**: **top**: Abhishek Verma: GODL – India/ President's Secretariat; **middle**: Satwiksairaj Rankireddy: GODL – India/Prime Minister's Office; **bottom**: Chirag Shetty: GODL – India/Prime Minister's Office; **346**: H.S. Prannoy: Kairosnapshots/Shutterstock; **347**: P.V. Sindhu: Abdul Razak Latif/Shutterstock.com; **348**: **top**: K. Srikanth: msyaraafiq/ Shutterstock.com; **bottom**: Thomas Cup men team: Hindustan Times; **349**: **top**: Nandu Natekar: Hindustan Times; **middle**: Prakash

Padukone: Hindustan Times; **bottom**: Jwala Gutta and Ashwini Ponnappa: Hindustan Times ; **350**: **top**: Vijender Singh: Paolo Bona/ Shutterstock.com; **bottom**: Amit Panghal: Hindustan Times; **352**: **top**: Nikhat Zareen: EvrenKalinbacak/Shutterstock.com; **bottom**: M.C. Mary Kom: Hindustan Times; **353**: Pravin Thipsay: Niklesh Jain/ChessBase India; **355**: **top**: Viswanathan Anand: Niklesh Jain/ChessBase India; **middle**: Mir Sultan Khan: CC by SA 4.0/Unknown Cameraman of 1932; **bottom**: Dibyendu Barua: Hindustan Times; **356**: P. Harikrishna: PD; **357**: **top**: R. Praggnanandhaa: Hindustan Times; **middle**: D. Gukesh: Hindustan Times; **bottom**: K. Humpy: Hindustan Times; **359**: **top**: Mithali Raj: GODL – India/President's Secretariat; **bottom**: Jhulan Goswami: Hindustan Times; **360**: **top**: Harmanpreet Kaur: GODL – India/President's Secretariat; **middle**: Poonam Yadav: GODL – India/President's Secretariat; **361**: Sachin Tendulkar: Hindustan Times; **362–63**: **background**: Virat Kohli: Hindustan Times; **365**: Suryakumar Yadav: Hindustan Times; **366**: **left**: All-India team: PD/India; **right**: Vinoo Mankad stamp: GODL – India/India Post; **367**: **top**: 1983 World Cup team: Hindustan Times; **bottom left**: ODI World Cup: Hindustan Times; **bottom right**: Rahul Dravid: CCA 3/ 0 Unported/Bollywood Hungama – http://www.bollywoodhungama.com/more/photos/view/stills/parties-and-events/id/1341543; **369**: **middle**: Geet Sethi: Hindustan Times; **bottom**: Pankaj Advani: Hindustan Times; **371**: Mohammedan Sporting: GODL – India; **372–373**: Sunil Chhetri: Hindustan Times; **375**: I-League winners: by courtesy of I-League; **376**: **middle**: 1956 Olympics: PD/ Unknown author; **bottom**: Chuni Goswami: PD/The Hindu; **377**: Neville D'Souza: PD/India; **378**: Bhaichung Bhutia: GODL – India/Ministry of Youth Affairs and Sports; **379**: S. S. Hakim: GODL – India/ President's Secretariat; **380**: Ali Sher: Hindustan Times; **381**: **top left**: Arjun Atwal: Yu Chun Christopher Wong/ Shutterstock.com; **bottom left**: S.S.P. Chawrasia: Isogood_patrick/ Shutterstock.com; **top right**: Jeev Milkha Singh: mooinblack/ Shutterstock; **382**: **top**: Aditi Ashok pendakisolo/Shutterstock; **bottom**: Jyoti Randhawa mooinblack/Shutterstock.com; **383**: Anirban Lahiri: Isogood_patrick/Shutterstock.com; **385**: **top**: Dilip Tirkey: GODL – India/Ministry of Youth Affairs and Sports; **middle**: Harmanpreet Singh: by courtesy of PIB; **bottom**: Savita Punia: GODL – India/President's Secretariat; **386**: PD/International hockey game: Corepics VOF/Shutterstock.com; **387**: **top**: Berlin Olympics: Unknown author - Bharat Hockey; **middle**: Dhyan Chand: PD/India; **bottom**: Hockey team 1932: Wikimedia Commons/Bhartiya Hockey; **388**: Gender balanced team: Hindustan Times; **389**: 1928 Olympics team: PD/United States; **390**: Varinder Singh: GODL – India/ President's Secretariat; **392**: **top**: Shushila Devi Likmabam: GODL – India/Prime Minister's Office; **bottom**: Powerlifting: sportpoint/ Shutterstock.com; **394**: **top**: Rahi Sarnobat: CCA-SA 4.0/BBC World Service India Pvt. Ltd; **middle**: Saurabh Chaudhary: GODL – India/ Ministry of Youth Affairs and Sports; **bottom**: Esha Singh: CCA-SA 4.0/BBC World Service India Pvt. Ltd.; **395**: **middle**: Manu Bhaker: GODL – India/Rajya Sabha TV; **bottom**: Jaspal Rana: GODL – India/ Ministry of Petroleum and Natural Gas; **396**: Ronjan Sodhi: GODL – India/President's Secretariat; **397**: Dipika Pallikal: CHEN WS/Shutterstock.com; **398**: Saurav Ghosal: CHEN WS/ Shutterstock.com; **399**: **bottom left**: Shikha Tandon: GODL – India/ President's Secretariat; **bottom right**: Sandeep Sejwal: CCA-SA 2.0/ Free for use/ Korea.net/Korean Culture and Information Service; **400**: **top**: Bula Choudhury: GODL – India/Government of India; **bottom**: A. Sharath Kamal: Hindustan Times; **401**: **top**: Mouma Das: Hindustan Times; **bottom**: Manika Batra: Stefan Holm/ Shutterstock.com; **402**: Poulomi Ghatak: Hindustan Times; **403**: G. Sathiyan: CC by SA 4.0/Sathiyan Gnanasekaran - Own work; **404**: **top**: Karman Kaur Thandi: Mai Groves/Shutterstock.com; **bottom**: Ankita Raina: Teo Wei Keong/Shutterstock.com; **405**: **top**: Sania Mirza: Mai Groves/Shutterstock.com; **bottom**: Mahesh Bhupathi: Chris Harvey/Shutterstock.com; **406**: **top**: Leander Paes: Rena Schild;/Shutterstock.com; **bottom**: Saikhom Mirabai Chanu: GODL – India/Ministry of Youth Affairs and Sports; **407**: Yumnam Renu Bala Chanu: GODL – India/President's Secretariat; **408**: **top**: Sakshi Malik: CCA-SA 3.0/Bollywood Hungama – http://www.bollywoodhungama.com/news/parties-and-events/sonakshi-sinha-sakshi-malik-grace-promotions-whisper-likeagirl-campaign/sonakshi-sakshi-grace-the-promotions-6/; **bottom**: Anshu Malik: CCA-SA 4.0/ Jørgen Løken; **410**: **top**: Vinesh Phogat: Azamat Mukanov/Shutterstock.com; **bottom**: Bajrang Punia: Azamat Mukanov/Shutterstock.com.

ADVENTURE 411–430

Opener pic, 411: Shutterstock.com; **413**: **top**: Vijay Kumar Devarkhyani: by courtesy of the record holder; bottom: Highest skydive landing team: by courtesy of the record holder; **414**: Usha Mahajan: by courtesy of the record holder; **415**: New Aero sports policy: by courtesy of PIB; **416**: Nitin Gadkari: by courtesy of PIB; **417**: **background**: by courtesy of the record holder; **insets**, **top**: North – South expedition – group: by courtesy of the record holder; **bottom**: Dhruveer Singh Gandhi: by courtesy of the record holder; **419**: **top to bottom**: by courtesy of the record holders; **420**: Bharat Pannu: by courtesy of the record holder; **422**: Water sports centre: by courtesy of PIB; **423**: Bhakti Sharma: GODL – India/President's Secretariat; **424**: Deepa Malik: GODL – India/President's Secretariat; **425**: Cape2Rio team: by courtesy of the record holder; **426**: Marathon: Shutterstock.com; **427**: Abhishek Singh Pandher: by courtesy of the record holder; **428**: Nanda Devi: Shutterstock.com; **430**: Trekking: sugitas/Shutterstock.com.

STATES AND UNION TERITORRIES 431–455

Opener pic, 431: Shutterstock.com; **432**: Talakona Falls: Shutterstock.com; **433**: **top**: Healthcare drone: Shutterstock.com; **bottom**: Golden Langur: Shutterstock.com; **434**: glass bottles: Shutterstock.com; **435**: **top**: Danteshwari temple: Hari Mahidhar/ Shutterstock.com; **bottom**: Palolem Beach: Shutterstock.com; **436**: Solar Power: Shutterstock.com; **437**: **top**: Morni Hills: Shutterstock.com; **bottom**: Kalka – Shimla train: Amit kg/ Shutterstock.com; **438**: Sir Dorabji Tata Park: Arnav Pratap Singh/ Shutterstock.com; **439**: **top**: Anegundi: Filip Jedraszak/ Shutterstock.com; **bottom**: Houseboat: Shutterstock.com; **440**: Bhimbetka: Shutterstock.com; **441**: **top**: Ganesh Chaturthi: Snehal Jeevan Pailkar/Shutterstock.com; **bottom**: Manipur cityscape: Shutterstock.com; **442**: River Umngot: Ujjayan Purkayastha/ Shutterstock.com; **443**: **top**: Hume's Pheasant: Shutterstock.com; **bottom**: Rhododendron: Shutterstock.com; **444**: Sun Temple: Shutterstock.com; **445**: **top**: Wagah border: Elena Odareeva/ Shutterstock.com; **bottom**: Udaipur city palace: Shutterstock.com; **446**:Red Panda: Shutterstock.com; **447**: **top**: IIT Madras: Hindustan Times; **bottom**: Kakatiya Rudreshwara temple: Shutterstock.com; **448**: **top**: Green Imperial Pigeon: Shutterstock.com; **bottom**: Forest Research Institute: Ultimate Travel Photos/Shutterstock.com; **449**: Imambara: Shutterstock.com; **450**: Darjeeling tea estate: Ron Ramtang/Shutterstock.com; **451**: **top**: Indian Grey Mongoose: Shutterstock.com; **bottom**: Scuba Diver: Shutterstock.com; **452**: Fort Diu: Shutterstock.com; **453**: **top**: Delhi University: Hindustan Times; **bottom**: carving on walnut wood: Shutterstock.com; **454**: Changthang Plateau: Shutterstock.com; **455**: **top**: Lakshadweep: Shutterstock.com; **bottom**: Matri Mandir: Shutterstock.com.

A

B

C

D

E

F

G

H

I

J

K

L

M

N

O

P

Q

R

S

T

U

V

W

ABBREVIATIONS USED IN THE BOOK

b. = born on
in. = inch/inches
ft = feet
cm = centimetre/centimetres
m = metre/metres
g = gram/grams
kg = kilogram/kilograms
hr = hour/hours
min./mins = minute/minutes
sec./secs = second/seconds
Mt = Mount

PREAMBLE

Limca Book of Records ('*LBR*') as a record-keeping publication, has been compiling records since 1987 and has seen over 30 editions. It is India's first and longest continuously published book of records.

It is, however, a private book, run and managed by a private organization with no public funding whatsoever. The retail price is also subsidized by the owner Coca-Cola India Private Limited ('CCIPL'). The *LBR* also accepts absolutely no funding or payment or any other charges from record applicants or record holders for entries or for processing or for publication acceptance.

Consequently, it is important to understand that all decisions are taken by applying a set of standards that are specific and stringent, but equally are subjective, and based on what the editors and staff of *LBR* and Consultants ('*LBR* Team') think are most suitable for the book. And that decision is solely *LBR*'s and is not answerable to or affected by any other individual, entity or by what another entity may do or accept.

I. INTRODUCTION

1. *LBR* is a catalogue of achievements made by Indians. It catalogues unique milestones and landmarks including, but not limited to, firsts, bests, mosts, inventions, discoveries, and honours and awards received by Indians at home or abroad in all fields – both human and natural – that can be qualified in superlatives and that conform to the prevailing editorial policy in force during any year.

While this is primarily a catalogue of superlatives and achievements, it is also a book of records, and a work of reference, and therefore in the spirit of empirical record-keeping, it will record other milestones that may be negative or not celebratory or laudatory but are notable, such as 'longest trial in a court of law' or records pertaining to disasters or crime. Any such record is a statement of fact on record, and is not meant to downplay any entity, nor encourage anyone to attempt to beat such records.

LBR encompasses an extensive range of information and is thus divided into several chapters and record categories. Prospective entries under these chapters and categories may include, but are not limited to, any of the following headings: a record, a quantifiable skill, a superlative or historical landmark/ phenomenon/ man-made or natural event/ process/ structure considered as remarkable as a record by the *LBR* Team.

2. Anyone with a reasonable claim for a record may write to *LBR* for possible inclusion (subject to acceptance under *LBR* criteria).

3. Entry into *LBR* and attempt of any record are subject to compliance with the general Terms and Conditions (the 'Terms') as well as the specific rules and guidelines applicable to each type of record attempt or claim (the 'Attempt'). Where pre-existing terms do not exist to cover a particular record or Claim, a relevant policy shall be decided by the *LBR* Team and that shall be binding. Earlier policies and parameters go under continuous review and modifications, and the *LBR* Team is not bound to any previously existing parameters.

4. Individuals or groups interested in attempting to set or break a record must understand and accept general policy and study the Terms and the specific rules and guidelines applicable to the Attempt, and sign the Disclaimer and Indemnity Form (available before the commencement of any Attempt) in order to be considered for inclusion in *LBR*. Records already set and sent for inclusion post-facto are also bound by all the rules and guidelines; and acceptance of all Terms and Conditions is a necessary qualifier to any record being accepted.

5. All Terms, rules and guidelines apply to a person/ persons making a record Attempt ('Applicant'/ 'Applicants') who sends an Application to *LBR* as well as any and every person/ persons ('Participant'/ 'Participants') part of such an Attempt (for example, in an Attempt by a group or organization).

6. *LBR* is owned by CCIPL, which reserves the right to modify these Terms and any other rules and guidelines established in relation to an Attempt or general policy. CCIPL does not implement or involve itself in editorial policy and does not process submissions. *LBR* is collated and published by publishers Hachette Book Publishing India Pvt. Ltd/ Hachette India, who will process the entries, make all decisions on acceptance and inclusion, and publish the book autonomously as is required for an independent book of records. Publication dates and content design are decided and implemented in conjunction with CCIPL.

All such modifications of the Terms and Conditions, and policy, will be updated (i) on the website: https://www.coca-colaindia.com/limca-book-of-records; and (ii) on the webpage: https://www.hachetteindia.com/home/rulesandguidelines (for the latest rules and guidelines, and updates) and anyone attempting to enter their record in *LBR* must review the Terms and the corresponding rules for each Attempt regularly to remain informed of any changes or modifications therein.

7. *LBR* and its representatives do NOT charge any fee or accept any money for the application, review, processing or acceptance of records [please see clauses III.17 and III.18 of 'General Guidelines' pertaining to certificates and discount on sale of copies to Applicants].

II. ELIGIBILITY CRITERIA

1. To be eligible for consideration by the *LBR* Team for a successful Attempt, 'Applicant' must fulfil the following conditions:

a. The Applicant should be a resident Indian or non-resident Indian (NRI)/ overseas citizen of India (OCI), and must submit ID and residence proofs and other documents as required by law to establish this.

b. The Applicant must have read and consented to the Terms, the specific rules and guidelines applicable to the Attempt, and must have signed and submitted the Disclaimer and Indemnity Form before undertaking the Attempt

c. *LBR* does not accept applications of children below 13 years except in certain memory-related categories, select skill and art-based categories, and those under certain national and international Sports categories as decided by the *LBR* Team, and as per certification by relevant national and international sports organizations and authorities. The Applicant must fall in one of the two age groups, as specified below, and must adhere to the eligibility criteria for that age group.

2. The Attempt must be corroborated by a valid proof of age:
   i. Age Group I – Between 13 years and up to 18 years
   ii. Age Group II – Above 18 years

3. Age Group I:
   a. An Applicant undertaking an Attempt under this age group must be older than thirteen (13) years and younger than or up to eighteen (18) years at the time of the Attempt
   b. Consent from a parent or legal guardian must be submitted, after such parent or legal guardian has read the Terms as provided and consented to the same. The parent or legal guardian is also required to have read and consented to the Disclaimer and Indemnity Form, and provide a Certificate of Medical Fitness, signed and stamped by a certified doctor, in certain Attempts as decided and indicated by the *LBR* Team, and any other rules specified in relation to the category of the Attempt, before undertaking the Attempt.
   c. Certain categories of records may not be permitted for Applicants from this age group, as may be notified by CCIPL and/or *LBR* from time to time. Any record in this age group must be cleared with *LBR* before it occurs to see if it will be considered suitable as a record entry and *LBR*'s decision shall be final regarding its own criteria for inclusion and safety.
   d. Attempts that are detrimental to the health of such persons, or that are potentially dangerous, or that are in violation of any law in force, will not be accepted for entry in *LBR*.
   e. Any Attempt by minors beyond 15 minutes will be considered as endurance and would lead to the rejection of the claim. Any record attempt below that time duration (or even if the activity is strenuous within that time frame) that the *LBR* Team deems as stressful or strenuous for a minor, or as dangerous, harmful or injurious in any other way, may also be rejected at the discretion of the *LBR* Team.
   f. Guardians/ parents must sign a Disclaimer and Indemnity Form assuring against any exertion, stress or harm caused to the minor record Applicant and indemnifying *LBR* and CCIPL against any such occurrence.
   g. Memory records are available to this age group and subject to the decision of the *LBR* Team and representatives of *LBR*.
   h. Certain records, such as the lightest/ heaviest baby born or a medical feat performed on a child below 13 years may be accepted at the discretion of the *LBR* Team under the Medical Sciences chapter, wherein the child/ baby itself is not an active actor in the record.

4. Age Group II:
   a. The Applicant must be above eighteen (18) years of age.
   b. The Applicant must have carefully read and consented to the Terms, and the specific rules and guidelines set down for the Attempt, and submitted the Disclaimer and Indemnity Form before engaging in the Attempt as well as a Certificate of Medical Fitness (with the medical practitioner's registration number mentioned on it) to attempt any physical feat or one involving mental exertion, or one deemed so by the *LBR* Team.

III. GENERAL GUIDELINES

1. Standard norms and rules should be adhered to while setting national and world records. In some cases there may be additional event-specific norms that need to be observed.

2. The onus of proving a record claim rests on the Applicant. The claim, signed by the Applicant, should be backed by adequate and satisfactory documents without which it will not be accepted. Materials submitted as supporting evidence, such as press clippings, audio/ videotapes, flash/ pen drives, CDs, DVDs. hard drive and photographs, become the property of the publisher Hachette Book Publishing India Pvt. Ltd/ Hachette India and the Copyright Owner, but only copies should be submitted with the originals kept safe by the claimant for Life after the claim has been accepted (see also Section V {Evidence]). Forms such as the Application Form duly signed by the Applicant and validating/ witnessing authorities as indicated by the representatives of *LBR* and/ or the rules and guidelines need to be submitted in the original (hard copy) and a copy retained by the Applicant/ Applicants for Life after the claim has been accepted. *LBR* does not take any responsibility for lost material/s if the record is questioned or objected to by any person. In case of a query or objection raised, the responsibility of providing the evidence again for reverification (see also Reverification of Evidence clause V.15) and all expenditures therein lies with the Applicant.

3. It is not necessary or binding for someone from *LBR* to be present at the record-making event, but proper authentication of the same must be ensured. Authentication should be by someone who is competent and in a responsible position, such as a Gazetted Officer, District Magistrate or Principal of a school/ college, unless specified otherwise.

4. The Applicant/s must update themselves with the latest record before making any Attempt to break it. Potential record-breakers should inform *LBR* at least 30 days in advance about the record Attempt details and procedure in order to avoid disqualification on technicalities.

5. Confirmations from Consultants are not to be treated as final. The final confirmations are only issued by the LBR Editorial Team. You are advised to check the existing record with the LBR Team just prior your attempt as well, so that you may be intimated of any updates.

6. While breaking an existing record, the Applicant/s must follow the rules, technical specifications and set precedents. For example, if the needle-threading record specifies a no. 13 needle, no other needle may be used.

7. Records should be absolute and not technical offshoots. For example, if one is setting a typing record, it is assumed that it is normal typing. One-finger or two-finger typing will not be registered as separate records. Records have to be quantifiable and comparable, and overly specific variables may not be considered.

8. While *LBR* does accept new categories, these will have to be of high interest value and have definable and comparable parameters, and these are entirely subject to the *LBR* Team's decision. For example, even if no record exists, a 'two-hour marathon for guitar playing' will not be accepted.

9. Not every record set by women is eligible for entry as the subcategory 'First woman to ... '

10. Collections should have a basic 'standard'. Limited numbers of obscure articles may not be accepted unless of exceptional interest value, and that shall be decided upon by the *LBR* Team.

11. For distance records, only basic types of vehicles are recognized: four-wheelers and plus, two-wheelers, geared bicycles, gearless bicycles, tandem bicycles and electric vehicles. No differentiation is made by the *LBR* Team between engine capacities of one kind of vehicles for speed or 'fastest' records. In terms of endurance, for instance, if the category is Four Corners of India by a two-wheeler, then motorcycles of any cubic capacity (cc) and scooters are considered under the same category.

To ensure measurability, distance against time will be the criterion. Cross- country or intra-country motoring/ cycling or other vehicular records must get prior clearance from the *LBR* Team for inclusion. In non-speed records, vehicles may be categorized according to engine capacity: up to 60 cc; 61—100 cc; 101—350—500 cc; and above 500 cc.

12. Before attempting any driving record, Applicants have to submit a copy of the following document/ documents, as applicable, attested by a Gazetted Officer or Notary Public: their valid driving licence/earlier experience certificate in case of motor sport or bicycling record; pilot's licence/ aero-sports course certificate/earlier experience certificate in case of aero sports record; mountaineering/mountain sports course certificate/ earlier experience certificate in case of a mountain sports record; and water sports course certificate/ earlier experience certificate in case of a water sports record to the *LBR* office for prior approval.

13. All claimants must send in send in supporting photographs for their Claim to the *LBR* Team. In physical evidence with documents or photographs, these should not be stapled them to the entry. Detachable clips should be used. In cases where applicable and as indicated by the *LBR* Team, time- and date-stamped video recordings of the Attempt must be provided.

14. Attempts that may result in physical harm, such as 'hitting head against a wall' or mental/ emotional duress for the applicant, such as 'isolating oneself for 100 days' will not be considered and are entirely the decision of the *LBR* Team.

15. Any record in the book may be reconsidered or dropped without prior intimation.

16. Certificates issued are valid only for the date or period specified and will be considered ended if surpassed by a new record, and/ or change in criteria, measuring methods, or if disputed and found to be erroneous on reverification (see clause V.15).

17. For reasons of space or any other reasons, a confirmed entry may be dropped at the time of going to press. The *LBR* Team may inform the Applicant of the change in status but is not bound to do so.

18. Record holders within India are entitled to ONE complimentary copy of their certificate and its postage, if eligible, and further copies need to be ordered by writing to the *LBR* Team and on payment (including GST) as indicated. Record holders outside India are entitled to ONE complimentary copy of their certificate but will need to pay courier and/ or postal charges (including applicable taxes/ surcharges). Requests for the reissue of older certificates issued in previous years are considered on a case-by-case basis and such certificates reissued on payment within reasonable time as per printing schedules provided the record is accessible in *LBR*'s archived editions.

19. Record holders are not entitled to any remuneration or free copies of *Limca Book of Records*. They may, however, avail a 30 per cent discount on the cover price of the book by writing to the *LBR* Team and following the payment process.

20. If new record holders do not receive their certificate within two months after the release of the book, they should contact the *LBR* office.

21. The *LBR* Team reserves the sole right to decide on the suitability of all records for inclusion in the book. The Team's decision on all such matters is final. Any attempt to browbeat or threaten the *LBR* Team or representatives shall result in instant disqualification.

22. ATTEMPTS BY MINORS:
Records by minors below 13 years are not accepted, except under certain memory-related categories, select skill and art-based categories, and certain recognized national and international tournament categories as decided by the respective Consultants for specific sports.

23. Records that are against the law (e.g., driving at an age not qualified for licence) or those that require excessive physical exertion (like a marathon) detrimental to a minor's health will not be accepted.

24. OBJECTIONS/ DISCREPANCIES

a. Any typographical error or inaccuracy in the statement of a record or certificate should be pointed out by the record holder immediately.
b. Objections raised by any person regarding any published entry shall be entertained only within a period of three (3) years from the date of publication or acceptance/ certification of a record/ entry. However, discrepancies identified by the *LBR* Team suo moto shall be addressed regardless of passage of time. Applicants must note that, in accordance with the prevailing laws, there is no limitation in respect of criminal liability should it arise.

A. CHAPTERS AND CATEGORIES

LBR reserves the right to include or exclude any chapter or category, or section or record category as otherwise listed below and is under no obligation to publish all or any of the listed chapters or categories in *LBR* or any of its publications.

The list provided here is only for illustrative and explanatory reasons, and for the clarity of persons seeking to engage in an Attempt. Further, the following list consists only of chapters and categories that have been published in previous editions and is non-exhaustive. *LBR* may, at its sole discretion, include additional chapters or categories, delete a chapter or category, or even merge two or more chapters or categories as the *LBR* Team deems appropriate. Any such addition, deletion or merging of chapters or categories creates no obligation on the part of *LBR* Team and/ or CCIPL to inform any person making an Attempt of such addition, deletion or merger. Records after acceptance may also be changed or deleted if suitable circumstances warrant it, and this also shall be the sole decision of the *LBR* Team.

1. THE HUMAN STORY

This chapter contains records, talents and information, and includes, but is not limited to, unique achievements, uncommon talents, collections, community development initiatives and other human feats. Applicants under this category are required to not break any laws, and must sign and submit the Disclaimer and Indemnity Form, Self-Declaration of Medical Fitness and Certificate of Medical Fitness, as applicable, at least one month prior to the Attempt. *LBR* prohibits and will not accept any Attempt that is likely to cause harm or be of nuisance to the general public, or is likely to cause unnecessary waste of essential goods or resources such as food items, or is likely to harm the environment; and of course possible physical, mental or emotional harm to oneself.

a. Records involving alcohol consumption as an event or performance measure will not be considered.
b. Yoga or endurance, or speed or strength records are only for Age Group II unless specifically permitted otherwise in writing.
c. Applicants from Age Group I can perform for a maximum of 15 minutes in mass participation records involving strength, speed or performance. Any Attempt longer than that will be considered endurance on the part of minors and rejected. In such records attempting mosts in terms of numbers, minors will not be counted, such as in a two-hour-long dance performance. The allowance may depend upon the nature of the Attempt. For example, minor Applicants/ Participants might participate in an Attempt involving reading for more than 15 minutes but will not be allowed at any mass physical feat claim for more than that time period, such as most Participants performing the plank together. Such applications, if accepted by the *LBR* Team, will need a Medical Fitness Certificate confirming that no harm will be caused to the Applicant/ Participant by such an Attempt.
d. A new section for virtual records has been added from this edition onwards. The current categories are for single sessions conducted on a single platform.
e. *LBR* does not have categories related to religious traditions and ceremonies, unless they form general records.
f. Records indicating or involving harm to physical or mental health, such as 'most blood donated in a day', or 'starving for the most number of days', or 'isolating oneself for the longest period' will not be considered.

2. STRUCTURES

This chapter contains records related to general, modern, residential, religious, mechanical and historical structures, bridges, dams and flyovers, and various other specialized structures.

a. There are no set parameters of the claim regarding fastest construction as each construction would have multiple aspects of difference and the *LBR* Team does not wish to encourage the fastest construction of public services or private buildings.

3. EDUCATION

This chapter contains records and information related to literacy, schools, higher education, archives, libraries, museums and quizzes. *LBR* has discontinued the 'youngest' category as a record claim. Record claims with qualifications beyond postgraduation are considered. Record claims pertaining to online courses, or qualifications based on the University Grants Commission (UGC)-National Eligibility Test (NET), or publication of research papers will not be considered.

4. MEDIA AND COMMUNICATIONS

This chapter contains records and information related to the broad fields of (a) media and (b) communications, and may be divided into six sections: (i) print, (ii) radio, (iii) television, (iv) post and philately, (v) telecom, and (vi) Internet, social media and apps (applications). Applicants wishing to undertake an Attempt under this chapter must ensure compliance with the specific guidelines provided by the *LBR* Team.

5. AGRICULTURE

This chapter contains records and information, and the chapter may include, but shall not be limited to, topics such as agricultural crops, farm machinery, milk and milk products, poultry, animal sciences, fisheries, agricultural research and awards. Specific rules are to be complied with for Attempts under this chapter.

6. DEFENCE

This chapter contains records and information pertaining to all the branches of the armed or paramilitary forces and related military records. This chapter does not accept entries unless routed through the appropriate defence authority/ organization with the understanding that no official secrets, or confidential information, are being revealed in the process. An independent entry by current or former defence personnel should be accompanied with a self-declaration that no official secrets or confidential information is being revealed. The chapter is otherwise compiled by the *LBR* Team from news sources originating with government ministries and information sources such as the official websites of the Indian Navy, Army, Air Force and Coast Guard as well as the Press Information Bureau, Government of India.

7. TRANSPORT

This chapter contains records and information, and the sections under this chapter include road, rail, water and air transport. Applicants who claim records under any of these sections shall provide evidence of the same, including authentication documents as required by the *LBR* Team.

8. SCIENCE AND TECHNOLOGY

This chapter contains absolute records like oldest planetarium and first nuclear reactor along with discoveries and records in, but not limited to, mathematics, physics, chemistry, biology, engineering, environmental sciences, computers, information technology and space technology. All Attempts under this chapter are required to follow the specific rules for both types of events as provided by the *LBR* Team. For a new invention to be considered as a record, it must be patented with a recognized national/ international body. This chapter also includes records and relevant information compiled by the *LBR* Team.

9. VISUAL ARTS

This chapter contains records and information related to cinema, photography, painting and some categories of drawing and cartooning. The records related to national and regional commercial and art cinema is based on information collected from the National Film Archive of India (NFAI), public domain, magazines and national newspapers. The records about box-office collection are obtained from the website www.boxofficeindia.com, the standard source in India for collecting such details, or similar sources.

a. Individual record claims may be submitted for consideration under this chapter, subject to compliance with the basic criteria laid down:
   i. The film should have been cleared by the Central Board for Film Certification (CBFC) and given a censor certificate.
   ii. Certification requirements for Over the Top (OTT) content/ films/ drama series will be decided on a case-by-case basis and as per the laws of the land and relevant authorities/ organizations.
   iii. The film should be screened at film festivals or at public theatres/ auditoriums.

b. Information related to painting and photography is collected from newspapers, magazines, the Internet and any other verified source. Individual record claims may be submitted for consideration under this chapter, subject to compliance with the basic criteria laid down:
   i. No miniature paintings in any medium are considered in this chapter currently. They may be eligible for entry in the Human Story chapter depending on parameters.
   ii. All rangoli, *alpana* and *kolam* records have been categorized under one category of 'Traditional floor art'.
   iii. Considering that art is a subjective concept, the *LBR* Team reserves the final decision regarding the artwork so produced. Random repetition of patterns, block colour patches, strokes of paint, or smearing paint randomly on the canvas would lead to the rejection of the claim. Similarly, geometric shapes, haphazard lines and arbitrary usage of colour would also lead to rejection. The artwork so produced should have a coherent sense of pattern, colour and tone. It should depict a certain level of skill and creation of aesthetics. For photography claims, repetitive, fragmented and haphazard images would not be considered. The images should have a coherent sense of posture, alignment and lighting.
   iv. The largest art competition would be a single-day category following the rules of continuous events and being a maximum of 12 hours.
   v. Portrait categories: A portrait should have only a single person in the painting/ mosaic. A portrait is considered to be a drawing/ painting of the head and shoulder of a person for the purposes of record claims.
   vi. Origami claims have been sorted into the following categories:
      1. Largest origami mosaic – solo/ group
      2. Single-item origami (single sheet, single item)> A) Tallest/ Longest; B) Widest
      3. Multiple-item origami (multiple sheets, multiple items)> A) Tallest - solo/group; B) Widest – solo/ group
      4. Marathon origami (single day, single venue) – solo
      5. Most towel origami made – solo/ group – in 1 hour
   vii. Claims regarding pencil carvings (graphite) have been sorted into the following categories:
      1. Largest collection of carved pencils
      2. Most pencil carvings done – single day
      3. Most pencil carvings done – 1 hour
      4. Smallest pencil carving

10. PERFORMING ARTS

This chapter contains records related to talent and information in the fields of dance, music and theatre (including but not limited to puppetry and other local theatre types depending on parameters), and dance drama and dance–martial arts crossovers. The records are further divided into marathon events or group events. All Attempts under this chapter are required to follow the specific rules for both types of events as provided by the *LBR* Team. Record claims pertaining to fastest performances will not be considered.

11. ADVENTURE

This chapter may be divided into various sections, including but not limited to, aero sports, mountaineering, road expeditions, water sports, marathons (those not classified internationally as athletics track and field events) and other adventure activities. A person undertaking an Attempt under this category may seek the *LBR* Team's guidance/ assistance for specific guidelines. Potential Applicants are advised to note that such guidelines or safety advice provided by the *LBR* Team shall merely be explanatory, non-exhaustive and will not create any responsibilities or liabilities on behalf of the *LBR* Team and/ or CCIPL, whatsoever.

a. For all claims related to Ironman triathlon, *LBR* refers to the International Triathlon Union and the Indian Triathlon Federation.
b. For swimming records, only solo as well as up to three-person relay crossings (each covering at least 10 km) will be considered. For marathon swimming – with permitted breaks – breaks of only 1.5 minutes will be allowed for each completed hour. Exceptions

may be made for para swimmers or extremely remarkable records, subject to the discretion and decision of the *LBR* Team and Consultants.

c. A minimum altitude of 6,000 m is required to review any mountaineering claim. Claims regarding Mt Kilimanjaro (5,895 m) will not be considered in accordance with this limit. All mountaineering claims must be verified by the Indian Mountaineering Foundation or a similar credible international body.

d. For road expeditions, there are separate categories for women in solo attempts and group attempts where Applicants and, if present, Participants are women. e. Our categories for expedition records for two-wheelers will now be sub-divided as:
   - Up to 150 cc
   - 151 to 450 cc
   - Over 451 cc

e. Adventure/ Marathon and Endurance Claims
   i. A detailed logbook must be maintained with entries in chronological order. All entries in this logbook must be witnessed and authenticated by reputed individuals/ competent authorities (a Gazetted Officer, District Magistrate or Principal of a school/ college, unless specified otherwise). A sample sheet will be given by the *LBR* Team on request. Emphasis will be on events that highlight special skills.
   ii. In cases where applicable and as indicated by the *LBR* Team, time- and date-stamped videos of the Attempt must be provided.
   iii. All adventure/ endurance events come under five categories. Special instructions on rest breaks for each of them follow:
      1. Marathon (non-stop): A five-minute break for rest after every completed hour is allowed as per prevailing international norms. These breaks may be accumulated (e.g., a 15-minute break may be taken after 3 hours of non-stop action) but not added to the tally. The logbook must clearly indicate the rest breaks.
      2. Virtually non-stop: Minimal breaks permitted for medical/ toilet purposes but no rest breaks. Breaks are to be indicated in the logbook.
      3. Continuous: Performed on a rotating or relay basis.
      4. Normal: Breaks permitted as and when necessary.
      5. Absolute non-stop: No breaks at all.
   iv. Attempts jeopardizing individual or public safety and public property are not encouraged.
   v. All adventure feats/ stunts/ sports, etc., require prior written approval from authorities concerned.

12. GOVERNMENT

This chapter contains information and records. This category may include, but shall not be limited to, such subjects as nationhood, parties, elections, the Parliament, states, administration, government officials, civics, judiciary, and law and order.

13. MEDICAL SCIENCES

This chapter contains records and information from the field of medical sciences such as medical breakthroughs, medical camps, 'firsts' and 'mosts' in selective medical procedures, mass participations, medical tests, medical devices and equipment.

Claims are acceptable only from registered medical practitioners and related to government-approved medical practices and institutions, such as those affiliated to the Indian Medical Association, the Ministry of Health and Family Welfare, and any others as deemed eligible by the *LBR* Team.

The *LBR* Team will reject any Attempts that may potentially or otherwise harm or endanger persons/ patients, e.g., speed-related records, such as 'most kidneys transplanted in a day' or 'most LASIK surgeries performed in a day', whether at a medical centre or in camps, charitable or otherwise.

LBR may accept camp-related statistics that turn out to be records, but may not process or encourage any camps set up to create records, especially speed-related medical science Attempts because such Attempts may jeopardize patient safety and health.

14. THE NATURAL WORLD

This chapter contains information and records, and the entries are compiled from multiple and deemed verified reports in magazines, newspapers and Internet resources available to *LBR* on topics including, but not limited to, geographical features, flora, fauna, environment and conservation. Information related to flora and fauna is verified with nature conservation authorities, well-known wildlife institutions, government websites and relevant international websites.

All claims related to rainwater harvesting and pollution control are counterchecked with government sources and/ or authoritative expert bodies. Gardening records relating to non-agricultural production and claims, such as largest pumpkin, will require scale-comparative photographs as well as other indicated documentation.

15. LITERATURE

This chapter contains records and information from the field of literature. Applicants willing to undertake an Attempt under this chapter must ensure compliance with the basic criteria laid down.

a. Only published works will be considered unless the work created is an art installation, or superlative or an artefact.
b. No long ghazals/ poems, rewriting of religious texts, or anthologies will be considered.
c. A work infringing copyright or violative of any other prevailing laws will not be considered.
d. General category claims – book(s) self-published or published by a publishing house, should be available for purchase online or at bookshops. Sales records must be certified by publishers who have audited accounts or by Nielsen BookScan.

16. BUSINESS AND ECONOMY

This chapter contains records and information, and the sections under this chapter may include, but shall not be limited to, the economy, financial institutions, financial instruments, banking, industries and companies, workforce, housing and real estate, and advertising.

Applicants who claim records under any of these sections shall provide proof of the same, including authentication letters from independent observers including at least one expert in the field. Industry company data must be from authentic authorized bodies such as the Registrar of Companies and the Securities and Exchange Board of India (SEBI), or in the case of own company figures, audited figures must be submitted.

17. SPORTS
The Sports chapter of the *LBR* primarily, contains records, sports-related statistics and information. It is prepared by independent Consultants, who are well-established journalists and/ or authorities in particular sports. The Consultants in conjunction with the *LBR* Team are the final authority on all records under this chapter. In cases where an uncommon sport is involved, the decisions will be made in consultation with an expert in the field.

IV. PROCEDURE FOR ATTEMPT

1. *LBR* recognizes two types of Attempts:
  a. an Attempt to break a previously existing record; and
  b. an Attempt to set a new record.

2. The following procedure must be followed by any person willing to undertake an Attempt to be considered for entry in *LBR*:

An application by the person attempting the record should be either emailed to **lbr.entries@hachetteindia.com** or couriered/ mailed by registered post (see clause IV.3: Application Procedure):
  a. Such application should contain details regarding the unique achievement, or proposal to set a record, for the consideration of the *LBR* Team, along with the complete address and contact number of the person attempting the same, at least one (1) month before the Attempt in order to avoid disqualification on technicalities. For specific requirements in the procedure for an Attempt please refer to Section III of these Rules and Guidelines/ Terms.
  b. The person undertaking the Attempt must approach the *LBR* Team regarding the proper procedure and information or documents required for consideration of a successful Attempt.
  c. On completion of an Attempt, the Applicant must provide the *LBR* Team detailed and accurate documentation, as required by the *LBR* Team, and these then be scrutinized by the *LBR* Team.
  d. All entries to an edition are confirmed only after the deadline, i.e., the last date for submission of entries. Any Application made after such a date may be considered for a subsequent edition of *LBR*.
  e. On confirmation of an entry, a certificate shall be mailed to the Applicant who carried out the successful Attempt. Such certificates shall be sent after the particular edition for which the Attempt has been considered is printed or released.
  f. For all Attempts to be undertaken, the person undertaking such an Attempt must sign and submit the Disclaimer and Indemnity Form and Certificate of Medical Fitness (in hard copy) as and when required to the *LBR* Team, prior to the Attempt. The acceptance of any application for entry in *LBR* shall be conditional on the signing of and adherence to the Disclaimer and Indemnity Form, the Terms, and any other specific rules and guidelines established by *LBR* in relation to a particular category of Attempt.
  The following rules will apply to Disclaimer Forms:
    i. Disclaimer forms should have only one party mentioned, i.e., the record claimant. The second party is not applicable.
    ii. Applicants may choose to get the form notarized instead of adding witnesses. Or witnesses can be used, but verification from the notary holds more value.
    iii. Disclaimer forms have to be on a stamp paper of minimum value of Rs 10.

3. APPLICATION PROCEDURE
  a. All applications must be sent to the following addresses: Limca Book of Records (Editorial); Hachette Book Publishing India Pvt. Ltd; 4th/5th Floors, Corporate Centre; Plot No. 94, Sector 44; Gurugram 122003, Haryana, India; Ph: (Board) +91-124-4195000; Fax: +91-124-4148900
  Email: **lbr.entries@hachetteindia.com**
  Hachette Book Publishing India Pvt. Ltd is a company incorporated under the Indian Companies Act, 1956, with CIN U22222DL2007PTC164081.
  b. *LBR*'s primary mode of communication is email (and only via its formal email IDs), which is both retrievable and transparent as well as a formal record. No Attempt should be made based on phone or other verbal conversations, or communication on social media/ messaging platforms.
  c. There is no need for personal visits to the *LBR* office to hand over record-related applications, documentation or evidence, and in case the Applicant does visit personally, then the application and requisite documents may be handed over at the Reception. Since all claim formats devised are such that they need written submission, everything should be clear from written communication.
  d. Submissions must be in English since *LBR* is currently published in the English language (submissions in other languages shall be accepted, but they should be accompanied with an English translation).
  e. The primary application shall consist of the following:
    i. Name of the Applicant;
    ii. Complete postal address of the Applicant;
    iii. Contact details of the Applicant;
    iv. Description of the record the Applicant wishes to apply for; and event plan.
    v. Confirmation of acceptance of *LBR* procedures, Terms and Rules and Guidelines via a formal statement on email or signed hard copy.
  f. These applications shall be perused by the *LBR* Team, and further correspondence shall take place between the Applicant and the *LBR* Team member concerned, from the assigned chapter/ section.
  g. On acceptance of the initial application, the general guidelines and record-specific guidelines shall be emailed or couriered to the Applicant by the *LBR* Team along with the procedure and documentation required.
  h. On receipt of the correspondence from a member of the *LBR* Team, the Applicant shall send the following documents (in both soft and hard copies) to the

addresses mentioned in clause IV.3(a) above:
  i. A covering letter stating the Attempt details;
  ii. A signed copy of the Disclaimer and Indemnity Form sent to the Applicant;
  iii. A self-attested copy of the Applicant's government-approved identity proof (such as passport, voter ID card, PAN card, Aadhaar, etc.);
  iv. A self-attested copy of the Applicant's government-approved age proof (such as passport, birth certificate, ration card, etc.) together with the 'Required Documents' as indicated by the *LBR* Team.

i. On authentication and verification of the Required Documents, the Applicant shall obtain a confirmation from the *LBR* Team to proceed with the Attempt.

j. After completing the Attempt in accordance with the provisions of Sections III and IV, and collecting evidence of the Attempt in accordance with the provisions of Section V, the Applicant shall send the following to claim a record (the 'Claim'):
  i. Details of the supposed record, duly authenticated by Gazetted Officers, or relevant public authorities, or relevant authorities in charge, or other competent authorities. Such authentication must be on the basis of personal verification of every detail of the Claim.
  ii. Material evidence of the event, consisting of all the evidence collected by the Applicant during the Attempt. All CDs/ DVDs, flash/ pen drives and other data storage media/ devices sent to the *LBR* Team, as part of the application process, should have the Applicant's name and the record category written legibly on it.

k. A Claim that is successfully submitted shall be considered for entry in the *LBR*.

l. The application procedure should be completed within the last date of submission. Entries submitted after the deadline may be considered for the subsequent edition unless extension was granted in writing or on email for extenuating circumstances, or at the discretion of the *LBR* Team.

m. In addition to the aforementioned rules, specific requirements provided under the relevant categories must be fulfilled.

V. EVIDENCE

1. The onus of proving a record is on the Applicant. The Claim, signed by the Applicant, should be backed by adequate and satisfactory documentation without which it will not be accepted by the *LBR* Team.

2. The Applicant must, as part of the verification process, submit all supporting documents including at least two authentication letters (originals) on stamp paper, photographs (or CD/DVD/ flash drive containing still photos), personal details of the Applicant, including residential address and contact details, along with a covering letter, without which the Claim will not be considered for entry.

3. Outside of moral and creative ownership rights, which will vest in the creator/artist/ author, etc., the assigned copyright/publishing rights and any other intellectual property rights in and to any such material evidence shall, to the extent permitted by law, be waived unconditionally by the Applicant and transferred to *LBR* and CCIPL by the submission.

4. The evidence must only be sent after the Required Documents, as indicated by the Rules and Guidelines, have been verified and the primary application has been duly confirmed and evidence asked for by the *LBR* Team.

5. Only the Claim may be supplemented by evidence of the record with the following to be submitted on the currently prevailing and commonly available and accessible data storage media from where it is easily retrievable, such as a flash/ pen drive or hard drive, with the onus of providing a back-up copy/original being on the Applicant:

a. Press clippings of local, national or international newspapers, or press cuttings, or news reports in an electronic form, furnishing direct evidence of the record; or
b. Audio recordings from radio, or any such fact of record which could be heard, furnishing direct evidence of the record; or
c. Direct evidence/ audiovisual recording of the record; or
d. Any other fact of record that may be in audio, visual or audiovisual format, furnishing direct evidence of the record; or
e. Photographs of any such fact of record documented by photographs furnishing direct evidence of the record. (It is advisable to submit high-resolution photographs only that are pictures 1,500 pixels wide for horizontal images and 1,500 pixels high for vertical images, of 1 Mb or more.)

6. If any of the evidence mentioned above is in a local language, it must be sent along with a copy of an English translation of the said document attested by a Gazetted Officer/ Notary Public.

7. The evidence must be clear, distinct and unambiguous.

8. *LBR* reserves the right to refuse the Claim if evidence sufficient to prove the record act beyond reasonable doubt is not furnished, or for any other reason whatsoever at *LBR*'s discretion.

9. For categories where specific evidence is required, a reference is invited to the respective category, mentioned in this document on Rules and Guidelines, for the requirements.

10. The material evidence provided by the Applicant shall NOT be returned. The Applicant is advised to keep all original evidence along with copies.

11. Wherever possible, a person from the *LBR* Team may also visit for verification. In such cases also, the evidence shall be sent along with the Claim.

12. In case of records where giant structures are put in place or super-sized objects are involved, the measurements shall be taken in the presence of appropriate observers and authenticators, such as Gazetted Officers, Principal of a school/ college, an engineering expert, or others as approved by the *LBR* Team.

13. Originals must not be sent, unless specifically requested by *LBR* for scrutiny. *LBR* will not keep copies longer than twelve (12) months after acceptance of the Claim, but record holders should keep their evidence to be produced for disputes for Life (see below V[15]: Reverification of Evidence). Evidence and documents of rejected records will be destroyed immediately after informing the Applicant of the decision.

14. All records and evidence are accepted in good faith and normal deep scrutiny. Any submission of fake evidence shall be met with a charge of cheating and other offences as mentioned in the Indian Penal Code and other applicable laws.

15. REVERIFICATION OF EVIDENCE:

a. In case a discrepancy in the record comes to light, as pointed out by any person or independently detected by the *LBR* Team, the onus of providing the evidence again for reverification of the record entry lies entirely with the record holder. If, in the opinion of the *LBR* Team, the discrepancy for whatsoever reason that has come to light is genuine, the same shall be communicated to the record holder and evidence sought for reverification; in the meantime, the record will be frozen/ suspended and the certificate considered withdrawn until the evidence is reverified by a panel consisting of an *LBR* Team member and a legal consultant. Announcement of such a suspended/ frozen record will appear only on the *LBR* website publicly and nowhere else. Subsequent to reverification, the record may either be restored, or amended or struck off completely.
b. *LBR* will not keep any data or records longer than one year (12 months) from acceptance in writing, In the event of any objection or discrepancy needing reverification (see clause V.15[a] above), the record holder must keep all supporting evidence safe and readily accessible.
c. In all matters pertaining to reverification of records/ evidence, the *LBR's* decision shall be final and binding.

VI. ACCEPTANCE CRITERIA

1. Each Attempt must be categorized within one of the chapters or categories listed under Section II and III[A]. However, *LBR* reserves the right, to be exercised at its sole and absolute discretion, to accept applications for Attempts.

2. Records must be absolute and not technical offshoots and they must be quantifiable, comparable and measurable.

3. No Claim shall be considered valid unless it is sent, along with the required evidence, in the manner prescribed in Sections IV and V.

4. *LBR* reserves the right to publish or delete any chapter, section, category or record in the present or any future edition of *LBR*, without any notice to the Applicants. *LBR* is under no obligation to inform record holders when a record may be dropped. Such decisions shall be the sole prerogative of the *LBR* Team in the larger continuing interests of the book.

5. Records shall be considered for publishing only on the grounds of their interest value and general public acceptance.

6. *LBR* will not consider potentially dangerous Attempts by Applicants, particularly those belonging to Age Group I, being up to thirteen (13) years of age.

7. Further, no entries in violation of any law, rule, regulation, guideline or any other statutory instrument shall be accepted.

8. Entries for the new edition of *LBR* will be confirmed only after the annual deadline, which is usually 31 May.

9. In all matters pertaining to the *Limca Book of Records*, the *LBR* Team's and/ or CCIPL's decision shall be final and binding.

10. Record claims are accepted in good faith and may be considered records and published in the book as such unless disproved with appropriate evidence.

11. It should be borne in mind, that *LBR* by its rejecting a Claim is not stating that the Claim may not be a record, or that the achievement, if any, is belittled. It is merely stating that for its purposes and within the framework of the book, as run by its editorial policy, it does not think the Claim suitable to feature.

12. Harassment of staff, including overt or covert threats, including threats of legal process for rejecting a Claim, or for any other reason whatsoever, or defaming *LBR* or the *LBR* Team on public platforms will not be acceptable and will be met with all the measures under law. Any such behaviour will also result in automatic disqualification of the Claim.

VII. STATUTORY COMPLIANCE

1. It is mandatory for Applicants to abide by all local, state and national laws, rules and regulations applicable in relation to the Attempt. *LBR* expressly prohibits any Attempt that involves violation of any local, state or national laws, rules or regulations. Applicants are under an obligation to ensure that all activities related to the Attempt are neither unlawful, nor against public decency and morality.

Applicants must note that *LBR* strongly discourages Attempts that are likely to offend the sentiments of any community. *LBR* also discourages Attempts that may cause harm to the public or animals, or cause any damage to the environment, and Applicants are requested to refrain from making such Attempts. Applicants shall bear sole responsibility for any consequences arising out of any non-compliance with any applicable laws, rules or regulations insofar as they relate to the Attempt. *LBR* shall not be liable for any harm caused to the public or the environment in the course of the Attempt, and *LBR* shall not be responsible for any noncompliance with any applicable local, state or national or international laws, rules and regulations insofar as they relate to the Attempt.

2. With the submission of any Claim a record holder agrees to abide by the Terms and Conditions, and Rules and Guidelines, in full and is thereby covenanting that the submission is true with no falsifying of evidence or no mala fide intent of any sort whatsoever.

VIII. SAFETY PRECAUTIONS

1. The Applicant is requested to take all reasonable safety precautions prior to the Attempt including, but not limited to, the testing of all equipment used for the Attempt, the utilization of prescribed safety equipment in relation to the Attempt, the presence of requisite medical personnel and treatment facilities, and any applicable safety permits required under local, state or national laws, rules and regulations.

2. The Applicant understands that the Attempt may be dangerous to them, other Participants and spectators, and that they must identify such risks, with the help of professional advice, such as the risk of accident, illness, paralysis, injury, loss or death that may be caused by negligence, forces of nature, or other agencies, known and unknown. The Applicant knowingly and freely assumes all such risks, both known and unknown, and assumes full personal responsibility for the Attempt and its consequences.

3. The Applicant shall bear sole responsibility for taking all such safety precautions and acknowledge that CCIPL, the *LBR* Team and/ or their respective directors, publishers, editors, officers, appointed representatives, Consultants, or agents shall not, in any manner whatsoever, be responsible for making any safety arrangements for the Attempt.

IX. PUBLICITY

1. The Applicants undertake and irrevocably and unconditionally permit CCIPL and *LBR* to cover any Attempt through various media including newspapers, radio, television (news and other channels), Internet, mobile apps, social media, etc., and shall not raise any objection, protest or demur whatsoever to such coverage or in this regard. Whilst *LBR* shall make all reasonable efforts, there is no obligation on the part of *LBR* to air or otherwise engage in publicizing any Attempt. The Applicants must, at the request of CCIPL/ *LBR*, participate in all promotional activity (such as publicity and photography) in relation to a successful Attempt, free of charge, and consent to CCIPL and *LBR* using their name and image in all promotional materials, free of charge, should CCIPL/ *LBR* Team wish to do so as mentioned under Section X below.

2. In the case of publicity-related interview and other occasions/opportunities and/ or events where the participation or presence of the Applicant may be required, the *LBR*/ CCIPL Team will contact the Applicant/s in writing/ on email for their consent and willingness for such an interview and/ or event.

X. LICENCE TO USE NAME, IMAGE, LIKENESS, RECORD

Applicants hereby grant in perpetuity to CCIPL and *LBR*, their authorized agents, successors and assigns, the worldwide licence to use the name, image, likeness, pictures, video recordings, audio recordings, etc., of the Applicants in relation to any Attempts undertaken by the Applicants (the 'Licensed Property'). Applicants agree and grant to CCIPL and Hachette Book Publishing India Pvt. Ltd/ Hachette India a waiver of their privacy and personality rights, and grant the right to use any element of the Licensed Property for any purpose in connection with *LBR* including, but not limited to, the publication and distribution of *LBR*, the promotion of *LBR*, CCIPL, and any of its divisions or products, and the filing of copyright, trademark and other similar registrations in relation to *LBR* that involve the Licensed Property. All material submitted in connection with a potential entry in *LBR* (whether in written, audio, electronic or visual form, or a combination of these) or any photographs, video and/ or film footage and/ or audio recording taken of Applicants are assigned to *LBR* and CCIPL upon submission and become the property of *LBR* and CCIPL exclusively. *LBR* and CCIPL may use the material in any medium in any reasonable manner they deem fit. Copyright in any such material remains the sole property of *LBR* and CCIPL.

XI. INTELLECTUAL PROPERTY RIGHTS

The name 'Limca' and the 'Limca' logo are registered trademarks of The Coca-Cola Company, USA, and should not be used for any publicity in relation to an Attempt, or after a Claim has been accepted, without the express permission of CCIPL. All rights, titles and interests including, but not limited to, the Intellectual Property Rights, in *LBR* and in any and all entries received, shall vest solely and exclusively in CCIPL at all times. CCIPL or any person or entity permitted by CCIPL in this regard shall be entitled to use any information in connection with the entry in any media for future promotional, marketing, publicity and any other purpose, without any permission and/ or payment to the Applicant.

XII. RESPONSIBILITY FOR ALL ASSOCIATED COSTS AND INSURANCE

The Applicant understands and acknowledges that all expenses incurred in relation to the Attempt shall be borne solely by the Applicant. CCIPL and/ or *LBR* Team shall in no manner be responsible for reimbursing any expenses incurred in the course of the Attempt, or even in the event that the Applicant is successful at the Attempt. CCIPL/ *LBR* shall not be responsible for providing any kind of insurance in relation to any Attempt, and shall not be responsible for any emergency medical expenses or any subsequent medical expenses in the event of any incident/ accident, illness or incapacity arising out of the Attempt.

XIII. WAIVER OF CLAIMS AND INDEMNITY

1. Applicants acknowledge and consent on behalf of themselves, their heirs, successors, assigns, personal representatives and next of kin, to WAIVE ALL CLAIMS AND RELEASE AND HOLD HARMLESS the *LBR* Team, Hachette Book Publishing India Pvt. Ltd/ Hachette India and all its employees, directors, parent or affiliate organizations, Consultants, representatives, partners, CCIPL, its directors, publishers, editors, officers, employees and representatives, and its partners, affiliates, subsidiaries, advertising agencies, agents and their respective directors, officers, employees and representatives (the 'Released Parties'), with respect to any and all injury, disability, paralysis, death, or loss or damage to person, property or reputations, arising out of the Attempt, to the fullest extent permitted by law. The Applicants agree to indemnify and hold the Released Parties harmless from all losses, liabilities, damages, costs or expenses (including but not limited to reasonable legal fees and other litigation costs and expenses) incurred by any of the Released Parties as a result of any claims or suits that any Applicant/s (or anyone claiming by, under or through such Applicant/s) may bring against any of the Released Parties to recover any losses, liabilities, costs, damages or expenses that may arise during or result from the Attempt.

2. Further,
   a. *LBR* retains an indemnity for human error or typographical error, and the right to revise a record because of that; and the right to withdraw or modify a certificate because of such error lies with the *LBR* Team.
   b. The right to suspend records/ certification on receipt of disputes or objections lies with the *LBR* Editorial Team. In such cases the record verification will be revisited, and the Claimant of the record must provide reverification (see clause V.15) and, if necessary, further detailing to answer such objections. If the Claimant is not able to furnish a copy of the evidence as per the original claim, the record and certification may be cancelled.
   c. The principle of acceptance is basic verification and acceptance in good faith, so records should be clear and detailed. *LBR* reserves the right to do forensic examination or reopen a record case later if found to be suspect.
   d. Faking of records and evidence is a criminal offence and shall be dealt with strictly under the prevailing laws. The application/ Claim/ record shall be cancelled and the Applicant/ record holder shall be immediately blacklisted and no further applications/ claims from them shall be entertained; and the rights to legal prosecution shall be reserved.
   e. For records involving mass participation/ huge numbers, for example, 'most people at a concert' or 'most vehicles in a rally', the simple principle of sequentially numbered badges should be there with a logbook of a unique identifier (licence/ registration number, individual ID card or any similar clearly visible device).
   f. *LBR* is a private body and its editorial criteria solely belong to it alone and its decisions shall be the ones solely binding on any record.

XIV. SEVERABILITY

Each of the provisions contained in these Terms/ Rules and Guidelines is considered to be reasonable by CCIPL, *LBR* and the Applicants, and each clause, subclause, paragraph and sub-paragraph shall be construed as independent of any other provision. If any provision of these Terms/ Rules and Guidelines proves to be invalid, void or illegal it shall not in any way affect, impair or invalidate any other provision and the remaining provisions shall remain in full force and effect.

XV. DISPUTE

The courts of competent jurisdiction at Delhi shall have exclusive jurisdiction to determine any and all disputes arising out of, or in connection with, any Attempt undertaken or entry made for the purpose of *LBR*. Further, all issues and questions concerning the construction, validity, interpretation and enforceability of these Terms/ Rules and Guidelines, or the rights and obligations of the Applicants and/ or CCIPL and/ or partners of *LBR*, shall be governed and construed in accordance with the laws of the Republic of India.
Note: For specific guidelines all Applicants are requested to contact the *LBR* Team by email at **lbr.entries@hachetteindia.com**

APPENDIX 1

The clauses below are subject to ongoing review and modifications, and applicants may check this section from time to time to update themselves on categories that may have been discontinued, modified or changed.

1. SPECIAL NOTE FOR PROSPECTIVE ATTEMPTS

a. For young children: No marathon records or dangerous records will be considered for children. They can attempt records in mental mathematics, collections and Rubik's cube. The pre-approved categories are as follows:

Main categories:
i. Mental Mathematics (without using pen and paper)
ii. Calculation (using pen and paper)
Spoken or visual or flashing numbers (for calculation purposes) will be considered as mental maths. Both the major categories have the following subcategories for attempting records:

- Five-minute event: The Applicant will be given five (5) minutes to attempt the event. The time will be the major benchmark for making and breaking records.
- Marathon event: The Applicants set the quantum of calculations for attempting the record. The time will not be considered for attempting a new record. However, for breaking the record in this category both time and the quantum will be considered as parameters.
- Sprint event: The Applicant will be given one (1) minute to attempt a record. Time cut-off will be the major benchmark for breaking records.

The Attempt must be made in the approved categories only. The age criteria are U-18 and above 18 only. The documents submitted/ record attempted will not be considered on their face value and will be only considered for review after the *LBR* Team approves it. Calculations with or without decimals will be considered as the same.

- The following events will not be considered for records:
  i. Multiplication and division by a single digit.
  ii. Writing/ speaking of multiplication tables.
  iii. Squaring of 1-, 2- and 3-digit numbers.
  iv. Multiplication of 2-digit numbers.
  v. Any record Attempt with even a single error.
  vi. Multiple claims under the same category.

b. There are categories in the book, marked with a double asterisks, indicating that they are one-time categories. These categories will not be carried forward into our subsequent editions and are not contestable.

c. Certain categories in the book are marked with a single asterisk, to indicate that the age group/s of Participants in the record have been modified. These entries too shall not be carried into subsequent editions and are not contestable. Applicants may, on a case to case basis, undertake an Attempt in the category under the modified specific rules and guidelines as informed by the *LBR* Team.

d. Additional pointers to remember before sending the documentation or claims:
   i. Applicants should not send any documents unless requested by the *LBR* Team, post-approval.
   ii. Applicants should not send any documentation if their event has not been approved for consideration by the *LBR* Team.
   iii. Documents received by *LBR* for events that are not pre-approved (in writing or on email) will not be reviewed by the *LBR* Team.

2. A NOTE FOR PAST, PRESENT AND POTENTIAL RECORD HOLDERS

a. The name Limca and the Limca logo are registered trademarks of The Coca-Cola Company, USA, and should not be used for publicity when a record is being attempted or after the Claim has been accepted, without written permission of the publisher.

b. When records are being attempted, it is not obligatory for the *LBR* Team to provide invigilators. However, where possible they may do so.

c. All Attempts at breaking old records and setting new ones are undertaken entirely at the risk of the Applicant. Neither the *LBR* Team nor CCIPL can be held responsible by the Applicant/ person undertaking an Attempt or any third party for any liability that may arise out of such an Attempt.

d. Applicants may use the name '*Limca Book of Records*' while attempting the record as long as:
   i. they do not use the logo of the *Limca Book of Records* or Limca brand or any Licensed Property of CCIPL;
   ii. they do not receive or give money in the execution of such an Attempt using *LBR* as a party or implied party or endorser; and
   iii. they do not offer Participants/ partners any kind of inducement using *LBR* as a party. **This is strictly prohibited and will result in the Applicant's name being blacklisted and rejected for any future application/ attempts.**

e. The *LBR* Team reserves the complete and incontestable right to decide which chapters, sections, photographs, categories and records to publish or delete in future editions. *LBR* will not consider potentially dangerous record Attempts by minors or any Attempt that violates a law.

f. *LBR* strives to be completely authentic. However, it sometimes happens that an earlier record may come to light or be applied for after the book is released. In such cases corrections/ updates will be carried out in the next edition or as deemed fit by the *LBR* Team.

g. Records that are 'firsts' are not entitled to perpetuity and can be dropped from the book without any prior intimation.

h. For reasons of space or any other reasons whatsoever, a confirmed Claim may also be dropped. *LBR* Team members may inform the Applicant of the change in status but are not bound to do so. Such decisions are the sole prerogative of the *LBR* Team in the larger continuing interests of the book.

i. The record holders are not entitled to any prize money, gift(s) or free copies of *LBR*.

j. **In case the record is subjected to reverification, the onus to prove the same is on the Applicant, so the Applicant must retain copies of documentary, images, audio and video evidence with them should such a situation arise. *The Limca Book of Records* holds the right to revoke any record that fails reverification and to cancel the issued certificate.**

k. In all matters pertaining to *Limca Book of Records*, the *LBR* Team's decision is final.

3. DISCONTINUED CATEGORIES

a. A few categories have been discontinued and will not be featured in any subsequent editions. The website is updated regularly regarding such categories.

b. Youngest category: The youngest category has been dropped. The only exceptional cases are sports, art and creative skills and any other reputed competitions where there is a quantifiable group. The age categories are specified only to ensure that no records are created against the law (for example, driving at an age not legally permissible) and to ensure that minors do not try to attempt records that require excessive physical exertion (like marathon events or climbing high mountains) and/ or those that may be detrimental to their physical, mental or emotional well-being.

c. Most surgeries/ medical procedures within a time duration: The category for most surgeries/ medical procedures has been discontinued as the quality of the procedure may be compromised during such claims.

d. Tractor service camps: The category for most tractors serviced has been discontinued as such claims are difficult to monitor and make it an industry-specific claim.

e. Largest blood/ organ donation drives

f. Wrist cracking/ wrist rotation
g. Most couplets written
h. Holding most burning candles in the mouth Fastest construction of structures
i. Fastest yoga asanas
j. Collection of error coins
k. Longest interview
l. Limbo skating
m. One-hand claps
n. Most postcards sent in a day – solo/ group – single/ multiple venues
o. Largest packers and movers of household goods
p. Most people screened/ diagnosed – single/ multiple venues
q. Most postcards sent in a day – individual/ group – single/ multiple venues
r. Largest anthology
s. Collections for '786' notes.

4. WHY WAS YOUR RECORD REJECTED?

Unfortunately, many applications are rejected. The following are the general reasons that lead to the rejection of applications:

a. Not accepted the Terms and Conditions and/ or Rules and Guidelines and/ or incomplete form
b. Insufficient documentation: The details provided do not suffice for verification purposes.
c. Not met criteria: For record purposes, *LBR* has certain criteria and set categories. For instance, in physical feats we only have categories for 1 minute or 1 hour claims. Any claim that does not follow the format (e.g., most push-ups in 40 seconds instead of 30 seconds) will not accepted.
d. Specific titles: Generally, *LBR* measures record titles by one single parameter so that anybody can attempt and break/ surpass that record. If the record claim is too specific or has multiple variables, the LBR Team would not consider such claims. For example, 'most push-ups in one minute' would be considered whereas 'most push-ups done in 1 minute by a teacher' will not be accepted.
e. Inappropriate/ Offensive: *LBR* does not accept or encourage inappropriate or offensive claims.
f. Claims involving alcohol/ smoking/ substance usage: *LBR* does not encourage or accept claims involving alcohol, smoking or substance use.
g. Animal welfare: Any claim that is not in accordance with animal rights laws or involves any mistreatment of animals is neither encouraged nor accepted in *LBR*.
h. Personality-related claims: Claims related to famous personalities, such as 'most people dressed as' or 'most times performing as' will only be considered for internationally recognized, iconic and universally acknowledged personalities. The *LBR* Team reserves the right of discretion in any such claim.
i. Record claims involving wastage of food/ medical supplies, e.g., artworks made with fresh food materials would not be considered.
j. Environmentally harmful claims: *LBR* does not support any claim that may have any sort of adverse effect on the environment.
k. Fastest musicians: *LBR* does not consider claims such as fastest guitarist, fastest piano player, etc., as it is not possible to judge the quality of music produced in such claims.
l. Firsts: The firsts in a field are generally not accepted unless they mark change in trend, beginning of a new era or change the traditional way for the matter. The *LBR* Team reserves the right to accept or reject any such claim.
m. Poetry: *LBR* does not accept claims pertaining to poetry due to its subjective nature.
n. Originality/ Uniqueness based claims: Uniqueness/ originality cannot be a parameter of competence for a record. The *LBR* Team reserves the right of discretion in any such claim.
o. Sports achievements: For records directly involving performance in sports, *LBR* only accepts those which occur at a top-level professional, international, or pre-eminent amateur levels, or as per the decision of the relevant Consultant in specific cases.
p. Largest anthology
q. Longest preservation of food items/ articles.
r. Claims relating to number of research papers written or published will not be accepted.

Limca Book of Records

NEXT EDITION: 2024

The last date for new entries and applications (complete with relevant documentation) for the *Limca Book of Records* 2024 edition:

31 May 2023

Please address all correspondence to:

Limca Book of Records (Editorial)
Hachette Book Publishing India Pvt. Ltd
4th/5th Floors, Corporate Centre
Plot No. 94, Sector 44
Gurugram 122003, Haryana, India
Phone: (Board) +91-124-4195000
Fax: +91-124-4148900
Email: lbr.entries@hachetteindia.com
Website: https://www.coca-colaindia.com/limca-book-of-records

Note: In order to have an accessible, credible and reproducible record of interactions, email (and where it is unavailable, registered postal mail or courier service) is the preferred form of communication and correspondence.